Preventing Conflict in the
Post-Communist World

Brookings Occasional Papers

Preventing Conflict in the Post-Communist World

Mobilizing International and Regional Organizations

ABRAM CHAYES
ANTONIA HANDLER CHAYES
Editors

THE BROOKINGS INSTITUTION
Washington, D.C.

Brookings Occasional Papers

THE BROOKINGS INSTITUTION is a private nonprofit organization devoted to research, education, and publication on important issues of domestic and foreign policy. Its principal purpose is to bring knowledge to bear on the major policy problems facing the American people.

On occasion Brookings authors produce research papers that warrant immediate circulation as contributions to the public debate on current issues of national importance. Because of the circumstances of their production, these Occasional Papers are not subjected to all of the formal review procedures for the Institution's research publications, and they may be revised at a later date. As in all Brookings publications, the judgments, conclusions, and recommendations presented in the papers are solely those of the authors and should not be attributed to the trustees, officers, or other staff members of the Institution.

Copyright © 1996 by
THE BROOKINGS INSTITUTION
1775 Massachusetts Avenue, N.W., Washington, D.C.

Library of Congress Cataloging-in-Publication data:
Preventing conflict in the post-communist world : mobilizing
    international and regional organizations / Abram Chayes
    and Antonia Handler Chayes, editors.
        p.   cm.
    Includes bibliographical references and index.
    ISBN 0-8157-1385-1 (alk. paper)
    1. Civil war. 2. International organization. 3. Regionalism
(International organization) 4. Security, International.
I. Chayes, Abram, 1922– . II. Chayes, Antonia Handler, 1929– .
JX4541.P74   1996
327.1'72'094—dc20   95-36259
                                                          CIP

The editors wish to acknowledge support for this project from the Carnegie Corporation of New York.

Contents

Part Six

Introduction

Abram Chayes and Antonia Handler Chayes

THIS BOOK is concerned with preventing violent conflict in eastern and central Europe (ECE) and the former Soviet Union (FSU). By now it is clear that the many violent conflicts erupting in this area have a very different meaning for the international community than conflicts and civil wars during the era of superpower competition and nuclear stalemate. It is not that the *nature* of conflict has changed. Ethnic and tribal wars have raged throughout history. But their significance, understood (and misunderstood) only within the simple framework of superpower rivalry and cold war risk a few years ago, is now far more difficult to grasp. The East-West stalemate no longer stabilizes an uneasy peace among nations. The governments emerging from communism lack both the authoritarian will to suppress intrastate differences that may have simmered for generations and the democratic power to manage them. With the end of forced homogeneity and repressed ethnic differences, old conflicts have resurfaced and new ones have been kindled in virulent form from Bosnia to Chechnya. The stability of governments and the status quo of borders are thrown into question. Actual and threatened disintegration of states in the area is widespread. No reference points have emerged to replace the cold war paradigm. Nor is there a way of knowing which conflicts will be contained within accepted borders, threatening only the participants, and which may spill over, igniting discontents and imitations on a wider scene. The prospect not only of widening conflict, but also of new precedents challenging old certainties of international life, causes deep concern in western Europe and the United States, with their recent memories of the cold war following on the heels of two world wars.

The prospect of destabilization, spillover, and proliferation of weapons of mass destruction presents new risks that have caused a radical change in

1

context and provided the impetus for earnest rethinking. But the beginnings of reorientation in efforts to cope with the changes have provided little comfort or assurance that the direction is sound or can help reduce the risks or bring a measure of stability. The last decade of this century produced a number of tentative approaches to this poorly understood and rapidly changing context. The efforts involve both traditional diplomacy and a less familiar multilateralism. They are based upon historic ties among states as well as new relationships. They involve international and regional institutions, singly and in concert. The private sector, including both business and nongovernmental organizations (NGOs), is playing a significant role.

In this book we examine only one crucial aspect of the effort to deal with the sea change that has taken place in this geographic area: how are international and regional organizations attempting to deal with the many forms of internal conflict that are both the cause and result of the end of communism and the East-West confrontation? We do not deal directly with the radical reorientation of economic systems, nor the humanitarian plights and flow of refugees caused by the change, except in the context of actual and potential violent conflict. We do not consider as such the feared rise of Islam in Eurasia, except as it colors the input of states into institutional responses. Nor is this a book about the development of civil society, except as one strategy for preventing and reducing the effects of violent conflicts. All these issues may be relevant to understanding internal conflicts and developing appropriate and effective strategies to manage them. In that context they are discussed within the essays that make up the chapters of this book.

The Uncertain Causes of Internal Conflict

We do not propose any unique causal explanation of intrastate break-down and strife. Like all major social movements, these deeply troubling phenomena have a complex and varied etiology. In one sense, they are the consequence of all of previous history. Three of the authors try to come to grips with this complexity: Keitha S. Fine, Jean Manas, and Wolfgang Reinicke. But all of the authors recognize that the international community is seeking solutions to a set of problems that are not (and perhaps cannot be) fully understood in any simple causal sense.

Keitha S. Fine draws an existential picture of the conflicts and chaos in terms of transition, noting that no single approach to transition from author-itarianism "can alone repair long-lived economic-structural, political-social, or individual dysfunctionality." She points out that the former regimes have a longer reach than anyone was prepared to admit, and new governments contain many of the old actors who continue practices that were rejected and are a built-in opposition to change. "The old is not yet dead: the new cannot be born."

The unstable climate existing during the early phases of transition is fertile ground for violence. Former dissidents who may have stimulated the shift withdraw from government or are marginalized. Ethnic politics seems to offer a "clean new identity" that promises a break with the recent past—with both communism and the forced homogenization of its government. Instability is compounded by the flow of refugees and the breakdown of law and order. "Ethnic and racial incidents appear from nowhere," helping to create new social divisions. These divisions are exacerbated by the outbreak of racism, anti-Semitism, and xenophobia. In ECE, ethnic conflict is fanned by a new generation of neofascists. And not unlike the west, the cities have become hotbeds of violence and crime. Some transitional governments deny or ignore these problems, and in some, the policies may exacerbate them and permit conflict to grow.

Jean E. Manas, writing about the "democracy mission" of the Council of Europe (COE), questions whether any approach that tries to craft solutions to ethno-national conflict in terms of establishing minority rights can get at some of its deepest causes. Unlike fundamental individual rights, there is no consensus on the content of minority rights sufficient to legitimize the suppression of secessionist or irredentist demands. Against the multiculturalism of minority rights stands the French ideal of republicanism. The state and ethnic identity are decoupled, and there is no distinction in the treatment of citizens, regardless of ethno-national characteristics. In theory, "neutrality" can be achieved. But Manas also rejects this as a universal solution. "No state is neutral as a matter of fact."

Ultimately, Manas questions all approaches that rely on the current status quo of states and borders: ". . . this commitment to majoritarianism within current borders has advantaged ethno-national majorities to the detriment of ethno-national minorities. Unhappy with this bargain, the more powerful of those minorities have . . . tried to change that situation, generally by struggling for the creation of new states in which they are in the majority (secessionism) or the alteration of borders so that they would become part of states in which they are in the majority (irredentism)."

Manas argues implicitly for "a conception of democracy that does not sanctify either territorialism or majoritarianism." Since most states are the product of past secessions and consolidations, "Drawing the line at today's map is as unprincipled (or principled) as drawing the line after tomorrow's secession." In his analysis of the activities of the Council of Europe and its underlying assumptions, he calls upon the nations of Europe to face cleavages so deep that apparent success in creating an electoral democracy can be only a palliative. Despite the fear of the "bottomless pit" of precedent, he maintains, the search for solutions to ethno-national conflict cannot be limited to those that refuse to contemplate actual secession. "The conceptual difficulties with the three models—minority rights, republicanism, and secessionism—do not suggest that all three are inherently bad ideas—or that the uneasy balances they offer will necessarily come to a quick end," but that there is no grand solution, and rigid structures may solidify conflict, not resolve it. "A good first step would be to appreciate the complexities associated with ethno-national conflict."

Wolfgang Reinicke, like Fine, sees the transition, or the period of "deconstruction and reconstruction" of state structures, as creating the opportunity for ethnic mobilization and violent conflict, since rapidly changing social, political, and economic norms have created an economic and cultural power vacuum. Following Joseph Rothschild, he identifies three forms in which ethnic relations can be organized in a society: (1) vertical hierarchy, in which one ethnic group dominates over others; (2) parallel segmentation, a society whose principal fragmentation runs along ethnic lines, without any group being dominant; and (3) a reticulate society, in which patterns of social and economic stratification cut across ethnic groups. The transition in ECE and the FSU is a movement from the vertical hierarchy of the old communist regimes to the reticulate society of democratic and market-based systems. The problem is that, on the way, the process often traverses a phase of parallel segmentation, which is vulnerable to political and social mobilization along ethnic lines, since there are no alternative bases of identification and the coercive apparatus that prevented it before is gone. Like Fine, Reinicke stresses how susceptible individuals are to ethnic mobilization at a time of economic deprivation in the course of transition, when new norms have not replaced the old one, and violence is endemic in the society. He distinguishes five principal forms that such mobilization may assume—cultural revivalism, political autonomy, self-determination, separation, irredentism—and observes "that ethno-national conflict in the ECE and FSU is prone to conflict resolution by violence rather than compromise . . . as competing groups attempt to divide and claim for themselves what not long ago seemed indivisible and was considered common to all."

Leaderships of emerging ethnic elites develop and solidify their political power on the basis of "mobilization and even conflict," by using the levers of "control of the means of production, finance, and communication in a society." Reinicke is particularly concerned about "the development of institutional exclusion in the reconstruction process," for denying other modes of identification for people emerging from vertical hierarchies will foster violent ethnic mobilization. Ethnic cores must be incorporated into the debates over system transformation, he argues. Thus it is crucial to assure "the existence of societal or subsystemic structures and institutional networks, both ethnic and nonethnic." Based on this analysis, he argues for an economic strategy, led by the international financial institutions (IFIs), the World Bank family and the International Monetary Fund (IMF), whereby IFIs must abandon their pretense of political neutrality and invest in projects that sustain or promote a peaceful transition to reticulate society.

Analysts and policymakers perceive the causes and the risks of internal conflict differently, and not all focus equally on ethnic aspects. Some, for example, find the nature of conflict to be predominantly a form of new politics, with ethnicity, religion, race, and xenophobia as levers to be exploited, rather than root causes. To some extent, proposed solutions will differ accordingly, but there is far from complete correlation. Responsive strategies depend as much on what is feared, by whom, and the intensity of concern, which in turn may depend on internal factors in individual states acting alone or in the context of international organizations. The international community is concerned about violent state disintegration and its effects as precedent in other situation, whatever the causes. Such disintegration is most threatening when it is close by, or when it mirrors states' own internal problems and a chain reaction seems likely. This is as true in Europe as it is in India and Pakistan.

States also fear the expansion of conflict and its spillover, which bring into play traditional security issues. A related concern is the impact of massive refugee flows attendant on destabilization of once-stable states. There are some whose major concerns are humanitarian. In the background is the fear of a revived Soviet superpower, less stable and "rational" than its predecessor—or its opposite, a dangerously disintegrating Russia. Finally, there is the other background fear of Islamic fundamentalism.

These concerns lead to different priorities, from encouraging rapid transition to western-type democracies in ECE and FSU nations, to conflict suppression endorsing any kind of stabilization to avoid violence. No one can say now which of these concerns should predominate in policymaking, or whether any is even valid. But any one of them may lead to a different set of policy choices than would be reached from a different starting point. One of the purposes of this book is to accept the uncertain understanding of the causes of conflict while helping to define available approaches to prevention.

Definitions and Scope

This book does not limit its discussion of conflict prevention to preventive diplomacy in traditional terms—a focus only on preventing the outbreak of violent conflict. That is essential, especially during a period in which there is growing reluctance by third parties to involve themselves in the dangerous business of violence and to commit the resources to be effective in quelling it. A major conclusion is the need for the investment of much larger resources, not only of money, but of time, imagination, and energy, in finding and using better ways of early intervention to prevent bloody conflict from erupting.

We expand this traditional concept in two dimensions. First, conflict prevention can also occur in the course of violent confrontation. Such an effort can prevent horizontal or vertical escalation and can often provide the parties with breathing space in which there is a chance to compose the differences that led to conflict. Second, conflict prevention is concerned with preventing the recurrence of conflict after a settlement is reached. These phases cannot be kept entirely separate. A situation can move from one to another and back again. Often the same forces operate in each, and the same instruments must be used. However, the different phases may call for different approaches or emphases.

Why International Organizations?

International and regional organizations are the established vehicles through which consensus for action to address internal conflict is established by the relevant international community. Europe offers the richest environment for exploring the actual and potential effectiveness of international and regional organizations. Western Europe is the locus of a thick web of powerful, affluent, and historically successful organizations. The editors and most of the authors of this volume could be considered "institutionalists." We have come to believe that institutions matter, and that they have the capability of bringing greater power, legitimacy, and expertise to bear on complex international problems than any one state or ad hoc grouping. It is a truism that international organizations are made of states and that the decisions of the members are an ultimate limit on what the organization can accomplish. Yet organizational structure, processes, and resources lead to conclusions different from those that would be reached by less formal modes of communication. Some of the organizations studied— the Organization on Security and Cooperation in Europe (OSCE), the European Union (EU), the IFIs, for example—display a notable autonomy of initiative and action. The study of the growth of international and regional organizations in Europe reveals a broad range of approaches to conflict prevention.

This being said, it remains true that thus far the effectiveness of international organizations in coping with internal conflict has been disappointing and their potential elusive. Although it is common and true to cite limitations of resources in explanation of these deficiencies, it is also true that a considerable commitment has been made—the annual budget of the major international organizations in the former Yugoslavia alone comes to $3.5 billion—with not very much to show for it.

Yet it is far too early to reach conclusions about the longer-term capability of these organizations or to be confident about potential strategies that might be effective. Most of the international and regional organizations here considered were created and developed after World War II and during the cold war, and were designed to address the problems of those eras. Both the problems and the geographic focus today are different. The concern is now with all of Eurasia, and the cold war and problems of economic recovery from World War II seem a distant memory. Most of the organizations have been making serious and fundamental attempts at reorientation and adaptation.

Adaptation, however, is not automatic or simple. As almost all the chapters show, these organizations are slow to enter the fray and, in general, offer blunt instruments to address the problems. In what is still a state system, international organizations must operate by consensus. But for the very reason that consensus is important, it is slow and cumbersome in coming. Thus intervention is often too little, too late, or too tentative. International organizations are sometimes better positioned to concentrate and amass needed resources than a single nation, but the consensus to bring resources to bear on a problem is very hard to achieve. This is true of financial and far truer of military resources, but the alternatives do not appear to be much better.

Careful analysis of the record to date, however inadequate it has been, and the juxtaposition of the performance of all the relevant organizations suggest some ways in which their contribution could be improved over that of the first half decade since the cold war. We discuss the major organizations that operate or seem to have potential to prevent conflict in ECE and the FSU. We examine intermediation by formal international organizations in traditional and newer guises. We explore the tangible inducements that regional and international financial institutions can offer, and the intangible inducements of belonging to the community of democratic nations that is the imprimatur of membership in the Council of Europe. We analyze in depth the powerful magnets of admission to the European Union and NATO that affect patterns of behavior among potentially conflictual communities. We examine the potential and, more important, the limits of the threat and use of military force. We also consider the contribution organizations can make to reconstruction after conflict subsides.

This comparative view begins with the trans-European regional organizations, OSCE and the Council of Europe. They are also the ones that pursue the lowest-key and least coercive form of intervention. A major section is devoted to the EU and the effect of its example and the aspiration for membership as conflict inhibitors. The book then turns to economic organizations, which have power and influence to mount a conflict prevention strategy, but are only beginning to do so. We look at the conflict prevention potential of the regional security organizations. Finally, although the UN is present throughout the volume as actor, foil, or *primus inter pares,* we conclude with three chapters on the efforts of the United Nations in this region "to save succeeding generations from the scourge of war."

The Organization (formerly Conference) on Security and Cooperation in Europe

Diana Chigas and her coauthors argue that a "settlement-and-enforcement" model for conflict resolution cannot be transposed to the earlier stages in a conflict. Instead, they claim, the OSCE has developed a new model for conflict prevention that does not focus on substantive settlement of the underlying dispute. In the early stages of a conflict, neither the parties nor the issues are likely to be crystallized.

Traditional methods . . . [using] confrontation, pressure, and advocacy will frequently only exacerbate conflict, while traditional strategies for traditional international mediation of conflicts, with their emphasis on "carrots" and "sticks" to induce settlements, are inadequate to deal with the long-term psychological, social, economic, and political problems at the root of ethno-national conflicts. . . . They implicate the most fundamental of human aspirations and needs (such as identity, recognition, security, meaningful participation in political processes), and cannot be "solved" through negotiation of legally binding and enforceable agreements.

The problem is to help set up processes that will get at underlying strivings and discontents before they harden into intractable and violent conflict.

Ironically, the requirement for consensus among the fifty-two nations that comprise the OSCE, so often cited as an impediment to action, may be its greatest strength, according to Chigas. It makes action requiring large resources, such as enforcement, nearly impossible. "[OSCE's] strategy has been to build on its existing structures for multilateral discussion, and especially its inability to undertake any enforcement action." It has proceeded by dialogue and 'jawboning' at early stages of conflict where large-scale intervention would be inappropriate. The resulting intervention is quiet and low-key. The primary mechanisms are "the missions of short and long duration" and the High Commissioner on National Minorities (HCNM).

The OSCE innovation is to substitute a "management" for an "enforcement" mode of intervention. As a result, it becomes what Chigas characterized as an "insider third party." In contrast to the classic model of mediation, the intermediary operates within the state structure, putting pressures (even though gentle) upon government while attempting to win its confidence and that of the other parties. "Insider" does not imply less neutrality but more continuous involvement closer to the ground than a typical international mediator might achieve. The objective is not a one-shot attempt at conflict resolution, but to start processes going, whether in politics, in the legislative forum, or through intense round table dialogues, in which the contending parties can begin to know and trust each other, thus creating the time and space for managing conflict.

Despite the consensus rule, formal fifty-two-nation approval of these missions is not required. The HCNM has the authority to initiate country visits, and he has exercised it. The "missions" can be stimulated by the OSCE Chairman-in-Office and are informally supervised by the Permanent Council. These missions may cover a broader subject matter and be less localized geographically within a country than the activities of the HCNM.

But they share the same goals, and both serve as early warning to the OSCE, as well as providing transparency within and outside the country and working with governments and parties in conflict to prevent escalation. The basis for successes achieved, for example, in Estonia, described at length in chapter 2, is not power but persuasive influence and the ability to offer alternatives to escalation.

Nevertheless, the OSCE processes are far from an ideal solution. They seem to succeed in relatively low-level situations, but homeopathy does not work to cure pneumonia. The then-CSCE was ineffective in dealing with the raging conflict in the former Yugoslavia, as Mario Zucconi points out in chapter 5. It is pitifully underfunded, with a total budget of $27 million. Moreover, the processes established may not take permanent root by the time OSCE missions leave. And already there is some backlash, as in the Baltics, which express concern that they are being singled out. But the power of focus on conflict prevention, the willingness to become deeply involved as a quasi-insider, the modest goals, and the absence of bureaucratic sclerosis make the OSCE a very important model.

The Council of Europe

The focus of Council of Europe activities is only indirectly conflict prevention. Its mandate is to establish and to some degree enforce norms of civilized and democratic national behavior. Jean Manas' chapter questions the COE's assumption of a peace mission, and particularly its strategy of emphasizing formal minority rights as a cure for secessionist tendencies.

By sanctifying existing state borders, the Council, all of whose members, predictably, are established or emerging states, begs the question of disagreement over what is the appropriate "self" for democratic self-determination. In Croatia is it the inhabitants of the former Yugoslavia or only those who live in Croatia? If so, why are not the Serbs of Krajina equally entitled to their own space?

The COE's traditional emphasis on individual human rights did not come to grips with the issues of governance in an ethnically divided society. A policy of nondiscrimination as among individuals does not assure governmental neutrality as among groups. The shift to a minority rights emphasis was motivated by post–cold war realities and a search for answers to secessionism. "The multicultural conception, which rises in opposition to the republican conception, conceded that ethno-nationalism and public life cannot be decoupled, and substituted a vision of a multicultural nation-state."

The new vision is by no means unopposed in the Council, and there is disenchantment elsewhere, as exemplified by Vaclav Havel in the wake of the dissolution of Czechoslovakia. Nevertheless, chapter 3 underscores the power of norm development and elaboration, efforts shared with the OSCE, though less emphasized in chapter 1. The assumption is that western-type democracies operating under the rule of law and protecting fundamental human rights are effective in preventing internal conflict. The combination of recognized norms on these matters and more stringent application of admission requirements may have long-term effects on the way states address ethno-national conflict. Recent Council outreach in its modest confidence-building projects, workshops, and technical assistance are designed to reinforce these norms. Like the OSCE, Council of Europe activities are low-key and cost little. They depend upon the power of persuasion, prestige, and the pressures of members to induce conformity with Council norms—-but these are not trivial.

Economic Power: The Draw of Membership in the European Union

The next three chapters, all written by Europeans with close knowledge of the European Union, examine in depth its conflict prevention potential. John Pinder focuses on its history, its federalist characteristics, and its extraordinary economic power, implying that, with little more, the desire to enter this community will serve as a lever to prevent conflict in many of the former ECE nations and perhaps in those western areas of the FSU where membership may be within reach. Membership in the EU is premised upon liberal democracy, respect for human rights, the rule of law, and a market economy. As with the COE, the assumption is that this will go a long way toward creating a climate in which peace can be maintained or restored. "The combination of prosperity, peace, and freedom that central and east Europeans saw embodied in the Community was attractive and it encouraged them to throw off the Soviet system." Business managers understand that democracy and the rule of law are essential for their ability to function. Although, "since its instruments are mainly economic, the Community's main target has been the establishment of effective market economies," Pinder argues that "the significance of this for the consolidation of constitutional democracies should not be underestimated."

The chapter traces the history of the current EU institutions, explaining how the organization arrived at its not inconsiderable powers and the building blocks that are now in place for a federal union. Although its quasi-federal budget is small, its political powers are embryonic, and common currency remains a receding ideal, the Union has enormous power over internal and external trade.

There has been some direct economic and political assistance, but by far the most important assistance given to ECE and the FSU is in the form of trade. Both exports and imports have grown rapidly, especially between the EU and the Visegrad countries, where economic reform was faster paced than elsewhere in ECE. A network of trade agreements has been concluded, the most important of which are the Europe Agreements, which are conceived as the critical first step toward ultimate membership, much as the Partnership for Peace in NATO, discussed below. Nonetheless, protectionism remains serious, particularly in agriculture, steel, and other products of interest to ECE countries. It has embittered relations and hampered growth and transition to market economies.

There have been a number of initiatives for direct assistance to marketization. The EU provided much of the impetus and funding for the European Bank for Reconstruction and Development (EBRD), described in chapter 8. The Poland and Hungary Aid for Economic Reconstruction (PHARE) and Technical Assistance for the CIS (TACIS) programs for ECE and the FSU respectively have made a modest contribution (approximately 1.5 billion ECU per annum each) to the institution of market democracies and the building of infrastructure.

It is widely accepted that membership itself will be the most powerful guarantor of democracy and a market economy. "Membership is a cast-iron guarantee that the member states maintain market economies with the contribution that such economies make to pluralist democracy and to alleviating some of the economic causes of ethno-national conflict." But the very attraction of membership explains why it may be unlikely to happen in the near term. Agricultural and other forms of protectionism will not die easily. The effort to assure democracy in transitional states may be beyond the political capacity of the EU, unless they have solidified into mature democracies before entry—and that will take some time. The idea of early admission with the hope that membership criteria can be met once inside has not been viewed favorably. And each additional member complicates the EU's internal problems—its capacity to make decisions, take action, and develop its institutions.

Reinhardt Rummel's chapter deals with EU *political* initiatives to prevent conflict in ECE and the FSU. He argues that the attraction of integration for ECE and FSU nations is not only economic, but also reflects the high degree of stability and opportunity for peaceful resolution of conflict they see in the Union. Rummel develops the steps that the EU has taken in its own transition from "an economic giant but a political dwarf" to a political power capable of establishing regional peace and stability—an intervenor and mediator on the global stage. Maastricht created the Common Foreign and Security Policy (CFSP) as a framework to coordinate and ultimately unify EU foreign policy. "Theoretically CFSP can draw on economic sticks and carrots of the Union and on military support from the WEU [Western European Union] [and] NATO. . . . [In practical terms] this is the exception rather than the rule." Thus far, it has resulted more in coordination than in unity, more in declarations than action. Nevertheless, a structure is in place for more ambitious concerted foreign and security policy undertakings in the future.

The EU has focused outreach efforts to offer assistance to ECE and FSU nations to build democracy as a conflict prevention strategy. The economic cooperation agreements with ECE and some FSU nations contain provisions for regular political dialogue as well. Rummel also discusses the technical assistance and funding provided by PHARE and TACIS. The projects range from assistance in creating free media to election monitoring, with varying degrees of success. More directly, the Balladur Plan of 1993 was a mechanism to get ECE and FSU countries to address their own border and minorities problems in preparation for membership in the Union. Although at first it was regarded as paternalistic, the initiative has been seriously engaged. Fifty nations attended the opening conference in May 1994. Two regional round tables, one in the Baltic and one for the Visegrad countries, have held five meetings at which boundary problems and transborder issues have been discussed. Settlements and agreements on these issues are to be consolidated in a "Stability Pact," signed at the final meeting of the initiative in spring of 1995. The final document includes a declaration of principles emphasizing, *inter alia,* respect for rights of minorities and 124 bilateral and multilateral agreements, some of which settled minor disputes; others promoted cooperation and exchanges. Most important, the process has been started, with the impetus of eventual EU membership to keep the momentum going. The hand-off from EU to OSCE for implementation is an important phenomenon of inter-organization cooperation to be followed closely.

Although the EU's signal failure in the former Yugoslavia is addressed in chapter 5, Rummel describes two instances of CFSP action that offer modest promise: the intermediation that helped lower tensions over the Gabcikovo-Nagymaros dam between Hungary and Slovakia and funneled the dispute to the International Court of Justice (ICJ), and the assumption of responsibility for the administration of the town of Mostar in Croatia to stabilize an uneasy peace.

Because of the EU's power and its draw for ECE and FSU nations, Rummel sees an unrealized potential for it in orchestrating the efforts and strategies of other European organizations. At the same time, he emphasizes the difficulties of achieving consensus even within the EU for CFSP action. And he provides no easy solutions to institutional rivalries and the difficulties of aligning complex international bureaucracies, with overlapping but not congruent membership, that wish to pursue their own policies in conflict prevention and otherwise.

Zucconi, however, holds the mirror of failure up to the performance of the CFSP in the former Yugoslavia. He shows that the CFSP, far from generating a well-designed and deliberated common policy, permitted Germany to hijack the EU by insisting on recognition of the breakaway republics before Croatia and Bosnia had met the requirements for protection of minorities laid down in the EU's own documents, and in disregard of the conclusions of the distinguished Arbitration Commission it had constituted to pass on the issues. Recognition removed the room to negotiate that might have truncated, if not averted, the war in Bosnia. The CFSP, said the Italian foreign minister, was more important than Bosnia. Greece achieved the same result with respect to its dangerous embargo on Macedonia by vetoing any contrary CFSP decision.

The International and Regional Financial Institutions

The IFIs and the EBRD are different in that they have substantial funds to offer. Both sets of institutions are deeply involved in attempting to facilitate structural reform, with a strong emphasis on the area of ECE and the FSU. Given their mandates and history, how can they participate in the complex work of conflict prevention? Wolfgang Reinicke argues that since the IFIs are already deeply involved in system transformation, and are likely to be asked to pay the cost of reconstruction in the aftermath of conflict, business considerations alone dictate closer attention to the effect of their investments on ethnic conflict and conflict prevention. He shows that it will require a considerable change in the culture of the IFIs to bring them to contemplate a conflict prevention strategy, and in some cases perhaps changes in mandate and charter. Despite the reputation of institutional rigidity, however, the IFIs have shown some flexibility in broadening their agenda to take account of the economic impact of such problems as environmental pollution, resource depletion, and population growth.

The International Bank for Reconstruction and Development (IBRD or World Bank) has traditionally insisted that it can consider only the economic soundness of projects it funds, and cannot be diverted by political or social considerations. This purist perspective has already changed. Over the past decade, as the Bank has entered the field of structural adjustment lending, it has begun to pay attention to "enabling conditions" without which sound economic development is impossible. In addition to matters such as environmental degradation, it looks at the soundness of governance as well as poverty and income distribution. Indeed, it has begun to address the issues of undue military expenditure. The introduction of these heretofore extraneous criteria has led the World Bank into a far greater participatory process, involving publics and NGOs.

The International Monetary Fund advances resources not for projects but to provide reserves to protect the currencies of its members in times of balance-of-payments difficulties. In order to ensure repayment of these advances, however, it conditions them on economic reform in the borrowing country. Traditionally, these conditions were standard monetarist prescriptions with little attention paid to social and political impacts of the policies. In recent years, however, along with the IBRD, the IMF has acknowledged the importance of these aspects to the problem of successful structural adjustment. Its four reform goals for ECE are primarily associated with economic system transformation, but it too has begun to include enabling conditions. The issues of poverty, good governance, and levels of military spending, though applied more narrowly than by the Bank, have become part of the Fund's policy-based criteria.

If these enabling conditions are relevant to the soundness of IBRD funding, it seems hard to deny that the issues of ethnic relations are equally significant. Reinicke, in an elaborate matrix distinguishing analytically among indirect-direct and active-passive strategies, argues for such seemingly obvious moves as requiring nondiscrimination among ethnic groups in Bank projects, or ensuring that its resources do not go exclusively to the ruling majority or the regions where it is concentrated.

The European Bank for Reconstruction and Development

The EBRD was organized in the euphoria after the fall of the Berlin Wall to be the premier financial instrument through which European resources would be channeled into ECE and the then transforming but still united Soviet Union. Unlike the traditional IFIs, its charter contained an expressly political element. Article 1 enjoins the Bank "to foster the transition towards open market-oriented economies and to promote private and entrepreneurial initiative in Central and Eastern European countries committed to and applying the principles of multiparty democracy, pluralism and market economics."

The first president of the Bank, Jacques Atali, not only tried to take this injunction seriously but applied these principles with a flamboyant disregard for the sensitivities of his European shareholders. Ethno-national conflict was high on his agenda, and he made a number of strong moves, not only in connection with the EBRD's investment activities but as an independent political spokesman. After little more than two years, however, he departed in quasi-disgrace, to be replaced by Jacques de Larosier, a former managing director of the IMF, an impeccably conservative IFI bureaucrat. Since then, the EBRD's financing activities have gone forward with only the minimum legally required attention to the criteria specified in article 1. Melanie Stein argues that there is room, if not legal obligation, for sensitive attention to democracy-building and conflict prevention considerations, along lines similar to those advocated by Reinicke, without falling into the trap of overt intervention in political affairs.

These two chapters suggest that the enormous power of international financial institutions can be harnessed to conflict prevention, even though that is not their primary purpose. The efficiency argument made by Reinicke is by no means spurious, although there are no guarantees of the results of these strategies. The investment made in the former Yugoslavia—the sixth largest user of IMF funds—has been substantially lost. If consciousness of their impact on potential conflict informed IFI and EBRD strategies more self-consciously, the leverage for conflict prevention might be increased significantly, especially in combination with the magnet of membership in the EU.

The Role of Security Organizations

Traditional European security organizations have played but little part in the effort to prevent ethno-national conflict, but under certain circumstances they might be critical in the prevention and mitigation of conflict and its recurrence. In their chapter on NATO, Antonia H. Chayes and Richard Weitz describe NATO's efforts at policy reorientation and its participation as a partner of the UN in peace operations in the former Yugoslavia, which came early in its post–cold war mission review.

Although Bosnia has barely tested the coordinated military potential of NATO, the establishment of a headquarters unit in Zagreb and its participation in the Adriatic embargo gives some sense of its capability. The experience in enforcing the "no-fly" zones and safe havens in the former Yugoslavia, described in the chapter, illustrates both the potential and inherent difficulties of a UN-NATO partnership. Though not exacting operationally, these operations too have been conducted satisfactorily. However, tensions arose from time to time over the objectives and implementation of policies announced by the UN Security Council. Yet the limitations of both the UN Charter and the North Atlantic Treaty require that NATO perform its peace operations in ECE or the FSU at the request of the UN or the OSCE, rather than on its own initiative, unless there were a direct threat to NATO territory. "For NATO to have operational credibility, intensive training focused on peace operations must begin in earnest." Unfortunately, a combination of internal political disagreements over the integrated command structure and the enormous obstacles to enlargement have slowed the process down.

The largest dilemma facing NATO is the issue of the enlargement of its membership. It has created a number of devices to begin to include ECE and FSU nations, starting with the North Atlantic Cooperation Council (NACC) and evolving into the more individualized contracts under the rubric of the Partnership for Peace (PfP). NATO officials and those of individual members have led some of the ECE states to believe that they are on a "fast track," and they have increased their pressures for membership. However, the prospect of extending NATO eastward to the borders of Russia has stirred opposition especially from nationalist forces in Russia, contributing to the fragility of the present government. President Yeltsin's outburst at the December 1994 Budapest (OSCE) summit and Russia's refusal once again to join PfP were almost predictable manifestations of the problem. Thus enlargement presents a serious dilemma, and has been put off to a vaguer future consummation, while the relevance of NATO and its ability to participate in the actual conflicts of ECE and the FSU continue to be in doubt.

David Huntington's examination of the "European pillar" of the alliance questions whether the WEU will ever develop into an effective security force for Europe or will continue to be a shadow conception of the French, seeking an alternative to the U.S.-dominated NATO. He describes the efforts to build an all-European force from what is now a bare-bones structure. Although the WEU would be free to act under circumstances when NATO may not, either because of legal restrictions or choice (presumably pressures from the United States), it has neither forces, command structure, nor capabilities of its own. It must rely entirely on contributions of its members—who are the also the members of NATO and the EU—or of NATO itself.

The WEU is interesting as a security organization because in theory it may provide a halfway house for ECE and FSU nations through its "associate partner" status or some other device earlier than the current pace of integration in NATO or the EU will allow. But because it has no military forces, it cannot now offer the security guarantees that these nations are seeking. Such halfway houses are likely to be seen by the intended beneficiaries as yet another device to delay entry into both the EU and NATO.

The WEU has engaged in some peacekeeping activities under its own banner: mine sweeping during the Iran-Iraq War, involvement in naval operations during the Gulf War, and enforcement of the embargo against Serbia in the Adriatic. But it remains "an inexperienced institution struggling to assert itself in the face of deep political divisions among its members." The key to its present ineffectiveness is the unwillingness to commit the resources necessary to make WEU into an actual military force. In the end, a significant part of NATO assets, such as airlift and C4I, are U.S. strengths, and so, as the French have ruefully come to recognize, a WEU operation of any size would probably need to be approved by the North Atlantic Council. The key relationship to watch is that of the WEU and the EU as the latter develops its CFSP.

The result is that there is no capable and willing military force in Europe ready to shoulder the burdens of peacekeeping, should the situation require one to prevent or mitigate conflict in ECE or the FSU. As creatures of the western alliance and the cold war, both NATO and WEU have not yet completed the transition that would allow them to be of use in the FSU. The Commonwealth of Independent States (CIS), even in combination with the inexperienced OSCE, has yet to gain legitimacy. Thus there is nowhere for ECE and FSU nations to look but the UN. With all of its gropings in the immediate past, it has a long history of peace operations, and it is truly international.

The UN in Conflict Prevention:
Its Scope and Capacity for Learning

The UN is the only organization capable of orchestrating all the strategies that might be necessary to mount an effective effort at conflict prevention including humanitarian, economic and peace operations and peace building—one that might be timely and with enough resources to make a difference. Boutros Boutros-Ghali's *Agenda for Peace* dutifully gives pride of place to "preventive diplomacy," but beyond the most formal of intermediation through the instrumentality of diplomatic representatives of the secretary-general, there is little to report.

Shashi Tharoor, the UN's second-ranking official for peacekeeping, in his canvass of the UN record in Europe, remarks that until Yugoslavia, the true internationalism or "United Nations-ness" of UN peace operations has been its hallmark. Since then, conditions have changed. The United Nations Protection Force (UNPROFOR) is predominately composed of troops of the Security Council's Permanent 5 and has relied on NATO, an independent organization, for enforcement. This has further complicated a difficult situation in which several different kinds of peace operations have been undertaken simultaneously, and the classic element of consent is dangerously eroded. He defines the challenges that he believes must be met if the current sense of pessimism and frustration about UN capabilities is to be overcome. He calls them "the eight Cs."

1. The challenge of capacity. The UN must be able to support what it mandates. This requires steps from improved command and control, to better staffing and planning, to force inventories and availability.

2. The challenge of cooperation. Europe, above all, offers opportunity for effective partnerships with capable regional organizations, but differences of outlook and culture must be worked through, and the UN's impartiality must not be compromised by seeming alignment with a partisan organization.

3. The challenge of command. There must be a balance between UN command and the "legitimate concerns of governments who are politically accountable to their publics for the risks taken by their soldiers." Tharoor considers the range of NATO issues in this light.

4. The challenge of coercion. This section raises the knotty problem, posed by both former Yugoslavia and Somalia, of performing humanitarian missions for which there is consent, simultaneously with enforcement missions that lack total consent. This issue is also dealt with in chapters 12 and 13.

5. The challenge of choice. How is the UN to decide which of the many demands for intervention to meet? Is either political choice driven by public

pressures or triage morally sustainable? If not, can the UN act in all conflicts worldwide at the same time?

6. The challenge of credibility. Whichever choice it makes—whether self-limitation or trying to do everything everywhere and failing—how can the UN remain a credible institution?

7. The challenge of contribution. Insufficient resources of money, time, and talent is a major and still growing problem, even when action is mandated.

8. The challenge of the common cause. Tharoor makes a final plea for maintaining the true universality of UN efforts to prevent conflict and restore peace.

To Jarat Chopra and Thomas G. Weiss, the demands on the UN for maintaining peace in the conflict-ridden "former second world," when added to pressures of conflicts elsewhere in the world, suggest a new model for complex, new generation peace operations. "Subcontracting the implementation of international decisions to powerful states" may be a pragmatic solution to situations that may require the use of force, but only if accountability is ensured "by joint control mechanisms composed of belligerents, regional states, multilateral, and nongovernmental organizations, as well as interested and disinterested states to provide leverage and a modicum of confidence in the peace process."

There are historical precedents. The United States managed Korea in 1950, the Gulf War, the United Nations Task Force (UNITAF) phase of Somalia, and Haiti. The British patrolled the sea lanes to prevent the shipment of oil to Beria in violation of the sanctions against Rhodesia. The French assumed the burden in Rwanda, and acquitted themselves well. Russian troops police the cease-fire in Georgia. In all these cases, there was Security Council authorization and coalitions on the ground, but the control remained with the initiating state. The issue of whether to anoint the CIS—read Russia—with the UN seal of approval remains the most sensitive. The force proposed for Nagorno-Karabakh with Russian troops predominating, but tempered with CIS contingents and OSCE political review, represents an experiment in subcontracting with added accountability.

Even the secretary-general, in a follow-up position paper to the *Agenda for Peace* at the end of 1994, recognized the practical necessity of empowering states to carry on enforcement actions under certain circumstances. According to Chopra and Weiss, accountability is the key to ensuring that this recourse does not become a disguise for neoimperialism. They propose three stringent criteria: (1) states act as clear agents of the UN, with continuing links; (2) the UN gives clear and incontestable instructions to its "agent"; and (3) ongoing accountability is maintained. In the end, they recognize that these conditions may be difficult to impose as the situation on the ground evolves on a minute-by-minute basis, but they insist that pragmatism must not be an excuse for abdication.

Michael Doyle completes this trilogy on UN peace operations, also taking as a point of departure the unprecedented demands that post–cold war state disintegration places on the UN. He focuses not on the enforcement end of the spectrum, for which he questions both UN capability and suitability, but on a range of peace-making and peace-building operations to create, maintain, and sustain consent. He remains convinced that some kind of formal peace agreement between the parties is essential and is worth the time, effort, and pressure it takes to achieve one. The new device of "Friends of the Secretary-General," an ad hoc grouping of states interested in the particular situation, is an important means of mobilizing these pressures. Nevertheless, the peace agreement is "an obsolescing bargain." The position and power of the UN are strongest at the moment it is signed. Therefore, time is of the essence; delay in deploying the peacekeeping mission, as in Cambodia, can dissipate the initial momentum for compliance. In any case, the mission cannot simply assume that the consent embodied in the agreement will continue. It must have a "flexible political strategy to win and keep popular support and create the support of local forces of order." And in order to relieve the UN of some of the burden of political responsibility in failed states, Doyle recommends the creation of a "semisovereign mechanism," like the Supreme National Council in Cambodia, to act in the name of the state. But in the end, the UN must "leave behind a legitimate and independently viable political sovereign," and to do so calls into action the panoply of peace-building measures and programs elaborated by the secretary general and that make up much of the argument of this book.

A Final Question: Are Effective Strategies Available?

The three chapters on the UN deal in important ways with the full range of UN peace operations. The UN High Commissioner for Refugees (UNHCR) has had a major role in the former Yugoslavia and has been the only UN presence in many of the bloodiest conflicts in ECE and the FSU, such as Tajikistan. But the UN, at least in theory, also has capabilities over a far greater array of potential strategies than it has thus far brought to bear on conflict prevention. UN agencies have not only provided humanitarian assistance, but work in the fields of health, education, human rights, and development, and it has some connection with the organizations that promote economic growth. All of these areas are essential building blocks for peace and for the prevention of conflict in the first place.

Despite the UN potential in so many fields and the rich array of regional organizations available in Europe, the traditional pleas for "coordination" and "interlock" have achieved little in the way of concerted efforts. There has been some cooperation (and much tension) between the UN, the EU, and NATO in the former Yugoslavia. But some highly relevant actors, such as the IFIs, are only beginning to recognize the importance of the contribution they might make to conflict prevention and mitigation, and how important their capabilities could be if they were to exercise their potential leverage.

This book offers an extended view of how each of these potential players in a more multifaceted, concerted approach now operates. It lets us understand how difficult it is to achieve effective joint action on a sustained basis. They are highly centralized and slow-moving bureaucracies. They are all institutions in transition, trying to adapt to a radically changed environment. The states that comprise them have not provided clear direction, and for each of them, it is problem enough to reach a consensus among members without trying also to reach agreement with other international organizations. Yet many of them must contribute to any successful effort to control ethno-national conflict.

Thus a concerted strategy is needed. But the experience of putting together this book, if not the book itself, leaves us with the conviction that joint action is not achievable with the existing ways of doing business. It seems relevant that the successes we have been able to report, such as the OSCE High Commissioner on National Minorities, are the result of flexible, nonhierarchical processes, working close to the ground in direct contact with the parties in conflict. This suggests that useful "coordination" is unlikely to be achieved across the board among organizational headquarters, but ad hoc among particular missions—and NGOs as well—working in particular situations. A concerted effort of imagination to discover how to achieve joint action at that level is the necessary next step in mobilizing international organizations for preventing ethno-national conflict.

Part One

Preventive Diplomacy and the Organization for Security and Cooperation in Europe: Creating Incentives for Dialogue and Cooperation

Diana Chigas, with Elizabeth McClintock and Christophe Kamp

RATHER THAN ushering in a new world order of democracy and peace, the end of the cold war brought new tension and violence throughout Europe and the former Soviet Union. Wars are raging in Bosnia, Nagorno-Karabakh, Moldova, Georgia, and Tajikistan, inter alia, and escalating tensions in many more countries have caused serious concern in the international community. At the same time, the end of the cold war has reduced the importance of and the threat posed by regional conflicts to the major powers' basic security interests. In an environment of shrinking resources, the major powers are no longer willing to bear the economic and political costs of sustained large-scale intervention to stop regional conflicts that do not seem to affect their national interests directly.

The question of how to respond to emerging ethno-national conflicts in this new international environment is not simple. Neither military action or threats to stop or deter violence, nor economic sanctions, two traditional approaches to dealing with potentially violent conflicts, are likely to be appropriate in post–cold war conflicts. They are too costly for the sanctioners, too difficult to organize and maintain, and it is not clear that they will produce the desired results.[1]

Consequently, governments have increasingly turned to efforts to stem potential conflicts through softer and less costly strategies of mediation. "Preventive diplomacy" has become the watchword of the 1990s, as the international community, and international organizations in particular, struggle to find alternatives to coercion for dealing with the ethno-national conflicts spreading in Europe. Still, three years after the UN secretary-general called for greater emphasis on preventive diplomacy in his *Agenda for Peace,* it is not yet clear what "preventive diplomacy" is and, more critically, how it should be implemented.

International discussion about preventive diplomacy has conceived the issue largely in politicomilitary terms. The *Agenda for Peace* proposes to strengthen preventive diplomacy through strengthening the information-gathering and deterrent instruments available to the United Nations. It defines the requirements of preventive diplomacy as consisting of early warning, fact-finding, and preventive deployment. And, although confidence building also constitutes an integral part of a preventive diplomacy strategy, it too is conceived in politicomilitary terms, as arms agreements and information, or in terms of "minipackages," largely scaled-down versions of more comprehensive packages on which agreement was not possible. International intervention and intermediation is conceived in terms of settlement and enforcement: beginning with a fact-finding mission, whose findings are aired in the Security Council or other political decisionmaking body, followed by an authoritative decision directing the parties to undertake certain actions (such as cease hostilities) and frequently providing for high-level intermediation under a specific mandate. Decision and intermediation efforts are to be backed and reinforced by coercive military or economic measures, if needed.

Underlying this treatment of preventive diplomacy is the tacit assumption that the settlement-and-enforcement-centered model for international intermediation, prevalent during the cold war, can be transposed to earlier stages in a conflict. The first basic premise of this chapter is that it can not. These methods, which were highly appropriate in well-defined politico-military disputes, are not appropriate to deal with earlier intervention in the complex internal, ethno-national conflicts that are endemic to the post–cold war period. They do not provide a mechanism to initiate a process and quickly gain the cooperation of the parties once a conflict is foreseen. Nor are they adequate to address the early stages of a conflict in which the parties may not be ready for settlement. Finally, coercive military and economic measures, generally used to generate a willingness to settle, are difficult to assemble and maintain, and thus cannot provide the deterrent (or incentive) for which they are designed.[2] As the conflict environment and issues change, as well as the timing of involvement, so will the institutional responses and the strategies needed to deal with them. A new model and a new methodology for third-party intervention are needed.

Our second proposition is that the Organization for Security and Co-operation in Europe (OSCE) has developed an alternative strategy that is proving to be very effective in preventing escalation of conflict. Many have expressed disappointment at its failure to become Europe's collective security umbrella, and have criticized it as unable to act decisively or redundant of the United Nations. The OSCE's tools and methods, however, are based on an entirely different philosophy that has grown out of its own peculiar structure and its historical focus on nonmilitary means to influence the behavior of its member states. Rather than settlement and enforcement, it looks to cooperative management and dialogue as the framework for intervention and the means for preventing escalation and violence. This approach has proven to be an effective alternative in an environment in which expectations of quick and comprehensive settlements or of coherent coercive international action against noncompliance are likely to lead to disappointment.

What has been characterized as the OSCE's greatest weakness—the need for consensus decisionmaking and the lack of coercive powers—in this context has evolved into its greatest strength. The OSCE has responded effectively to changing international conditions, and has created new roles and approaches for preventive diplomacy. A better understanding and systematization of the OSCE's experience can help to clarify its role and contribution to the interlocking system of international organizations active in conflict prevention and management. It also provides a more generally applicable model of preventive diplomacy.

The Need for a New Approach

The world has changed. The major conflicts threatening European peace and security have changed. The parties involved in the conflicts have changed. The international environment has changed. And the relationship of international organizations to the parties to a conflict has changed. These changes have serious implications for the role of international organizations in the prevention and management of conflict. In particular, three new developments in the post–cold war international order put into question the traditional approaches to conflict mediation practiced by international organizations during the period of the cold war.

Dealing with New Issues and Circumstances: The Diminishing Relevance of "Solutions"

Ethno-national conflict is not a new or strange phenomenon for the international community. With the end of the cold war, however, the international political environment in which these conflicts are taking place and the nature of the threat they pose to international peace and security have changed, and with them the conditions and requirements of effective international responses.

First, conflicts during the cold war were framed as issues of security, defined in politicomilitary terms. The overwhelming threat to international and national security was nuclear war, and security depended essentially on the behavior of two main players: the United States and the Soviet Union. Interethnic conflict was of concern primarily insofar as it implicated or escalated the larger U.S.-Soviet confrontation. It was sufficient to avoid escalating U.S.-Soviet tensions. The United States and the Soviet Union needed only to agree on how to manage the conflict, and they had the resources and the will to "enforce" their agreement on the disputing parties. As the U.S.-Soviet rivalry receded, the former bloc leaders lost the willingness and capacity to impose peaceful solutions to conflicts. No longer willing to devote human and material resources to stopping conflict, they have also diminished their own ability to influence the behavior of conflicting parties, as the political influence they once had over "client" states diminished in proportion to the diminishing nuclear threat and cutbacks of aid and resources.

At the same time, the nature of the threat to international security has changed. Ethno-national conflicts no longer threaten to unleash a U.S.-Soviet nuclear war. It is no longer the U.S.-Soviet relationship that is at issue; the international community now is forced to deal with core causes of these conflicts, and neither the traditional processes for enforcing human rights obligations nor the traditional processes for resolving conflict during the cold war provide an effective guide to dealing with them. Traditional methods for dealing with human rights compliance issues through confrontation, pressure, and advocacy will frequently only exacerbate conflict, while traditional strategies for international mediation of conflicts, with their emphasis on "carrots" and "sticks" to induce settlements, are inadequate to deal with the long-term psychological, social, economic, and political problems at the root of ethno-national conflicts. What is at stake in these conflicts is not "measurable," quantifiable, or even negotiable, as arms, missiles, or borders were during the cold war. They implicate the most fundamental of human aspirations and needs (such as identity, recognition, security, meaningful participation in political processes), and cannot be "solved" through negotiation of legally binding and enforceable agreements. Post–cold war conflict-resolution strategies will need to focus not on conflict "settlement" but on conflict "management," and pay greater attention to developing structures and processes for dialogue, for rebuilding confidence and relationships, and for enabling the parties to deal constructively with their differences over the long term.

The need for longer-term and less settlement-focused strategies is heightened by the fact that by becoming involved much earlier in the course of a conflict, international organizations are now becoming involved in situations that frequently are not yet "ripe" for resolution.[3] At this stage, parties are often not ready to give up their unilateral strategies and to seek a negotiated outcome jointly with their adversary, because they believe they have the military or political upper hand, and that their unilateral policy options are both achievable and more attractive than any outcome a negotiation process might produce.[4] The search at this stage for agreements, commitments, or a final settlement may not only fail, but could be counterproductive. "If 'not ripe' is the diagnosis . . . getting people in a room together and employing all sort of careful procedural means to foster negotiation will likely be to no avail. The basic condition for a negotiated agreement will not be met since possible agreements appear inferior to at least one side in comparison with its unilateral alternatives. When this is the case, strategy should focus *not* on the negotiation process but instead on actions *away* from the table that can reshape perceptions in a manner that generates a zone of possible agreement."[5] In other words, agreements or settlements may not be an appropriate goal at early stages. The third party often will need to focus its energies not on producing comprehensive settlements, but on "ripening" the situation through building trust, opening communication and correcting distortions in perceptions, helping to build mutual understanding of underlying interests, or shaping attitudes within relevant governments, particularly concerning the feasibility and value of unilateral alternatives.

The Challenge of Gaining Entry

Early intervention in conflicts that, by their nature, touch on such sensitive issues as the essence of the state's identity, sovereignty, and independence significantly heightens the importance and difficulty of process initiation and entry issues for the third-party. Traditionally, third-party mediation has awaited invitation by the parties. At incipient stages of a conflict, however, disputants are less likely to invite the third party to mediate. Earlier intervention generates a number of barriers to entry that do not exist or are muted when warring parties are exhausted, unable to achieve their aims unilaterally, and ready and able (in domestic political terms) to look for a negotiated solution.

Even if early third-party assistance is viewed as potentially helpful for the parties concerned, inviting or publicly accepting third-party involvement is politically costly, a sign of weakness or disgrace or a stimulus for demands and pressures for harmful concessions. At the same time, imposition of an intermediary on the situation at such early stages of a conflict is not likely to succeed. Concerns about infringement of sovereignty and loss of control over their own affairs, as well as of undesired pressure or blame by the third party, are likely to loom higher in the minds of disputants early on, when they have not yet had the opportunity to test the viability of their unilateral policy options.

Worse yet, involuntary interposition of the third party at early stages of the conflict may actually cause the escalation that the intervention was designed to avoid. Impositional measures at this stage are likely to provoke rather than alleviate a conflict. Even mere attention by international organizations, traditionally reserved for serious situations or crises, could inadvertently send a message that a dispute has deteriorated into a serious crisis of international concern and encourage the parties to exploit the attention to gain favor for extreme positions rather than resolve their differences quietly. Post–cold war intervention strategies must not rely on formal invitations and acceptance of mediation, and must be lower-key, flexible, and nonthreatening if they are to be effective.

The Demise of the "Mediator?" The Relationship of the International Organization to the Parties

As international organizations become involved in post–cold war ethnonational conflicts in a system that remains largely intergovernmental, they will find it more and more difficult to undertake pure "intermediation" of the kind practiced by Jimmy Carter at Camp David or by Cyrus Vance, David Owen, and Thorwald Stoltenberg in Bosnia. Although the conflicts and issues affecting international security have international implications, and often interstate aspects, they are no longer interstate conflicts. Today's conflicts are between an internationally recognized government, which is the international organization's main interlocutor, and a nongovernmental group (or groups) not entitled to (and constantly struggling for) such recognition. Any international organization will necessarily think twice before placing itself squarely in the middle of such a conflict and potentially exacerbating the conflict by bolstering the position of the minority group and leading it to harden its demands. More fundamentally perhaps, member governments are reluctant to undermine the legitimacy of other governments by conferring international status on a nongovernmental competing group.

Even when willing to assume the intermediary's role, international organizations run into trouble in the new political landscape. They are obliged to deal formally with only one of the parties, the recognized government, and thus their ability to be a neutral outsider in the conflict is inevitably compromised. A new conception of the third-party role is therefore necessary in order for international organizations to play an effective part in reducing conflict.[6]

The situation is further complicated because international organizations are getting involved in potential conflicts earlier, before the positions of the parties have been clearly defined and hardened, and frequently before the minority population is even well organized, or before it is possible to identify the key parties and their legitimate representatives. If the goal is to forestall a conflict rather than resolve a dispute, there is no need for "mediation" per se. The international organization thus finds itself in the position more of an "adviser" to the government, though not a partisan adviser, on actions it might take to mitigate or prevent escalation of tensions with members of its own population. In this role of nonpartisan advisor, the international organization must fulfill several functions, often simultaneously:

as an *adviser,* recommending to the government actions it might take;

as a *negotiator* with the government, representing the interests of minorities (though not necessarily the parties themselves) and of the international community, and ensuring that these are taken into account in any legislation or other decisions adopted; and

as an informal *intermediary,* between the "kin" state of the minority and the home state, or between government and minority. These multifaceted demands mean that there must be a different definition of the third party's role and approach.

The Emergence of a New Approach: The Organization for Security and Cooperation in Europe

The OSCE began as a fairly traditional security process in 1975, when thirty-five European and North American states signed a declaration, known as the Helsinki Final Act, establishing the Conference on Security and Co-operation in Europe (CSCE).[7] Its origins can be traced back to a Soviet initiative in 1954 to create a pan-European security conference that would legitimize and stabilize the post–World War II bloc divisions. Rejected for nearly twenty years by the West, which viewed the proposals as an attempt to divide the North Atlantic alliance, the Soviet proposal finally gained acceptance during the period of détente in the 1970s, after the Soviet Union agreed to include the United States and Canada, begin negotiations on mutual and balanced force reduction, and include human rights and human-itarian issues in an overall approach to European security.

1975–90: Unrealized Potential

Despite its cold war origins and traditional focus on politicomilitary aspects of security, the OSCE from the outset had several unique character-istics that would later enable it to meet the challenge of developing new instruments and methods for conflict prevention and management in the post–cold war international order.

First, due primarily to United States and western insistence, the OSCE adopted a comprehensive concept of security that included not only military and interstate political relations, but also economic cooperation and human rights within states as well. The Helsinki Final Act established basic princi-ples governing the relations between the participating states, divided into three categories or "baskets": (1) questions relating to security in Europe; (2) cooperation in the fields of economics, science, technology, and the environment; and (3) cooperation in humanitarian and other fields. By including respect for human rights and fundamental freedoms alongside territorial integrity and inviolability of borders as principles of European security, the OSCE was the first interstate forum to define respect for human rights as an essential factor for peace and a basic ingredient of friendly relations among states. Especially after 1980, when the Soviet

Union attacked the United States record on African Americans and Native Americans, thereby abandoning its argument that human rights was solely a matter of internal affairs, the OSCE's jurisdiction has been well established, and its approach from the start has focused on how human rights issues affect peace and security. This concept gave the OSCE broad jurisdiction from the outset, making it particularly appropriate to deal with the ethno-national conflicts that have plagued Europe since the end of the cold war.

Second, the OSCE was established as a political agreement, not a legal treaty, and as a process rather than an organization. It is essentially a regime for cooperative, not collective, security, designed to promote security through ongoing dialogue and persuasion, not coercion. It has no enforcement powers nor any power to issue decisions that legally bind its members. Commitments made by participating states are only politically binding, and the OSCE did not and does not have any mandate for enforcement of the commitments through sanctions, military enforcement action, or collective response against aggressors or other violators of OSCE norms.[8] In addition, until very recently, the OSCE had no institutional home. The Helsinki Final Act established a process of follow-up meetings to review implementation of OSCE commitments, set new norms, expand cooperation, and maintain political dialogue. Its recent transformation from a "Conference" to an "Organization" for security and cooperation in Europe has not changed its character as a political process.[9] Set up as a forum for multilateral discussion, the OSCE has been forced by its very nature to develop alternative methods for inducing compliance with its principles, based on persuasion rather than coercion. This political character gave the OSCE a special advantage in dealing with sensitive internal issues after the end of the cold war, for which judicial or enforcement processes would neither be appropriate nor feasible.

Finally, from the outset, the Helsinki Final Act established a decision-making process based on consensus, defined as the absence of any objection that would constitute an obstacle to taking the decision in question.[10] The consensus principle ensures that the big powers would not be subject to the tyranny of the smaller states, and that the latter would have a guarantee that their own views would matter in the final substance, at least in respect to those issues about which they cared the most. The consensus principle not only gave the OSCE the flexibility to change its structures and procedures dramatically when circumstances changed after 1990, but would be the source of significant, yet noncoercive, peer pressure on governments to act. While limiting the OSCE's ability to judge or sanction violators of its norms and procedures, the consensus rule gives great legitimacy and weight to OSCE norms, especially those concerning human rights, and has generated a significant amount of pressure on governments to respond and comply with norms to which it, too, has agreed. The consensus rule, while potentially paralyzing, turned out to be a significant source of power and persuasive influence for the OSCE, permitting it to *induce* compliance rather than enforce it.

These three elements form the core of a fundamentally different approach to dealing with conflict, one based on complexity and comprehensiveness rather than simplification of issues, on politics and dialogue rather than law and enforcement, and on moral rather than legal authority. The full potential of the approach, however, was not realized until after the end of the cold war. During the first years of its existence, the OSCE process consisted of a number of follow-up review meetings and intersessional meetings to address specific topics. Following the traditional "settlement-and-enforcement" paradigm of negotiating decisions and evaluating and pressuring states to comply with OSCE norms, the OSCE developed into what has been described as "an amorphous process of diplomatic brinkmanship—once likened to a 'floating crap game'—moving from city to city with no fixed beginning and no fixed end."[11] The OSCE would continue to suffer from U.S.-Soviet confrontation, accusations, and denunciations, leading to considerable disappointment that led the United States in particular by 1986 to consider ending the process altogether.

Nonetheless, although the OSCE process produced no "results," the standards embodied in the Helsinki Final Act, agreed to by all OSCE states, set the agenda for international discussions and did spawn and sustain the growth of dissident groups such as Charter 77 in Czechoslovakia and Helsinki monitoring groups in the Soviet Union and the Baltic states, whose championing of the principles of the Helsinki Final Act contributed to the collapse of communism in the East. By 1986, as Gorbachev's reforms were taking hold, and U.S.-Soviet relations were improving, the atmosphere and dynamics within the OSCE changed. Confrontation was replaced by cooperation, and Soviet intransigence faded in tandem with the release of many political prisoners and easing of other oppressive practices. From 1986 to 1990 the OSCE realized significant achievements, expanding human rights norms and establishing procedures for raising issues of noncompliance, especially in the area of the rule of law and human and minority rights, as well as advancing negotiations on reduction of conventional armed forces and beginning talks on confidence- and security-building measures (CSBMs). Since the fall of the Berlin Wall, it has also served as the basis for an innovative approach to conflict prevention and management.

A brief look at the recent historical evolution of the OSCE will illustrate the significance and originality of these principles as the basis and catalyst for the OSCE's evolution into one of the primary instruments for preventive diplomacy in Europe.

1990–92: Transition to a New Approach

1990 marked a turning point for the OSCE. It was catapulted into center stage following the fall of the Berlin Wall, and many looked to it to be Europe's new security umbrella. However, as the nature of the conflicts within and among states changed, it was clear that it either had to create new structures and mechanisms to deal with the new challenges or risk being rendered obsolete. With the breakup of the Soviet Union and Yugoslavia, the OSCE's membership increased to fifty-three states, making the creation of new and more efficient structures even more urgent.[12] Western Europeans and the United States also looked to the OSCE to provide eastern Europeans with a substitute for greater integration into western Europe through membership in the European Union or NATO.

Enhancement and institutionalization of the OSCE met with significant opposition, especially from the United States, which was concerned that it might eclipse other European forums and rival NATO as Europe's primary security organization. Consequently, as the OSCE moved toward greater institutionalization at the Paris Summit of 1990, what emerged was a rudimentary and limited structure with mandates that clearly reflected the serious compromises that were required to reach agreement.

The "Charter of Paris for a New Europe," adopted in November 1990 by the OSCE heads of state, aimed at "defining the OSCE's identity in a new international environment."[13] It set up a three-tiered process of consultation to provide greater frequency and continuity to its political dialogue.

—*Follow-Up Meetings and the Council of Foreign Ministers (Ministerial Council).*[14] The OSCE heads of state or government would meet every two years in "Follow-Up Meetings,"[15] and foreign ministers would meet at least once a year as the "Council of Foreign Ministers" to mandate and prioritize the activities of the OSCE for the following year, prepare the summit ("Follow-Up") meetings every other year, and address issues brought up by the Committee of Senior Officials.[16]

—Committee of Senior Officials (CSO; now Senior Council). The third
tier of political consultation, the Committee of Senior Officials, was composed of senior diplomats who would meet several times yearly to "prepare
the work of the Council, carry out its decisions, review current issues, and
consider future work of the CSCE including its relations with other international fora."[17] The CSO was also given overall responsibility for managing crises.[18]

—Chairman-in-Office (CIO). The affairs of both the Council of Foreign
Ministers and the Senior Council would be coordinated and managed by the
Chairman-in-Office, the minister of foreign affairs of the country holding
the Chairmanship of the OSCE, who would also carry out much of the
follow-up to CSO decisions.[19] (The Chairmanship of the OSCE is held by
the country hosting the preceding Council of Foreign Ministers and Senior
Council meeting.)

Concerns expressed by the United States and some others ensured that the
consultations, although seemingly ambitious, would be in no way comparable
to the frequent meetings of EU officials or the UN Security Council.[20]

The Charter of Paris also set up three OSCE institutions. Kept rigidly
separate, and located in separate cities, they were designed and structured to
foreclose the emergence of powerful, independent OSCE bureaucracies:

—Secretariat. A Secretariat was established in Prague to service CSO
meetings, maintain documentation, and provide information to the public.

—Conflict Prevention Centre (CPC). Located in Vienna, the CPC was
established to "assist the Council in reducing the risk of conflict."[21] Its
primary function lies in the military realm, supporting military aspects of
conflict prevention. Because of disagreement about whether the CPC should
take on more political conflicts, its role was confined to helping to implement confidence- and security-building Measures and to coordinating the
exchange of military information.

—Office of Free Elections (OFE). Located in Warsaw, the OFE was set
up at the insistence of the United States primarily as a short-term venture to
monitor elections in the new democracies of eastern Europe and the former
Soviet Union, and to ensure that human rights issues would remain on the
OSCE's agenda.

The Charter of Paris effectively transformed the OSCE from a forum for
confrontation and pressure to an organization for security through cooperation and promotion of democracy. It succeeded in ensuring that more
frequent dialogue would take place, and provided the administrative support necessary to support it. It did not, however, effect any fundamental

change in the way the OSCE operated nor give the OSCE the capacity to play a significant role in dealing with Europe's new security challenges. When political consultations began in January 1991, the limitations of the OSCE's structures and process, and of its basic approach to dealing with conflict, quickly became apparent. Inability to agree even to convene a special meeting, much less to take concerted action, to respond to the Soviet actions in Latvia and Lithuania left many delegations frustrated and discouraged. Frustration only increased as the OSCE tried in vain to address and contain the rising violence in the former Yugoslavia.

The first response was to try to strengthen the OSCE's coercive "enforcement" capacities through development of mandatory processes aimed at compelling states to observe its norms and decisions. These mechanisms proved to be largely ineffective. OSCE emergency meetings and decisions reached by "consensus-minus-one" had no effect on the worsening conflict in the former Yugoslavia. Some mechanisms were never even used. It became increasingly apparent that the basic approach to issues of compliance and conflict, carried over from the cold war days, was less relevant to the ethno-national conflicts in post–cold war Europe. It was reactive, waiting until something had happened before taking action, and it was purely declaratory, without any operational effect. By the beginning of the Helsinki Review Conference in the spring of 1992 (Helsinki II), the OSCE states were realizing that the consensus rule was not the main problem. Rather they needed to find a new philosophy and approach to dealing with conflict.

1992 and Beyond: The Development of a New Approach

Beginning at Helsinki II, the OSCE began to turn away from the "settlement-and-enforcement" paradigm toward developing and strengthening its processes for political dialogue and developing a clear operational capacity to respond quickly, flexibly, and noncoercively to emerging conflicts. The new OSCE was consolidated at Budapest in 1994 under a new name, and its change of approach affirmed. It would be "a primary instrument for early warning, conflict prevention and crisis management in the region,"[22] with a "flexible and dynamic" approach.[23]

Helsinki II and subsequent Council meetings created several institutions and instruments that would form the cornerstone of the OSCE's preventive diplomacy and conflict management approach. These included: (1) the High Commissioner on National Minorities (HCNM); (2) the Permanent

Committee; (3) an expanded role for the Chairman-in-Office; and (4) the long-term in-country mission. Along with the long-term missions, the HCNM is perhaps the most important and innovative of the OSCE's new preventive diplomacy instruments. It was created explicitly as an "instrument of conflict prevention at the earliest possible stage," to provide early warning and early action on tensions involving national minorities that could escalate into conflict endangering peace and security.[24] It is the first and only OSCE institution with authority to initiate preventive diplomacy activities on its own judgment and without a prior mandate. The establishment of the High Commissioner was both controversial and formative of what would be the core of the OSCE's new approach to preventive diplomacy.

The creation in 1993 of the Permanent Committee formally gave the OSCE a permanent body for political consultation for the first time.[25] The Permanent Committee, based in Vienna, evolved into the OSCE's primary decisionmaking body, and by 1994 there was hardly any practical difference between the Permanent Committee and the CSO. This situation was recently codified at Budapest, where the Permanent Committee, renamed Permanent Council, was designated the "regular body for political consultation and decision-making."[26] The Permanent Council conducts comprehensive and regular consultations, and takes decisions on all issues relevant to the OSCE. The CSO, renamed "Senior Council," now acts as a broad policy forum for the OSCE, with representation at a higher level.[27]

Along with the enhancement of the political consultation process came the strengthening of the role of the CIO, who at Helsinki II was given the broad task of "coordination of and consultation on current CSCE business."[28] The CIO was given authority to dispatch personal representatives, on his or her own initiative, to assist him or her in dealing with a crisis or conflict, and could obtain assistance from the preceding and succeeding Chairmen, operating together as a Troika, or from ad hoc steering groups, to carry out entrusted tasks.[29] Since 1992 the CIO has evolved into the OSCE's executive branch, and is currently entrusted with "overall responsibility for executive action."[30]

The fourth instrument developed after 1992, the "long-term mission," was created to provide an on-the-ground OSCE presence and support in troubled regions. These missions, mandated by and accountable to the Permanent Council (formerly to the CSO), reflect a wide spectrum of conflict-management roles, tasks, and objectives, as each is designed to address the specific situation in the region in which it is deployed. Along with the other three new or expanded institutions, these would be the heart of the OSCE's system of conflict prevention and management.

In addition, in the period following the Helsinki II summit, the functions of the OFE and the Secretariat, originally extremely limited, were expanded. The post of secretary-general was created in December 1992 to support the CIO and to act as Chief Administrative Officer charged with managing the budget and overseeing the OSCE institutions in Prague, Vienna, and Warsaw, as well as maintaining contact with other intergovernmental organizations.[31] Fears, again expressed most loudly by the United States, of creating another United Nations Secretariat, led the OSCE states to limit the secretary-general to a purely administrative function, but the heavy burden on the CIO, coupled with the need for continuity between CIO terms, has resulted in a slight relaxation of the proscription on political activities.[32] The OFE, expanded and renamed the Office of Democratic Institutions and Human Rights (ODIHR) in January 1992, assumed additional responsibilities in supporting democratization and monitoring compliance with OSCE human rights norms and serving as the OSCE's liaison with nongovernmental organizations.[33] As concerns grow about the slow pace of democratization and continuing human rights abuses in many countries, greater efforts have been made to integrate human rights considerations into the preventive diplomacy activity of the OSCE. ODIHR currently assists in the preparation and support of long-term missions and, working closely with the Chairman-in-Office, participates in discussions of the Senior and Permanent Councils.[34]

An organigram depicting the basic structure and formal relationships among the various OSCE organs is presented in Figure 1-1. The organigram cannot capture the complex web of informal relationships and interactions that have been the hallmark of the OSCE, nor the dynamic, continually evolving character of its institutional structure. Yet the OSCE's unique capacity for conflict prevention lies precisely in these informal and flexible interactions among the institutions, and with and among the OSCE governments of the member states.

Implementing Preventive Diplomacy

The 1992 Helsinki Document marks the OSCE's recognition that the traditional regimes and instruments for compliance and for the peaceful

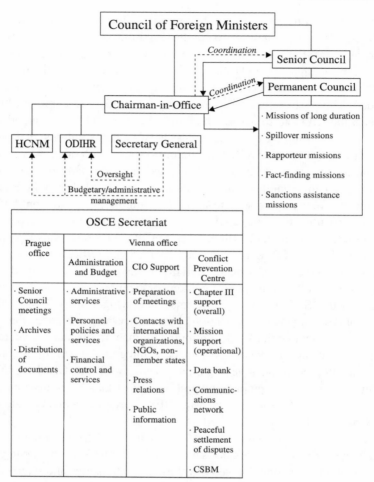

Figure 1-1. OSCE Institutions

settlement of disputes were not effective to deal with the conflicts that emerged after the cold war. It established a framework for an innovative and unique alternative approach that tries to respond to new conditions and conflicts in Europe. The defining feature of this approach is that it seeks to influence governments' behavior through dialogue and persuasion, and that redefines the role and activities of the "mediator."

A Structure for Politics: Managing Compliance and Preventing Conflict through Dialogue and Consultations

After a brief flirtation with compulsory mechanisms allowing some decisions to be taken without consensus, the OSCE chose to retain the political consultation process at the center of its preventive diplomacy machinery. To date, the OSCE has not developed a UN-type secretariat, nor does it have any plans to do so. And there have been no serious attempts since 1992 to dilute the consensus rule.

The OSCE's choice to retain its essential character as a political process with consensus decisionmaking, even among fifty-two participating states, and to build its conflict-prevention strategy around that, turns two pieces of conventional wisdom on their head. The first is that to be more effective and credible and to eliminate the influence of vested interests, international organizations need to develop stronger independent powers (for example, a stronger secretary-general, greater right of independent initiative and control of policymaking and resources by international civil servants) and become truly supranational. The second is that achievement of effective conflict prevention and resolution requires the development and application of instruments with "teeth," such as binding legal obligations, obligatory procedures, and coercive enforcement measures, such as sanctions or military action.

The OSCE's challenge to these basic tenets reflects a different perspective on the realities and possibilities for the role of international organizations within the international political system. It assumes that coercive enforcement strategies will be too costly and ineffective in a large number of cases, and that it is impossible to insulate international organizations from the structure of an international system in which some states are more powerful than others or from the influence of states' pursuit of their own self-interest. The likelihood of states accepting any procedure that imposes on them binding decisions on issues touching on national and cultural identity and sovereignty is low. Even if it were possible to "enforce" desirable behavior in ethno-national conflicts, assembling the broad international consensus necessary to legitimize such action and implement it will be difficult. Finally, with the OSCE's growing emphasis on earlier intervention and prevention after 1992, coercive options became inappropriate instruments, likely to escalate rather than reduce tensions.

Conflict-prevention and management policies of international organizations are controlled ultimately by the member states. States decide whether to devote time and resources to settle a conflict. They decide whether to act alone or through an international organization. They decide through which organization to act and how much financial and material support to give to a conflict-resolution effort.[35] And it is the member states, as parties to conflicts, who decide whether the interests at stake are important enough to risk the consequences of refusing to accept the decision of an international organization, or even to cooperate with it.

Consensus is the world the way it is, at least with regard to issues that implicate core national interests. In this realm, states will not be forced to change their behavior; they will need to be persuaded to do so. Consistent with its own pragmatic focus, the OSCE has accepted this political reality for what it is. Rather than try to prevent or suppress the influence of politics and of member states' pursuit of their own fundamental interests, the OSCE has chosen to try to harness and channel the political process to become an effective instrument of preventive diplomacy. Its strategy has been to build on its existing structures for multilateral discussion and especially its inability to undertake any enforcement action or even to impose any decision on a participating state. Instead, it has replaced the traditional "enforcement" or "punishment" model that seeks to induce proper behavior through coercive measures with what Abram Chayes and Antonia H. Chayes have termed a "managerial model" of compliance.[36] The "managerial model" relies on "jawboning" and political discussion to persuade governments to comply with OSCE norms or to behave in ways that reduce conflict. The OSCE's institutional reforms since 1992 have been directed toward strengthening this dialogue process.

THE PERMANENT COUNCIL AND THE CIO: CREATING AN EFFECTIVE ENVIRONMENT FOR "JAWBONING." Since 1975, political dialogue and the consensus rule, as a fair and noncoercive process for rule making, has been a source of the OSCE's power to regulate state behavior and deter undesired behavior. The consensus requirement drives the dialogue process and has been critical in the establishment of an effective managerial system. It gives great legitimacy to the OSCE's norms, especially those on human rights and minorities issues, which form the basis for the OSCE's involvement in internal conflicts. It sets a tone of persuasion rather than coercion and ensures that governments have a significant say in the formulation of policies that affect them. Consensus decisionmaking not only makes it difficult to refuse to engage in the process, but its inclusiveness can encourage conformity and "buy in," thereby deterring noncompliance with the resulting norms and decisions, even though they are not binding. In fact, within the OSCE process, states withhold their consensus only on those very few items on which they feel so strongly that they are willing to "cash in" political credibility and capital that might have been used to obtain support for future policies and, in the extreme case, risk isolation. This essentially political process creates a tremendous amount of "peer pressure" to conform—not become the spoiler—and in this way acts as an effective and valuable instrument of preventive diplomacy and conflict resolution. Even in situations of violent conflict, such as Chechnya, it has proven to be a useful tool to gain entry into highly sensitive situations and to exercise a restraining influence on the parties to prevent further escalation or widening of the conflict. In Chechnya, this political process has facilitated Russian participation in a Permanent Council resolution condemning the "disproportionate use of force by the Russian Armed Forces" in Chechnya,[37] as well as unprecedented Russian acceptance of an on-site "OSCE Assistance Group" to monitor human rights and promote dialogue and negotiation—the first time Russia has accepted an international presence on her territory and international mediation of an internal dispute.[38]

The creation of the Permanent Committee (now Permanent Council) in December 1993 enhanced the OSCE's capacity to manage compliance by giving it a *permanent* forum for political dialogue and decisionmaking. It also gave the OSCE additional capability to detect, monitor, and respond quickly to emerging and rapidly evolving conflicts. The Permanent Council performs a number of important functions in conflict prevention. At the simplest level, mere participation in the Permanent Council's discussions can provide an incentive to governments to moderate behavior that may escalate conflict, by drawing international attention to incidents or issues at an early stage, and by communicating the degree and intensity of concern by the international community. The continuous presence of the issue of Russian troop withdrawal from the Baltic states on the agendas of the Permanent Council week after week served this function, and it reinforced other OSCE and state efforts to broker an agreement.

The Permanent Council also serves as a forum for the generation and wide dissemination of information about OSCE norms and expectations, which frequently can in itself be an effective deterrent for governments contemplating further escalatory action. This has ranged from information sharing and further discussion on Russia's peacekeeping operations and the implications of the Greek decision to cut trade with Macedonia through Greek ports, to raising of specific incidents, such as the expulsion of three Canadian journalists from Azerbaijan, or an incident in Latvia relating to two generals.[39] The recent adoption of provisions at the Budapest Council Meeting mandating that "human dimension issues will be regularly dealt with by the Permanent Council" expands this transparency-maintenance function by giving it a clear role in monitoring and discussing compliance with the OSCE's human rights norms.[40]

Finally, and perhaps most important, the creation of the Permanent Council allows the member governments to raise small issues or incidents that may escalate conflict and to "deal with questions when they are small and to keep them small."[41] The Permanent Council's working methods have tried to ease fears of states that raising concerns about the internal situation of another country might escalate the situation or provoke an unwanted confrontation. A regular agenda item, entitled "current issues," has made it possible to raise issues in a more low-key and discreet fashion, without calling public attention to the situation or sending a message that the situation has deteriorated into a crisis. On delicate topics on which countries have been reluctant to initiate a discussion, active interventions primarily by the United States, Sweden, Russia, and Turkey, have ensured that the political discussion within the Permanent Council has remained current and dynamic.

The role of the Chairman-in-Office also facilitates the raising of potentially contentious issues at early stages. Often items will be put on the agenda by the CIO, who manages and proposes items for the agenda of the Permanent Council and the Senior Council and provides discussion papers on the basis of which decisions are made. In addition, delegations frequently will address their concerns informally to the CIO. The CIO may act as an informal channel of communication, able to explore participating states' concerns quietly with the party concerned, giving it a "last clear chance" before an issue is raised in the Permanent Council's plenary session.

By all accounts, the Permanent Council has developed into an effective problem-solving forum. The Permanent Council meets once a week in plenary session, and informal briefings by mission heads or meetings of subgroups or working groups concerned with particular OSCE activities ensure daily consultation and dialogue.[42] The sessions have been described by participants as very frank, open, and "undiplomatic," leading some experienced diplomats to remark that the Permanent Council holds the most detailed and substantive international discussions held anywhere on conflicts in the OSCE region.[43]

A CUMBERSOME PROCEDURE? STREAMLINING AND OPERATIONALIZING POLITICS. The risk of relying on such a complex multilateral process as a primary instrument of preventive diplomacy is that decisionmaking will be slow and based on the lowest common denominator. It is also said to be inflexible and difficult to modify in the face of rapidly changing circumstances, resulting in rigidity and incoherence of policy responses. In an attempt to minimize these drawbacks of consensus decisionmaking, the OSCE has increasingly devised ways to delegate both the formulation and implementation of policy initiatives to smaller groups or individuals. This alleviates the need for the OSCE to act as a whole all the time while still retaining the advantages of an ongoing, consensus-driven "jawboning" process.

Formulating policy in smaller groups. The Helsinki Document goes quite far in trying to streamline and speed up the operation of the consensus rule in decisionmaking. It anticipates the transaction of a great deal of OSCE business in groupings smaller than fifty-two states and provides for the creation of ad hoc steering groups to assist the Chairman-in-Office in carrying out conflict prevention, crisis management, and dispute resolution.[44] These smaller groups have been an important feature of the OSCE's policy formulation process, and have helped considerably to rationalize the decisionmaking process in the OSCE. Smaller working groups and steering groups have been established to address institutional issues (for example, a Group on Budgets, Finance Committee, Working Groups to prepare for follow-up summit and review conferences), to develop recommendations for decisions by the Permanent Council on specific issues (for example, on coordination with the United Nations in Bosnia), and to assist in the implementation of OSCE policy. A steering group of ten states continually helped to refine the mandate of the OSCE's Spillover Mission in Macedonia, and to give it ongoing guidance, and in Nagorno-Karabakh, a small group of nine countries, known as the "Minsk Group" has been responsible for managing the negotiation process.[45] At an informal level, the creation of ad hoc "friends" groups to facilitate discreet discussions among member states involved in a particular situation has become a common means of undertaking political discussion and preventive activity.[46] These practices, of course, do not eliminate the need for consensus decisions, which in some cases may be necessary to ensure that conflict prevention activity has sufficient political support and credibility. However, they do open a space for significant political activity within the OSCE involving less than the full contingent of fifty-two participating states in the phases before or in preparation of consensus decisions.

"Delegating" implementation. In implementing or operationalizing preventive diplomacy, the trend toward giving small groups of people considerable discretion for day-to-day management of OSCE issues has been marked. The OSCE's philosophy and standard operating procedure is to address larger political questions and decide on guiding principles and frameworks in the Permanent or Senior Council, while leaving day-to-day implementation to the in-country missions or the Chairman-in-Office. Mission mandates agreed upon in the Permanent Council are often vague and lacking in operational specificity. OSCE members rely on the mission heads to develop and refine the mandate on the ground, subject to reporting requirements to the Permanent Council and day-to-day supervision and guidance by the Chairman-in-Office.[47]

The discretion afforded to implementing bodies has often been broad, at times extending to actions that go beyond, or even contravene, the strict terms of the mandate, when they make practical sense. In the Latvian case, for example, the mission's activities evolved in a way not specifically foreseen in the mandate. Although it was mandated to advise the Latvian government on citizenship issues, provide information and advice to institutions, and to report on the situation to the OSCE,[48] the mission also became involved in facilitating negotiations between Latvia and Russia over the disposition of the Skrunda military base. It is also helping to monitor the international aspects of Russian withdrawal from the base.[49] Similarly, in Macedonia, the Spillover Mission has organically expanded its initial military mandate. When internal tensions began to threaten Macedonia's stability as much as, if not more than, the possibility of spillover of the Yugoslav conflict, the mission turned its attention and resources to facilitating disputes between the government and Albanian minority.[50]

The Role of the Chairman-in-Office. The OSCE's primary "delegatee" and the prime force in the transformation of its multilateral dialogue process into an operational instrument for preventive diplomacy has been the Chairman-in-Office. The Helsinki Document and subsequent Council decisions give the CIO a clear role as leader, facilitator, and coordinator of the political consultation process and as the primary agent responsible for implementing Senior Council and Permanent Council decisions.[51]

The role of "political executive" is a significant innovation in the realm of international organizations, and has been an important factor in the OSCE's success. It has helped the OSCE streamline the cumbersome consensus rule without losing the advantages of a highly political, consensus-driven consultation process. The CIO has also served as a link between the OSCE as international *organization* and the OSCE participating states in a way that maximizes the likelihood that any action taken by the OSCE has the political support and resources needed to make it effective.

Unlike the secretary-general of the United Nations, who is accountable to the Security Council but independent of it, the CIO is not only accountable to the political structure but is a representative of it and, moreover, has a vested interest in it. The CIO is the embodiment of the political process: a foreign minister, based in a state's capital, with direct access to political decisionmakers in capitals, acting as chair, facilitator, and implementer of a political process, but without any formal independence from it. There is little risk that the CIO will try to set up a competing authority to the OSCE's political bodies or act contrary to their interests. On the contrary, the CIO provides a credible link to political capitals, and often plays the role of catalyzing the political process and mobilizing resources for OSCE action.

The CIO has much latitude, both formally and informally, to initiate and guide OSCE policymaking, in order to help avoid lengthy and arduous multilateral negotiations that had previously resulted in too little action taken too late in the former Yugoslavia. Complaints are frequently first addressed informally to the Chairman-in-Office, who then may decide to request the High Commissioner to take on the issue, or initiate informal mediation or negotiation him or herself with the parties concerned, thereby completely bypassing the formal procedure of the Permanent Council.[52] The CIO may also send a "personal representative" to investigate situations, prepare recommendations for action, and engage in informal mediation efforts.[53] Since 1992 personal representatives of the CIO have visited, often more than once, Estonia, Latvia, Georgia, Moldova, Tajikistan, Nagorno-Karabakh, Ukraine, Uzbekistan, Armenia, Azerbaijan, Russia, Macedonia, Bihac, and Chechnya. In some cases the recommendations of the personal representative have served as the basis for the establishment and definition of a mandate for an OSCE mission of long duration. In Nagorno-Karabakh and in the Transcaucasian states, the appointment and visit of the personal representative was used to try to mediate a political solution to the conflicts in those areas, and in the case of Latvia the appointment of a personal representative helped to overcome the reluctance of that country to allow any OSCE presence.[54]

An active CIO will also take the initiative to mobilize OSCE institutions (such as the High Commissioner or ODIHR) to act, as well as to marshal the necessary political support for preventive diplomacy action. During the Swedish chairmanship in 1992, for example, foreign minister Margaretha af Ugglas' 1992 trip to central Asia helped to draw the OSCE's attention to the situation there and stimulated a number of significant OSCE activities in the region. The High Commissioner's involvement in Kazakhstan and Kyrgyzstan beginning in April 1994 was also undertaken in large part due to CIO af Ugglas' urging. The current CIO, Hungarian foreign minister Laszlo Kovacs, has taken the initiative to involve the OSCE in Chechnya, where only UNICEF, and now the Red Cross, have been allowed to go. The CIO has initiated several missions to Chechnya and Moscow in early 1995 that explored possibilities for humanitarian assistance, discussed future democratic developments, and examined the human rights situation in Chechnya.[55] Kovacs was personally involved in the negotiation of the terms of reference of the missions to Grozny, in particular the on-site "OSCE Assistance Group" that has been mandated to promote human rights and democratic institutions, facilitate humanitarian assistance, and facilitate negotiations between the parties.[56] He continues to provide active support to the mission's mediation efforts, through bilateral contacts with Moscow and mobilization of European Union and OSCE political support. These activities have positioned the OSCE as mediator of the conflict, have helped to prevent further escalation of the violence, and have contributed to some improvements in the humanitarian situation in the region.

The CIO's role as *political* executive has also made possible the Senior Council's willingness to delegate policy formulation to smaller subgroups of states, and to take a "hands-off" approach to implementation of preventive diplomacy, as carried out by the High Commissioner, the missions, the ODIHR, or the CIO him or herself. The CIO effectively now oversees the accountability of all subgroups, missions, and independent OSCE institutions to the political process.

The CIO acts as the primary contact and oversight for the long-term missions in the field. The CIO is in weekly telephone contact with the missions, and is responsible for giving them day-to-day guidance on their direction and activities. In addition, formally, the CIO is the High Commissioner's only interlocutor during his or her pre-early warning involvement.[57] The CIO also sits on *all* the ad hoc steering committees and frequently acts as a mediator between them and the full Senior Council to facilitate approval of the committees' recommendations. Thus the CIO is able to perform the dual function of ensuring that the OSCE's political bodies are kept abreast of developments and activities, and of obtaining political feedback and input to the operation of the smaller groups quickly, efficiently, and informally.[58] The CIO's status as a *political* executive, who cannot act credibly without the Permanent Council's political backing (at least in the face of states' opposition), and who, moreover, rotates every year, seems to have alleviated participating states' concerns about losing political control over OSCE preventive diplomacy and made them more willing to accept a considerable amount of independence by ad hoc subgroups and by operational missions. These practices have greatly simplified and improved the OSCE's decisionmaking process and its ability to provide effective and timely early warning and action.

The New Mediation: The "Insider Third Party"

The most important and innovative contribution of the OSCE to the theory and practice of preventive diplomacy has been its development of a new role and methodology for conflict prevention that we call the "insider third party." The role combines some of the basic characteristics of traditional mediation by international organizations with those of an "insider" to the conflict working for change from within the governmental and political processes in the state concerned, and in some cases actually becoming part of the government process. It maintains two essential characteristics of an outside mediator of the conflict: impartiality and lack of vested interests in the substantive issues at stake. This allows the third party to move easily back and forth among the parties. The "insider third party" role also maintains the traditional function of the international organization as watchdog and monitor of the conflict, while ensuring transparency and providing an impartial analysis of the situation, as well as exerting by its very presence pressure on the government to modify its behavior.

At the same time, the insider third party is not a mediator. It benefits from the advantages that insiders to the conflict enjoy: in particular, an "insider's" special knowledge and understanding of the situation and concerns of the parties; knowledge of and access to policymaking circles within the country; influence not based solely on the status of representative of an international organization, or on the capacity of the international organization to exert pressure on the country; and, finally, a capacity to take the initiative to identify and address issues that could lead to greater conflict between the government and minority. The insider third party acts as a trusted adviser and partner-in-dialogue, rather than a detached mediator. It operates with the government primarily, but also with the various minority groups and others involved in the conflict. In this role, the third party seeks not to resolve the conflict but to improve all parties' policies and actions regarding the ongoing relationship among them. The process serves to empower moderate parties inside the conflict itself and to resolve the conflict by strengthening the voices of moderation on all sides and creating and preserving a space within which they can sustain a dialogue and jointly develop and carry out policies without being undercut by extremist elements on their flanks. This may include providing political and other support for moderation of government policies or of minority reactions to the government, or serving as a scapegoat for attacks on potentially unpopular policies. It may also include stepping in as an "insider" to fill gaps in the democratic system of a country, actively working to ensure that moderate, conflict-reducing government policies function effectively, and in many cases even performing governmental functions whose absence would surely escalate the conflict.[59] At times, as is evident in the OSCE's experience in Estonia, the "insider third party" can become a true insider, a quasi-formal part of the governmental process.[60]

For the OSCE, it became abundantly clear after 1990 that the traditional intermediation role and strategies were not appropriate for internal ethnonational conflicts. The role of the outside, neutral facilitator was neither practically nor politically feasible. Although the OSCE, more than any other international organization, had clearly established its own jurisdiction to deal with such conflicts,[61] and consequently was in a better position to intervene as an intermediary, concerns about undermining the legitimacy of the government and establishing an unsettling precedent that ethnic minorities could circumvent constitutional policymaking processes weighed against assuming such a role. In addition, the OSCE's emphasis on preventive diplomacy undertaken *before* a conflict erupts, and its own adoption of cooperation and persuasion, rather than coercion, as its basic approach made it politically difficult for the OSCE to become an outside neutral mediator. Governments were sure to resist early intervention in internal affairs by the OSCE, and the OSCE was not prepared to impose a process on them against their will.

The "insider third party" role emerged almost organically from the OSCE's need to respond pragmatically and immediately to post–cold war international relations in an atmosphere of quickly escalating tensions in a number of eastern European countries. The innovative conception of a mediative role without being a true "mediator" was developed in two new instruments: the High Commissioner on National Minorities and the in-country "missions of long duration."

THE HIGH COMMISSIONER ON NATIONAL MINORITIES. The history of the office of the High Commissioner on National Minorities is one of the development and evolution of the adviser-facilitator role. The written mandate contains a fairly traditional, linear process for engagement and subsequent mediation of conflict: an information-gathering stage leading to "early warning" alerting political bodies of an impending dispute, followed by a political decision authorizing and defining the parameters of a mediatory effort, and finally, implementation of a formal program of "early action."[62] Experience quickly proved, however, that the model was unworkable in practice. The distinction between "early warning" and "early action," although conceptually clear, is frequently blurred in practice, and it is often quite difficult to determine when tensions have evolved beyond the "early warning" stage to merit a formal notice to the Senior Council.

In practice, the first High Commissioner, former Dutch foreign minister Max van der Stoel, has chosen to view the mandate as a living mandate and to develop a customary practice where the mandate is silent or insufficient to deal with the situation at hand. He quickly recognized that the core of the High Commissioner's role had to be the promotion of "dialogue, confidence and co-operation" between the parties,[63] and he has never provided an "early warning" notice or requested authority to conduct early action. The High Commissioner has even said that he would consider his efforts to have failed should he feel obliged to issue an "early warning" notice under the mandate.[64] Rather than encouraging deescalation of tensions, an early warning notice would only operate to increase them, since at that point parties may be unable to retreat publicly from their positions.

The mandate, however, provides no guidance on when and how to "promote dialogue, confidence and co-operation" among often ill-defined parties without escalating the conflict, nor on how to overcome a fundamental dilemma of the insider third party: to fulfill such a mediative role when the only formal interlocutor, and the only party over which the OSCE may have any formal authority, is the government of the state concerned.[65]

Van der Stoel has built on the High Commissioner's right of initiative, and the independence it gives him, to manage this dilemma. The High Commissioner enjoys discretion to decide which situations he will address, what approach he should take, and when the "early warning" stage has ended. In making these decisions, the High Commissioner consults informally with the CIO especially, and with interested OSCE states as well as the governments concerned.[66] Nonetheless, subject only to minor restrictions and an obligation to consult with the CIO, the High Commissioner needs no prior approval or instructions from the Permanent Council. The High Commissioner is able to operate quite independently from the rest of the OSCE, a faculty reinforced by the location of his office in The Hague, far from the Permanent Council in Vienna.

The HCNM is also independent of the government and minority population. Unlike other OSCE instruments, the High Commissioner does not directly represent the governments of the OSCE states, and consequently is not beholden to the government concerned. At the same time, as an independent "instrument of conflict prevention," the HCNM is not an advocate for minorities, an international ombudsman, or an OSCE human rights "policeman." His role has not been merely to judge or remedy issues of compliance with OSCE obligations. Van der Stoel has been quite clear: he is the High Commissioner *on* National Minorities, not *for* National Minorities: "If OSCE commitments such as contained in the Copenhagen Document are violated, the High Commissioner has, of course, to ask a government concerned to change its line, reminding it that stability and harmony are as a rule served best by ensuring full rights to persons belonging to a minority. However, he has also to remind the members of a minority that they have duties as well as rights."[67] This independence has not only facilitated early intervention and rapid response to evolving circumstances, but has allowed the High Commissioner to establish his credibility as an *impartial* third party vis-à-vis *all* interested parties, including the OSCE itself. As such he is well positioned to develop a role as a preventive "mediator" to "promote dialogue, confidence and co-operation" and help the parties search for mutually satisfactory solutions.

In the implementation of his role, van der Stoel has created an approach and methodology for the insider third party that reflects a clear conception of the nature of the conflicts with which he is dealing and the limitations of his own role in preventing and resolving them. His goal is not to "resolve" complex ethno-national disputes. Instead, he has seen his main task to be in the realm of short-term conflict prevention, to prevent acute escalation of tensions, and, looking to the longer term, to help set in motion a process of dialogue between the government and minority that will address the long-term relationship between them and deal with the root causes of the tensions.[68]

Building credibility and influence: getting to know the parties. Van der Stoel's involvement has generally encompassed a process of visits and regular telephone communication for purposes of familiarizing himself with the situation, developing of relationships with the parties, communicating of recommendations to the governments concerned, and follow-up to address issues or tensions that arise during the course of his involvement or during the implementation phase of his recommendations.

The first visit or two to a country is principally aimed at getting to know the different actors, listening to their points of view, and becoming familiar with the major issues of concern, the apparent obstacles to resolution, and the potential dangers of nonresolution. His strategy is one of developing personal relationships with the major interested parties in order to engage them in a cooperative process of conflict reduction and implementation of commitments. This reflects van der Stoel's own belief that durable solutions require meaningful and voluntary consent by the parties and that "cooperative implementation of commitments and recommendations will in the end be more fruitful than enforcement."[69]

Conferring international recognition on a particular party or leader as the legitimate representative of the minority's interests in a mediated dialogue with the government may be difficult and could escalate the conflict. Therefore, the High Commissioner engages in consultations with a wide range of affected parties. He typically meets with the highest-ranking government officials, including the president, prime minister, foreign minister, other ministers (those for interior, education, culture, and so on), members of parliament, and other government officials responsible for minority-related policy. The HCNM also meets with opposition party leaders, a wide array of minority representatives including appointed or elected officials, heads of nongovernmental organizations, and religious leaders, as well as a number of individuals. Outside actors, such as "kin states" of minority populations, who have significant interests and influence over the evolution of the conflict, are also consulted. The informal consultation format has been quite useful, particularly in providing a structure in which necessary parties, who for political and other reasons cannot sit "at the table," can be included and engaged in the larger conflict-prevention process.[70]

Making cooperation easy: a low-key role. Consistent with the confidentiality provisions of his mandate,[71] the High Commissioner has preferred to take a low-key and confidential approach to his role, in order to gain the trust and cooperation of the parties, as well as to discourage maintenance of strong demands and exploitation of outside attention that could escalate the conflict. He has eschewed both formal characterization of his efforts as "mediation," "early action," or "early warning," and he has avoided interacting at a formal level with the CIO or the Permanent Council, in order to avoid escalating the conflict by forcing the parties to make public declarations or initiate "negotiations" over sensitive internal affairs. With some limited exceptions,[72] the High Commissioner has eschewed extensive contacts with the press, and when approached by media representatives, he has limited himself to general comments on the importance of reasonableness. More extensive contact or commentary in the media would endanger his status as an impartial party and could impair his ability to gain the cooperation of the parties in his process.

"Mediating" with one party: advising the government. Ultimately, the High Commissioner can interact officially only with the government concerned. He has prepared recommendations to the government in question, usually in the form of a letter to the foreign minister, suggesting specific changes in the substance of the government's minorities policy on issues such as language, education, and citizenship, in order to address pressing minority concerns that might lead to further escalation of the conflict.

The preparation of policy recommendations is not foreseen in the mandate, which contemplates a more traditional fact-finding and mediation role for the High Commissioner. However, given the structural constraints on the High Commissioner's relationship to the parties, it is the only *formal* instrument available to the High Commissioner (aside from the early warning notice) for carrying out his preventive diplomacy functions.

Van der Stoel clearly does not view his recommendations as an end in themselves, nor merely as benchmarks for compliance, but as a framework within which the government and minority can begin to address their long-term problems constructively.[73] The very specific legal, policy, and institutional changes suggested are intended to "address minority concerns and thereby improve conditions for dialogue."[74] They are an instrument in a multiparty dialogue process rather than a judgment or "court order." In addition, because the impact of the juridically nonbinding recommendations rests on their power to persuade, they must demonstrate an understanding of the underlying interests at stake and propose solutions that meet those interests.

The tone and content of the HCNM's recommendations reflect their mediative purpose. They seek to build positive incentives for government action by emphasizing the government's own interest in addressing issues that concern its minority population. They frequently also address the responsibilities and obligations of minority groups to refrain from actions or positions that can exacerbate tensions, although they are formally addressed to the government. In Estonia and Latvia, for example, the HCNM emphasized the political risks of treating noncitizens, who are predominately ethnic Russians, as less than full members of society, a situation that, van der Stoel pointed out, could increase the danger that Estonia's Russophone population could become alienated and radicalized.[75] At the same time he stressed that reduction of tensions would require an equal "contribution on the part of the non-Estonian population," namely, that Russian-speakers achieve mastery of the Estonian language at a simple conversational level.[76]

In nearly all cases, the HCNM has supplemented his recommendations on minority policy with suggestions on measures either the government or the OSCE might take to initiate or institutionalize dialogue on underlying causes of tension. These typically have included the establishment of round tables, ombudsmen, or minority rights offices to hear individual complaints.[77] This reflects van der Stoel's belief that it is not sufficient to address the short-term causes of escalation and that, ultimately, real resolution must happen within the framework of the state itself, in dialogue between the state and the minority. Although the High Commissioner has neither the resources nor the mandate to manage such a long-term process of dialogue and negotiation, he cannot ignore these fundamental long-term issues. Consequently, the launching of a process that can deal with the root causes in the long term has been an important component of his approach.

Keeping the conflict tractable: crisis prevention. In addition, and as part of his long-term preventive diplomacy approach, the High Commissioner has intervened on occasion as an informal mediator to contain and deescalate crises that might polarize the general relationship between a government and minority population, or interstate relations between the state and the kin state. The High Commissioner intervened in Estonia in mid-July 1993 to facilitate the resolution of an impending crisis that had been sparked by the call for referenda on "national-territorial autonomy" by the Russophone-dominated city councils of Narva and Sillamäe following the Estonian parliament's passage of a controversial law on aliens in June 1993.[78] Similar interventions took place in Macedonia, Ukraine, and Albania to help cool emotions and prevent further escalation. These interventions have frequently involved consultations with the minority's kin state as well.

Ongoing involvement and follow-up. Finally, the High Commissioner's involvement does not stop with issuance of the recommendations. The recommendations have been the start of a longer-term process of dialogue between the High Commissioner and the parties, in which he can nudge them step-by-step to implement his recommendations. In spite of the mandate's clear provision for limited interaction with the parties in the early warning stage, the High Commissioner has made multiple visits to all the countries in which he is involved, and has not yet ended his involvement in any situation.[79] In some cases he has suggested the creation of expert teams to provide ongoing attention and advice on the implementation of his recommendations and the general improvement of dialogue.[80]

THE IN-COUNTRY MISSIONS. The "missions of long duration," as the in-country missions are commonly called, were not foreseen in the Helsinki Document. They were developed organically by the OSCE to respond to the perceived needs of specific situations, such as initially the situation in the former Yugoslavia.[81] There are currently nine local missions operating within the OSCE region. Four missions, operating in Estonia, Latvia, Macedonia, and Ukraine, have been characterized as preventive diplomacy missions. The remaining missions are deployed in areas in which armed conflict has broken out: in Georgia, Moldova, Tajikistan, Chechnya, and Sarajevo.[82] Missions sent in 1992 to Kosovo, Sandjak, and Vojvodina (Federal Republic of Yugoslavia) have not been operative since the Serbian government withdrew its consent in June 1993.[83]

Although the conditions in which they operate differ significantly, the purposes of the missions—preventive diplomacy and crisis management alike—are essentially the same and similar to those of the High Commissioner: to deescalate tensions and keep the conflict tractable in order to permit negotiations and longer-term conflict resolution to take place. Their structure and functions, however, differ significantly from those of the HCNM, giving them a special and complementary role to the HCNM in the OSCE's conflict-prevention activity.

First, the missions intrude far more into the internal affairs of the country in question than the HCNM or any other instrument of conflict prevention. They are resident in the country for at least six months and in practice for considerably longer, as the Senior Council has extended all the missions' mandate once or several times beyond the initial six-month period.

Second, they are also visible and operational *throughout* the country. They usually have a main office in the capital, but spend a great deal of time traveling to remote areas to gather information, monitor developments, and talk to officials and residents, at both the national and local levels. These include not only the head of state and government ministers, but also members of parliament, local political leaders, media, nongovernmental organizations, and individual residents. In the words of the Estonian head of mission, "the contacts should be adequate on all levels and in every direction in order to make it possible for the Mission to warn the OSCE but also the Government, if in the opinion of the Mission a crisis or confrontation were to develop."[84] Some missions also establish additional local offices outside the capital to maintain a presence and capability for ongoing observation of particular trouble areas.[85] This has allowed the missions to become involved with the practical implications and implementation of policy decisions that may have been taken at the urging of the High Commissioner. Although the Head of Mission frequently interacts with the highest levels of government on sensitive policy issues, the bulk of the mission's activity involves monitoring, advice on legislative drafting and implementation of regulations, and pleading the cases of individuals with local officials charged with enforcing rights or implementing regulations.

Third, the scope and reach of their activities are also broader than those of the High Commissioner. Where the High Commissioner's mandate limits his activity to issues involving national minorities, both by mandate and in practice, the missions address a broad range of issues, from military, economic, social, and political issues to issues of minority policy.[86] In addition, for missions with apparently narrow written mandates, broad language and a shared emphasis between the missions and the Senior Council have allowed them to become involved in areas not originally contemplated.[87]

Fourth, unlike the HCNM, the long-term missions have no independent authority. Created and mandated by the then CSO, and recently by the Permanent Council, they are an instrument of the political process and consequently are dependent upon the continuing consent of the government concerned, which can withdraw it at any time. And although governments are constantly under pressure in the Permanent Council not to withhold consent to the missions' activities, even more than the High Commissioner, the missions are forced to work cooperatively with the government and refrain from too much criticism of it, so as not to jeopardize their continued existence. The missions walk a fine line: if they are seen too much as advocates for the minority population, they may be terminated by the government, but if they fail to raise and pursue sensitive issues, they will lose the confidence of the minority population. In either case they lose their ability to act in a mediative role as facilitators of dialogue and reduction of conflict.

The most effective missions have overcome this dilemma through careful definition of their role and function, turning themselves into "insiders"
to the conflict, acting as full participants in the situation or as a voice to
catalyze moderating influences within the conflict itself. Rather than remain detached from the parties and the conflict, they have become a player
involved with *all* the parties, from the national and local governments to the
various minority groups. In this way the most successful missions have
managed to *build* an effective third-party role because of the knowledge and
confidence the parties have gained from the breadth and depth of those
relationships.

Mission members are selected by the Chairman-in-Office in consultation
with the host government based on their knowledge and experience of the
area and of the issues causing tensions between minority and majority
populations in the country. They all are required to speak the relevant
languages of the country, an obvious qualification that frequently has not
been met in United Nations missions in the former Soviet Union.[88]

Although differing widely on tasks and activities, the mandates specifically order the missions to establish and maintain contact with affected
parties as one of their primary tasks, in order to establish a base for
promoting dialogue and solving problems.[89] They spend most of their time
either on the road traveling from town to town to talk with officials,
nongovernmental organizations, and citizens, or receiving private individuals who come to the local offices to register their complaints of mis-
treatment. The relationships thus developed have been a key source of
credibility and influence. These relationships give the missions access and
a knowledge and understanding of the situation that no single actor in the
situation has, the High Commissioner included.

The core of the missions' methodology is to build on these relationships
and the access to information they provide to persuade, prepare, and assist
the parties to deal with their conflict through dialogue and negotiation
rather than violence. They allow the missions to fill certain missing functions within the society and the international community that would normally serve to moderate behavior or allow the parties to deal with conflicts
constructively.

Information for early warning and deterrence. "Transparency—the generation and dissemination of information about the requirements of the
regime and the performance of the parties under it—is an almost universal
element of management strategy."[90] One of the primary tasks of the missions is to maintain the transparency of the conflict situation, by gathering

and disseminating accurate information on the situation to the OSCE, as well as to ensure that parties are well informed of OSCE standards and views. This in turn contributes to the effectiveness of the Permanent Council's "jawboning" process as an instrument of conflict prevention. The availability of reliable information on the situation facilitates coordination and consensus-building among the fifty-three OSCE states.[91] It enhances the quality and timeliness of the resulting decisions, by ensuring that the Permanent Council receives early notice of brewing tensions and that the decisions are well informed and relevant to what is happening on the ground. It also can operate as an effective deterrent for actors contemplating noncompliance or escalatory behavior.[92]

The missions submit weekly (or sometimes biweekly) confidential reports to the CIO, frequently with extensive detail about the activities of the mission, the discussions and interactions with a wide range of people affected by the tensions, and about the situation at the given moment in the area. These are usually circulated to the other OSCE institutions and to the Permanent Council.[93] In areas where the High Commissioner is involved, the missions act as his eyes and ears, following progress on implementation of his recommendations and reporting back to the HCNM and the Permanent Council on progress made. Although the missions are typically quite small, averaging eight people,[94] the mere presence of the missions serves as a reminder that the international community is closely monitoring developments, and has served as a deterrent to escalation.[95] In some cases, decreases in the level of human rights abuses have been attributed to the presence of the missions. In others the OSCE missions have established themselves as the only source of impartial information, and in this way have contributed directly to diffusing tension.[96]

Information: facilitating communication and decisions about negotiation.
A second, critical function filled by the missions is the provision of reliable information *to each of the parties* about the conflict and about the other parties. The role is not one of an intermediary carrying messages back and forth, but of a "partner-in-dialogue" who provides information that may influence the party's decision whether or not to escalate. Parties' decisions about whether to negotiate or escalate are influenced by their perceptions of each other's interests and intentions, the viability of their own unilateral strategies, and of the possible existence of negotiated options that could satisfy their interests. Yet in tense situations of ethno-national conflict, effective and useful communication and information are frequently the first to be compromised, as partisans seek to present evidence to support their

positions, distrust breeds rumors and myths, and the internal (often local) nature of the tensions makes it difficult to get a full picture of the situation. The task of the third party is frequently, at least initially, one of restoring communication and helping to correct distortions and misperceptions that escalate emotions. The relationships and special access to information of the missions have given them special influence and credibility, enabling them to open up communication and calm emotions by helping the parties understand the perceptions and interests of the others. Moving easily from one side to the other, they can decrease suspicions, lessen mutual fears, and help parties get unstuck from bargaining positions. The missions have also been active in disseminating information to the public about existing rights and procedures for minorities or about legislative changes within the state itself. The Estonian mission, for example, took out a full-page ad in the newspaper encouraging noncitizen residents to register to vote in the local elections that took place in October 1994.

A voice and force for moderation: the mission as "ombudsman" for minorities and adviser to the government. Where voices of moderation are silenced and credible mechanisms for peaceful settlement of disputes or complaints of the minority do not exist, the missions frequently step in to fill that function within the host society. Several in-country missions have developed an open door policy for "walk-in visitors" to register complaints and seek the OSCE's advice about government activity with respect to minorities.[97] Listening to individuals' cases constitutes a major part of the mission staff's work. Where a valid case can be made, the mission will frequently take up the matter with appropriate officials, and although there is often nothing the mission can do about an individual's case, the mere fact of their having listened and been concerned about the minority's plight is often enough to satisfy the individuals, particularly in a system that has no office or mechanism for listening to minority concerns and does not seem concerned to hear them. This kind of activity has helped to prevent a buildup of grievances that could escalate tensions at the national level if not dealt with or channeled appropriately.

At the same time, "the missions are, and must be, seen to be supportive and helpful in the efforts of the host country to come to terms with internal problems."[98] They provide ongoing advice and cooperative assistance to the government on a broad range of issues, including formulation and implementation of legislation concerning constitutional law, citizenship, aliens, minority rights, and the establishment of councils for interethnic dialogue.[99] In areas in which the High Commissioner is also involved, the missions have assisted the governments to implement his recommendations. In Estonia, for example, the mission, working closely with the Council of Europe, is helping to establish a system for language training.[100] In Latvia the mission has assumed a key role in the negotiation and implementation of the Russian withdrawal from the Skrunda military installation, and the Estonian mission has become the third member of a commission in charge of implementing a Russian-Estonian agreement on social guarantees for Russian military pensioners.

Local crisis diffusion. Finally, at times the missions will be called upon to mediate specific crises that could escalate the general level of tension within a country. In Macedonia, for example, the OSCE mission facilitated an agreement between the government and Albanian leadership to defuse a riot that had broken out in Skopje in November 1992 as a reaction to what Albanians thought was excessive police force against an Albanian boy who was smuggling cigarettes. OSCE missions have helped to negotiate the release of hostages in Moldova and the pullback of tanks in both Moldova and Kosovo. As an on-the-ground presence with extensive contacts, the missions are in the best position to detect developments that might lead to escalation of tensions and to intervene quickly and effectively with all sides as a moderating influence.

Creating conditions for effective conflict resolution. One of the most important roles of the missions is to lay the groundwork for negotiation and conflict resolution. In some cases, notably in Georgia, Moldova, Tajikistan, and Chechnya, where fighting has broken out, they assume a mediation function between the parties, but without great success. The preventive diplomacy missions in Estonia, Latvia, and Macedonia continue to be the OSCE's "success stories." In those situations three factors existed that are not likely to be present in the crisis management missions: (1) the timing of the missions—their involvement at incipient stages of conflict, when the situations are still conducive to dialogue and policy changes are less costly; (2) significant political support and cooperation from influential countries such as the Scandinavians and the United States, which have also engaged in significant parallel bilateral contact in support of the missions' activity; and (3) the host governments' willingness (or perceived need) to cooperate with the OSCE. In Georgia, Moldova, and Tajikistan, where violence has already broken out and the situation is less amenable to dialogue, the more influential and active OSCE members have been reluctant to confront Russia or to invest the greater resources and political capital needed to support the missions' activities effectively, and consequently these "crisis

management" missions have not been able to bring parties to the negotiating table and to fulfill what is ostensibly their primary task: to promote an
overall settlement of the conflict.[101]

The failure of the crisis management missions to broker settlements
obscures an extremely valuable prenegotiation or premediation role the
missions play in preparing the ground for later negotiation: changing
parties' perceptions and reducing fears, exploring options for settlement,
and helping governments to set up legislative and regulatory frameworks
that could, for example, make it easier for breakaway republics to consider
a nonsecession alternative, in short, opening a space in which the forces of
moderation might eventually take hold. All the missions have succeeded, to
some extent, in exerting a moderating influence on the parties, and in some
cases have been able to stimulate dialogue. At times they have served as the
only point of contact between the parties, and have served as ombudsmen
and mediators to settle individual grievances or crises that could further
escalate the conflict.

The mission to Georgia has recently been given a specific mandate to
"promote respect of human rights and fundamental freedoms and assist in
the development of legal and democratic institutions and processes" and to
coordinate with the HCNM and ODIHR in these matters.[102] Working with
ODIHR, it has also developed a proposal for special status for Ossetia,
which, according to the secretary-general, "is receiving attention in political
circles in Georgia" and has sponsored direct talks between the parties that
resulted in agreement to cooperate in fighting organized crime, restoring
rail and road communications, economic reconstruction, housing, and refugees.[103] The Ukraine mission's "Locarno Conference" and proposals served
as a basis for agreements between Kiev and Simferopol that led the Crimean parliament to cancel a referendum on Crimean independence, thus
significantly deescalating tensions in Ukraine. Similarly, the mission to
Moldova has been particularly successful in engaging the breakaway
"Trans-Dniester Republic" in intensive dialogue, with a view to trans-
mitting information about the other parties and on the possibilities of a
negotiated process, and recently formally opened an office in Tiraspol (the
Transdniestrian capital). Since mid-1994 the mission head has been active
in facilitating an Expert Group on the future status of the breakaway
republic within Moldova, which has reported some progress toward the
development of a single text and, more recently, in facilitating a summit
between Moldovan and Transdniestrian leaders.[104] The mission has also
organized a seminar on, *inter alia,* principles of a democratic constitution,

and on decentralization, autonomy, and federalism. It also provided significant support for delegations that had gone to observe the parliamentary elections on February 27, 1994, and has been quite active in advising the government on language legislation and other human rights issues.[105] These activities have helped to lay the groundwork and create an environment for an effective conflict-resolution process to take place once the parties decide to come to the table.

The OSCE as "Insider Third Party"

The HCNM and the missions differ greatly in structure, stature, scope of action, and approach. It is not a coincidence, however, that these two instruments have become the OSCE's main success stories and its main instruments of conflict prevention. Despite their differences, they share a basic approach and method that has been able to gain the cooperation of the parties concerned, especially of governments, and to persuade them at least to avoid conflict-escalating actions, if not to adopt policies that can establish a long-term dialogue between the government and minority population. Both instruments have turned away from the view of the third party as a "resolver" of conflict. They are both concerned less with using power than with using persuasion as a means for inducing changes of policy, less with judging compliance with legal obligations than with generating practical decisions, and less with formality than with acting with the flexibility needed to address the situation at hand and as a facilitator and adviser over the long term.

This does not necessarily mean that they are liked. Indeed, in the Baltic states, the HCNM, if not also the missions, are seen as advocates for the Russian-speaking minority population. Nonetheless, both the HCNM and the missions have become "insiders" to the situations in which they are involved, in the sense that they have "insider" relationships and understanding of the issues and societies, as well as influence that is more characteristic of an insider than of a "mediator." Finally, they act *in cooperation* with the parties concerned, especially the governments, as partners-in-dialogue to facilitate and provide support for the emergence of moderate voices and actions within the society itself. A close examination of their experiences reveals four basic structural and methodological characteristics that define the High Commissioner's and the missions' role as "insider third parties."

LIMITED MANDATES. Ironically, limited mandates of both the HCNM and the missions are a source of great "power" and influence and, indeed, would seem to be an essential condition for an effective "insider third party." Both the High Commissioner and the missions do not rely on their authority to bind the parties, but on their ability to persuade. Their influence is based on their power to develop close relationships with a wide range of parties and engage them in an ongoing process of dialogue. Coercive strategies of shaming, publicity, or sanctions can prevent the functioning of this process. The parties themselves can also stimulate resistance by governments to early OSCE involvement in conflict situations because of the political risks of backing down from their previous positions on highly emotional issues, or of entering into a process that may lead to international criticism, pressure, or imposition of an unsatisfactory or biased solution. For an international third party to gain entry into a conflict at early stages of its development and work cooperatively with the parties to prevent further escalation, the action will need to be seen by the parties concerned, at least initially, as exploratory, nonbinding, and noncoercive.

At the same time, any effective strategy must recognize that a purely cooperative approach, with no "teeth," such as that represented by the High Commissioner and the missions, will not provide sufficient incentives to the parties to bring about deescalation and improvement in government-minority relationships. Indeed, much of the legitimacy and authority of the HCNM and the missions derive from their relationship to the OSCE, and the success of their activities has been due to a large extent to the unequivocal support from the OSCE participating states and to parallel actions by the CIO and individual OSCE members with the governments concerned.[106] What is new and effective in the OSCE's approach is its *separation* of the coercive and mediative functions and its casting of the HCNM and the missions as clear and unambiguous facilitators for positive action. This strategy has made the role of "insider third party" possible, while at the same time enhancing its persuasive power. It has empowered the cooperative, problem-solving role by providing a pressure incentive for action by the parties without affecting the parties' relationship with and confidence in the HCNM and the missions.

If a government follows HCNM or mission recommendations, it is less likely to be accused of giving in or backing down to unfair pressure. The HCNM's and missions' lack of authority to bind or judge allows them to offer the parties a face-saving manner to take deescalatory actions. At the same time, the pressure generated by publicity, shame, and bilateral activity by influential countries is always present. It is, however, kept in the background, allowing the OSCE to create "friendly," rather than coercive, pressure on the parties to cooperate with the HCNM or the missions. The HCNM and the missions remain untainted by the more coercive strategies. *They* do not possess or exercise any coercive authority, and pressure that may be applied is not tied directly to their activities. The OSCE's political organs, for their part, have also refrained from interfering with or linking their discussions of substance of the disputes, or their more coercive activities, to the High Commissioner or the missions. Indeed, at the recent Budapest review meeting, a proposal to have regular reviews and discussions of governments' implementation of the High Commissioner's recommendations failed because of concerns that the prospect of such action would make governments less cooperative and open with the High Commissioner. The Permanent Council has in practice "delegated" supervision of the missions to the Chairman-in-Office and has refrained both from interfering in the missions' implementation of their mandates and from involving the missions in their discussions and debates on those countries.

The significance and effect of the OSCE's approach can better be appreciated by comparison with similar mediative efforts undertaken by the United Nations. For example, the United Nations secretary-general has been mandated by the Security Council to offer his good offices in the search for a resolution to more than thirty years of intercommunal strife in Cyprus. The mandate under which the secretary-general's representative operates, however, also condemns the Turkish intervention on the island in 1974 and the continued presence of Turkish troops on nearly 40 percent of the island. It calls for the withdrawal of Turkish troops and refuses to recognize the Turkish Cypriots' unilaterally declared state. In the same breath, the mandate attempts to create a mediative role for the United Nations and condemns the behavior of one of the parties, thereby bringing pressure for it to change its policy. This has in effect made the United Nations a party to the conflict in alliance with one side. By taking a stand on the substantive issues in the dispute, the mandate limits the flexibility of the UN mediator and makes it more difficult for him to gain the confidence and openness of at least the Turkish parties.

In contrast to the "power" of the OSCE, and particularly of its member states, which remain in the background providing pressure for moderation in a nonthreatening way, the coercive "power" of the United Nations overshadows the mediation process. It reduces the persuasive power of the UN representative, his ability to develop a cooperative, problem-solving relationship, and thus the attractiveness of the options or recommendations he may offer.

PROCESS AND POLICY VS. SUBSTANCE AND SETTLEMENT. The second characteristic of the "insider third party" role shared by the HCNM and the
missions is their focus on policy and politics, rather than rights, and their
concern with the *process* by which the parties are dealing with their conflict, rather than the substance of the legal, economic, and social issues
regarding treatment of minorities. Both the HCNM and the missions have
made clear that although their work involves human rights issues, they are
conflict-prevention, not human dimension, instruments. This is to underline
that their aim is not to determine whether there has been "compliance" or
whether the government's actions are "legal." Although international legal
standards and OSCE norms serve as indispensable points of reference for
them, as "insider third parties," the HCNM and the missions have steered
away from determinations or interpretations of rights and have focused
on satisfying the interests and alleviating the fears of all the parties
concerned.[107]

In addition, any recommendations are very operational and realistic, and
suggest a step-by-step approach supported by ongoing assistance (mainly
by the missions) on the formulation and implementation of policy initiatives. The tone and content of the recommendations emphasize the effect
that current policies have on the government's ability to command the
loyalty and cooperation of the minority population, and the political risks of
the policies toward minorities, in an attempt to help the government see
how it is in its own interest to adopt policies more favorable to their
minority populations. Indeed, in some cases (notably Estonia), the HCNM
and the missions have clearly and explicitly determined that although there
has been no systematic violation of human rights, further action by the
government would be necessary and constructive. The High Commissioner's and the missions' repeated reminders to the minority population
that they, too, have responsibilities to the state and to the government sends
a clear message that they are not merely seeking to pressure the government
to change its policy. Instead, they are seeking to address the interests and
fears of all parties, including the government.

Coupled with this policy-oriented and interest-based approach is an
emphasis on process rather than settlement. This is what makes the "insider
third party" different not only from the traditional judge-policeman role
frequently played by international organizations, but also from the mediation or good offices role. Both the High Commissioner and the missions
have a process orientation focused on communication and building better
relationships. They do not aim for short-term solutions, nor for a com-

prehensive settlement of the conflict. Their approaches focus heavily on the promotion of dialogue between the parties and on building and strengthening the moderate voices within the societies themselves. On the other hand, they have not shied away from addressing the substantive issues that have led to government-minority tensions or from mediating settlements to specific disputes. Indeed, especially in Estonia and Latvia, they have made quite specific and concrete suggestions for legislative and regulatory changes. These activities, however, are viewed as part of a broader approach to establish a long-term process of dialogue and moderation on both sides.

INITIATIVE AND PARTY CONTROL. The coexistence of an independent right of initiative with significant party input and control over the process is perhaps the *sine qua non* of the insider third party role. Independence and freedom to act allow the High Commissioner and the missions to remain flexible and to respond quickly in a timely fashion to emerging tensions. Independence is also essential to the maintenance of their impartiality and their ability to separate their own mediative role from the more coercive activities of the OSCE and its constituent members. The OSCE "insider" can take the initiative to deal with escalating situations without first having to gain the formal approval of the parties or the OSCE states. For the HCNM, this right is formally inscribed in his or her mandate.[108] Although the missions operate directly under the instructions of the Permanent Council or CIO, in their day-to-day functioning they work in a fashion similar to that of the HCNM. Independence is the key to impartiality. Together they allow the "insider" to act as a third party and to interact with a wide range of actors.

On the other hand, their position as instruments within the formal framework of the OSCE creates significant moral pressure on the parties, and especially the host government, to act responsibly and to cooperate, precisely because, given the consensus procedure, the chances of their being forced to accept something they do not like are so low. And indeed, although the Baltic states and Albania, for example, have expressed some dissatisfaction with the lengthy involvement of the High Commissioner and the missions and have tried to persuade the OSCE to withdraw them, they have not been prepared to refuse them.

The final factor in the equation is that the parties have significant input and control over the process. The host government can at any time withhold or withdraw consensus for a mission's mandate or financing, and although the High Commissioner's independence is well established in the mandate, there are several ways in which the host government can limit involvement.[109] And the nongovernmental parties can thwart the process by simply failing to participate. Such party control over the HCNM and the missions would seem, at first glance, to undermine their independence and impartiality and potentially turn them into a tool of the government. In practice, it seems to enhance the influence of the insider and may even be the most important factor making it possible for these OSCE instruments to achieve insider status. The parties' retention of ultimate control over the process alleviates fears of loss of control over internal policymaking on issues of such importance as identity and security and fears that unfavorable substantive results will be imposed, both of which tend to incite resistance by parties to third-party involvement. It is easier for the host government to cooperate when it knows that it will be kept informed and have significant input on an ongoing basis and that it can terminate the activity at nearly any time.

INFORMALITY AND DISCRETION. Although both are well known and followed by the press in the countries in which they are involved, the HCNM and the missions maintain a low-key and informal approach to their role. Their reports to the OSCE are confidential (the HCNM's recommendations are eventually released, but only later, and his or her trip reports to the CIO are strictly confidential), and their contacts with the parties, as well as with the OSCE, remain informal where possible. This informality and discretion have allowed them to remain flexible, while still fulfilling their obligations of accountability to the OSCE. And because it allows the parties to engage in dialogue and cooperate with the OSCE without immediately backing down from their positions, it is also essential to the HCNM's and the missions' ability to engage the parties in exploring creatively and seriously whether and how they might reduce tensions and resolve their differences.

The Way Ahead

The OSCE has been characterized as the "most creative organization today in the field of preventive diplomacy."[110] It has consistently been able to gain entry into situations traditionally considered to be highly sensitive internal affairs, and governments have shown a willingness to cooperate with the OSCE and consider its recommendations seriously. In all of its preventive diplomacy interventions, the OSCE has succeeded at a low cost in preventing escalation and in keeping alive efforts to manage tensions through dialogue. It has also made some progress, albeit small, in some of the most difficult ongoing conflicts in Europe, with which no organization—the United Nations, the European Union, NATO, the Western European Union, or the Council of Europe—has been able to cope. It has again, albeit slowly, been able to engage Russia cooperatively on hard issues such as Moldova, Georgia, Nagorno-Karabakh, and Chechnya, and to provide a role and influence for international institutions where Russia may otherwise have chosen to go it alone. After two years of undermining the OSCE's process, Russia has now agreed to co-chair the "Minsk Group" mediating a solution in Nagorno-Karabakh and has accepted limited OSCE involvement in Chechnya. Similarly, the missions in Moldova and Georgia, experiencing better cooperation and support from Russia, have been able to make progress after a long period of exclusion and stalemate.

At the same time, the OSCE faces serious limitations and challenges to maintaining its effectiveness in the future. There is a general feeling of disappointment in its perceived inability to deal with the fundamental problems facing Europe today, a feeling only reinforced after the failure of the OSCE states to agree on a common declaration on Bihac at the Budapest summit meeting in December 1994. Some policymakers see the OSCE as the second, third, or fourth choice for security matters, behind NATO, the UN, and the European Union.[111]

The OSCE faces a basic dilemma: its greatest strength is also its greatest weakness, and just as the strengths have led it to become Europe's, and perhaps the world's, premier preventive diplomacy organization, the limitations and problems it faces threaten its relevance to future European security problems.

The Problems

CONSENSUS AND COOPERATION IN A LESS SUPPORTIVE ENVIRONMENT. The consensus rule and the cooperative, nonbinding, dialogue-based managerial approach to compliance and conflict flowing from it have been key to the OSCE's success in preventive diplomacy. However, it also limits the OSCE's ability to play anything other than a preventive diplomacy role and, some claim, limits its relevance to the most difficult and intractable violent conflicts affecting European security such as Georgia, Tajikistan, Nagorno-Karabakh, or Turkish action against the Kurds, to say nothing of the continuing war in Bosnia. The OSCE has few instruments at its disposal, other than its noncoercive, flexible methodology, to give parties incentives to cooperate with it in reducing conflict, or to come to the negotiating table once a conflict has escalated beyond an early warning stage. For nearly two years the "Minsk" process, led by the OSCE, was consistently undermined by Russia, which set up a parallel process of its own. The OSCE was similarly unable to have much impact, and indeed was excluded from the negotiation and peacekeeping oversight processes in Moldova and Georgia, until the Russians decided to cooperate.

Fundamentally, the success of the "jawboning" and the managerial model for conflict prevention depends heavily on political support from and good relations among the OSCE's most influential members, as well as on the desire of host governments to remain in good standing with the international community. In particular, although the OSCE's success stems largely from its ability to engage Russia's cooperation in international conflict-resolution efforts on some of the most pressing and difficult problems in eastern Europe and the former Soviet Union, it has also to a certain extent been "hostage" to Russia's attitude and relationship to the West. As long as Russia sees the OSCE as the primary organization for European and its own security,[112] the OSCE will flourish. As the relationship between the West and Russia becomes uneasy, the necessary cooperation and political support for conflict prevention may become more difficult, and the OSCE's ability to become involved and influence the course of a conflict may diminish.

The OSCE is likely to see its influence wane even in countries in which it has experienced success. The incentives that led the Baltic countries, Slovakia and Hungary, Romania and Macedonia, to cooperate with the OSCE even when they would not have been inclined to do so are diminishing. These states followed OSCE recommendations in part because of their desire to become integrated into western Europe, and as their relationship to western European organizations becomes more settled (or problematic), they are becoming more assertive. After two years of willingly accepting visits and attention by the HCNM, missions, the Permanent Council, and the ODIHR, the Baltic governments are now complaining that they are being singled out unfairly and are pushing for the HCNM and the missions to leave. Albania has also pushed for a final "bill of health" from the HCNM, ending his involvement on the issue of the Greek minority in that country. The changing relationship between Russia and the West, the diminishing pull of integration into western institutions for nations of the former Soviet Union, and diminishing hopes for early integration by east central European nations make it more difficult for the OSCE to fulfill its preventive diplomacy and crisis management efforts. It has led some to argue that the OSCE should develop its capacity to sanction noncooperative behavior.

FLEXIBILITY AND FLUIDITY: LACK OF CONTINUITY AND STAYING POWER.   The small, fluid organizational structures, and especially the role of the "political executive," are innovative and important assets permitting the OSCE to bridge what is often a huge gap between an international organization and the political process among member states, and allowing it to respond rapidly, flexibly, and appropriately to varied and rapidly evolving conflicts. However, the price for the flexibility and fluidity afforded by this institutional structure is that the OSCE depends heavily on leadership by individuals, such as the CIO, and by individual delegations, especially powerful delegations like the United States and Sweden. The officials and the national policies change frequently. And foreign ministries of members who are active in two or more major European institutions, such as the European Union, frequently cannot support the high level of activity required for an effective chairmanship. The Troika provides some continuity in leadership and resources,[113] but the OSCE's capacity for sustained and consistent action suffers.

In addition, the limited financial resources available to the OSCE affect its capacity to have a long-term impact. The OSCE's overall budget for 1994 was a mere $27 million, of which only approximately $550,000 was dedicated to the HCNM's activities and just $6 million for nine in-country missions.[114] The missions are mandated and budgeted on a six-month basis, a policy that facilitates their acceptance by host governments but that also limits their ability to plan and execute longer-term activities. Mission staff is also frequently inadequate and underqualified, leading the secretary-general to complain in his 1993 Annual Report that participating states "have been slow in ensuring that a sufficient number of qualified personnel is available to fill vacancies."[115] Missions are frequently not even staffed up to their small mandated strength, and in many cases activities are designed and implemented by nonspecialists and staff is made available only for limited periods of time.[116]

As a result, the OSCE has not been able to establish processes and infrastructure within the countries themselves for long-term dialogue and transformation of the conflict. With the possible exception of the mission to Estonia, which participated in the formation and ongoing support of an interethnic round table, the missions have not established any effective, self-sustaining institutions or processes to promote interethnic dialogue and deal with tensions when they arise. The Kosovo mission expressed regret that it did not leave anything behind to continue its facilitation work after it left. Again with the possible exception of the Estonian round table, the interethnic round tables recommended by the High Commissioner have fared no better than the missions in establishing long-term dialogue in practice.[117] Plagued by disputes over the round table's scope of authority and representation, by long speeches, posturing and accusations, and by lack of support or responsiveness by the governments or parliaments in each country, they have not made much headway in addressing issues of fundamental concern to the parties.[118]

PROCESS OR INSTITUTION? A BINARY CHOICE. Perhaps the most serious challenge to the future development and effectiveness of the OSCE is its lack of clarity and consensus on how to deal with the basic dilemma. Should the OSCE remain a "process," redesigned to fit the new realities of post–cold war Europe? Or should it be transformed into a more traditional intergovernmental organization similar to the United Nations, the Organization of American States, or NATO? There are powerful arguments on both sides. The OSCE's small bureaucracy, politically based approach, and flexible third-party mechanisms have made the OSCE a leader in preventive diplomacy. However, the weaknesses associated with consensus decisionmaking and the lack of independent institutional structures and resources have led many to push for greater institutionalization and legalization.

Those favoring greater institutionalization are concerned that the OSCE will be marginalized in a future European security architecture if it does not transform itself into a collective security arrangement. While falling short of advocating that the OSCE become a full-fledged security organization with enforcement powers,[119] they believe that limiting itself to preventive diplomacy alone would abdicate an important part of its professed responsibilities as a regional arrangement under chapter 8 of the UN Charter. In the process, it would lose its credibility even in its preventive diplomacy role, as "any strongman could call its bluff with impunity."[120] Although they acknowledge the obvious legitimacy and power of decisions taken by consensus, they also have lingering concerns about the efficiency of the process, as well as about follow-up of OSCE decisions to which states have committed themselves. Accordingly, they seek to strengthen the legal and coercive tools available to the OSCE, and emphasize the development of legally binding commitments, mandatory conflict resolution and security mechanisms, and peacekeeping capabilities. France and Russia in particular seem to support transforming the OSCE into a treaty-based organization.

The recent Budapest review meeting saw a renewal of efforts to do away with the consensus rule. Russia proposed to create an OSCE Executive

Committee of ten members, both permanent and rotating. A less drastic proposal by Austria and Hungary would have permitted the adoption of recommendations and statements without the consent of the violators of OSCE commitments,[121] while the Parliamentary Assembly proposed an across-the-board 90 percent consensus rule.[122]

The move for greater institutionalization, legalization, and development of coercive instruments has been blocked by a few states, led by the United States. They argue that the weaknesses perceived by those favoring greater institutionalization are not real. Despite its enforcement powers and non-consensus-based decisionmaking structure, they argue, the United Nations has been no more effective than the OSCE in dealing with the ongoing conflicts in the former Yugoslavia, Georgia, Tajikistan, Moldova, or Chechnya. Indeed, the OSCE could be said to have been *more* effective by having succeeded in engaging the parties and Russia in continuing dialogue on issues that have been left untouched by other organizations. They point to the OSCE's involvement and presence in Chechnya and its ability to secure Russian acceptance of resolutions condemning Russian use of force as evidence of the power of political dialogue and cooperative approaches. And although it is clear that no mission will be sent to Turkey to deal with the difficult issue of Turkish action against the Kurds, the issue has been raised quite frankly on the Permanent Council's agenda week after week. If consensus is the world the way it is, they argue, adding a legal (treaty) basis, coercive instruments, or more independent institutional structures would be pointless, and even harmful, as it could limit the OSCE's political flexibility. Their arguments have been aptly summarized by a member of the U.S. Congress's Commission on Security and Cooperation in Europe: "Gains from creating a more bureaucratic, legalistic and expensive structure when even the existing entities lack both financial and political support are difficult to imagine. Moreover, it is not clear that a larger bureaucracy would garner more support from participating states, or that the bureaucracy would serve to commit states more deeply to lengthy or costly conflict management endeavors. On the contrary, the salary of each new highly-paid CSCE official takes away weeks' worth of financing for missions in the field."[123]

This debate goes to the heart of the OSCE's definition of its own identity and role in conflict prevention and European security and reflects the depth of concern about the negative aspects of the OSCE's politically based cooperative process, and the difficulty of developing strategies that can minimize (though probably not eliminate) the weaknesses of the OSCE's approach. As the Netherlands Helsinki Committee observed before the Budapest meeting, "Their rhetoric notwithstanding, states do not seem too sure about the particular role of the CSCE in Europe, or, if they are, how far they want to take that role."[124] The Budapest decisions, purporting to clarify the OSCE's mission and structure, retain these contradictory trends. The CSCE states agreed to change the name to "Organization" in deference to Russian and U.S. wishes, but at the same time were at pains to state that "the change in name from CSCE to OSCE alters neither the character of our CSCE commitments nor the status of the CSCE and its institutions. In its organizational development, the CSCE will remain flexible and dynamic."[125]

Meeting the Challenges: Streamlining and Operationalizing Politics (Again)

It is true that the results of OSCE activity are not immediately apparent or always measurable. It is also true that the OSCE's success is, to a large extent, "hostage" to the relations and attitudes of the most powerful participating states. And under its current structure, the OSCE is not well equipped to play a significant peace-making or peacekeeping role, except in very special circumstances. However, it is equally true that the perceived limitations of the OSCE are the source of great opportunities for OSCE action, and the proposed "cures"—dilution of consensus decisionmaking, greater institutionalization, and legalization of obligations—may be worse than the "disease." The price of greater institutionalization and legalization is very steep: at stake are the OSCE's strengths.

The challenge for the OSCE is to find new ways to deal with the weaknesses without undermining the advantages of a consensus- and politically based institutional structure. Despite the disappointment expressed by many at the limited achievements of the OSCE, it does, and will in all likelihood continue to play an important, if not central, role in the European arena. Indeed, the OSCE may be the only international institution that is able to engage Russia and provide an alternative to Russian-dominated peacekeeping and purely Russian influence in its "near abroad." Russia itself encouraged this idea during the December 1994 Budapest Summit.

While the OSCE's relevance and unique importance within the multi-institutional system for conflict prevention and management should not be questioned, there is much that can be done to improve its effectiveness, within the current framework of a process- and cooperation-oriented strategy.

STRENGTHENING INCENTIVES FOR COOPERATION: DEFINING INTER-INSTITUTIONAL ROLES AND RELATIONSHIPS. The OSCE will need to identify and capitalize on practical incentives for states to be "good citizens" of the OSCE. It will also need to strengthen the credibility of the background "threat" of negative consequences that could result from failure to cooperate with the OSCE. This can allow the OSCE to focus on what it does best—conflict prevention—and strengthen the effectiveness of its cooperative, problem-focused approach by positioning it as a government's last clear chance to meet its interests before more coercive measures will be applied.

Especially in Russia and central Asia, but also in eastern Europe where hope for early European Union integration is diminishing, the OSCE might consider closer cooperation with the international financial institutions operating in those regions. If their policies are coordinated with the OSCE's conflict prevention and management efforts, these institutions, and bilateral or multilateral aid programs more generally, can play a role as a background factor motivating these countries to cooperate with the OSCE. The OSCE's experience in Chechnya and the Baltics illustrates the power of such a multitrack coordinated approach. Providing aid for conflict-reducing policies (such as language education programs, infrastructure projects that benefit less well-off minority populations, and others mentioned in chapter 6 in this volume) could make possible the implementation of policies supportive of a minority's rights. Similarly, tying the disbursement of loans and aid to conformity with certain OSCE norms, or cooperation with the OSCE in conflict-prevention efforts in the case of the central Asian states, could serve as a more compelling "carrot" than membership in any of the traditional European economic and security organizations. Indeed, these countries' lack of interest in such organizations is precisely the reason that the OSCE, as the only regional organization of which these countries are members, should explore alternate means of exercising their influence in the region.

This, of course, requires a clearer and more rational division of labor among the various international organizations involved and processes for coordination and "hand off" so that each organization's activity in a particular country can reinforce the message and policy of the others. A clear understanding of roles and processes for coordination and collaboration among international organizations can help avoid dilution of the credibility and influence not only of the OSCE but also of other institutions by eliminating the opportunities for "forum shopping" and minimizing the risk of inconsistent messages from different international organizations. Despite frequent calls for "synergy of effort," "interlocking," and "mutually re-inforcing" institutions,[126] however, no serious effort has been made to implement a rational division of labor. The creation of the North Atlantic Cooperation Council (NACC), the NATO-led Partnership for Peace, and the European Union-initiated Stability Pact has confused the European security landscape, and it is not clear how each will work with the other or with the OSCE. A framework agreement for cooperation exists between the OSCE and the United Nations, and the OSCE consults regularly with the United Nations, NATO, and the Council of Europe (which also participate in OSCE meetings as observers).[127] Mutually supportive relationships between UN and OSCE missions in the field have also developed in Macedonia and Sarajevo, and in Latvia the UN Development Program and the Council of Europe have worked with the OSCE to develop a system for protection of human rights. However, despite an agreement that there would be a "practical division of labour between the two organizations, with one taking the lead on each issue of common interest, and the other playing a supporting role,"[128] the division of labor has been far from practical. In Tajikistan and Abkhazia, for example, where the UN takes the lead, the OSCE has also been active. OSCE representatives have made several monitoring trips to Abkhazia, leading UN officials to complain privately of OSCE interference. The OSCE, for its part, has complained that the UN is assuming responsibilities that the OSCE, at least in theory, could carry out and, where both organizations are involved, that there is little contact, not to mention coordination or mutual support. In Georgia, for example, there have been complaints that the UN has refused to become involved in South Ossetia, and has rejected high-level representation to coordinate action on the two (related) conflicts.[129] "There were no joint reports, a very limited exchange of information, and consequently no substantive diplomatic break-throughs by either organization."[130] Clearly, more is needed to ensure that the organizations develop a common understanding of their roles, strengths, and weaknesses, and work synergistically at an operational level.

An initiative at Budapest by the Dutch and German foreign ministers attempted to address this issue through a "CSCE first" policy. "CSCE first" would have designated the OSCE the "instrument of first choice" (in the words of the U.S. delegation) in dealing with regional conflicts, which could then be referred to the UN, by a consensus-minus-the-parties deci-sion, if necessary.[131] Although this proposal represents a much-needed effort to clarify the division of labor between the UN and the OSCE, and could have created a useful "hand-off" mechanism from the OSCE to the

UN, it did not base the definition of role on the organizations' apparent strengths, and would likely have weakened both the UN and the OSCE. The OSCE would be obliged to take on more than it could deal with, both in terms of the number and, more significantly, the nature of the tasks required, such as peacekeeping, peace-making, and enforcement of decisions, tasks for which it is ill-equipped. To compensate for its weaknesses, then, the OSCE would have to refer more and more situations to the UN, which, in turn, would not only undermine the OSCE's own credibility, but also increase the burden on the UN.[132]

Ideally, a division of labor based on comparative advantage would have the OSCE focus on the conflict-prevention and premediation or prenegotiation activities, while limiting its peace-making and peacekeeping activities, where the weaknesses of its structure and approach are most pronounced. As a practical matter, however, such a strict division of labor would not be possible, nor desirable. Because of its privileged status with Russia, the OSCE has been and will frequently be thrust into a peace-making or peacekeeping role. Its challenge, therefore, is to undertake these activities in a way that preserves its unique ability to gain the cooperation of the parties in preventing or reducing conflict through a political, noncoercive approach. This will not be easy. The OSCE's entry into peacekeeping could lead to the creation of large bureaucratic structures, or more stringent oversight and management by the member states, or divert too many resources from preventive diplomacy.[133] The OSCE's credibility as an organization is also at stake if it fails in peace-making or peacekeeping, and its ability to engage in preventive diplomacy could thereby be undermined.

The OSCE will need to choose carefully which peace-making operations it will undertake, and ensure they have the financial, and especially political, backing essential for any OSCE initiative to be effective. It will also need to develop appropriate and efficient arrangements for "hand off" to other international organizations and individual countries in case of weak political consensus or failure of the mission. There are some signs that the OSCE is headed in that direction. Although unable to reach a consensus decision on the "CSCE first" proposal, the Summit Declaration in the Budapest Document provides for the referral of issues to the UN Security Council if the OSCE is not competent to deal with them, or "in case CSCE efforts are frustrated and enforcement action is required."[134]

If it is forced to undertake peacekeeping operations, the OSCE should focus on those operations that, for whatever reason, cannot be undertaken in the traditional peacekeeping format. The relationship between the United

Nations and the United States in Haiti, or with the coalition in the Gulf War, could serve as a model for the OSCE. The OSCE's jawboning process may make it a better oversight body in these cases, where consensus decision-making and a large membership may permit more in-depth and substantive discussion and make it more difficult for those undertaking such operations to escape ongoing OSCE review.[135]

The development of ground rules under which the international community would sanction or participate in Russian "third-party" peacekeeping efforts, as begun at the Rome Ministerial Council meeting and endorsed and mandated by the Budapest meeting, could also be a fruitful area in which the OSCE's strength in norm creation and compliance-by-persuasion through a "jawboning" process may be useful. Where Russian intervention in a "peacekeeping" capacity in the former Soviet republics will likely be undertaken with or without international approval, the OSCE can provide a forum in which dialogue about these issues can take place on a continuing basis, and that offers an opportunity to the member states to negotiate the principles by which all such operations will function and monitor their ongoing implementation.

Nagorno-Karabakh will be the test. The OSCE has demonstrated creativity and flexibility in constituting the peacekeeping operation mandated at Budapest for Nagorno-Karabakh. As in Haiti, the primary peacekeeper is an interested outsider who is not prepared to submit to the control or direction of an independent international bureaucracy. At the same time, the international community is not prepared to sanction a purely Russian "peacekeeping" force. The framework negotiated at Budapest suggests a reconciliation of these interests that acknowledges Russia's need to have a larger say in operations that affect its vital interests and to which Russia will be contributing more than one-third of the troops, while providing for some international political oversight.[136] As of mid-1995, there is still much that must be worked out. It is likely that operational control and decisionmaking will be left to the contributors of forces, dominated by Russia, and the jawboning process will be relied on to ensure political accountability, with a small, Vienna-based group taking responsibility for day-to-day monitoring and guidance for the peacekeeping operations.

MAKING PREVENTIVE DIPLOMACY LAST. If the OSCE is to retain its focus primarily on preventive diplomacy and premediation activities, it will need to strengthen its ability to sustain preventive diplomacy initiatives in an ongoing and consistent fashion, and enhance its long-term impact.

Some initiatives have already been taken. The High Commissioner has developed an informal practice of suggesting and at times undertaking follow-up activities on implementation of his recommendations, and in establishing expert missions in Slovakia, Hungary, and Ukraine.[137] In addition, he has encouraged nongovernmental organizations (NGOs) to undertake parallel activities to provide expertise and assistance to the parties in developing and implementing minority policies. NGOs, for example, are advising the interethnic round table in Romania, and are providing expertise on minority language and education policies in several countries. These NGOs remain in regular contact with the HCNM as they plan and implement their programs, and have provided valuable follow-up that the resource-poor OSCE has not been able to supply.

Within the OSCE, longer-term follow-up activities have largely been undertaken by ODIHR. Its recent narrowing of focus has enhanced its capacity to support long-term conflict prevention through strengthening the voices of moderation and building the society's internal capacity to avert polarization and conflict in times of tension. Its programs have provided an important reinforcement and support of the High Commissioner's and missions' activities. Working with the missions, ODIHR has assisted countries in drafting constitutions and, indeed, in Georgia took the initiative to develop and help the various parties reconcile different constitutional drafts.[138] Through its regional seminars in central Asia, it has increased awareness of OSCE norms and procedures at the grass roots and among the domestic officials responsible for implementing them and provided often the only forum in which government officials and local NGOs meet and engage in dialogue. The establishment of an OSCE liaison Office in central Asia should add significant capacity for longer-term monitoring and assistance.[139]

Despite significant progress since 1992, the OSCE's capacity for leadership and sustained attention to policy initiatives can be strengthened, in particular with respect to the role of the Chairman-in-Office and the missions. The instability and lack of continuity of the CIO's role will require that OSCE states overcome their hesitation and allow the secretary-general to assume a bigger political role in the OSCE of the future. As yet, the office has not been exploited to its full capacity, despite the qualifications and political credibility of the secretary-general, German ambassador Wilhelm Hoynck, who managed Germany's tenure as CIO in 1991. Granting a limited right of political initiative to the secretary-general to contribute to discussion of regular agenda items of the Permanent Council, and allowing the secretary-general to act as the CIO's political adviser, could greatly enhance the effectiveness of OSCE conflict-prevention initiatives. This might include giving the secretary-general the authority to undertake fact-finding missions under the direction of the CIO or to represent the CIO with individual states.

In addition, the resources available to the OSCE, both financial and human, must be increased. The High Commissioner is overworked, and it is becoming increasingly difficult for him to address the number of situations that need his attention. Moreover, his mandate does not include many potentially dangerous interstate territorial and political disputes, such as the Greek-Macedonian dispute over the name, symbols, and constitution of the former Yugoslav republic, or the Turkish-Russian dispute over regulation of shipping through the Bosporus strait. While responsibility for dealing with these situations would, logically, fall to the CIO, in practice, the CIO has not been active in these areas, and his or her ability to deal with them, except through informal channels in Vienna, may be limited because of the CIO's direct accountability to the Permanent Council. The creation of a deputy or similar position of high stature to enhance the HCNM's capability, and expansion of the use of Personal Representatives of the CIO (for example, by appointing higher-stature people, and appointing them for a six-month or one-year period) to address those issues not within the HCNM's authority, will be needed in the future to ensure that the successful experience of the High Commissioner can be continued and replicated in other areas.[140]

The missions could benefit from professionalization and training of their staffs, as well as political follow-up to their reports, which are often not even read by many of the diplomats in Vienna. The secretary-general's office could be given more responsibility and authority to recommend to the Permanent Council follow-up action on the information provided, when necessary.[141]

Finally, the funding available for OSCE activities must also be increased. Of course, a substantial increase in financial contributions by the participating states carries certain disadvantages. The independence, flexibility, and political support given to the OSCE, particularly by powerful countries like the United States, has flowed in part from its low cost. The United States pays only about $3 million to support the entire organization, a tiny sum compared to its contribution to other international organizations, and is prepared to allow less ongoing oversight and control of its operations as a result. Nonetheless, some increase in the financial resources available to the OSCE for conflict-prevention and management activities would significantly enhance its capacity.

Cooperation with NGOs, in particular those specializing in conflict resolution and democratization, could allow the OSCE to expand its resources and ensure sustained, long-term initiatives, at little or no extra cost or bureaucracy. Parallel informal actions can both support and enhance the official efforts, but also help to establish relationships and a process that can continue after OSCE active involvement is ended. The OSCE might consider drawing on NGO resources to help design and implement ongoing dialogue forums, and develop procedures for lending critical political support to NGO efforts to bring parties together in dialogue.

The OSCE has traditionally been reluctant to involve NGOs in its activities or to deepen contacts with them. This has been the result largely of a failure to distinguish between "insider" NGOs (for example, advisers, conflict-management NGOs, and so on) and "outsider" NGOs (such as Amnesty International) who operate more on the basis of information-gathering and more confrontational pressure for action. NGO "insiders"—capacity builders concerned with promoting better management and resolution of conflicts—could provide direct support and assistance to conflict-resolution efforts undertaken by the OSCE. Again, the High Commissioner has been a pioneer in this area, drawing on NGOs to help him prepare for his missions. The secretary-general has also initiated contact with NGOs to develop a database and resource list of NGOs with expertise and knowledge in the geographical areas in which the OSCE is involved and in conflict resolution generally. These may provide good models for future cooperation.

Conclusion

Is the OSCE an organization with a "bright past, fuzzy present, and uncertain future," as one leading expert has claimed?[142] Can it survive a possible deterioration of relations between Russia and the West? The answers to these questions depend on the participating states themselves. The OSCE is still in search of an identity. Or rather, its member states, with some difficulty, are still seeking a consensus on its proper role and identity in the new European security "architecture."

The OSCE's future can be "brighter" if it can focus on two elements of the post–cold war order that have made the OSCE useful and effective despite its cumbersome structure and lack of "teeth." First, in an era in which the international community is seeking to address new security risks arising from social, ethnic, and economic problems within states themselves, and to do so before conflict breaks out, the need for "cooperative," that is, noncoercive, rather than collective, security has become more pressing. Second, ultimately, in a system still made up of sovereign states, international organizations will only be as effective as their constituent members allow them to be. And the end of cold war confrontation neither means that states will want more effective or powerful international organizations, nor that they will have the political (and economic) will to deal effectively with conflicts when they arise. Indeed, in the post–cold war era, as security threats have become multifaceted and the security needs of the OSCE states no longer uniform, political will may become a scarcer commodity than it was in the days of confrontation.[143]

The OSCE's innovation and effectiveness lie in its implicit recognition of these two realities and its construction of an organization that provides a process and environment for generating political will and making action more feasible and effective in the absence of strong political will. The OSCE has recognized that conflict prevention requires new instruments and methods, and it has given new meaning to the phrase "cooperative" security by building a new methodology and tools for prevention that rely on cooperative engagement of the parties in conflict.

In this context, ironically, the OSCE's greatest weakness—its consensus decisionmaking and its lack of "teeth"—is also its greatest strength. Rather than reduce its power, it has enabled the OSCE to gain the cooperation and confidence of the parties in reducing conflict. Many organizations are able to generate binding decisions, impose sanctions, or supply the threat of coercive action. Few have the ability to gain the cooperation of the parties concerned in a search for a way out of further escalation. The OSCE's structure and mechanisms give it that power. To induce parties to deescalate and deal with their disputes productively requires both the threat of sanction and the promise of a "way out." Neither is sufficient in itself, yet when one organization carries out both functions, it may make cooperation less attractive to the parties concerned. Where parties tend to evaluate procedures in terms of the potential risks they entail rather than of the potential contribution to the conflict-resolution process, initiatives by organizations that rely on legally binding instruments, or that have the capacity to inflict greater pain on the parties for noncompliance, are likely to meet with great resistance.

The political nature of the OSCE reflects the political reality in the world at large. The relevance of such a process increases the OSCE's ability to address especially difficult issues and to get movement on such issues that would be completely out of the purview of most international organizations. The real challenge for the OSCE is how to retain this advantage while strengthening the coherence of the coercive power in the background through cooperation with other international organizations and individual participating states.

Notes

1. For an extensive discussion of the limitations of military action and economic sanctions in the post–cold war era, see Antonia H. Chayes and Abram Chayes, "Alternatives to Escalation," paper presented at the August 1994 meeting of the Aspen Strategic Group.

2. Ibid.

3. Zartman is the originator of the "ripeness" idea. Richard N. Haas defines "ripeness" as a point at which "there exist the prerequisites for diplomatic progress, that is, whether particular circumstances are conducive for negotiated solution or even progress. Such prerequisites may include characteristics of the parties to a dispute as well as consideration about the relationship between or among the parties." Richard N. Haas, "Ripeness and the Settlement of International Disputes" *Survival,* vol. 30, no. 3 (1988), pp. 232–49.

4. Hass, "Ripeness," p. 233. Fisher and Ury define these unilateral policy options as the Best Alternative(s) to a Negotiated Agreement, or BATNA: Roger Fisher and William Ury, *Getting to Yes: Negotiating Agreement without Giving In* (Houghton Mifflin, 1981).

5. D. Lax and J. Sebenius, *The Manager as Negotiator: Bargaining for Cooperation and Cooperative Gain* (New York: The Free Press, 1986), p. 59.

6. The OSCE's experience in Ukraine is a good illustration. The OSCE has established a small mission to take up residence in Ukraine, with the explicit mandate of mediating the dispute between the Kiev government and Crimea, yet it has neither consulted with nor obtained the consent of the Crimean government for such a role. Nor could the OSCE formally do so. As a result, the mission, which became operational on November 24, 1994 (three months after the Permanent Council agreed on its terms of reference), reported that Crimean authorities had "considerable reservations" about allowing an OSCE presence in Crimea. "Report from the OSCE Missions," *OSCE Newsletter,* vol. 2 (February 1995), p. 7; "News from the Field," *OSCE Newsletter,* vol. 2 (January 1995), p. 5.

7. Since January 1, 1995, the *Conference* was changed to the *Organization* for Security and Cooperation in Europe. For the sake of readability, the term OSCE is used throughout this article, except when referring to OSCE publications and quotations before 1995.

8. The OSCE did, however, suspend the participation of Yugoslavia (Serbia and Montenegro) in 1992 for failure to comply with the principles, commitments, and provisions of the OSCE, as well as OSCE decisions. 13th CSO, Journal 7, Annex 1 (1992).

9. The recently adopted Budapest Document 1994 makes clear that "the change in name from CSCE to OSCE alters neither the character of our CSCE commit-

ments nor the status of the CSCE and its institutions. In its organizational development the CSCE will remain flexible and dynamic." Budapest Decisions, Chapter I (29) (1994).

10. The practice was formulated in this way to mitigate the paralysis difficulties that could result from a requirement of unanimity by encouraging states to withhold consensus only when they categorically rejected a matter.

11. Conference on Security and Cooperation in Europe, *Beyond Process: The CSCE's Institutional Development, 1990–92* (Washington, 1992), p. 3.

12. The Federal Republic of Yugoslavia (Serbia and Montenegro) was suspended from the OSCE in 1992, bringing the number of active members to fifty-two.

13. OSCE "Fact Sheet" (Department of Chairman-in-Office Support, Secretariat, 1994), p. 2.

14. At the December 1994 Budapest Review meeting, the name of the organization was changed from Conference on Security and Cooperation in Europe. The names of several of the component institutions were changed as well. The new names are placed in parentheses. The post-Budapest names will generally be used to refer to the institutions.

15. Charter of Paris for a New Europe, "New Structures and Institutions of the CSCE Process," (1990), pp. 21–22; Supplementary Document to Give Effect to Certain Provisions Contained in the Charter of Paris for a New Europe (1990), Chapter I (D).

16. Ibid., Chapter I (A).

17. Ibid., Chapter I (B).

18. Ibid.

19. Ibid., Chapter (A) (5). The CIO generally maintains a large staff and center of operations within the ministry of foreign affairs in his or her own country. A representative of the CIO, with a staff, is based in Vienna to manage Permanent Council and Senior Council meetings and affairs.

20. CSCE, *Beyond Process*, p. 5.

21. Charter of Paris for a New Europe, p. 22; Supplementary Document, Chapter I (F).

22. Budapest Document, "Towards a Genuine Partnership in a New Era," Summit Declaration, para. 8 (1994).

23. Ibid., Summit Decisions, Chapter I, para. 29 (1994).

24. Helsinki Document, "The Challenges of Change," Summit Decisions, Chapter I (15) (1992).

25. Rome Document, "CSCE and the New Europe—Our Security Is Indivisible," Decisions, CSCE/4-C/Dec.1, para. 7.1 (1993). Neither the 1990 Paris Charter, nor the subsequent Helsinki Document, foresaw the need for an ongoing consultative body on political matters. The only formal permanent consultative body was the CPC's Vienna-based Consultative Committee, established by the Paris Charter to give support to the implementation of the confidence- and security-building measures (CSBMs) negotiated in the Treaty on Conventional Armed Forces in Europe. This group evolved into a group for ongoing political consultations, which was quasi-formalized at the December 1992 Stockholm Ministerial meeting as the "Vienna Group." The Vienna-based representatives met regularly but did not acquire any formal status until the Vienna Group became the Permanent Committee (now Permanent Council) a year later.

26. Budapest Decisions, Chapter I (18) (1994).

27. Budapest Decisions, Chapter I (17) (1994). At Budapest the Senior Council was given a direction-setting function to "discuss and set forth policy and broad budgetary guidelines." The Budapest Document encourages states to "be represented at the level of political directors or at a corresponding level."

28. Helsinki Decisions, Chapter I (12) (1994).

29. Ibid., Chapter I (15).

30. Budapest Decisions, Chapter I (19) (1994).

31. Summary of Conclusions, Third Meeting of the Council (Stockholm, December 14–15, 1992), Annex 1.

32. The most recent decisions taken at Budapest permit the secretary-general to participate in Troika ministerial meetings, and mandate the secretary-general to "be more actively involved in all aspects of the management of the CSCE." Budapest Decisions, Chapter I (20) (1994).

33. "Prague Document on Further Development of CSCE Institutions and Structures," 2d Council of Ministers Meeting (Prague, January 30–31, 1992), Chapter III (9)–(11). At Helsinki II, ODIHR was mandated to. . . . ["assist the monitoring of implementation of commitments in the Human Dimension" (by participating or consulting to on-site missions, for example), "act as a clearinghouse for information," and "assist other activities (..), including the building of democratic institutions" (by arranging seminars at the requests of states, providing facilities to other OSCE institutions, and consulting with other inter-governmental organizations), Helsinki Decisions, Chapter II (5–(6) (1992).]

34. Budapest Decisions, Chapter VIII (29) (1994).

35. See S. Touval, "Why the U.N. Fails," *Foreign Affairs,* vol. 73, (September–October 1994), pp. 44, 46.

36. Abram Chayes and Antonia H. Chayes, *The New Sovereignty: Compliance with International Regulatory Agreements* (Harvard University Press, 1996), pp. 3, 31. The Chayes refer to this model in relation to efforts to ensure compliance with international treaty obligations. While efforts to deal with and reduce simmering tensions are not directly issues of compliance, the comparison is still useful, as both issues of compliance and conflict prevention entail persuading a government to change its behavior in order to conform to some generally accepted standard, whether it be a treaty obligation or general expectation regarding how parties should deal with their differences. Moreover, emerging conflicts between a government and a minority population in a country frequently are sparked, or fueled, by alleged noncompliance with OSCE human rights norms.

37. "Russia Accepts OSCE Call for Immediate Cease-fire in Chechnya," OMRI Daily Digest, no. 26, part 1 (February 6, 1995).

38. As the OSCE spokesperson commented: "there was no need to employ confrontational tactics against Russia. Invoking the OSCE Human Dimension mechanism and despatching a mission to Chechnya without Russia's consent would have done just that. Now we have Moscow's cooperation," Basic Reports, no. 42 (January 31, 1995), p. 4.

39. *OSCE Newsletter,* vol. 1 (February 4, 1994); vol. 1 (March 1, 1994).

40. Budapest Decisions, Chapter VIII (5) (1994). The new provisions, aimed at enhancing compliance with OSCE commitments, move away from the traditional OSCE process of intermittent "review conferences" to begin to establish a permanent and continuous review of implementation, as well as to strengthen the

organization's capacity to take action in cases of noncompliance. It also gives the CIO the authority, and the responsibility, to raise issues of human rights violations, thereby bypassing states' traditional reluctance to raise the question of human rights violations in other countries in all but the most serious cases. See also Chapter VIII (6).

41. R. Fisher, *Improving Compliance with International Law* vol. 14, Procedural Aspects of International Law Series (Charlottesville: University Press of Virginia, 1981), p. 15.

42. These might include subcommittees or working groups to discuss financial matters, review and make recommendations on the budget or on the further development and streamlining of OSCE institutions, or to study and prepare recommendations for Permanent Council action in specific conflicts.

43. Wilhelm Höynck, "CSCE Works to Develop Its Conflict Prevention Potential," *NATO Review,* vol. 42 (April 1994), pp. 16–22.

44. Helsinki Decisions, Chapter I (16)–(21) (1992) (ad hoc steering groups to be established on a case-by-case basis to assist the Chairman-in-Office). The ad hoc groups are to be composed of a restricted number of participating states (including the current, former, and succeeding Chairman-in-Office); their general mandate stresses impartiality and efficiency. In urgent cases these ad hoc groups may be established by a "silence" procedure, allowing a decision to be taken after the lapse of a stated amount of time with no objections.

45. Members of the in-country mission in Macedonia comment that the steering committee established to monitor that situation was useful as a sounding board to help them deal with a broad and ambiguous mandate, as well as to develop political backing for the activities that the mission undertook. Since 1992 many of the functions of this steering committee have been taken over by the Chairman-in-Office, and by the Permanent Council, which now provides a regular and permanent interlocutor for the mission members. Nonetheless, smaller groups continue to be used widely in the OSCE for the formulation of Senior Council decisions and for review and recommendations on ongoing OSCE activities.

46. Conflict Management Group, "Methods and Strategies in Conflict Prevention: Report of an Expert Consultation in Connection with the Activities of the CSCE High Commissioner on National Minorities," (December, 1993), p. 16.

47. Missions prepare bimonthly reports to the Permanent Council and are in nearly daily contact with the Chairman-in-Office. Mission heads also make frequent trips to Vienna to brief interested Permanent Council members on the activities of the missions, test their own thinking about future activities, and receive political input from OSCE states.

48. See 23rd CSO, Journal 3, Annex 3 (September 23, 1993).

49. Following a request by the Permanent Council on June 30, 1994, the Chair-in-Office appointed on April 6, 1995 an OSCE representative to assist the Joint Russian-Latvian Committee on the Skrunda Radar Station with the implementation of the agreement. The OSCE representative is co-located with the OSCE mission in Latvia, and able to benefit from the advice and assistance of the mission. During its 9th session on February 23, 1995, the Permanent Council decided on the mandate for an OSCE Inspection Regime. As of May 1995, the members of the Inspection regime have not yet been selected by the Chair-in-Office.

50. See 17th CSO, Journal 2, Annex 3 (November 6, 1992) for the text of the original mandate of the Spillover Mission to Macedonia.

51. Helsinki Decisions, Chapter I (12)–(13) (1992). When the Council of Foreign Ministers later established the "Vienna Group" to consult regularly between CSO meetings, they designated the CIO as its chairman and instructed it to "undertake preliminary discussion of items suggested for the agenda of the CSO by the Chairman-in-Office." Stockholm Meeting of the Council of Foreign Ministers, Summary of Conclusions, Decision 7 (December 1992). Although the Council decision establishing the Permanent Committee in December 1993 makes no explicit mention of the CIO's role, one may infer from the Council's silence on the matter that the Stockholm provisions delineating the CIO's role with respect to the Vienna Group have been carried forward. The Permanent Committee's practice has borne this out.

52. "The CSCE Mechanism of Conflict Management," address by Dr. Piotr Switalski, Chairman of the Department of Chairman-in-Office Support, OSCE Secretary-General, at the OSCE Seminar on Negotiation and Conflict Management Techniques, Helsinki, Finland, January 25, 1994.

53. Budapest Decisions, Chapter I (19) (1994). In some cases the Senior Council (CSO) has requested the appointment of a Personal Representative to facilitate dialogue among conflicting parties and to negotiate and make recommendations on the establishment of long-term on-site missions. See, for example, 17th CSO, Journal 2, Annex 2 (mandating the CIO's Personal Representative to begin discussions with the parties in the Georgia-Ossetia conflict to reduce tensions and extend civil order and to "initiate a visible CSCE presence in the region"); 17th CSO, Journal 2, para. 5 (November 16, 1992) (requesting the CIO to appoint a Personal Representative to "explore the modalities of a possible mission to Estonia").

54. Margaretha af Ugglas, "Conditions for Successful Preventive Diplomacy," in S. Carlsson, ed., *The Challenge of Preventive Diplomacy* (Ministry of Foreign Affairs of Sweden, 1993). Margaretha af Ugglas served as Chairman-in-Office from December 1992 through November 1993.

55. CIO personal representative Istvan Gyarmati visited Moscow on January 9–10 to solicit support from Russia for OSCE involvement in the political settlement of the crisis in Chechnya. A first mission of four people, accompanied by the Russian minister of justice and other Russian officials, was sent to Chechnya on January 26–29, and on February 22 a second human rights mission was sent to examine the human rights situation there. The first mission was instrumental in facilitating an agreement among the parties to allow the International Committee of the Red Cross to visit prisoners. See Report on the Talks on the Situation in Chechnya, Doc38/95 (January 12, 1995), reprinted in *Helsinki Monitor,* vol. 6, no. 1 (1995), p. 118; "OSCE Sends Human Rights Group to Chechnya," *OSCE Newsletter,* vol. 2, (February 1995), p. 1; "OSCE Sends Mission to Chechnya," *OSCE Newsletter,* vol. 2, (January 1995), p. 1.

56. The terms of reference were approved at the first meeting of the Senior Council on March 31, 1995, which was opened by Kovacs himself.

57. Helsinki Decisions, Chapter II (17)–(21) (1992).

58. Höynck, "CSCE Works to Develop its Conflict Prevention Potential," pp. 16–22.

59. In Estonia, for example, the OSCE in-country mission was invited to participate in the drafting of the statute of the Presidential Roundtable for dialogue

between government and Russophone minority groups, and it has been a very active observer and supporter of the round table process.

60. In this sense, the "insider third party" closely resembles and builds on William Ury's concept of an "outer third force" which seeks to empower and mobilize the "inner third force" in a conflict—those parties and forces of moderation that are willing to work together resolve the conflict. William Ury, "Conflict Resolution Among the Bushmen; Lessons in Dispute Systems Design," *Negotiation Journal*, vol. 11, no. 4 (October 1995), pp. 365–75.

61. The OSCE was the first interstate forum to define respect for human rights as a basic ingredient of friendly relations among states. "The participating States recognize the universal significance of human rights and fundamental freedoms, respect for which is an essential factor for the peace, justice and well-being necessary to ensure the development of friendly relations and cooperation among themselves as among all States." Helsinki Final Act, Chapter 1 (8) (1975).

62. Helsinki Decisions, Chapter II (1992).

63. Ibid., Chapter II (12). The High Commissioner is currently involved in Estonia, Latvia, Kazakhstan, Kyrgyzstan, Ukraine (all mainly regarding the position of the Russophone population), Slovakia (mainly the Hungarian minority), Hungary (mainly the Slovakian minority), Romania (mainly the Hungarian minority), Albania (the Greek minority), and Macedonia (the Albanian minority).

64. Conflict Management Group, "Methods and Strategies in Conflict Prevention, p. 6.

65. This is left completely to the discretion of the High Commissioner, who is authorized to discuss the issues with the parties and, "where appropriate," promote dialogue. Helsinki Decisions, Chapter II (12) (1992).

66. Indeed, it appears that where possible, the High Commissioner prefers *not* to act completely independently, especially when it comes to initiating a visit. He is fully aware that many states were reluctant to issue a "blank check" to an international authority to intrude unchecked into sensitive internal affairs, and that he needs to gain the confidence of these states if he is to maintain their political support for his role. R. Zaagman, "The CSCE High Commissioner on National Minorities: An Analysis of the Mandate and the Institutional Context," in Arie Bloed, ed., *The Challenges of Change: The Helsinki Follow-Up Meeting and Its Aftermath.* For an account of the Helsinki II deliberations and the concerns of the OSCE states, see H. Zaal, "The CSCE High Commissioner on National Minorities," *Helsinki Monitor,* vol. 3, no. 4 (1992), pp. 33–37.

In the case of Romania and Ukraine, the countries themselves invited the High Commissioner to visit. His involvement in Macedonia followed a formal request by the CSO to visit the country before to an OSCE rapporteur mission that was to evaluate the government's application for admission to the OSCE. In Kazakhstan and Kyrgyzstan, the High Commissioner became involved on the recommendation of then-CIO Margaretha af Ugglas of Sweden, who had visited several central Asian countries in 1993.

67. M. van der Stoel, "The Role of the CSCE High Commissioner on National Minorities in CSCE Preventive Diplomacy," in Carlsson, ed., *The Challenge of Preventive Diplomacy*, p. 44. The HCNM's title in the French version of the official text, however, does use the word "for" (*pour*).

68. See Intervention by Max van der Stoel at the Human Dimension Implementation Meeting (Warsaw, September 28–29, 1993), p. 5: "Immediate de-

escalation of a situation can only be a first step in the process of reconciling the interests of the parties concerned. The goal is to start, maintain and enhance a process of exchanges of views and cooperation between the parties, leading to concrete steps which would de-escalate tensions and, if possible, address under-lying issues." See also Conflict Management Group, "Methods and Strategies in Conflict Prevention," p. 6.

69. Max van der Stoel, Keynote Speech to the CSCE Seminar on Early Warning and Preventive Diplomacy (Warsaw, January 1994), p. 10.

70. It would have been impossible, for example, for Estonia or Latvia to be seen as negotiating with Russia over their treatment of Russian-speakers in their coun-try. See Konrad Huber, *Averting Inter-Ethnic Conflict: An Analysis of the CSCE High Commissioner on National Minorities in Estonia, January–July 1993* vol. 1, no. 2 (Occasional Paper Series, Conflict Resolution Program, Emory University, 1994), p. 37. Similarly, Greece has consistently repelled international intervention in its relationship with Albania over the issues of Albania's treatment of its Greek minority and Greece's treatment of Albanian migrant workers. In both cases the High Commissioner's informal consultations with Russian and Greek officials permitted him to assure them that their interests and concerns would be taken into account, and persuade both governments to refrain from actions that could further escalate the tensions in the Baltics or Albania.

71. On the issues of confidentiality, the High Commissioner's mandate is quite clear: the High Commissioner is to work in strict confidence. Not even the Perma-nent Council must be informed until after the HCNM terminates his involvement; the HCNM consults and reports to the CIO in strict confidence. Helsinki Decisions, Chapter II (4), (18). See also Zaagman, "The CSCE High Commissioner on National Minorities," p. 10.

72. In Estonia, for example, a public statement by the High Commissioner on National Minorities about assurances given to him by the Estonian Prime Minister and by the Russian leaders of Narva and Sillamäe, who had called for a referendum on autonomy for those cities, helped to deescalate tensions and prevent the issue of the referenda from provoking a crisis, Conflict Management Group, "Methods and Strategies in Conflict Prevention," (1993), p. 13.

73. "The most essential contribution to the elimination of minority problems as destabilizing elements in Europe is the promotion of a better and more harmonious relationship between majority and minority within the state itself." M. van der Stoel, "The Role of the CSCE High Commissioner on National Minorities in Preventive Diplomacy," in Carlsson, ed., *The Challenge of Preventive Diplomacy,* p. 46.

74. Intervention by Max van der Stoel at the Human Dimension Implementa-tion Meeting, Warsaw, September 28–29, 1993, p. 5.

75. "Recommendations by the CSCE High Commissioner on National Minori-ties upon his visits to Estonia, Latvia and Lithuania," CSCE Communication 124 (April 23, 1993). In Romania the High Commissioner made a point of emphasizing that he was aware "that in a country which has gone through a process of funda-mental transformation in the last few years, the Government has to cope with many other pressing problems." At the same time, he noted, the recommendations were designed to "allay concerns which apparently exist among some minority groups" and to "contribute to the stable development of your country." "Letter from the

CSCE High Commissioner on National Minorities to the Minister of Foreign Affairs of Romania," CSCE Communication 253 (September 21, 1993).

76. "Recommendations by the CSCE High Commissioner on National Minorities upon His Visits to Estonia, Latvia and Lithuania," CSCE Communication No. 124 (April 23, 1993).

77. In Estonia, Romania, Slovakia, and Macedonia, the High Commissioner has supported and closely followed developments in round tables that have been established to promote government-minority dialogue. The High Commissioner recommended the establishment of an ombudsman in Lithuania, a National Commissioner on Ethnic and Language Questions in Estonia and Latvia, and a Special Office for Minority Questions in Albania.

78. For a detailed description of the High Commissioner's efforts in Estonia, see Huber, *Averting Inter-Ethnic Conflict*. See also Conflict Management Group, "Methods and Strategies in Conflict Prevention," pp. 13, 27–28.

79. Paragraph 11c of the mandate provides for the High Commissioner to "pay a visit" to a country in connection with his information-gathering activities, and although it appears to contemplate the possibility of further site visits by experts (paragraph 33) accompanied by the HCNM, it is silent on the possibilities for follow-up activity. Since the start of his functioning in January 1993 until May 1995, the High Commissioner has paid several visits to the countries where he is involved: Estonia (10), Latvia (3), Slovakia (6), Hungary (5), Romania (5), Macedonia (11), Albania (7), Kazakhstan (2), Kyrgyzstan (2), Moldova (1), Ukraine (5), Russia (2), and Greece (5).

80. A team of three minority rights experts has been set up to visit Slovakia and Hungary regularly in order to analyze the situation of Hungarians in Slovakia and Slovaks in Hungary and make recommendations for improving policy in this area. 21st CSO, Journal 3/Corrected Re-issue (1993) 8–9. In Ukraine, on the suggestion of the HCNM, the CSO has mandated another team of three to explore possible constitutional arrangements for economic autonomy of Crimea within Ukraine. 27th CSO, Journal 3, Annex 2 (June 15, 1994.)

81. The first in-country mission was established on August 14, 1992, to the former Yugoslavia. 15th CSO, Journal 2, Annex 1 (August 14, 1992).

82. The Sarajevo mission was established to support the ombudsmen for Bosnia-Herzegovina, who are charged with protecting human rights and dealing with violations of international law arising out of "ethnic cleansing." The most recent mission, an "OSCE Assistance Group," has been established for Chechnya. It has primarily a human rights and humanitarian focus, but its mandate includes fostering the development of democratic institutions and promoting dialogue and negotiations for a political settlement of the crisis.

83. These missions were deployed in September 1992, but following the suspension of Yugoslavia from the OSCE, the Serbian government refused to extend the Memorandum of Understanding that formed the basis for the missions, and they had to be withdrawn in July 1993. To remain involved and share information from these areas, an informal, open-ended ad hoc group was established in Vienna, and the CPC Secretariat continued to compile weekly surveys of events in these areas. 1993 Annual Report on CSCE Activities, Office of the Secretary General. In addition, the CIO Troika has undertaken short-term visits to Belgrade and other territories in Serbia and Montenegro, and as recently as June 1994, the CSO has

pressed for the return of the missions of long duration to Kosovo, Sandjak, and Vojvodina. 27th CSO, Journal 3, Annex 1 (June 15, 1994).

84. Statement by Ambassador Timo Lahelma, former Head of the OSCE Mission to Estonia, in the Opening Plenary of the CSCE Implementation Meeting on Human Dimension Issues, Warsaw, September 27–October 15, 1993.

85. The Estonian mission, for example, has offices not only in the capital Tallinn, but also in Johvi and Narva, two towns where the significant populations and political activity of Russian-speakers has been a source of tension in that country.

86. The Estonian mission's mandate, for example, covers a range of issues relating to the "status of the communities," including citizenship, language, migration, social services, and employment, as well as a catch-all category of contribution to the "efforts of Estonian national and local authorities to re-create a civic society." Terms of Reference for the OSCE Mission to Estonia, 19th CSO, Journal 2, Annex 1 (February 3, 1993). Similarly, the Ukrainian mission's mandate requires reporting "on all aspects" of the situation in the Crimea, and provides for the mission to analyze the current situation in Crimea and submit "suggestions to the appropriate authorities for the solution of existing problems." OSCE Newsletter, vol. 1 (September 7, 1994), p. 1.

87. The Macedonian mission built on language tasking it to "engage in talks" and establish contacts with government officials, political parties, and citizens to broaden its original activities of preventing spillover of the Yugoslav conflict into Macedonia, to focus on alleviation of ethno-national tensions between the government and the Albanian minority, while the Latvian mission, tasked with providing advice on citizenship issues, played an important role in facilitating negotiations over Russian withdrawal from the Skrunda military base.

88. There have been complaints, however, that mission members have turned out not to have the language capabilities claimed in their résumés.

89. The language of the mission mandates on this issue is remarkably similar. In Macedonia the mission is tasked "to engage in talks with the Governmental Authorities of the Host Party, to establish contacts with representatives of political parties." In Estonia the mission is mandated to "establish and maintain contacts with competent authorities on both the national and local level," while in Kosovo, Sandjak, and Vojvodina, it is supposed to "establish contact points for solving problems."

90. Chayes, and Chayes, The New Sovereignty, p. 32.

91. Although the information contained in the OSCE mission reports may not be as complete or accurate as the intelligence gathered by some of the larger western countries, they have served a valuable function, both in keeping smaller countries with more limited intelligence-gathering capacities up to date on developments, and especially in providing early warning of brewing tensions and an impartial source of information on which consensus for some kind of action might later be built.

92. See Chayes and Chayes, "Alternatives to Escalation," p. 12; The New Sovereignty, p. 32. The authors describe three ways in which the transparency of a regime can influence the strategic interaction among treaty partners in the direction of compliance: (1) by facilitating coordination among independent decisionmakers converging on the treaty norm; (2) by reassuring actors that others are complying, that is, that they are not being taken advantage of; (3) by exercising deterrence

against actors contemplating noncompliance. The arguments are equally relevant to the government-minority relationship. Transparency and information facilitate coordination among a number of government agencies charged with formulating and implementing policy, and may even catalyze high-level government action to ensure implementation of certain norms.

93. Some delegations complain that too much information comes in from the missions, and have proposed institutionalizing the establishment of small groups to oversee missions, and instituting guidelines that would limit the frequency and length of reporting and provide only summaries to the full Permanent Council.

94. The largest, the three missions of long-duration to the minority-populated regions of Serbia-Montenegro, had been authorized for forty persons, but never exceeded a total number of twenty members. The OSCE mission to Georgia is now authorized up to seventeen members, as of March 1994. See *Modalities of the CSCE Mission to Georgia,* Permanent Committee Journal 14, Annex 1 (March 29, 1994). The remaining missions range from four members (Tajikistan) to ten members (Macedonia, including two European Union Monitoring Mission staff). For a good summary of the mandates and institutional and financial development of the missions, see Conflict Prevention Centre, *Survey of CSCE Long Term Missions and Sanctions Assistance Missions* (Vienna, January 20, 1995).

95. The significant reduction in the number of beatings and deaths caused by Serbian police brutality in Kosovo in 1992–93 has been attributed to the presence of the OSCE mission there. Referring to the OSCE Mission to Kosovo, now withdrawn, former mission member Larry Butler comments: "Missionaries were effective in the first instance simply by their very visible presence. Although we had no special vehicle markings or clothing, we were immediately noticed by both parties wherever we went, and we went everywhere. This acted both to reassure the ethnic Albanian population and to warn the Serbian authorities of direct foreign interest in the situation." "CSCE Kosovo Mission: Preventive Diplomacy in Action," intervention by Lawrence E. Butler at the Conference on Kosovo and the Balkans (December 6, 1993). The Permanent Council and the Senior Council also have taken note of increases in suppression of human rights, police brutality, and rising tension in Kosovo, Sandjak, and Vojvodina since the withdrawal of the missions. See, for example, Permanent Council, Journal 14, Paragraph 4 (Statement on Agenda Item 3) (March 29, 1994); 27th CSO, Journal 3, Annex 1 (June 15, 1994).

96. In Kosovo and Moldova, where government (Serbian and Moldovan) authorities were concerned that the information reaching the international community was biased against them, the OSCE missions gained a reputation as impartial collectors of information, and in this way were able to forestall further escalatory action by parties (especially government authorities) who might have felt that they needed to be on the defensive because the entire international community did not understand them. Specifically, the Serbians viewed most international observers as advocates for the minority populations, and in Moldova, where most information reaching the international community came from Moscow or Bucharest, the Moldovan government felt that it was biased against it. Interview with Larry Butler, former member of Kosovo OSCE Mission, March 25, 1994; Lord Lucas of Chilworth (rapporteur), *The CSCE Human Dimension: Principles, Mechanisms and Implementation,* Draft Interim Report of the Sub-Committee on the Conference on Security and Cooperation in Europe, North Atlantic Assembly (May 1994), para. 33.

97. The term is that of the former Head of Mission of the mission to Estonia, Ambassador Timo Lahelma. In Kosovo the mission served a similar function by taking up and investigating individual complaints about abuses. Mission members report that prompt investigation of all allegations of human rights abuses helped to restrain Albanians from exaggerating Serbian action, lowered propaganda levels on both the Albanian and Serbian sides, and dampened Serbian militia activities, leading to a significant reduction of interethnic tension. "CSCE Kosovo Mission: Preventive Diplomacy in Action," intervention by Lawrence K. Butler at the Conference on Kosovo and the Balkans.

98. Statement by Ambassador Björn Elmér, Head of the Delegation of Sweden to the OSCE, at the OSCE Seminar on General Issues, Tashkent, Uzbekistan (September 29, 1994), p. 4.

99. In Estonia the mission's influence played an important role in the government's decision to issue travel documents to its mostly Russophone noncitizen population, who were considered stateless and unable to travel without documentation, and later in the government's decision to extend the deadline for registration of noncitizens applying for Estonian residence. See OSCE Annual Report 1994 (November 14, 1994), p. 8.

100. Ibid.

101. See 19th CSO, Journal 3, Annex 3 (February 4, 1993) (mandate of mission to Moldova); Decisions of the Rome Council Meeting, CSCE 4-C/Dec. 1, para. 2 (Georgia); Permanent Council, Journal 14, Annex 1 (March 29, 1994) (modalities of mission to Georgia). The one exception to this trend is the OSCE mission in Chechnya, which from its modest humanitarian beginnings, came to host the negotiations between the Chechen leaders and Moscow, and assume the role of mediator in those talks. Unlike the other "crisis management" missions, the Chechnya mission has benefited from Moscow's strong interest in promoting the OSCE as Europe's security organization, and from intensive interest and activity by the OSCE's political organs, especially the CIO and France, as president of the EU, in support of the mission's initiatives.

102. Modalities of the OSCE Mission to Georgia, Permanent Council, Journal 14, Annex 1, section 3.C (March 29, 1994).

103. OSCE Annual Report 1994, p. 5.

104. See "News from the Field," CSCE Newsletter, vol. 1 (December 1994), p. 4; "Report from the OSCE Missions," OSCE Newsletter, vol. 2 (February 1995), p. 4.

105. OSCE Mission to the Republic of Moldova, 19th CSO, Journal 3, Annex 3 (February 4, 1993). See also Lord Lucas of Chilworth (rapporteur), The CSCE Human Dimension, para. 33–35; CSCE Newsletter, vol. 1 (December 1994), p. 4.

106. In Estonia, for example, the Chairman-in-Office's intensive dialogue with the government and with other OSCE governments both on Russian troop withdrawal and the situation of the Russophone population contributed greatly to progress in this situation. Similarly, the Moldovan mission's efforts have received a boost from the parallel activity of the CIO's personal representative, and current CIO Laszlo Kovacs's personal intervention in the negotiations with Russia over Chechnya were critical to the establishment of a long-term mission and to OSCE involvement in the political negotiation process there. OSCE Press Release, 19/95 (Vienna, March 20, 1995).

107. Their interest-based approach does, of course, have its limits, as both the HCNM and the missions cannot sanction any policies that would violate the provisions of the Copenhagen Document or other OSCE norms. Within these limits, however, they have taken advantage of the broad and frequently imprecise nature of the rights and obligations enumerated in these documents. Rather than try to define and clarify further the rights of the minority population, they have tended to focus on issues of how the general standards enunciated should be implemented in the particular situation at hand. Where there are few clear responsibilities or stipulations as to how the principles should be implemented, the "insider third party" can more easily fashion a package that satisfies the interests of all parties concerned.

108. The right of initiative of the High Commissioner is expressed by his independence toward the OSCE participating states. According to the mandate, the High Commissioner "will provide "early warning" and, as appropriate, "early action" at the earliest possible stage in regard to tensions involving national minority issues which have not yet developed beyond an early warning stage, but, in the judgement of the High Commissioner, have the potential to develop into a conflict within the CSCE area, affecting peace, stability or relations between participating States, requiring the attention of and action by the Council or the CSO," Helsinki Decisions, Chapter II (3). The High Commissioner consults in confidence and provides strictly confidential reports after a visit. The mandate states further that the High Commissioner may decide to hand a particular case over to the Council of Senior Officials if he concludes that the situation is escalating beyond the High Commissioner's possibilities for effective intervention. The fact that the High Commissioner (and not the CSO) decides when or if at all to hand over a particular case to the CSO, gives the High Commissioner great independence and initiative. Helsinki Decisions, Chapter II (17)–(20).

109. Paragraph 7 requires a CSO mandate for HCNM involvement in an issue that "has been brought to the attention of the CSO," which, of course, the host government can veto. Paragraph 11c of the mandate allows the High Commissioner to "pay *a* visit" in order to assess the nature of the tensions in a particular country (emphasis added). The language of this paragraph appears to contemplate only limited involvement by the High Commissioner, at least without a formal "early action" mandate by the CSO, and a state desiring to end HCNM involvement could raise objections to ongoing HCNM involvement on this basis.

110. Ambassador John Maresca in the United States Institute of Peace *Special Report: The Future of the Conference of Security and Cooperation in Europe,* Report of Proceedings of a Roundtable Convened on September 26, 1994, p. 5.

111. Ibid. Summary of comments of Ambassador James Goodby, p. 8.

112. Writing in *Foreign Affairs* magazine, Andrei Kozyrev commented: "The creation of a unified, non-bloc Europe can best be pursued by upgrading the CSCE into a broader and more universal organization. After all, it was the democratic principles of the 53-member CSCE that won the cold war—not the NATO military machine. The CSCE should have the central role in transforming the post-confrontational system of Euro-Atlantic co-operation into a truly stable, democratic regime." Andrei Kozyrev, "The Lagging Partnership," *Foreign Affairs* vol. 73, no. 3 (May–June 1994), p. 59–71. The consensus rule's preventing any

outvoting of Moscow, and diminishing United States influence, as compared with the United Nations, only reinforces this belief.

113. As part of the Troika, the Swedes, for example, continued to lead the OSCE's efforts in the Baltics under the Italian chairmanship, because of their interest in the region and their experience and availability to undertake the effort.

114. CSCE Annual Report 1994, p. 27. The missions also receive in-kind support from participating states, primarily in the form of personnel seconded to serve on mission staff. By contrast, NATO's overall budget for 1994 was $900 million.

115. CSCE Annual Report 1993, p. 4.

116. H. Hurlburt, "CSCE Conflict Resolution in Practice," *Helsinki Monitor,* vol. 5, no. 2 (1994), p. 37.

117. The High Commissioner has recommended or supported ongoing council and round table structures in Estonia, Macedonia, Slovakia, Romania, Kazakhstan, and Kyrgyzstan. He recommended the establishment of an ombudsman in Lithuania, a National Commissioner on Ethnic and Language Questions in Latvia, and a Special Office for Minority Questions in Albania.

118. For an extensive discussion of the round tables, their functioning, and their drawbacks, see A. Johannsen, *Optimal Formats for Institutional Mechanisms that Promote Government-Minority Input into Policy-Making and Increase Confidence between Authorities and Community Leaders: A Study of Inter-Ethnic Councils and Roundtables,* unpublished working paper, available through the Foundation on Inter-Ethnic Relations, The Hague, Netherlands.

119. Address by Peter Kooijmans, minister for foreign affairs of the Netherlands, to the Permanent Committee, May 17, 1994.

120. Ibid.

121. "A Roadmap from Vienna to the CSCE Summit in Budapest," Proposal presented by the Foreign Ministers of Austria and Hungary, Vienna, June 1994, para. I (b).

122. The Parliamentary Assembly's General Committee on Political Affairs and Security recommended "To adopt a decision-making procedure which no longer requires consensus or consensus-minus-one. A starting point could be a rule requiring a consensus of 90% of both membership and financial contributions." Vienna Declaration, July 1994 (65).

123. Hurlburt, "CSCE Conflict Resolution in Practice," p. 36.

124. Netherlands Helsinki Committee, *A Focus on the Future: Using an Enhanced Conference on Security and Cooperation in Europe—A Contribution to the Budapest Review Conference,* Utrecht, August 15, 1994.

125. Budapest Decisions, Chapter I (29).

126. Statement of Manfred Wörner, NATO secretary-general, to the Rome Meeting of the CSCE Council, November 30, 1993, quoted in British-American Security Information Council, Report 94.3, *Deciding the CSCE's Future: Prospects for the 1994 Budapest Summit* (September 1994), p. 5.

127. The ODIHR and the Council of Europe have started to collaborate in giving specialized seminars in the central Asian states. The Seminar on Human Dimension Issues, held in Kazakhstan in April 1994, was jointly moderated by an ODIHR and Council of Europe representative. Competition between the OSCE and the Council of Europe, however, still remains strong.

128. Resolution A/48/549 (Cooperation between the UN and the CSCE, November 1, 1993). It was agreed that the UN would take the lead in Tajikistan, Abkhazia, and Bosnia, while the OSCE would take the lead in Nagorno-Karabakh, Moldova, South Ossetia, and Macedonia.

129. For a useful summary of the current state of the relationship between the UN and the OSCE after Budapest, see W. Kemp, "The OSCE and the UN: A Closer Relationship," *Helsinki Monitor,* vol. 6, no. 1 (1995), p. 23.

130. Ibid.

131. A more elaborate and operational proposal, the "CSCE first" proposal, was presented by the Dutch and Germans at Budapest. This policy would have given the OSCE the capacity to refer issues to the United Nations Security Council by a consensus-minus-the-parties decision. German-Dutch Proposal, "An Agenda for Budapest," Part II (2)–(3) (1994). The initiative failed at the last moment in negotiations with Armenia and Azerbaijan over whether and how the consensus-minus-the-parties provisions would apply to Nagorno-Karabkah. The issue was referred back to the Permanent Council in Vienna for further work. The participating states declared in Budapest "their political will to provide, with an appropriate resolution from the United Nations Security Council, a multinational CSCE peacekeeping force following agreement among the parties for cessation of the armed conflict." Budapest Decisions, Chapter II (4). At the time of writing in May 1995, no agreement has been reached between the parties of the conflict in Nagorno-Karabakh, and the Senior Council has therefore made no decision to send a peacekeeping mission.

132. Ibid., p. 30.

133. Even if the countries contributing troops assumed all the costs of their upkeep in a CSCE peacekeeping operation, the development of a serious peacekeeping capability within the CSCE would entail a significant increase in resources and bureaucratic infrastructure for oversight and management of operations. This, in turn, is likely to lead to greater concern, interest, and oversight from capitals, as well as a greater demand for involvement in decisionmaking, which would not only hinder the OSCE's flexibility but also, as the U.N.'s difficult experience persuading countries to contribute troops suggests, its credibility.

134. German-Dutch Proposal, "An Agenda for Budapest," Part II (2)–(3) (1994).

135. The veto power flowing from the consensus rule will permit the United States, Russia, or any other powerful country to reject OSCE involvement in areas in which they do not want it, but also permits smaller, less powerful countries to challenge their proposals and policies.

136. In the Budapest document, the OSCE states "declared the political will" to deploy, with an appropriate UN Security Council Resolution, a multinational peacekeeping force following an agreement on cessation of armed hostilities, and set up a high-level planning group to make recommendations on such issues as command control, logistics, allocation of resources, rules of engagement, and "arrangements with contributing states." Budapest Decisions, Chapter II (4) (Regional Issues: Intensification of OSCE action in relation to the Nagorno-Karabakh conflict) (1994). The basic framework for undertaking OSCE peacekeeping operations is laid out in the Helsinki Decisions, Chapter III (17–56) (1992).

137. See above, *note 70,* for a description of the expert missions.

138. An ODIHR Expert Working Group on the Georgian Constitution was established to assist the Georgian constitution-drafting process. The working group met for a week in May 1994, visited Tbilisi to evaluate drafts of the proposed constitution, and hosted a round table in Warsaw in September to help reconcile differences between different constitutional drafts in circulation in Tbilisi. In Tajikistan, ODIHR provided the OSCE mission with comments on the draft constitution, and coordinated solicitation of comments and advice by the European Commission for Democracy through Law and several leading constitutional experts. See OSCE Annual Report 1994, Sec. 4.2, p. 17.

139. The task of the office, located in Tashkent, Uzbekistan, will be to promote information exchange between the OSCE and the central Asian states, to establish and develop contacts with local universities and NGO's, to promote OSCE principles, and to assist the OSCE in developing activities in the central Asian states. 27th CSO, Journal No. 3, Annex 4.

140. Austria and Hungary have proposed the creation of a post of "Adviser on Issues of Stability and Security" with a mandate similar to the HCNM, but aimed at providing early warning and early action in situations outside the HCNM's jurisdiction. At this juncture, a High Commissioner with as broad a mandate as that suggested by the Austrians and Hungarians is not realistic; states are unlikely to accept a self-initiating and independent office similar to the High Commissioner without certain clear limits regarding the areas of involvement.

141. Germany and the Netherlands have argued for the creation of ad hoc groups to provide day-to-day guidance to missions. Such involvement by groups of states in the day-to-day operation of the mission would likely have reduced the missions' flexibility to respond to circumstances as they arise. "A Joint Agenda for Budapest," Proposal presented to the CSCE by the Foreign Ministers of Germany, Klaus Kinkel, and the Netherlands, Peter Kooijmans, Section II (6) (May 1994).

142. "The OSCE Process: Bright Past, Fuzzy Present, Uncertain Future," *The International System after the Collapse of the East-West Order,* edited by Armand Olesse, Richard Cooper, and Y. Sakamoto (Dordrecht: Nijhoff, 1994), pp. 770–80.

143. See Victor-Yves Ghebali, "Sécurité collective ou défense collective? Les choix de l'Europe post-communiste," in *L'Etat du Monde, Edition 1995* (Paris: La Découverte, 1994), pp. 615–18.

TWO

The Council of Europe's Democracy Ideal and the Challenge of Ethno-National Strife

Jean E. Manas

THE STRASBOURG-BASED Council of Europe is not in the business of preventing or resolving intrastate conflicts. "[Its] aim is, without impairing the territorial integrity and national unity of states, to achieve . . . a higher degree of mutual understanding and respect, giving all peoples a chance to rid themselves of frustrations."[1] The Council's primary mission is to ensure that European states become and remain western-style parliamentary democracies, respectful of human rights and the rule of law. Nevertheless, Council officials believe the Council's work in democratization has applicability to internal conflicts. Putting a prime value on democracy serves a peace function by helping international actors identify "correct" resolutions of these conflicts and by creating a moral momentum in favor of actions supporting those resolutions. In many internal conflicts, the valuation of democracy carries this burden well. It allows, for instance, the outside actor to condemn powerful elites resisting democratization and to support pro-democracy forces fighting oppressive regimes.

This chapter describes and evaluates the Council's democracy mission. In particular, it explores the limitations of that mission and how it does not always succeed in providing clear moral guidance. The Council, like most other democrats, subscribes to a territorial-majoritarian conception of democracy. Under this conception, democracy is the rule of the majority of the population of a clearly defined territorial unit. Since different borders give rise to different majorities and different majorities lead to different policy outcomes, a territorial-majoritarian conception of democracy invariably begets a questioning of the borders within which the majority is to be constituted. In its extreme, the questioning takes the form of ethno-national conflict.[2]

Ethno-national strife poses a formidable challenge to the moral guidance that the Council's democracy mission aspires to provide; this challenge undermines the peace function the mission is designed to serve. If the democracy mission is to meet the challenge of ethno-national conflict, it must provide a justification of borders. Avoiding that impossible task, the Council, like all other intergovernmental organizations, has always responded to the questioning of borders by simply assuming that existing states are the appropriate territorial units. As expected, this commitment to majoritarianism within current borders has advantaged ethno-national majorities to the detriment of ethno-national minorities. Unhappy with this bargain, the more powerful of those minorities have, time and again, tried to change that situation, generally by struggling for the creation of new states in which they are in the majority (secessionism) or the alteration of borders so that they would become part of states in which they are in the majority (irredentism).

International organizations have been generally unwilling to meet the secessionist logic that results from their territorial-majoritarian conception of democracy by tinkering with borders. Instead, they have advocated conceptions of democracy intended to neutralize the adverse impact that the constitution of majorities within existing borders has on ethno-national minorities. As this chapter indicates, the Council has been no exception to this pattern. Throughout the cold war, the Council worked on rendering states ethno-nationally neutral. Principally, it pressured states not to discriminate against citizens on the basis of ethno-national characteristics, at least in areas affecting fundamental rights.

Post–cold war ethno-national conflicts have drawn attention to what was obvious all along: nondiscrimination does not translate into ethno-national neutrality. Many laws are nondiscriminatory on their face, but significantly disadvantage certain groups. Recognizing this fact, the Council has recently shifted its focus from working to render states ethno-nationally neutral to working to create "legal safe havens" for members of ethno-national minorities. A favored means has been the promulgation of an international legal framework that recognizes and institutionalizes the status of minorities and places strict limits on what ethno-national majorities can do to ethno-national minorities. These limits to majoritarianism have been collectively identified under the catch-all label of "minority rights"; the conception of democracy supplemented by minority rights has been termed "pluralist democracy."

Much of this chapter is devoted to mapping and evaluating the Council's embrace of minority rights, which received its greatest official recognition in the promulgation and adoption of the Framework Convention on the Protection of National Minorities agreed upon in November 1994 and formally signed in February 1995. The chapter argues that the notion of minority rights does not meet the fundamental challenge posed by ethno-national conflict. First, minority rights fails to meet the secessionist objection. So long as the Council's conception of democracy retains a majoritarian pillar, however weakened that pillar may be, advantages will accrue to the majority. Accordingly, a minority will continue to have an incentive to demand its own separate state. Certainly, many minorities might settle for "pluralist democracy" or some other similar "grand solution." The point is that the Council has no basis for condemning the minorities that refuse to do so. After all, a secessionist minority might embrace the notion of pluralist democracy, but insist that it be implemented within the confines of the new borders *it* proposes. There simply is no basis for portraying a secessionist minority as being any more territorialist or any less pluralist than an antisecessionist majority.

Second, minority rights institutionalizes the very differences that are at the roots of ethno-national conflict. Minority rights represents a total capitulation to a way of seeing these conflicts in terms of majorities and minorities. It elevates that outlook to official dogma, thus affirming a logic that contains the seeds of its own undermining.

Both difficulties suggest that the challenge posed by ethno-national conflict is much more fundamental than the Council's democracy mission has taken it to be. What is needed is a conception of democracy that does not sanctify either territorialism or majoritarianism. We have barely begun thinking about such a conception of democracy. A good first step would be to appreciate the complexities associated with ethno-national conflict. We can then begin the process of imagining flexible structures that allow these complexities to play out in full force.

Because the Council does not have a monopoly over the democracy mission, this chapter's analysis has implications beyond the Council. From the Conference on Security and Cooperation in Europe (CSCE) to US

Agency for International Development (AID), from Helsinki Watch to the International Federation of Human Rights, many entities also value democracy and further believe that their valuation of democracy provides clear guidance in situations of ethno-national conflict. Coming to terms with the fundamental challenge posed by ethno-national conflict necessitates, then, some serious reflection, not just in Strasbourg, but in many other capitals as well. This chapter hopes to contribute to that deliberation.[3]

The chapter is divided into three parts. The first part provides background. It describes the Council and its work, paying particular attention to the democracy mission, both from the Council's foundation in 1949 to the end of the cold war in 1989 and from the end of the cold war to the present. Although time and again the Council and its critics have strongly disagreed on whether the Council has implemented its democracy mission effectively, this disagreement only helps to underscore the agreement on the clarity of that mission. The second part deals with the challenge that ethno-national conflict poses to that clarity. It discusses the ways in which the Council has approached ethno-national strife since its founding, and focuses on the post-1989 developments, in particular the notion of minority rights. A concluding part explores the difficulties that the Council and its fellow democrats face, discusses some possible courses of action, and offers a few tentative recommendations as a basis for stimulating further conversation about the potential of the Council and other international actors in this domain.

The Council of Europe's Democracy Mission

Ten European states (Belgium, Denmark, France, Ireland, Italy, Luxembourg, the Netherlands, Norway, Sweden, the United Kingdom) founded the Council of Europe in 1949,[4] in the immediate wake of World War II and at the outset of the cold war. For these states, the Council at its founding was a vehicle to mark their distaste for authoritarianism and communism and to consolidate their common commitment to western-style parliamentary democracy and to values, such as respect for human rights, that they associated with that system of governance. To show that they meant business, the founding states endowed the Council with a unique and very elaborate legal mechanism for managing compliance with human rights in Council member states. Over time, the Council's human rights monitoring mechanism took on a life of its own.

Throughout the cold war, the Council remained a second-tier international organization, partly because some west European states (the United Kingdom and Scandinavian states) were suspicious of its federalist tendencies and partly because East bloc states, dismissing the Council as a western propaganda ploy, shunned membership. Things changed dramatically in 1989. With the ascendance of the western democratic ideology, the Council was called upon to play an important role in the effort to help east European states consolidate the transition from communism to democracy. Although there has been much debate over whether the Council has fulfilled its role well, there has been little disagreement over the clarity of the ultimate goal.

The Council of Europe during the Cold War: A Beacon for Western-Style Democracy and Human Rights

The Council's founding is credited to the convergence of two different ideological forces. On the one hand, there were the Europeanists, who, wishing to avert another pan-European war, urged the creation of a pan-European organization that would provide a forum for all European states to settle their disputes peacefully. On the other hand, there were the Westernists, notably Churchill and a number of other conservative politicians, who, more concerned with the threat of communism than the threat of war, wished to create a union around the values they identified with the West. Churchill's statement in 1942 summarizes most succinctly the Westernist agenda pivotal to the Council's founding: "It would be a measureless disaster if Russian barbarism overlaid the culture and independence of the ancient States of Europe. Hard as it is to say now, I trust that the European family may act unitedly as one under a Council of Europe."[5] At the Hague Congress of 1948, which was convened by the European Movement, the Europeanist and Westernist forces converged. The Congress was a resounding success[6] and was followed by the founding of the Council of Europe the following year.[7]

Since the Council was founded by western states, it never experienced a tension between the two ideologies (Europeanism and Westernism) that were critical to its founding. From the beginning, the Council was located firmly on the western side of the cold war ideological divide. Its member states used the Council and its founding to declare the moral superiority of western-style liberal parliamentary democracy to the system in place in communist countries. The Council member states viewed pan-European unity or even cooperation, by and large, as a mere aspiration not worth the compromise of western values. European unity, if it was to come, was going to be based on western values. This aspirational character of the attachment to Europeanism helped further to consolidate the Westernist agenda: by taking it for granted that Europe constitutes a natural unit, the Europeanist ideal helped portray the bloc system as unnatural.

Because the Council was so firmly planted in Westernism, it did not make an effort to reach out to East bloc states. Although the western states recognized that the true solution to interbloc rivalry lay in doing away with the opposition between the systems in place in each bloc, they also understood that the likelihood that East bloc countries would embrace western-style democracy was quite slim. Therefore, the Council's immediate work with respect to eastern Europe amounted to the issuance of a few condemnations.[8] Recognizing that these condemnations were part of the cold war's ideological battlefront, the east European states brushed them aside, maintaining that the western-style democracy championed by the Council of Europe was a mockery of true democracy, which was to be found under communism. Given this rhetorical climate, it is not surprising that the Council did not count a single East bloc state among its members.

Although the Council's founding fulfilled the ideological goal of asserting the primacy of western values and the political goal of consolidating some kind of unity around those values, the member states wanted to indicate that they had more than a symbolic association in mind. Some states urged the creation of "a political authority with limited functions but real powers."[9] This federalist drive, however, was met with stiff opposition from the United Kingdom and Scandinavian states and was abandoned within two years of the Council's founding. More than any other event, the creation of a separate European Coal and Steel Community in 1951 by six European states ("the Europe of Six") marked the end of the Council's federalist aspirations. During the remainder of the 1950s, some federalist aficionados of the Council pursued a more modest effort of establishing the Council as "the general framework of European policy," but that effort did not amount to much either.[10] The signing of the Treaty of Rome establishing the European Economic Community in 1957 signaled the definite demise of the Council's federalist potential.

Although the member states failed to transform the Council into a meaningful suprastate political authority, they did not abandon the body completely. They established a special niche for it when they endowed it with a unique and elaborate mechanism for managing compliance with human rights in member states. The sole motivation here was not ideological, that is, to show Soviets that the West was serious about certain values. With the Nazi and fascist experiences of World War II having made it clear that no liberal democracy was immune to totalitarian tendencies, many western governments welcomed a suprastate human rights watchdog to guard against the possibility that their state would undergo that experience again.

Although the Council has worked on increasing links among member states in the social, cultural, and scientific domains, the Council has historically been best known for its human rights work. Many international observers who have never heard of the Council of Europe are familiar with the European Convention on Human Rights (ECHR) and the European Court of Human Rights, respectively a Council instrument and a Council organ. The Council has viewed its human rights work as the central pillar of its more general democracy mission. Recognizing that few nondemocratic states would agree to democratize overnight, the Council has thought that inducing these states to respect human rights would place them on a slippery slope from authoritarianism to democracy. Accordingly, the Council has seen its task as fourfold: first and foremost, promulgating human rights norms (norm elaboration); second, getting states to agree to abide by human rights norms; third, increasing compliance with these norms; and finally, augmenting gradually the number of human rights norms binding on states.

The Council set itself to this task soon after its founding. The initiation of a project for the drafting of a convention on human rights was one of the first acts of the Committee of Ministers, the executive and legislative branch of the Council. The Committee of Ministers convened a Committee of Experts for that purpose in its second session in 1949. The goal was to prepare an instrument that would render legally binding on signatory states the guarantees contained in the UN Declaration on Human Rights, which, being a "mere" declaration, was aspirational in character and had no legal force. The European Convention on Human Rights, officially called the Convention for the Protection of Human Rights and Fundamental Freedoms, was signed by most Council of Europe member states a year later on November 4, 1950, and it entered into force on September 3, 1953, once a sufficient number of signatories had ratified it. The Convention also created the European Commission of Human Rights and the European Court of Human Rights, perhaps the two most important suprastate human rights enforcement bodies in the world. During the following four decades, the Council built on its norm elaboration work with the adoption of several additional protocols to the European Convention on Human Rights, as well as more than one hundred instruments and conventions, including the Social Charter of 1961, enumerating social and economic rights and putting in place a mechanism for supervising states' compliance with those rights, and the European Charter of Local Self-Government of 1985, designed to encourage states to strengthen institutions of local government.

MANAGING COMPLIANCE WITH HUMAN RIGHTS. Although the Council was quick to promulgate norms and put in place a supervisory mechanism, the Council has never had any material powers for forcing states to abide by these norms or to place themselves under supranational supervision. Unlike NATO or even the UN, the Council cannot appeal to military might to fulfill its mission. Nor can it impose any type of material sanctions. Unlike the international financial institutions, for instance, the Council does not dispense economic aid that it can condition on compliance with its norms. The Council's powers are limited to granting the imprimatur associated with membership and compliance with its norms. Moral condemnation is the worst sanction that the Council may impose on a state, such as the rump Yugoslavia, that openly flouts human rights norms.

The Council's lack of the material powers that other international organizations possess does not place the Council in a significantly worse position relative to those organizations. This is because many of the organizations possessing such powers are very hesitant to use them. As Abram Chayes and Antonia H. Chayes explain in *The New Sovereignty: Compliance with Treaties in International Regulatory Regimes,*[11] international organizations do not so much "enforce" compliance as "manage" it (the term is theirs) through a strategy that is quite fluid. Diplomatic pressure, public shaming, even interpersonal relationships play important roles in enhancing state compliance with international norms. This strategy can be criticized for being little more than a defeatist lowering of expectations, yet, in the absence of other plausible alternatives, the strategy will continue to attract adherents.

The Council's work provides an excellent illustration of this approach. The most important component of the Council's strategy for getting states to comply with Council norms has been to use the leverage implicit in membership. Nonmember states have wanted to join the Council to get the imprimatur of membership. States have sought that imprimatur either because they valued it for its own sake or because they thought it would render it easier to silence domestic or foreign critics. Since membership is conditioned on minimum respect for human rights, the Council has been able, with varying degrees of success, to use the admission process to pressure candidates to make certain changes. Moreover, as a general rule, admission has been accompanied by the state's signing and ratification of several Council instruments, including the European Convention on Human Rights.

Once admitted to the Council, a member state comes within the purview of the Council's human rights supervisory mechanism. The most important *formal* component is spelled out in the European Convention on Human Rights, applicable to all signatory states. The Convention provides for a process through which an offender state can be brought first before the European Commission of Human Rights, either by other states or by aggrieved individuals, and subsequently before the European Court of Human Rights. Other components of the human rights supervisory mechanism include the work of the Parliamentary Assembly. Its various committees have the power to send fact-finding missions to member states. The Assembly Committees may also issue critical reports or positive recommendations. The Assembly's work has complemented that of the Commission and the Court, because the Assembly has been capable of acting more swiftly than those two bodies and has had fewer constraints on its jurisdiction. For instance, the Court's jurisdiction may be triggered only if a state has consented to it. No such limitations govern the Assembly's work. The Committee of Ministers has powers similar to the Assembly's, though it has been less quick to use them. The final component is the work of the Secretariat, which is more informal and cooperative. The Secretariat provides technical advice to member countries that are working on bringing their legislation and policies into line with Council norms.

EVALUATION OF THE COUNCIL'S HUMAN RIGHTS WORK. Throughout the cold war, the bulk of the Council's everyday work was focused on its member states, particularly those states in which human rights violations were systematic. These states included both member states that underwent periods of semi-authoritarian governance, such as Greece in the late 1960s and Turkey in the early 1980s, and member states that departed from their general respect for human rights in particular areas, such as the United Kingdom in Northern Ireland.

To its defenders, the Council's work in the field of human rights is exemplary. The Council pioneered human rights norm elaboration and enforcement, and it has remained at the cutting edge of that work. The European Convention and its additional protocols constitute the most advanced international legal framework for human rights in the world. The

Convention was the first international instrument to expose a state to international judicial action, either on the complaint of another state or of an aggrieved individual, for human rights violations. Although no longer unique, the Council human rights organs are still the busiest in the world. In 1991 the European Commission on Human Rights declared 217 applications admissible.[12] That same year, the European Court handed down judgment in seventy-five cases.[13] The Court has condemned many states for human rights violations, and many states have made the required changes in their legislation or policies. The docket of the European Court of Human Rights has grown to the point where the Council has decided to reform the Convention system: the Commission is to be abolished, and in the majority of cases there will be one, final court decision so as to streamline the current overloaded two-level system. Finally, both the Parliamentary Assembly and the Committee of Ministers have put unprecedented pressure on member states in which democracy and human rights received major, albeit temporary, setbacks. The Committee of Ministers threatened to suspend Greece for seriously failing in article 3 obligations, which include respect for fundamental human rights, and the Parliamentary Assembly condemned Turkey on several occasions.[14]

The Council's critics acknowledge the Council's pioneering work in the domain of human rights, but they fault the Council for granting its imprimatur all too easily. In the first place, the critics accuse the Council and its organs of allowing member states to flout human rights norms whenever it has been in those states' interest to do so. The Committee of Ministers invoked the article 8 suspension mechanism only once, against the Colonels' Greece. Turkey lived through a period of military rule in the early 1980s without a single condemnation from the Committee of Ministers, let alone a threat of suspension. Ignoring several Parliamentary Assembly resolutions calling on the Committee to condemn Turkey,[15] the Committee contented itself with the ritual of requesting Turkey's minister of foreign affairs to inform it of the status of the democratization effort in the country.[16]

The critics also fault the human rights supervisory mechanism for not being as strict as it could be. Indeed, the Convention does not require that a signatory state agree to the Convention's individual petition provision, which permits an aggrieved individual to bring a case directly before the Commission. Nor does it require that a signatory state agree to the compulsory jurisdiction of the European Court; as recently as in 1980, Cyprus, France, Greece, Malta, Spain, and Turkey did not agree to the individual petition provision of the European Convention. Thus, historically, the only way grievances against some offender states could be brought before the Commission was through a complaint filed by another member state.[17] Since states are very reluctant to bring formal proceedings against each other, particularly when they have little to gain from such proceedings, many violations ended up never coming before the Commission.

Critics also point out that, even if a state were to file a complaint against another state, this action might not amount to much. Although the Commission has important investigative powers and it may put pressure on a state, its proceedings are not public and its mandate provides that it try to resolve all cases amicably.[18] If amicable means fail, the Commission has only two options. On the one hand, the Commission can make a recommendation to the Committee of Ministers, the executive body of the Council.[19] The recommendation, however, is not binding; the Committee of Ministers is free to ignore it or to take a less confrontational route. On the other hand, the Commission itself can bring the case before the European Court of Human Rights, but only if the accused state has agreed to the Court's jurisdiction.[20] If not, and if the Committee of Ministers declines to act on the basis of the Commission's recommendation, a state may, once again, escape condemnation, despite violating European Convention norms.

For the Council's defenders, this criticism of the human rights supervisory mechanism both overlooks the Council's significant achievements and overestimates the possibilities for human rights in the aftermath of World War II and during the height of the cold war. Had the Council pushed harder, the Council's defenders contend, it might not have achieved even as much as it did. Critics counter, however, that it is easy to tell a success story for an international organization if the organization never requires more than the minimum that states have been willing to deliver. Critics accuse the Council of precisely this type of lowering of expectations.

The critics are correct that the Council was reluctant during the cold war years to be very tough on its member states. Yet the cries for more muscular approaches to human rights are also problematic. Very tough stances may make the international organizations look righteous, but it is unclear to what extent they further the asserted goal of increasing compliance with human rights norms and improving the prospects of democratization. The risks with a soft approach are obvious: an authoritarian state is let off the hook too easily; it is not pushed as far as it would be willing to go. Perhaps, for instance, the Council could have forced Turkey to democratize more quickly. But the risks with a tough approach are just as great: an authoritarian state is pushed too far and, as a result, the hard-liners within the regime lose any incentive to accommodate the liberals. Accordingly, they take back or withhold even the little that they would have been willing to give. Had the Council been tougher, Turkey might have taken longer to return to democracy.

In the last analysis, the tension between the tough and soft approaches to democratization that has plagued the Council's work turns out to be fundamental. It is the same tension that we witness in the enforcement of a whole range of international norms: norms in the field of trade, the environment, nuclear nonproliferation, and so on. Regardless of whether the hawks or the doves have the better of the argument in general or whether the Council or its critics are right in this particular case, this tension ought not to obscure the underlying consensus to which both the Council and its critics subscribe. Both sides are in complete agreement on the clarity of the Council's democratization mission. Their disagreement is limited to whether the Council has implemented its mission most effectively.[21]

The End of the Cold War and the Eastward Expansion of the Council of Europe: All-Around Democratization

Because West bloc states did not invest much in operationalizing the ideological aspects of the interbloc struggle, the Council remained a second-tier international organization throughout the cold war. The western states preferred to put their energies into what they considered to be more realistic and immediate concerns, such as solidifying military alliances and improving internal economic unity. Accordingly, NATO and the European Economic Community, respectively the quintessential military and economic organizations, quickly eclipsed the Council on the international organization scene.

The year 1989, however, marks a turning point in the Council's fate. As the East bloc crumbled, a Europewide consensus emerged around the western-style democratic ideology that the Council of Europe cherished and had championed for four decades. As securing the triumph of that ideology became a top priority both for the west European states and for many of their former adversaries, the Council found itself with a major share in this Europewide effort to encourage and consolidate democratization.

For the Council, the most immediate consequence of the end of the cold war has been the rush of membership applications from eastern Europe. Many of these states desire membership because their new governments are committed to upholding human rights and democratic principles and they want to mark that commitment through admission to the club of democracies. All applications are not motivated by pro-democracy impulses alone, however. Some states seek membership in the Council because it promises to give them an important boost in legitimacy. As members of the Council, these states can silence both internal and, more important, external critics by pointing out that their human rights record is at Council of Europe levels. Since the Council has a track record of cutting semi-authoritarian states some slack, as with Turkey in the early 1980s, the newly democratizing states considered Council supervision a not-too-heavy price to pay to silence internal and external critics. Finally, for former East bloc countries, membership in the Council has the additional benefit of being a quick and easy way of marking and thus consolidating both the end of Europe's division into two blocs and, more important, their break from Russian domination. With NATO and European Union (EU) membership unavailable, the Council of Europe has been the best alternative in the short run.

The Council has been delighted at the boost of stature associated with the flood of applications. Consistent with its traditional democracy mission, however, the Council, unlike the Conference on Security and Cooperation in Europe, did not immediately admit all applicants. On the contrary, it has tried to use the application process as a tool for effecting changes in applicant states. To date, roughly half of the applicants still have not made the cut.[22] Furthermore, the Council has undertaken a not insignificant effort to help former East bloc countries mold themselves in the image of their western counterparts, a process that has continued after admission. These democratization aid programs are collected under the name of *Demosthenes*.

In carrying out both sets of democracy promoting activities—conditioning admission on democratic reforms and providing democratization assistance—the Council has experienced intense ambivalence. Reflecting the tension between the tough and soft approaches toward semidemocratic states discussed in the previous section, the Council has been uncertain how strict it ought to be with respect to the requirements it imposes on applicant states. Similarly, in administering the democracy aid programs, the Council has been unsure to what extent it should be working *with* semi-authoritarian governments rather than in slight opposition to them.

ADMISSION OF NEW MEMBERS. The Statute of the Council of Europe makes clear that membership in the Council is open to all European states,[23] but it subjects membership to the important requirement that "every Member of the Council of Europe . . . accept the principles of the rule of law and of the enjoyment by all persons within its jurisdiction of human rights and fundamental freedoms."[24] During the cold war, this requirement was interpreted in a way that excluded states that were not western-style democracies. Under current Council practice, an applicant country, in addition to guaranteeing human rights and fundamental freedoms, must have "held free and fair elections by secret ballot and universal suffrage, resulting in the constitution of a parliament composed of representatives of political parties enjoying freedom of organization and expression and having real powers" and must "provide for the holding of such elections at regular intervals."[25]

The flood of applications from east European states has posed an acute dilemma: how strict ought the Council be in interpreting and applying the requirements of democracy and respect for human rights as prerequisites for admission? On the one hand, the Council could take a relatively loose approach to these requirements, which would lead to the immediate admission of east European states. This, in turn, would consolidate these states' break from authoritarianism. With these states incorporated into the Council's human rights regime, the Council could more effectively influence their conduct. The loose approach has, however, a significant drawback: since membership is the biggest incentive the Council has to offer, easy admission deprives the Council of its most important tool to effect changes in applicant countries.

On the other hand, the Council could take a stricter approach to the admission requirements. This stricter approach would ensure that the prize of membership would be granted only to the truly deserving. States interested in membership therefore would first have to make a genuine effort toward compliance with Council norms. Although this approach constitutes a good use of the membership tool, it risks depriving the Council of leverage over borderline states where the leadership is open to democratization and human rights, but is unwilling or unable to move too rapidly in that direction.

The Parliamentary Assembly, the Council organ with the most extensive role in the admission process, has dealt with this dilemma by displaying a flexible attitude. In the first place, the relevant committees of the Parliamentary Assembly have not reviewed applications mechanically, approving the deserving and rejecting the undeserving. Instead, the Assembly committees and their rapporteurs have made specific recommendations to applicant states and have held up their reports to give those states the opportunity to implement those recommendations. To date, the committees have issued no negative reports; rather, they have shelved many applications in anticipation of some event or another (for example, the holding of elections, the adoption of a citizenship law, and so on).

With respect to admission itself, the Assembly loosened the requirements and opted to tighten the postadmission monitoring mechanisms. Thus the Assembly has shown a willingness to admit states (such as Romania) with mediocre human rights records, provided that those states make specific commitments to certain changes soon after admission and appear to be making substantial progress toward democracy. At the same time, the Assembly has announced that it will closely monitor new members to ensure that they honor those specific commitments.[26] The Assembly declaration that "the honouring of these commitments is a condition of full participation of parliamentary delegations of new member states" suggests that the Assembly may sanction a state that rests on the laurels of its admission.[27]

Finally, the Parliamentary Assembly has also made sure that nonmembers are not left without any supervision or inducement to effect changes. The Assembly created a "special guest status" for nonmember states. Many current members held this status for a preliminary period before their admission, and today all pending applicants hold that status. Guest status has allowed the Assembly to institute a formal and continuous link between the Council and nonmember states and has provided a forum for the application of informal (and formal) pressure on those states. In Order no. 485 (1993), for instance, the Assembly instructed its Political Affairs Committee to report regularly on the situation of human rights in states with guest status. Moreover, because applicants do not automatically obtain guest status, the Assembly has also used the carrot of guest status to induce states to implement certain minimum changes at once. For example, to obtain guest status, a state must accept the Helsinki Final Act and other CSCE declarations, as well as the two United Nations Covenants on Civil and Political Rights and on Economic, Social, and Cultural Rights. Recently, the Assembly has further strengthened these conditions by requiring a state with guest status to have *ratified* the UN Conventions.[28]

The Assembly, in conjunction with the Council of Ministers, has also moved in the direction of promulgating alternative human rights monitoring mechanisms for nonmember states. A March 9, 1993, resolution, for instance, authorizes the Committee of Ministers, if invited to do so by a nonmember state, to "appoint specially qualified persons to sit on a [domestic] court or other body responsible for the control of respect for human rights" in that state. The Committee would agree to such an arrangement only if it (the Committee) were granted the power to appoint the majority of such a court's members and if the law to be applied by this court were to include the substantive provisions of the European Convention on Human Rights. The Committee of Ministers created this extraordinary option in response to Lord Owen's prodding and repeated calls by the Parliamentary Assembly to create some kind of mechanism for the protection of human rights in nonmember states. The Assembly had initially suggested that the Committee of Ministers open up the Council of Europe human rights supervisory organs, such as the European Court on Human Rights, to nonmember states.[29] When that suggestion went unheeded, the Assembly made a more general call in 1993.[30] To date, no state has taken up the Committee of Ministers on this extraordinary offer, which raises serious sovereignty issues. However, that might change in the unlikely event that the Parliamentary Assembly follows up on a suggestion to render the "special guest status" contingent on a state's acceptance of the terms of this resolution. The Council is also considering the possibility of opening up the European Convention on Human Rights and its supervisory mechanism to certain nonmember states.

All these measures—adopting a less rigid approach to the application review process, loosening admission requirements in return for tightening postadmission monitoring, creating a guest member status, and so on— have been designed to grant the Assembly more flexible and adaptable leverage over applicant states than the on-and-off switch of membership, without debasing the value of membership in the Council. These interim measures have generated a heated debate quite analogous to the debate, summarized in the previous section, over whether the Council was as tough on member states during the cold war as it could have been. To the Council's defenders, the Council has displayed unprecedented sophistication in dealing with this novel situation. To its critics, the Council squandered wildly the little leverage that it had. The pivotal point of the debate is Romania's admission, which, for the advocates of the "tougher" approach to human rights enforcement, constitutes a sacrifice of democratic and human rights principles in the face of intense political pressures.

COOPERATION AND TRAINING PROGRAMS IN FORMER EAST BLOC COUNTRIES. Soon after the events of 1989, the Council of Europe undertook a program of cooperation and assistance in eastern and central European (ECE) countries designed to help these countries put in place democratic state institutions.[31] The basic philosophy of *Demosthenes,* as this undertaking has come to be known, is the transmission of democratization expertise from western officials or experts to their eastern counterparts. *Demosthenes* carries out this goal through a range of activities. In some instances, Council of Europe officials or western human rights experts have visited ECE countries for the purpose of providing advice on issues of democratization, providing an opinion on the compatibility of a state's legislation with Council norms, or for training ECE government officials in such issues. In other instances, ECE officials have come to the West for internships or study visits in western institutions. The Council of Europe has either organized or helped fund these visits. Under *Demosthenes,* the Council has also organized or funded seminars, workshops, and conferences bringing together western and eastern European officials and experts. Finally, the Council has created a democratization information network by issuing specialized publications, translating fundamental human rights texts into ECE languages,[32] setting up libraries of basic human rights material in a number of ECE states and expanding the jurisdiction of its Human Rights Information Centre to include those states.[33] Complementing the *Demosthenes* program have been three smaller programs: *Lode,* for the development of local government and democracy,[34] *Demo-droit* for legal cooperation,[35] and *Themis* for the development of law focusing on the following subjects: the police, the prosecutor's office, the judiciary, the prison system, the ministry of justice, and the drafting of legislation.[36]

These aid programs have been extremely limited in scope. The programs have targeted for the most part mid- to high-level government officials: for example, ministry officials, appellate judges, police chiefs, prison governors. They have not been able to reach officials involved in the day-to-day operation of the state system (cops on the beat, prison guards, and so on). Although there have been some efforts to target central and east European journalists, that endeavor has been quite modest. Even the effort directed at high-level officials has involved only a handful of officials. Take, for instance, a training program implemented by the Association of European Judges for Democracy and Freedom (MEDEL) and supported financially by the Council of Europe. This program places ECE judges with their west European counterparts for a period of about one month. In 1991 the program placed fourteen judges; in 1992 it placed thirty.

These limitations are not surprising in light of the restricted budget under which these programs have been operating. In its first year (1990), *Demosthenes* had a budget of only 13 million French francs ($2 million). The 1991 budget was 22 million francs, an insubstantial increase given the increased demands placed on the programs that year. Although the *Demosthenes* budget was increased to 50 million francs (roughly $9 million) in 1993[37] and to 54 million francs in 1994 (roughly $10 million),[38] it is still quite modest, particularly since much of this money is spent on the transportation and lodging of government officials. Since 1992 these meager resources have had to be stretched to cover the republics of the former Soviet Union, including the Central Asian republics.

The lack of funding is not a problem limited to the aid programs. Although the member states have increased the Council's budget substantially in order to enable it to meet some of the demands arising from the effort to incorporate the former East bloc countries, the increase is small given the task at hand. In 1991, for instance, the Council's budget increased by close to 50 per cent. In dollar terms, however, the increase was a mere 210 million French francs (at the time, $40 million).

Although the Council has tried to raise funds elsewhere, it has not succeeded. The European Bank for Reconstruction and Development (EBRD) has declined to fund the training and legal aid programs. Significant funding is unlikely to be forthcoming from any other source, particularly since the European Union, comprised of the wealthiest Council members, has decided to engage in this type of assistance through its own program, Poland and Hungary Aid for Economic Reconstruction (PHARE). PHARE has provided some funding to Council of Europe programs, but the funds are small and have been limited to projects designed to develop the legal framework, a question of particular interest to the EU, which is keener on the emergence of a pro-market legal framework than on the development of human rights. It is unlikely that the situation will change dramatically any time in the near future. In the interim, the Council's training and education programs will, at most, be minor complements of the PHARE program.

A more fundamental question than the question of funding relates to the basic premise of *Demosthenes* and related aid programs. The programs presuppose that east European government officials are eager to uphold democratic principles, but that they have a limited idea what democracy means in practice. The programs, therefore, dispatch western "experts" to teach "easterners" all about democracy. This presupposition, a critic may argue, is doubtful (apart from being offensive). Although there are certainly instances where a government official is willing to do the "right" thing, is unsure what the right thing is, and can use help from more experienced westerners, these instances are more likely to constitute the exception than the rule. More often than not, the eastern government official will know exactly which course of action is consistent with democratic principles. If the government official is not following that course of action, it is because she or he has opted not to, for political or other reasons. In the critics' eyes, *Demosthenes* provides an unwarranted boost of legitimacy to these antidemocratic government officials; programs appear to further the goal of democracy without doing much. The critics suggest as an alternative that the Council direct its efforts toward nongovernmental organizations (NGOs) and help them develop creative strategies for resisting authoritarianism.

The Council has been increasingly aware of this line of criticism and has tried to be at least partially responsive. Until mid-1993 all initiatives undertaken under the democratization and legal aid program were carried out either at an intergovernmental level or in conjunction with entities suggested by governments. That year the Council decided to branch out in the direction of NGOs. It accordingly added a new component to *Demosthenes* entitled "civil society," aimed at developing and reinforcing the role of NGOs.[39] The activities under that heading have remained quite limited, however, with only a handful of seminars and information meetings in a number of countries on the role of NGOs in a democratic society.[40] Even those activities have taken place with the approval of the governments of the state in question.

The political explanation for exclusive dealing with or through governments is that the Council is an intergovernmental organization. Its member states want it to work with and through governments, and the Council finds it easier to do so. However, the exclusive dealing also has a more principled defense. The critique of exclusive dealing may underestimate the number of instances where good-intentioned east European government officials truly do not know what course of action is the correct one. How is a lawyer schooled in communism supposed to know, after all, how to draft habeas corpus legislation? Moreover, these programs may also affect behavior in more subtle ways. If the Council were to cease working with government officials, it would lose some opportunities for affecting behavior, however modest these changes might appear. Even worse, it might affect the course of actions adversely, by alienating potential converts. Working with opposition NGOs, which are frequently staffed with communists-turned-democrats, might have exactly that effect.

In sum, since the end of the cold war, the Council has engaged in a major project to help East European states transform themselves into western-style democracies. Critics have raised serious questions about various aspects of this undertaking. Just as during the cold war, however, both the Council's critics and its defenders agree on the clarity of the

Council's democratization mission. They disagree only over whether the Council has made the greatest use of its potential to implement that mission.

Democracy and the Challenge of Ethno-National Conflict

Given that the Council subscribes to a territorial-majoritarian conception of democracy, ethno-national disputes challenge fundamentally the clarity of purpose that the Council's valuation of democracy presupposes. First, the democracy mission assumes the units within which democratization is to take place. Ethno-national conflict, however, reveals serious disagreements over those units. In situations of ethno-national conflict, both sides might be fully committed to "demo-cracy" (rule of the people). Yet they might have incompatible definitions of the applicable "demos" (people). Thus, for instance, one side might argue that the appropriate "demos" is "Yugoslavs," while another side argues that the appropriate "demos" is "Croats," and still another side argues that it is "Serbs of Krajina."

Second, the approach assumes that the concept of democracy has a clear and precise content. Ethno-national conflict, however, involves strong and deeply felt differences over the content of the concept, even in instances where parties have been able to agree on the definition of the appropriate "demos" ("we" are all French or Bosnian or Lebanese or American or whatever). Should democracy entail the rule of the majority (which can alternatively be characterized as the *tyranny* of the majority), or should it entail some protection for a minority (which can be alternatively characterized as the *tyranny* of the minority)? The question—what type of democratic governance is appropriate in an ethnically divided society—is unresponsive to the suggestion that the question be settled democratically. What procedural rules would govern the process to decide the appropriate form of governance?

These two difficulties suggest that the valuation of "democracy" may constitute vacuous posturing when the term is kept sufficiently abstract that two conflicting groups may both comfortably adopt it as their banner. If, to remedy this problem, the term is rendered sufficiently specific, then the mission ends up favoring one conflicting side over another. This bias would not be a problem if one could comfortably declare the demands of the disfavored side to be illegitimate. The following discussion examines whether the Council has found a basis for doing so.

The Council's Traditional Approach to the Challenge of Ethno-Nationalism: Nondiscrimination

As one would expect, the Croats of Croatia or the Serbs of Krajina were not the first to question the integrity of the unit within which democratization is to take place. Ethno-national conflict has challenged the Council's mission of democratizing existing state units from the beginning. Many Council members were colonial empires; they had to deal with independence struggles in their colonies. Other Council members had to face secessionist movements in the metropolis: the Irish of Northern Ireland, the Basques of Spain and France, the Kurds of Turkey are some of the many groups that challenged the integrity of the state unit within which democracy is to reign.

This challenge to the democracy mission—the questioning of the unit within which democratization is to take place—has not been historically of great concern to Council officials. They have always viewed existing states as the operational units for purposes of democratization. Not that the Council has officially ruled out secessionism. Rather, in most instances, the Council officials have simply taken existing maps for granted. When confronted with a strong secessionist claim, they have taken sides against secessionism in subtle ways: first, separatists—whether Kurdish, Basque, Irish, or Corsican—have not received a hearing in Strasbourg; second, states (such as Turkey) involved in intense antisecessionist struggles have been permitted to depart from some human right norms for the duration of the combats.

The political explanation for this attitude is straightforward. The Council is an organization made up of state members. Every state considers its borders and its unity to be sacrosanct. Accordingly, an organization that is at the service of states can never regularize secessionism. It has to take existing states for granted. Indeed, the Council's attitude is not an exception; it mirrors the attitude of all other international organizations, including the United Nations.

This political explanation certainly helps us understand why it is that the Council has taken a position disfavoring secessionism. It does nothing, however, to justify or legitimize that position. To the contrary, the acceptance of existing borders appears initially like a wholly unprincipled act that carries no moral force and that cannot be legitimately foisted upon a regionalized minority intent on creating its own separate state.

Aware of this line of reasoning, Council officials and other supporters of existing maps have tried to ground their hostility to secessionism in a more principled basis, namely, the principle of territorial integrity, which forms the bedrock of the post–World War II international legal order. This move fails, however, for two reasons, the first doctrinal, the second rhetorical. First, territorial integrity does not prohibit secessions. It merely forbids state-on-state aggression. The principle frustrates secessionism only indirectly, insofar as most secessionist movements would likely be unsuccessful in the absence of outside help. Even assuming the wisdom of a ban on outside support for secessionist struggles, that specific ban does not translate into a general ban on secessions. Second, and more important, even if the principle of territorial integrity were interpreted as banning secessions, that interpretation would simply move the justificatory burden one level up. What is the justification for interpreting the principle in that manner?

One justification is that secessionism is a bottomless pit. If one were to allow for one secession, one would have no principled way of blocking others. Since every secession comes with a terrible human cost, the opening of the door for secessionism would be a tragic mistake. This justification, however, can be stood on its head. The fact is that we have already allowed many secessions: every single existing state is the product of some type of secession or other violent border change. Drawing the line at today's map is as unprincipled (or principled) as drawing the line after tomorrow's secession. Moreover, there is no reason to think that the ban on secessions carries any lower human costs than the regularizing of secessions. If regularizing secessionism encourages secessionists, prohibiting it solidifies the resolve of antisecessionists.

In the absence of a principled justification for the hostility to secessionism, most defenders of current borders have tried to secure the existing map by appealing to a conception of the nation-state that renders the location of borders irrelevant. This conception, which the French call the "republican" conception,[41] recognizes that when the nation-state is conceived as having a specific ethno-national identity, there is no principled basis for condemning secessionism. Any ethno-national minority has a legitimate basis for wanting to secede from the state whose predominant identity does not correspond to its own and to form a separate state. As a result of this recognition, republicans propose to decouple the state and ethno-nationalism through a conception of the nation-state as devoid of any ethno-national identity. They accordingly expect the state to be fully neutral among all the ethno-national groups that make up its population. So long as the state is neutral, an ethno-national minority has no legitimate basis for secession.

Republicans have found such neutrality in the principle of formal nondiscrimination. If a state treats its citizens without any distinction based on ethno-national characteristics, then ethno-national neutrality is achieved. The Council has subscribed to this notion. The European Convention on Human Rights, for instance, has mandated that all persons be allowed to enjoy the enumerated fundamental rights without any distinction based on ethno-national characteristics.[42] Although the Convention has limited this formal equality mandate to the exercise of fundamental rights and has not extended it to all types of legislation, Council officials have pressured states to rid their legislation and policies of instances of formal discrimination.

One objection to republicanism is that no state is ethno-nationally neutral, as a matter of fact. This empirical picture, however, does not pose a major conceptual challenge to republicanism. In the republican mission, states that have an ethno-national identity become the target of moral condemnation as part of an effort to render them ethno-nationally neutral.

The more fundamental objection to republicanism questions the very possibility that a state may be rendered ethno-nationally neutral. Formal nondiscrimination can simply not deliver what it promises. Many state laws and policies may be ethno-nationally neutral on their face, while in fact substantially disadvantaging ethno-national minorities. Take, for instance, legislation and policies establishing an official language for the state and governing its use. Is formal nondiscrimination violated when France adopts French as its official language? Is it violated when France requires that all official business be conducted in French and that public schooling take place in that language? For most republicans, the answer has traditionally been negative. Even the most staunch republican has not advocated the idea of a state without an official language or languages. Republicans have only tried to justify the choice of a particular language by appealing to the fact that it is the language of the majority. But that presupposes the borders within which the majority is constituted. Why cannot the official language be Breton in Brittany and Corsican in Corsica?

Some secessionists accept the republicans' ideal of an ethno-nationally neutral state, but insist that it be implemented within the new borders proposed by secessionists. The secessionists are right. If ethno-national neutrality were attainable, a republican would not be antisecessionist. She or he would be agnostic with respect to borders. That the republican cares about the location of borders only buttresses the secessionist's point that borders do matter.

The Emergence of Minority Rights in the 1990s: The Copenhagen
Document and the Venice Draft

Although the republican conception's inability to render secessionist
claims illegitimate has always been apparent, the Council did not feel
compelled to reconsider its stance until the explosion of ethno-national
conflicts in eastern Europe and the former Soviet Union in the post–cold
war era. In the midst of these conflicts, the Council along with other
international actors openly recognized that it was unfair to expect a regionalized minority to give up claims for an independent state in return for
nothing more than a promise of formal nondiscrimination. Perhaps what
sent the message home was the dissolution of Yugoslavia. As the breakup
became inevitable, international actors decided to recognize the breakaway
republics. They also realized, however, that such recognition would make it
impossible to take a stance against a spiraling logic of secessionism. If
Croats of Yugoslavia were considered to have a legitimate basis for not
wanting to be part of Yugoslavia, Serbs of Croatia would have to be
considered to have a legitimate basis for refusing to remain in a Croat
Croatia.

The international actors, and notably the Council, thought they could
break this logic by appealing to a different conception of the nation-state,
the multicultural conception. The multicultural conception, which rises in
opposition to the republican conception, concedes that ethno-nationalism
and public life cannot be decoupled. As a result, it permits the state to have
a predominant ethno-national identity. It requires, however, that the state
put in place official mechanisms for the recognition and protection of
minority ethno-national identities. Thus, for instance, a state is free to adopt
a particular language as its official language, but it must create mechanisms
for a minority to be able to enjoy its language to the fullest. Because, under
the multicultural conception, a minority rights framework satisfies all the
legitimate demands of a minority, there is no basis for advocating secessionism. As is readily obvious, crucial to this structure are two beliefs: that
a minority rights framework does in fact satisfy all the legitimate demands
of minorities, and that a state's opposition to minorities is illegitimate.

In the early 1990s the notion of minority rights took international circles
by storm. International legal scholars heartily embraced the notion.[43] So did
states. As early as 1990, the Conference on Security and Cooperation in
Europe adopted a pathbreaking document, the *Document of the Copenhagen Meeting of the CSCE,* that included an unprecedented list of minority
rights. A year later the European Community announced that it would

recognize only those new ex-Yugoslav republics that respected the rights of their minorities.[44] The Council of Europe Parliamentary Assembly echoed the same theme. Indeed, the Parliamentary Assembly's Resolution 969 on the crisis in Yugoslavia (1991) provides an excellent illustration of an attempt to secure borders by appealing to minority rights. Article 6 acknowledges the right of the Yugoslav republics "to secede from the federation" and it "calls upon the Council of Europe member states to consider recognizing those republics which have declared independence." The same article, however, also "stresses that any right to self-determination must be accompanied by full respect for human and minority rights."

LEGAL BACKGROUND OF THE DEVELOPMENTS IN THE 1990s.   The international actors' embrace of minority rights in the post–cold war era signals not the discovery but the rediscovery of minority rights. Minority rights were very much in vogue during the post–World War I League of Nations era. The League system contained several bilateral and multilateral treaties with minority rights provisions.[45] However, partly because the League minorities system was assigned part of the blame for World War II, the postwar international legal framework shunned the notion of minority rights.[46] For some critics, the principle of minority rights was a harbinger of trouble because it institutionalized a state's internal division. Although the prewar League of Nations system contained several bilateral and multilateral treaties with minority rights provisions, a UN Committee investigating the continuing vitality of these minorities instruments thought the postwar framework was so much at odds with the notion of minority rights that it declared that those instruments were no longer binding on the signatory states.[47]

The strict anti-minority rights position softened slightly in the 1960s. In 1966 the UN General Assembly adopted the International Covenant on Civil and Political Rights, whose Article 27 provided: "In those states in which ethnic, religious, or linguistic minorities exist, persons belonging to such minorities shall not be denied the right, in community with other members of their group, to enjoy their own culture, to profess and practice their own religion, or to use their own language." This general provision appeared to be an important first step in the direction of minority rights. But the first clause of article 27 was expressly inserted so that a state could easily avoid the application of that article by asserting that it did not have any minorities. States (such as France) that subscribed to the republican conception did just that.[48] Thus the principle of minority rights, like the principle of self-determination, entered international law only to find itself inapplicable in those states that denied it.

The Council was definitely closed to the idea of minority rights through-out the cold war years. In 1961 the Council ignored the first serious proposal for the adoption of a minorities instrument.[49] In 1973 it took a harder look at the question. It formed a Committee of Experts to investigate the need for a minorities instrument. The Committee of Experts solemnly announced, however, that there was no such need,[50] and the issue was dropped. In the years that followed, the Council dealt with the minorities question primarily under the human rights rubric.

During these years the Council also engaged in a number of other activities that it viewed as proxies for advancing the cause of minorities, proxies that did not challenge the republican conception of the nation-state. First, the Council worked on strengthening institutions of local govern-ment, which had the effect of strengthening the hand of minorities in instances where minorities are regionally concentrated. Second, the Coun-cil sponsored cooperation among border provinces. Although limited, this work has been at times a surrogate for minority rights where border regions in neighboring states are heavily populated by groups having a cultural kinship.

In the early 1980s the mood began to shift in Strasbourg. This shift was attributable in large part to a new pro-multiculturalist ideological climate in Europe. The importance of the larger ideological developments to the legal developments cannot be overstated. As of the early 1980s, even France, the erstwhile bastion of republicanism, began experimenting with multi-culturalism, under the semi-official slogan of "le droit à la différence."[51] In the late 1980s the French parliament went so far as to pass legislation recognizing the distinct status of a "Corsican people." Although the legisla-tion was struck down as unconstitutional,[52] its mere passage was indicative of a major shift in the ideological climate. International legal circles could not help but be influenced by these larger developments.

These west European developments had their expected effect in Stras-bourg. Consistent with this new thinking, the Council began work at the beginning of that decade to draft a European Charter for Regional and Minority Languages. The Charter was adopted in 1989. The adoption of the Charter, however, was a very small step in the direction of minority rights. First, the Charter does not lay down binding norms, but merely enumerates a series of aspirations for the preservation of these languages. Second, the Charter has no enforcement mechanism. Third, and most important, it does not grant any rights to linguistic *groups,* but rather protects languages as such. Situated in the Council's traditional work aimed at the preservation of cultural heritage, the Charter has little applicability to the salient issues at stake in ethno-national disputes, issues that involve the distribution of power among conflicting groups.

The CSCE and the Copenhagen Document

The issue of minority rights made its full entrance into intergovernmental forums in Europe in 1990, in the wake of the dissolution of the East bloc and as the Soviet Union and Yugoslavia were coming apart. This is easy to explain politically. With the Soviet Union gone, several European states (notably Austria, Germany, Greece, Hungary, and Turkey) felt free to champion the cause of their ethnic brethren in former East bloc countries. Equally important, Russia, with substantial Russian-speaking minorities in the so-called near abroad, became an important advocate.

Early in 1990 the Venice Commission on Democracy through Law, a commission of legal experts with consultative status to the Committee of Ministers, formed a Working Group to start drafting such an instrument. By late spring the Commission had already adopted a list of principles. The first major step in this field, however, was not taken by the Council but rather by the CSCE. While the Venice Commission was still at work, the CSCE took the lead by issuing its far-ranging declaration on the rights of national minorities, the Document of the Copenhagen Meeting of the CSCE. Issued on June 29, 1990, it is the first post–World War II European document to articulate and develop the notion of minority rights; it remains the major document of reference on this subject.[53]

The Copenhagen Document is remarkable in that it articulates, for the first time, a detailed program for the recognition of minority *identity* rights. Resolution 32, for instance, declares that "Persons belonging to national minorities have the right freely to express, preserve and develop their ethnic, cultural, linguistic or religious identity and to maintain and develop their culture in all its aspects, free of any attempts at assimilation against their will." The same resolution goes on to enumerate a number of particular rights that give substance to this broader declaration. On the surface these rights are "individual rights," granted to *members* of minority groups, rather than to groups as such. Yet most of the rights can, by their very nature, be exercised only collectively. These rights, granted to persons belonging to national minorities, are the following:

—The right to use freely their mother tongue in private as well as in public.

—The right to establish and maintain their own educational, cultural, and religious institutions, organizations, or associations, which can seek voluntary financial and other contributions as well as public assistance, in conformity with national legislation.

—The right to profess and practice their religion, including the acquisition, possession, and use of religious materials, and to conduct religious educational activities in their mother tongue.

—The right to establish and maintain unimpeded contacts among themselves within their country as well as contacts across frontiers with citizens of other States with whom they share a common ethnic or national origin, cultural heritage, or religious beliefs.

—The right to disseminate, have access to, and exchange information in their mother tongue.

—The right to establish and maintain organizations or associations within their country and to participate in international nongovernmental organizations.

Not only does the Copenhagen Document grant a number of substantial linguistic and cultural rights to members of national minorities, but it also places important affirmative duties on the states. It requires that states recognize minorities as such and "adopt, where necessary, special measures for the purpose of ensuring to persons belonging to national minorities *full* equality with the other citizens in the exercise and enjoyment of human rights and fundamental freedoms."[54] The Document further requires that states "protect the ethnic, cultural, linguistic and religious identity of national minorities."[55] To that end, the states are asked to "endeavor to ensure that persons belonging to national minorities . . . have adequate opportunities for instruction of their mother tongue or in their mother tongue, as well as, wherever possible and necessary, for its use before public authorities." The Document also recognizes that some states have sought to fulfill some of these aims by establishing "appropriate local or autonomous administrations corresponding to the specific historical and territorial circumstances of such minorities."[56] It stops short, however, of requiring such an arrangement.

Although uncharacteristically generous in recognizing identity rights, the Copenhagen Document is not a total celebration of minority grievances. To the contrary, it strikes a particular compromise between recognition of minority ethno-national identities and preservation of state integrity. Thus, while detailing minority identity rights that are unprecedented in international legal instruments, the Document strongly reaffirms the inviolability of a state's territorial integrity and the ability of the state to impose minimum uniformity, including one or more official languages of communication. Resolution 35, for instance, states clearly that "None of these commitments may be interpreted as implying any right to engage in any activity or perform any action in contravention of the purposes and principles of the Charter of the United Nations, other obligations under international law or the provisions of the Final Act, including *the principle of territorial integrity of States.*" In the same vein, Resolution 34, detailing the linguistic rights to which members of linguistic minorities are entitled, recalls the "need to learn the official language or languages of the State concerned."

The Council and the Venice Draft

The CSCE's Copenhagen Document had a mixed reception in Strasbourg, but not for its content. Council of Europe aficionados had troubles with the CSCE's aggressive move in a field—norm elaboration—that they thought ought to be within the exclusive domain of the Council. Accordingly, at its first meeting after the CSCE's Copenhagen meeting, the Parliamentary Assembly of the Council of Europe hastily adopted a recommendation to the Committee of Ministers to "draw up a Protocol to the European Convention on Human Rights or a special Council of Europe Convention to protect the rights of minorities."[57] However, the Committee of Ministers did not rush to act, in part because it thought the Council of Europe could claim some involvement, albeit very indirect, in the issuance of the Copenhagen Document. As noted above, the Venice Commission, a Council organ, had collaborated with the CSCE on preparation of the Copenhagen Document. And the Document incorporated many of the principles that the Venice Commission had adopted a month before the Copenhagen meeting. Thus, from the perspective of the Committee of Ministers, the Copenhagen Document could be viewed as a good example of CSCE-Council cooperation. The Committee of Ministers also recognized that the Copenhagen Document was a mere nonbinding declaration with no enforcement mechanism and therefore did not preempt the Council's traditional work in the elaboration of legally binding documents with enforcement mechanisms.

Indeed, by February 1991, six months after the Parliamentary Resolution and less than a year after the Copenhagen Document, the Council of Europe was back in the lead. On that date, the Venice Commission presented a

Draft European Convention for the Protection of Minorities (the Venice Draft) to the Committee of Ministers. For the rest of that year, the Venice Draft became the central document of the minority rights project.

In light of the close cooperation between the Commission and the CSCE, it is not surprising that the principles embodied in the Venice Draft are, in broad outline, very similar to those embodied in the CSCE's Copenhagen Document. Several articles require the state to recognize and respect the distinctness of a minority ethno-national identity. Article 3, for instance, grants minorities "the right to the respect, safeguard and development of their ethic, religious and linguistic identity." Article 6 grants "persons belonging to a minority . . . the right to freely preserve, express and develop their cultural identity in all its aspects, free of any attempts at assimilation against their will." Like the Copenhagen Document, many of the remaining articles of the Venice Draft provide more specific rights. Article 5, for instance, guarantees the right to form group-based associations including associations that cross national borders. Article 5 further guarantees the right to international travel. Article 7 guarantees the right to use one's mother tongue in public and in private. Whenever a minority reaches a substantial percentage of the population of the region or of the country, article 8 grants its members the right to communicate with the political, administrative, and judicial authorities in the minority language. Article 9 also provides for the teaching of the minority language and the provision of schooling in that language. Article 10 reaffirms the right to religious free-dom. The Venice Draft is also careful to pay homage to the integrity of existing states. Article 1 (2) reaffirms the commitment to the state's territo-rial integrity. Article 12 permits limitations on the exercise of minority rights "in the interests of public safety, for the protection of public order, health or morals, or for the protection of the rights and freedoms of others." The Venice Draft differs from the Copenhagen Document only in an ex-pected way: it contains a detailed enforcement mechanism, in the form of a proposed European Committee for the Protection of Minorities.[58]

The Council's Venice Draft consolidated the ascendance of minority rights. European states embraced minority rights as a solution to the immin-ent breakup of Yugoslavia and the former Soviet Union. The European Community (EC), for instance, announced that it would recognize only those former Yugoslav republics that put in place legislation and policies guaranteeing the rights of minorities living within their borders. These republics' respect for minority rights would, in turn, justify the EC's refusal to endorse any further secessions.[59]

While the EC and many other international actors seized upon the idea of minority rights, the Council of Europe plodded along with norm elaboration work in this domain. Upon receipt of the Venice Draft, the Committee of Ministers of the Council of Europe, in October 1991, asked its Committee on Human Rights to examine the question of a minorities instrument, as well as the possibility of the Council becoming involved in preventive diplomacy. In early 1992 the Committee reported back. It recommended against the Council taking the more political role of engaging in preventive diplomacy. It announced, however, that some type of minorities instrument seemed both desirable and feasible.[60] In the spring of 1992 the Committee of Ministers formed a Committee of Experts to start drafting an instrument to be completed by December 1993.

Doubts about Minority Rights: The Vienna Summit and Its Aftermath

The minority rights paradigm peaked in 1992, when the United Nations General Assembly adopted a Declaration on the Rights of National Minorities and the Council of Europe Committee of Ministers passed a resolution inviting all member states to fulfill all their obligations and commitments to persons belonging to national minorities.[61] Significantly, however, the Committee of Ministers did not specify what obligations or commitments it had in mind. Nor did that year see the emergence of a European instrument for the protection of minorities.

As the Committee of Experts took its time and the Committee of Ministers did not send out signs of urgency, an irate Parliamentary Assembly voted, on February 1, 1993, to approve a Proposed Protocol on the rights of national minorities.[62] Since the Parliament has only consultative powers, the Proposed Protocol could not go into effect unless adopted by the Committee of Ministers. Accordingly, the Parliament forwarded the Proposed Protocol to the Committee of Ministers along with a strongly worded recommendation that it be adopted. At the time, therefore, expectations were high. Many observers predicted that a protocol would be opened for signature at the much-trumpeted first summit of the heads-of-state of the Council of Europe scheduled for October 1993 in Vienna. Indeed, the Committee of Experts was given a new deadline, September 1993.

If the fall of 1991 and the spring of 1992 were when the minority rights paradigm peaked, the Vienna summit is when it crashed. At Vienna the minority rights paradigm ran into heavy republican criticism. Led by Czech president Vaclav Havel, many east European states resisted strongly the idea of minority rights. Republicans made the persuasive case that minority rights, by institutionalizing internal differences, constituted a wedge in the efforts to forge together a nation around certain unities. How could the Council condemn unitarians when it has historically rubber-stamped the practices that so many western European states have employed in consolidating their own unities? The double standard is not only historical, but also contemporary. If Germany may insist that all non-Germans speak German as a precondition for naturalization, why cannot Estonia require knowledge of Estonian from its "aliens"? For many east Europeans, the double standard is most obvious in the efforts to exclude immigrant minorities in western Europe from the scope of any minority rights instrument, as the proposed drafts do.

The critics further buttress their case by attributing the breakup of Yugoslavia to the Tito regime's staunch multiculturalism and its institutionalization of intranational differences. The critics also warn that minority rights could become a banner in the hands of Russian expansionism in the near abroad. Indeed, they have a point; Russia has invoked the status of Russian speakers in the former Soviet Republics to justify an intrusive role there.

Finally, republicans launch the fundamental critique that the principle of minority rights represents a total capitulation to a way of seeing these conflicts in terms of majorities and minorities. They point out that the principle elevates that outlook to official dogma, thus affirming a logic that contains the seeds of its own undermining. Republicans think that the correct course of action is a continuation of efforts to render states ethno-nationally neutral.

Given the frontal attack on minority rights at Vienna, one could have easily expected the Vienna summit to signal the end of the minority rights experiment. It did not, for the simple reason that all states at Vienna recognized the dangers of returning to the unabashed republicanism of the cold war era. If the Council were to excise minority rights from its vocabulary, it would be hard pressed to dismiss the secessionist struggles of ethno-national minorities.

As a result, although the Vienna summit dashed the hopes of minority rights advocates, it ended with a nod in the direction of minority rights, a nod from which Council bureaucrats could draw some comfort. The declaration produced at the Summit instructed the Committee of Ministers to draft an additional protocol to the European Convention on Human Rights. This protocol is to be "in the cultural field" and will contain "provisions guaranteeing individual rights, in particular for persons belonging to national minorities." Further, the declaration instructed the Council to draft a more general framework convention "specifying the principles which contracting States commit themselves to respect, in order to assure the protection of national minorities." Finally, the declaration approved a minority-conscious policy for the Council Secretariat to follow in its everyday work of helping member states and applicants consolidate their system of democratic governance.

These points notwithstanding, it is easy to see why this declaration cannot achieve its purpose of rendering secessionist claims illegitimate. An advocate for an ethno-national minority could easily proffer a legitimate critique of the Vienna summit declaration as republican window dressing. The additional protocol, the only instrument that is expected to have a meaningful enforcement mechanism (the European Court on Human Rights), will likely grant very little to national minorities. Because the protocol will include provisions that will be applicable to all persons regardless of their status as a minority, it is unlikely that those provisions will be of the type that will satisfy the demands of powerful minorities. The most one could expect to see in such a protocol are general minimalist provisions guaranteeing everyone the right to speak his or her native tongue. It would be prohibitively expensive for a document, which would be invocable by, for instance, all residents of Krajina—regardless of whether they are Serbs or Americans—to require that everyone has a right to receive public education in one's native tongue.

Although this critique is fair, it falsely suggests that had Vienna mandated a more substantive minorities framework, it would have met the secessionist challenge. A minority rights framework, however, cannot meet that challenge in either its strong version or its weaker version. The problem with minority rights is not simply that it frustrates the secessionists' demands for a separate state. Minority rights is, after all, a compromise, and no compromise is expected to satisfy all sides. The problem with minority rights is more fundamental: it proffers no basis for dismissing as illegitimate the secessionist demands that the minority rights arrangement frustrates. Or, stated more modestly, minority rights offers no basis for rejecting these demands within the confines of a territorial-majoritarian conception of democracy.

So long as the Council's conception of democracy retains its majoritarian pillar, advantages will accrue to the majority. Accordingly, a minority will continue to have an incentive to have its own separate state. Certainly, many minorities might settle for minority rights. The point is that the

Council has no basis for condemning the minority that refuses to do so. Since pluralist democracy subscribes to the territorialist-majoritarian logic underlying ethno-national conflict, pluralist democracy cannot condemn secessionism. From the perspective of multiculturalism, it is not readily apparent why it is preferable for a Serb of Krajina to enjoy minority rights in a unified Croatia, rather than for a Croat of Krajina to enjoy minority rights in a separate Krajina. There simply is no basis for portraying a secessionist minority as being any more territorialist or any less pluralist than an antisecessionist majority. The conclusion is unavoidable: a territorial-majoritarian conception of democracy contains its own conceptual seeds of destruction.

The preceding discussion shows the difficulties attending both the efforts to establish the superiority of multiculturalism to republicanism and the efforts to use minority rights as a way of rendering secessionist challenges to current borders illegitimate. The discussion does not suggest, however, either a retreat to republicanism or an embrace of rampant secessionism. The difficulties that plague the first option have already been explored; they have moved the Council in the direction of minority rights in the first place.[63] The difficulties with the second option are equally obvious; if one were to embrace secessionism, where would one legitimately draw the line? The conclusion follows inescapably that, in a world divided into *nation-states,* it is difficult, if not downright impossible, to articulate an incontestable "grand solution" to ethno-national disputes, without at least bringing into question the very nation-state system itself. The problems with any one of the three models—republicanism, multiculturalism, and secessionism—are simply the flip side of the problems with the other two models.

This point suggests that the challenge posed by ethno-national conflict is much more fundamental than the Council's democracy mission has taken it to be. Where "pluralist democracy" fails to meet the challenge of ethno-nationalism, no other grand solution that preserves territoriality and majoritarianism as its hallmarks may succeed. Yet one cannot even begin to think of a conception of democracy devoid of either. The difficulty with ethno-national conflict, then, is not practical, but conceptual.

Conclusion: Coping with the Challenge

The conceptual difficulties with the three models—minority rights, republicanism, and secessionism—do not suggest that all three are inherently bad ideas or that the uneasy balances they offer will necessarily come to a quick end. Some parties, for instance, might certainly be persuaded that a bundle of minority rights in the hand is better than whatever they might find in the bush after a protracted conflict. The conceptual difficulties point to a more modest, but ultimately quite important, conclusion: the Council's democracy mission does not provide a basis for identifying the "correct" resolution of ethno-national conflicts.

Council aficionados are likely to object that this line of reasoning is addressed to a straw man, that the Council is not in search of a "correct" resolution but something much more modest: a—any—reasonable resolution that achieves peace. Since this chapter suggests that minority rights, republicanism, and secessionism are all equally reasonable, the Council would see in this chapter no obstacles to choosing the model that is most likely to be peaceful. Consistent with this mind-set, Council officials are progressing with their wide-ranging work in the domain of minority rights, confident that their work is contributing directly to the restoration of *pax Europa*. In the domain of norm elaboration, an Ad Hoc Committee for the Protection of National Minorities has been focused since November 1993 on carrying out the instructions contained in the Vienna declaration. In the fall of 1994 the Committee issued a Draft Framework Convention for the Protection of National Minorities. The Committee of Ministers adopted the Framework Convention in November 1994 and opened it for signature in February 1995. As of July 1995, twenty-seven member states had signed the Convention and one had ratified it.

In its basic philosophy, the Framework Convention is unequivocally the product of the minority rights paradigm. Indeed, the Convention is substantially similar to the texts discussed in the previous section; if anything, it is more protective of minority rights than those other texts. Surprisingly, the Convention also includes an enforcement mechanism. Article 24 provides that the Committee of Ministers shall "monitor" the implementation of the Convention. Article 25 requires that signatory states provide "full information on the legislative and other measures taken to give effect to the principles set forth in the Convention" both initially and thereafter periodically or at the request of the Committee of Ministers. Finally, article 26 establishes a committee of experts to assist the Committee of Ministers in monitoring compliance with the Convention. Despite its strong pro-minority provisions, however, the Convention continues to acknowledge republicanism. Article 5, for instance, makes clear that a state is free to pursue general integration policies.

The adoption of the Framework Convention does not signal the end of the norm elaboration work. The Ad Hoc Committee on National Minorities is continuing its efforts to promulgate an Additional Protocol to the ECHR. Not all Council organs are awaiting the outcome of the Committee's work. The Parliamentary Assembly, for one, has announced that the Proposed Protocol it adopted in February 1993 is binding on its future work.[64] Thus the Parliament will condition the admission of new states on compliance with the norms outlined in the protocol.[65] The Parliament may also condemn member states for violating those norms. The Parliamentary Assembly has indeed started to pay increasing attention to the status of minorities in both applicant and member states. Although no state has been denied admission because of a failure to comply with the Additional Protocol, Romania and the Slovak Republic were admitted with the understanding that they would bring their legislation into compliance with the minority rights norms. Under the Assembly's recent decision to monitor newly admitted states to ensure that they comply with their preadmission commitments, the Assembly is certain to follow closely the developments in the field of minority rights in those two countries. More recently, the Assembly has also put significant pressure on Turkey for its actions in the predominantly Kurdish-speaking southeastern provinces. The Socialist group went so far as to call for the suspension of Turkey's membership.

The Secretariat is also busy with work intended to dampen ethnonational tensions. The Secretariat is now empowered to provide technical assistance to efforts by European states to negotiate bilateral minorities instruments. Although the Secretariat has done no work to date in this field, this inactivity may be attributed to a great extent to the European Union's stealing the initiative in this domain with its so-called Balladur plan.[66] Thus, if European states decide to engage in bilateral or multilateral negotiations on the status of minorities, they might request the Secretariat's help.

The Secretariat has also continued with its traditional work in transborder cooperation and creation of euroregions. To date, the Secretariat has helped form two euroregions: the Carpathian euroregion, consisting of provinces in Hungary, Poland, Slovakia, and the Ukraine, and the Neisse euroregion, composed of provinces in Germany, Poland, and Czechoslovakia.[67] Additionally, the Secretariat has begun to provide legal advice to east European states on legislation potentially affecting the minorities question: citizenship laws, language laws, local government laws, and so forth. Such advice has already been given to Estonia, Moldova, and the Slovak Republic.

Perhaps more important, the Secretariat has begun to sponsor a number of confidence-building projects in ethno-nationally sensitive areas. These projects, primarily in the field of culture, education, the media, and so on, are intended to increase mutual comprehension among conflicting groups.[68] So far such efforts have been modest: the Secretariat has provided support for bilingual radio stations in Croatia (Italian-Croat) and Estonia (Estonian-Russian) and for the creation of an intercultural teacher education center in Romania. More projects, however, are scheduled for the near future. Finally, since 1993 the *Demosthenes* project has been funding minorities and nationalities seminars, such as the conference on nationalities and minorities held in Budapest in September 1993. The 1994 program included, for the first time, a "minorities" heading, listing workshops and study visits for Albania, Croatia, Estonia, Hungary, and Slovakia.[69]

It is too early to gauge the peace potential of all these activities. Ultimately, much will depend on the reception that a potential minorities instrument receives in states experiencing ethno-national tensions. Confidence-building measures or minorities seminars may lay the necessary groundwork. Indeed, there are signs that some modest successes are in the making.

In the face of the extreme suffering that accompanies violent conflict, the peace effort carries a strong appeal. Nevertheless, the fixation with peace poses two substantial difficulties. First, the abandonment of the search for the "correct" resolution of ethno-national conflicts and the embrace of *any* reasonable resolution that secures peace ironically jeopardize peace. Cognizant that the international actors have no preference for one solution over another, parties acquire every incentive to make clear that any resolution other than their preferred one will result in the continuation of hostilities. As the parties outperform each other, ethno-national conflict rages on in full force. The Bosnian conflict best illustrates this point. In Bosnia the international community's signal that it is willing to take any negotiated settlement has perversely hardened the resolve of the conflicting parties. Both Bosnian Serbs and the Sarajevo government have since made it a priority to provide previews of the type of costs that would be associated with any peace that does not satisfy their basic demands. Having given up any claim to be advocating a "correct" resolution of the Bosnian dispute, the international actors have lost the basis for telling either side that their stand is illegitimate.

Second, when we respond to the ultimate failure of republicanism, secessionism, and multiculturalism by suggesting that any one of these three models will do, what is lost is the possibility of putting into question the fundamental assumptions that all three models share: a world divided into nation-states with distinct national identities, a territorial majoritarian conception of democracy, and so on. These presuppositions are not that innocuous: through their belief in the stability of borders, both of territories and of group identities, they display an eerie similarity to the way of thinking that animates ethno-national conflict. The defeatist lowering of expectations leads us to call off a search that might ultimately burst the limits imposed by these presuppositions.

A handful of democrats have already started the questioning of the rigid structures—the nation-state, the minority group—that we all take for granted, that we all employ and apply in coming to terms with these conflicts.[70] One can only hope that something will snap one of these days and that we will all join the questioning. Clearly, the solution to the conceptual challenge of ethno-nationalism, if one may use the term solution, lies in such a shift in thinking, a shift that is only frustrated by the affirmation of rigid structures by grand solutions of the minority rights type.[71] In the specific context of democratization, our best hope, perhaps our only hope, is to start sketching a conception of democracy that refrains from sanctifying territorialism and majoritarianism (*and* minoritarianism). This might sound crazy and perhaps it is unattainable, but we will never know unless we try. A good first step would be to appreciate the complexities associated with ethno-national conflict. We can then begin the process of imagining flexible structures that allow these complexities to play out in full force.[72]

Suggesting a vague search for a new conception of democracy as an alternative to the Council's work in minority rights might strike some as utopianism run amok. How can we talk in such vague and speculative terms, one may object, when the fighting and the suffering rages in Sarajevo and elsewhere? Implicit in that objection is the belief that "realists" are somehow carrying out activities that are effective in lessening the suffering. That possibility cannot be excluded a priori. Yet neither can the possibility that "realists" are merely apologists for an ugly present and that the little immediate benefit that they offer, if any, does not justify the tremendous loss associated with the abandonment of the quest for a significantly better future. It is beyond the scope of this chapter to resolve this tension between realism and idealism, a tension that one international legal scholar has recast in terms of apology versus utopia.[73] Given the number of people who have embraced realism without much apparent success in resolving these conflicts, however, one might not go terribly wrong in erring on the side of utopia.

The preceding discussion is not meant to suggest that there is no room for certainty and decisive action. Decisive action is warranted in the enforcement of fundamental norms. The Council ought to continue that work, regardless of what it does in the contested field of ethno-nationalism. If the Council persists, as it is likely to, in elaborating norms in the contestable domain of ethno-nationalism, it would be well advised to separate that work from its work in the incontestable domain of human rights. There is some type of behavior that is definitely beyond the pale; why paint that behavior with the same brush as all other proscribed behavior?

In an effort to create a distinct niche for the Council's work in enforcing fundamental norms and to enhance the Council's effectiveness in this domain, I would propose that the Council adopt a list of minimum criteria, a sort of "Declaration of Fundamental Norms," that any actor, whether it be a "state" or a "group," must follow. These criteria should then be applied very strictly, far more strictly than any of the other norms promulgated by the Council.

To enhance the Council's powers in enforcing these fundamental norms, the Council should consider appointing a Commissioner (or Commission) for Fundamental Norms entrusted with the task of identifying violations. A separate Commissioner or Commission is necessary because all existing Council organs, for one reason or another, are less than ideal candidates for the task. Because the enforcement body must offer an unsullied image of immunity to political pressures, both the Committee of Ministers and the Parliamentary Assembly fail the test. The European Court on Human Rights has an excellent image in this respect, but is otherwise ill equipped for this task. The identifications of the violations ought to take place with the shortest possible delay; Court proceedings take substantial time. The Court proceedings could be radically speeded up, but such a move might have undesirable side effects. In any case, it is certain to run into financial obstacles. Although the European Court is not an ideal candidate, a Council Commission for Fundamental Norms could be composed of members of that Court. It could also be composed of members of the European Commission of Human Rights, which is scheduled to be abolished once the proposed revisions of the European Convention are adopted.

The Commissioner or Commission entrusted with the task of enforcing the Declaration of Fundamental Norms ought to be given full powers of access to all persons and organizations. She or he ought not be limited to the intergovernmental level. Wide access would ensure that the Commissioner would be very quickly appraised of any potential violation and would be informed of all sides of the story. It would also increase the Commissioner's legitimacy. Although proposals for involving NGOs in intergovernmental activities generally meet with resistance on sovereignty grounds, this particular proposal of linking the Commissioner with NGOs is unlikely to be significantly opposed because few states question that sovereignty must yield when truly fundamental norms are at stake.

The greatest difficulty with this set of recommendations is identifying the list of fundamental norms. There is a wide disagreement over what is fundamental and what is not. For some, the right to an independent state is fundamental. For others, it is not. Minimalists would limit a declaration of fundamental norms to the most basic rights, such as the right to be free from torture.

The difficulty presented by the disagreement over the fundamental norms is not one to be avoided, but rather one to be engaged. It points, after all, to the necessity and desirability of initiating a spirited public debate and self-examination over what values it is that we consider fundamental. Such a debate will only complement the debate over a new conception of democracy that rises to the challenge of ethno-nationalism. As we get ready to construct the "new world order," both debates are only to be welcomed.

Notes

1. Council of Europe, Contribution of the Council of Europe to the CSCE Meeting of Experts on National Minorities 5 (1991).

2. Most analysts have used the term "ethnic" to label these struggles and conflicts. I have found that term unsatisfactory primarily because it implies a determinative distinction between statal identities or entities, which are labeled "national," and substatal identities or entities, which are labeled "ethnic." In this scheme, national identities are taken for granted; they are stable, rational, and acceptable, if not desirable. By contrast, ethnic identities, are challenged or questioned; they are irrational and suspect. I consider this opposition to be unhelpful, first because I see both an ethnic dimension in national identities and a national aspiration in ethnic identities, and second because I do not consider one type of identity more (or less) stable, rational, or acceptable than the other type. Consistent with this view, I have preferred to use the term "ethno-national," which collapses the distinction between the national and the ethnic. In so doing, I think I have found a term that is truer to the origins of the term "ethnic," the Greek word *ethnos,* signifying "people," which did not incorporate the limiting connotations that the

later English incarnation has acquired. I am not the first to use the term "ethno-national." See Walker Connor, "The Politics of Ethnonationalism," Journal of International Affairs 27 (1973) p. 1; see also Walker Connor, *Ethnonationalism: A Quest for Understanding* (New York: Center for International Relations, New York University, 1993). Connor, however, uses the term to emphasize the ascriptive basis of nationalism, rather than to collapse the distinction between the ethnic and the national.

Although, in problematizing the distinction between the ethnic and the national, this chapter differs from much of existing scholarship, it shares with that scholarship the conceptualization of these conflicts in terms of identity struggles. Why else would it use the term "ethno-national" to describe these conflicts? For some critics, this fixation with identity constitutes misguided idealism (in the philosophical sense of the word) because these conflicts are socioeconomic in nature. Insofar as the critics desire to relegate all culture to some superstructure that is driven by some economic base, I plead guilty to subscribing to some type of idealism. The chapter operates at the level of "phenomena." Insofar as the conflicts present themselves as ethno-national in nature, I believe that they can be fruitfully described and analyzed internally as such, even if these conflicts often, if not always, have a socioeconomic dimension.

3. This chapter constitutes an application, within the context of the Council's democracy mission, of a more general thesis that I am developing in a forthcoming work entitled "Doing the Right Thing in the Face of Ethno-National Conflict."

4. The ten governments signed the Statute of the Council of Europe on May 5, 1949. The Statute entered into force on August 3, 1949. Greece and Turkey became members later that year. The Council of Europe was headquartered in Strasbourg.

5. See A. H. Robertson, *The Council of Europe: Its Structure, Functions and Achievements* (London: Stevens, 1961), p. 1 (citing F. L. Schuman, "The Council of Europe," *American Political Science Review* 45 [1951]), pp. 725 and n. 1).

6. See Susan Strange, "The Council of Europe," *World Affairs* 3 (1949), pp. 246, 247.

7. See George Powell, "The Council of Europe," *International Law Quarterly* 2 (1950), pp. 164, 165.

8. See generally Robertson, *Council of Europe,* pp. 238–40 (discussing Council of Europe measures indicating that the Council viewed the system in place in east European countries as incompatible with the values it cherished).

9. See ibid., pp. 82–94.

10. See ibid., pp. 99–108.

11. Cambridge, Mass., Harvard University Press, 1996.

12. See "Council of Europe," in 1991 European Year Book, vol. 39, The Hague, p. 25.

13. See ibid., pp. 26–27.

14. See Jean-Paul Pancracio, "La Turquie et les organes politiques du Conseil de l'Europe," *1984 Annuaire français de droit international* (Paris: Centre national de la Recherche Scientifique, 1985), pp. 161, 162–63.

15. See ibid., pp. 173–75.

16. Ibid., pp. 171–73.

17. See ECHR, article 24.

18. See ECHR, article 28.

19. See ECHR, article 31.

20. See ECHR, article 48 (1) (a).

21. There are some indications that, since the end of the cold war, the Council has done some important work to make its human rights supervisory system tougher. First, the Council has pressured all member states to agree to the individual petition provision of the Convention. By now, almost all have. Similarly, member states have been pressured to agree to the compulsory jurisdiction of the European Court. Almost all have. The Council has also adopted an additional protocol to the European Convention, which provides that, in signatory states, an individual may bring a case before the Court, without a Commission recommendation to that effect. See Protocol no. 9 (September 6, 1990). Protocol no. 9 entered into force on October 1, 1994, the necessary number of ratifications having been reached. Finally, the Committee of Ministers has adopted an additional protocol to the European Convention on Human Rights, that abolishes the European Commission and permits an aggrieved individual to bring a case directly before the Court. See Protocol no. 11 to the Convention for the Protection of Human Rights and Fundamental Freedoms, article 1 (May 11, 1994). Under the proposed protocol, the screening function of the European Commission would be taken on by three-judge panels of the European Court called Committees. If the three-judge panel does not declare a case inadmissible, it will be submitted to a seven-judge Chamber, which will have the power to hand down a decision on both admissibility and the merits. All but one of the member states have signed Protocol no. 11. If the remaining state gives in, and once a sufficient number ratify the protocol, the changes would go into effect.

One may dismiss these improvements as largely cosmetic or deny the Council credit for them, but one cannot deny that the Council has been moving in the direction of toughening its human rights supervisory mechanism. These improvements should not be exaggerated, however. Perhaps the best proof that the Council has not yet departed from its traditional soft approach to managing compliance with human rights norms is the relaxed attitude that the Council has taken toward the aggressive way in which Turkey has been fighting a Kurdish armed insurgency in its southeast. The Parliamentary Assembly was galvanized into action only after Turkey's Constitutional Court banned a pro-Kurdish political party with more than twenty elected deputies and the Turkish parliament lifted the parliamentary immunity of those deputies, opening the way for a trial in which they would be exposed to the death penalty for speeches delivered in parliament.

22. Finland, traditionally committed to strict interbloc neutrality, joined the Council in 1989, as soon as the cold war came to an end. In 1990 Hungary became the first East bloc country to be admitted. Czechoslovakia and Poland followed suit the next year. Subsequently, all east European countries applied for membership. At the time of writing, however, only Bulgaria, Czechia (the Czech Republic), Estonia, Lithuania, Romania, the Slovak Republic, and Slovenia had joined the ranks of those early admits (Czechia and Slovakia joined after the breakup of Czechoslovakia). As of October 1994 the remaining applications (those of Albania, Belarus, Croatia, Latvia, Moldova, Russia, Ukraine, and Yugoslavia) are all pending. Macedonia has non-voting membership. With the exception of the rump Yugoslavia, all those countries were granted guest status at the Parliamentary Assembly. On October 8, 1991, the Committee of Ministers voted to suspend any cooperation with the rump Yugoslavia. Bosnia-Herzegovina has not applied. For a history and the current status of all applications, see Office of the Clerk of the Assembly,

"Relations Between the Council of Europe and the Countries of Central and Eastern Europe" (February 23, 1994).

With respect to the remaining former Soviet republics, the Bureau of the Parliamentary Assembly has clearly indicated that, unlike the CSCE, the Council is not inclined to admit the Asian republics of the former Soviet Union. See Parliamentary Assembly, "The Geographical Enlargement of the Council of Europe," reprinted in *Human Rights Law Journal* 13 (1992), pp. 230, 231. These countries might be eligible, however, for a yet-to-be established associate membership status and are definitely eligible for the Council's democratization aid programs. See ibid., p. 233. The Council has still not reached a decision on the membership eligibility of the Caucasian republics (Armenia, Georgia, and Azerbaijan), all three of which have requested guest status at the Parliamentary Assembly. See ibid.

23. See Statute of the Council of Europe, article 4.

24. Ibid., article 3.

25. See Andrew Drzemczewski, "The Council of Europe's Co-operation and Assistance Programs with Central and East European Countries in the Field of Human Rights," *Human Rights Law Journal* 14 (1993), pp. 229, 248.

26. See Order no. 488 on the honoring of commitments entered into by new member states (1993).

27. See ibid. For a list of commitments, see Report on the honouring of commitments entered into by member states (March 7, 1994) (Rapporteur Masseret). This order appears to be most relevant to the situation in the Slovak Republic and in Romania.

28. See Parliamentary Resolution 1009 (September 3, 1993) (doc. 6875).

29. See Recommendation 1183 on access by European nonmember states to institutions operating under certain Council of Europe conventions relating to human rights (1992).

30. See Recommendation 1204 on the creation of a transitional mechanism for the protection of human rights for European nonmember states of the Council of Europe (1993); see also Resolution 993 on the general policy of the Council of Europe (1993) (calling on the Committee of Ministers to set up "transitional machinery for the protection of human rights in European states which are not members of the Council of Europe"); Recommendation 1219 (1993).

31. See Directorate of Political Affairs, "Council of Europe Cooperation and Assistance Programs with Central and East European Countries: 1993 Annual Report" (March 4, 1994) [hereafter *1993 Annual Report*]; Directorate of Political Affairs, "Council of Europe Cooperation and Assistance Programs with Central and East European Countries: Programme 1994" (1994) [hereafter *Programme 1994*]. Annual reports are also available for the preceding years.

32. See *1993 Annual Report,* pp. 51–53 (listing the Council of Europe documents available in translation).

33. See "Information and Documentation Centres on the Council of Europe" (March 3, 1994) (stating that centers have been set up in Warsaw, Prague, Budapest, Moscow, Bratislava, and Sofia, within existing institutions, and that two centers are planned in Bucharest and Vilnius).

34. See Directorate of Environment and Local Authorities, "The Lode Programme" (1994).

35. See Directorate of Legal Affairs, "Demo-Droit Programme" (March 21, 1994).

36. See Directorate of Legal Affairs, "Themis Plan for the Development of Law: Proposed Implementation Activities for 1994" (January 18, 1994); Directorate of Legal Affairs, "Themis Plan for the Development of Law" (March 11, 1994).

37. See *1993 Annual Report,* p. 5.

38. *Programme 1994,* p. 2.

39. Directorate of Political Affairs, "Co-Operation and Assistance Programs with Central and East European Countries: Bi-annual Report" (September 1, 1993), p. 5.

40. See *Programme 1994,* p. 34.

41. Ernest Renan's seminal piece *Qu'est-ce qu'une nation?* is considered to be the founding text of this conception of the nation-state. See Ernest Renan, *What Is a Nation?* in Homi K. Bhabha, ed., *Nation and Narration* (New York: Routledge, 1990), p. 8. Renan articulated the republican conception in the course of a major intellectual debate with two German writers, Strauss and Mommsen, over the status of the German-speaking French province of Alsace. Espousing an ethnic conception of the nation-state, the latter submitted that Alsace had to be part of a unified Germany. Espousing a political conception of the nation-state, Renan viewed Alsace as French. See generally Alain Finkielkraut, *La defaite de la pensée: essai* (Paris: Gallionard, 1987). The ideological debate went, of course, hand in hand with a military-political struggle over Alsace that was not resolved until the end of World War II.

42. See ECHR, article 14.

43. See, for example, Isse Omanga Bokatola, *L'Organisation des Nations Unies et la protection des minorités* (Brussels: E. Bruylant, 1992); C. Brolmann, ed., *Peoples and Minorities in International Law* (Dordrecht; Boston; Norwell, Mass.: M. Nijhoff, 1993); Yoram Dinstein and Mala Tabory, eds., *The Protection of Minorities and Human Rights* (Dordrecht; Boston; Norwell, Mass.: M. Nijhoff, 1992); Henri Giordan, ed., *Les minorités en Europe: Droits linguistiques et droits de l'homme* (Paris: Editions Kimé, 1993); Hurst Hannum, *Autonomy, Sovereignity and Self-Determination* (Philadelphia: University of Pennsylvania Press, 1990); Natan Lerner, *Group Rights and Discrimination in International Law* (Dordrecht; Boston; Norwell, Mass: M. Nijhoff, 1990); Patrick Thornberry, *International Law and the Rights of Minorities* (Oxford University Press, 1991); Université Libre de Bruxelles, Institut d'Etudes Européennes, *La protection des minorités et les droits de l'homme* (1992); Addeno Addis, "Individualism, Communitarianism and the Rights of Ethnic Minorities," *Notre Dame Law Review* 66 (1991), p. 1219; Henry Steiner, "Ideals and Counter-Ideals in the Struggle over Autonomy Regimes for Minorities," ibid., p. 1539.

44. See European Community, "Declaration on the Guidelines on the Recognition of New States in Eastern Europe and in the Soviet Union" (December 16, 1991), reprinted in *International Legal Materials,* 31 (1992), pp. 1486, 1487.

45. See generally Thornberry, *International Law.*

46. See Patrick Thornberry, "Is There a Phoenix in the Ashes?—International Law and Minority Rights," *Texas International Law Journal* 15 (1980), pp. 421, 443.

47. See "Study of the Legal Validity of the Undertakings Concerning Minorities" (April 7, 1950), p. 71, E/CN.4/367 ("Between 1937 and 1947 circumstances as a whole changed to such an extent that, generally speaking, the League of Nations system of international protection of minorities should be considered as having ceased to exist").

48. Yves Plasseraud, *Qu'est-ce qu'une minorité en France aujourd'hui?*, in *Groupement pour les droits des minorités: Les minorités à l'age de l'Etat-nation* (Paris: GDM, 1985), pp. 271, 274.

49. See Peter Leuprecht, "Le Conseil de l'Europe et les droits des minorités," *Les cahiers de droits* 27 (1986), p. 203.

50. See Committee of Experts on Human Rights, "Rights of National Minorities" (November 9, 1973), p. 5.

51. See Henri Giordan, *Démocratie culturelle et droit à la différence: Rapport au ministre de la culture* (Paris: La Documentation Français, 1982).

52. See Decision no. 91–290 (May 9, 1991), in *Journal Officiel* (May 14, 1991), p. 6350. See generally Bruno Genevois, *Le controle de la constitutionalité du status de la collectivite territoriale de Corse, Revua français de droit administrat* (1991), p. 407.

53. The CSCE founding document, the Final Act of the Helsinki Conference of 1975, contained a brief statement on the minorities issue. This provision, however, was squarely located in the republican tradition of formal equality: "The participating States on whose territories national minorities exist will respect the right of persons belonging to such minorities to equality before the law, will afford them the full opportunity for the actual enjoyment of Human Rights and fundamental freedoms and will, in this manner, protect their legitimate interests in this sphere." Final Act, Principle VII. The Helsinki Final Act went to great lengths, moreover, to emphasize each state's right to territorial integrity and to freedom of choice with regard to its political, social, economic and cultural systems.

In "Minority Rights in the CSCE Context," in Dinstein and Tabory, eds., *The Protection of Minorities and Human Rights,* Mala Tabory notes that an annex to the Final Act provides that "The participating States, recognizing the contribution that national minorities or regional cultures can make to cooperation among them in various fields of culture [education], intend, when such minorities or cultures exist within their territory, to facilitate this contribution, taking into account the legitimate interests of their members" (p. 187). Tabory points out, however, that "this provision is weak in that it is only a statement of 'intention'" (p. 193).

54. See Resolution 31 (emphasis added).

55. See Resolution 33.

56. See Resolution 35.

57. See Parliamentary Assembly Recommendation no. 1134 (October 1, 1990).

58. See articles 18–30. The Committee would be composed of one member from each Council of Europe state (see article 19). The Committee would have the power to review "reports on the measures [states] have adopted to give effect to their undertakings under this Convention" and to "make any necessary recommendations" (see article 24). If so empowered by a State, the Committee will also be able to hear petitions brought against that state, either by another state signatory of the instrument (see article 25) or by individual members of national minorities (see article 26). The Committee is instructed to try to find a friendly settlement of the matter (see article 28). If no such settlement appears possible, the Committee may prepare a report with specific recommendations that will be transmitted to the Committee of Ministers of the Council of Europe (see article 29). The Committee of Ministers will decide on the appropriate course of action (ibid.).

59. The EC did not follow the recommendations of the Arbitration Commission that it had established to apply the guidelines. Citing the inadequacy of safeguards

for the Serb minority under the laws of the newly independent Croatia, the Arbitration Commission recommended against the recognition of that state. It recommended in favor of the recognition of Macedonia. For purely political reasons, the EC ignored both recommendations. Under German pressure, Croatia was recognized. Under Greek pressure, Macedonia was not recognized. See chapter 5.

60. See Petter F. Wille, "Minority Questions in the Council of Europe," *Helsinki Monitor* 5 (Utrecht, The Netherlands: Netherlands Helsinki Committee, 1994), pp. 26, 29.

61. See Resolution (92)10 (May 1992).

62. From a substantive point of view, the Proposed Protocol is very similar to the Venice Draft. The sole significant difference is in the enforcement mechanism. Because the Proposed Protocol takes the form of an additional protocol to the European Convention on Human Rights, a violation by a signatory state would trigger the full ECHR mechanism, including the jurisdiction, where applicable, of the European Court of Human Rights. Thus the Protocol would not necessitate the creation of a separate mechanism.

63. See the section on the Council's traditional approach to ethno-nationalism above.

64. See Heinrich Klebes, "Draft Protocol on Minority Rights to the ECHR," *Human Rights Law Journal* 14 (1993), pp. 140, 14.

65. See Order no. 484 (instructing the Committee on Legal Affairs "to make scrupulously sure when examining requests for accession to the Council of Europe that rights included in this Protocol are respected by the applicant countries").

66. The goal of the Balladur plan was to encourage east European states to resolve all sensitive interstate issues, including those concerning borders and national minorities, through bilateral and multilateral treaties. These treaties would form the basis of a Europewide settlement, the Pact on Stability in Europe. The European Union would try to convince all central and east European countries to join this effort to elaborate the Pact through a combination of incentives (aid, future membership) and disincentives (cessation of cooperation). See chapter 4.

67. See Institute of EastWest Studies, *Carpathian Euroregion Newsletter* (November 1992).

68. See Secretariat, "Mesures de confiance dans le domaine des minorités: Propositions de projets-pilotes pour 1993.

69. See *Programme 1994,* pp. 34–35.

70. See, for example, Gidon Gottlieb, *Nation against State: A New Approach to Ethnic Conflict and the Decline of Sovereignty* (New York: Council on Foreign Relations Press, 1993). For a succinct summary of the book, see Gidon Gottlieb, "Nations without States," *Foreign Affairs* 73 (May–June 1994), p. 100; Dov Ronen, *The Quest for Self-Determination* (New Haven: Yale University Press, 1979).

71. I develop this thought at greater length in the work cited above in note 3.

72. I have found Gerald Frug's "Decentering Decentralization," *University of Chicago Law Review* 60 (Chicago: University of Chicago Press, 1993), p. 253–338, a very helpful start along those lines. The call for flexible structures should not be interpreted as a call for abandonment of borders, both territorial and ethno-national. As Frug reminds us (pp. 337–38), we have reasons to want to affirm borders even though we question them.

73. See Martti Koskenniemi, *From Apology to Utopia: The Structure of International Legal Argument* (Helsinki: Finnish Lawyers' Publishing Company, 1989).

Part Two

THREE

Community against Conflict: The European Community's Contribution to Ethno-National Peace in Europe

John Pinder

THE MAASTRICHT TREATY has established the European Union (EU), with the European Community (EC), founded nearly a half century ago, as its central pillar. Alongside the Community, the Treaty set up the Common Foreign and Security Policy (CFSP) and the Cooperation in Justice and Home Affairs. The ways in which the CFSP can contribute to ethno-national peace in Europe are considered in chapter 4. This chapter concerns the specific contribution of the Community, with its largely economic competences and its institutions comprising significant federal elements. The Community contributes in two main ways: through its external policies, involving mainly trade and aid; and through the special relationship among its member states and the prospect of membership among those that wish to join. While the Community and the Union are coterminous and membership of one implies membership of the other, the Community's characteristics require a separate analysis. In what follows, the term Community will be used unless the reference is to the Union's composite structure as a whole.

Many thanks are due to Katrijn Otten, who obtained much of the information which is the basis for the section on Community policies toward central and eastern Europe and the CIS countries.

Conflicts and the Influence of Membership or
Prospective Membership

The Community is a polity based on the rule of law and respect for
human rights, including equality before the law. Member states of the
Community must be democratic. This has been made clear since the first
approaches with a view to accession were made in the early 1960s; [1] and it
is explicit in the Maastricht Treaty, which affirms that the member states'
systems of government "are founded on the principles of democracy."[2] The
Community also embodies significant elements of representative government, and thus it is not only composed of liberal democracies but also itself
has characteristics of liberal democracy. This is highly relevant to the
resolution of ethno-national conflicts, one condition of which is equality of
rights before the law, contradicting the nationalistic principle that "the
nation is . . . the fundamental ethical category" which overrides private
rights and "rejects the rights of other nations living in its territory."[3]

Liberal democracy is also conducive to peaceful resolution of conflicts
through the practices of mutual accommodation that derive from the processes of representative government in constitutional democracies based on
citizens' rights and the rule of law. Of course the liberal democratic formula
does not guarantee that conflicts will be peacefully resolved. Within the
Community are Northern Ireland and the Basque country, and there is
potential for violence also in Corsica, Alto Adige or Sud Tyrol, and elsewhere. But there is no interstate violence in the Community. In the cases of
both Northern Ireland and the Basque country, the pairs of member states
involved have cooperated with some success to try to end the violence. The
equality before the law, together with the processes of political accommodation at the level of both the Community and member states, can be seen
as removing potential causes of violence.

The combination of prosperity, peace, and freedom that central and east
Europeans saw embodied in the Community was attractive, and it encouraged them to throw off the Soviet system. Many now aspire to join.
Bulgaria, the Czech Republic, Hungary, Poland, Romania, and Slovakia,
which have Europe Agreements of association with the Community, have
already lodged their applications for membership. The peoples of the eastern countries have a good impression of the European Union: opinion
surveys have shown that among the central and east Europeans, over four
times as many have a positive impression as have a negative one; and
among European countries of the Commonwealth of Independent States

(CIS)—that is Russia, Ukraine, Belarus, and Armenia—the ratio is over six times. Furthermore, 33 percent of the central and east Europeans feel that their country's future lies with the EU, which is over two and a half times as many as see their future in any other affiliation.[4]

The democratic character of the Union influences the business community, among others, because businesspeople know that they will not secure a place on the inside track of the integrated market unless their country can pass muster as a democracy. The Iberian enlargement of the Community provided evidence of this. The business interests, which might have been afraid that national democratic governments could take populist actions inimical to business, were confident that Community law would ensure fair treatment, and hence supported the new democracies in Spain and Portugal, which could, as such, accede to the Community.[5] The Community has also made it clear that protection of human rights, including those of people belonging to minorities, is a prerequisite for membership.

Accession, when it comes, should provide a more definitive guarantee of democracy and human rights. For the former East Germany, this came about through its incorporation into the Federal Republic, a textbook example of what has been called democracy-through-incorporation. Accession by means other than merger with an existing member state would, on the other hand, offer democracy-through-convergence, illustrated by the accession of Greece, Portugal, and Spain, whose democracies were supported by the enlargement of a "democratic community of sovereign states."[6] But particularly since the Community has been strengthened by the Single European Act and the Maastricht Treaty, accession contains an element of incorporation as well as convergence, for although the Community lacks the means of physical coercion, its institutions do constrain member states in areas where they were previously completely sovereign. It has become yet stronger as a guarantor of democracy and human rights.

Membership and, before that, prospective membership, are the Community's most powerful contribution to the resolution of conflicts between the states concerned, including those conflicts that involve minorities across their mutual frontiers, and the guarantees of rule of law and democratic government should help to alleviate ethno-national conflict even where there is no cross-border element. A major part of this chapter is therefore devoted to explanation of the Community's institutions, powers, and methods of working, as a basis for evaluating the operation of this incentive.

The Influence of the Community's External Policies

The Community combines the strength of all its member states in its common instruments of external trade policy. It makes a substantial collective effort in the field of aid and finance. These economic instruments are given a coherence and an additional political dimension by means of agreements with partner countries. In the case of the eastern neighbors, this process begins with trade and then trade and economic cooperation agreements and moves on to the Europe Agreements for central and east European states and Partnership and Cooperation Agreements for states of the CIS.

The economic weight of the Community, which is, along with the United States, one of the world's two greatest trading powers, lends influence to its external economic policy. This can be brought to bear directly on ethno-national, or, as the Community itself puts it, minority problems, and in support of the rights of "members of minorities," as the Community prefers to express it.[7] But the Community's major contribution to the resolution of such problems is less direct and consists of the help it can give in the building of structures of a market economy, constitutional democracy, and civil society. Since its instruments are mainly economic, the Community's main target has been the establishment of effective market economies. But the significance of this for the consolidation of constitutional democracies should not be underestimated. Constitutional democracies cannot survive apart from an active civil society, which balances and supports the political and judicial institutions with a diversity of independent associations and institutions. Together, constitutional democracy and civil society may be called pluralist democracy. Civil society has many aspects: social, educational, religious, cultural, and so on. Among the latter, by far the most important is the economic aspect of civil society, which is indeed the market economy. The market economy is an essential support for constitutional democracy. There appear to be no cases of such democracies without a market economy. India may come closest to having been an exception, but there were always substantial market elements in the Indian economy. Otherwise, there seems to be complete empirical confirmation of what theory should indicate: that civil society in one of peoples' most important activities, that is to say in the economy, is an essential support for constitutional democracy. While the Community has instituted policies intended to support democratic institutions directly as well as elements of civil society, by far the most important element of its external policy in this area is its contribution to the development of market economies.

In the following section, therefore, the explanation of the Community's powers, institutions, and methods of working includes particular reference to its external economic instruments and their use by the institutions, as a basis for subsequent analysis of the Community's influence on the central and east Europeans and the CIS.

The European Community: Federal Elements in the Government of the Economy

This section explains the character of the Community so that its capacity to exert influence on countries of central and eastern Europe and of the CIS can be understood. Since the Community is still in the process of developing, and since the problems among its eastern neighbors, including the ethno-national problems, will remain of concern for some time to come, a static snapshot is not enough. It will be helpful to observe the dynamics of the way in which it has developed up to now: the enhancement of its institutions, powers, instruments, and policies, and the forces that have helped to bring this about. In essence, this has been done by putting in place successively a number of building blocks, which may be termed federal because each such block could be an element in the structure of a federal union—as, indeed, some of the most important sponsors of these developments have intended the Community to become. While it is possible that the Maastricht Treaty was the last such building block, and that its most important element, the economic and monetary union, may not be realized in any effective form, it is in the writer's view more likely that further federal elements will be put in place during the period in which central and east European countries may expect to become member states. So it is useful not only to know where the Community stands today, but also whither it may go during that period.

The Fundamental Motive for Establishing the Community: Peaceful Resolution of Conflicts

The Community was established in the wake of World War II, which had torn Europe's people and physical fabric apart. The fundamental motive was to ensure that such violence would not occur again.

THE FEDERAL IDEA. The most influential idea in devising the method for ensuring peace was that of a federal union, based, sometimes no doubt naively, but often entirely rationally, on the examples of the United States and Switzerland. The significance of this idea was greater than is usually realized today.[8] In the late 1940s when the scene for establishment of the Community was set, not only was there "a rising tide of opinion" in favor of European political institutions,[9] but this opinion was crystallized at the highest political level. Following his speech at Fulton, Missouri in March 1946, in which he introduced the concept of the Iron Curtain and at the same time said that "the safety of the world requires a new unity in Europe,"[10] Churchill went on, in a speech at Zurich in September, to assert that "we must build a kind of United States of Europe," toward which "the first step must be a partnership between France and Germany."[11] Although Churchill was vague about the institutions to be envisaged, his words electrified opinion on the continent and made the idea of strong political institutions at a European level appear operational. It soon became evident that Churchill, like other British political leaders, had little intention of committing Britain to take part in any institutions of federal type. But many leaders on the Continent, and in particular in the six founder states of the Community—France, Germany, Italy, and the Benelux countries—did have that intention. They made this clear by insisting on inclusion of the term *federation* in the resolutions of the Congress of Europe at The Hague in May 1948, which had been convened by Churchill to launch a movement for uniting Europe.

REALIZATION BY STEPS. The problem with the federal idea was that governments were not prepared to make the leap from their status as completely sovereign nation-states to members of a multinational federation. Yet a conventional international organization at European level would not have provided a firm enough guarantee that relations between European states, and particularly between France and Germany, would not deteriorate again as dangerously as they had before. It was Jean Monnet, combining a vision of a united Europe with deep practical knowledge of governmental processes, who devised the concept of achieving a federal system through a series of steps, each of which would take the participating states part of the way. As he put it in the statement he and his collaborators drafted for Robert Schuman, the French foreign minister, to announce the initiative that launched the first great stride, the creation of the European Coal and Steel Community (ECSC), the intention was to "build the first concrete foundation of a European federation which is indispensable to the preservation of peace."[12] Although only a first step, the Community that Monnet initiated was built to last. Much of its institutional structure remains in the Community of today, though with the subsequent addition of further federal elements. The motives behind its construction have also persisted until now, at least as far as the Franco-German partnership is concerned.

EC 1950–85: Foundation, Development, Stagnation

Monnet's first draft of what was to become Schuman's declaration on May 9, 1950, defined the essential political objective as being "to make a breach in the ramparts of national sovereignty which will be narrow enough to secure consent, but deep enough to open the way towards the unity that is essential to peace."[13] Consent was to be forthcoming because the proposal would solve an urgent political problem facing governments and because the federal elements in it did not seem excessive; yet it would open the way to the unity necessary for peace because those federal elements were nevertheless significant. The first application of this formula in the creation of the European Coal and Steel Community was a resounding success.

THE EUROPEAN COAL AND STEEL COMMUNITY. The urgent problem facing the French government was to ensure French security following the revival of German coal and steel production. The recovery of this production had been severely controlled in the aftermath of the war because it was seen as the industrial basis for German military power. But the hot war was now being succeeded by the cold war, and the United States was determined that West Germany should provide an example to the East of what a capitalist economy could achieve. Alarmed by the specter of what could become a revival of German military might, the French government was extremely anxious to find a way of ensuring control of its potential industrial basis. Unilateral control was hardly practicable since France did not control the Ruhr, Germany's industrial heartland. Monnet was in any case convinced that attempts to dominate Germany unilaterally would not endure, any more than they had done following World War I. The answer could only be a framework within which the coal and steel industries of both Germany and France would be controlled on an equal basis, along with those of Italy and the Benelux countries, the other European democracies that wished to take part. Britain preferred to stand aside.

The institutions that Monnet and his advisers designed for the ECSC provided in effect a government for these countries' coal and steel industries. Monnet had, as the deputy secretary-general of the League of Nations, experienced at first hand the weaknesses of an international organization that depended for its decisions and actions on the agreement of several member states' governments. He was determined that the ECSC should have an executive that would not be under the control of the governments for every step it took. So he secured the establishment of the High Authority as an independent executive for the ECSC. His advisers realized that, since the member states were parliamentary democracies based on the rule of law, such an executive should be supervised by a parliamentary and a judicial body, hence the addition of the Common Assembly (later to become the European Parliament) and the Court of Justice. During the negotiations for the ECSC Treaty, representatives of partner governments insisted on the need for a Council in which ministers of the governments could seek to ensure that the activities of the Community were compatible with their own. The result was the structure of institutions much as it stands now: executive (now the European Commission), Court, Parliament, and Council. In presenting this design to the inaugural session of the Common Assembly, Monnet took pains to underline its federal characteristics.[14]

This institutional structure governed the member states' coal and steel industries in a satisfactory way, reaping through free trade the benefits of the transborder complementarities and competition that had been frustrated by the protectionism of the past. Above all, it provided a framework within which Franco-German reconciliation could begin to flourish. Striking evidence of this came in the peaceable settlement of what had previously been the apparently insoluble ethno-national problem of the Saar.

FRANCO-GERMAN RECONCILIATION: THE SAAR. The Saarland had, like the other frontier regions, Alsace and Lorraine, long been a bone of contention between Germany and France, part of the cause of the terrible violent conflicts between the two countries. Following World War I, France had wanted to annex the Saar. But Woodrow Wilson opposed, and a compromise was agreed among the victorious Allies: the Saar was to be under the aegis of the League of Nations, administered by an international commission with a Frenchman as its head and with French ownership of the coal that was the heart of the Saar's economy and was complementary with the French steel mills in the Lorraine. In 1935 the future of the Saar was to be decided by a plebiscite. Meanwhile France for a time occupied a substantial part of Germany when the Germans failed to pay the impossible burden of reparations that the Allies had imposed after World War I. But the hard French line evoked bitter reactions among the Germans. When the plebiscite was held, under League of Nations auspices, the Saarlanders, who are German-speaking, voted by a huge majority for incorporation into the German Reich.

Jean Monnet had been the deputy secretary-general of the League of Nations in 1922 when the international regime for the Saar was devised and was keenly conscious of the error the Allies had then imposed upon the League.[15] He observed with concern the French government's attempt to repeat the pattern after World War II, incorporating the Saar into the French economy and securing its government by a French High Commissioner "in proconsular style." He was convinced that a "system of indefinite domination" would be no more sustainable after World War II than it had been after World War I. It was with growing alarm that he saw the French government, troubled by the evidence that the United States was going to insist on the revival of the German steel industry, intensifying its efforts to annex the Saar politically.[16] Thus Monnet envisioned the proposal for the European Coal and Steel Community as "radically transforming the political context" within which problems such as the Saar would become soluble.[17]

Indeed, after the ECSC Treaty entered into force in 1952, no more was heard of the idea of political annexation of the Saar. But, as was to be expected, opposition to the "proconsular" regime became rife among the Saarlanders and grew in Germany too. By 1954 it was evident to all that the reason for the economic annexation had been superseded by the ECSC. Franco-German reconciliation was, moreover, proceeding apace in the context of the Community. By October 1954, when discontent among the Saarlanders was becoming acute, the two countries were able to agree that the citizens of the Saar could choose between a new European statute, which federalists hoped might eventually become a District of Columbia for Europe, and incorporation into the Federal Republic of Germany. Neither government was to interfere in the campaign, and despite a somewhat virulent performance by some German nationalists in the Saar, the French government as well as the German refrained from doing so. When the referendum was held in October 1955, one-third of the Saarlanders voted for the European statute and two-thirds for incorporation into the Federal Republic. So profoundly had French opinion changed in the context of the Community, as had the French government's calculation of the national interest in the new, European regime for coal and steel, that the result was received in France "with a good grace, which bordered on indifference."[18] Thus was one of Europe's most dangerous ethno-national problems resolved.

FAILURE OF THE EUROPEAN DEFENSE COMMUNITY. Only six weeks after Monnet and Schuman launched the project for the ECSC in May 1950, North Korea invaded South Korea. As this followed a series of expansionist moves by Stalin in Europe, the United States became seriously concerned about the defense of Western Europe and insisted that a German military contribution was required. Just as Monnet had reacted to the revival of German industrial power with his proposal for the Coal and Steel Community, so he and some other French leaders reacted to the prospect of reviving German military power with the proposal for a European Defense Community (EDC), with a European Army in which the German troops would serve on an equal basis with those of the other member states. A treaty was signed by all six governments and a constitutional document was drafted by a constituent body based on the Assembly of the ECSC.[19] But although the treaty had been signed, the European Army was a step too far for some politicians of the French center as well as being bitterly opposed by the Gaullists and Communists. The French National Assembly voted in August 1954 not to approve the project.

THE EUROPEAN ECONOMIC COMMUNITY AND THE CONSEQUENCES.   Many felt that the Community experiment had been killed at the same time as the EDC Treaty, but the political and economic motives for continuing it proved stronger than the temporary mood of Euroskepticism. In less than a year the Community process was relaunched. Franco-German reconciliation and the prospect of a permanent peace were by now associated with this process, and serious statesmen were not going to abandon it just because the proposal for defense integration had proved, for the time being, not feasible. Soon after the collapse of the EDC project, the Benelux countries sponsored a proposal for a common market or economic community. The resurgent European industries were going to need a wider market than those of the existing small or medium-size European states, if they were to compete with American industries. Such, at least, was the argument that convinced the more forward-looking among policymakers and the more dynamic among industrialists in the member states of the ECSC.[20] At the intergovernmental conference of these states at Messina in June 1955, a fair wind was given to the Benelux proposal as well as to a parallel project, initiated by Monnet, for a European Atomic Energy Community (Euratom).

The Benelux proposal was developed into the treaty establishing the European Economic Community (EEC), which in effect gave wide-ranging economic powers to Community institutions on the pattern of the ECSC. The common market was to offer free movement among the member states for goods, services, capital, and people going about their business. The backbone of the common market was the customs union, to be established gradually according to a detailed timetable over a period of twelve to fifteen years. Along with this came the common agricultural policy (CAP). The Community also established arrangements for tariff preferences and economic aid for the then "associated overseas territories" of the member states, and since developed for a much wider range of purposes. All of these elements are today of much significance to the central and east Europeans.

Alongside the main elements, the EEC and Euratom treaties, which entered into force in January 1959, provided for a wide range of economic cooperation to be organized by the Community institutions. As with the ECSC, these institutions comprised a Council of Ministers, a Commission (which, however, was less strongly placed in its relationship with the Council than was the High Authority), the Court, and the Assembly, which were now shared by all three communities.

The Community, as the combination of the three communities came to be called, was now no longer an experiment, but a solidly based institution with competences that included virtually the whole of the member states' mutual and external trade. It was consolidated by its economic success in the 1960s, a prosperous decade for the member states in which their mutual trade grew twice as fast as world trade and their economies twice as fast as those of Britain and the United States. While this occurred in the framework of the customs union, and surely in part thanks to the liberalization of the Community's internal trade, the external impact of the customs union was at least as impressive. Faced with the common tariff of what now amounted to an equal trading power, the United States could have reacted defensively and instituted protectionist measures. Instead, the American response was the Kennedy round negotiations under the General Agreement on Tariffs and Trade (GATT), concluded in 1967, which resulted in a general reduction of tariffs on industrial goods by the United States, the Community, and other industrialized countries by an average of about one-third, a liberalization unprecedented in the history of international negotiations. The Community, in the course of the Kennedy round, showed itself to be a great trading power, generally on the side of liberal trade, but with strongly protectionist reflexes in the fields of agriculture, textiles, and some other "sensitive" sectors.

During the 1960s and 1970s, the Community developed a number of practices of potential significance in relation to central and eastern Europe. It broadened its preferential arrangements in the early 1970s through a Generalized System of Preferences (GSP), giving tariff preference to a wide range of imports from almost all developing countries, which was subsequently also adopted by the other industrialized countries. Already in

1962 it had concluded an association agreement with Greece providing for the elimination of tariffs and quotas from trade between Greece and the Community over a transitional period of twelve years, with up to twenty-two years allowed for the abolition of protection for some of Greece's sensitive industries. The agreement established a ministerial Council of Association, a Committee of Association for senior officials, and a committee to associate Greek and Community parliamentarians, in rough parallel with Community institutions.

The agreement also stated that Greek accession to the Community was the ultimate aim, and that was accomplished twenty years later. The experience with the subsequent association agreement with Turkey was less happy, because the Community has not followed through on the reference to future membership. As we shall see, this experience led to some reluctance to include such a reference in association agreements with central and east European countries, and it was not until 1993 that the aim of membership for these associates was explicitly endorsed.

Meanwhile the first application of the British, along with the Danes and the Irish, for membership, was vetoed by President de Gaulle in 1963. The three countries were not admitted to the Community until 1973, after de Gaulle's death. De Gaulle wanted neither the British as rivals for leadership in the Community, nor the constraint of the Community institutions, in which he found the federal elements particularly objectionable. Indeed, in 1965 he refused to accept majority voting in the Council, as foreseen by the EEC Treaty, and withdrew his ministers from conducting Community business. He allowed them to return only after he had made it clear, in the so-called Luxembourg compromise, that he would not be bound by a majority vote on matters that he deemed important for France. There was very little majority voting in the Council for the next twenty years. National ministers and officials were thereby able to retain their grip on Community business, and the result was a prolonged period of relative stagnation in the Community's development that was to last until the mid-1980s.

When the French government lifted its veto, allowing the admission of Britain, Denmark, and Ireland, it devised a formula that it called "completion" and "deepening" to go with the widening. The aim of the completion was to conclude unfinished business of particular interest to France: the common financing of the common agricultural policy, ensuring that all member states would share in the support for agriculture, which was especially beneficial for French farmers. The other aim, of deepening, was intended by France to lock not only Britain but also Germany firmly into the Community with a monetary union and a common foreign policy. But the Germans insisted that monetary union must be accompanied by the guarantee of strict economic policies to prevent inflation and stronger Community institutions to ensure this. The French government, however, in the early post–de Gaulle period still highly resistant to majority voting in the Council or more power for the European Parliament (as the Assembly was to be renamed), refused such economic and institutional rigor. Only tentative steps toward monetary integration were taken. France likewise was not prepared to consider majority voting for the cooperation in foreign policy, which became the rather weakly performing European Political Cooperation. But although the attempt to deepen was not immediately effective, both monetary integration and foreign policy cooperation became steadily more important, culminating in the major provisions of the Maastricht Treaty twenty years later. The concept that widening should be accompanied by deepening remains a powerful one, which is highly likely to condition the enlargement of the Community and Union to include the countries of central and eastern Europe.

Despite the difficulties and only modest progress during the 1970s and early 1980s, the Community survived and accomplished some significant things: enlargement to include not only Britain, Denmark, and Ireland but also, in 1981, Greece and, in 1987, Portugal and Spain; the creation of the European Monetary System with its Exchange Rate Mechanism; direct elections to the European Parliament; and the establishment of the European Council of heads of state and government, with the participation of the president of the Commission. Thus the Community remained in good enough shape to launch a strong phase of development between 1985 and 1992.

EC 1985–92: Regeneration

In the early 1980s many thought that the Community was incapable of significant further development. Mrs. Thatcher was blocking such development until she got Britain's "money back," as she somewhat crudely expressed her reaction to the poor hand dealt to Britain as a result of the predominance of agriculture on the expenditure side of the Community budget. There was an agri-budgetary crisis, with huge stocks of unsaleable foodstuffs in the Community's storehouses and a budget deficit that could not be covered from existing resources. Spanish and Portuguese negotiations for entry had been hanging fire, largely because of pressure from the farm lobbies in France. As was to occur again in the 1990s, the political difficulties accompanied a poor economic performance. These were the circumstances in which the idea gained ground that both European industry and the Community itself could be regenerated by an ambitious program to complete the single market by the end of 1992.

THE SINGLE MARKET AND SINGLE EUROPEAN ACT.   The Franco-German partnership and political motives were again important, as they had been when the Communities were founded in the 1950s. But more strongly than in the launching of the common market proposal in 1955, business interests were pressing for the single market program. Whereas in the 1960s tariffs and quotas had been seen as the main protectionist devices, nontariff barriers and distortions had become increasingly important through the bad times of the 1970s and were now seen as the main cause of the fragmentation of the Community's internal market which was impeding the development of European industries, and particularly of those that depended most intensively on the new technologies.

Jacques Delors, who became president of the Commission in 1985, skillfully steered the project to the top of the Communities' agenda and to the center of the Intergovernmental Conference which adopted the Single European Act. The central feature of the Single Act was the program to complete the single market in 1992, with the amendments to the Community's treaty necessary to bring it about. Along with this there was the provision for "economic and social cohesion," code words for substantial funds from the Community budget to help the development of the economically weaker member states.

The Single Act also gave the Community competence to deal with pollution having cross-border effects. While the CFSP is in the province of chapter 4, it is pertinent to observe here that its institutionalization has accompanied major developments in the Community's economic powers, with respect to both the single market and the single currency.

The single market should in principle have been established through the EEC Treaty's original provisions for the common market. But the key measures were frustrated by the application of the unanimity procedure in the Council. Laws to remove the nontariff barriers that fragmented the market had been enacted by the Council, but at so slow a rate that the proliferation of the barriers overtook them. When it became clear that nearly three hundred new laws would be required to complete the single market, it was obvious that only majority voting in the Council could bring this about. Thus the Single Act provided for majority voting with respect to almost all the legislation required. Laws, in the form of Community Directives or Regulations, were then enacted at a rate of about one a week between 1987, when the Single Act came into force, and 1992, when the legislation for the single market was virtually completed. The principle of majority voting now governs most of the Community's legislation, and this was a major cause of the Community's regeneration in the five years following the entry into force of the Single Act.

The Single Act also strengthened the role of the European Parliament. Under the "cooperation procedure" now applicable to most of the single market legislation, the Parliament has powers of amendment which, although not decisive, have enabled it to get the Council to accept more than half the numerous amendments that it has proposed to the single market measures. Significantly for the central and east Europeans, the Parliament was also given the power of assent over association agreements and treaties of accession, which enables it to say yes or no to them but does not provide a procedure for amendment beforehand. The Court of Justice, with its growing workload, which was to be further charged by the cases arising from the single market measures, was supplemented by a Court of First Instance, to deal with certain fields of Community legislation.

THE MAASTRICHT TREATY 1989–91: A MASSIVE BUILDING BLOCK. The Single Act and single market program both strengthened the federal aspects of the institutions and launched an economic boom that continued for some five years, until 1992. In the context of that prosperity, more people were open to the arguments of Delors and others that the integration of financial markets which was part of the single market program would, through the newfound ease of capital movements across frontiers, lead to instability of exchange rates unless the Community moved to monetary union with a single currency. The stage was set for the next big building block in the Community's development, the Maastricht Treaty, with the program to establish the economic and monetary union at its heart.

There was powerful business support for the single currency project. The motive was not so much to eliminate the substantial transaction costs of changing money, but rather to remove the inhibition to long-term investments of uncertainty about the future course of exchange rates. The French government had acquired a new economic motive to confirm its long-standing predilection for monetary integration: European monetary policy was run mainly by the German Bundesbank, although France had, through rigorous monetary policies, for some time kept its fundamentals in at least as good shape as had the Germans. France saw the single currency as a means of securing its due share in the making of monetary policy through joint European policymaking. But it was a political event that gave the decisive impulse to the project. In 1990 the former East Germany was absorbed into the Federal Republic; and, with the collapse of the Soviet empire, the new and larger German state would have every opportunity to exert its influence on its eastern neighbors and thus to increase yet further its weight in European affairs.

Just as in the 1950s, France wanted to anchor Germany as securely as possible in the Community framework. The single currency would be one means of doing this, a common foreign and security policy with moves toward a common defense another. German leaders too, fully aware of the benefits that the Community's safe anchorage had brought to Germany in terms of stability and reconciliation with its neighbors as well as prosperity due to the economic integration, agreed that the Community should be strengthened. Their interest was more in the CFSP and in institutional reform, particularly to enhance the role of the European Parliament. But they were willing to accept the single currency project provided that it was to be the responsibility of an independent European Central Bank dedicated to price stability and that the participating states would be bound by strict anti-inflationary "convergence criteria."

The program to establish the Economic and Monetary Union (EMU) was the backbone of the Maastricht Treaty, which was agreed by the heads of EC governments in December 1991. The Treaty provided for a three-stage process to introduce the single currency, the ecu, by 1999 at the latest, with a European Central Bank to manage it, at the center of a European System of Central Banks, all of which were to be independent of their governments. The convergence criteria were designed to ensure that the member states kept their budget deficits, government debts, inflation rates, and exchange rate fluctuations within strict limits before full participation in the EMU. Those that were not ready when the single currency was introduced could have a derogation until such time as they should meet the criteria, a provision that may be important for some central and east European states when they join the Community. Britain and Denmark, the reluctant integrators, secured the right of opting out.

Among many lesser provisions for Community competences, those that may be of most significance to the central and east Europeans are the provisions concerning the Trans-European Networks (TENs) for transport, telecommunications, and energy infrastructures; development aid; and research and technological development. Among the Treaty's many provisions for institutional reform, the most significant were those giving the Parliament the right to approve appointment of the Commission and the right of codecision, a complicated procedure giving the Parliament a nearly equal role with the Council in enacting Community legislation in fifteen fields including the free movement of workers and the single market. The Treaty also recognizes the status of citizen of the Union for all the nationals of the member states.[21]

The Maastricht Treaty 1992–93: Birth Pains

In a context of recession following the boom of 1987–92, of high unemployment, instability in eastern Europe, war in Bosnia, German difficulties in assimilating its new eastern Länder, and what the French have called an atmosphere of "morosity" that ensued, the birth of the Union, as the Treaty called the Community plus the two new pillars, has been a troubled one.

DIFFICULT RATIFICATION AND MONETARY INSTABILITY. The Danes were the first to move to ratify the Treaty, with their referendum in June 1992. Although the mainstream political parties campaigned in favor, the citizens voted against, even if only by 50.7 to 49.3 percent, the narrowest of margins. The French followed with a referendum in September, voting by a margin of only 51 percent in favor and 49 percent against. Even though opinion polls indicated that two-thirds were satisfied with the result (many had doubtless cast their votes against the president who had called the referendum rather than the Treaty itself), it was, given France's leading role in the development of the Community, deeply disquieting. The British parliament, beset by a determined group of opponents in the governing Conservative party, which had only a narrow majority in the House of Commons, experienced a year of trench warfare over the bill for ratifying the Treaty, before it was finally enacted in August 1993. The Federal Republic ratified even later, in October, after its Constitutional Court in Karlsruhe completed its deliberations and judged that the Treaty was not incompatible with the German constitution. The Treaty entered into force in November 1993, nearly two years after it had been agreed by the heads of government at Maastricht. But confidence had been shaken by the disquiet that it evoked among many of those who were to be, after November, the Union's citizens.

Loss of confidence by the money markets had striking effects. When, following the Danish voters' no, the French voters approved the Treaty by such a narrow margin in September, the markets lost their confidence entirely in the prospect of exchange-rate stability. They attacked the currencies that they saw, with some justification, as overvalued, forcing the pound and the lira to float down, out of the Exchange Rate Mechanism. By August 1993, doubting that the French government would sustain its hard money policy in the face of rising unemployment, they did the same to the French franc. The margins of fluctuation permitted by the Exchange Rate Mechanism, originally fixed at 2.25 percent on either side of the central rates, were widened to 15 percent. Public opinion, particularly in countries where the Treaty or the single currency project was not popular, tended to conclude that the EMU was finished and that because the single currency project was so central to the Treaty, the Treaty itself was now of little consequence. Because this attitude could crucially affect the Community's influence on the aspiring candidates for membership from central and eastern Europe, it is important for this study to assess whether or not such a conclusion is justified.

PROSPECTS FOR FURTHER DEVELOPMENT OF THE EC-EU. France remains determined that the single currency will be established as provided by the Maastricht Treaty. Not long after the speculators had forced the franc through the floor of its band in the Exchange Rate Mechanism, the French government restored it to its former relationship with the mark. This French tenacity in the face of unemployment had become somewhat easier to sustain with the beginning of recovery from the recession and the consequently lower level of German interest rates. The German rates, which had been high because of the Bundesbank's insistence on controlling inflation despite the heavy costs of unification, were reduced as the risk of inflation abated. But the earlier deepening of the French recession owing to the high interest rates, imposed in Germany for domestic reasons and transmitted through the integrated money markets, had served to confirm the French determination to gain a due share in the control of European monetary policy through the EMU. The German government, for its part, knows that the commitment to the EMU in the Maastricht Treaty must be respected if it is to maintain its partnership with France and the solidity of the EC-EU, which it sees as vital elements of stability in Europe. In case Germans might be tempted to waver, they will have to accept that French agreement to the accession of central and east European countries—an essential German interest in order to ensure permanent stability among the eastern neighbors—is likely to be conditional on the introduction of the single currency. French determination and German acceptance are, moreover, bolstered by influential business support, on the grounds that the recent instability of exchange rates has underlined the urgency of a real guarantee of future stability through the single currency.[22]

The likelihood that at least a core group of member states, centered on Germany, France, and Benelux, will establish the EMU has been strengthened by the renewal of economic expansion, which, once again, improves the political prospects for continued integration. There is also some recognition of the merits of the proposals of President Delors for tackling the longer-term problem of the competitiveness and dynamism of the European economy.[23] While much of the emphasis is on flexibility of labor markets, which is mainly a matter for the member states rather than the Community, the proposed program for investment in Trans-European Networks is an action on which the Community is embarking and that could both lay the foundations for a physically integrated and attractive European economy in the next century and underpin the economic revival that should follow the recent recession. TENs that reach into and across central and eastern Europe and the CIS are a part of the program that could have a major impact on the health of the eastern economies and their integration into the west European economic and political system, and hence on their capacity to deal with their ethno-national problems.

With the continuation of the EMU project, the Franco-German partnership holds. This implies that, while Germany accepts the single currency and participates in moves toward a common defense such as the Eurocorps and a strengthening of the Western European Union, France accepts further growth in the powers of the European Parliament and the accession of central European countries without undue delay. The Intergovernmental Conference convened in 1996 should ensure at least some installments among the items on this agenda. But a further critical mass of reforms will be required before the central Europeans accede, if the Franco-German partnership and the Community are to remain in good enough shape to face the challenge of the enlargement.

Britain, however, has thus far refused to join the parade. In response, Alain Lamassoure, the French minister for Europe, articulated a concept that has been known as Europe at differing speeds or tiers, or even as variable geometry. He proposed the creation of a core group of member states that would accept all the commitments of the Treaty, including the new developments. Others could stand aside from this or that commitment, at least for a time. But until they accept each commitment, their vote in that field would be suspended. A similar proposal was made by Wolfgang

Schäuble and Karl Lamers, respectively chairman and foreign affairs spokes-man of the German Christian Democrat Parliamentary party.[24] When faced with the prospect of being left out of the club, British governments have in the past sooner or later decided to participate. This may well happen again, particularly if a government is returned at the next election, by May 1997 at the latest, which is less resistant to the developments in question. If the British government decides not to participate and tries to block reform, there are two possibilities: either the EC-EU remains, formally, as it is, with the prospect that stagnation will reduce its effectiveness; or, as seems more likely, other member states find a way, as the French and German proposals implied, to proceed without Britain.

The forces favoring further integration are strong: France, Germany, most other member states, the European Commission and Parliament, busi-ness associations and the more dynamic firms, and the general need to respond to the requirements of growing interdependence. These have car-ried the Community to the point it has reached today, and they remain as compelling as they were before. Although further integration is by no means inevitable, it is reasonable to think about the relationship with central and eastern Europe in the light of such development.

The Community in 1995: Federal Elements and Capacity for Action

It will doubtless have become evident to the reader that what have been called the federal elements in the institutions and powers (the elements that could comprise parts of the structure of a federal union if one is finally achieved) are regarded with favor by this writer. The reason is a conviction that institutions and powers with these characteristics are likely to be more effective in dealing with the manifold challenges that arise from the inter-dependence among states, including the challenges relating to the Com-munity's eastern neighbors. So it is reassuring to be able to observe that, when all the building blocks so far created by an incremental process are put together, the structure of the Community is short of that of a federal union in only a few, if crucial, respects.

POWERS AND INSTITUTIONS. The Community now has the powers over both internal and external trade that a federation would require. It has a quasi-federal budget, limited however to a rather small proportion of gross domestic product (GDP). When the Maastricht Treaty's provisions for the EMU have been implemented, it will have a federal currency. With that, together with its capacity to provide aid and assistance, the Community will have all the essential powers over external economic policy. Defense and defense-related foreign policy remain, however, almost entirely dependent on the policy instruments of the member states and on unanimity in decisions on their collective use: still far from a federal system in that field.

The Community's judicial system is broadly federal.[25] Its legislature, too, might be called federal where, as for most legislation, the Council is subject to a majority voting procedure, and the Parliament has powers of approval, assent, or codecision, which, as we have seen, cover a number of important matters. The Parliament has influence but not power through the cooperation procedure in most other legislative fields, so that here it remains quite some distance, though not remote, from a federal model. The Commission has some of the attributes of a federal executive but cannot be classed as such so long as it remains subject to the present degree of detailed control by the Council. Here the Parliament's new power to approve the Commission's appointment may, together with Parliament's powers over the budget, legislation, and cases of alleged maladministration, tilt the balance toward a federal executive. In addition to these institutional features, the establishment of a Union citizenship, given that all the institutions except the Council have a direct relationship with citizens, points toward a further federal characteristic.

As regards the Community's powers, it has only to complete the process, stipulated in the Maastricht Treaty, for establishing the single currency and the European Central Bank, to have the essential federal powers in the economic field. Without further transfer of power over foreign policy, and in particular the responsibility for the control of armed forces, to the Community's putatively federal institutions, the Community, or Union, would not become a federal state. Although there have been proposals, including from the German government, for placing the CFSP under the aegis of the Community institutions, the idea of a common defense force subject to federal institutions is doubtless still futuristic. But the reform of the institutions so as to be essentially federal, with responsibility for the federal economic powers that have already been allocated to the Community, is not so remote. It is quite feasible that the Parliament will have moved considerably farther in the direction of general codecision by the time the first central Europeans enter the Community, which it might then be legitimate to call a federal union.[26]

The significance of this for the central and east Europeans is that a Community that is more federal will be a safer anchorage for their still relatively new pluralist democracies and hence also for their capacity to deal with their ethno-national problems. The process of joining will have moved from the less definitive democracy-by-convergence toward the more definitive democracy-by-incorporation. The stronger the Community, moreover, the greater will be the influence of prospective membership on aspiring countries preparing themselves to join.

COMMUNITY INSTRUMENTS FOR POLICIES TOWARD EAST CENTRAL EUROPE AND CIS COUNTRIES. In the field of trade, and increasingly in the field of finance, the Community has common instruments of policy, which render its actions much more effective than they would be if, like most international organizations, it had to rely on the separate instruments of its several member states.

For trade policy the Community disposes of the normal instrumentarium of tariffs, quotas, and contingent protective devices such as antidumping duties, countervailing duties, and safeguards that usually take the form of quotas. Its single market legislation, directed against distortions of trade between member states, also has major external implications and is the subject of international and bilateral negotiations. The Community also provides aid and technical assistance, financed from its budget, for the Poland and Hungary Aid for Economic Reconstruction Program (PHARE) and the Technical Assistance for the CIS (TACIS) program. The Community's European Investment Bank is a source of loans for development projects, some at low rates of interest, subsidized from the Community budget. Loans are also available from a long-established ECSC facility, for purposes connected with those industries. Also in the field of finance, there is coordination of the terms for export credits; and the single currency will be an instrument of great significance.

The various agreements with partner countries discussed below are also a form of instrument, including the Trade and Economic Cooperation Agreements and the Europe Agreements as well as the Partnership and Cooperation Agreements. The ultimate instrument is the accession to the Community and Union. I shall return to this later, after considering the use of the Community's instruments of external policy.

Community Policies toward East Central Europe and CIS Countries

Community policy toward the East has quite a long history, since the Community's foundation in the 1950s. But until the cold war melted away and the transformation to market economies began, the Community's main activity in relation to Europe's eastern part was to restrict the Soviet attempts to reinforce the economic hegemony over east central Europe.[27] This did, however, set the scene for the radical changes starting in 1989.

Community Policies to 1989

Despite the Community's opposition to the Soviet-style regimes, it was favorable to what was then known as East-West trade. The political problems did not prevent business from carrying on this trade; and there was a widely held official view that the linkage between trade and security was positive, because it gave the eastern regimes an interest in stable relations and might work in favor of pluralism through the contacts of economic agents on the eastern side with those of the West. There was a sharp difference between European and American views of this. U.S. administrations tended to suspect that what looked to Europeans like interdependence was in fact dependence on an unscrupulous Soviet leadership. Europeans, and most of all the Germans,[28] sought to encourage the economic interdependence, which they saw as more likely to reduce the risk of conflict and to impose some dependence on the part of the economically weaker Soviet side.

Both the resistance to Soviet hegemony, manifested in the Community's refusal to negotiate a trade agreement with the Council for Mutual Economic Assistance (COMECON) through which the Soviet Union exercised economic hegemony over central and east Europeans, and the trade, which demonstrated the economic superiority of the western side, made a good impression on many of the people who were to lead their countries out of the Soviet system and into the new relationship with the West. This impression was strengthened by the Community's performance in the Helsinki negotiations to establish the Conference on Security and Cooperation in Europe (CSCE), because the Community's member states did much to ensure that the human rights provisions were enshrined in the Final Act in 1975. This was a considerable help to the human rights activists who set up the Movement for the Defense of Human Rights and the Committee for the Defense of the Workers (KOR) in Poland, and Charter 77 in the then Czechoslovakia, as well as to the like-minded editors of *The Chronicle of Current Events* in Russia.[29] These things, on top of the demonstration effect of a free, prosperous, and democratic Community, gave it a flying start when a new relationship became possible from 1989 onwards, and helped give the more independent-minded people in the East the courage to throw off the Soviet constraint.

Community Policies from 1989

Partly because of the overriding desire to detach east central Europe from the Soviet Union, the Community responded remarkably swiftly to the assertion of independence on the part of its eastern neighbors, using its instruments of trade and aid policy and developing economic agreements and political relations.

THE COMMUNITY'S AIMS. The aim of Community policy was to help the central and east Europeans toward pluralist democracy and market economy.[30] There were rational grounds for this aim. Market economies make better economic partners. Geography is not an adequate explanation of the fact that the Community's trade with Sweden or with Switzerland has been of the same order of magnitude as that with the whole of COMECON. The greater economic dynamism and aptitude for trade of the market economies is the more convincing reason. Pluralist democracies likewise make better neighbors. Mature liberal democracies seldom if ever go to war with each other.[31] They also, over the long run, have a greater capacity for political stability because of the ingrained habits associated with the rule of law based on human rights and the practices of political accommodation that sustain the system. For similar reasons they are, in ways that are germane to this study, more capable of resolving their ethno-national problems peacefully. For the Community, all these things are of great value because, apart from feelings of solidarity with fellow Europeans, instability in central and eastern Europe or the CIS, which might degenerate into violent conflict, could bring much grief to the Community's citizens.

The Community's main contribution to the resolution of ethno-national problems in the East is its effort to help create successful pluralist democracies and market economies there. The Community makes specific interventions to help deal with particular ethno-national problems. But its policies that aim to improve the democratic and economic structures are the more significant, both in terms of the resources and policymaking effort that is put into them and probably in the impact on the ethno-national problems themselves. The EC is by far the largest economic partner of the central and east Europeans and the CIS countries. Even if it is impossible to measure the benefits of the relationship in terms of ethno-national peace, it is an illusion to suppose that things must be more important just because they can be measured.

PROBLEMS OF POLITICAL AND ECONOMIC TRANSFORMATION. The transformation into a pluralist democracy of a polity based on the monopolistic control of political activity by a centralized party is an enormous task. Free elections are not easy to arrange, and the creation of an effective multiparty system is yet harder. The representatives in parliament must assume their role of enacting laws and controlling the executive in a satisfactory way, and this requires properly functioning party organizations and parliamentary staffs. Equally essential are government officials ready to work for governments of differing complexions, and media that are independent or at least multiparty. The rule of law requires independent courts and a legal profession with the skills and attitudes to make it work. And beyond these formal aspects of pluralist democracy lies the civil society without which it cannot survive: associations and institutions in the social, educational, cultural, and religious or moral fields, together with those of the market economy, which are independent of the government yet at the same time supportive of the democratic polity.[32] The Community and the Union seek to help the consolidation of the democracies through general agreements and through political dialogue, which is in the field of chapter 4. There are some Community policies that have particular relevance to democracy in general or the ethno-national problems in particular, such as its Democracy Program and its policies on human rights, minorities, and regional cooperation. But the Community's main contribution is made with its powerful economic instruments of trade, aid, and financial policy. As economic instruments, these have their effect largely in the field of market economy with its powerful relevance to the establishment of a solid pluralist democracy.

The transformation from command economy to market economy is likewise a vast undertaking.[33] Enterprises that formerly took their instructions from the central authorities now have to make their own decisions on prices, production, purchases, sales, work force, investment, and research and development. Privatization is the way to ensure that this happens. That, too, is a huge job, as is the creation of a culture of small and medium enterprises on a scale to provide the jobs that will be shed from incompetent state enterprises. Capital markets and financial institutions have to be established from scratch. Labor market institutions, including those for training and for social security, have to be adapted to the new environment. External trade has to be liberalized and redirected toward the market economies. Currencies have to be made convertible. Budget deficits and monetary policy have to be controlled so as to provide a stable currency. The whole legislative infrastructure for the institution and regulation of a market economy has to be put in place. The physical infrastructure of transport, communications, and energy supply has to be brought up to standard, not to mention the sadly polluted environment. Most of this has to be done by the transforming countries themselves. Particularly for those that were first with their reforms, there has been time to form a view as to how successful their efforts appear to be.

RESULTS OF THE REFORMS SO FAR AND THE PROBLEMS AHEAD. The central European countries in particular have proceeded far with their reforms. Some of the east Europeans and Russia have made important, if patchy, progress. Most other CIS countries have made little progress so far. The major elements of the policy of reform that has been advocated and supported by the West are macroeconomic stabilization and privatization. The form of macroeconomic policy has been determined by the International Monetary Fund (IMF), whose lead the Community and its western partners accepted in this field. A strict control of monetary and fiscal policy and progress toward currency convertibility have been the main features. In central Europe this policy has succeeded in moving the economies toward monetary and price stability. Stable currencies, together with the other reforms so far achieved, are certainly a necessary condition of healthy economic development. Whether they are also sufficient is not yet clear.

There has been considerable success in controlling inflation in central Europe. From the brink of hyperinflation at the start of its reforms, Poland brought its rate of increase of consumer prices down to 37 percent in 1993. Slovenia, without such a dangerous starting point but at an earlier stage in its reforms, had a rate of 33 percent. The Czechs, Hungarians, and Slovaks were all within the range of 21–23 percent. Bulgaria, however, suffered 73 percent, Romania 257 percent, and the CIS states all had rates of more than one thousand percent, except Azerbaijan with 981 percent, Russia with 911 percent, and Uzbekistan with "only" 533 percent.[34] Russia's anti-inflation efforts have brought its rate down toward double digits in the course of 1994. But the costs of the transition, both where inflation has been controlled and where it has not, have been enormous.

Between 1989 and 1991, the statistics show a fall of real GDP by nearly one-fifth in Poland, followed by growth of 5 percent in the next two years. This was the best performance among the eastern countries. In the Czech Republic, Hungary, and Slovenia the fall was also about one-fifth, spread between 1989 and 1993, with an apparent bottoming out in the last year of the period. These four are the countries that made most progress with their reforms. In Slovakia the fall over that period was one-quarter, in Bulgaria and Romania about one-third, and in Russia and Ukraine about two-fifths.[35] Industrial production has fallen yet more sharply, which will bear very hard on employment in the large state sectors. The growing private sector, on the other hand, is not well measured by the statistics, which may therefore exaggerate the fall in production and the rise in unemployment. But the economic pain has been extremely serious, of an intensity not seen in the West since the great slump of 1929–33, when it had politically disastrous consequences except in the solid and mature democracies.

Unemployment in 1993 was in the range of 10–16 percent in Bulgaria, Hungary, Poland, Romania, Slovakia, and Slovenia. The only country with a serious reform program that has escaped such unemployment is the Czech Republic. Despite Prime Minister Klaus's fiery neoliberal rhetoric, his prudent policy has kept the rate down to no more than 3.5 percent. Throughout the CIS, too, the rate was still very low, but this was due to the lack, or in the case of Russia, incompleteness of reforms, not to a prudent conduct of them.[36]

Unemployment and the extent to which production has fallen remain dangerous problems in the reforming countries. Even if the recovery is fast from now on, the risk of political reactions against the reforms remains. In Poland and Hungary the recent elections have returned former communists to power. They seem inclined to continue on the path of reform. But elsewhere the return of people associated with the old regime might have a different result; and extreme nationalists remain a threat in a number of countries. Economic recovery is urgently required. What could the Community do to help bring it about? A starting point for an answer is what the Community has already done with its trade, aid, and financial instruments, and that is the subject of the following sections.[37]

The Community's Trade Policy

Trade may be the most important contribution that the Community can make to the development of the eastern economies. Its imports from the central Europeans have made a significant impact on their GDP, offsetting the loss from the collapse of trade with the former COMECON partners. Qualitatively, the trade provides their economies with modern equipment and offers markets to their more dynamic and competitive firms. The chance to export to the Community from low-cost neighboring countries is, moreover, a major incentive for private foreign investment, which is the most effective vehicle for the transfer of technology and management skills and for access to channels of distribution in the western markets.

EXPORTS FROM THE EASTERN COUNTRIES TO THE COMMUNITY. The qualitative impact on the composition of their exports is shown by the rate of growth of sales to the Community by key sectors of industry in eastern economies. For the six countries with Europe Agreements taken together—Bulgaria, the Czech Republic, Hungary, Poland, Romania, and Slovakia—the exports to the Community of transport equipment were 58 percent higher in the period January–August 1993 than a year earlier, and those of machinery and electrical equipment 25 percent higher. Textiles and clothing exports grew by 22 percent, more than balancing the imports in this category from the Community which were sent for "outward processing" and return as eastern exports. The growth for "miscellaneous manufactures" was 20 percent. These are very high rates of growth by any standards, particularly in view of the fact that the exporters were selling into a market beset by recession. These six countries have raised their share of the Community's imports by two-thirds between 1989 and 1993, from 2.7 percent to 4.2 percent, while their share of the Community's exports has doubled, to 5.3 percent.

This export performance is the more significant in that the Community is by far their largest trading partner, taking some half of their total trade. It is likewise the main trading partner for the CIS countries, accounting again for nearly half the total. But changes in the Community's trade policy have so far made little difference to the latter trade, for the exports from the CIS are mainly of raw materials and energy products which do not encounter any protective devices on entry into the Community. It is the turbulence in the CIS economies that has prevented any dramatic development of their exports, not the Community protection.

The countries most advanced in reform increased their exports as a whole to the Community extraordinarily rapidly between 1990 and 1992, before the recession began to bite. The four countries party to the Visegrad agreement, the Czech Republic, Hungary, Poland, and Slovakia (often termed the V4 countries), managed an export growth of no less than 54 percent over that two-year period. Bulgaria, which had also pressed ahead with reform, achieved almost exactly the same result, while Romania, where reforms were delayed, suffered a decline of 14 percent.

By 1993 Romanian exports had hit the bottom and begun to recover, gaining 19 percent in the period January–August over the year before. But the swift progress of the V4 countries was checked, with a growth of only 3 percent, and the experience of Bulgaria was about the same. The surge in Albanian exports during the same period was remarkable, with a gain of 84 percent; but this followed a loss of 29 percent between 1990 and 1992, and reflected the quite unusual extent of the damage done by Enver Hoxha to the Albanian economy. For Albanians, there is nowhere to go but up.

Part of the stagnation in the exports of the V4 and Bulgaria in 1993 may be due to their efforts to hold their exchange rates stable while their inflation continues. But more important has been the recession in the Community, and to some degree the partly consequent protection of the Community's market.

COMMUNITY TRADE POLICIES. The bad news about Community trade policy toward the eastern countries is that considerable protection remains, most particularly in agriculture. Indeed, agricultural exports from the six associated countries fell by 25 percent between January–August 1992 and the same period in 1993. Even if other factors played their part, there can be little doubt that this trade would be a great deal larger if the CAP protection were removed. There has also been a recourse to antidumping duties to the benefit of the Community's hard-pressed steel industries and to the detriment of central European producers. The same device has been used in cement, magnesium, urea, and some chemicals. While the amount of trade involved is not very large, the use of this weapon deters exporters from making the effort to develop a market, which they fear may become restricted in this way. Textiles and clothing, too, have been restricted by quotas, though these are due to be eliminated in 1997.

The good news is that the liberalization has outweighed the protection, and continues to do so. Challenged by the extraordinary events of 1989–90, the Community quickly undertook a considerable reduction of tariffs and relaxation of quotas on imports from the reforming countries. The quotas imposed specifically on imports from COMECON countries were abolished, and many of the quotas that applied also to imports from other regions were suspended. Tariffs were cut by granting the Generalized System of Preferences, which allowed a wide range of imports to enter free of tariffs, although this privilege was restricted to a given quantity of imports for so-called sensitive products where the competition for Community industries was too uncomfortable. As the whole of central and eastern Europe entered the category of reforming countries, these measures were applied to all of them, apart from Serbia and Montenegro where they were withheld because of sanctions. Trade and economic cooperation agreements were concluded with all these countries too, although they contained more form than substance.

Much more important were the Europe Agreements, concluded so far with the six countries mentioned above, and entering into force for the first two—Poland and Hungary—in February 1992.[38] Because some parts of these Agreements concern matters that are beyond the competence of the

Community, they have to be ratified by all the member states. This took no less than two years from the date of signature of the Agreements. But because the trade aspects were within the exclusive competence of the Community, Interim Agreements were devised[39] so that the trade elements have not suffered the dilatory ratification by member states and have by now been applicable for some time. In July 1994, moreover, the Community initialed free-trade area agreements, seen as forerunners of Europe Agreements, with Estonia, Latvia, and Lithuania. With Slovenia, preliminary discussions went well enough for the Commission to seek a mandate from the Council in the spring of 1994 to start formal negotiations.[40] The Berlusconi government, however, giving way to nationalistic pressures, required the grant of the mandate to be suspended during its period in office on the grounds that certain problems connected with property rights claimed in Slovenia by Italian nationals should first be resolved.

The Europe Agreements provide for the establishment of industrial free trade between the Community and its partners over a period of five years on the side of the Community, but allowing the partners up to ten years before all their tariffs and quotas have to be removed. The possibility for either side to apply "safeguards," which allow quotas or other protection to be imposed if imports of a product cause serious disruption of markets or threaten to do so, will however remain. Home country treatment, which is the equivalent of free trade, is to be applied to services and the right of establishment. Capital movements, already freed by the Community, are to be freed by the partners during the transitional period, though if this creates difficulties they may be imposed again. For agriculture, there are a number of specific relaxations of quotas and reductions of tariffs for each partner country, but the CAP protection is not scheduled to be phased out like the industrial protection.

These arrangements are comprehensive, but they made little difference at first to the trade, because the first stages of liberalization had been preempted by the measures of 1989–90. They should, however, offer encouragement to foreign firms to invest in productive facilities in the associated countries, because there is a fair assurance that the Community market will be tariff-free for them by the time their investments begin to result in substantial production.

The time when trade will be free is, moreover, approaching, particularly since the European Council, at its meeting in Copenhagen in June 1993,[41] decided to accelerate the liberalization of trade. As a result, almost all industrial goods are to enter the Community tariff-free by 1995. The tariffs on textiles and clothing will be removed by the end of 1996, and quantitative restriction of those imports by the end of 1997. Quotas on steel have already been removed, and tariffs are to disappear by the end of 1995, though the associated countries are not likely to forget the imposition of antidumping duties when the recession combined with the growth of imports hit the Community's steel industry hard. For agriculture, there are some further tariff and quota concessions, but the basic stance of protection by the Community has not changed. However, provided that the Community does not make a habit of imposing antidumping duties or safeguards, the virtually complete freeing of industrial imports from the associates is now imminent, or, for textiles, not far ahead. The European Council also underlined the importance of the alignment of laws of the associated countries on those of the Community, to the extent needed for their full participation in the single market.

The states of the CIS, which remain behind the associated countries in their reforms, have up to now had only trade and economic cooperation agreements, ensuring that the most favored nation treatment they already enjoyed de facto is secured de jure and providing for some other benefits. Most of these benefits were marginal, much less significant than the GSP which the Community extended to Russia and other members of the CIS in 1993. But Partnership and Cooperation Agreements were signed with Russia and Ukraine in 1994 and are under negotiation with Belarus, Moldova, Kazakhstan, and the Kyrgyz Republic. Agreements tailored to the circumstances of other CIS members states are to follow. These agreements offer a relaxation of quotas and, for Russia and Ukraine, specific provisions regarding textiles, nuclear products, coal, and steel. Services, the right of establishment, and capital movements are treated similarly to the provisions of the Europe Agreements. The approximation of laws is, as in the Europe Agreements, also envisioned: the partner countries are to align their laws on the Community's single market legislation. The major difference from the Europe Agreements is that a free-trade area is to be considered only when the partner country is further advanced in reform.

After the surge of liberalization in 1989–90, the Community rested on its oars until 1993. By then, however, the Community realized that a big challenge remained to the east, in the danger that instability could get out of hand. The European Council therefore took the decision in June not only to accelerate trade liberalization but also to make an explicit offer of future membership for the countries with Europe Agreements. With recovery from the recession, this positive disposition may last for some time. But given that there will be no really important liberalization of agricultural trade, it remains doubtful whether the trade measures will be enough to ensure that the regeneration of the eastern partners is as rapid and strong as it needs to be.

The Community's Aid Policy

It is useful to take a broad view of the flows of funds from public sources to the countries of central and eastern Europe and the CIS. Financial assistance includes the standby loans that have been made, under IMF leadership, to countries that need support to enable them to take the risk of moving their currencies toward convertibility. Such loans have been provided to most of the central and east European countries. Financial support is also involved in the debt reduction for the benefit of Poland and Bulgaria. In Poland's case, half the total debt of some $44 billion has been forgiven, removing what was an intolerable burden from the Polish economy, if at the cost of making the capital markets more wary about loans to Poland in future.

Support by way of investment from the Community includes loans at favorable rates for central and east European countries from the European Investment Bank (EIB), amounting to ecu 1.7 billion ECU (ECU 1 = $1.2) in 1990–93, mostly for infrastructure projects and in some instances with the help of interest rate subsidies from the Community budget. There is also the European Bank for Reconstruction and Development (EBRD), established on the initiative of the Community, with 51 percent owned by Community institutions and member states and the remainder by other European countries, the United States, Japan, and some other countries and international institutions. The EBRD is intended to finance mainly private investments in the countries of central and eastern Europe and the CIS, which has not proved easy at the early stage of their transformation (see chapter 7 in this volume). Then there are official export credits which amounted to 8.2 billion ECU, or nearly one-half of the total assistance commitments in 1990–93 from EU member states, mostly France and Germany.[42] These are intended for repayment over the short or medium term, but are meanwhile of considerable use as they are linked with imports that are wanted in the recipient countries' economies.

The PHARE program was launched by the Community and the other advanced industrial countries of the Organization for Economic Cooperation and Development (OECD), with the role of coordinator given to the

European Commission. The aim of PHARE is to help economic reform and structural adjustment, although it has also some subsidiary aims such as the support of democratic institutions and the protection of minorities. The primary means is technical assistance, but there is now a trend toward support for investments, particularly in infrastructure. The European Council in June 1993 decided that "the EIB, the EBRD and the other international financial institutions" should "take the leading role in this process."[43]

PHARE PROGRAM FOR THE EAST CENTRAL EUROPEAN STATES. The PHARE program is financed predominantly, as far as the Community is concerned, from the Community budget, at a current rate of appropriations of 1 billion ECU a year. From 1990 to 1993 3.3 billion ECU was appropriated in the Community budget, though, because the rate of disbursement lags behind that of appropriations, only 1.4 billion ECU had been paid out during that period. Poland was the largest recipient, with 25 percent of the total, followed by Hungary (13 percent), Romania (11 percent), the Czech Republic plus Slovakia, which were a single state for much of the period (10 percent), Bulgaria (8 percent), with the rest distributed among five other countries (Albania, Estonia, Latvia, Lithuania, Slovenia) and for multicountry projects (10 percent) and humanitarian aid (8 percent). The fields for assistance are chosen by the recipient countries. During that period the development of the private sector was the first priority, followed by education and training, agricultural reconstruction, and environment and nuclear safety.[44]

The PHARE program has its critics. Among them have been the Community's Court of Auditors, whose annual reports have criticized the efficiency, though not the probity, of the Commission's administration of the program. Among the criticisms have been slowness of payments, unsuitability of some of the humanitarian aid, and lack of coordination with other donors.[45]

The Commission has responded with reforms to take account of some of the criticisms.[46] From 1993 onward, three-year indicative programs are drawn up for each recipient country, in order to ensure more stability and continuity. Another change has been the decision to allocate up to 15 percent of the budget for infrastructure programs. With the importance given to the Trans-European Networks of transport, telecommunications, and energy distribution in the Maastricht Treaty and the Commission's White Paper on regenerating the Community's economy,[47] there is an opening for a very ambitious program to reach these networks across central and eastern Europe and into the CIS. This is in principle the intention, at least of the

Commission. But there has not so far been evidence of the political will on the part of the governments to launch such a program on a major scale. The Marshall Plan has been used as a standard of comparison for what the Europeans are doing, and it has been suggested that, even if the will to show such generous self-interest were present, the projects on which to spend the money were not. But the Community's eastern neighbors sorely need a modern infrastructure. They also need to be integrated physically as well as mentally into the Community. A strong impulsion from the expansion of viable investments to create an infrastructure to integrate the whole of Europe would help to ensure healthily growing economies in these countries. It would also help the Community itself to become more dynamic and competitive. The case for launching a great program for that purpose is very strong.

TACIS PROGRAM FOR THE CIS COUNTRIES. By March 1994 it could be claimed that the "aid" of the Community and its member states to the CIS states amounted to 53 billion ECU, some two-thirds of total western "aid" of 85 billion ECU. As much as 38 billion ECU of the Community's contribution, however, of which 27 billion ECU came from Germany alone, consisted of credits or credit guarantees; and a further 9 billion ECU was the German contribution to Russian troop withdrawals. While doubtless a significant help for the Russian economy, these sums were not aid in the normal sense of the word. Humanitarian aid amounted to nearly 2 billion ECU, three-quarters from the member states and one-quarter from the Community itself. A similar sum had been allotted to technical assistance, about one-third of it from the member states and two-thirds from the Community's budget, under the label of the TACIS program. Unlike PHARE, in which the OECD governments together with international organizations participate, TACIS is financed solely from the Community budget.

The aims of TACIS are similar to those of PHARE, and the method is to pay for experts to transfer their knowledge and advice to the CIS countries. A major difference is that, with reform in the CIS coming later, TACIS was slower to get off the ground, being launched only in mid-1991. By the end of 1993, the appropriations for it had amounted to 1.4 billion ECU. Of this about one-fifth was for nuclear safety, one-sixth for enterprise restructuring and development, 13 percent for public administration reform, social services, and education, with most of the rest for agriculture, energy, transport, telecommunications, and policy advice. Russia was allocated 497 million ECU, multicountry programs 395 million ECU (help for nuclear safety being a substantial part of that), Ukraine 119 million ECU, and the other smaller CIS states much smaller amounts. Like PHARE, from 1993 there are three-year indicative programs for each country. For 1993–95 the main priorities are much the same as for 1991–93.[48]

Most of the CIS countries have not so far been prepared for usefully receiving large amounts of aid. But Russia in particular has made much progress with reforms, and the case for much bigger aid programs is becoming stronger. The extension of the TENs program into Russia would in particular be of enormous benefit, psychologically and politically as well as for the economy.

Democracy, Human Rights, Minorities, Regional Cooperation

Democracy and human rights, with their relevance to the resolution of ethno-national conflicts, receive some attention from EC policies of aid and, in the case of human rights, trade. Minorities themselves are also a concern of the Community's aid programs, as is regional cooperation among recipient countries, which can help to alleviate transborder ethno-national problems.

THE DEMOCRACY PROGRAM. Following an initiative of the European Parliament in 1992, a pilot Democracy Program was launched in 1993, leading to the second Democracy Program in 1994. The allocation in the Community's 1994 budget was 10 million ECU for central and east Europeans, through the PHARE program, and 10 million ECU to the CIS countries through TACIS.[49] The rather small amount is to be spread over a wide field: parliamentary practice, human rights, independent media, development of structures for nongovernmental organizations and representative channels, local community participation, and public education. The method is to link nongovernmental organizations in the EC with similar organizations in the eastern countries, and also to create networks among the latter. The program is being managed by the European Human Rights Foundation, an independent charitable foundation that has some experience of cooperation with the Commission.[50] Closely associated with the Democracy Program is a "civic society" program, helping to create and promote nongovernmental organizations in the eastern countries. The priorities seem to be appropriate for the aim of supporting the procedures and practices of pluralist democracy, together with the rule of law, in the partner countries, even if a sharper focus might be desirable at this early stage of the program's development.

HUMAN RIGHTS. In a declaration on human rights in June 1991, the European Council affirmed that "the protection of minorities is ensured in the first place by the effective establishment of democracy," which is valid provided that the democracy is of the liberal and constitutional variety. The declaration also referred to "the cultural identity as well as rights enjoyed by members of minorities which such persons should be able to exercise in common with other members of their group."[51] Caution about the concept of minority rights as such was reflected in the use of the phrase "rights enjoyed by members of minorities."

The declaration by the heads of state or government in the European Council was developed by the foreign ministers meeting in the Council into a policy resolution giving guidelines for its implementation. The Community was to give graduated responses to "grave and persistent human rights violations or serious interruption of democratic processes," through confidential or public démarches, changes in the content or channels of cooperation programs, or the deferment of signatures or decisions in the cooperation process or, when necessary, the suspension of cooperation with the states concerned.[52] This was, to some extent, a formulation of practices that the Community had already adopted. Thus negotiations for a trade and economic cooperation agreement with Romania were suspended both in July 1989 and, after the change of regime, in June 1990, following blatant acts of repression. The Community delayed the entry into force of the agreement until it had, by January 1991, received reports on the events from both the government and the opposition. Negotiations with Bulgaria for a similar agreement were suspended from May 1989 to March 1990 because of infringement of the rights of the Turkish minority. The repression in the Baltic republics by the Soviet Union in January 1991 was followed by the suspension of technical assistance and of meetings of the joint committee that supervised the trade and economic cooperation agreement.

The case of Yugoslavia is much graver. Here, following indefinite suspension of the preferential trade and economic cooperation agreement, sanctions were applied to Serbia and Montenegro because of their support for Serb aggression within Bosnia. But the sanctions were imposed far later than they might have been, so that their undoubted impact on the economy did not bear timely political fruit. The economic weight of the Community should be a powerful weapon. But while the relatively strong Community institutions are responsible for the execution of sanctions, the decisions to impose them are taken through the weaker procedures for cooperation in foreign policy. These need to be strengthened beyond the Maastricht provisions for the CFSP if such instruments are to be used more effectively.

Whereas human rights were mentioned only in the preambles of earlier agreements, the more recent agreements give the parties "the right to suspend this Agreement in whole or in part if a serious violation occurs of [its] essential provisions."[53] This gives the Community firmer ground on which to withdraw benefits associated with the agreements. In addition to such sticks, the Community also employs the carrot of some modest funding for promotion of human rights protection, for example through grants to nongovernmental organizations working in this field.

MINORITIES. The protection of minorities is mentioned in the preambles to the Europe Agreements with Bulgaria and Romania and the Trade and Economic Cooperation Agreements with Albania, Estonia, Latvia, and Lithuania. The PHARE program also provides support for activities intended to improve the position of minorities. For the Roma community, for example, there is training in leadership and management, a trust for land settlement, provision for legal defense and local language training programs. PHARE funds have been used to finance a newsletter on rights relating to minorities, conferences on minorities, and, where there are evident problems, investigating missions. The Democracy Program contains a separate part in its budget for programs for minorities, to help them with know-how for participation in the democratic process. The Union has also declared itself ready to provide aid from its budget to support the stability pact that resulted from the Balladur plan to help alleviate cross-frontier minority problems in Europe.[54] (See chapter 4.) On the other hand, although adequate constitutional provision for protection of minorities was one of the conditions laid down for the recognition of the Yugoslav republics, Croatia and Bosnia were recognized by the Union without having fulfilled that condition.

REGIONAL COOPERATION. Since 1991 the promotion of regional cooperation among the recipients has been a growing element in the PHARE program. These activities emphasize common problems in the core areas of energy, environment, transport, and human resources including distance learning such as educational television programs, and education more generally. The programs are based on sectors within this core and led by a coordinator in one of the recipient states, who works with representatives of other recipients and of the Community. These regional cooperation activities create networks that should help overcome suspicions among the eastern countries, which can be particularly acute where there are transborder

ethno-national problems. There is also a provision for transborder cooperation between adjoining regions in partner countries and Community member states, such as Poland and Germany, in fields such as infrastructure,
pollution control, tourism, and business. The PHARE budget in 1994 for all
the transborder activity was 150 million ECU.[55]

The Europe Agreements foresee also greater cooperation among associated countries with respect to trade; and help is available for groups of
countries that wish to build on the experience of Benelux or the Community
itself. The most significant result so far has been an agreement committing
the Czech Republic, Hungary, Poland, and Slovakia to form a central
European free-trade area by January 1998, eliminating by three stages the
tariffs and quotas from their mutual trade.[56]

The TACIS program has allocated 395 million ECU, or 29 percent of its
budget over the period 1991–93, for multicountry programs.[57] The largest
share of this goes to nuclear safety. But there is also support for sectors of
interdependence such as the transport, telecommunications, and energy
networks, the environment, financial services, and action against the trade
in drugs.

Agreements and Their Institutions

While the trade and economic cooperation agreements are relatively
simple and are supervised by joint committees, the Europe Agreements and
Partnership and Cooperation Agreements have a more complex structure
and contents. The institutions as well as the content of the Europe Agreements are now regarded as vehicles to help carry the partners along the road
to accession to the Community and Union.

Apart from the trade provisions, the more elaborate Agreements provide
for extensive economic, financial, and cultural cooperation, which in fact
embodies the activities of the PHARE and TACIS programs, and for political dialogue. Each Agreement also provides for an Association Council,
comprising ministers and commissioners responsible for the subjects under
discussion; an Association Committee for senior officials, to prepare the
meetings of the Council and carry on the work between times; and a
Parliamentary Committee of Association, comprising members of the parliament of the associated state and of the European Parliament. The purpose
of these institutions is not just to facilitate a smooth operation of the
Agreements but also to provide a context for a close and settled relationship
with the partner countries. With the partners in the Europe Agreements the

function now goes beyond this, toward preparation for future membership. At its meeting in June 1993, the European Council decided to promote a structured multilateral dialogue of the twelve member states with all the Europe Agreement partners, which should help induct these countries into some aspects of the Union's way of doing business.

The Future Accession of East Central European States to the Community

Acceptance of east central European states as new members will be the most powerful contribution the Community and Union can make to the resolution of their ethno-national problems. Membership is a cast-iron guarantee that the member states maintain market economies, with the contribution that such economies make to pluralist democracy and to alleviating some economic causes of ethno-national conflict. Membership also goes far to guarantee the democratic character of member states' governments. It removes, as the case of the Saar shows, some of the most dangerous economic causes of transborder ethno-national conflict. Because of the danger to the Community itself of any transborder conflicts between member states, it gives the other member states a very strong motive for putting what resources they can at the service of efforts to resolve any such ethno-national conflicts. Although there is also another side to the argument, as has been demonstrated by the Danish resistance to the purchase of properties in Denmark by Germans, against the background of the historic ethno-national conflict over Schleswig-Holstein, and as Czech resistance to a similar phenomenon likewise indicates, the positive side predominates by a long way. If the proposition that pluralist democracy based on human rights and equality before the law promotes the peaceful resolution of ethno-national conflict is accepted, then the Community's contribution to conflict resolution in new or aspiring member states must be seen as highly positive.

EC-EU Policies toward Enlargement

When the central and east Europeans began their transformations and the Community initiated the concept of Europe Agreements of association with them, member states were hesitant about the idea of membership for these countries. France in particular was unenthusiastic, fearing it would further increase Germany's weight in the Community and move the center of gravity away from France and toward the East, while also suspecting that the coherence and strength of the Community could be diluted and that competition with French agriculture could become more intense. Several other member states shared some of these concerns, and the European Commission was also at first hesitant. But the central European partners were insistent, and the Commission itself warmed to their case. The member states relented to the extent of accepting, in the preambles to the Europe Agreements, that membership was an objective for these countries, which the Agreements could help to bring about.

Two of the larger member states soon began to press for a more positive approach, if with somewhat divergent motives. Both Britain and Germany saw enlargement to the East as a contribution to prosperity and stability there. But Germany wanted the Community to be strengthened through institutional reform so that it would accommodate the new members without losing any of its political strength and capacity for action, whereas the British government hoped that the increase in the number and diversity of the member states would help to loosen the constraints of the Community which, for reasons dating back to World War II and beyond, British governments had tended to resist. The result of British and German pressure, together with the growing conviction throughout western Europe that the integration of central and east Europeans was necessary for the future stability of the continent, led by 1993 to the important change of policy promulgated at the meeting of the European Council at Copenhagen in June of that year.

The European Council decided at that meeting that the "associates in Central and Eastern Europe that so desire shall become members of the Union." This was to be accomplished as soon as each of them is able to satisfy the political and economic conditions: stability of institutions guaranteeing democracy, the rule of law, human rights, and "respect for and protection of minorities"; a functioning market economy and the capacity to cope with competitive pressures and market forces in the Union; and "ability to take on the obligations of membership including adherence to the aims of political, economic and monetary union."[58]

CONDITIONS OF MEMBERSHIP FOR CENTRAL AND EAST EUROPEANS.   The Maastricht Treaty affirms that the member states' "systems of government are founded on the principles of democracy." But in addition to the general principle, there are a number of specific reasons why member states must be pluralist democracies.

The representatives that member states send to the Council and their citizens send to the Parliament have to come from soundly democratic systems. It would not be possible for other member states to accept that laws enacted through the votes of representatives of authoritarian systems should override their own laws, as Community law must do if it is to provide equality before the law for all the Union's citizens. The votes of nondemocratic representatives would inevitably sometimes swing the outcome in their favor, and thus bring Community law, which is the foundation of the whole enterprise, into disrepute. The judges of the Court of Justice must emanate from polities where the rule of law applies. Equally significant, the judicial systems of the member states, which have the task of judging most of the cases that arise under Community law, subject to the authority of the Court of Justice, must be able to do so to a standard that satisfies the other member states, whose citizens and companies will be parties to many of the cases. The laws of member states and the practice of their courts must also respect human rights, including those of the citizens belonging to minorities, or the citizens of other member states will suspect that they too will, in an integrated economy and polity, suffer from the impact of unfair economic or political practices. Finally, the officials of all member states have the task of executing Community law and policy, much of which is delegated to them, and must do this according to the standards of public service of liberal democracies, or the other member states will again find their interests prejudiced. Thus there are sound practical reasons why the standards of democratic government of member states should be high enough in all these respects. But such standards are not easily or quickly attained, and the challenge they pose for internal political development in central and eastern European countries will not be easy to meet.

Ability to compete on equal terms in the single market likewise requires a market economy in which all the vast range of single market legislation is the framework. The judicial systems have to digest the legislation and the economic agents have to work competitively in the type of economy that it shapes. The same will apply to the regime of the single currency. Transitional periods, perhaps long ones, are normal Community practice, enabling member states to be eased into the rigors of the system. But there must be a realistic prospect that any state which accedes will be able to make the grade within a period that is not excessively long.

THE CONCOMITANT EVOLUTION OF THE EC-EU. The obligations of membership mentioned by the European Council include what our multilingual Community calls the "acquis": the accumulated mass of treaties, laws, declarations and resolutions, international agreements, and agreements among member states connected with the Community's activities.[59] Those obligations are vast and complex, but quite precise. There is little doubt as to what the new member state's political, judicial, and economic system has to take on board. Economic and monetary union, also mentioned by the European Council, is likewise a precise concept, with the obligations delineated by the Maastricht Treaty. There may be doubts about the timetable for achieving it or about some of the detail, but the aim, which the European Council in Copenhagen stipulated that new member states must accept, is clear. The same cannot be said of the other aim that was enunciated: political union. Here the words cover serious differences of view between present member states.

The term political union has two main aspects: common foreign and security policy and institutional reform. The obligations of new member states in the field of the CFSP have been defined in a report of the Commission to the European Council as being to accept and implement that policy "as it evolves."[60] But that is a vague definition. How the policy evolves will depend on the member states, and since the CFSP is the responsibility of an intergovernmental arrangement in which unanimity is likely to be the rule, at least until further amendment of the treaty, a member state can control the way in which it evolves. What new member states have to accept is the "acquis" of existing agreed policies. Beyond that, their obligation is to accept the fairly unconstraining rules of the game. Since the decision to admit a new member state has to be taken by the existing member states unanimously, however, a candidate for accession could be blackballed by one or more of the Union's governments which found that candidate's orientation in foreign policy unacceptable. If majority voting is introduced for the CFSP, or an integrated defense system is developed, as the French promotion of a "common defense" could imply, then the obligations in this field would become more precise and more onerous.

The divergence among member states about institutional reform is fundamental to the future of the Community and Union and of great significance to the aspiring member states from central and eastern Europe and to the capacity of the EC-EU to help resolve their ethno-national problems. The view of the majority of member states, and of Germany in particular, is that the Union should have "a federal goal" and that the Intergovernmental Conference to be convened in 1996 should "strengthen the federal character of the Union." They wanted to insert these words in the Maastricht Treaty to imply enhancement of the instruments, and reform of the institutions in a federal direction.[61] Britain and Denmark, to the contrary, opposed the introduction of further federal elements, whether powers, instruments or institu-

tional reforms. Britain in particular fought successfully to have the word
federal deleted from the final version of the Maastricht Treaty; fought a
rearguard action against more legislative power for the Parliament, though
finally accepting the modest degree of codecision that the Treaty provides;
and resisted the extension of majority voting in the Council, especially with
respect to the CFSP. The British government's view of political union is an
association of freely cooperating independent sovereign states, far removed
from the federal pattern that Germany and a number of the other member
states envisage.

Amendments to the Treaty have to be ratified by all member states; and
the accession of new member states requires not only ratification by all the
existing member states but also the assent of the European Parliament. The
case for making the institutions stronger and more democratic will gain in
force as the entry of central European states, to be followed by east Europeans, becomes imminent. A number of governments, Germany in particular,
will fear that the EC-EU would be weakened and could eventually disintegrate if that entry is not preceded, or at least accompanied, by substantially
strengthening the Union. Deadlock is conceivable, with Britain refusing
amendments to strengthen the Union and the Parliament and some governments withholding approval of accession without such amendments. But a
positive outcome is probable, whether through a change of British policy or
a core group moving ahead to closer integration, in the expectation that the
others will eventually follow. Thus widening is likely to be accompanied by
deepening, at least on the part of some member states; and if there is a core
group, most of the central and east European states may well join it, after a
transitional period, rather than remain in an outer tier.

The European Council, at its meeting in June 1993, also underlined the
importance of the Union's "capacity to absorb new members, while maintaining the momentum of European integration."[62] Like political union, the
"momentum of integration" was not defined. Each member state can decide
for itself what it means. For France, with its concern to anchor Germany
and keep the EC-EU intact, the single currency is central and progressive
defence integration also very important. For Germany, with its desire for
more solidly based institutions and for securing the central and east Europeans within a thoroughly democratic structure, institutional reform, and in
particular codecision for the European Parliament, is necessary. The Commission, in its report to the European Council on the criteria and conditions
for membership, likewise stressed the need for a "more solid democratic
basis" for the Community, through strengthening the role of the European

Parliament; and by pointing to the difficulty of reaching unanimous decisions in a Council with an increasing number of members, implied that more majority voting would be required.[63] The British government, on the other hand, has lacked enthusiasm for maintaining the momentum of integration in any respect except the action required for full completion of the single market.

The Community also has to make some more mundane preparations for the entry of central and east Europeans. It has been estimated that the support of these countries' extensive agriculture would be beyond the reach of the financial resources that could possibly be available for the common agricultural policy.[64] The CAP, only recently reformed to bring the prices in the Community to a significantly lower level, will have to be reformed again, bringing them much closer to the world level and supporting farmers in other ways, not related to the volume of their production. Much has already been done in this direction, but if the central and east Europeans are to be accommodated, much more needs to be done, including the transfer of at least some of the income support received by farmers from the Community's to member states' budgets. The difficulty of securing agreement on such a reform, from France in particular but also from other member states, is not hard to imagine. The central and east Europeans, being far poorer than the Community average, with economies requiring much structural adjustment, will also become a major burden on the structural funds, and hence on the Community budget. Here the Germans, as the biggest contributors to the budget, are heavily involved; and the present main recipients from the funds, Greece, Ireland, Portugal, and Spain, will fear that they may lose some of their share. The difficulty of these problems, the time they can take to manage, and the aggravation to both existing and aspiring new members should not be underestimated.

The conditions that the EC-EU will have to fulfill, both economic and political, will affect the central and east Europeans in a number of ways. The economic conditions—the reform of the CAP and of the, probably much expanded, structural funds—will influence both their material circumstances when they join and the impression they get of the Community, probably in an unfavorable direction, while they are waiting for membership. The political conditions may be the subject of conflict among the existing member states and hence convey another bad impression; and the outcome will determine whether the EC-EU that is available to join is a loose association of states or more like what might be called a federal union.

Conclusion: The Community's Contribution to Ethno-National Peace

The east central European states that aspire to membership have to satisfy the present member states and the European Parliament that they are going to remain sound liberal democracies. This involves not only their institutions and social structures, or civil society, but also their behavior, including, as the European Council stated, their treatment of minorities. They also have to make it clear that their market economies are in good enough shape.

But a prolonged period either of disillusion with democracy and market economy among central and east European citizens or of vacillation or poor performance on the part of the EC-EU could lead to the conclusion that membership may not be so attractive after all. Although the balance among central and east Europeans remains predominantly favorable to the Union, some ground has been lost since 1990. Seven percent fewer among the central and east Europeans had a favorable impression in 1994 than in 1993, with a rise of 4 percent on the opposite side; and there was a swing of 4 percent from favorable to unfavorable among the citizens of European countries of the CIS (Armenia, Belarus, Russia, Ukraine). Since 1990, 12 percent fewer in Hungary, Poland, Slovakia, and the Czech Republic had a favorable view, with a rise of 6 percent among those with a negative view and 8 percent among those who were neutral.[65] These were declines from extraordinarily high levels of enthusiasm; and the impression is still good. But the relative decline may be a warning to the EC-EU that the central and east Europeans could walk away if the performance of the Community and Union does not improve; and that would be good for neither the ethno-national nor any other of Europe's problems.

Part of the decline in enthusiasm for the Community and Union is doubtless due to the western recession and attendant morosity, not to mention the disunity demonstrated in the process of ratifying the Maastricht Treaty. But shortcomings in the policies toward central and eastern Europe and the CIS states have also contributed. Since the heady days of 1989–90, the EC-EU has indulged too much in protection against imports from the East, allowed too many inadequacies to persist in its programs of assistance, been slow to decide that the accession of eastern neighbors would be a good idea, and failed to put its economic weight to good political effect in relation to the former Yugoslavia. But the message of this chapter is that the Community's structures and economic powers give it a remarkable potential to help resolve ethno-national problems in Europe.

The Community is, through its PHARE and TACIS programs of technical assistance, making a modest contribution toward alleviating ethno-
national problems by actions in the fields of minorities, human rights, and
support for democracy and civil society. It has also gone far to remove
protection against industrial imports from countries with Europe Agreements, though it remains protectionist in agriculture as well as with respect
to imports of sensitive products from other eastern countries. But the
Community's outstanding contribution to the peaceful resolution of ethno-
national conflicts comes from the influence of its structures and its characteristics as a polity on countries that become member states or expect to do
so. The rule of law removes discrimination from much of economic life for
all citizens of the Union and entrenches liberal as against exclusive nationalist values. The elements of representative government in the processes of
legislation and policymaking of the Community provide a new dimension
for the concepts of self-determination and self-government. For the "self,"
in matters of Community competence, becomes the Community as a whole,
reflecting the interdependence among member states that makes the citizens
members of a wider society as well as of their ethno-national group. The
idea that there can be government for the wider society as well as for
narrower groups renders ethno-national problems more soluble.

While the value of the Community's structures should be appreciated,
the difficulties of ensuring that they help to resolve ethno-national conflicts should not be ignored. The pressure in central and eastern Europe
may just be too strong to be contained by institutions that do not dispose
of armed force—or even by institutions that do. The Community may
fail to adjust its policies and institutions in ways that are required for the
eastern enlargements. It will be hard to reform the common agricultural
policy yet again, cutting prices to world levels and limiting the Community's contribution to farmers' income support. Yet this has to be done
if enlargement to the East is to succeed. The structural funds will have to
be increased. The resistance from protectionist, import-sensitive industries will have to be overcome. Awkward questions about voting rights
in the enlarged Union will have to be answered. Interest in enlargement
to central and eastern Europe may not be sustained, although the membership of Austria, Finland, and Sweden will lend support to Germany's
undoubted commitment. Despite the widespread desire to move in the
federal direction, resistance to strengthening the Community may prevail, and the complications of enlargement, if it then takes place, may
lead to a period of disintegration.

Against such dangers, the will to unite and enlarge remains strong. France does not look as if it is abandoning its drive for the single currency and a common defense. Germany will continue to insist on the need for enlargement to the East and more powers for the European Parliament. Most other member states will accept all these things, and some will press hard for them. Reluctance on the part of the British or other governments, or various unforeseen accidents, could stand in the way of progress toward such a federal union and thus diminish the Community's capacity to deal with ethno-national problems as well as with many of the other challenges that will confront it. But the record of putting in place successive building blocks, recounted earlier in this chapter, lends credibility to the belief that the Union is more likely to continue to move in that direction than to regress toward becoming a more conventional international organization, particularly when the economic and political objectives that have motivated its progress up to now remain as strong as they have been shown to be. While there can be no certainty about the outcome, it is not unreasonable to expect that the Union will, through deepening as well as widening, help to resolve the ethno-national problems of central and eastern Europe, and make a significant contribution to alleviating them among the countries of the CIS, acting as a valuable partner of the United States in doing so.

Notes

1. *Political and Institutional Aspects of Accession to or Association with the EEC,* the Birkelbach report (Political Committee of the European Parliament, January 1962); see also Stanley Henig, *External Relations of the European Community: Associations and Trade Agreements,* European Series 19 (London: Chatham House and PEP, 1971), pp. 37–39, 130.

2. Article F, European Union Treaty.

3. Peter Andras Heltai and Zbigniew Rau, "From Nationalism to Civil Society and Tolerance," in Z. Rau, ed., *The Reemergence of Civil Society* (Boulder, Colo., Westview Press, 1991), pp. 134, 137.

4. European Commission, *Central and Eastern European Eurobarometer: Public Opinion and the European Union (16 Countries' Survey),* 4 (March 1944), Annex fig. 10, 14.

5. Laurence Whitehead, "Democracy by Convergence and Southern Europe," in Geoffrey Pridham, ed., *Encouraging Democracy: The International Context of Regime Transition in Southern Europe* (Leicester: Leicester University Press, 1991), pp. 50–52.

6. Ibid., pp. 48–49.

7. Declaration on Human Rights by the European Council, June 28 and 29 1991, cited in Commission of the EC, *The European Community and Human*

Rights (Luxembourg: Office for Official Publications of the European Communities, 1993), p. 49.

8. See, for example, Walter Lipgens, ed., *Documents on the History of European Integration,* vols. 1–3 (Berlin and New York: de Gruyter, 1984–88); and Lipgens, *A History of European Integration 1945–1947: The Formation of the European Unity Movement* (Oxford: Clarendon Press, 1982).

9. Alan Milward, "The Committee of European Economic Cooperation (CEEC) and the Advent of the Customs Union," in Lipgens, ed., *A History of European Integration,* p. 568.

10. Cited in Lipgens, *A History of European Integration,* p. 181.

11. The speech is reproduced in Walter Lipgens and Wilfried Loth, eds., *Documents on the History of European Integration, Vol. 3: The Struggle for European Union by Political Parties and Pressure Groups in Western European Countries 1945–1950* (Berlin and New York: de Gruyter, 1988), pp. 662–66, citations from pp. 664–65.

12. Statement by Robert Schuman, French foreign minister, May 9, 1950.

13. Jean Monnet, *Memoirs* (London: Collins, 1978), p. 296.

14. Jean Monnet, *Les États-Unis d'Europe ont commencé* (Paris: Robert Laffont, 1955), pp. 51–54.

15. Monnet, *Memoirs,* pp. 86, 90–92.

16. Ibid., p. 283–84.

17. Ibid, p. 92.

18. Henri Brugmans, *L'Idée européenne 1918–1945* (Bruges: De Tempel, 1965), p. 171.

19. For an account of this episode see Carl J. Friedrich, "Introduction," in Robert R. Bowie and Carl J. Friedrich, eds., *Studies in Federalism* (Boston: Little Brown and Company, 1954).

20. Comité Intergouvernemental créé par la Conférence de Messine, *Rapport des Chefs de Délégation aux Ministres des Affaires Etrangères,* the Spaak report (Brussels: April 21, 1956), pp. 9–10; and John Pinder, *European Community: The Building of a Union* (Oxford: Oxford University Press, 1991), pp. 60–63.

21. For a full explanation of the Maastricht Treaty, see Andrew Duff, Roy Pryce, and John Pinder, eds., *Maastricht and Beyond: Building the European Union* (London: Routledge for the Federal Trust, 1994).

22. Samuel Brittan, "Single Currency Rises Again," *Financial Times,* May 12, 1994; Martin Wolf, "Emu May Not Be Dead, After All," *Financial Times,* August 1, 1994.

23. European Commission, *Growth, Competitiveness, Employment: The Challenges and Ways Forward into the 21st Century,* White Paper (Luxembourg: Office for Official Publications of the European Communities, 1994).

24. Alain Lamassoure, *Le Monde,* May 30, 1994; *Überlegungen zur Europäishcen Politik* (Bonn: CDU/CSU Fraktion des Deutschen Bundestages, September 1, 1994).

25. See T. C. Hartley, *The Foundations of European Community Law* (Oxford: Clarendon Press, 1988), p. 47.

26. For a fuller analysis, see John Pinder, *The Community after Maastricht: How Federal?* special issue of *New European Quarterly Review,* vol. 5, no. 3 (1992).

27. For a review of the history of this and other aspects of the relationship until 1991, see John Pinder, *The European Community and Eastern Europe* (London: Pinter Publishers for the Royal Institute of International Affairs, 1991).

28. See, for example, Timothy Garton Ash, *In Europe's Name: Germany and the Divided Continent* (London: Jonathan Cape, 1993).

29. See John Pinder, "The European Community and Democracy in Central and Eastern Europe," in Geoffrey Pridham, Eric Herring, and George Sanford, eds., *Building Democracy? The International Dimension of Democratization in Eastern Europe* (Leicester: Leicester University Press, 1994), pp. 121–22.

30. See for example Commission of the EC, *Action Plan: coordinated assistance from the Group of 24 to Bulgaria, Czechoslovakia, the German Democratic Republic, Romania and Yugoslavia,* SEC (90)843 final (Brussels, May 2, 1990), and *Association Agreements with the Countries of Central and Eastern Europe: a general outline,* COM(90)398 final Brussels (August 29, 1990).

31. Literature on this theme is summarized in Eric Herring, "International Security and Democratisation in Eastern Europe," in Pridham, Herring, and Sanford, eds., *Building Democracy,* p. 103 and n. 10 on p. 115.

32. See Ernest Gellner, *Conditions of Liberty: Civil Society and Its Rivals* (London: Hamish Hamilton, 1994).

33. See Pinder, *The European Community and Eastern Europe,* chap. 4.

34. Consumer price indices, from Economic Commission for Europe, *Economic Survey of Europe in 1993–1994* (New York and Geneva: United Nations, 1994), p. 75, table 3.3.1.

35. Calculated from ibid., p. 68, table 3.2.5.

36. Ibid., p. 86, table 3.4.4.

37. Where no references are given, data in these sections have been obtained from general sources given in Pinder, *The European Community and Eastern Europe,* and from internal documents of the European Commission and interviews with its officials.

38. 93/742 Euratom, ECSC, EC, *Official Journal of the European Communities* (L347), December 31, 1993; 93/743 Euratom, ECSC, EC, *Official Journal* (L348), December 31, 1993.

39. See, for example, 92/228 EEC, *Official Journal* (L114), April 30, 1992; 92/229 EEC, *Official Journal* (L115), April 30, 1992; 92/240 EEC, *Official Journal* (L116), April 30, 1992.

40. *Euro-east,* May 24, 1994, p. 8.

41. "Copenhagen European Council, 21 and 22 June 1993," *Bulletin of the European Communities,* 6 (1993).

42. Calculated from *G24 Assistance Commitments: Type by Donor* (Brussels: European Commission Directorate-General 1, July 12, 1994).

43. "Copenhagen European Council, 21 and 22 June 1993," p. 19.

44. *PHARE in 1993—Improvements, Innovations and Continuity* (Brussels: European Commission PHARE Information Office, December 2, 1993); *What Is PHARE?: A European Union Initiative for Economic Integration with Central and East European Countries* (Brussels: European Commission PHARE Information Office, May 1994).

45. "Cooperation with the countries of Central and Eastern Europe and the Soviet Union," *Official Journal* (C309), November 16, 1993, pp. 177–99.

46. *Independent,* October 10, 1994.

47. European Commission, *Growth, Competitiveness, Employment: The Challenges and Ways Forward into the 21st Century* (Luxembourg, 1994).

48. *What Is Tacis? Partnerships and Cooperation with the New Independent States* (Brussels: European Commission Tacis Information Office, May 1994).

49. *The European Union's Phare and Tacis Democracy Programme: Guidelines* (Brussels: European Human Rights Foundation, 1994).

50. *Annual Report 1994* (Brussels and London: European Human Rights Foundation, 1994).

51. Commission of the EC, *The European Community and Human Rights.*

52. *Resolution on Human Rights, Democracy and Development,* by the Council and Member States, meeting within the Council, November 28, 1991, cited in Commission of the EC, *The European Community and Human Rights,* p. 52.

53. Commission of the EC, *The European Community and Human Rights,* p. 24.

54. *Stability Pact in Europe: The Documents Adopted by the Paris Conference,* Europe Document 1887, Atlantic Document 86, *Agence Europe,* May 31, 1994.

55. *Together in Europe,* May 15, 1994, p. 4.

56. *East-west,* February 21, 1994, pp. 26, 27.

57. *What is Tacis?,* p. 4.

58. "Copenhagen European Council," p. 13.

59. European Commission, "Report on the Criteria and Conditions for Accession of New Members to the Community," Europe Documents, *Agence Europe* 1730, July 3, 1992.

60. Ibid.

61. Drafts of the Treaty on European Union Presented by the Luxembourg and the Dutch Presidencies to the Intergovernmental Conference, Europe Documents, *Agence Europe* 1722–23, July 5, 1991, and 1750–51, December 13, 1991, Articles A.W.

62. "Copenhagen European Council," p. 130.

63. "Report on the criteria."

64. See Richard E. Baldwin, *Towards an Integrated Europe* (London: Centre for Economic Policy Research, 1994).

65. *Central and Eastern European Barometer,* pp. 29–30.

FOUR

The European Union's Politico-Diplomatic Contribution to the Prevention of Ethno-National Conflict

Reinhardt Rummel

IT HAS BEEN obvious from the beginning of the new era in Europe that the challenge of ethno-national conflict in the eastern part and the objective of union building in the western part of the continent are intertwined. The character and scope of the new conflicts in Europe, and the circumstances under which they have come about, had an impact on the rationale of west European integration.

The European Union's Adaptation to New Security Challenges

During the cold war the Community had been an instrument to stabilize the West. Brussels was part of this process of reducing tensions in critical regions of the world and specifically in Europe.[1] Starting in the 1970s and 1980s, the European Community (EC) and the European Political Cooperation (EPC) had some experience with the mitigation of ethno-national disputes such as the Arab-Israeli conflict, the Cyprus conflict, and the conflict in South Africa.[2] Yet almost no concepts or instruments existed for the type of issue that has become the most common security challenge in today's Europe.[3] In many ways the response to potential conflict on their doorsteps has been a cold start for the west Europeans and their collective organizations. As the European Union (EU), which was designed to cope primarily with controversies and conflicting interests among its member states, moved into a position of conflict management in eastern Europe, a new type of policy mix was required, new internal structures of decision-making, and a new level of international sharing of responsibilities. These demands contributed to the idea of enriching the external component of the Community, of moving from EPC to Common Foreign and Security Policy (CFSP), and of establishing a political union alongside the economic union. The Treaty on the European Union (Maastricht Treaty), in force since November 1, 1993, codified the idea.[4]

After the proposed European Defense Community aborted in 1954, the European Community developed as an economic giant but remained a political dwarf with relatively little influence on Europe's security. Something needed to be done about this asymmetrical development. In 1970 EPC was created as a system of mutual information, consultation, coordination, and concerted diplomacy among the EC member states, directed toward the goal of a common European foreign policy, primarily in support of EC trade policy. Ten years later, in the London Report of 1981, the foreign ministers took measures to improve the still embryonic administrative structures and political decisionmaking processes of EPC. They defined joint action as the goal of EPC and expressly mentioned for the first time the political aspects of security as a subject of cooperation. Although the EC Commission was now allowed to participate in the deliberations and common activities of the EPC member states, EC and EPC remained two legally, institutionally, and sometimes politically separate bodies. EPC itself remained primarily a consultative process.

Gradually during the 1980s EPC was connected with the EC. After the Single European Act of 1987 incorporated EPC in an international treaty, economic instruments such as financial aid or trade embargoes could be used by EPC for foreign policy purposes. In institutional terms the establishment of a secretariat in Brussels helped to assist the Presidency in coordinating common policies and in acting as a spokesman and representative of the member states. The foreign ministers met regularly, at least six times a year. The Political Committee and the European Correspondents' Group met at least once a month. In addition, there were regular meetings of some twenty working groups, as well as countless meetings of ambassadors of the member states.

EPC's main areas of activity during the 1980s encompassed East-West relations, including the work of the Conference on Security and Cooperation in Europe (CSCE), cooperation within the United Nations, the trouble spots in the Middle East, southern Africa, and Central and Latin America, and the fight against international terrorism. A considerable part of EPC policy was devoted to the observation of human rights worldwide. Yet in spite of an ever more sophisticated internal infrastructure, the member states as a group had continuous difficulty in speaking with one voice and acting in common. An Atlanticist fraction built around the United Kingdom tried to strengthen close relations with Washington, a Latin group led by France looked mainly southward to ensure its interests, and a third orientation, led by Germany, was primarily concerned with stability in eastern Europe. Bonn was more inclined than its fellow EPC partners to take President Gorbachev at his word when, in the second half of the 1980s, he promised a move toward the reduction of tensions in Europe and developed the concept of a "common European house."

There was a larger common denominator among the member states in the economic sphere. All of them were facing the need for industrial modernization at home as well as growing competition in the international market. EC Commission president Jacques Delors's concept of "Single Market 1992" seemed to be the perfect answer. The creation of an Economic and Monetary Union (EMU) required a substantial extension of the Rome Treaty. An intergovernmental conference (IGC) of the heads of state and government of the EC-EPC was projected for the end of 1991 to hammer out the EMU. Fairly late in the preparatory process, at the end of 1990, politicians as well as experts noticed that other, more political issues were rapidly increasing in relevance: the United States and the USSR stopped regarding themselves as enemies, the importance of military assets in Europe was dramatically downscaled, the strategic transformation of Europe was in full swing, German unification set new terms for European countries, and open borders toward the East (combined with the soon to come large space of the single market) raised the problem of an uncontrolled inflow of refugees, asylum seekers, and international criminals.

Most important was the rise of ethno-national tension in the sense of ethnic groups, living together in one country or in neighboring countries, beginning to assert their interests and seeking to change their status. The potential for armed conflict following from such unrest has been high and has caused security concerns in western Europe and elsewhere. The physical spillover of violence to neighboring regions may occur in many ways. The fighting may be extended to neighboring countries to internationalize the conflict. A fighting party may hide in adjacent areas and organize its attacks from a safe place (which may cause the adversary to carry the war across the border), or it may terrorize a noninvolved but influential country to mount political pressure for its cause. The clandestine infusion of weapons may be channeled through neighboring countries. Embargoes may have to be imposed by force. Armed conflict may cause large numbers of refugees that may become a challenge to the social and political stability of the recipient country. Countries may be affected by some of these contaminations even if they are not directly bordering the conflict area. Perhaps most worrisome is that the resolution of a conflict by force may be misread as a tolerated method of realizing political objectives. Beyond human miseries and material burdens, it is the political culture that is at stake.[5] All this seemed to need early and thorough attention to avoid the eruption of violence, spread of instability, and contamination leading to unrest in the West.

In response to these challenges a second IGC was launched to deal with political problems, to be convened and synchronized together with the first IGC on the EMU. The negotiations of both IGCs resulted in the Maastricht Treaty in December 1991. This Treaty consists of three pillars: the communitarian EMU, the intergovernmental CFSP, and the cooperation in areas of justice and home affairs.

However, when CFSP was designed, during 1991, a large part of the new conflict-ridden world had not yet unfolded. Germany was united, but the Soviet Union remained intact until December 1991; the Gulf War continued through the spring of 1991, and its aftermath lingered in the UN; Yugoslavia, still calm at the beginning of 1991, began to disintegrate when the fighting started in June, and the crisis of recognition came in December, just as the Maastricht Treaty was being concluded. The Treaty, and especially its second and third pillars, reflects change, but only a first stage. While the member governments felt the push toward fundamental adaptation, they were also uncertain about the outcome of innovation. The provisions on CFSP therefore mention the strategic fields of adaptation, but most of the provisions are more an extrapolation of the line of evolution of EPC than a qualitatively fresh start. (These provisions are discussed more fully below in "Structural Measures of Conflict Prevention.")

The one exception is defense. The word had not figured in any of the texts of European unification since 1954 when the European Defense Community foundered in the French Assemblée Nationale. The Maastricht Treaty seeks to implement a security policy including the eventual framing of a common defense policy, which might in time lead to a common defense. The Union is to request the Western European Union (WEU), which is recognized as the military arm of the EU, to elaborate and implement decisions and actions of the Union that have defense implications. The provisions on defense are potentially important innovations in the security sector of the unification process, though they will certainly need further qualification given the new range of security tasks after the end of the cold war. The WEU Petersburg Declaration talks of some new responsibilities such as crisis management, peacekeeping, and humanitarian actions. But conflict prevention has not yet become one of the new components of this modernized notion of defense and security.

What international role did the member states have in mind when they tried to strengthen the second pillar of the Union? What is the new division of labor in the security field with other organizations, particularly NATO? While the political-military challenges of the East-West conflict had been the prerogative of NATO and particularly the United States, the Community, according to Christopher Hill,[6] specialized in a number of functions in international relations, among them (1) stabilizing western Europe, (2) managing world trade, (3) forming a principal voice of the developed world in relations with the underdeveloped world, and (4) providing a second western voice in international diplomacy. A more self-confident and maturing European Union, again in Hill's view, could now move on to the following functions and become potentially (1) a replacement for the Soviet Union in the global balance of power, (2) a regional pacifier, (3) a global intervenor, (4) a mediator of conflicts, (5) a bridge between rich and poor, and (6) a joint supervisor of the world economy.

Except for the function of replacing the Soviet Union, which is a bit optimistic, the EU has staged actions in all of these roles since the inception of the Maastricht Treaty.[7] Unlike the UN and the Organization for Security and Cooperation in Europe (OSCE), the EU, as of now, has not had a strategy designed specifically to prevent ethno-national conflict in the world or in a particular region such as eastern and central Europe and the CIS. Only recently have part of its objectives and external activities been directed toward this goal, for example, the Balladur Initiative which provides elements of a more comprehensive EU philosophy of how to promote conflict prevention. Although, as would be expected, the EU mostly pursues economic strategies and relies least on military approaches of conflict prevention, the rest of this chapter addresses neither of these. Instead, it focuses on Brussels's attempt to use political-diplomatic means and to develop norms and institutions that enable a peaceful settlement of ethno-national clashes.

The European Union's Paradigmatic Quality: An Instrument of Conflict Prevention?

West Europeans have been largely successful in avoiding armed conflict and war in the past fifty years. Many factors have joined to create such relatively peaceful circumstances. Among them are economic stability and NATO-guaranteed security. Two other elements of the existing political system in western Europe are also key: democracy and integration. Developing democracy within the states of eastern and central Europe and the CIS as well as integration among these states is therefore regarded as a road to peace in that region as well. Some of the EU's most promising strategies to deal with violent conflict lie in promoting democratic and integrative structures in the East.[8]

Democracy

The EU has been making specific efforts toward developing democracy in the eastern and central European and CIS region without, however, making it a strategic concept comparable to the scope of the 1992 project. In Brussels the support of systemic transformation in eastern and central Europe and the CIS was motivated by the bad experience with communist ideology and totalitarian rule in the former socialist camp and the good experience with the western political systems based on law, human rights, pluralist government, and market economy. All of these western values culminate in liberal democracy, which in the view of the EU and its member states has a built-in quality of peaceful conflict resolution, respect for minorities, and high potential of participation of the citizen in public policy. This is why the politicians of the member states of the EU as well as the representatives of the Union and its institutions, especially the European Commission and the European Parliament, regard the establishment of full democracy in the east of the continent as a safeguard to their own vital interest.

For the West, liberal democracy is a systemic framework that assists with the prevention of both intra- and interstate conflicts.[9] As to transborder conflicts, Brussels's foreign and security policy follows implicitly the experience that "the absence of war between democracies comes as close as anything we have to an empirical law in international relations."[10] Moreover, the evidence suggests that democratic states, when in conflict with another state, are more inclined to accept third-party mediation than authoritarian states are.[11]

The EU's strong faith in democracy as a route to peace was illustrated by Brussels's reaction to Moscow's military intervention in Chechnya. While President Yeltsin was blamed for the violation of human rights and the rights of minorities in the Caucasus, understanding was voiced concerning the sensitive situation of the Russian democracy. In other words, the continuation of democratic reform in Russia was rated higher than the compliance with human rights norms and standards as enshrined in the UN Charter and the documents of the OSCE. This example also demonstrates some of the side effects and dilemmas in promoting democracy. The situation is particularly complicated concerning intrastate conflict.

Of course, there is no guarantee that democracies will always be successful. Violence in critical regions within the EU, for instance in Northern Ireland, is the exception to the rule and illustrates some of the limits of liberal democracy. It also demonstrates its strength: as the past twenty-five years of Irish terrorist behavior indicates, ethnic conflict within democracies neither dramatically escalates nor spills over in significant ways. Rather, the assumption is that the context of democratic rule in the British Isles constrains the smoldering conflict and eventually will allow peaceful resolution. Thus leaders in the EU are convinced that democracies provide, at least theoretically, a better systemic environment for conflict mitigation and peaceful settlement, mechanisms of political solution, and education in the use of peaceful means.

What then has the EU done to promote democracy in eastern and central Europe and the CIS area? How strong was the EU's faith in democracy as a route to peace? How does the EU act on that faith?[12] In fact, the EU as such has not designed a massive program of democratization, but has included some support for the establishment of democratic infrastructure in the Poland and Hungary Aid for Economic Recovery (PHARE) and Technical Assistance to the CIS (TACIS) programs.[13] It has been rather the member states than the EU proper that have been transferring direct expertise from West to East in terms of helping to organize the ingredients of a democracy, elaborating a constitution, and developing the necessary institutions. The two most visible and direct engagements of the EU have been diplomatic support for democratic transformation and assistance for the development of democratic rules and infrastructure.

DIPLOMATIC SUPPORT FOR DEMOCRATIC TRANSFORMATION. In all its official relations and communiqués with countries in the East, the EU has made reference to the principles of democracy. The EU has not gone so far as to make democracy an explicit precondition for economic and other support, but it has been clear to all eastern countries that without democracy there will be only limited interaction. In specific cases the EU has been prepared to press actively for the introduction of or the compliance with democratic rules.

One such attempt was made with Slovakia at the end of 1994 when a delegation of the EU in an official démarche expressed its concerns to President Gasparovic of the Slovak parliament over the undemocratic behavior of the governing coalition and reminded him to carefully bear in mind Slovakian external interests while reforming the political system. The démarche was unsuccessful. Mr. Gasparovic flatly rejected the criticism from Brussels, and the leader of the Slovakian National party (SNS), Slota, resented the "interference in internal affairs of a sovereign state."[14] Both men as well as Prime Minister Meciar were likewise unimpressed by the move of the Committee on External Relations of the European Parliament to halt a credit of $246 million raised by the EU and twenty-four donors earlier that year. If the interruption or withdrawal of foreign aid should turn out to be unsuccessful too, will the institutions of the EU then contemplate banning Slovakia from the list of candidates for EU membership?

Membership in the EU is excluded for nondemocratic states.[15] This has been stressed many times over by EU officials and is required by the Treaty of Rome as well as the Maastricht Treaty, which specifies that the "Union shall respect fundamental rights as guaranteed by the European Convention for the Protection of Human Rights and Fundamental Freedoms and as they result from the constitutional traditions common to the Member States as general principles of Community law."[16] The Europe Agreements and the Partnership and Cooperation Agreements[17] make reference to democracy. The June 1993 decision on EU enlargement puts forward strict criteria for accession by the associated states: as a precondition for membership a state must have reached an institutional stability as a guarantee for democracy and the rule of law, for the preservation of human rights, and the respect and protection of minorities.[18]

The attractiveness of EU democracies, their stability, and their efficiency certainly is an asset the member states can count on when dealing with states in transformation. There has not been much open objection on the part of the eastern countries to the western demand for democracy. Rather it seems to coincide with eastern aspirations. Whether in practical terms it is regarded more as a help than an obstacle that the EU has based its relations with the East on the promotion of democratic rights and rules in those countries is open for assessment. It will be a burden to comply with many western systemic standards at the same time. Social needs, educational deficiencies, as well as national pride may stand in the way of accepting and understanding western models of democratization. In the case of the démarche in Bratislava, some of the Slovakian leaders apparently retorted that the representatives from Brussels did not understand the particular circumstances of the local situation as well as the need for stability in Slovakia.[19]

ASSISTANCE FOR THE DEVELOPMENT OF DEMOCRATIC RULES AND INFRA-STRUCTURE. More than declarations are needed to establish a democracy successfully. Essential preconditions include economic progress, social justice, a free media, and a certain level of education. The West and more specifically the EU have been active in all these areas, on the level of states, international organizations, and nongovernmental organizations (NGOs). The scope and record of these activities vary considerably from case to case.[20] The EU has engaged in election monitoring in several states of eastern and central Europe and the CIS. Observation of the Russian election in December 1993 was conducted as a so-called Common Action of CFSP.[21] Several hundred monitors, most of them volunteers from EU member states, were dispatched to various places in Russia during the voting to observe whether the election process was fair and the vote was secret and free. Russian authorities were informed beforehand and gave the monitors access to the election sites. The monitors had been briefed in advance by the European Commission and reported back to Brussels. The overall tenor of those reports was that the elections had been by and large correct, but that it was doubtful how well the voters understood what they were doing.

The development of democracy from scratch is a long and complex process that has to engage many layers and sections of the society. At the initiative of the European Parliament, the EU has incorporated a Democracy Program in both PHARE and TACIS. It supports nongovernmental organizations in the PHARE partner countries in their effort to promote democratic principles and the rule of law. The PHARE Democracy Program for 1995 will make available some 8 million ecu ($10 million) for more than fifty macroprojects and more than one hundred microprojects.[22] The macroprojects range from helping to draft laws against racism to holding a history competition to promote greater objectivity in the teaching of Hungarian history; from the creation of an agency for local democracy in the Maribor region of Slovenia to human rights education in Albania; from a study tour of elections in Germany for young parliamentarians from east European countries to the support of the establishment of a negotiating

structure among trade unions, employers' associations, and governmental
bodies in Poland. The microprojects are a new category within the Democracy Program, which allows direct funding for NGOs in the partner countries without a partner based in the EU being required. The projects
recommended for funding in 1995 were in areas ranging from human rights
and the translation of teaching materials on democratic principles, to supporting the transparency of local government activities, or the retraining of
union shop stewards in the steel industry.

What can the EU achieve in terms of conflict prevention in countries of the
East by trying to promote democratic transformation and support the development of democratic rules and structures with numerous projects? These efforts
can be evaluated as both short-term measures to guide initial reform and as a
long-term structural investment that may pay off only over a long time. For
both purposes it is important that the EU appears as a convincing agent by
making a good case for democracy and providing essential help.

Precisely because of existing ethno-national conflict and other deficiencies of societies in eastern Europe, it is very difficult to introduce democracy, build the necessary institutions, and educate the electorate as well as
the political leaders. Yet the EU policy of democratic transformation in the
East does not convey much determination.[23] While the support for building
up democratic infrastructure, interparliamentary cooperation, and election
monitoring are initial contributions to the stabilization of democratic values
in the society of formerly socialist countries, it may still be a long time
before democracy is understood and firmly implanted there. So far, democratization has advanced only halfway, partly it is even retreating. In half of
the eastern and central European and the CIS states, former communist
leaders are back in power.

Moreover, the western democratic systems are not always convincing in
their performance. They show limits in dealing with local ethnic conflict as
demonstrated by Greece in Cyprus, Spain in the Basque area, France in
Corsica, and Great Britain and Ireland in Ulster.[24] And ironically, the EU
itself sometimes does not pass as a showcase of democracy, as illustrated by
the opposition to the Maastricht Treaty on grounds of democratic deficiencies of the EU.

Integration

The Community very rapidly became a pole of attraction for most of the
countries in the former Soviet orbit, mainly because of its relatively high

socioeconomic standard, but partly also because of its political stability and its peaceful forms of dealing with ethno-national conflicts. The EU can be seen as a security system that exemplifies the second law of international relations: countries that freely engage in a union-building process reach a point where they will not use force anymore against each other. In this sense, for some countries and ethnic groups in the East, close connection, if not membership, with the EU is regarded as a guarantee for their own stability and a quasi-automatic insurance against the emergence of ethno-national conflict among them. However, just as in the case of democracy, integration is less effective in dealing with intrastate violence.

Moreover, the relationship between integration and peace could potentially be conflict producing.[25] Arguably, the expectation of faster integration into the EU precipitated Slovenia's declaration of independence, which, together with other factors, produced a domino effect in Yugoslavia in 1990–91 leading to outright war. Integration of eastern and central European states into the EU may also be conflict producing in that states admitted first are more likely to take an uncompromising attitude in their disputes with states applying for membership later. A good example has been Greece's policies toward Turkey in the past and toward Albania and Macedonia more recently.

Moreover, Moscow has already made it plain that NATO's enlargement would be regarded as a hostile act. Is the enlargement of the EU a different story? Brussels is well aware of the sensitivity of this question and has tried to deal with Russian concerns by offering a partnership and cooperation agreement and inviting Moscow to participate in other western forums such as the Economic Summit. But nobody can be sure whether these confidence-building measures will be strong enough.

Intra-East integration also may have disadvantages. If Russia is excluded, it threatens to contribute to intra-East tensions and could be taken as a vehicle for reassertion of Russian authority in the neighborhood. Moreover, it is not easy for countries and ethnic groups in eastern and central Europe and the CIS, who after several decades of suppression are free now to speak out and assert their identity, to join in such an integrative process. Psychologically they are asked to act against their instincts and to compromise their newly acquired freedom.

Despite these negative outcomes, the conviction remains strong in Brussels that on the whole integration has been successful in keeping peace among west European countries and that the relation of eastern countries with the EU allows them to study the integration model, its techniques, difficulties, and blessings. It will take time and good examples to convince the politicians and populations of central and eastern Europe that in the modern interdependent and civilized Europe no country can expect to have it one hundred percent its own way. Rather, it is the rule that everybody has to compromise, comply with common standards, and accept "supranational" authorities. The member states of the EU have been trained in that type of thinking, they have internalized the sharing of sovereignty, and they have achieved promising results. It takes a good deal of confidence to rely on such a strategy. The fact that the EU exists and prospers on the basis of such a regime may help countries in the East to commit to the same behavior.

There are two basic forms that integration could take. The first is integration into the EU by accession. The second is integration among the eastern European countries themselves. These two paths are not entirely consistent, but the EU has encouraged both.

MEMBERSHIP? Almost all countries of eastern and central Europe and the CIS have expressed their wish to become members of the EU. Poland and Hungary, in mid-1994, were the first to apply officially. The EU has not made up its mind who will be accepted and when. While this decision is pending, Brussels is asking the candidates to continue to qualify according to the Copenhagen criteria. These include the above mentioned democratic requirements as well as preconditions for market economies and economic competition. Moreover, the candidate countries have to accept the goals of the EMU and political union and be prepared to shoulder the obligations that derive from these commitments.[26]

Candidate countries have argued against these criteria and asked for early accession. "Early" means that they want to prepare for meeting the criteria of democracy and market economy inside rather than outside the Union. Brussels fears destabilization of the Union and therefore favors the opposite sequence. A more refined debate has referred to the view that, although early accession, may not be feasible in the economic or, more specifically, in the communitarian sectors of the Union, there are fewer obstacles in the spheres of intergovernmental cooperation. At one point, Commissioner Andriessen expressed the idea of scaled accession inviting newcomers to participate in the foreign policy aspects only, but the concept was never turned into an official plan. On the eastern side some politicians have also launched the idea of becoming early members in those sectors of the EU where the requirements can be met more easily.[27] If all easterners persist in wanting to join the Union and Brussels keeps up its preconditions of entry, then the EU will by definition dominate the international politics of Europe.

A MODEL TO COPY? The EU has long promoted cooperation and integration in other regions of the world. In principle, it has adopted this policy also in eastern and central Europe and the CIS, but it has not done much in practical terms to foster interaction there. The most prominent attempts at regional cooperation are the Central European Initiative (former Pentagonale),[28] the Visegrad,[29] the Baltic Sea[30] and the Black Sea cooperation,[31] as well as the cooperation within the CIS.[32]

All these regional groups of countries (with the possible exception of the CIS) are cooperative enterprises with functional agendas without any ambition of forming a community or union à la Bruxelles. Yet some of the political laws and their benefits are the same in regional cooperation and regional integration. In some respects the CIS has the best preconditions for making progress with integration and transnational exchange. On the other hand, historical factors and the unavoidable dominance of Russia in the group make it difficult to copy the EU model.

Theoretically, circumstances in this regard are more promising among the Visegrad Four, but ironically the very magnetic forces of the EU that attract these countries also work to undermine their drive for integration among themselves. They are presently engaged in a competition for the first to be accepted as an EU member. They also fear that a successful eastern cooperation or integration would undermine their chances of becoming members of the EU.[33]

In practice the paradigm of the EU is hard to reproduce or apply in other, less favorable circumstances. Regional cooperation has been fairly successful in eastern and central Europe and the CIS without, however, reaching anywhere near the achievements of the EU. These attempts will need time, despite the carrots and sticks deployed by Brussels.

WHICH PATH? The more promising approach for the states of eastern and central Europe (though less so for those of the CIS) seems to be accession to the EU, even though it will not be soon. The example in this case is the southern enlargement of the Community by Greece, Spain, and Portugal in the first half of the 1980s. They all left dictatorships behind and joined the core group of the European Community, Madrid and Lisbon ardently, Athens with some temptation to overstate its role. The critical period with countries in eastern and central Europe is from now to entry. Can the EU be kept attractive?

The ambitions of the Maastricht Treaty and the circumstances of its ratification procedure, which provoked more criticism of the technocratic

Brussels machine than ever before in national debates and referenda, have sent mixed signals to the East.[34] Some, like Poland and Hungary, have applied for membership, and most of the others will, but many have expressed doubts and do not want to join in an unconditional way. The Czech prime minister, Vaclav Klaus, has repeatedly stated that some of the rules in the EU have to be changed if Prague decides to enter. These are brave if not arrogant words. The Swiss population, in 1993, could afford to reject incorporation into the European Economic Area (EEA), just as the Norwegians preferred in 1994 (against the advice of their government) to stay outside the EU.[35] Both countries are rich, and Norway is a longtime NATO member. But none of the eastern countries is in an economic and political situation to refuse an offer of accession from Brussels if it were made in the near future.

Meanwhile, improving democracy in the EU and continuing integration are regarded by Brussels as building leverage through investing in its own credibility. This is seen as an essential asset when it comes to the mediation of conflict or the enforcement of solutions. As shall be seen below, in cases like the Slovak-Hungarian dispute over the Gabcikovo-Nagymaros project, the attractiveness of the EU has been claimed as crucial in transforming a conflict and enhancing the leverage of other international organizations within which the Fifteen form part of the membership.

Structural Measures of Conflict Prevention: Creating Networks and Commitments

While democracy and integration shape the systemic environment within which countries and their people in eastern and central Europe and the CIS can play out ethno-national conflicts, more direct means are available to the EU to work on the prevention of conflict. The strategy consists of diplomatic tools such as dialogues, discussion rounds, and multilateral cooperation to create a framework within which a given or potential conflict can be dealt with in a preventive and peaceful way.

Since Maastricht, this task is carried out within the framework of the CFSP. As designed by the Treaty, CFSP is rather a process than a policy. It is also not a *common* policy in the sense of a single external policy of the Union. The member states continue to have their own foreign policies which, it is true, should support the CFSP line, but there is no obligation to do so. The Union conducts external relations in its own right in the sectors of trade, technological and financial cooperation, as well as foreign aid. These communitarian polices dispose of a budget of their own and are part of a separate decisionmaking and implementation process within which the European Commission plays a central role as the initiator of action. CFSP, on the other hand, remains, at least for the time being, basically an intergovernmental framework focused on coordinated diplomatic activities. The European Commission's position within this framework is weak. The Commission does not have the exclusive right of initiative as in the communitarian sphere. It shares this function with the Presidency and the member states, which decide by consensus whether and how they want to be active in a joint manner.

The minimum of cooperation within CFSP is mutual information and consultation among the Fifteen plus the European Commission, but they can go beyond this stage and act together in two specific procedural fashions: common positions and common actions. Once the Council establishes a Common Position on a subject, for instance, the support of Ukrainian transformation and independence, then this position will serve as a reference for all further action in this field, be it individual national policies or policies of the group, whether in bilateral relations or in the context of international organizations or conferences. If the Council decides on a Common Action, such as the EU monitoring mission of the general elections in Russia, the details of the action, including financial implications, will be determined in common. While in all activities under the heading of CFSP, unanimity or at least consensus is required, the Common Action regime provides for majority voting in the implementation of the action. During its short experience since November 1993, about a dozen Common Actions have been established, and in none of the cases was the majority voting rule applied. As will be discussed below, a conflict-prevention connotation can be attributed to most of the Common Actions even though only a few have been officially marked by this name tag. Examples are monitoring elections in Russia and South Africa, providing humanitarian assistance in the former Yugoslavia and establishing an administration in Mostar, support for the Middle East peace process, support for the extension of the Non-Proliferation Treaty (NPT), and promotion of the Stability Pact to tackle problems concerned with borders and minorities in central and eastern Europe.

Theoretically CFSP can draw on economic sticks and carrots of the Union and on military support from the WEU, NATO, or an ad hoc group of member states. In practical political, administrative and legal terms, this is the exception rather than the rule. Therefore most CFSP activities are limited to common political declarations, to démarches of the Presidency or the Troika, and to diplomatic initiatives such as proposals to develop the OSCE or to extend the NPT. The combined position of the Fifteen is certainly a point of orientation for many countries, but substantive action would create more credibility and a better standing for CFSP. CFSP also lacks the planning capacity needed for conflict prevention: early warning machinery, careful and comprehensive analysis, joint assessment, and the preparation of operational options from which to choose. Finally, CFSP lacks a broad political base. Conflict prevention needs public support to justify the investment in the mitigation of a conflict that has not yet proven it will affect the interests and the security of the people in an essential way. The European Parliament plays only a consultative role in CFSP. The EU as such is not a democratic system. Given all these deficiencies, which the Maastricht Treaty has not been able and not been intended to change, it is surprising, as will be seen below, that CFSP nevertheless has contributed to enhance the conflict-prevention capacity of the EU as a whole.

In general the EU has developed two prime avenues to entice countries in eastern and central Europe and the CIS into structured relations designed to improve preconditions for conflict prevention. The first activity tries to establish a network of cooperative links directed at political-diplomatic aspects of local or regional conflicts all over the east central European and CIS area. The second, the Balladur Initiative, is more specifically focused on potential border and minority conflicts and, for the time being, is limited to east central Europe.

Networks

The Europe Agreements, which the EU has already concluded with the six east central European countries and is preparing with the three Baltic countries and Slovenia, deal extensively with economic matters, but one component is reserved for the so-called political dialogue. Similar provisions are also to be found in the Partnership and Cooperation Agreements with Ukraine, as well as the one with Russia. In contrast to the Europe Agreements, which associate eastern countries to the EU and are designed to prepare them for eventual membership, the Partnership and Cooperation Agreements do not open up a perspective of accession. In each case, however, the "political dialogue" is similar and permits discussion of all kinds of foreign policy and security matters on which the parties involved want to provide or receive information. The dialogue is not a consultative instrument, let alone a place for negotiations. Rather it helps to put economic cooperation into a political context. It can involve heads of state, ministerial meetings, and high-level or expert working group meetings. One of its limiting features is that it runs on a rigid calendar with two rounds of meetings a year, and does not allow for continuous exchange of views or for the treatment of issues as they emerge.

The dialogue provides a framework within which factors can be discussed that have an impact on conflict prevention. It also can be used as a contractual reference point that serves to establish more specific bilateral initiatives in the field of external relations. To mention one of many examples, the 1994 Corfu European Council used the occasion of the signing of the EU–Ukraine Partnership and Cooperation Agreement to ask the Council to develop a more comprehensive policy with Kiev, which should include "cooperation with Ukraine in multilateral fora in support of regional and international stability and the peaceful settlement of disputes."[36]

In December 1993 the Italian foreign minister, Beniamino Andreatta, went further. On behalf of himself and his British colleague, Douglas Hurd, he presented to the Council of the Union an initiative designed to broaden this consultative process so as to hasten the development of closer relations between the then Twelve and the countries of central and eastern Europe. In a letter to Willy Claes, the Council President, the ministers suggested that the EU should respond positively and imaginatively to the desires in the East for closer consultation and to develop "new links between the associate countries and the work of the two intergovernmental pillars of Maastricht, CFSP and justice/home affairs."[37] Such links, says the letter, "would enable the associate countries to align their policies and practices more closely with those of the European Union and thus help to prepare them for eventual accession." Recalling that the separate discussion on the development of an enhanced military relationship with the countries of central and eastern Europe is beginning in the WEU,[38] the two ministers stressed that "although there is provision in the agreements for regular political dialogue with the European Union, relations with these countries tend to be dominated by economic issues" and that the waiting candidates had "consistently expressed a desire to develop a closer political relationship with the European Union." Mr. Andreatta said he felt that the Anglo-Italian initiative would be a "signal to nationalist forces of the Russian Federation because of the fact that the ex-COMECON countries are integrating" into the EU.[39]

The Andreatta-Hurd idea was discussed during the June 1994 Corfu European Summit, and the Commission was asked to elaborate a plan which it presented to the Council one month later. Aspects of foreign and security policy, including conflict-prevention matters, play a significant role in the plan: "The Union and the associated countries have a common interest in preventing conflict related to issues such as borders and frontiers, and should consult frequently on foreign and security policy issues of mutual concern."[40] The Commission presented two specific proposals: "Gradually joint meetings of the Union and the associated countries should replace the present troika format, as these provide a far greater opportunity for participation and a feeling of belonging"; and "Joint meetings should take place on the occasion of regular Council meetings and, where appropriate, through coordination meetings in the framework of relevant multilateral fora (the United Nations General Assembly, the CSCE Budapest review conference and summit, the stability pact and other fora)."[41]

On the basis of these recommendations the December 1994 Essen Summit agreed on a strategy for preparing central and east European countries for future accession to the EU. The core element of this strategy is a structured relationship between the governments of the associate countries and the institutions of the EU to enable the countries of central and eastern Europe to play a positive role in discussions on matters of common interest. The structured dialogue covers Community areas, especially those with a trans-European dimension (including energy, environment, transport, science, and technology), Common Foreign and Security Policy, as well as home and judicial affairs. The dialogue should be effective also at the level of the parliaments of the participating countries and the European Parliament. Making such cooperation a normal part of the life of governments and parliaments, so goes the reasoning in Brussels, familiarizes countries in the East with cooperative solutions to potential conflicts and will be an important preparation for accession.[42]

At its March 7, 1994, meeting, the General Affairs Council decided to open the possibility for the associate countries to align themselves with certain CFSP activities of the Union: statements, démarches, and joint actions. Practical guidelines on implementation were drawn up in consultation with the associated countries in October 1994. In its December 1994 strategy paper the Council summarized the motives and goals of this cooperative network:

> The structured relationship covering Common Foreign and Security Policy is especially important as a means for overcoming the widespread sense of inse-

curity in Central and Eastern Europe. It can reinforce efforts in the framework of the Western European Union, NATO and the partnership for peace, the Conference on Security and Cooperation in Europe and the stability pact, to increase security and stability throughout Europe. The Union and the associated countries have a common interest in preventing conflicts related to issues such as borders and frontiers, and should consult frequently on foreign and security policy issues of mutual concern."[43]

The Stability Pact for Europe

In the spring of 1993 the French prime minister, Edouard Balladur, presented a proposal for a process of stabilizing eastern Europe by diplomatic means, culminating in a Stability Pact for Europe. At the time, the initiative seemed as artificial as it was ambitious. The Pact was not to be an alliance against a common enemy but a commitment to peaceful conflict resolution within the group of participating countries. It would express the goal of the EU to reduce tension and potentially violent conflict in the region of the accession candidate countries; and by settling all potential conflicts of this type, it would pave the way for these countries to enter the Union. The slogan in Paris is "new members but no new conflicts."[44]

The goals and procedures of the plan were presented in a summary report annexed to the communiqué of the December 1993 European Council meeting in Brussels.[45] The official objective is to contribute to stability by preventing tension and potential conflicts in Europe. It is therefore not concerned with countries in open conflict. The prime intention is to promote good neighborly relations and to encourage countries to delimit their borders and to resolve the problems of national minorities that arise.

In principle, the project is geographically open-ended and evolutionary in character, but it has focused initially on the countries of central and eastern Europe that have the prospect of becoming members of the European Union: the six associate countries, the three Baltic countries, and Slovenia. Despite some hesitation by the other EU member states, particularly Germany and the United Kingdom, the Balladur Initiative was declared a Common Action under the rules of CFSP.[46] Three stages were projected: first a conference in Paris in May 1994 to set the agenda and terms for the enterprise; second, the organization of two Regional Round Tables, one for the Baltic region and one for the southeast European region, to discuss potential disputes among the member candidates and to initiate solutions; and third, a final conference in March 1995 to adopt the Stability Pact.[47]

The attitude of the participating east European countries has gradually shifted from flat rejection at the outset of the Balladur Initiative to full acceptance toward the end of its course. Skeptics saw the Initiative as an instrument of French domestic politics, designed to raise the prime minister's profile in external relations. Countries in the East and West were concerned about French motivations: was the Initiative a means to undercut the CSCE or to keep the United States away from the business of the "Europeans"? East European countries resented what they saw as the paternalistic attitude of the EU and its member states. And some were hesitant to negotiate sensitive bilateral disputes in a multilateral framework under the eyes of so many unaffected participants. Nevertheless, within a year, from May 1994 to March 1995, the atmosphere changed from cool reservation to eager interest.

More than fifty countries attended the inaugural conference in May 1994 in Paris, including those mainly concerned by the Initiative, their immediate neighbors, states able to make a particular contribution, countries with an interest in stability in Europe by virtue of their defense commitments, and countries having association agreements with the Union. Representatives of the CSCE, Council of Europe (COE), WEU, NATO, and the United Nations were also asked to attend.

The task of the inaugural conference was to set up the Round Tables to accompany the bilateral discussions. There was much confusion and uncertainty, but by dint of the determination of the EU and especially France to carry through,[48] the conference managed to set the process on track. The EU was to be the convenor of the Round Tables but left it to the east Europeans to decide whom they wanted to participate. The EU would actively oversee the process, encourage the parties to establish good-neighbor agreements among themselves, and undertake efforts to improve, de jure and de facto, the situation of national minorities. The EU was also to encourage regional cooperative arrangements and provide financial support.

The first of the Regional Round Tables was held for the Baltic region on September 21, 1994, and for the other countries of central and eastern Europe on September 22, 1994. Subsequent rounds were held in November and December 1994 and January 1995. The EU Troika made visits to the Baltic states in July 1994 and to Romania, Hungary, and Slovakia in November 1994. Last, in anticipation of forwarding the Pact to the CSCE, the EU Troika has also made contact with the CSCE Troika.

The "Baltic Round Table," consisting of Poland and the three Baltic states, seems to have made more progress than the "East Central European Round Table." As participants, they invited the OSCE (Troika and High Commissioner), the COE, the Baltic Council, and UN Development Program as well as Sweden, Finland, Iceland, Denmark, Norway, Germany, Russia, Canada, and the United States. Belarus began to take part as well, as of the fourth meeting. Russia and the United States participate as observers. From the beginning, the Baltic countries emphasized the practical side of the Pact and introduced proposals for projects targeting transborder cooperation and language training. In the second meeting, Poland proposed that its neighborhood treaties with the Baltic states and Germany should be included in the Pact. During the fourth meeting (January 19, 1995) the Round Table received information from Russia concerning minority and border questions in the region and a report on the treaty on border questions between Latvia and Belarus.

The four Visegrad countries plus Romania and Bulgaria organized the "East Central European Round Table," inviting Slovenia, Switzerland, Austria, and Ukraine to participate. As of the third meeting Turkey has taken part, and Moldova joined in the fourth meeting. By the fifth meeting the participating countries had reached agreement on which of the existing bilateral treaties they were prepared to include in the Pact. Hungary, Romania, and Slovakia hoped to conclude bilateral treaties before the beginning of the concluding conference in March 1995.[49] In each of these cases the EU has offered both political support and financial help. The EU-Troika visited Budapest, Bucharest, and Bratislava in October 1994 and February 1995 to review the progress of the ongoing negotiations. The Commission has established a checklist of projects to be sponsored by the EU to accompany the negotiation and implementation process.

At the final conference in Paris, on March 20, 1995, more than fifty states adopted the Pact on Stability in Europe as the result of the European Union's "common action."[50] Participants in the Paris conference have not signed a new treaty, but instead have endorsed a political declaration containing principles already enshrined in many previous agreements. Attached to this multilateral declaration is a list of bilateral agreements, arrangements, and political declarations consisting of some fifty documents concluded between east European states and individual member states of the EU, as well as some thirty-five documents concluded between east European states. Only a dozen of these documents were achieved during the 1994–95 negotiations of the Pact; the others had been signed between 1990 and 1993. In the EU's view, the compilation of all the bilateral documents and the parallel effort to codify solutions for remaining bilateral disputes was a worthwhile collective enterprise of preventive diplomacy and will contribute to stability in Europe by the establishment of good neighborly relations based, in some cases, on bilateral agreements between the countries principally concerned, in particular relating to the consolidation of borders and the problems of national minorities. According to the EU, the diversity of cultures, languages, religions, traditions, and origins must become the source of enrichment and a unifying factor, and cease to be a cause of tension and rivalries. These are fine intentions, but it remains to be seen how they will be implemented in practice.

To turn intentions and agreements into substance, the countries principally concerned need further encouragement as well as practical and financial support. The OSCE and the EU will have to play a major role in this regard. After its approval by all participants in the Paris conference, the Pact has been officially forwarded to the OSCE, which will act as its guardian and promoter in the future. Funding for cooperative projects would have to come out of the present budgetary and regulatory framework of PHARE, but a number of countries have insisted on the need to provide additional funds for the Pact. To that end, Prime Minister Balladur proposed the creation of a Fund for Good Neighborhood and Stability.[51]

As with the "structured relationship" described above, it is hard to predict the future value of the Pact. At a minimum, all sides have learned some lessons and have become more familiar with the objectives, possibilities, and limits of the enterprise. Brussels knows it has to avoid any hint of imposition or direct conditioning. The east European countries have become more relaxed and less suspicious. They have become accustomed to discussing bilateral matters before a multilateral audience. They know they can profit from the experience of others in comparable situations by raising disputes and difficulties early on. Although the financial means committed to Pact projects are very limited, they seem to have strengthened the credibility of the Initiative. Countries have used the procedures of the Pact as a platform to demonstrate their maturity in terms of handling border and minority problems, and thus that they are eligible for membership in the EU, the WEU, and NATO.

Case Studies in EU Conflict Prevention

During its relatively short experience of conflict prevention in countries of east central Europe and the CIS, the EU has had to address different types of challenges. To give a more concrete sense of this activity, I present two examples in some detail. One, the Gabcikovo-Nagymaros case, dealt with a dispute where violence had not yet erupted. The other, the EU administration of Mostar, is a case in which a settlement had been reached but remained shaky and in need of consolidation. A third important case, the European Community Monitoring Mission (ECMM) in the former Yugoslavia, which was an effort to prevent violence already under way from escalating or spilling over into neighboring areas, is discussed in chapter 5.[52]

Gabcikovo-Nagymaros: Taming a Dispute to Avoid Violence

The dispute between Hungary and Czechoslovakia over the Gabcikovo-Nagymaros dam on the Danube brings together some of the most troublesome issues in central Europe.[53] Originally agreed upon in 1977, the dam is a legacy of grandiose communist planning for a hydroelectric power station that took no account of environmental impact or popular feeling. It has aroused nationalist passions on both sides, exacerbated by its impact on the Hungarian minority of 600,000 in Slovakia.

Hungary stopped work on its side of the Danube as the Communists lost power in 1989. Indeed, the political opposition gained power with the help of the environmentalist protest. Czechoslovakia continued despite some environmental concern there, too. In the fall of 1992 Slovakia, shortly before becoming an independent state, said it regarded completion of the dam as a vital interest, while the fragile government of Hungary, beset by nationalist activists, saw it as a potentially mortal threat because of the major damage it would cause to the Hungarian landscape, water supply, and the utility of the Danube River as an important waterway. For the separatist Slovak government of Vladimir Meciar, the dam was a symbol of national identity and of the strength of the new state. Hungarian opposition to the project was interpreted as a strategy to undermine and weaken the new Slovakia. Budapest's political support of the Hungarian population in Slovakia, which was against the dam as well as antiseparatist, added to the suspicion in Bratislava. The quarrel was brought to a head when Slovakia unilaterally started to divert water from the Danube on October 24, 1992.

The Hungarian prime minister, Jozef Antall, asked for help from the Danube Commission, comprising all riparian countries on the Danube River, but received little response. Letters to world leaders in an attempt to internationalize the dispute and bring it to the International Court of Justice and appeals to the CSCE emergency procedure and the UN Security Council were also unavailing. The Slovaks defended their view that the imminent diversion of the Danube was justified by flood prevention and improvement of navigation.

The European Community had no formal standing in the matter since neither party to the dispute was a member of the EC. Its interest is obvious, however, since the dam is a large project in the heart of Europe involving natural resources, environmental protection, future energy supplies, an important navigable waterway, and political relations between two potential future members of the EU. Brussels therefore took on a mediation role not because it was asked to do so by the parties in conflict, but to serve its own interests. The occasion for diplomatic intervention was there each time the Community had to talk to or negotiate with the countries involved. While having a dialogue with the Visegrad countries on political, economic, and security matters, how could Brussels ignore the conflict between two of the dialogue partners?

In fact, it was at the margins of an EC–Visegrad Three meeting in London on October 28, 1992, immediately after diversion of the river had started, that the EC representative managed to defuse the conflict in a relatively unspectacular way.[54] The parties signed an agreement in principle stating that the construction of the dam would be stopped and the situation returned substantially to the status quo ante while a group of experts examined the environmental, shipping, and hydrological aspects of the problem and the case was submitted to the International Court of Justice for a final ruling. The details of the submission to the Court were agreed upon at a meeting with the prime ministers of Slovakia and Hungary, Meciar and Antall, in Brussels on March 4, 1993. At the end, EC Commissioner Van den Broek, who was in the chair, could claim that an emotional and potentially violent conflict had been at least temporarily defused. Today, while Slovakia and Hungary have concluded further agreements, the ruling of the Court is still pending,[55] and the question of the Hungarian minorities in Slovakia continues to be a matter of concern in the EU.[56]

Mostar: Stabilizing Peace on a Local Level

The idea of an EU administrator for the city of Mostar was first proposed on August 20, 1993, by Lord Owen and the former Norwegian foreign minister, Thorwald Stoltenberg, the EU, and UN mediators in the Bosnian conflict. Mostar, situated in the very south of Bosnia in an area dominated by Croats, has been a symbol of peaceful multireligious and multiethnic cohabitation for centuries, home to Catholic Croats, Muslim Bosnians, and Orthodox Serbs. During the recent fighting the city was first defended by Muslims and Croats against the Serbs before, in a second round, Croats and Muslims fought each other. The two wars have damaged the famous ancient town and destroyed normal life in the municipality, leaving all ethnic groups in disarray. Owen and Stoltenberg tried to find a solution that would not only avoid ethnic cleansing but enable the survival of the people of Mostar and set an example of multicultural coexistence. Their proposal was accepted by EU foreign ministers at their informal meeting in Alden Biesen on September 12, 1993, and Hans Koschnick, a German Social Democrat, a deputy of the Bundestag and former governing major of Bremen, was chosen for the job.

In March 1994 the governments of Bosnia and Croatia as well as the Bosnian Croats agreed to the establishment of a "Federation Bosnia-Herzegovina" and asked the EU to take over the administration of the largely destroyed city of Mostar situated within this Federation. The EU agreed to do this as part of the deal that ended the fighting between Bosnia's Croats and Muslims. In April 1994 a group of experts from the European Commission and from EU member countries began preparing to run the administration, and technical personnel started to clear the city of rubble. Croat and Muslim delegations from Mostar negotiated and signed the final agreement at the EU headquarters in Brussels on June 8–9, 1994.

Koschnick took office on July 23. The war-torn town, which had a prewar population of 126,000, is now mainly inhabited by Muslims and Croats. Koschnick's mandate is to reinstate the viability of the city, to repair the local infrastructure, to organize a unified police force of Croats and Muslims, and to build up the city administration. The project is an attempt to reconcile ethnic groups that only recently were locked in a fierce war against each other. The goal is also to bring back the Serbs that used to live in Mostar but had to flee during the Croat-Muslim battles. If the attempt is successful, Mostar may well be regarded as a model for a new beginning and as proof that the new federation can be viable and that peaceful cohabitation of various ethnic groups in Bosnia is still conceivable for the future.

Mostar is run as a CFSP Common Action combined with EU-WEU cooperation. The EU supported the project with 32 million ecu ($40 million) during 1994. A budget of 80 million ecu ($100 million) has been assigned for 1995. The costs of the forty-five experts who belong to various European nationalities are assumed by their home countries. The WEU has promised to send two hundred policemen from various member countries to help train the police force. There is to be a unified municipal administration consisting of seven departments each of which is codirected by an EU expert and a local administrator. They work with a local body consisting of five Croats, five Muslims, three Serbs, and two representatives from other groups. After two years the EU administration will be handed over to a freely elected municipal parliament.

Five months after he took over, Koschnick was still optimistic about achieving this goal but admitted that his team had run into major difficulties: EU nations have been slow in sending the proposed personnel, and some Croat leaders have been blocking reconciliation.[57] The WEU nations have provided only half the promised number of police: Germany 70, France 20, The Netherlands 12, Spain 10. Nevertheless, they form a buffer between the eastern (Muslim) and the western (Croat) sides of the Neretva River of Mostar. With two thousand local "policemen" (really militiamen) in each of the two parts of the town, their task seems quite delicate.

The Mostar operation is an example of an attempt from outside the conflict area to stabilize peace by preventing a resumption of the fighting. Success is likely to be dependent less on the local predisposition for peace than on developments in the wider theater of war.[58] The possibilities that the United States may unilaterally lift the arms embargo on Bosnia[59] or that UN troops may be withdrawn from Croatia are reminders that, despite local efforts for peace stabilization, recurrence of violence may always be triggered by the still unsettled wider conflict. To make Mostar a success will require the concurrence of many factors; this demonstrates the boldness as well as the desperation of the enterprise.

Though conflict-prevention activities of the EU on the ground have been limited, the Gabcikovo and Mostar operations must be regarded as successes, based on their contributions to the mitigation of conflict and to the development of a common foreign and security policy of the EU. Brussels participated for the first time actively and substantially in conflict management. The two cases, along with the EC Monitoring Mission in Yugoslavia, are representative of what the EU likes to promote: preventive action supported by all EU and WEU instruments. But they also reflect the still limited scope of CFSP's operation in conflict prevention. Other cases in recent years may have been more ambitious but also less successful. The former Yugoslavia is the most important example, where the premature recognition of Slovenia and Croatia had such far-reaching and generally negative effects, and continuing efforts at mediation have produced no results. Equally telling may be Macedonia and Albania, where Greece has vetoed constructive and preventive CFSP actions.

All these events demonstrate that the EU and CFSP lack influence and credibility because of self-imposed restrictions such as the consensus rule and the compartmentalization of its foreign policy process. The Fifteen need a very specific constellation to do business and to be able to disregard all these impediments. EU member states are not yet prepared to take on, in practical terms, the wider responsibility pronounced in their official documents. There may be more common *positions* on conflicts like Chechnya or Algeria, but hardly common *action*. The new European institutions and rhetoric are only a first step in the necessary process of adaptation to the post–cold war security challenge, but the mind-sets of the people within the fifteen nation-states have not changed. It will take more experience to develop a more enlightened outlook. In the meantime, the EU will have to use its influence as much as possible in the areas where it is relatively strong, such as the expansion of democracy, regional integration, and structural dialogue described earlier in this chapter.

The EU's Role in the Web of Organizations Engaged in Conflict Prevention

While it is important for the EU to develop mechanisms for bilateral interaction with potential conflicting parties, it is equally important for the EU to be able to interact effectively with the other international organizations and actors engaged in conflict prevention. International organizations consist of member states. The question to be asked is who educates and activates whom? Does the international organization educate the states, or do the states educate the international organization? Who within them has the motivation to act? No doubt the organization proper will be interested in being proactive in order to build up its influence and, as a by-product, help prevent conflict. What drives the EU into action? The communitarian institutions push the member states. But the member states may be de-motivated because they resist integration and therefore refuse to engage in multilateral action for conflict prevention. Or they may hide behind blaming the "inefficient" EU and do nothing at the member state level while referring instead to the duties of the EU or the obstruction from other members. Member states may push the EU to do something, only to have the EU refuse because such things are not in line with how it sees its role.

As the EU and its member states interact, the internal policy processes within member states are definitely an important element to understand, in order to be able to change the conflict-prevention capacity of the EU. As an example, France and the United Kingdom did not want to go too far in emphasizing ethnic self-determination because of their domestic problems in this regard; Paris and London also wanted to avoid giving Germany enhanced influence by taking roles in mediating disputes or building coalitions.

The Fifteen are members in all of the important multilateral institutions that have a bearing on conflict prevention. Within these organizations, the EU is the central decisionmaking and operational organization for its members. It is, at least theoretically, well suited to the orchestration of multi-actor conflict prevention. When the European Commission presented its strategy on preparing the accession candidates, it explicitly inserted its proposals into the broader structural relationship in an effort to overcome the widespread sense of insecurity in east central Europe: "It can reinforce efforts in the framework of the Western European Union, NATO and the Partnership for Peace, the Conference on Security and Cooperation in Europe and the stability pact, to increase security and stability throughout Europe."[60]

Most of the political-diplomatic aspects of conflict prevention are dealt with in CFSP, while economic aspects are part of the Community's external relations, and military aspects are treated outside the EU, either in the WEU or NATO. As conflict-prevention measures combine political, economic, and military components, CFSP tries to draw on other institutions or coordinate their work. For this purpose, CFSP can use the powers and provisions of Maastricht, mainly article J, where reference is made to all of these multilateral organizations.

EU Interaction with the UN and the OSCE

The UN is a reference for EU action, but also a forum to launch preventive initiatives. The Security Council has the primary responsibility for the maintenance of international peace and security, including preventive diplomacy, peacekeeping, peace enforcement, and peace-making.[61] The EU as such is not represented in the Security Council, but the permanent members, France and the United Kingdom, are asked to act in the sense of the Union's interests as stated in article J.5 of the Maastricht Treaty.[62] Initiatives of the EU may be launched via these two members, and in any case the EU is better off for having two of its members on the Security Council.[63]

For the implementation of its resolutions, such as sanctions against Serbia, the Security Council relies on the assistance of regional arrangements (like the OSCE) or organizations (like the EU). So Brussels will receive a mandate from New York to conduct an operation, or it will support the secretary-general in preventive action, election monitoring, or an observer mission. During the mediation efforts in the area of the former Yugoslavia, the EU originally built its action on a European mediator, Lord Carrington, but soon found out that it needed the UN framework to mount more comprehensive pressure. Mediation became a bicephalous UN-EU enterprise, and is now in the hands of the Contact Group within which the EU is only one of six members including London and Paris in their national capacity. The EU has moved a good deal away from Foreign Minister Le Poos's initial remark that Yugoslavia was the Community's responsibility.

Within the OSCE the EU has played major roles in developing both the institutional aspects of the organization and its code of conduct, as well as participating in conflict-prevention measures. With the active support of the EU, the OSCE has developed its primary function in preventive diplomacy, especially through the work of its High Commissioner on National Minorities and via its missions in crisis areas. Personnel of EU institutions as well as experts from EU member states have participated in these activities, including fact-finding missions on compliance with human rights standards.

The EU had to call on the OSCE as well as the UN to join in the task of monitoring in Yugoslavia and to try to find a settlement for the conflict. On the other hand it is also true that "the recognition of the EC's crisis management role in Yugoslavia was a clear indication that the Community was the principal actor in the CSCE process."[64]

Part of the relatively high relevance of the EU in both the OSCE and the UN may be explained by the sheer number of fifteen countries holding largely identical positions and exerting a rather extended co-optive power. Moreover, the EU as an organization offers a uniquely broad field of competence. If requested to participate in preventive measures by either the UN or the OSCE, it could contribute economic, political, or humanitarian actions and ask the WEU to join with military and police support. The real secret of the EU's influence (some regard it as its major deficiency) is that most of the EU member states are contributing in both incarnations, as part of the union of Fifteen and as individual states. It is hard to determine which line of operation is more influential.[65]

EU Relations with the WEU and NATO

The WEU, which was reoriented to new tasks including peacekeeping operations at Petersburg in 1992, may be requested by the EU to elaborate and implement decisions taken in CFSP. The understanding is that the military implications of all questions are part of the WEU's responsibilities. This has been the case in Yugoslavia in relation to embargo enforcement in the Adriatic and on the Danube, and also applies to Mostar. NATO has even intervened to enforce UN-protected zones in Bosnia. So the EU and the WEU-NATO have started to experience conflict management.

Both organizations join the EU also in developing the dialogue with countries from eastern and central Europe and the CIS, including the goal of creating networks of communication and cooperation between West and East in Europe. So far, however, as the De Gucht Report[66] on relations between the EU, the WEU, and NATO reveals, the division of labor among the three institutions reflects the individual struggle of each of these institutions for relevance rather than an orchestrated structure.[67]

The EU and the Council of Europe

Relations between the EU and the COE have expanded since the end of the cold war. Both organizations were confronted with a new scope of tasks in an enlarged Europe and had to adapt to these new challenges individually. At the same time they discovered a further need to coordinate their respective tasks of effecting systemic change in the former socialist countries. From different ends, both organizations worked in the same places with the same objectives. Ethno-national conflict prevention became part of their division of labor.

The EU shares with the COE the role of stabilizing democratic values and structures in countries of eastern and central Europe and the CIS. Although all EU member states are also members of the COE and the EU as such has an observer position, it seems that coordination between the two organizations could be improved. In comparison to the EU, the COE is more of a normative body than a foreign policy actor. The COE can refer to its thirty-three members and its experts in the field, while the EU can mobilize a wider range of instruments and engage in power politics. Beyond an intensified exchange of information and experience, the EU and the COE may want to coordinate some of their programs on the ground.[68]

As of now, the information flow among all of these organizations is relatively poor and needs to be improved. Which organization is engaged in which action? Which is best suited to take on an operation? How to mutually reinforce separate operations? The EU, being the spider in the web of international organizations, is predestined to coordinate closer cooperation among them.

Conclusion

There is no question that internal violence and ethno-national conflict present an increasing threat to stability in east central Europe and the CIS region. However, in analyzing the role of the EU in this endeavor, it is also important to keep in mind why these conflicts are an issue of international concern—for those of us not living in these regions and not directly affected. The questions of why the EU and other international organizations are motivated to intervene in these disputes in the first place and whether this kind of intervention is legitimate need to be constantly reassessed with each new initiative. Ethno-national conflicts in Europe come in all varieties and degrees of intensity, and correspondingly the proposals for solutions to them must differ widely. Not all of the many measures taken have had a stabilizing effect, and at times the very act of identifying an ethnic conflict as such may solidify the ethnic actors and marginalize other political voices.

Many of the states of east central Europe and the former Soviet Union are clearly under assault from voices within calling for national self-determination, an ideal that neither the EU nor its democratic member states can afford to disregard completely. However, at this stage it is hard to find a consensus on collective rights for ethnic minorities, especially if this includes the right of secession. Political leaders in both eastern and western Europe fear that putting too much emphasis on minority rights could revive dangerous and familiar strains of nationalism, and the questioning of state borders could unleash centrifugal forces on the European continent and undermine the integrationist process. Member states willing to yield authority incrementally to the EU have no interest in losing power to separatists at home. Part of the reason why France and the United Kingdom were reluctant to recognize the former Yugoslav republics was their concern that outright secession elsewhere would encourage separatist movements at home to claim similar rights. Such cautious calculations on the part of EU members have played a very large role in the EU strategies devised for dealing with ethnic conflicts in the East, strategies driven by the belief in the greater benefits of the preservation of stability of states and borders in a Europe moving toward greater integration.

This policy has borne some fruit thus far. Some of the conflicts addressed in this chapter have been mitigated or temporarily transformed. However, even these will need continuous observation and care. The potential for reescalation will remain as long as the basic claims of dissatisfied ethnic minorities are not met or mediated. For instance, this is the case with the Hungarian minority in Slovakia while the ruling of the International Court of Justice on the dam is still pending. The EU could do much to redress the situation in some of these cases and needs to adopt a differentiated approach that is sensitive to the particular needs in each case. In Estonia the need is to teach Estonian to the Russian-speaking population to help depoliticize the citizenship issue. In Slovakia there is a need for the state to allow broadcasting opportunities, schools, and newspapers to allow for the cultural expression of the Hungarian minority. In the case of the German minority in Hungary and Romania, the current financial support from Germany needs to be replaced by more "neutral" and less suspicious assistance from EU sources. All these measures and many more will have to be considered—and some of them already have been considered in the context of the Stability Pact—in order to shift the bulk of conflict-prevention measures from the abstract declamatory level to the more realistic practical level.

The EU's basic conflict-prevention asset is the example its members provide and the prospect of joining them in the common enterprise. In order to exploit this asset the EU must maintain a credible opportunity for new membership in the long run, while engaging in specifically targeted prevention and stabilization measures in the short run.

Notes

1. "Brussels" stands here and throughout this chapter for a number of incarnations of the EU. The Union may either act through the Presidency (position held by each member state for six months on a rotating scheme), a representative of the (supranational) European Commission, the Troika (which consists of the current presidency, the preceding and succeeding presidency, and a representative of the European Commission), a special envoy (like Lord Owen), or a group of principal countries (like France, Germany, and the United Kingdom in the so-called Contact Group together with the United States and Russia).

2. Some research has been done on the performance of European Political Cooperation in international crises; see Christopher Hill, "EPC's Performance in Crises," in R. Rummel, ed., *Toward Political Union: Planning a Common Foreign*

and Security Policy in the European Community (Baden-Baden: Nomos Verlagsgesellschaft, 1992), pp.130–50.

3. What does experience with the attempt of resolution of earlier conflicts tell us about the promise, prospects, and limitations of conflict prevention as a post–cold war strategy to promote peace? See David Wendt, "The Peacemakers: Lessons of Conflict Resolution for the Post-Cold War World," *Washington Quarterly,* vol. 17, no. 3 (1994), pp. 163–78.

4. For an account of the interaction between the change in East-West relations and the west European integration process, see Mathias Jopp, *The Strategic Implications of European Integration* (London: The International Institute for Strategic Studies, 1994).

5. Apart from this line of reasoning, other motivations have been put forth to justify early intervention in potential conflict. The soundness of reasoning for preventive action and its power of conviction decisive prerequisites for winning political acceptance and support at home as well as with the conflict parties. Conflict prevention is open to suspicious perceptions (outside powers may need a pretext to interfere). It has a strong taste of self-fulfilling prophecy. To declare and treat a conflict as potentially violent raises the stakes. The parties may immediately try to beef up their bargaining position and prepare for a fight. Such behavior may cause the opposing party to follow suit and thus trigger an escalation: a dormant conflict may erupt because of the good intentions of conflict prevention! Another twist of the same question is the view from the side of the conflicting parties: are their interests taken into account, and to what degree? Or do outsiders mainly impose their interests and their definition of security on the conflicting parties? All this determines the success of a conflict-prevention effort as well as the scope of an outsider's commitment to conflict-prevention policies.

6. The following two lists of present and conceivable future functions of the Community are taken from Christopher Hill, "The Capability-Expectations Gap, or Conceptualizing Europe's International Role," *Journal of Common Market Studies,* vol. 31 (September 1993), pp. 310–14.

7. See the "Report on the Likely Development of the Common Foreign and Security Policy with a View to Identify Areas Open to Joint Action, European Council, Lisbon 1992," in *Agence Europe,* Document 5761 (June 29–30, 1992), Brussels.

8. For further discussion of these and other lessons to be learned from the west European integration process, see John Pinder's contribution to this volume.

9. There is obviously a correlation between advanced democracies and peace, but the causal link is far from established. For all we know, a combination with some other factor (ethnic homogeneity, economic development, and so on) leads a society to be both democratic and peaceful. The EU does not debate these correlations. It acts on the assumption that the positive relationship between democracy and peace exists in principle and that it will be successful in the East in particular.

10. Jack S. Levy, "Domestic Politics and War," in Robert I. Rotberg and Theodore K. Rabb, eds., *The Origin and Prevention of Major Wars* (Cambridge, Mass.: Cambridge University Press, 1989), p. 88. The subject has been studied extensively with more or less the same result, that democracies do not tend to go to war with each other. See Michael Doyle, "Liberalism and World Politics," *American Political Science Review,* vol. 30, no. 4 (December 1986), pp. 1151–70. Zeev Maoz and Bruce Russett, "Alliance, Contiguity, Wealth, and Political Stability: Is

the Lack of Conflict among Democracies a Statistical Artifact?" *International Interactions,* vol. 17, no. 3 (1992), pp. 245–67. Stuart A. Bremer, "Democracy and Militarized Interstate Conflict, 1816–1965," *International Interactions,* vol. 18, no. 3 (1993), pp. 231–49.

11. See William J. Dixon, "Democracy and the Management of International Conflict," *Journal of Conflict Resolution,* vol. 37, no. 1 (1993), pp. 42–68. EU representatives are less outspoken than representatives from the United States on the strategic values of democracy. It would be hard to find a European statement like the following from Secretary of State Warren Christopher: "Europe's long-term security—like America's—requires that we actively foster the spread of democracy and market economies. Democracies tend not to make war on each other. They are more likely to protect human rights and ensure equal rights for minorities. They are more likely to be reliable partners in diplomacy, trade, arms accords, and environmental protection." Extracts from Christopher's speech to NATO on February 26, 1993, Europe Documents, no. 1828, March 3, 1993, p. 3.

12. Many blueprints have been produced in the West to bring about political transition in the East, for example, Samuel P. Huntington, *The Third Wave: Democratization in the Late Twentieth Century* (University of Oklahoma Press, 1991), and Larry Diamond, "Promoting Democracy," *Foreign Policy,* vol. 87 (1992), pp. 25–46.

13. For more details on these programs, see John Pinder's chapter in this volume. See also the record of the EU's policy on this subject, in European Commission, Annual Report, 1991–1994, Brussels.

14. Berthold Kohler, "Der Fingerzeig aus Bruessel," *Frankfurter Allgemeine Zeitung,* December 5, 1994, p. 6. According to Kohler, one of Brussels's major criticisms was that Mr. Meciar and his governing coalition had tried with rather unfair means to exclude former prime minister Moravcik's party, the Democratic Union, from the Slovak parliament. Kohler reports that Slota had reacted to the EU démarche by saying: "If we had to comment on resolutions of the French or the German Parliament, we would have to write diplomatic notes every month."

15. The process of admitting the Russian Federation as a member to the COE was halted early in 1995 because of Moscow's military intervention in Chechnya. The case was complicated in the sense that a majority of the Duma was either indifferent or against President Yeltsin's unpeaceful attempt at solving the conflict.

16. *Treaty of the European Union,* Article F.2.

17. The EU has concluded Europe Agreements with six east central European countries (Poland, the Czech Republic, Slovakia, Hungary, Bulgaria, and Romania) and is negotiating such agreements with the three Baltic countries and most likely also with Slovenia. A Partnership and Cooperation Agreement has existed with Ukraine since 1994, and another one is being negotiated with Russia.

18. European Council of Copenhagen, June 21–22, 1993, Conclusions of the Presidency, in *Agence Europe,* Document 1844–45 (June 24, 1993).

19. See Berthold Kohler, "Flotte Sprüche über EU und NATO," *Frankfurter Allgemeine Zeitung,* January 18, 1995, p. 10.

20. See the chapters by John Pinder and others in this volume. A record of the EU's major links with and activities toward east central Europe and the CIS is compiled in Barbara-Christine Ryba, "L'Union européenne et l'europe de l'est: L'évolution des relations de la Communauté—devenue Union européenne—avec

l'europe de l'est et les perspectives d'avenir," *Revue du Marché commun et de l'Union européenne,* no. 382 (November 1994), pp. 564–82.

21. This instrument of Common Action is discussed below. There is no good report on the Russian case, but for one on the South Africa mission of election monitoring, see Martin Holland, "The European Union's Common Foreign and Security Policy: The Joint Action on South Africa," *Basler Schriften zur europäischen Integration,* no. 3 (March 1994).

22. See European Commission, "Bringing Democratic Principles Closer to Home," *Info-PHARE,* no. 5 (December 1994), Brussels, p. 13. The Directorate General for External Economic Relations runs a PHARE Information Office which produces the brochure.

23. Instruments such as financial support for democratization, démarches in favor of democracy, and sanctions for noncompliance are all fine, but they need to be part of a more aggressive concept. Such a policy has been advocated for the CSCE in, Charles A. Kupchan and Clifford A. Kupchan, "A Concert for Europe," in Graham Allison and Gregory F. Treverton, eds., *Rethinking America's Security: Beyond Cold War to New World Order* (W.W. Norton, 1992), pp. 249–66.

24. When in July 1994 a new attempt was made by London and Dublin to reconcile the conflicting parties of Northern Ireland, the head of the Sinn Fein party, Gerry Adams, did not renounce violence. This aborted the attempt. Violent conflict continued, London and Dublin having few instruments at their disposal to halt the underground fighting. See "Sinn Féin Rejects UK Proposal over Ulster," *Financial Times,* July 25, 1994, p. 16. Then, only five days later, the IRA declared it would end the armed struggle starting September 1, 1994. Sinn Fein was included in serious discussions over Northern Ireland at Stormont Castle, in Belfast, on December 9, 1994. In effect, Sinn Fein "bombed" itself to the negotiation table. "It has once again been shown that violence pays; thus there is serious reason to fear that it will return. Northern Ireland would not have reached the point it is at today had the IRA not pushed aside the peaceful civil rights protests of the Northern Catholic minority, which began in 1968, and begun its terrorist campaign against Britain and the authorities in Northern Ireland. The IRA would not have agreed to end its violence had the Loyalist terrorists not repaid the IRA in kind for its killings. . . . The IRA has wanted power—power over the six northern counties of Ireland, to force them into union with the Republic of Ireland, against the will of those counties' Protestant majority population" (William Pfaff, "Northern Ireland: For a Political Settlement, Consider Condominium," *International Herald Tribune,* November 17, 1994, p. 4).

25. In the literature most authors attribute a positive connotation to federalist integration. To mention just one representative of this view: Heinz Gärtner, "Regionale Regime im Süden, Konfliktbearbeitung, Streitschlichtung, Kooperation und Integration," in Catherine Schiemann Rittri and Reiner Steinweg, eds., *Krieg und gewaltfreie Konfliktlösung,* (Chur, Switzerland: Verlag Ruegger, 1993), pp. 119–38. For an opposite view see the chapter by Max Frenkel in Kurt Mueller, ed., *Minderheiten im Konflikt. Fakten, Erfahrungen, Loesungsansätze* (Zurich: Verlag Neue Zuercher Zeitung, 1993), pp. 178–93.

26. For more details on these criteria see John Pinder's chapter in this volume.

27. In November 1994 Polish foreign minister Olechowski said that participation of Poland in the second and third pillars of the Maastricht Treaty could be envisaged before its entry in the Community pillar centered on economic

issues. Olechowski also thought that representatives from central European countries would have a say in the 1996 revision of the Maastricht Treaty. *Agence Europe,* no. 6359 (November 18, 1994), p. 3.

28. Alfred A. Reisch, "The Central European Initiative: To Be or Not to Be?" *RFE/RL Research Report,* vol. 2, (August 27, 1993), pp. 30–37.

29. David Shumaker, "The Origins and Development of Central European Cooperation: 1989–1992," *East European Quarterly,* vol. 27, (September 1993), pp. 351–73.

30. Jenonne Walker, "European Regional Organizations and Ethnic Conflict," in Regina Cowen Karp, ed., *Central and Eastern Europe,* Stockholm International Peace Research Institute (Oxford University Press, 1993), pp. 45–66.

31. Oemer Faruk Genckaya, "The Black Sea Economic Co-operation Project: A Regional Challenge to European Integration," *International Social Science Journal,* vol. 45 (November 1993), pp. 549–57.

32. Malcolm Chalmers, "Developing a Security Regime for Eastern Europe," *Journal of Peace Research,* vol. 30, no. 4 (November 1993), pp. 427–44. Caroline Kennedy-Pipe, "The CIS: Sources of Stability and Instability," in Karp, ed., *Central and Eastern Europe,* pp. 258–82. Boris Meissner, "Die GUS zwischen Integrationsplänen und Krisenerscheinungen," *Osteuropa,* vol. 44 (September 1994), pp. 833–54.

33. Christoph Royen, "Kein Nachruf auf die 'Visegrad'-Staatengruppe," *Europa Archiv,* vol. 49 (November 25, 1994), pp. 635–42.

34. How much and what type of democratic participation is needed to make a political system effective, and where is the line beyond which the system becomes ineffective? This question has accompanied the EU since its inception forty years ago. Robert A. Dahl, "A Democratic Dilemma: System Effectiveness versus Citizen Participation," *Political Science Quarterly,* vol. 109, no. 1 (1994), pp. 23–34.

35. Beginning in January 1994 the EU and the members of the European Free Trade Area (EFTA) formed the European Economic Area (EEA), an organization of close economic cooperation. Only one year later, three of the former EFTA countries (Austria, Finland, and Sweden) had become members of the EU, which reduced the number of the former EFTA countries in the EEA to three: Norway, Iceland, and Liechtenstein.

36. European Council at Corfu, June 24–25, 1994, Presidency Conclusions, *Agence Europe,* special edition, no. 6260 (June 26, 1994), p. 12. Other general guidelines comprise: "sustained support for the consolidation of democratic institutions, for respect for human rights and for the achievement of market oriented economic reforms; the promotion of good neighborly relations between Ukraine and its neighbors; support for the full implementation of nuclear and conventional disarmament agreements; acceptance by Ukraine of internationally accepted nuclear safety standards within an overall energy policy."

37. *Agence Europe,* (December 22, 1993), p. 6. Justice and Home Affairs do include a number of cooperative measures, such as the fight against international crime, which have implications for the subject of conflict prevention but have not been dealt with in the context of this research.

38. For more details, see David Huntington's chapter in this volume.

39. All quotations in this paragraph are taken from *Agence Europe* (December 22, 1993), p. 6.

40. European Commission, "The Europe Agreements and Beyond: A Strategy to Prepare the Countries of Central and Eastern Europe for Accession," *Agence Europe,* Documents, no. 1893 (July 21, 1994), p. 4. The twelve national European correspondents are the knots within the CFSP network of communication where virtually all information on foreign and security policy is concentrated and dispatched. It is also used as an on-line discussion pool.

41. European Commission, "The Europe Agreements and Beyond," p. 4.

42. For a full account of the strategy, see Report from the Council to the Essen European Council on a strategy to prepare for the accession of the associated Central and Eastern European Countries (CCEE), *Europe Documents,* no. 1916, (December 14, 1994). Beginning in 1995, there is agreement among the Fifteen to hold the following meetings:

—Heads of State and Government: annual meetings on the margins of a European Council meeting.

—Foreign Ministers: semi-annual meetings for discussion of the full scope of relations with the associate countries, in particular the status and progress of the integration process.

—Ministers responsible for internal market development, in particular Finance, Economics, and Agricultural Ministers: annual meetings.

—Transport, Research, Telecommunication, and Environment Ministers: annual meetings.

—Justice and Home Affairs: annual meetings.

—Cultural Affairs, Education: annual meetings.

In general, the meetings should take place in connection with the corresponding Council meetings. Preparations for all these meetings will be made at respective meetings at the working level.

43. *Europe Documents,* no. 1916, December 14, 1994, p. 5.

44. Jean François-Poncet, "Diplomatie préventive," *Le Figaro,* May 26, 1994, p. 1.

45. The Communiqué and the Annex I (Stability Pact: Summary Report) are reprinted in *Agence Europe,* no. 6127 (December 12, 1993), pp. 1–12.

46. This came about at the end of 1993 after President Mitterrand and Chancellor Kohl had sent respective letters on October 29, 1993, to the then holder of the EU Presidency, the Belgian prime minister Dehaene.

47. For a more extensive description of the idea of the Balladur Initiative, see Victor-Yves Ghebali, "Vers un pacte de stabilité en Europe," in *Défense nationale,* vol. 50 (October 1994), pp. 66–77.

48. See *Atlantic News,* no. 2626, May 27, 1994, p. 2, and no. 2627, May 31, 1994, p. 2.

49. The Hungary-Slovakia agreement was concluded in the last days before the final conference of the Pact. It grants "autonomy" to the Hungarian minority in Slovakia. The respective treaty between Hungary and Romania is still pending.

50. The Pact on Stability in Europe, in *Agence Europe,* Documents, no. 1927 (March 29, 1995), pp. 1–9.

51. See "Balladur präzisiert Vorstellung über Stabilitätspakt in Europa," *Frankfurter Allgemeine Zeitung,* November 22, 1994, p. 5.

52. The best published record of the ECMM is a report by a German diplomat who participated in this ongoing enterprise for a long period; see Johannes Preisinger, *Die EG-Beobachtermission im ehemaligen Jugoslawien. Bilanz und Zukunfts-*

perspektiven (Frankfurt/M.: Hessische Stiftung Friedens- und Konfliktforschung, 1994).

53. The following information is taken mainly from a newspaper report, "A Dam Too Far," *Independent,* October 30, 1992, p. 18.

54. Karoly Okolicsanyi, "Slovak-Hungarian Tension: Bratislava Diverts the Danube," *RFE/RL Research Reports,* vol. 49 (December 11, 1992), pp. 49–54.

55. Alfred A. Reich, "Hungarian-Slovak Relations: A Difficult First Year," *RFE/RL Research Report,* vol. 50 (December 17, 1993), pp. 16–23.

56. To mention one of the most recent events in this regard: the European Commission took steps with the president of the parliament of Slovakia and the (new) Prime Minister Meciar expressing "doubts and fears" about the parliaments deliberations on November 3, 1994, concerning in particular the rights of the Hungarian minority. The president of parliament, Mr. Gasparovic, responded that the Commission's fears were based on inaccurate information and reassured the European Commission officials that democratic principles would be respected. *Agence Europe,* no. 6372 (December 7, 1994), p. 5.

57. Jens Schneider, "Marathon-Mann in der geteilten Stadt," *Süddeutsche Zeitung,* December 19, 1994, p. 3. Schneider describes Koschnick's laborious enterprise of turning his local interlocutors away from fighting the battles of the past and useless ideological disputes toward shaping a common future and the pragmatic solution of day-to-day needs of citizens.

58. Ironically, the interrelation of reconciliation in a town like Mostar and reduced fighting in the region may turn out to be negative: soldiers returning from the battlefield home to Mostar and finding no job in the destroyed city are tempted to continue "a little bit of war." To mention one event: Koschnick's residence was attacked by a rocket on September 11, 1994. See "Where the EU reigns," *The Economist,* September 17, 1994, p. 38.

59. Koschnick expressed this concern when he stated, that in case the UN withdraws its Blue Helmets, the EU team will have to go, too. In his view the EU team, situated between the two parties, cannot sustain this operation on its own. Reinhard Voss, "Polizisten als Puffer zwischen den Parteien," *Frankfurter Rundschau,* December 20, 1994, p. 3.

60. European Commission, "The Europe Agreements and Beyond," p. 4.

61. Concerning the definition of these notions, see B. Boutros-Ghali, A*n Agenda for Peace: Preventive Diplomacy, Peacemaking and Peace-keeping, Report of the Secretary-General pursuant to the statement adopted by the Summit Meeting of the Security Council on 31 January 1992* (United Nations, 1992).

62. Article J.5 of the Maastricht Treaty reads: "Member States represented in international organizations or international conferences where not all the Member States participate shall keep the latter informed of any matter of common interest. Member States which are also members of the United Nations Security Council will concert and keep the other Member States fully informed. Member States which are permanent members of the Security Council will, in the execution of their functions, ensure the defense of the positions and the interests of the Union, without prejudice to their responsibilities under the provisions of the United Nations Charter.

63. For an analysis of the provisions of the Maastricht Treaty concerning the EU's policy in the UN, see Peter Schmidt, "A Complex Puzzle—the EU's Security

Policy and UN Reform," *International Spectator*, vol. 29 (July–September 1994), pp. 53–66.

64. This is the assessment of an official of the European Commission, Fraser Cameron, "The European Community and CSCE," in Michael A. Lucas, ed., *The CSCE in the 1990s: Constructing European Security and Cooperation* (Baden-Baden: Nomos Verlagsgesellschaft 1993), pp. 266, 267.

65. Case studies to attribute influence to overlapping membership or to the policy of the EU as EU would be as fascinating as complicated. The ambivalence of the two-level game, EU and members states, is built into the Rome Treaty and continued in the Maastricht Treaty. For example, to finance actions of CFSP (for instance, monitoring missions), the Maastricht Treaty leaves it open who will bear the burden; it reads in Title V, article J.11: "The administrative expenditure incurred by the Institutions through the provisions concerning the common foreign and security policy shall be charged to the budget of the European Community. The Council may also:

—either decide unanimously that the operational expenditure involved in the implementation of the said provisions is to be charged to the budget of the European Community; in this case, the budgetary procedures provided for in the Treaty establishing the European Union shall apply;

—or find that such expenditure should be charged to the Member States, possibly in accordance with a scale to be determined."

66. European Parliament, Report of the Committee on the Institutional Affairs on the Future Relations between the European Union, WEU and the Atlantic Alliance (rapporteur: Karel de Gucht), Session document A3–0041/94 (January 27, 1994).

67. The chapters in this volume by David Huntington on the WEU and by Antonia H. Chayes and Richard Weitz on NATO provide further suggestions for an improved interaction of these organizations with the EU.

68. For more suggestions concerning the improvement of the EU-COE interaction, see the chapter by Jean E. Manas in this volume.

FIVE

The European Union in the Former Yugoslavia

Mario Zucconi

"THIS IS the hour of Europe."[1] So said Luxembourg's foreign minister, Jacques Poos, to the press in the early phase of the European Community's attempt to bring the Yugoslav conflict under control.[2] The remark, though lapidary, became the paradigmatic expression of western Europe's hollow ambitions in the post–cold war international environment.

In the Balkans in 1991 the European Community (EC; later the European Union) took up a colossal task for which it was badly equipped and that in fact uncovered the flimsiness of the collective mechanisms through which that organization expected to deal with the new, fast unrolling panorama of international problems and pressures. Especially in the early phase of the conflict, the Community took up a broad commitment that went far beyond anything it had previously done in the global arena. In the end the Yugoslav conflict dealt a serious blow to the image and credibility of the organization, to its perceived weight as a major unitary actor, and to its aspiration to anchor the emerging political order on the European continent.

Yet the inadequacy and failures in the Balkans should not be attributed solely to the European Union (EU). Individual major powers and other multilateral institutions steered clear of the problem, proved unable to bring it under control (as was the case with the Conference on Security and Cooperation in Europe [CSCE] in the early phase), or were able to deal only with very limited aspects of it (as did the UN and NATO after the armed conflict broke out). In fact it is hard to separate the inadequacies and failures of the EU from the context of the broader inadequacies and limitations of present-day multilateralism. However necessary specific reforms of the EU may be at present, it is only one of the organizations that channel the collective action of the western countries.

The armed conflict that erupted in the Socialist Federal Republic of Yugoslavia (SFRY) in late June 1991 is the longest-lasting, most complex crisis the international community has had to deal with since the end of the cold war. The conflict caused a substantial evolution of the competencies and structure of a number of international institutions. It separated those that proved relevant in the present international environment from the irrelevant ones. It brought some of them, most notably the UN and NATO, to begin using their capabilities in a complementary way.

The Yugoslav conflict has also shown how the power structure of the international system has changed in just a few years and how multilateral organizations, for all their shortcomings, are increasingly becoming the only instruments available for managing international stability. Therefore the important issue seems to be not whether multilateral organizations are more or less relevant and capable of dealing with international instability, but rather how we can improve their effectiveness. This conclusion applies to the EU as well as to all the other institutions that played a role in the international response to the conflict in the former Yugoslavia.

After a chronological review of the record of the western European intervention in the crisis, the second part of this chapter analyzes the experience in terms of the objectives, competencies, structure, and instruments of the EC-EU. It also examines the pressures and expectations to which the organization tried to respond and why the performance fell short. The last part draws some conclusions about the conditions for a more effective use of EU capabilities in the framework of a new and evolving arrangement among the western industrialized countries.

The European Union's Intervention in the Conflict: A Chronology

Since June 1991 four multilateral institutions have dealt in a major way with the conflict in the former Yugoslavia: the CSCE, the EU, the UN, and NATO. This chapter focuses on the EC-EU experience, but analyzes that experience in the context of the overall response of the international community, and thus also of the actions—parallel, successive, and overlapping—of other international institutions.

In the late spring of 1991, with the political situation fast deteriorating and the probability of large-scale violence increasing, many looked to the

CSCE as the most suitable institution for dealing with the crisis. As major fighting broke out in late June, Austria asked that the CSCE's newly established emergency mechanism for crisis management be activated. The EU bloc supplied the twelve votes necessary to call a crisis meeting. However, although, as late as June 1992, the CSCE summit in Helsinki still claimed that the organization had prime authority with regard to security threats in Europe, from the very beginning it was unable to exert any influence on the evolution of the conflict, and more generally, it proved ill-equipped to deal with a crisis deriving from internal disputes and the breakup of a state.

In fact, frequent successive meetings of the organization, at the foreign ministers' level and as a Committee of Senior Officials, never took any action beyond calling on the contending parties to respect international rules, such as the unacceptability of the use of force, and supporting the "democratic development, unity and territorial integrity of Yugoslavia." In September the CSCE decided to expand to all its members the EU ban on exports of arms and military equipment to Yugoslavia. CSCE communiqués routinely offered the organization's endorsement to the most recent initiative of the Community.[3] These endorsements, together with the paralysis of the pan-European organization in the face of the Yugoslav crisis, reinforced for a while the impression that the Community was the only institution capable of effectively influencing developments.

The Community, in effect, had a free hand in the summer and fall of 1991. The United States was glad to see it take the central responsibility for dealing with the crisis. Moscow, for its part, was then in the midst of a political revolution that in a few months would lead to the collapse of communist rule and the breakup of the Soviet state.

Western Europe's attempt to influence events in Yugoslavia was a complex operation and moved through different phases. It was based on important economic relations with that country (more than half of Yugoslavia's trade in mid-1991 was with the EU),[4] on Yugoslavia's desperate need for international financial assistance (with an $18 billion foreign debt, in early 1991 Belgrade was negotiating the rescheduling of a $1 billion debt repayment and a $2.5 billion new loan from the World Bank and the EU), and, more generally, on the powerful gravitational force of the Community in post–cold war Europe.[5] Its response to the crisis derived also from the ambitions western Europe was developing in the new political context of the continent.

In the weeks and months that followed the Slovene and Croatian declaration of independence, western Europe was very active in trying to quell the armed conflict and find a political accommodation, despite its already crowded foreign policy agenda. Most European capitals held high expectations that they could decisively influence events. The early involvement and expectations clearly define the most important phase of the EU interaction with the conflict: June–December 1991. For the purposes of this chapter, two other phases are identified: the first phase in the months preceding June 1991, and the last in the period following the recognition of Croatia and Slovenia and dominated by the civil war in Bosnia and Herzegovina.[6]

Phase One: The Attempt to Maintain a United Yugoslavia

The few initiatives that came from the collective bodies of the western European countries in the phase preceding the outbreak of the armed conflict were aimed at maintaining a unified Yugoslav state. EU Commission president Jacques Delors and Luxembourg's prime minister Jacques Santer, as President of the Council of Ministers, reiterated this collective position on their visit to Belgrade of May 28–29 and offered aid and closer relations as rewards. The same position, enhanced by a number of specific incentives, had been presented in Belgrade two months earlier by the Community's "Troika" (composed of the representative of the country holding the Presidency, his predecessor, and his successor). Before that, the EU Commission had made the renewal of the economic cooperation agreement contingent on the country remaining united. The possibility of Yugoslavia acceding to the association treaties was another incentive repeatedly offered.[7]

The official Washington stand was no different. On June 21 in Belgrade, U.S. secretary of state James A. Baker strongly endorsed the position adopted two days earlier at the CSCE Berlin meeting and characterized the possible move toward independence of Slovenia and Croatia as "unilateral secession . . . illegal, illegitimate." He ruled out recognition of the breakaway republics. However, he also warned Belgrade about the need for democracy and a peaceful solution to the constitutional crisis of the country.[8] The possible repercussions that secessions in Yugoslavia could have on other areas of instability, and especially in the Soviet Union, was a foremost consideration in the minds of many western leaders. Baker warned during his visit to Belgrade that "Instability and breakup of Yugoslavia could have some very tragic consequences, not only here, but more broadly in Europe."[9]

However, while most western governments focused their strategies on maintaining a united Yugoslavia, signs of support for the secessionist positions were also coming from both sides of the Atlantic. Actions taken by the U.S. Congress generally reflected a growing preoccupation with the violation of political and human rights in different parts of Yugoslavia, and the European Parliament went so far as to indicate the possible recognition of internal borders.[10] A Resolution passed on March 13 declared that "the constituent Republics and autonomous provinces must have the right freely to determine their future in a peaceful and democratic manner and on the basis of recognized institutional and internal borders." The Parliament also temporarily blocked a plan for a $1 billion EU aid program, demanding that Belgrade respect human rights and implement economic reforms. The Commission itself drafted guidelines making aid conditional on respect for political and human rights.[11]

Reacting to the flare-up of violence in Croatia in early May, Austrian foreign minister Alois Mock spoke in support of a drive for independence of the two republics. Political pressure in favor of Slovene independence had been growing in Austria. As early as the end of 1990, the leader of the Austrian People's party, Erhard Busek, reportedly urged Ljubliana to secede.[12] In the spring of 1991 there were at least four countries leaning toward support for Slovene and Croatian independence: Hungary, Denmark, Germany, and Austria, although in late June Vienna moved to align itself with the EU's position. In addition, the Vatican was also supportive of the two republics' independence. While adhering to the collective EU stance, Italy also at times reflected domestic pressures favoring Slovene and Croatian independence. Of course, once the armed conflict broke out following the declaration of Slovene and Croatian independence, Germany especially took a much more forceful position in support of the two republics' move.

Phase Two: The EU Effort to Control the Crisis

When fighting broke out in Slovenia after June 25, the Community partners acted collectively but within an ill-defined institutional framework. Other western European countries generally followed the Community's lead. Throughout the second half of 1991 the EU was looked upon as the most suitable organization for dealing with the Yugoslav crisis and played an almost exclusive role. For much of that time the Community's strategy remained that of maintaining some form of unified Yugoslav framework, or at least, as explained below, trying to solve all the different aspects of the Yugoslav crisis contextually.

The EU Troika mediated an agreement in early July providing for a three-month freeze on implementation of the independence declarations while the parties tried to negotiate a political solution to the crisis. The agreement was formalized in the "Common Declaration for a Peaceful Solution of the Yugoslav Crisis," signed on the island of Brioni on July 7. It also envisioned the deployment of EU observers in Slovenia and, if possible, in Croatia to monitor the cease-fire. In the Croatian case, there were obstacles to the actual deployment.[13] On July 5 the Community suspended all financial aid and banned arms exports to Yugoslavia in the expectation that it could force the parties to accept binding Community mediation. Praising the European efforts, Washington quickly followed Brussels in imposing a ban on arms sales.

The organization of a peace conference, vetoed at the CSCE by Belgrade, was taken up by the Community after the war moved to Croatia. The August 27 and September 3 meetings of the EU ministers of foreign affairs, in the framework of European Political Cooperation (EPC),[14] drafted the mandate of the proposed conference. It included among its general principles "No unilateral change of borders by force, protection for the rights of all people in Yugoslavia and the need for full account to be taken of all legitimate concerns and aspirations."[15] In the attempt to overcome explicit Serbian resistance, the foreign affairs ministers threatened to impose broad economic sanctions against those who refused to accept the EU proposal.[16]

The Peace Conference opened at The Hague on September 7 with Lord Carrington, a former British foreign secretary and former secretary-general of NATO, as president. While at Brioni the solution of the crisis had been left to negotiation among the parties, at The Hague the EU mediators advanced a specific constitutional solution replacing the federal state with a confederation of sovereign states. As an inducement this time, the EU offered association status to the individual republics.

An Arbitration Commission first proposed by the EPC meeting of August 27 was to advise the Conference on legal matters. Although it was to be auxiliary to the Conference itself, the declaration seemed to imply that the Commission's decisions would be legally binding on the parties. The five members of the Commission were to be selected from among the presidents of the Constitutional Courts of EU member states. Since the Yugoslav Federal Presidency was unable to agree on the two appointments it was entitled to make, that selection was made by the three judges already appointed by the EU countries. French constitutional court judge Robert Badinter, the originator of the idea of the Commission, was chosen by the other members as president.[17] The Brussels declaration mandated that "relevant authorities," not specifically identified, were entitled to submit their differences to the Commission.

In an attempt to bring the deteriorating military situation under control, the EU gained agreement of the parties to accept a small team of observers and began to deploy them in mid-July. Eventually there were fifty observers in Slovene and Croat territory. But, as cease-fires continued to be signed and broken, a number of Community partners repeatedly put forward the idea of a European "interposition force" to separate the warring parties. As defined by the secretary-general of the Western European Union (WEU), Willem Van Eekelen, the mandate of the force would be "to isolate the sources of conflict" and "to ensure an orderly process of change."[18]

Originally proposed by the governments of Luxembourg and the Netherlands, the "interposition force" was strongly supported by France, which wanted it organized under the control of the WEU. And since the Maastricht Treaty negotiations were then under way, the "interposition force" proposal got caught up in the controversial issue of the Union's "common foreign and security policy." Many thought that a mission in Yugoslavia of a large and visible WEU-led force would settle many of the contentious points that were holding up the conclusion of the treaty.[19]

This symbolism may have been the main attraction of the proposal. In other respects, it appeared totally unrealistic, due, in the first place, to the lack of organizational and command structure and logistic capability of the WEU. Moreover, the proposal met with a strongly negative reaction on the part of the Soviet Union. And, most important, it could not overcome London's opposition. The German government, despite its enthusiastic support, was then bound by constitutional restrictions on the use of German forces out of the North Atlantic Treaty area.

The unreality of the idea of a large European interposition force is also demonstrated by Serbia's refusal to allow even cease-fire observers along its border with Croatia. There were those who supported the dispatch of such a force without regard to the consent of the warring parties. Indeed, Germany advocated a speedy recognition of Croatia, on the grounds that the consequent "internationalization" of the crisis would permit intervention without Belgrade's consent.[20] Then at the London extraordinary session of the WEU Council, on September 18–19, the proposal of an EU-WEU "interposition force" was thoroughly examined and, in effect, killed. At that point Paris insisted that the UN Security Council deal with the Yugoslav issue, initiating the action that led to the first UN intervention in the crisis.

After the Hague Conference failed to move the conflict to the negotiating table, Security Council Resolution 713 of September 25 tried to affect events by imposing "a general and complete embargo on all deliveries of weapons and military equipment to Yugoslavia." However, the Resolution did not prescribe any enforcement measure, and it would take until late November for the Security Council to accept the European proposal to deploy peacekeeping forces.

Thereafter, successive sessions of the Hague Conference produced important, if only temporary, results. Serbian president Slobodan Milosevic accepted the principle of independence of the republics that wanted it. The Conference also formally stated, for the first time at the October 4 meeting, that "recognition would be granted in the framework of a general settlement." Finally, a sort of autonomy status was envisioned for areas in which a national or ethnic group constituted a majority.[21] Washington and Moscow endorsed the ongoing peace process with a joint statement of October 18.

Lord Carrington, the chairman of the Peace Conference, acting as the EU's negotiator, made a detailed proposal on October 25, with the general agreement of five of the six republics. It included, among others, the following points:

> In the framework of a general settlement, recognition of the independence, within existing borders, unless otherwise agreed, of those republics wishing it.
>
> A free association of the republics with an international personality as envisaged in these arrangements.
>
> Comprehensive arrangements, including supervisory mechanisms for the protection of human rights and special status of certain groups and areas.[22]

In an attempt to meet Serbian concerns, the final draft Convention presented by Lord Carrington on November 4 included a more detailed list of the institutional elements, including demilitarization, that would characterize the "special status" of the areas in which a national minority constituted a local majority.[23] On November 8, after Serbia rejected Carrington's peace proposal, the EU Council imposed economic sanctions on Yugoslavia suspending the cooperation agreement and trade concessions, and asked the Security Council to order an oil embargo. Washington immediately joined in this action. The sanctions were later lifted and economic aid reestablished for Slovenia, Croatia, Bosnia and Herzegovina, and Macedonia, all of which had adhered to the Community's plan.

But as a massive offensive was launched against Dubrovnik, the main tourist city of the former Yugoslavia, and the Croatian Serbs moved to establish their own state in the Krajina region, the impression developed that the events on the ground and the peace negotiations were to a great extent proceeding independently. Then, in late November, the eastern Croatian city of Vukovar fell after weeks of artillery fire. The widespread impression was that the western Europeans were completely impotent.

To this point, the Community had consistently resisted pressures for the selective recognition of the independence of Slovenia and Croatia. The pressures that counted most were those coming from Bonn. For several reasons, which tended to feed on each other (that is, domestic politics and the ineffectiveness of the EU action), the German government was increasingly anxious to separate the Slovene and Croatian cases and to proceed with recognition. Yet, in their meeting of November 8 held in the EPC framework, the twelve foreign ministers once more restated the Hague position that recognition could be considered only in the framework of a general settlement.[24]

In the fall of 1991 Bonn was not completely isolated in its position. More and more people were connecting the Yugoslav crisis with the collapse of communism and the breakup of the Soviet Union. In that changed European security environment, they argued, there was no compelling need to keep the Yugoslav state united. The recognition position gained strength in the midst of persistent confusion about western European objectives, of ineffective intervention, of stalemate among the contending parties, and of continuing mixed signals from different western capitals. Lord Carrington's plan had stalled in the face of Belgrade's opposition. By the end of November no less than twelve successive cease-fires had been signed, often in the presence of EU mediators, but either had not taken effect or had lasted only hours.[25] And, especially in the early phase of its intervention in the crisis, the Community's attempt to safeguard a unified framework had been marred by inconsistencies, particularly in its political and legal approach.

Very early in the crisis London diluted its support for the territorial integrity of Yugoslavia. After the intervention of the Yugoslav National Army in Slovenia, Foreign Secretary Douglas Hurd felt "obliged significantly to qualify an early statement supporting the 'integrity of Yugoslavia' by adding that this should not include the use of force."[26] Similarly the United States, at the Security Council meeting of September 25, repeatedly characterized the situation as being one of "outright military intervention against Croatia."[27]

Both the negotiation of cease-fires and the insistence on rules such as the inadmissibility of the use of force or of territorial acquisition through force implied a de facto recognition of parties other than the Federal Republic of Yugoslavia. The obligation of nonintervention, for example, is an obligation directed at states. For the same reason, the rejection of territorial conquest by force implicitly acknowledged the existence of Croatia.[28]

The first opinion of the Badinter Commission on November 29 was further evidence of the failure of the effort to maintain some form of one-Yugoslavia settlement. It found that the federal governmental organs had become unable to function, and thus the SFRY no longer met the criteria of a "state" under international law. It concluded that "the SFRY [was] in the process of dissolution."[29]

In Germany, as early as July, a resolution of the Bundestag asked for recognition, reflecting the wide public support for the independence of Slovenia and Croatia. Chancellor Kohl increasingly committed himself to support recognition of the two republics. "When dialogue and harmonious coexistence are no longer possible," he declared on September 4, "we must . . . consider . . . recognizing under international law those republics which no longer wish to belong to Yugoslavia."[30] From July on, Minister of Foreign Affairs Hans-Dietrich Genscher repeatedly used the threat of a German unilateral move to pressure Germany's allies and as a means to deter Serbian aggression.

As other attempts to stem the violence failed, it was argued that the strategy of internationalizing the conflict—"preventive recognition"—was the only political lever western Europe could still use to restore peace. And, although Kohl had promised French president François Mitterand that any recognition of the two republics would be the act of the Twelve together,[31] in mid-November he was promising the Christian-Democratic Union convention in Dresden that Croatia and Slovenia would be recognized by Christmas. "The Croats will not be left alone," he pledged.[32]

A last-minute effort to derail German recognition was made in early December. Lord Carrington wrote to the then president of the Community, Foreign Minister Hans van den Broek of the Netherlands, on December 2, warning that a separate initiative by Germany "would undoubtedly mean breakup of the Conference" on Yugoslavia and lead to other dangerous developments. The president of Bosnia and Herzegovina, Ilija Izetbegovic, made known his deep concern to the Community governments. UN secretary-general Javier Perez de Cuellar warned that "selective recognition could widen the present conflict and fuel an explosive situation." Again, on the eve of the decisive December 16 meeting of the Community, Perez de Cuellar reminded the German government of the position agreed upon at the November 8 EPC meeting, that recognition "can only be envisaged in the framework of an overall settlement." Stern warnings also came from U.S. deputy secretary of state Lawrence S. Eagleburger (a former ambassador to Yugoslavia) that separate recognition of Croatia and Slovenia would damage the prospects for peace and "almost inevitably lead to greater bloodshed." Cyrus R. Vance, the UN mediator in Yugoslavia and former U.S. secretary of state, took the same position.[33] To all these démarches, Genscher responded with coolly worded letters that simply confirmed Bonn's determination to proceed, with or without agreement of its EU partners.[34]

Late in the day on December 14 the UN Security Council began debating a draft resolution warning that no country should upset the political balance in Yugoslavia by taking unilateral action. Although the French and British missions drafted the resolution with the object of thwarting Bonn's pledge to recognize Croatia and Slovenia by Christmas, in the Security Council debate they backed away from their position because of last-minute indications from Germany that it would stand firm despite any UN action. The Franco-British retreat was thought necessary to avoid a serious political crisis within the European Community.[35]

According to some accounts, Germany made some concessions in the last phase of the Maastricht Treaty negotiations, to sweeten the inevitability of recognition for London. In a recent interview, former minister of foreign affairs Gianni De Michelis maintained that, for tactical reasons, Italy moved toward recognition starting in late September, with the goal of keeping Germany "anchored to the EU [unitary] line."[36] Greece, traditionally Serbia's friend, was apparently won over with the assurance that the Republic of Macedonia would not be recognized.[37] Italy, Belgium, and Denmark also indicated their readiness to recognize Croatia and Slovenia in the days before the December 16 meeting of the EU ministers of foreign affairs.

The extraordinary EPC ministerial meeting in Brussels on December 16 was a tense and difficult one.[38] Prisoners of their own commitment to follow a common approach to the Yugoslav crisis, the EU ministers faced Germany's inflexible position. De Michelis credits himself with bringing his colleagues to realize, in the face of especially strong French objections, that the need to show unity a few days after the signature of the Maastricht Treaty was much more important than the differences among them over

Yugoslavia.[39] A late-night "compromise" accepted the German position but established a set of "Guidelines on the recognition of new States in Eastern Europe and in the Soviet Union." They included:

—Respect for the provision of the [UN] Charter and the commitments subscribed to in the Final Act of Helsinki and in the Charter of Paris.

—Guarantees for the rights of ethnic and national groups and minorities.

—Respect for the inviolability of all frontiers which could only be changed by peaceful means and common agreements.

—Acceptance of all relevant commitments with regard to disarmament and nuclear nonproliferation as well as to security and regional stability.

Then, in a "Declaration on Yugoslavia," they invited all Yugoslav republics to submit their application for recognition by December 23. The applicants were required to specify whether they accepted the commitments in the Guidelines and the provisions laid down in the draft Convention under consideration by the Conference on Yugoslavia, especially those on human rights and the rights of national and ethnic groups. Reflecting Greek sensitivities with regard to the possible recognition of the Republic of Macedonia, the Declaration asked for a commitment from each applicant republic "to adopt constitutional and political guarantees ensuring that it has no territorial claims towards a neighboring Community State and that it will conduct no hostile propaganda activities versus a neighboring Community State, including the use of a denomination which implies territorial claim."[40] The republics that were found by the Badinter Commission to have fulfilled the conditions would be recognized as of January 15, 1992.

A more in depth analysis of the implications of this decision is offered in the second part of this chapter, but it is useful at this point to define the main differences with the previous EU common position. The December 16 decision based recognition on the merit of the individual case without reference to the possible interdependence with other cases. The list of generalized conditions replaced the contextuality within which, until November, it was thought that the separate aspects of the Yugoslav crisis should be solved. Although one of the conditions was that the applicant should accept the continuation of the Conference on Yugoslavia, in fact the decision eliminated what had been the main purpose for the Conference since its creation. The only legacy of the previous peace process was that the principles it had established were now the conditions that the applicant had to avow. Lastly, some of those conditions, rather than adhering to traditional criteria for recognition of statehood, were political criteria, reflecting specific interests of individual EU countries.[41]

Despite the collective December 16 decision and without waiting for the Badinter Commission's opinions, Bonn recognized Croatia and Slovenia on December 23.[42] Shortly before the critical date of January 15, the Arbitration Commission gave its ruling: favorable for Slovenia and Macedonia, but against Croatia, and Bosnia and Herzegovina.

Bonn had pressed Croatia in early December to improve its legislation with regard to human rights and protection of minorities, and Genscher avowed that Croatia "has achieved the highest imaginable standard of respect for minority rights."[43] But, after asking Zagreb for further assurances, in its Opinion no. 5 (January 11, 1992) the Badinter Commission found that "the [Croatian] Constitutional Act of 4 December 1991 does not fully incorporate all the provisions of the draft Convention of 4 November 1991, notably those [concerning the] 'special status.' " In the case of Bosnia and Herzegovina, the Arbitration Commission asked, in Opinion no. 4, that, in view of the different positions taken by the "Serbian people of Bosnia-Herzegovina," further appropriate guarantees were needed in applying for recognition, "possibly by means of a referendum of all the citizens of the SRBH [Socialist Republic of Bosnia-Herzegovina] without distinction, carried out under international supervision."

Notwithstanding these negative opinions, on January 15, again in tow of the German unilateral initiative, the EU partners moved to recognize Croatia and Slovenia. They also accepted the Greek veto of the recognition of Macedonia because of the controversy over the name of the prospective independent state. Only France objected, as it had at the December 16 meeting, and put on record that its recognition of Croatia was conditional on Zagreb's fulfillment of the conditions set by the Badinter Commission. The Vatican had recognized Croatia and Slovenia two days earlier. Ukraine, itself still unrecognized internationally, had recognized them on December 12. Other countries as well, under the impetus of the action of the European Community, moved to recognize Croatia and Slovenia in mid-January, including Australia, Austria, Bulgaria, Canada, Estonia, Hungary, Latvia, Lithuania, Iceland, Malta, New Zealand, Norway, Poland, San Marino, Sweden, and Switzerland.

Initially, the decision of December 16 was seen as "a great triumph of German foreign policy," as Chancellor Kohl boasted, but this very fact created great apprehension internationally.[44] One commentator said, for example: "One year after reunification, and only days after moving to the fore economically at the European Community summit meeting in the Netherlands, Germany offered for the first time since World War II a display of political might. . . . By sweeping away British and French objections, the reunited Germany did for the first time what the rump West Germany never dared: It forcefully elbowed through an unpopular move that it perceived as crucial to its own interests."[45] And there was no lack of awareness in Germany itself on this point. "Germany is acting in a highly sensitive psychological environment," wrote Bonn's General Anzeiger. "The fear of German dominance and unilateralism has grown."[46]

Phase Three: Scaled-down Ambitions from 1992 on

The role of the European Union in the international response to the Yugoslav crisis greatly diminished after January 15, 1992. The decision it had come to one month before, while formally a common decision of the Twelve, had in fact uncovered the inadequacy of the Union's structure and mechanisms for pooling interests and capabilities and for producing collective policies with regard to international stability. Although Germany had demonstrated its weight in the new European political context, it also found itself, as a result, in profound diplomatic isolation.[47] In the coming months and years, while individual western countries maintained a high level of initiative, both Brussels and Bonn turned away from their earlier ambitions and were on the whole content with remaining on the sidelines.[48]

The abandonment of the search for an integrated (or contextual) solution compelled Bosnia and Herzegovina, and Macedonia also, to seek independence, and their independence in turn set free new centrifugal ethnic pressures within these two republics.[49] Thus, beginning in early 1992, western Europe and the international community in general faced an even more complex situation, to the creation of which they had contributed.

In Bosnia and Herzegovina, in particular, no one of the three ethnic groups had an overwhelming majority. Traditionally, Serbia and Croatia had coveted parts of its territory. Thus, once that republic became detached from the larger reality of federal Yugoslavia, the situation there was potentially explosive. Indeed, the Bosnian civil war became the most dramatic and harrowing aspect of the Balkan crisis in the following years. In addition, the issues the international community had to deal with at this stage changed. They were no longer political and legal, but humanitarian and military. This brought other international institutions to the fore, with the UN the most active, and with a new and growing role of NATO in support of the UN humanitarian operations.

As already mentioned, the need to involve the United Nations was first felt after the failure to create an EU-WEU "interposition force" for Croatia in mid-September 1991. After passing Resolution 713 (September 25) imposing the arms embargo, the Security Council responded to the western European pressure for sending peacekeeping troops to monitor the Geneva cease-fire agreement between Croatia and the Croatian Serbs. It first took up the issue at the end of November shortly after the Geneva cease-fire agreement in Croatia (Resolution 721 of November 23). Eventually, Resolution 743 of February 21, 1992, adopted under chapter 6 of the Charter, established the UN Protection Force (UNPROFOR) to be deployed in the "protected areas" of Croatia, areas with large Serbian populations outside the control of Zagreb. Subsequently the Security Council passed Resolution 758 (June 8, 1992) that extended the mandate of UNPROFOR to Bosnia and Herzegovina in connection with an agreement among the warring factions to permit the reopening of the Sarajevo airport. The early mission of protecting the humanitarian convoys organized by the UN High Commissioner on Refugees and other organizations broadened over time to include a multiplicity of tasks: silencing sniper fire, taking control of heavy weapons, monitoring the no-fly zone over Bosnia, and protecting six Security Council-designated "safe areas." These extensions of the traditional peacekeeping mission began a period of great difficulty and considerable confusion about UN military operations.[50]

Reflecting growing pressures on the part of European and U.S. public opinion that something be done at least to control the level of violence, in June 1992 NATO agreed to make itself available in support of the CSCE and UN operations. For the first time the Security Council invoked its chapter 7 powers in Resolution 770 of August 13, 1992, calling on member states "nationally or through regional agencies or arrangements" to help ensure the delivery of humanitarian assistance.

As time went on, NATO became the main enforcement structure and the main power factor in a number of Security Council decisions. The process began with the enforcement of the embargo along the Adriatic coast in 1992. Then, after a UN report of March 1993 found hundreds of violations of the no-fly zone, NATO started enforcing that decision under authorization of Security Council Resolution 816 (March 31, 1993). A few months later NATO began providing "close air support" on a case-by-case basis for UNPROFOR personnel operating in the safe areas, thus giving more substance to the decision establishing those special areas. The authorization for the operation was contained in Security Council Resolution 836 of June 4,

1993. In taking up those tasks, NATO carried out some high-profile operations, such as the downing of Serbian planes after a bombing raid, or
delivering and enforcing ultimatums to stop the bombing of Sarajevo and
Gorazde, or the destruction of the runway of the Ubdina airport in Croatian
Krajina, which was being used to support attacks on the Bosnian safe area
of Bihac. The visibility of those operations, and the expectations created by
the use of force and by NATO's role, further helped to push the Community
to the sidelines. At the same time, coming as a response to Western public
opinion's pressures rather than as part of any effective political and diplomatic strategy, the coercive use of military force remained episodic and
contributed to the growing inconsistency of the international response in
this phase. Moreover, as the pressure to use NATO's power against the
Serbs contrasted with the need for the consent of all parties on which the
UN officials conducting the operation on the ground insisted, a serious and
lasting divergence emerged between the two organizations, hampering the
effectiveness of their respective operations and, in the end, bringing serious
discredit to both of them.

For its part, the EC recognized Bosnia and Herzegovina on April 6, 1992.
A referendum, in which 99 percent of those voting supported independence,
had been boycotted by the Bosnian Serbs, almost a third of the population.
On March 27 the Bosnian Serbs proclaimed their own "Serbian Republic of
Bosnia-Herzegovina" with its capital in Pale, near Sarajevo. Only a few
days before the date of recognition, moreover, Bosnian Serb leaders had
repudiated a "Statement of Principles for New Constitutional Arrangements
for Bosnia and Herzegovina" negotiated by Portuguese diplomat Jose Cutileiro representing the EC Presidency. The Cutileiro Plan, to which the
Bosnian Serbs had originally adhered, defined Bosnia and Herzegovina as
consisting of "the citizens of the Muslim, Serb and Croat nations, and other
nations and nationalities."[51] In this phase the EC, hoping to contain the
spread of violence in Bosnia and Herzegovina, repeatedly stressed its
strong commitment to the territorial integrity of the republic.[52] The U.S.
administration, which in this case had urged swift recognition as a way of
avoiding the breakup of the country, followed the Europeans one day later.[53]
It also recognized Croatia and Slovenia on the same date. These actions
took place in the midst of a serious escalation of the fighting throughout the
republic and around Sarajevo.

With the violence increasingly directed at the civilian population and
reaching unprecedented levels of barbarity, much of the pressure of the
international community was now targeted specifically on Serbia as protec-

tor and supplier of the Bosnian Serbs. On May 11 the EU ministers of foreign affairs decided to recall their ambassadors from Belgrade, and a number of other countries followed the EU action, beginning with the United States on May 12. Resolution 757 (May 30, 1992) condemned the Federal Republic of Yugoslavia for its role in the Bosnian conflict and imposed a comprehensive array of mandatory sanctions upon it. Three days earlier, the EU had imposed a less comprehensive list of sanctions, with, among others, air links exempted at Paris's insistence.[54] In that same month the UN Security Council recommended that the General Assembly should admit Slovenia, Croatia, and Bosnia and Herzegovina to membership in the UN. Moreover, Security Council Resolution 777 (September 19, 1992) rejected the claim of the Federal Republic of Yugoslavia (Serbia and Montenegro) that it should succeed automatically to the membership of the former SFRY in the UN, and recommended to the General Assembly that it "should apply for membership in the United Nations and that it should not participate in the work of the General Assembly."[55] This action was technically neither an expulsion nor a suspension and thus fell short of the Union foreign ministers' call of July 20 that the country be expelled from the United Nations. France, the United States, the United Kingdom, and Belgium were among the sponsors of both Resolution 777 and 757. During the same period, the CSCE also acted to suspend the Federal Republic of Yugoslavia.

The Union now concentrated its scaled-down activities primarily on the attempt to stop the fighting in Bosnia through any kind of political settlement. To that end, a peace conference was called in London for late August, under the cochairmanship of Carrington's successor, Lord Owen (also a former British foreign secretary) and former U.S. secretary of state Cyrus Vance, who served as representative of the UN secretary-general. The cochairmanship inaugurated a phase of successful, if limited, partnership between the two institutions, following a period of polemical response of the new UN secretary-general, Boutros Boutros-Ghali, to the pressures exerted by the western Europeans for more decisive UN action. In one such instance, after Lord Carrington reported to the UN secretary-general on a cease-fire agreement and invited the Security Council to take enforcement action, Boutros-Ghali reacted testily, questioning the appropriateness of a regional organization telling the UN what to do.[56]

The International Conference on the former Yugoslavia opened on August 27 in the presence of the foreign ministers of a number of influential powers, including the United States, Russia, China, and Japan, and established the main reference framework for the subsequent Geneva negotiations. As part of this framework the regional parties underwrote a series of general principles such as the illegitimacy of frontiers changed by force, the renunciation of violence as a way to settle national grievances, and respect for individual and minority rights. It also set up six working groups: on Bosnia, minorities, the succession to Yugoslavia, economics, confidence-building measures, and humanitarian relief.

In addition to the principles already announced in London, all warring parties pledged not to interfere with the flow of humanitarian aid and not to violate the ban on military flights over Bosnia. However, "the shells and mortar bombs falling on Bosnia's capital," wrote *The Economist* in the days of the conference, "seemed mocking proof of the inability of diplomats to end this conflict."[57]

While paying tribute to those general principles, the attempt of the EU and UN mediators to reach some settlement in Bosnia had to fly much closer to the ground, to the real conditions determined by the fighting. As argued in the concluding part of this chapter, they had little choice, given the extremely limited and often ill-managed investment the international community was making in the attempt to stop the war. By the fall of 1992 the Serbs (31.5 percent of the population, according to the April 1991 census) and the Croats (17.3 percent) controlled 65–70 and 25–30 percent of Bosnian territory respectively, with the Muslims (43.8 percent of population) besieged in a number of urban areas.

Thus the plan that Vance and Owen circulated in the fall and officially submitted to the parties in January 1993 built on the Cutileiro Plan that had been agreed among the leaders of the three factions on the eve of the referendum. This agreement explicitly recognized Bosnia as being made up of three "national components" and accepted the principle of "cantonization" of the country, although, after recognition of Bosnia and Herzegovina, this notion was rejected by its President Izetbegovic.[58] The Vance-Owen plan envisioned three cantons for each group, reflecting the prevailing ethnic character of the different areas, with a tenth ethnically mixed canton around Sarajevo. In contrast with later plans, the qualifying feature of the Vance-Owen proposal was that it still provided for a central, multiethnic government that was to keep Bosnia from being dismembered and absorbed into a "Greater Serbia" and a "Greater Croatia."

The plan was backed by the EC Council of Ministers of February 2, 1993, and, after some initial criticism, by the new U.S. administration of President Bill Clinton. It was accepted by Serbia's president Milosevic and, subject to the approval of his group's Assembly, by the Bosnian Serb leader Radovan Karadzic. Tighter enforcement of the trade embargo on the Danube and Washington's pressures on its allies to launch air strikes against the Serbs and to lift the arms embargo on the Bosnian government (the "lift and strike" option) were, possibly, effective leverages. But in the end the plan was rejected by the Bosnian Serb Assembly of Pale in early May.

With the Vance-Owen plan dead and with Paris and London, which had the two largest contingents on the ground in Bosnia, opposing the use of air strikes against the Serbs, some western governments tried to present as an alternative option the creation of "safe havens" around six Bosnian cities. However, as General Philippe Morillon, the commander of the UN troops in Bosnia and the originator of the proposal, pointed out, the "safe havens" were solely an emergency plan to save human lives, not a substitute for the Vance-Owen plan.

Unlike the Vance-Owen Plan, which envisioned a leopard-skin distribution of the ethnic groups without territorial continuity between the Serb cantons and the Republic of Serbia—to which, of course, the Serbs had objected—the direction taken by the Geneva negotiations was toward a mere partition of Bosnia into three ethnic states. The version of the plan presented at the end of August gave 52.5 percent of territory to the Serbs, 17.5 percent to the Croats, and 30 percent to the Muslims. Lord Owen, still chairing the negotiations, now condemned the old Vance-Owen plan as "unrealistic"; Vance, who had stepped down from his assignment, judged the new partition plan as "completely wrong."[59]

On the other hand, all other strategies encountered the insurmountable resistance of the French and British governments. In Copenhagen on June 21, 1993, when Izetbegovic asked EU foreign ministers to lift the arms embargo against his government, British foreign secretary Douglas Hurd lectured him that the certain result would be intensified fighting and the suspension of the relief operation. And while the Twelve talked in Copenhagen of the need to avoid pressures on the Muslim side, after the meeting, senior officials acknowledged to the press that the EU's strategy was to force the Muslims to accept the *fait accompli* of the Serbian and Croatian territorial acquisitions.[60] From Copenhagen also came clear indication of the lack of a center of decision and of the hesitancy and timidity of the western action. Chancellor Kohl tried to convince his Community colleagues to lift the arms embargo on Bosnia by showing a letter President Clinton had sent him supporting the action. However, while Kohl was relying on the authority of the U.S. presidency, Clinton was trying to use

Kohl to restart an earlier U.S. initiative that had already cost Washington a serious diplomatic defeat.[61]

The EU's diplomatic influence became increasingly marginal in the summer and fall of 1993, as the intensified Serb offensive and growing pressures from Washington gave the use of military force, however occasional, the prominent role. In early August, when the U.S. administration threatened to act unilaterally to prevent the "strangulation" of Sarajevo and urged the allies to take appropriate measures, NATO approved a plan to attack the Serb positions around the city. In this case, as in Sarajevo and Gorazde in February and April 1994, the determination shown by the western allies contributed, with intense UN negotiations, to produce the desired effect.

However, because of its very effectiveness, the growing use of military force tended also to become increasingly a strategy of its own, increasing expectations and creating higher standards for assessing effectiveness. It pushed the negotiating process further into the background, and even came into conflict, at times, with the requirements of that process. Thus in August Lord Owen criticized the threat of military action because it tended to stiffen the Bosnian government's position. A month later, indicating his limited commitment, President Clinton disabused Izetbegovic of any expectation of western military action and urged him to go back to the negotiating table and strike the best deal he could.[62] In January 1994 the European Parliament asked that Lord Owen be replaced and that "another EU mediator be appointed, this time provided with an appropriate mandate and a new strategy for pursuing it."[63] The Council, however, rejected the proposal.

Then, in the first half of 1994, Greece succeeded to the presidency of the Union. The lack of confidence in the Greek presidency further contributed to the waning of Europe's collective role in the former Yugoslavia. London and Paris took the initiative to bring together all independently active countries, thus in effect bypassing the Greek presidency. Washington became increasingly active diplomatically, and much of the credit for the April 1994 Muslim-Croat agreement on the confederal plan for Bosnia went to the United States. At the same time, Moscow's domestic pressures pushed it to play a more active role. With the largest contingents on the ground in Bosnia, Paris and London were now the main conditioning elements behind the UN operation. In April those four powers plus Germany, which insisted on a place in the discussion, formed a "Contact Group" for Bosnia. With the creation of the Contact Group the peace process had been taken over by a sort of directorate, which further reduced the role for the collective mechanisms of the western European foreign policy.[64]

The result, however, confirmed the limited interest of the international community in the issue and, more generally, the lack of an adequate rationale for mobilization of the most influential countries around issues of international stability in the post–cold war environment. Meeting jointly in Geneva in mid-May 1994, the Contact Group and the EU Troika (Greece, Germany, and Belgium) announced a new peace initiative that they claimed aimed at the preservation of Bosnia and Herzegovina "as a single union within its internationally recognized borders."[65] The plan differed only marginally from the earlier ones, allotting 51 percent of the republic's territory to the Muslim-Croat federation, which had asked for 58 percent), and 49 percent to the Bosnian Serbs, who controlled over 70 percent of the territory and had a demonstrated capability for conquering even more. Despite various incentives directed at Belgrade in particular, during the second half of 1994 the Contact Group peace process remained stalled. What progressed were the differences emerging among the outside actors and between the United Nations and NATO over their respective roles.

When, after a harsh winter and what seemed then like an effective ceasefire, large scale fighting resumed in May and June 1995, the Contact Group's plan and the Croatian-Bosnian Confederation remained the basis on which to build the international initiative. Moreover, although some movement in the situation came from the growing difficulties between Bosnian Serbs and Belgrade and from the new military capabilities demonstrated by Croatia (who took control of Croatian Krajina away from the Serbs), such movement enhanced the role of only a few individual capitals—Washington, Bonn, and Moscow—making ever more irrelevant the efforts of other European states and of the Union itself.

What Common Foreign Policy?

Many commentators have criticized the EU for the "fiasco" in the former Yugoslavia. The focus of complaint has been the failure of the Community's attempt to bring the conflict under control in the second part of 1991.[66] Others have attempted to exonerate the EU by pointing out that the crisis caught the organization in a phase of institutional renovation. James B. Steinberg argues that "in many respects, the Yugoslavia crisis was 'premature'; it caught Europe in the act of self-redefinition."[67] Others emphasize the already crowded foreign policy agenda of the EU in the summer and fall of 1991, which included the fast deteriorating situation in the Soviet Union, the collapse of communism, the unification of Germany, and the Maastricht Treaty negotiations.[68] Still, rather than revealing the potentialities and capabilities of the EU, the efforts to deal with the crisis over the next three years instead confirmed its inadequacy in dealing with problems of international stability in Europe.

The Formal Structure for Foreign Policy Decisionmaking

A careful assessment of the EU response to the Yugoslav crisis must begin by examining the mechanisms and instruments available to the institution. Rather than exonerating it once more for its failure to achieve the goals it set for itself, this analysis is used to highlight the gap existing between the capabilities of the institution and the requirements deriving from a critical and complex situation such as the conflict in the former Yugoslavia.

The case has been made that, precisely because of the exceptional response required to meet the Yugoslav challenge, the EU greatly broadened its collective competencies and initiatives.[69] Unquestionably the countries of the Community tried to rise to the occasion and to adapt their capabilities and mechanisms to the circumstances. In a number of instances, such as the convening of the Hague Peace Conference, they demonstrated a considerable ability to exert influence. However, in the end, walking in the mine field of Balkan politics without adequate institutional equipment proved not only unproductive, but also harmful for the western European organization itself.

While the specific mechanisms of EU foreign policymaking or coordination are examined in another chapter of this volume, it is important to recall here that in June 1991 the twelve EU partners were in the final stretch of the negotiations for the treaty on European Union (the Maastricht Treaty), which was signed on December 11, 1991. A central feature of the treaty was title 5, providing for a "common foreign and security policy" (CFSP), in addition to the old "economic community" that had been established by the Treaty of Rome in 1958. Thus the search for new structures and mechanisms for a common foreign policy was very much in the minds of European leaders as they dealt with the conflict in Yugoslavia. In fact, as the attempt to create an EC-WEU interposition force and the December 16 recognition decision demonstrate, the desire to show communality of purpose and action in external affairs at times dictated the EU response to the Yugoslav crisis.

Technically, European Political Cooperation, practiced since the 1970s and given treaty form by the Single European Act of 1986, prevailed during the first part of the period under consideration, and the new CFSP after the ratification of Maastricht. Nevertheless, the format of CFSP that prevailed was not very different from the old EPC. It remained "intergovernmental cooperation" rather than a true common policy with binding mechanisms, moving beyond the unanimity rule. As in the EPC, the top decisionmaking body remained the Council. Much of the implementation function stayed with the Presidency, assisted if necessary by the Troika. The alternative of broader responsibility for the Commission was rejected.

The innovation of the Maastricht Treaty's CFSP was that the Council could now identify issues for "joint action." But even here the CFSP required a unanimous vote not only for selecting the issues on which to act, but also for defining those specific matters of implementation on which decisions could then be taken by qualified majority.[70]

The CFSP language in Maastricht echoes the loyalty obligation of article 5 of the Community Treaty: "The Member States shall support the Union's external and security policy actively and unreservedly in a spirit of loyalty and mutual solidarity." Although a violation of the Community Treaty can be brought before the Court of Justice, however, the Maastricht Treaty commits only the political responsibility of the member states before their own collective body, the Council. British foreign secretary Douglas Hurd, the main advocate of the approach adopted at Maastricht, defended it in a recent essay: "The Community is a community of law, and requires mechanisms for enacting, enforcing, and adjudicating legislation. But foreign policy is rarely implemented through national legislation. Other mechanisms are required. . . . The key to coherent and successful foreign policy cooperation is persuading your partners of the force of your arguments, not resorting to the procedural means of a vote to overrule their point of view."[71]

Thus neither the EPC nor the CFSP were, by themselves, mechanisms for producing a more "common" policy than the individual states were ready to agree on through bilateral or multilateral negotiations. The first of the two frameworks "exhorts," while the second "commits [the partners] to try" to reach agreement on common positions. Neither of them prescribes dimensions or geographical areas of common policy.[72] The formal framework within which the EU acted, whether EPC or the CFSP, seems to make little difference in explaining why the organization was able or unable to take particular actions in responding to the Yugoslav crisis. While formally acting within the EPC framework in the second part of 1991, the EU took initiatives and adopted mechanisms that in some cases were then still on the drawing board of the Maastricht Treaty. Thus, for instance, while the EU Observer Mission did not satisfy the CFSP requirement of formal, prior adoption of a "common position," it could be considered a "joint action." The interposition force also, had it been created, would have taken the form of a "joint action." And although the imposition of economic sanctions falls under the Community Treaty, the broader framework of the peace process and political objectives with which those sanctions were connected was another important issue on which the Twelve acted collectively. Moreover, the EU reacted swiftly to the outbreak of the conflict, moving much beyond what it had ever done before in the field of external affairs.[73]

Conversely, although the former Yugoslavia was selected as one of five areas of "joint actions" of the CFSP at the extraordinary European Council of October 29, 1993, that did not introduce any new element or greater resolve in the EU's response to the ongoing crisis. In short, both the activism of the early phase, under the looser EPC framework, and the lack of initiative in the most recent one, under the somewhat more formal CFSP, have little to do with the specific instruments for coordinating foreign policies in use at the time.

Goals and Conditions

The test of what would constitute a successful common EU policy toward a complex issue like the Yugoslav crisis is the ability to keep the different aspects of the issue under control. Among the diverse ramifications involved are instability in the southern Balkan region, the refugee problem, the pressures of public opinion related to humanitarian issues, implications for NATO and the WEU, the impact on Warsaw Pact countries and the former Soviet Union, and others. To maintain the necessary control, it is essential to contain the pressures to focus on particular interests or to align with one party or the other in the dispute.

With regard to Yugoslavia, in 1991 the main requirements of an overall solution were related to the cleavages among social groups there. Mobilization of ethnic differences in the context of noncontinuous distribution of the ethnic groups was the common feature of the different and successive aspects of the Yugoslav conflict throughout all the republics, although Slovenia and Montenegro presented the fewest problems in this respect. A most important factor further complicating the problem was that Serbia, which was both the largest and strongest of the republics, had an especially large national community, three million strong, outside its own territory. Thus the only hope of controlling the conflict itself was to maintain some political link among the different areas of the former Yugoslavia, or at least to establish conditions for a consensual and contextual separation of the different parts. The least expedient policy was to extract and separate specific parts of the problem, leaving the others on their own and neglecting the linkage effect of the scattered ethnic groups. As the issues and interests associated with the crisis multiplied, the EU tended increasingly to refer the other republics to general principles and general rules of international law without regard to the specific contextual situation.

Finally, most commentators do not seem to appreciate adequately the decisive value attributed by the contending parties to western European actions, in particular to recognition, and therefore the impact of those actions on the evolution of the conflict. Because of the controversial nature of secessionist action under international law, recognition of Croatia and Slovenia had and was intended to have what is called a "constitutive" effect. It formalized the existence of the state for purposes of international law.[74]

In the early phase of strong EU activism, however, the actions of the Community, the goals it set for itself, and the high expectations it had of influencing events, reflected the recent transformation of the structure of power on the European continent. Freed from the compelling security concerns of the cold war, the EU believed it could manifest its gravitational power as the most important, integrated economic pole on the continent. And if the Community had been conspicuously absent as a unitary actor in the recent Persian Gulf crisis, the Yugoslav crisis looked like an opportunity for letting that newly emerged power of western Europe cast its shadow on the continent. For in the absence of the zones of strategic interest dictated by the cold war, Yugoslavia seemed to be there for any willing influential country or international organization to take on.

Moreover, to some European capitals it seemed to offer the possibility of enhancing their power image and exerting political influence. France, in particular, saw the chance to counterbalance the increased weight of Germany by taking a leadership role in an institutional initiative. Coming soon after the end of the division of Europe and Germany, the early expressions of German support for the independence of Croatia and Slovenia provoked much concern in Paris about a possible "Teutonic bloc" emerging in central Europe.[75]

Finally, the western European willingness to take responsibility for the crisis suited the reluctance and difficulties other actors had in responding to it. In Washington, where the very glamor of the Gulf operation speeded up the profound transformation of the country's political priorities, a widespread attitude was that the conflict should be seen as a "European problem" for the EU and the CSCE to tackle.[76] In a series of speeches from 1989 on, U.S. leaders clearly defined the terms of a new arrangement with the western European allies, and in particular had assigned the allies the main responsibility for stability on the European continent. As mentioned above, a CSCE unable to take any operational decision was glad to leave the stage to the Community; and throughout 1991, at least, NATO maintained the same position, in part reflecting the U.S. reluctance to become involved with the issue.

In short, when the conflict broke out in June 1991, the EU took upon itself the task of dealing with it in response to a number of new pressures and in fulfillment of new internal and international expectations. But if the Yugoslav crisis presented a clear opportunity, the actual ability of the Community to bind together the will of its member states into a common foreign policy seems to have been too undeveloped for the task. And if the new post–cold war political environment created room to maneuver for a powerful collective actor such as the EU, so too did it provide opportunities for individual dominant states such as the new, united Germany.

The Drive to Recognize Croatia and Slovenia

Throughout the early period, support grew for the theory that "internationalization" of the conflict through recognition could ultimately bring it to an end. The only strong basis for the theory was that months of intense negotiations using different carrots and sticks produced no movement toward a stable solution of the problem. As already mentioned, German minister of foreign affairs Hans-Dietrich Genscher had threatened "preventive recognition" of the two republics as early as July. And, as Genscher noted again when the German position finally prevailed in mid-December, after months of diplomatic activity had failed to stem what he characterized as aggression by Serbia, it was now time to test alternative strategies.[77] It is true, of course, that any attempt to meet the desire of the Slovenes and Croats for independence through a consensual agreement for devolution of central power could always be frustrated by Serbia through the refusal to accept specific conditions.[78] It does not follow, however, that the separate recognition of Croatia and Slovenia was the only alternative. At that time,

Lord Carrington was still working on a possible confederal solution. Moreover, on December 20, in applying for recognition, the government of
Bosnia and Herzegovina still expressed its willingness to be part of a
possible new Yugoslav state.

But no one, neither international organization nor individual country,
was ready to act to impose a solution. Germany was particularly badly
placed in this regard because historical and constitutional constraints made
it impossible to participate in military operations against Serbia or even
give weapons to Bosnia and Herzegovina.

The decisive factor in the final political outcome was the steady and
determined German support for the recognition of Croatia and Slovenia. To be
sure, in the fall of 1991 frustration grew in proportion to the number of
cease-fires negotiated and abandoned, and to the repeated and failed attempts
to reach a peace agreement. But the recognition option was not devised as a
result of those failures and frustration. It developed independently, and it was
present from the very beginning. It was selectively directed at Croatia and
Slovenia. And from the start it had interfered to some extent with the attempt to
find an integrated solution to the conflict.[79] Germany simply developed a
policy of its own early on and grew increasingly determined to follow it no
matter what the position of its Community partners was. What was decisive
was not the merits of the policy, nor the confusion as to strategy and of lack of
determination on the part of the EU partners, but rather that the German leaders
were clearly more committed to that position than they were interested in
devising a collective position with the other Community partners.

The recognition policy had important roots in German domestic politics,
and it quickly gained the political center stage. De Michelis has stressed
recently, recalling the 1991 events, how "Bonn was compelled, solely for
domestic reasons, to take the path of a sped up recognition of Croatia and
Slovenia."[80] And those roots are also noted in the reconstructions of a
number of other observers.[81] German public opinion reacted strongly
against the level of violence and barbarity in the conflict, especially as EU
mediated cease-fires continued to be flouted. In the newly united Germany,
Croatians were the dominant group in the Yugoslav immigrant community
of 700,000. Part of the Social Democratic party (SPD) leadership was
lobbying for recognition of Croatia and Slovenia even before the two
republics declared independence. On July 1, 1991, echoing Chancellor
Kohl's statement on the same day, Christian Democratic Union (CDU)
party secretary general Volker Ruehe called on Germany and other Europeans to recognize the breakaway republics. "If we Germans think everything

in Europe can stay just the way it was, if we accept the status quo and do not recognize the right of self-determination of Slovenia and Croatia, then we have no moral or political credibility." He asked for the starting of a "movement in the EU to lead to such recognition," although then he warned that Germany could not act alone.[82]

The tide of recognition continued to rise inexorably in Germany throughout the fall months. John Newhouse quotes a German diplomat as saying that, although officials like himself were opposed to Germany going alone, all they could do was "dela[y] the decision quite a long time. . . from July to December."[83] Foreign Minister Hans-Dietrich Genscher, a Free Democrat, was concerned about moving in concert with the other European partners and about the possible repercussions of a recognition policy on the precarious Soviet situation. But he soon found himself under pressure from all directions and began to look at the internationalization of the conflict as an initiative that could stem what he saw as Serbian aggression.

Chancellor Kohl's boast that the December 16 Community decision allowing recognition of the individual republics was a "triumph" of German foreign policy, and, even more, Bonn's decision to move ahead with recognition before the date collectively set of January 15, are the final evidence, if evidence is needed, of German unilateralist disposition on this issue. Indeed, according to witnesses present at the December 16 meeting, Genscher made it clear that Bonn did not even consider itself bound by the finding of the Badinter Commission as to the applicants' compliance with EU mandated conditions for recognition.[84]

The German drive was not contained by any countervailing Community action. As noted above, the rhetoric of a European common foreign policy was not matched in the second half of 1991 by structures and mechanisms adequate to produce one. With the CFSP unable to compel the interests and will of the member states into a united policy, in the end they gave up the effort so as to be able to claim a unity of action that was in fact totally hollow. The so-called "compromise" reached in the December 16 meeting was simply an acceptance of the obligatory option of the recognition of Croatia and Slovenia. And at this point what was an institutional shortcoming turned into a much more serious problem of faulty political decision.

Only the Old Republics, and All the Republics

Two features characterize the December 16 decision: it selected the old republics of federal Yugoslavia, with the old borders as the only possible successor states to the SFRY; and it applied to all those republics the same set of criteria for recognition. Although the EU foreign ministers cast their action in terms of basic principles and rules of international law, it is hard to detect in their December decision any real possibility of contributing to bring the Yugoslav crisis under control.

As to the first point, the principle of the earlier collective EU policy of preserving the territorial integrity of the SFRY was now applied without discrimination to the individual republics, making their old borders the point of departure for defining the successor states. The U.S. administration moved along exactly the same line in early 1992 when it rushed the western Europeans into recognizing Bosnia and Herzegovina.[85] However, even accepting the de facto dissolution of the Federal Republic of Yugoslavia, it is hard to make a compelling legal or political case for the specific recognition of *all* the old republican borders as international borders.

The focus on the republican borders was not there from the beginning. Most of the early EU and CSCE statements were not specific when referring to "internal borders." The March 1991 Resolution of the European Parliament supported self-determination for both "constituent republics and autonomous provinces" of Yugoslavia.[86] In Resolution 713 the UN Security Council, always very cautious when approaching the matter of article 2(4,7) of the Charter, referred only to the unacceptability of "territorial gains or changes within Yugoslavia brought about by violence." And in September 1991 the CSCE declared that Kosovo had a right to self-determination, although it had never been a "republic" and its autonomous-province status had been revoked in 1990.

In addition, during the continuing effort to find an overall solution to the crisis, positions were taken, including a number of actual acts of self-determination, contradicting the notion that the old republics were the successor states. Thus Serbia's president Milosevic warned early on that the separation of parts of the old federal state could not be based on the old republican borders. In late September the Kosovo Parliament voted to declare independence and to hold a referendum. Again, in September, the Serbs of Croatian Krajina declared independence as soon as the Hague conference ended. In November the Bosnian Serbs stated their desire that Bosnia and Herzegovina remain within the Federal Republic and warned that, in case of secession, they would declare the independent Serbian Republic of Bosnia-Herzegovina. They actually did so on January 9. Even after the December 16 Community decision, Krajina and Kosovo applied for recognition together with the four republics. And, in applying for recognition, the Bosnian government itself stated that it was acting out of necessity and was willing to remain part of a federal state inclusive of both Serbia and Croatia.

The Arbitration Commission dealt with the issue of the republics as successor states and of the republican borders in a number of opinions. In its first opinion, of November 28, 1991, published on December 7, and the only one preceding the decision to recognize, it found that "the Socialist Federal Republic of Yugoslavia is in the process of dissolution." Consequently it found that the republics were now faced with "problems of state succession as may arise from this process."[87]

The second opinion, issued on January 11, 1992, clearly subordinated self-determination to the interest of safeguarding the territorial integrity of the republics. The question posed was "whether the Serbian population in Croatia and Bosnia-Herzegovina, as one of the constituent peoples of Yugoslavia, have the right to self-determination?" The Commission replied that, while international law does not spell out all the implications of the right to self-determination:

It is well established that, whatever the circumstances, the right to self-determination must not involve changes to existing frontiers at the time of independence (*uti possidetis juris*) except where the States concerned agree otherwise.

Where there are one or more groups within a state constituting one or more ethnic, religious or language communities, they have the right to recognition of their identity under international law.

The Serbian population of Bosnia-Herzegovina and Croatia must therefore be afforded every right accorded to minorities under international conventions as well as national and international guarantees consistent with the principles of international law.

In its third opinion, again issued on January 11, 1992, the Arbitration Commission replied directly to the question of whether the boundaries between Croatia and Serbia and between Bosnia-Herzegovina and Serbia could be regarded as international borders. It found that "once the process [of dissolution] in the SFRY leads to the creation of one or more independent States . . . the former boundaries become frontiers protected by international law," except when otherwise agreed. It based this finding on "the respect for the territorial status quo and, in particular, [on] the principle of *uti possidetis*," citing the International Court of Justice in *Burkina Faso* v. *Mali,* where it ruled that *uti possidetis* "is a general principle, which is logically connected with the phenomenon of the obtaining of independence, wherever it occurs. Its obvious purpose is to prevent the independence and stability of new states being endangered by fratricidal struggles."

Whatever the merit of the Badinter opinions as a matter of legal doctrine, for the purposes of this chapter it is relevant to note their overall consistency with the strong political pressure toward recognition of Croatia and Slovenia. Thus, for instance, after Croatia and Slovenia declared independence, the SFRY was unable to exercise control over its former territory. The Community, as early as November, and the Arbitration Commission on November 29 therefore drew the conclusion that "The Yugoslav Federal Republic no longer functions and the Federation itself, since 8 October, has been in the process of dissolution."[88] However, the same conclusion could have been reached for Croatia, since in October Zagreb had already lost control of more than 30 percent of the republic's territory,[89] and the Croatian government counted on an outside decision to legitimize its jurisdiction over the entire territory of the former Republic of Croatia.

The same can be said of the subordination of possible Serb "self-determination" to the territorial integrity of Bosnia-Herzegovina. The application of *uti possidetis* is problematic in light of the specific context of the post-1989 cases of state succession. The Serb population did not find itself scattered across colonial borders when an external colonial jurisdiction ended. Rather it was spread around a single sovereign state. And, as is discussed more extensively below, granting the Serbs "minority status" was a different matter in Croatia, with a Serbian population of 11.5 percent and a Croat population of 80 percent, than in Bosnia and Herzegovina, with a 31.5 percent Serbian and 43.8 percent Muslim population. Formally equal treatment was a poor reflection of reality.

As Marc Weller has noted, in charting its way between territorial integrity and the right to self-determination, the Arbitration Commission was trying to avoid a total disintegration of existing governmental structures and territorial definition. But when the Commission had to choose among different elements in what it defined as a "fluid" state of affairs, it opted for a way consistent with the direction in which the political decision of the EU countries was moving. Except for the first one, all the Commission's opinions were given after the decisive EU meeting of December 16, and the Commission was acting in a framework that was increasingly well defined politically and in which the decisions increasingly determined the path toward solidification of that early fluid state of affairs.[90]

The overwhelming influence of political factors is shown, above all, by the EU's disregard for the Badinter Commission's opinions when, in mid-

January 1992, it acted on recognition. The EU recognized Croatia, despite its failure to make the further constitutional amendments that the Commission had deemed necessary.[91] However, the Republic of Macedonia was not recognized, despite the Commission's favorable ruling on its eligibility. In particular, rejecting the views presented by Greece, the Commission found that Macedonia had "renounced all territorial claims of any kind in unambiguous statements binding in international law; that the use of the name 'Macedonia' cannot therefore imply any territorial claim against another State." However, apparently Bonn and Athens had agreed in December on mutual "back-scratching."[92] The value of the Arbitration Committee's work suffered no better a fate than the other nonbinding structures the partners created in the attempt to deal with the Yugoslav crisis.

Thus the EU decisions conformed to the general notion that recognition is more a political matter than one of legal doctrine. The focus on the republics derived from the origin of the issue in the Slovene search for independence, from Germany's domestic support for Croatian independence, and from the fact that, early on, the governments of those two republics necessarily became interlocutors of the western attempt to bring the crisis under control. Political choices were made on the basis of individual countrys' interests, rather than in response to general principles or with a view to keeping the whole crisis under control.

This brings us to the second point, the uniform treatment of all the components of the former Yugoslavia, regardless of specific circumstances. Because of the substantively different social and political character of the republics themselves, the decision to extend to all of them the same approach and basic rules, resulting in treating all six former republics identically as successor states, was in fact the cause of further problems.

The 1974 federal Constitution of Yugoslavia envisioned six republics and two autonomous provinces, Kosovo and Vojvodina, both parts of the Republic of Serbia. The 1990 revision of the Serbian Constitution abolished the administrative autonomy of the two provinces. All of these political entities differed in their history and ethnic composition, including the degree of ethnic integration. The Slovene government began to take steps toward independence in the mid-1980s. These steps were broadly supported within the republic, and it faced no challenges to its rule over the entire republican territory. In contrast, in Croatia 14 of 102 administrative districts had a Serbian majority. In areas such as Croatian Krajina the distribution of the Serbs was concentrated enough to make them contemplate regional autonomy, and they began to take steps in that direction as early as October 1990.

The principle of territorial integrity, although an easy answer for Slovenia, was thus problematic for Croatia. And it bore almost no relationship to the political reality that surfaced in Bosnia and Herzegovina as a consequence of the breakup of the federal state. The roots of Bosnia and Herzegovina as a distinctive political entity are not as deep and strong historically as those of other republics. Although the population was sufficiently integrated in the urban areas, it was still potentially separable into three communities, no one of which had an overwhelming majority. As noted above, the April 1991 census established that the population of Croatia was comprised of 43.8 percent "ethnic Muslims," 31.5 percent Serbs, and 17.3 percent Croats. In the runoff to the elections of 1990, Bosnian politics reorganized itself along ethnic lines. The existence of two strong republics acting as sponsors and protectors of the autonomy of the Serb and Croat communities made the creation of a unified political entity in Bosnia as unfeasible as was the survival of the Federal Republic in 1991. And the impossibility for this republic to survive outside a larger framework was clearly recognized, as indicated above, by the leadership of its different constituent groups on a number of occasions. In these circumstances, the territorial integrity of the old Bosnia and Herzegovina within its administrative borders was hardly imaginable, short of a massive international military intervention.[93] At the same time, the former province of Kosovo had, like Slovenia, an overwhelming majority composed of a single group (90 percent Albanian). However, since it had lost its autonomous status in 1990, according to the Community's approach, it was not eligible to be a successor state.

The twelve EU ministers who met on December 16, 1991, ignored these historical, social, and ethnic complexities. They regarded themselves as limited by two fixed points: the need to produce a "common policy" and the need to recognize Slovenia and Croatia within their old borders. They could not avoid the second point, if they wanted to satisfy the first, as long as they had no adequate mechanisms for imposing a less than unanimous will. Thus all they could do was to mask a selective political choice behind an appeal to general rights and principles of international law. It was, in other words, the need to recognize those two republics that molded their broader approach and the set of rules they established, not, as one would expect, the other way around. In the end they subordinated the Yugoslav reality to other needs, and so remained impotent before the problem.

The Tasks of the European Union and of the
International Community

The analysis in the previous pages has indicated that the EU's capabilities were inadequate in relation to the objectives that the organization set for itself and that it used those capabilities ineffectively. However, the potential influence of the organization, properly conceived, was and is enormous.

On the institutional side, it is important to remember that the crisis prevention and crisis management mechanisms available when the conflict broke out were mostly focused on cold war issues and antagonists. Yugoslavia's past position as a "gray area" between East and West, paradoxically, turned into a liability for the international community. Because it had not belonged to either of the two cold war military alliances, Yugoslavia was left out of the new regulatory framework of both the disarmament provisions and the confidence-building measures defined in the 1990 Treaty on Conventional Forces in Europe (CFE). Moreover, it benefited relatively little from the western political and economic investment in the normalization of relations on the European continent. It could not be included in the North Atlantic Cooperation Council, created in December 1991, because only former Warsaw Pact countries were eligible. The new European Bank for Reconstruction and Development did not start its operations until the Yugoslav crisis reached its most violent phase, in early summer 1991.[94]

In fact, to borrow a concept from Christopher Cviic's book *Remaking the Balkans,* the West was beset by increasing "Yugoweariness."[95] Yugoslavia was now of no strategic use for the West, and the costs of its special position of the past seemed increasingly unjustified in the new post–cold war context. Rather than appreciating the emerging threat, the West responded to it in the early phases with growing impatience. Yet, since the international community was in the end compelled to intervene, it is most important to understand the conditions of an effective intervention.

The first element that was missing—and amazingly is still missing to this day—was a clear, even if limited, approach to the problem. When the breakup of old states began in eastern Europe, nobody knew how to combine the right to self-determination with the need to avoid the total disintegration of governmental structures and related interstate relations. The main preoccupation in the mind of western leaders was the fragility of the Soviet state. And of course the position taken by western governments could not help but affect the evolution of the situation there, since some of the constituent republics aspired to separate from their old association in the expectation of joining a new one.

From the beginning of the Yugoslav political and constitutional crisis, the only approach taken was support for the territorial integrity of the federal state. When that proved unfeasible, the territorial integrity criterion was unthinkingly applied, as discussed above, to the old republics, disregarding that politics in the federal state had structured itself around ethnic lines and only in part coincided with the territorial subdivisions. In other words, the strategy the West selected focused solely on the territorial factor and identified self-determination with the integrity of the republican territories. In this way it strengthened the position of those political elites that made territory, and war over territory, the issue. Also to the extent that the recognition of Croatia meant support for Croat rights without regard to democratic guarantees, it strengthened and even encouraged revisionist claims on parts of Bosnia and Herzegovina that threatened the very existence of the state. In contrast, an approach that focused on individual and human rights, procedures, and rules of the game would have deemphasized the value of territory and the legitimacy of those ethnically based political elites.

A second striking feature of EU member states' response in the second half of 1991 is that they tried to do everything by themselves, although a wide array of instruments and massive intervention was obviously required. The second half of Jacques Poos's declaration is as revealing as the first half. "This is the hour of Europe; *it is not the hour of the Americans.*" But if he meant to suggest that Yugoslavia was Europe's "Gulf," he was drawing a farfetched parallel indeed. Whatever the state of exaltation created by the end of the division of the continent, the countries of Europe had little tradition of looking beyond the defense of their own territory. In fact they had grown accustomed to relying on the United States, an outside power, for their own stability and the defense of their own interests.

Instead of pooling capabilities with other actors and creating the critical mass necessary for dealing with such a complex issue, the western Europeans used Yugoslavia to gratify their vanity. And Washington was glad to oblige. NATO, the only capable collective military structure available, was kept away from the stage because Paris wanted it to be an all-European act. Thus it was not used in the early phases of the armed conflict when its intervention might have made a difference.

Even when considered by itself, the Community had plenty of capability and influence to use in the Yugoslav crisis, but its specific capabilities seem more suited to the earlier phases of a crisis, before "hard," especially military, instrumentation became necessary. In the Yugoslav context, the pre-June 1991 phase was the most appropriate one for a massive nonmilitary western European intervention to disperse the gathering clouds. There were plenty of warnings. In the second half of the 1980s Slovenia directed a number of acts of defiance at federal institutions. There were increasing manifestations of Serbian arrogance. The Croatian constitution was revised in mid-1990, in effect demoting the non-Croat residents of the republic to the status of minorities. The economic power of the EU would have been much more influential in that early phase, against precisely circumscribed objectives. In that phase it could have been used much more as a carrot, offering economic rewards for good behavior. Had its response taken this path, the Community might have influenced then the very character of the dispute.

In the absence of a broader strategy and power instruments, the EU mostly wielded the stick of economic sanctions at a time when the stakes were already too high to deal with the crisis. This belated approach meant that the EU intervention had to contend with the most extremist groups, rather than interacting with the broader range of political interests represented in the population at large before the bloodshed narrowed everybody's options. And, in dealing with the extremist groups as the parties in conflict, the western Europeans in effect legitimized and strengthened their position.

From the institutional perspective, the EU is better equipped to act collectively in deploying economic instruments. As its actions in the second half of 1991 indicate, the EU has had great difficulty in trying to act as a unitary political actor once the anticipatory phase of a crisis had passed. The political pressures of the hot conflict tended to diversify the responses. Old national policies were bound to reemerge, although in more limited guise, in the absence of the compelling security discipline of the cold war and the special global-power role of the United States.

As the issues of a crisis grew in complexity, the scale of the intervention required increased, and the range of necessary instruments broadened. It was a mistake to expect the EU to play the role of a regional power, implying, among other things, a sphere of influence of its own. Instead, its specific capabilities should have been deployed in a context of a more advanced global strategy of shared responsibility and complementary use of the competencies and capabilities of different international institutions.

The lesson of the EU involvement in the Yugoslav crisis, then, is the importance of early preventive action. In a world that needs long-term strategies for stability, the capabilities of the EU are enormously relevant. But the attempt to use them without careful attention to the limitations outlined above is a dangerous illusion that could recapitulate the failures and tragedies of western Europe's efforts to deal with the Yugoslav conflict in the fall of 1991.

Notes

1. Alan Riding, "Europeans Send High-Level Team: 'The Hour of Europe,'" *New York Times,* June 29, 1991, p. 4. Jacques Poos spoke to the press on leaving for the first EC ministerial mission to stop the war in Yugoslavia on June 28.

2. The events discussed in this chapter span the period of the conversion of the European Community to the European Union under the Treaty of Maastricht. The Treaty establishing the Union was signed on December 11, 1991, and came into force on November 1, 1993. EU is used throughout the text, with the understanding that it refers to the EC before November 1, 1993.

3. See, for instance, the Communiqué of the Berlin meeting, June 19–20, 1994.

4. Judy Dempsey, "Yugoslavian Government Seeks $4 bn Boost," *Financial Times,* June 3, 1991, p. 2.

5. For an overview of Yugoslavia's economic relations with western Europe, see Susan L. Woodward, *Balkan Tragedy: Chaos and Dissolution after the Cold War* (Brookings, 1995), and Christopher Cviic, *Remaking the Balkans* (London: Royal Institute of International Affairs, and New York: Council on Foreign Relations Press, 1991).

6. The most informed accounts of the EC response to the crisis in the former Yugoslavia are Jonathan Eyal, *Europe and Yugoslavia: Lessons from a Failure* (London: Royal United Services Institute for Defence Studies, 1993), and Marc Weller, "The International Response to the Dissolution of the Socialist Federal Republic of Yugoslavia," *American Journal of International Law,* vol. 86, no. 3 (July 1992), pp.569–607. For additional information and analysis, see also Woodward, *Balkan Tragedy;* Henry Wynaendts, *L'engrenage: Croniques yougoslaves, juillet 1991-août 1992* (Paris: Editions Denoel, 1993); John Zametica, *The Yugoslav Conflict,* Adelphi Papers 270 (London: Brassey's for the International Institute of Strategic Studies, Summer 1992); James Gow and James D. D. Smith, *Peace-making, Peace-keeping: European Security and the Yugoslav Wars,* London Defense Studies 1992 (London: Center for Defence Studies, Brassey's, 1992); John Newhouse, "The Diplomatic Roundup: Dodging the Problem," *New Yorker,* August 24, 1992; James B. Steinberg, "International Involvement in the Yugoslavia Conflict," in Lori Fisler Damrosch, ed., *Enforcing Restraint: Collective Intervention in Internal Conflicts* (New York: Council on Foreign Relations Press, 1993); Gabriel Munuera, *Preventing Armed Conflict in Europe: Lessons from Recent Experience,* Chaillot Papers 15–16 (Paris: Institute for Security Studies, WEU, June 1994).

7. *Europe,* no. 1725, May 27–28, 1991.

8. U.S. Embassies, *Wireless File,* "Baker Confers with Yugoslav Leaders," June 24, 1991.

9. Alan Riding, "Europeans War on Yugoslav Split," *New York Times,* June 26, 1991.

10. European Parliament Resolution on Yugoslavia, March 13, 1991. Among other initiatives of the U.S. Congress were the Nickles Amendment attached to the Foreign Appropriations Act of late 1990, dealing with human rights, and the Rohrbacher Amendment to the Direct Aid to Democracies Bill in 1991, dealing with aid to Slovenia and Croatia.

11. David Gardner, "Commission Ties Strings on EC Aid," *Financial Times,* March 20, 1991, p. 2.

12. Gianni De Michelis, "Così cercammo di impedire la guerra," *Limes* (Rome, 1994), no. 1, p. 231.

13. Brioni agreements in Europe Documents, no. 1725, July 16, 1991.

14. This mechanism of cooperation among the Community members is discussed in more detail in the next section.

15. EPC Declaration, EPC Press Release (September 4, 1991).

16. On the Serbian cold attitude toward the EC intervention after June 1991 see Wynaendts, *L'engrenage: Croniques yougoslaves,* pp. 58, 67.

17. Alain Pellet, "Note sur la Commission d'arbitrage de la Conférence européenne pour la paix en Yougoslavie," *Annuaire français de droit international,* vol. 37 (1991), pp. 329–45.

18. Weller, "The International Response," p. 575.

19. See Eyal, *Europe and Yugoslavia,* pp. 32–33.

20. See Weller, "The International Response," p. 575.

21. See ibid., pp. 581 and 583.

22. UN Document S/23169 (1991).

23. See Weller, "The International Response," p. 583.

24. French president François Mitterand had also obtained from German chancellor Helmut Kohl the promise that any recognition would have been acted upon only by the twelve together. See Newhouse, "The Diplomatic Roundup," p. 63.

25. For the record of this frustrating story, see Gow and Smith, *Peace-making.*

26. Michael Wise and Sarah Helm, "New-look CSCE's First Test," *The Independent,* June 28, 1991, p. 13.

27. UN Document S/PV.3009.

28. On this see Weller, "The International Response," p. 572.

29. *International Legal Materials,* vol. 31, no. 6 (November 1992), p. 1494–1500.

30. Cited in Weller, "The International Response," p. 586, no. 115. On the emerging German position, see also David Binder, "Some Western Nations Split Off on Yugoslavia," *New York Times,* July 2, 1991.

31. See Newhouse, "The Diplomatic Roundup," p. 63.

32. John Tagliabue, "Germany Sets Fast Pace on Recognition," *International Herald Tribune,* December 18, 1991.

33. David Binder, "U.N. Fights Bonn's Embrace of Croats," *New York Times,* December 14, 1991. Paul Lewis, "U.N. Yields to Plans by Germany to Recognize Yugoslav Republics," *New York Times,* December 16, 1991.

34. On Bonn's determination see, for instance, De Michelis, "Così cercammo," p. 234.

35. Lewis, "U.N. Yields to Plans by Germany." A strong difference with Washington with regard to military observers to deploy in Yugoslavia apparently was also another reason for the French and British giving up their original positions. The *International Herald Tribune,* with wide circulation in European capitals but mostly based on the *New York Times's* and *Washington Post's* services, did not reproduce the well-informed and names-naming Lewis article and gave only a compilation of agency dispatches about the Security Council debate.

36. De Michelis, "Così cercammo," p. 233. If somewhat uncertain in their edited form, the statements and revelations of this interview have not been disavowed by De Michelis.

37. Heinz-Jüergen Axt, "Hat Genscher Jugoslawien entzweit? Mythen und Fakten zur Aussenpolitik des vereinten Deutschlands," *Europ Archiv,* vol. 48, (June 25, 1993), pp. 351–52.

38. Besides the newspaper accounts, see De Michelis, "Così cercammo," pp. 234–35, and Wynaendts, *Croniques yougoslaves,* pp. 149–52.

39. De Michelis, "Così cercammo," p. 234.

40. EPC Press Release, December 15, 1991.

41. See Weller, "The International Response," p. 588.

42. John Tagliabue, "Kohl to Compromise on Yugoslavia," *New York Times,* December 18, 1991, p. A3.

43. Cited in Stephen Kinzer, "Europe, Backing Germans, Accepts Yugoslav Breakup," *New York Times,* January 16, 1992.

44. Steve Vogel, "Germany Recognizing New States: Slovenia, Croatia Must Accept Terms," *Washington Post,* December 20, 1991, p. A39.

45. John Tagliabue, "The New and Bolder Germany: No Longer a Political Dwarf," *International Herald Tribune,* December 18, 1991, p. 2.

46. Cited in Kinzer, "Europe, Backing Germans."

47. Axt, "Hat Genscher Jugoslawien entzweit?"

48. Among other developments, the resignation on December 20, 1991, of the federal government's prime minister, Ante Markovic, a Croat and for long the preferred interlocutor of the western Europeans, completed the Serbian takeover of the national government.

49. On the warnings given the EC by the other republics about the consequences of the recognition of Croatia and Slovenia, see, besides the Izetbegovic letter to Genscher, Wynaendts, *Croniques yougoslaves,* p. 54.

50. See P. Clesson and T. Findlay, "Case studies on Peacekeeping: UNOSOM II, UNTAC and UNPROFOR," SIPRI, *SIPRI Yearbook* (Oxford University Press, 1994), pp. 62–80, and M. Zucconi, "The Former Yugoslavia: Lesson of War and Diplomacy," SIPRI, *SIPRI Yearbook* (Oxford University Press, 1995), pp. 211–29.

51. Text in *Review of International Affairs* (Belgrade), April 1, 1992.

52. EPC statement on Bosnia and Herzegovina, April 16, 1992.

53. David Binder, "U.S. Recognizes 3 Yugoslav Republics as Interdependent," *New York Times,* April 8, 1992.

54. Security Council Resolution 757 also rejected for the first time Serbia's and Montenegro's claim to be the successors to the SFRY. The EC stated this position as its own on July 20.

55. The UN General Assembly adopted the Security Council recommendation with its Resolution 47/1.

56. UN Secretary-General, Letter to the UN Security Council of July 17, 1992.

57. "Barrage of Words," *Economist,* August 29, 1992, p. 18.

58. On this see Eyal, "Europe and Yugoslavia," pp. 61–62.

59. William Drozdiak, "EC Rejects Bosnian Appeal on Arms Ban," *International Herald Tribune,* June 22, 1993.

60. "Direr and Emptier," *Economist,* June 26, 1993, p. 55.

61. Elaine Sciolino, "Arm Bosnians? Clinton Didn't Mean It," *New York Times,* June 23, 1993. In considering the possible relevance of the lifting of the arms embargo on Bosnia, it is worth recalling that on September 25, 1991, among those asking the UN to impose a complete embargo on all the republics was the Federal Republic of Yugoslavia itself.

62. On Lord Owen, see Michael R. Gordon, "Leading NATO in Bosnia," *New York Times,* August 3, 1993, and David B. Ottaway, *International Herald Tribune,* August 3, 1993, p. 6. On Clinton, see Thomas L. Freedman, "Clinton Rebuffs Bosnian Leader in Pleas for Help," *New York Times,* September 11, 1993, p. A1.

63. *Nouvelles Atlantiques,* vol. 28, (January 22, 1994), p. 1.

64. From interviews with EU Commission officials.

65. *Nouvelles Atlantiques,* vol. 28, (May 18, 1994), p. 2.

66. See, among the most recent ones, Eyal, *Europe and Yugoslavia,* especially the Conclusions.

67. James B. Steinberg, "The Response of International Institutions to the Yugoslavia Conflict: Implications and Lessons," in Steven Larrabee, *Europe's Volatile Powder Keg: Balkan Security after the Cold War* (RAND Corp., 1994).

68. Interview with EC Commission officials.

69. For instance, then Italian foreign minister De Michelis offered an inventory of these innovations to define the EC's successes, in an interview in *La Repubblica* (Rome), October 27–28, 1991. Like other policymakers of that time, he has maintained the same position in later articles and interviews. Another response to the charge of failure comes from those who believe that, in fact, an important success of western Europe was, according to Douglas Hurd, that the "Europeans have avoided the disastrous rivalry of the western powers in the Balkans which caused such harm in the first years of this century." See D. Hurd, "Developing the Common Foreign and Security Policy," *International Affairs,* vol. 70, no. 3 (July 1994), p. 424. See also Roland Dumas (French foreign minister in 1991), in *Liberation,* December 6, 1991, pp. 17–18. But, while this thesis at best relies on the success of the EU as integrative structure rather than explaining its ability or inability to create stable policies around it, it also skirts the fact that there were expectations by the international community and the EU itself that it could do what it will not succeed in doing.

70. Treaty on the European Union, Articles J.3 and J.4.

71. Hurd, "Developing the Common Foreign and Security Policy," vol. 70, no. 3, p. 422.

72. CFSP refers to "the eventual framing of a common defense policy, which might in time lead to a common defense."

73. On an early occasion, in response to some perplexity among his colleagues about how to proceed, De Michelis reportedly invited the Troika to go on his plane. From interviews with EU Commission officials.

74. For a concise discussion of the legal effects of state recognition, see Michael Akehurst, *A Modern Introduction to International Law,* 6th ed. (London: Routledge, 1992), pp. 59–61.

75. William Drozdiak, "Crisis Cleaves EC," *International Herald Tribune,* July 5, 1991, p. 1.

76. David Buchan, Lionel Barber, and David White, "Yugoslav Crisis Thrusts EC into Role of Mediator," *Financial Times,* June 29–30, 1991, p. 3.

77. John Tagliabue, "European Ties for Slovenia and Croatia," *New York Times,* December 18, 1991.

78. Such criticism of the Carrington Plan is offered, among others, by Weller, "The International Response," pp. 586–87.

79. On the inflexibility of the Croatian president, Franjo Tudjiman, in the face of what he perceived as support from western Europeans, see Wynaendts, *Croniques yougoslaves,* chapter 9.

80. De Michelis, "Così cercammo," p. 233 (emphasis in text).

81. See Newhouse, "The Diplomatic Roundup."

82. Stephen Kinzer, "Kohl Warns Belgrade on Action in Slovenia," *International Herald Tribune,* July 2, 1991, p. 3.

83. Newhouse, "The Diplomatic Roundup," p. 64.

84. Tagliabue, "Germany Sets Fast Pace."

85. See Robert W. Tucker and David C. Hendrickson, "America and Bosnia," *The National Interest,* vol. 33 (Fall 1993), especially pp. 18–19.

86. European Parliament Resolution on Yugoslavia, March 13, 1991, clause 8.

87. The text of the three opinions cited can be found in *International Legal Materials,* vol. 31, no. 6 (1992), pp. 1494–1500.

88. "Decision relative à la suspension des accords entre la Communauté européenne, ses Etats membres et la Yugoslavie," cited in Weller, *The Internatoinal Response,* cit. pp. 582–83. The Slovene and Croatian decision created a new situation also according to UN representative Cyrus Vance, as he recognized in his report at the end of October to the UN secretary-general. UN Document S/23169.

89. It was not temporary loss of control, as some regions to this date remain outside Zagreb's (and the UN's) control, and in some cases they were, from the beginning, areas with large majorities of Serbian population. The areas are Croatian Krajina, Osijek, and Vukovar, parts of eastern and western Slavonia, and the region of Nova Gridiska and Novska. The issue cannot be eliminated simply by stating that it was a case of external aggression (also in part factually wrong), as does Weller, "The International Response," p. 604.

90. In four opinions (numbers 4 to 7, all issued on January 11, 1992), dealing with the application for international recognition submitted by four constituent republics of the SFRY, the Commission simply verified the existence of the conditions for recognition as spelled in the "Declaration on Yugoslavia" and the "Declaration on the Guidelines on the Recognition of New States in Eastern Europe and in the Soviet Union," issued by the EC on December 16, 1991.

91. In July 1992 the Commission eventually ruled that amendments introduced in May 1992 into the Croatian Constitution were satisfactory. For the text of Opinions 4–7, dealing with the request for recognition of the republics of Bosnia

and Herzegovina, of Croatia, of Slovenia, and of Macedonia, see *International Legal Materials,* vol. 31, no. 6 (November 1992), pp. 1501–02.

92. Axt, "Hat Genscher Jugoslawien entzweit?" p. 325.

93. Instead, in March 1992 Washington urged the recognition of this republic, using the same "prevention" argument that Bonn had used in the case of Croatia.

94. In the framework of the CFE Treaty, negotiations were to be initiated. Such negotiations never took place.

95. Cviic, *Remaking the Balkans,* p. 61.

Part Three

Can International Financial Institutions Prevent Internal Violence? The Sources of Ethno-National Conflict in Transitional Societies

Wolfgang H. Reinicke

THIS CHAPTER considers the potential contribution of international financial institutions (IFIs) to the prevention of ethno-national conflict. There are two reasons for such an examination. First, the unprecedented socioeconomic and political transformation of the former East bloc may force the international community to adopt new and innovative strategies to cope with that challenge. Among these, a shift in the approach of IFIs when getting involved in the domestic affairs of one of their new members from the countries of eastern and central Europe (ECE) and the former Soviet Union (FSU) should not be excluded a priori. Second, unlike large-scale interstate conflict, the origins and sources of ethno-national conflict as well as the efforts to prevent its outbreak point in the direction of international organizations whose purpose is not (or at least not exclusively) to intervene in armed conflict but to ensure that disputes, including those involving ethnic groups, can be resolved by addressing them at an early stage and by other than violent means.

The author is grateful to David Germroth, Jennifer Mitchell, James Schoff, and Sylke von Storck for their assistance in preparing this chapter.

Besides the obvious need to alleviate human suffering and deprivation, an inquiry into the role that IFIs could play in this process is also warranted because of the enormous financial costs that occur to these institutions once conflict breaks out. First, IFIs are usually asked to assist in the reconstruction of a country that has been embroiled in conflict, be it of an ethnic or other nature. The costs of these efforts could have been avoided had the prevention of armed conflict been successful. Second, most IFI programs in countries that are involved in conflict are likely to experience severe setbacks, if not outright destruction, as a result of armed conflict. From an efficiency and management perspective it would therefore appear rational for IFIs to do everything possible within and outside their organization to ensure the sustainability of their efforts to support the process of system transformation in ECE countries and the new republics of the FSU, or any society that is undergoing rapid and fundamental change due to internal and external developments. The fact that by the time Yugoslavia disintegrated in late 1992 it had become the sixth largest user of funds of the International Monetary Fund (IMF) and that the World Bank had lent a cumulative total of more than $6 billion before the outbreak of hostilities illustrates that point.[1]

While both antagonists and champions of IFIs have used the accusation of institutional rigidity and conservatism to support their case—the former by pressing for more rapid change, the latter by insisting on the status quo—a review of the institutional history of both organizations over five decades reveals some flexibility in responding to the need to adjust their mandates and goals and in some cases even their charters. During the past decade IFIs have had to contend with what were initially considered competing goals, such as responding to the rising threat, locally and globally, of environmental pollution, natural resource depletion, and population growth while at the same time promoting economic development. These and other more recent goals, such as poverty reduction and good governance, have been internalized by now in the agenda of the IFIs and continue to change the institutions' positions and policies on economic adjustment and development.

However, considerable debate remains among industrialized and between industrialized and developing member countries, as well as among officials within both institutions, about the degree to which the Bank and the Fund should revise their definition of economic development and fully internalize some or all of the factors mentioned above. In the wake of the end of the bipolar world and the developments in the world political economy over the last decade, both of which have been no less than dramatic and revolutionary, this debate has only intensified and further raised doubts about the ability of IFIs to respond to the rapidly changing global environment.

Linking IFIs and the prevention of ethno-national conflict requires: first, a delineation of the mandates and goals of the institutions; second, the identification of the causes of the conflicts; third, an analysis of the degree to which causes and remedies overlap; and fourth (if they do), the development of a set of policy responses that promotes the prevention of ethno-national conflict. This chapter is organized around these four themes and will demonstrate that many of the sources associated with internal violence do not originate in primordial ethnic tensions but are located elsewhere, increasing the need for a preventive strategy.

Before proceeding with the analysis, however, two caveats are in order: first, this analysis should be considered exploratory and preliminary in nature. Linking ethno-national conflict and the mandates and activities of IFIs combines two very large topics for which there is no actual precedent. Therefore, the policy responses that are discussed below require further and more detailed elaboration which lies beyond the scope of this chapter.

Second, ethno-nationalism, in particular ethnic conflict, is an extremely sensitive issue in international politics, not the least because it challenges to varying degrees at least one central form of social organization that societies have relied upon and that continues to represent the fundamental basis for the international system—the nation-state. Thus, despite the fact that there are good reasons to examine the relationship between IFIs and ethnic conflict, such an examination must keep today's limited political mandate of the IFIs in mind (notwithstanding the fact that this could change in the future).

The IFIs: Structure, Instruments, and Purpose

For the purposes of this study, the World Bank and the International Monetary Fund are considered representative of IFIs. This choice is driven not only by their important leadership roles among IFIs in general but also by their extensive involvement in the process of system transformation in ECE and the FSU.[2] Indeed, considering that most countries of the former East bloc were not even members before 1990, today's IFI engagement in the region is striking, not the least when compared to their activities in other regions of the world. Lending by the IMF to the former East bloc countries increased from 13 percent of Fund disbursements in 1989 to 55 percent in 1994.[3] The primary vehicle for these funds has been the Systemic Transformation Facility, against which eighteen states had drawn about $4.9 billion by the end of 1994.[4] The World Bank, too, has shifted its resources to meet the challenges of system transformation in the former East bloc, with the International Bank for Reconstruction and Development (IBRD) channeling almost a quarter of its lending to this area in 1994 (up from a level of only 8.1 percent in 1989).[5]

When the World Bank and IMF took up their work in 1947, their goals, mandates, and policy instruments reflected a compromise struck during the Bretton Woods negotiations of two fundamentally different approaches to managing the international economy.[6] The World Bank was given the immediate mission of helping rebuild the war-torn nations of Europe as well as a "second primary duty," as Lord Keynes put it, "to develop the resources and productive capacity of the world, with special reference to the less developed countries."[7] The basic task assigned to the IMF was to discourage nationalistic monetary policies and manage a fund to promote exchange stability and protect against countries' balance of payments problems.

The fiftieth anniversary of these two institutions has become an occasion to reevaluate their roles and missions. Without doubt the IMF and World Bank have changed a great deal from their original design. Indeed, as one participant of Bretton Woods recently noted, "there is little resemblance between the present functions and operations of the Fund and Bank and the way they were conceived at Bretton Woods."[8] This is particularly evident when one looks at some of the powers and prerogatives some sought to give these institutions in the 1940s but that were rejected in the context of the negotiations at Bretton Woods. For example, Harry Dexter White's original plan contained provisions that would give the International Stabilization Fund (later the IMF) the power to disapprove of a "monetary or banking or price measure or policy" that would cause serious disequilibrium in the balance of payments of a member, or the power to approve or disapprove any changes in exchange rates governing transactions among member countries.[9] The Bank was to become involved in the political sphere of members by requiring that they subscribe to a "magna carta of the United Nations," that would protect human rights and freedoms.[10] It was also proposed separately that the Bank should be able to lend directly to the private sector, without a government guarantee.[11]

A brief examination of the Articles of Agreement of both institutions leads to the conclusion that these proposals were rejected at the time. Yet, as will be shown further below, most of these activities or powers and a substantial number of other policy goals and mandates have become an integral part of IFI activities today, indicating that a considerable reorientation of policy goals and instruments has taken place. In most cases this was done by broadening or even redefining such basic themes as "development" or "growth and stability," in some instances by amending the IFI's charter. In retrospect this should not be too surprising. Not only has the international political economy undergone many important changes (and continues to do so), but both the Fund and in particular the Bank, at times somewhat reluctantly, have responded to critics within and outside the institutions calling for reorientation of their policies.[12]

It remains to be seen whether IFIs can keep pace with the dramatic changes that have taken place in the international political economy during the last decade. These changes should be seen in the context of not only the end of the bipolar order, but also the globalization of the world economy and the resulting political and social challenges.

Membership and Operations

THE WORLD BANK. The World Bank originated as one institution with a simple organizational structure to reflect its relatively clear-cut mission. It encouraged all countries to join, but decisionmaking was heavily weighted in favor of the most economically powerful nations, most notably the United States. This is because each member of the Bank has 250 votes plus one additional vote for each $100,000 share of capital stock. By the end of 1993, the ten richest (as measured by per capita GNP) industrialized countries continued to control an absolute majority (52 percent) of the votes. (The U.S. vote in the Bank originally counted for 36 percent of total votes, though it had declined to 17.4 percent by 1993.) Except for certain designated exceptions, all matters before the Bank are decided by a majority of votes cast.

Under the Articles of Agreement, membership in the IMF is a prerequisite for admission to membership in the Bank. Consequently Bank and IMF membership has been virtually identical. In the IMF, membership is open to every state that "controls its foreign relations" and is able to fulfill the obligations set forth in the Articles of Agreement.[13] Members can leave the organization whenever they wish, and indeed some countries (Cuba, Poland, Indonesia, and others) have done so in the past.

The Bank had forty-four members when it commenced operations. Its most important decisionmaking organs consist of the following: the president, the Board of Governors, and the executive directors.[14] By 1954 the Bank had fifty-five members, 16 executive directors (up from 12 in 1944), and the staff numbered 434 persons of thirty-one different nationalities. As of fiscal year 1994 there were 178 members, 24 executive directors, and approximately 10,000 staff members.

The Bank began with a very simple organizational structure. By 1954 the Bank was divided into five operational departments, including three that were regionally focused: Asia and the Middle East; Europe, Africa, and Australia; and the western hemisphere.[15] In addition, there was a Department of Technical Operations, which assessed the merits of both projects proposed to the Bank and ongoing projects. There was also an economic staff, a technical assistance and liaison staff, a treasurer's department (to execute financial procedures), and various administrative offices.

Any member that failed to meet its obligations could be suspended by decision of a majority of the governors (and a majority of the total voting power). This was the case with Czechoslovakia in 1953, when its request for a second postponement of payment was rejected by the executive directors in 1951 and the country refused to make payments. The Board of Governors then voted to suspend Czechoslovakia and threatened the country with expulsion. Czechoslovakia subsequently left the institution in 1954.[16]

The executive directors must approve every loan and major policy of the Bank. Any action to change the Articles of Agreement requires the approval of at least three-fifths of the members and 85 percent of the total voting shares (originally only 65 percent of the total votes were required to amend the charter; the "85 percent rule" was introduced in 1989 and effectively maintains the U.S. ability to veto any proposed amendment).[17]

The Bank is funded in small part by members' paid-in capital. The Bank originally intended to promote lending by guaranteeing securities issued by other institutions, but investors were more interested in buying securities issued directly by the Bank. This is how the Bank now funds the majority of its projects.

In procedural terms the so-called project cycle is the principal instrument of the Bank. It consists of six stages through which a project has to pass before approval: identification; preparation; appraisal; negotiation and board preparation; implementation and supervision; and evaluation.[18]

(1) Identification: A project can be proposed by the member governments themselves or be recommended by Bank officials, UN agencies, or nongovernmental organizations (NGOs). In this first phase, planners an-

swer questions such as: Who will benefit from the project? What are the costs involved? Are there other solutions to the same challenge? The project is also compared to other national or regional programs to determine priorities.

(2) Preparation: This is primarily the responsibility of the borrower, after the bank and member government have agreed on the objectives. Technical, economic, financial, social, and institutional aspects of the project are readied, and a timetable is established. The borrower prepares the plan with Bank oversight and help.

(3) Appraisal: The Bank makes its own independent assessment of the project. This includes "on-site appraisal missions." Assessment teams look at the technical, institutional, economic, and financial aspects of a project in detail.

(4) Negotiation and board presentation: The Bank's appraisal report forms the basis for negotiation with the borrower over terms and conditions. After give-and-take negotiations, all decisions and related reports and materials are submitted for approval.

(5) Implementation and Supervision: Once the loan is approved, funds become available. Project implementation is the responsibility of the borrower, as is procurement. The Bank supervises implementation and ensures that the project is proceeding as agreed.

(6) Evaluation: An independent department within the World Bank, the Operations Evaluation Department, is responsible for assessing project results. It reports directly to the executive directors and the Bank's president. It recommends means of improving performance in the future.

THE IMF. The Fund commenced financial operations on March 1, 1947. Bretton Woods delegates created the IMF to guard against the failure of the international payments system, hoping to prevent another calamity such as happened in the 1930s, when international trade and prices collapsed and a global economic depression ensued.[19] The IMF was given three main functions: "1) to administer a code of conduct with respect to exchange rate policies, payments associated with current account transactions, and convertability of currencies; 2) to provide members with financial resources to enable them to observe the code of conduct while correcting or avoiding payments imbalances; and 3) to provide a forum in which members could consult with each other and collaborate on international monetary matters."[20]

The Fund started operations with forty-four member countries. Four nations, including the Soviet Union, took part in the negotiations but did not sign the final agreement. As of the end of fiscal year 1994, the IMF had 178 members. Eligibility for membership is similar to that for the World Bank. Today the IMF has a staff of about two thousand, small when compared to the World Bank but much larger than the one hundred people working at the Fund in 1947.

The IMF Board of Governors is the senior decisionmaking body. Each member country appoints one governor (usually the minister of finance or central bank governor) and an alternate to the Board, which meets about once each year. Admission of new members, determination of quotas, and the allocation of special drawing rights (SDRs) can be executed only by the Board of Governors. All other powers, however, have been delegated to the Executive Board. The Executive Board is responsible for conducting the day-to-day business of the Fund and consists of the executive directors together with the managing director, who is its chairman. The members with the five largest quotas in the Fund (the United States, Germany, Japan, France, and the United Kingdom) each appoint an executive director. Nineteen other executive directors are elected by the remaining members.

Each IMF member has a quota which is expressed in SDRs. A member's quota determines its subscription to the Fund and its share allocations. It also affects the member's voting power and maximum access to the Fund's resources. The Board of Governors periodically reviews members' quotas and may propose certain adjustments. Voting power in the IMF is weighted as in the Bank. Each country has a basic allotment of 250 votes. In addition, it has one vote for each part of its quota that is equivalent to SDR 100,000. In the beginning, the United States and the United Kingdom together accounted for almost 45 percent of all IMF votes. As more countries joined, however, the proportional share of the U.S. and U.K contribution declined, and voting strength was more evenly distributed among the top five or six donors. Today the U.S. and U.K. share has shrunk to a little more than 22 percent. Still, the five largest members (the United States, Germany, Japan, France, and the United Kingdom) hold nearly 40 percent of the votes. Voting strength ranges from about 265,000 votes for the United States to just 290 votes for the republic of Kiribati.

The IMF is required to oversee both the international monetary system, in order to ensure its effective operation, and the observance by each member of its obligations. To accomplish this, the Fund exercises so-called surveillance over the exchange rate policies of members, who are required to provide the necessary information. The Fund has regular consultations with member countries to collect data and discuss domestic policies. The information enables the Fund to give prompt consideration to requests for use of its resources and thus gives members an incentive to cooperate fully with the IMF. The Fund may also provide the member country with advice and technical support to help identify emerging problems and implement corrective policies.

The main sources of the Fund's general resources are (1) subscriptions (quota payments by members) and (2) borrowing (from members at market-related interest rates). The Fund usually provides financial assistance to members by selling currencies or SDRs to them in exchange for their own currencies. For example, in the case of so-called Reserve and Credit Drawings, members may draw upon IMF reserves temporarily to solve balance of payment problems, provided they demonstrate reasonable efforts to overcome their difficulties. There are no performance criteria, and repurchases are made in three and one-half to five years. For Fund-administered facilities, however, assistance is available in the form of loans or grants. The Extended Facility, for example, is available when balance of payments difficulties are the result of structural factors such as production and trading patterns and might require more time to correct. In exchange for undertaking policies to promote stable growth, the IMF will extend its resources for longer periods of time. Performance criteria are applied and repurchases are made in four and one-half to ten years. As will be discussed in more detail below, the nature and purpose of these facilities have evolved over time, reflecting changes not necessarily in the Fund's goals but in how those goals can best be achieved.

Policy Goals and Mandates in History and Practice

THE WORLD BANK. The *original* purpose of the Bank was to help finance the reconstruction and economic development of its member countries.[21] The Articles of Agreement establish the Bank as an intergovernmental institution, corporate in form, all of whose capital stock is owned by its member governments. Initially the emphasis was less on what the Bank could lend directly out of its paid-in capital and more on the concept of the Bank providing a "safe bridge" over which private capital could move into the international field. Sharing the risk on an international basis was a unique feature at the time.

The loans had to be for "productive" purposes. The borrower could be a member government, a political subdivision, or a business or agricultural enterprise, but if the borrower was not a government, the loan had to be guaranteed by the member government in whose territories the project was located. The Bank had to be satisfied that under prevailing market conditions the borrower would be unable to obtain the loan from private sources under reasonable conditions. At the same time, however, the Bank was forced to be conservative with its lending, since it had to earn the trust of potential investors in the Bank's securities or guarantees. These were difficult requirements to meet, and a strict interpretation of them left the Bank with relatively few "bankable" projects.

As a matter of general policy, the Bank concentrated its lending on projects designed to contribute directly to the *productive capacity* of a country, region, or specific industrial sector and did not finance community projects of a primarily social character, such as sewage systems, street paving, water supplies, housing, and health and education facilities.[22]

Although the Articles require the Bank to give "equitable consideration to projects for development and projects for reconstruction alike," the early focus was on reconstruction. Once the European Recovery Program began operations, the Bank turned its attention to its other major field of responsibility, the financing of productive projects in the less developed areas of the world.

In theory, the majority of the Bank's operations were to take the form of guarantees by the Bank of loans made by private investors, as opposed to direct lending from the Bank. In the beginning, the Bank did not have well-established credit, and many investors thought that World Bank-guaranteed loans would sell in the market at varying interest rates depending on the credit of the borrowing country. Securities guaranteed by the Bank were also less easily transferable, which added to the cost of borrowing.

Over the years the Bank has fundamentally altered the way in which it lends money. The original vision for Bank lending proved unworkable in practice.[23] Today the Bank raises most of its money on the world's financial markets, selling bonds and other debt instruments to pension funds, insurance companies, corporations, other banks, and individuals. In addition, the organizational chart has mushroomed over the years. There are now six regional and six policy-related departments. Moreover, lending comes no longer just from the World Bank but from the "World Bank Group," a collection of specialized agencies. In addition to the Bank, the Group includes the International Finance Corporation (created in 1956), the International Development Association (1960), the International Centre for Settlement of Investment Disputes (1966), and the Multilateral Investment Guarantee Agency (1988).

In addition to this changing institutional structure, the Bank has undergone several cycles of change that led to an alteration of its policies. These changes were the result of a continuously, though not unidirectionally, evolving concept of development, economic, political, and social trends in both the donor and recipient countries, new scientific knowledge, and other factors. As one participant of the Bretton Woods conference recently noted, "Although the White plan had recognized a role for the Bank in supplying capital for specific projects in developing countries, the conservative nature of the Bank's charter, which emphasized not only the soundness of projects, but their bankability in terms of the borrowing country's ability to repay, deterred the Bank's early administrators from making large loan commitments for development. Furthermore, the Bank's articles made no explicit provision for lending to support the process of economic and social development, and it would take more than twenty years for the Bank to become a development institution."[24]

But the concept of development itself was subject to cycles of change, the latest of which became evident in Bank policies in the early 1990s.[25] The collapse of the East bloc not only allowed the donor countries and thus the Bank to alter the focus of their policies, but also presented IFIs with a formidable challenge for which there was no precedent—system transformation. Yet the uniqueness of this challenge also allowed IFIs to reflect upon and subsequently alter their strategies in light of policy failures. The consequences of that have been greater flexibility and transparency in the Bank's operations. Moreover, stagnant and in some cases even deteriorating conditions in many recipient countries worldwide, especially in Africa, raised new questions about the effectiveness and more recently also the efficiency of the Bank's internal and external operations.[26]

The changes in the Bank's policies and operations since the beginning of this decade reflect not only a broadened development agenda but, equally important, a definition of development that recognizes its interdisciplinary character by integrating different disciplines and acknowledging the complexity of the process itself. Thus, while on earlier occasions the broader political, social, cultural, and environmental framework of development was often considered secondary, and negative externalities—corruption, poverty, pollution—in any of these areas were seen as temporary and presumed to disappear with economic development, they have now become an integral part of, if not precondition for, sustained progress toward development. What was once considered incidental to development has become instrumental for development.

Poverty reduction, environmental protection, good governance, and reduced expenditures for arms provide the core of these enabling factors of
development. Although poverty reduction was never really abandoned, it
was the Annual Development Report of 1990, *Poverty,* that indicated a new
approach.[27] The Bank issued lengthy guidelines requiring the integration of
poverty concerns into its program planning as well as country and sector
analysis. According to the Bank, "The volume of lending should be linked
to country efforts to reduce poverty. Stronger government commitment to
poverty reduction—as measured by the adequacy of the policy framework
for growth plus human development and/or willingness to reform—warrants greater support; conversely, weaker commitment to poverty reduction
warrants less support."[28] Broad-based social sector programs, such as social
safety nets in the form of unemployment compensation, job creation schemes,
retraining programs, support in targeting health and nutrition spending, and
the financing of investments specifically designed to attack deep-seated
poverty, are central aspects of this approach. Another dimension that has
found increasing attention is the implications of involuntary displacement
of people in the context of economic development. According to the Bank,
an estimated 80–90 million people have been forcibly resettled by investments in infrastructure, irrigation projects, urban growth, and others.[29]

The second enabling factor, environmental protection, has been on the
Bank's agenda since the mid-1980s but gained momentum in the early 1990s
due to pressure from NGOs, increasing scientific evidence of global environmental problems ranging from the depletion of fish stocks to the ozone layer,
and especially in the wake of the UN Conference on Environment and Development (UNCED) summit in the summer of 1992. Environmental protection
has become a key component of sustainable development. Without it, long-
term development is undermined. Conversely, without development it is difficult to generate the resources needed for environmental protection. The Bank
supports projects for reforestation, pollution control, and land management,
and promotes national environmental action plans and economic policies that
help to conserve natural resources. The Bank goes even further to point out that
effective policies against environmental pollution have to counteract strong
political pressures, perhaps even by "taking rights away from people who may
be politically powerful."[30] The poor and the weak "may be less potent politically than the polluters whom governments must challenge."[31] As in the case of
poverty, the Bank has in place so-called environmental assessment procedures
whose purpose is to evaluate projects in terms of their environmental
soundness.

Good governance is the third enabling factor. According to the Bank, "governance is defined as the manner in which power is exercised in the management of a country's economic and social resources."[32] Good governance encourages governments to create the legal and institutional framework for transparency, predictability on the part of officials, and competence in the conduct of public affairs and the management of economic development.[33] From the Bank's perspective, good governance is an essential precondition for a country's effectiveness and efficiency in the application of resources and capital, including Bank loans. In practical terms this implies improving public sector management, ensuring economic and financial accountability, maintaining predictability in applying rules and regulations, and ensuring the availability of and access to information about the economy.

While all of the above applications of good governance refer to the economy of a country, it is difficult to see how a rigorous application of these goals will prevent the Bank from getting involved in a country's political affairs, which is prohibited under article 4 of its Articles of Agreement. It is difficult to imagine how an independent judiciary, freedom of organization, speech, the media, and even elections, all of which are preconditions for good governance but also elements of democracy, could be operated only with reference to economic efficiency and effectiveness criteria.[34]

Last, reduced military expenditures is seen as an enabling condition.[35] With the end of global superpower rivalry, what has been an economic reality for a long time has now also become politically more feasible. Proposals to reduce military budgets have recently regained their prominence, with two former World Bank presidents endorsing such a policy. The Bank has estimated that military expenditures in many countries exceed combined government expenditures on health and education, which contradicts the Bank's emphasis on poverty reduction and is in conflict with its framework on controlling public expenditures. Most certainly this issue is now being raised during the Bank's public expenditure review process, which is part of its new emphasis on poverty.[36] Furthermore, the Bank is considering the inclusion of a category dealing with military-related debt in its debt reporting system. Several countries, including China and the Czech and Slovak republics, have already sought assistance with conversion, and a number of African states, including Uganda, are receiving advice on demobilization and demilitarization from the Bank.

As can be seen from the discussion in the previous paragraphs, these factors are not only considered important in and of themselves but taken together they support each other and further improve the conditions for sustainable development. For example, a decrease in military expenditures allows governments to divert badly needed resources to poverty reduction programs. A reduction in poverty levels is one important condition for lower levels of pollution. Accountability, transparency, and the rule of law make a direct contribution to the objectives of sustainable growth and the reduction of poverty. Finally, all four enabling factors are subject to a policy approach that emphasizes participatory development. Participation is defined by the Bank as a "process through which stakeholders [the Bank, governments, and especially individuals] influence and share control over development initiatives, decisions and resources which affect them."[37] The incentives created by a participatory approach to development improve the chances that a development effort will be successful.

One important implication of participatory development is the increasing emphasis on decentralizing the development efforts by the Bank. In recent years this effort toward greater decentralization has led to a much greater involvement of NGOs in the activities of the Bank. In fiscal year 1993, 30 percent of all Bank projects included provisions for NGO involvement.[38] The Bank has identified four basic reasons why the participation of NGOs may help its efforts: (1) they reach poor communities and remote areas with few basic resources or little infrastructure, and where government services are limited or ineffective; (2) they promote local participation in designing and implementing public programs by building self-confidence and strengthening organizational capability among low-income people; (3) they generally operate at low cost; and (4) they identify local needs, build upon existing resources, and transfer technologies developed elsewhere.[39]

THE IMF. Thus far the IMF has gone through two distinct phases in its history, and all indications speak for the fact that it is about to enter another one. During its first phase, ending in 1973, the IMF oversaw the adoption of general convertability among major currencies, supervised a system of fixed exchange rates tied to the value of gold, and provided short-term financing to cover balance of payments problems. After five years of analysis and negotiation, the second phase began with the amendment of its constitution in 1978, broadening its functions to enable it to grapple with the challenges that had risen since the collapse of the par value system.[40] These functions are: (1) to promote the unrestricted exchange of members' currencies; (2) in place of monitoring members' compliance with obligations under a fixed system, to play a role in supervising economic policies that influence their balance of payments in the flexible exchange rate environment; and (3) to provide short- and medium-term financial assistance to members in such a way that it eases a country's painful transition to living within its means rather than subsidizing further deficits.[41]

Although the IMF's Articles have been amended only twice, this does not accurately reflect the extent to which the institution has changed over time. This is particularly true since the abandonment of the fixed exchange rate regime, when the IMF lost the power to approve or reject changes in the exchange rate. The principle of oversight was carried over into the amended Articles of Agreement, which call for the IMF to "exercise firm surveillance over the exchange rate policies of members."[42] But the creation of the Group of Seven, where from the late 1970s to the mid-1980s the most important international initiatives took shape, in many ways preempted the IMF's deeper involvement in policy coordination and implementation. The IMF was reduced to an advisory role in international policy and thus became more involved with developing countries, initially during the oil crisis[43] and later in the context of restructuring the debt for many Latin American countries in the 1980s.[44] This prompted another change in the Fund's operations. It no longer limited itself to providing short-term loans to ameliorate balance of payments imbalances, but began to provide medium- to long-term assistance for structural adjustment.[45]

Moreover, recognizing that developing countries are often more severely affected by external disturbances than are industrial countries, the Fund provides special assistance to developing countries through facilities that are legally separate from, but operated by, the Fund. The Structural Adjustment Facility (SAF) provides loans or drawings at a discount to support medium-term macroeconomic adjustment and structural reforms in low-income countries facing systemic balance of payments problems. The member develops and updates, with the help of the Fund and the World Bank, a three-year "medium-term policy framework" that governs the amount and strategy of the funding. The rate of interest on SAF loans is 0.5 percent, and repayments are made in five and one-half to six years. The Enhanced Structural Adjustment Facility (ESAF) is similar to the SAF in objectives and conditions for eligibility. The ESAF differs, however, in the scope and strength of structural policies and in terms of access levels, monitoring procedures, and sources of funding. In this context the Fund has increasingly relied on the advice of the staff of the World Bank in preparing medium-term policy measures designed to address the social aspects of SAF- and ESAF-supported programs.

In the wake of the disintegration of the Soviet Union and changes in other countries of the former East bloc, the Systemic Transformation Facility (STF) was founded in April 1993. It was created to help the economies in transition deal with the challenges posed by disruptions in their trade and payments arrangements due to a shift from trading at nonmarket prices to market-based trade. The STF was a temporary facility intended as a transitional step to other arrangements, such as standby and ESAF agreements. It was extended once, but expired in April 1995. Access to this facility was conditional on the adoption of certain types of monetary policies and institutions. By the time it expired, eighteen countries, including Russia, had drawn on the STF for a total of close to $5.5 billion; at least six did so in conjunction with regular Standby Agreements.[46] Like the Extended Facility, repurchases were made in four and one-half to ten years.

According to the Fund, the reform programs in eastern Europe share four goals: first, the wholesale replacement of central planning and management by a market-oriented system characterized by market-determined prices, flexible capital and labor markets, the legalization of private property, and adoption of open trade and investment policies toward the rest of the world (that is, convertible currencies); second, establishment of a viable financial system founded on market-based interest rates; third, measures to liberalize the operation of firms and markets, including privatization; fourth, creation of a viable social safety net, including funds for unemployment insurance and job retraining.[47]

The Fund has also begun to include enabling conditions (discussed earlier in the context of the Bank) in its policy formulation and procedure, though to a lesser degree. The issue of poverty entered the IMF in the early 1980s.[48] Again, as in the case of the Bank, this was in large part due to mounting external criticism that called for the IMF to consider the distributional and social implications of its lending.[49] As part of its support for adjustment programs, and in particular to mitigate the adverse effects they might have on the poor, the Fund started to address poverty issues through the SAF and especially through the ESAF. In fact some recent letters of intent have dealt specifically with poverty issues.[50] This has involved identifying those who would be least able to absorb the transitional costs of adjustment, assessing the effects of conventional macroeconomic adjustment programs on the disadvantaged, and finding alternative strategies that could ameliorate the short-term effects on the poor without sacrificing the longer-run macroeconomic benefits. Policy measures designed for such a purpose can be divided into four categories: targeted subsidies for essential goods; cash transfers to vulnerable groups; direct support for wages, producer prices, and targeted public works; and protection of education and health expenditures.

External pressure from both NGOs and member countries was also instrumental in raising environmental awareness in the Fund.[51] For example, the U.S. Congress has passed legislation calling on the U.S. executive director in the Fund to persuade the Fund to carry out a systematic review of the impact of its policies on the environment and sustainable management of natural resources and to encourage the Fund to eliminate or reduce potentially adverse impacts of its programs on the environment. Contrary to the Bank, the Fund is unlikely to get directly or actively involved in environmental protection.[52] At the same time there has been an increasing awareness that the issue cannot be separated from structural adjustment. Take the case of a country that hopes to improve its trade deficit via an increase of timber exports. To do so it proposes a sharp devaluation of its currency. The Fund should consider whether in the long term such a policy, which would result in greatly increased logging activity, is in the interest of sustainable growth. As a result it may actually advise against such a policy or at least require some form of environmental guarantee or safeguard before proceeding with a credit arrangement.[53] In other words, if the Fund "feels strongly about the environmental aspect . . . it might show itself less than forthcoming with a credit arrangement unless the member undertakes to adopt adequate environmental safeguards."[54]

Good governance has also become part of the Fund's policy-based criteria. However, the application is much more restricted than in the case of the Bank. Issues of governance have arisen for the most part in the Fund's efforts to establish market-based financial systems, particularly in the former East bloc. It is now recognized that private financial markets must be accompanied by an appropriate framework of regulations and prudential supervision of their institutions. However, as stated above, it is not quite clear how such an institutional network and its rules can be unlinked from the rest of the society and the economy, raising the question to what degree good governance can be treated individually along functional lines.

Finally, the issue of military expenditures has also been given increasing attention by the Fund. By demonstrating the waste and inefficiency of military expenditures, the Fund hopes to induce countries to reduce their overall spending on military hardware and to reallocate these resources to productive expenditures.[55]

The IMF also implemented a new reporting system to collect data on military spending. It works with countries to improve their data collection methods and reporting through technical assistance and policy talks, including discussions under article 4, which is now being interpreted to include military spending in the realm of "promoting stability" and "fostering orderly economic growth" and lending negotiations. As of September 1993, 105 members had reported defense data to the Fund in the context of regular article 4 consultations.

To summarize, IFIs have undergone substantial change over the last decades, especially since the mid-1980s. The Bank and to a lesser degree the Fund are no longer just concerned with the traditional goal of promoting output growth but in addition to that pursue a large number of sociopolitical objectives ranging from the reduction of poverty and environmental protection to the promotion of an infrastructure for transparent and efficient public policy. They do so in two ways: indirectly, by conditioning a project on the various factors considered vital for enabling sustained and equitable economic growth, and directly, by designing programs that are targeted toward the formation of a social, legal, and political framework within which economic growth can flourish. This by no means should imply that there is no further need for adjustment in the outlook, policies, and practices of the IFIs. To the contrary, the very question that this chapter addresses raises that issue. For that reason both indirect and direct strategies to promote sustainable development will be considered in preventing the outbreak of ethnic conflict.

Conceptualizing Ethno-Nationalism: Definition, Manifestation, Mobilization, and Sources of Ethno-National Conflict

This section conceptualizes the term ethno-nationalism and places it in the context of the system transformation currently under way in ECE and the FSU. It goes without saying that a thorough treatment of ethno-nationalism, whether in general or with a particular focus on the former East bloc, goes much beyond the scope of this chapter.[56] Keeping the central question to be addressed by this chapter in mind, this section starts by defining ethno-nationalism and its most prominent manifestations in ECE and the FSU. With that background, this section analyzes the circumstances under which individuals are more likely to define their interests along ethnic lines and are also able to voice those interests collectively. This discussion of ethno-national mobilization is then placed into the specific context of ECE and the FSU, which continue to struggle with the political, economic, and social transformation of their societies. The simultaneous occurrence of system transformation and ethno-national mobilization is thus seen as the primary potential source of violent ethno-national conflict.

Definitions

The term *ethnic* has its origin in the Greek words *ethnikos,* which can denote different things such as "national" or "foreign," and *ethnos,* which refers to a group, company, herd, tribe, people, or nation but which also means heathen.[57] The vagueness of the term has led authors to refer to what Anthony Smith has identified as "a social group whose members share a sense of common origin, claim a common and distinctive history and destiny, possess one or more distinctive characteristics, and feel a sense of collective uniqueness and solidarity"[58] as "ethnic community," "ethnie," "ethno-nationalists," "minorities," or "communal groups."

Ethno-nationalism, as opposed to its territorial, civic version embodied in the concept of the nation-state, envisions the nation as a "genealogical and vernacular cultural community."[59] While territorial and civic nationalist definitions of a "nation" center on a community of shared culture, common laws, and citizenship, ethnic nationalists define a nation *solely* on the basis of the genealogy of its members.[60]

Manifestations of Ethno-Nationalism

Based on this definition of ethno-nationalism, this study distinguishes between five types of ethno-nationalism currently found in ECE and the FSU: cultural revivalism, political autonomism, self-determinism, separatism, and irredentism.

Cultural revivalism is a phenomenon that is particularly noticeable among *ethno-classes.*[61] These small or ethnically, religiously, or regionally dispersed minorities usually direct their demands toward more equitable treatment. Despite no or limited experiences with sovereignty or statehood, their leaders may request the freedom and resources to build or enhance their social, cultural, religious, and educational institutions; to redefine their history; to reinforce their identity; and to revive their dialect or language. These objectives are usually formulated in terms of increasing minority participation in the existing regional and national politics system, rather than posing a challenge to the integrity of the existing nation-state.[62] Comprehensive cultural revivalism is clearly visible among the Roma population throughout eastern Europe.[63]

Ethnic nationalism can also manifest itself in demands for *political autonomy*. Although political autonomy movements demand a change in the structure of the nation-state, they do not advocate its disintegration. The notion of autonomy is the recognition of a group's right to be different and left alone, to protect and maintain a value system which is in some form contrary to the rest of society. Autonomy does not necessarily mean partition or secession. Rather, it manifests itself in the desire for protection from discrimination against an ethno-national language, cultural, and value system.[64] Movements of political autonomism can currently be found among Hungarians in both Slovakia and Romania.

In cases where ethnic or subethnic groups form a relative or absolute majority of the population and are territorially concentrated, political objectives most likely are framed in requests for territorial *self-determinism*. Ethnic leaders may seek to reorganize the administration of the state from a unitary to a federal or confederal structure in which specific regions gain some degree of provincial autonomy or full republican status. In recent years a movement of this kind has emerged in Moravia, one of the two principal historic regions of the Czech Republic.[65] A more dramatic instance can be found in Crimea, where ethnic Russians (who comprise roughly 70 percent of the population) have increasingly demanded greater autonomy from Ukraine and closer ties with Russia.

Separatism can be seen as a gradual extension of territorial self-determinism. It also manifests itself among ethnically and territorially compact populations, and the ethnic group usually opposes any form of inclusion in the existing federal or unitary state in which they find themselves living and campaigns to create their own independent state. In recent years such movements have included the Slovenes and Croats in the former Yugoslavia, the Abkhaz region of Georgia, Russians in the "Dniester Republic" in Moldova, and the Chechen and Tatar ethnic regions in Russia.[66]

Irredentism, the fifth manifestation of ethno-national conflict, occurs when an ethnic movement in one state seeks to unite its territory and population with another state of the same ethnicity, either in the form of an autonomous region or an integral administrative unit. Irredentist aspirations can take on two separate forms: active and passive. In active irredentism, a state encourages members of the same ethnicity residing in another state to separate from their current state structure and in many cases be incorporated. For example, Romania has vigorously opposed Moldova's attempts to assert a national identity and has openly cooperated with opposition forces in Moldova who advocate unity with Romania. Passive irredentism describes a situation where an ethnic group in one state seeks to separate from its current structure and unite with another state of the same ethnic origin that, however, does not favor such a move. For example, majorities in both Crimea and eastern Ukraine have called for greater ties to Russia, which apparently has no real interest in adopting two economically devastated regions and risking violent conflict with Ukraine. The distinction between active and passive irredentism may seem inconsequential, but it provides another marker in determining the extent and form of IFI involvement in ethno-national conflict. The active involvement of a third party (the second state) in ethno-national conflict can dramatically alter the landscape of crisis prevention.

These five variants are of course not mutually exclusive, and have been interpreted as potential stages of development depending on several inter-related variables, such as the response of the government to minority demands and the policies of foreign governments in supporting or discouraging secessionist movements. Others have referred to the evolutionary character of ethno-nationalism, with regard to changing aspirations of the ethnic group. Ultimately the relationship between different types of manifestations cannot be defined in general terms but requires an examination of the political system, the ethnic balance of power, the strategies adopted by the state, and the historical ethno-group relation in each particular country.[67]

Ethno-National Mobilization in ECE and the FSU

The blurred differentiation between the various manifestations or stages of ethno-nationalism creates a need to qualify the concept further. This qualification needs to keep in mind that the principal purpose of this analysis is to explore if and in what way ethno-nationalism in ECE and the new republics of the FSU, and the efforts to prevent it from erupting into violent conflicts, can be linked to the mandate and goals of IFIs.

For example, while IFIs may respond to each manifestation of ethno-nationalism with a different set of strategies, they themselves, and for that matter most other international organizations, should not and cannot be involved in determining which particular manifestation of ethno-nationalism will emerge as individuals and collectives mobilize along different ethnic identities. In addition, given that the emphasis here is on prevention, IFIs should use their mandate and power as early as possible. They should focus on the stage where ethnic grievances are becoming politically salient and help ensure that they do not turn violent, without specifying whether this occurs in the form of cultural revivalism, separatism, or any of the other manifestations mentioned above.

This conceptualization focuses on the phase of ethno-national mobilization, when an ethnic group has decided and is able to take political action in support of its collective identity and interests.[68] The crucial point for the question raised in this chapter is that this approach to the concept of ethno-nationalism allows an examination of its evolutionary character. It is thus better suited to capture the dynamics currently under way in ECE and the FSU and can point to the timing and strategies of early intervention central to any preventive effort by IFIs.

To identify under what circumstances individuals can and do mobilize along ethnic lines, this analysis relies on models of ethnic stratification or ranking. Such models characterize the way in which ethnicity does or does not structure social relations in a society. Joseph Rothschild, for example, distinguishes three models: *vertical hierarchy, parallel segmentation,* and *reticulate.*[69] In a society characterized by *vertical hierarchy,* one ethnic group dominates one or several others. Often the same power structure is matched in other social dimensions—political, economic, and cultural. *Parallel segmentation* characterizes societies whose principal fragmentation does run along ethnic lines. Each parallel segment, however, is characterized by an internal hierarchy based on socioeconomic criteria and by an elite that represents its interests vis-à-vis ethnic collectivities.[70] In a *reticulate* society, patterns of social, economic, and political stratification cut across ethnic groups, that is, each ethnic group pursues a wide variety of economic and political functions, and each economic class or political faction includes different ethnic groups.

It goes without saying that such models are ideal cases and do not always focus on all formal or informal aspects of the legal, political, and economic organization of ethnicity. As such they tend to oversimplify the actual situation in a particular country. However, for this study's purpose, which is merely to accentuate the conditions under which individuals are likely to mobilize along ethnic lines and which of the three models meets those conditions best, they are helpful.

The possibility or likelihood of ethno-national mobilization in each of these models can be determined by applying the following two questions to each: first, do groups find it necessary—for political, economic, or other reasons—to mobilize along ethnic lines? Second, does a country's political and economic system permit them to do so? Both must be answered in the affirmative for ethno-national mobilization to occur in a systematic and sustained way such as is currently observed in some parts of ECE and the FSU.

While individuals often find it necessary, in a country characterized by vertical hierarchy, to mobilize along ethnic lines in order to improve their socioeconomic status or gain access to political decisionmaking, the structure of the system does not permit them to do so.[71] Nor do they have the economic resources to sustain mobilization over a longer period of time. Any attempt to mobilize is crushed by those that hold political and economic power. The reticulate model represents a contrasting image. Individuals are free to mobilize along ethnic lines, but they seldom feel that it is necessary to do so. They are more likely to define themselves in terms of economic criteria, such as income or occupation, political allegiances, or other values. In a society characterized by parallel segmentation, individuals do feel the need to mobilize along ethnic lines and there are no or few structural or systemic impediments to do so. Each ethnic segment has its own internal political and economic hierarchy.

The above discussion can be placed into the current context of ECE and the FSU, whose societies are all undergoing fundamental changes driven and dominated by a process of political and economic transformation. In light of the nonethnic—in particular the political, economic, and cultural—modes of stratification in the East bloc as recently as the mid- to late 1980s, and their role in suppressing the ability to mobilize along ethnic lines, it is apparent that these societies were characterized by a system of vertical hierarchy.

Focusing again on a country's nonethnic (political, economic, cultural) means of stratification, the reticulate model contains many elements that ECE and the FSU are currently striving for in the context of system transformation—usually summarized under the rubrics of political democracy and a market economy. While the particular form of democratic and economic governance will differ across countries having fully developed reticulate structures, they still possess a common link: although democracy guarantees individuals the right to mobilize along ethnic lines, the market system, and in particular the way in which property relations are structured, encourages them to form identities (both political and economic) along nonethnic dimensions.

Thus, paying particular attention to the role of and implications for ethnic stratification, system transformation in ECE countries and the new republics of the FSU is best conceptualized as a transformation of a society characterized by vertical hierarchy to one structured by cross-patterned reticulation. But although both of these forms of social organization exhibit low levels of ethnic mobilization where the probability of conflict is low, they are separated by a process of ethno-national mobilization characterized by the emergence of what has been described earlier as parallel ethnic segmentation, which is prone to violent conflict. The following section examines this process in greater detail.

Ethno-National Mobilization and the Sources of Ethno-National Conflict in ECE and the FSU

A more detailed examination of ethno-national mobilization in the context of system transformation in ECE and the FSU can be made by considering the impact of this dual dynamic on the level of societal integration in a particular country.

Notwithstanding the fact that it represented a form of *forced* integration, the vertical model in the East bloc generated, through the prevailing ideology administered by the central hegemonic state, the perception of a relatively high degree of socioeconomic integration.[72] Similarly, cultural integration, in the sense of acculturation to a dominant, putatively "rational" norm in the socioeconomic and politically essential areas of life while tolerating ethnocultural particularities in supposedly marginal, private areas, was high in Eastern Europe and the Soviet Union. Moreover, if deemed necessary the system could always enforce ethnocultural assimilation and thus increase the degree of societal integration even further. Political integration was also high as constituent ethnic groups were coerced into acknowledging the system's legitimacy by the subtle (and sometimes less subtle) power of the dominant group's authority and the state apparatus. All three dimensions tended to legitimize and reinforce each other, increasing the level of societal integration across ethnic groups.

At the other end of the spectrum of ethnic stratification, the reticulate model is also characterized by relatively high levels of socioeconomic, political, and cultural integration, even though the political and economic structures by which this integration is sustained and legitimized differ radically from the model of vertical hierarchy in the former East bloc. The lower emphasis on ethnic stratification is less the result of enforcement from the top but more due to the fact that it is irrelevant both for the functioning of political democracy and to the performance of a market economy.

The degree of societal integration, however, does not remain constant as ECE and the FSU transform their political and economic systems and move from vertical ethnic stratification toward societies structured by cross-patterned reticulation. Rather, system transformation is characterized by a considerable degree of political, socioeconomic, and cultural disintegration. In the political realm this is reflected by the fact that the prevailing system of governance has been seriously delegitimized among the general population, including large segments of the dominant ethnic group. Moreover, the state structure and the institutions through which political integration across ethnic groups was enforced and administered have largely collapsed, and trust and confidence in new and still emerging structures of governance is low.

Political disintegration is accompanied by considerable socioeconomic disintegration. The centrally planned economic system has been discredited, and its failure is seen as one of the principal sources of systemic collapse. In addition, the economic and social hardships caused by the transformation process toward a market economy, heightened by overly optimistic initial expectations, further contribute to declining confidence in the economic outlook of individuals, fueling the forces of disintegration as economic corruption and crime take on an increasing significance. With the collapse of the political power structure and the economic system that was used to rationalize and legitimize its existence, acculturation and cultural assimilation have also lost their integrative attributes, further stimulating societal disintegration.

From the perspectives of the different ethnic group(s), with the likely exception of the one group that was in control of the system, the political and economic structures as well as the dominant culture are now openly recognized as unjust and illegitimate instruments of ethnic subordination. At the same time, new systemwide structures and institutions, if existing at all, are still in their formative stages and viewed with suspicion. They lack integrative power not the least because competing ethnic elites find it easy to discredit any emerging systemwide political or economic structure as yet another form of forced integration.

Indeed it is this forced nature of societal integration across ethnic lines under vertical hierarchy and its sudden delegitimization in the wake of system collapse that leads to a strong resurgence of ethnic identity, exemplified by an emerging structure of parallel segmentation. In the absence of fully developed political and economic structures and institutions characteristic of cross-patterned reticulation, which deemphasize the role of ethnic identification, ethnicity is becoming the principal basis of societal integration, subordinating the political, economic, and cultural components of an ethnic collective.

This dynamic—the systemwide political, economic, and cultural disintegration and subsequent attempts at reintegration along ethnic lines—is the principal source for the emergence of ethno-national conflict. More specifically, while vertical stratification was characterized by a set of strong centralizing principles and institutions that enforced ethnic integration, system transformation is characterized by the absence of systemwide functioning and newly legitimate political and economic structures. Such structures could either defuse ethnic mobilization or respond appropriately, incorporating ethnic demands into the operational aspects of the political system. Their absence leads to strong pressures and incentives for political, economic, and cultural segregation. Different ethnic segments of society strive to redefine political, economic, and cultural boundaries along ethnic—that is, societal—lines, generating the various ethno-national manifestations discussed above.

Which particular manifestation (or what combination thereof) emerges depends of course on each country's historical and contemporary circumstances. Common to all, however, is that successful ethnic segmentation first and foremost demands the reestablishment of economic and political structures within each ethnic group. For ethno-nationalism to have its segmenting effects it must permeate all important aspects of society. More specifically, what has been referred to as subordinating the political, economic, and cultural components of societal integration to different ethnic identities in a multiethnic state leads to the development of intense competition among those groups over a country's political power, economic resources, and cultural heritage.

In the political realm, when state institutions have or are perceived as having lost their autonomy, they themselves become the target of competition and "a prize to be occupied and exploited by contending ethnic groups."[73] In many instances, however, competition over political power also implies competition over space, that is, the appropriation of territory. Competition is particularly intense over those territories that are populated by more than one ethnic group. Spatial competition may also occur, when a territory populated by a single ethnic group is contested by another one. The basis for such a claim is often historical, such as an externally imposed decision that had or has lost legitimacy for the competing group. This second type of competition over space does not necessarily have to occur within a single state, but could also be the subject of interstate competition, adding a further dimension to the dynamics of ethno-nationalism and providing a source for potential interstate ethnic conflict.

In the economic realm, competition primarily occurs over property, such as a country's natural resource and environmental endowments, infrastructure and fixed capital, financial assets, and other goods that might enhance the economic resource base of an ethnic group.[74] This competition has to be seen against the background of the difficult transformation toward a market economy which creates not just a general feeling of insecurity but also a sharp contraction of the economy and declining living standards among large segments of the population. Moreover, even if these countries manage to halt the collapse of economic output, which in some ECE countries has already occurred, it is by no means assured that ethnic competition will abate. Economic expansion often tends to increase ethno-national mobilization and competition as resources and opportunities increase.[75]

Competition in the cultural realm for the most part is meant to support an ethnic group's territorial or economic claims. This leads to a strong resurgence of each ethnic group's cultural tradition, that is, an increased emphasis on the anthropological rather than sociological elements of culture. What was once considered a diverse and multicultural heritage becomes the source of competition whereby each ethnic collective's own culture is synonymous with its identity. Competing cultures and their symbols, in the form of architecture, art, literature, and music, are perceived not just as a threat to one's own identity but to territory and property alike.

Considering the kinds of issues over which economic competition takes place, it is evident that it cannot be separated from political, that is, territorial, competition. The same applies to the realm of culture, which is used not just to promote political and economic integration but to justify territorial seizure and economic confiscation. Thus, for example, while competition may originate in the realm of politics, it will quickly spill over into the economic and cultural arenas, the latter of which in its anthropological manifestation is most often used to reenforce the other two dimensions by supporting competing claims, heightening the intensity of competition.

The exception to the dynamic outlined above would be a country that, although composed of more than one ethnic group, already exhibits a relatively high degree of segregation along ethnic lines with respect to territory and the economy. Czechoslovakia is a case in point, though ethnic segregation was not the only reason for the peaceful dissolution of the country.[76]

Given the issues that are the focus of ethnic group competition and the absence of a well-established and legitimate framework to regulate such competition, it is no longer difficult to see that ethno-national conflict in ECE and the FSU is prone to conflict resolution by violence rather than compromise, as competing groups attempt to divide and claim for themselves what not long ago seemed indivisible and was considered common to all—territory *and* property alike. However, keeping in mind that the goal here is to target the expertise, experience, and resources of IFIs in such a way as to resolve competition in a peaceful manner, it is helpful to specify the causes of ethno-national conflict in greater detail. And although difficult to separate in reality, for analytical purposes it is helpful to differentiate between systemic and societal (subsystemic) causes of ethno-national conflict. At each level of analysis one can further distinguish between institutional and sociopsychological causes. Taken together these distinctions (systemic vs. societal and institutional vs. sociopsychological) lead to four potential sources of ethno-national conflict, all of which must be addressed during the process of system transformation in ECE and the FSU.

Considering first the institutional sources of ethno-national conflict, the absence of a strong, legitimate set of systemwide political and economic structures and institutions during the process of system transformation stands out.[77] Regarding the systemic level, note that as discussed earlier a conventional definition of ethno-nationalism is a group's attempt to gain "greater *access to* or *control of* political, economic, or cultural institutions *within the framework provided by the existing state.*" Putting this definition into the context of ECE and the newly independent states of the FSU, the structural and institutional vacuum at the system level becomes immediately apparent, and raises the questions access to what? control of what? within which framework? and provided by what state?

The sources of conflict are manifold and are present during the deconstruction and reconstruction phase of state structures. The widespread erosion of the power and authority of the central state and its established institutions, in particular the party organization, provides an opportunity for groups that feel deprived or disadvantaged to organize themselves and propound grievances and demands. Ethnicity is highly effective in performing this task because it has the ability to bring together a particular interest with an effective bond.[78] This is especially the case in the context of system transformation in ECE and the FSU, where rapidly changing social, political, and economic norms have created an economic, ideological, and cultural power vacuum. In the absence of institutional means of controlling the energetic competition to fill these vacuums, violence is highly likely.[79] The likelihood of ethno-national mobilization turning violent is particularly high once states have lost effective political control over substantial segments of the population but have maintained a monopoly over organized means of coercion, a scenario that can be found in many countries of the former East bloc.[80]

While one source of conflict at the systemic level can be identified during the period of dismantling and deconstructing old institutions and structures of authority, the process of reconstruction is equally prone to conflict once individuals have been mobilized along ethnic lines. Thus the failure to permit all ethno-national groups within the territory to share power in the center is likely to heighten ethnic rather than national identification not only of groups that are excluded but also of those that were able to appropriate a disproportionate amount of political power and now are tempted to justify that position along ethnic lines. The institutionalization of exclusion will increase the likelihood of spatial competition, tendency toward segregation, and thus the threat of violence.[81] Moreover, incorporation must generate tangible benefits for elites and followers so that an identification with the emerging structure can be legitimized. Finally, if necessary the emerging structures of governance must be able to absorb demands for limited political autonomy and separatism.[82]

System-level institution building alone, however, will not suffice to effectively prevent the outbreak of ethnic conflict. Of equal importance is the existence of societal or subsystemic structures and institutional networks, both ethnic and nonethnic. Political parties, business organizations (defined along sectoral lines or according to the size of the enterprise), labor unions, environmental groups, and interest groups are all vital for the emergence of cross-patterned reticulation, giving their members a sense of representation and rewards.[83] Moreover, these organizations not only aggregate and formulate interests but ensure that those interests can inform system-level structures through established channels of communication open to all.

The presence of an extended network of political, economic, and cultural institutions at the systemic as well as societal level is a necessary condition for the prevention of ethno-national conflict, but it is by no means sufficient.[84] Ethno-national mobilization and the subsequent competition over territory, the economy, and a country's cultural heritage is not an automatic process that surfaces by itself, nor is the mere presence of reticulate institutional structures sufficient to achieve societal support for system transformation.

Rather, at the systemic level ethnic segmentation or cross-patterned reticulation is organized and dominated by elites (political, economic, intellectual), whether they are defined along a single ethnic identity or encompass multiple ethnic groups.[85] These elites will play a decisive role in determining the degree, intensity, and direction of ethno-mobilization.[86] Even in instances where ethnic segmentation remains peaceful, such as the former Czechoslovakia, elites play a decisive role. The political elites of both the Czech and Slovak nations supported and realized the federation's dissolution in defiance of the majority of the people in both republics who wanted to maintain it.[87]

In most cases it is an organized effort by an emerging ethnic elite, an ethnic core, that uses mobilization and even conflict to legitimize competition and the establishment of hierarchical political and economic structures within each segment.[88] The ethnic core determines the pace, shape, scope, and intensity of the mobilization process. In addition, the makeup of the ethnic core will further reveal the form and direction of ethno-national mobilization that the formerly passive ethno-national community will take. Ethnic elites tend to intensify ethnic differences to solidify their power and position of leadership by awakening dormant feelings of ethnic identity or by "implanting a sense of ethnic identity among populations that were long forgotten."[89]

An ethnic core is gradually built up and derives its original means of power through the manipulation of premodern and modern variables of ethno-national crystallization.[90] They not only wield great power in deciding to initiate, approve, or veto policies within the scope of their influence, but also exercise power by preventing issues from being considered. The elite core of an ethnic group is thus not only the promoter but also the principal benefactor of ethno-national mobilization.[91]

If system transformation is to succeed within the confines of the current state, different ethnic cores must be incorporated into the debate over system transformation. Their demands must be given serious consideration and be reflected in the institutional network—political and economic, systemic and societal—that is being built. A strategy of exclusion will almost certainly increase mobilization and can be used to justify the use of violence to achieve complete segmentation. It is this broad representation and co-optation of multiple ethnic groups into a society's elite structures that defuses ethnicity as a strong means of social identity.[92]

Since elites tend to derive their power through control of the means of production, finance, and communication in a society, they will seek to use these resources to advance their unique interests, establish the legitimacy of their rule, and maintain their position of power. A diffusion of economic, financial, and communicative power at the societal level across different ethnic groups as well as widespread access to them are thus other important elements for cross-patterned reticulation.[93]

But while elites are powerful, they are not omnipotent. Elites are only as powerful as the degree to which they can rely on the sustained support and loyalty of their followers, whether it is to advance ethnic segmentation or in an effort to establish cross-patterned reticulation. It is true that the rapid disappearance of social, political, and economic norms that were the source of identification and social orientation has made it relatively easy for ethnic cores to advance their cause of segmentation.[94] But it is also true that new norms have not yet gained broad acceptance in society, and trust in the system is low.[95] Acceptance of such norms and the system that represents them is usually associated with deriving tangible benefits from it. For large segments of the population in ECE and particularly in the FSU, these benefits have not materialized yet. To the contrary, in the wake of system transformation, large-scale economic deprivation accompanied by a sudden sharp increase in levels of inequality, as well as widespread economic corruption and crime, have raised doubts about the virtues of the new system and the elites that support transformation. It has also made individuals susceptible to ethnic indoctrination and thus an easy target for the goals of ethnic elites. The frustration caused by economic hardship can easily be channeled into aggression and the use of violence.[96] A strategy of system transformation must take into account the implications of economic and social deprivation for the support of those elites that advocate segmentation.[97]

To summarize, in a multiethnic state, ethno-national mobilization is likely to be an integral part of system transformation as countries emerge from the vertical mode of ethnic stratification. Any efforts to suppress mobilization would not only be met with violence but would also risk reversing the process of system transformation. Therefore, the international community should accept the high probability of ethno-national mobilization in the transitional societies of ECE and the FSU manifesting itself in the various forms discussed earlier. For IFIs, given their deep involvement and interest in system transformation, this implies that they cannot divorce themselves from the phenomenon of ethno-national mobilization and the possibility that it might turn violent.

The above analysis has shown that for the purpose of the question this chapter raises, system transformation is the critical link between IFIs and

ethno-national conflict. IFIs are deeply involved in the political and economic transformation of ECE and the FSU. At the same time, the risk of
ethno-national conflict as depicted in the parallel segmentation paradigm is
an integral part of that transformation as countries attempt to pass from an
ethnic stratification characterized by vertical hierarchy to one that resembles cross-patterned reticulation. IFIs should have great interest in ensuring
that ethno-national mobilization remains peaceful. How they contribute to
the prevention of conflict is discussed below.

IFIs and Ethno-National Conflict: Strategies for Conflict Prevention

Based on the two previous sections, it is now possible to develop a set of
strategies that IFIs could use to prevent ethno-national mobilization in
transitional societies from turning into violent conflict. To do so, it is
helpful to make two additional distinctions that specify the nature of IFI
engagement in conflict prevention in greater detail.

This analysis first distinguishes between *indirect* and *direct* engagement.
Indirect measures are designed to ensure that IFIs do not inadvertently initiate
or intensify tensions among ethnic groups. What were referred to earlier as the
more traditional activities of the Bank and the Fund, that is, promoting economic development and ensuring the successful macromanagement of a
country's economy, are primarily scrutinized. Given their deep involvement in
the economic aid and transformation of ECE and the FSU, IFIs might find it
necessary to modify a particular aid or adjustment program once the ethnic
environment in which it is to be embedded is taken into consideration. (While
such a strategy may be suboptimal from an economic perspective in the short
run, the economic costs of conflict and destruction are so high that it is
optimal in the long run, even if considered from a purely economic perspective.) Thus, while indirect engagement does not target the causes of conflict
themselves, it ensures that IFI engagement in a country does not unintentionally increase ethno-national mobilization and possibly precipitate ethno-
national conflict.

By contrast, *direct* IFI engagement relies on a strategy that specifically
targets potential causes of ethno-national conflict, systemic or societal,
institutional or sociopsychological, or any combination thereof. The purpose of direct IFI engagement in conflict prevention is to give additional
support to system transformation, especially during the difficult and volatile transition period. The greater the ability of IFIs to deal directly with the

sources of conflict, the less the need to alter their ongoing economic aid and adjustment programs. While the Bank and the Fund may sponsor such activities, they do not necessarily have to be implemented by IFIs themselves. Instead, the nascent (but also contentious) relationship between IFIs and NGOs could be put to use toward such a cause.

A second distinction that helps to further specify IFI strategies for conflict prevention is based on a differentiation between *passive* and *active* engagement. *Passive* strategies are designed to prevent the violent disintegration of societies along ethnic lines but are not aimed at actively supporting societal integration across ethnic groups within the sovereign territory of an existing state. In other words, ethnic segregation has progressed to the degree that it dominates ethno-national mobilization and competition is likely to be resolved by territorial division. *Active* strategies presume the continued territorial integrity of the state and are formulated so as to encourage the establishment of cross-patterned reticulation, deemphasizing ethnic identities and encouraging alternative modes of identification characteristic of a system governed by political democracy and an economy based on market principles.

The choice of strategies (passive or active) will differ for each individual country in ECE and the FSU and may change over time. Active engagement by IFIs is likely to dominate in the early stages of ethno-national mobilization, when ethno-national aspirations manifest themselves predominantly in the form of demands for some degree of cultural or political autonomy and for self-determinism. While pressures for separatism and irredentism cannot be excluded, the preservation of the territorial integrity of a country is not in question at this time. In such circumstances, the role of IFIs is vital, and the process of system transformation becomes the principal instrument available to IFIs and the international community in preventing ethno-national conflict.

To be successful, system transformation must be sensitive to the four sources of ethno-national conflict outlined above. This requires first of all a strong emphasis on institution building, both at the systemic and societal level, to support the establishment of a framework within which cross-patterned reticulation can take place. Second, system transformation must ensure both the participation and support of a country's elites, including ethnic elites, and their supporters. This presupposes a relatively broad identification among the population with the emerging structure of democracy and a market economy.[98] This identification is not only important to ensure the sustainability of the new political and economic structures once they have been established; of equal importance are the stabilizing qualities of broad-based public and elite support during the volatile and difficult transition period, when the possibility of mobilization and conflict is particularly high.

In pursuing an active strategy, IFIs do not have to get directly involved in such sensitive domestic political issues as determining the particular institutional structure of cross-patterned reticulation. For example, the degree of political and economic centralization will depend on the particular set of circumstances at hand, such as how much ethnonational mobilization has already taken place as well as its particular manifestation. Given the legacy of centralized political authority and economic planning in ECE and the FSU, a more dispersed institutional network is likely to gain greater legitimacy. In addition, political systems based on federalism and consociational democracy tend to have a relatively successful record in responding to and absorbing ethnonational aspirations. In devising their strategy of transformation, IFIs should therefore be sensitive to such domestic developments.

Passive engagement is likely to dominate IFIs' efforts at prevention if all mobilized parties have taken the position that the territorial integrity of the country in question can no longer be preserved, or if the country has already experienced large-scale ethnic violence but is currently engaged in negotiating a peaceful settlement, often with the help of the international community. In these cases, the degree of ethno-national mobilization is high and manifests itself solely in the form of separatism, irredentism, or both by all parties involved. Prevention here is focused on peacefully resolving competing claims over territory, property, and so on. Successful passive engagement would lead to a division of territory and thus property between new, separate sovereign political entities. System transformation remains a dominant goal for IFIs in each of the new countries, but their capacity to prevent the outbreak of ethno-national conflict is no longer relevant within the old borders. The sovereign territory that was to be transformed either no longer exists or is likely to disintegrate, forcing IFIs to reconsider their strategy in light of the new environment, especially the new distribution of sovereign territory.

Peaceful resolution of ethno-national mobilization requires extensive mediation and arbitration procedures, most likely sponsored by countries or international organizations responsible for political and security affairs, as covered by other chapters in this book. The negotiations have to culminate in a series of binding agreements, often guaranteed by outside parties, among the different ethnic groups. The strong political and security component contained in this particular strategy of conflict prevention relegates IFIs to a secondary, though still important, role.

Several important points concerning the relationship between passive and active strategies need to be kept in mind. First, it is not inconceivable that IFIs could be engaged in both passive and active strategies at the same time. For example, while a separation agreement for a country is being negotiated, IFIs should lend their support to ensure that the process remains peaceful and succeeds—passive engagement. But they should also begin to develop a comprehensive strategy of system transformation for each of the newly independent states, which are still likely to consist of multiple ethnic groups. The "new" strategy of system transformation must take this into account—active engagement.[99]

Second, while the possibility that IFIs would get involved in the prevention of ethnic conflict only via a passive strategy cannot be ruled out, in most cases passive engagement is likely to follow some prior active engagement by IFIs.[100] The abandonment of an active strategy does not automatically imply a failure of the IFIs and their approach to system transformation; there are numerous other external and internal factors that could be responsible for the disintegration of a country. Still, for future reference, it would be helpful for IFIs to consider their need to switch to a passive strategy and examine to what degree their policies contributed to the increase in ethno-national mobilization and the subsequent disintegration of the country.[101]

However, it is highly unlikely that a single country would be the beneficiary of both passive and active strategies *at the same time*. In fact, given the definition of these two strategies—promotion of *peaceful disintegration* and promotion of continued *integration* in the context of system transformation—they are mutually exclusive. A joint application would be counterproductive and waste scarce resources of the IFIs. This raises the difficult question of when to switch from an active to a passive strategy, which amounts to an acknowledgment that prevention of ethno-national conflict within the confines of the current sovereign territory is no longer a realistic option. The appropriate timing of such a decision is vital for IFIs because ethno-national mobilization can take on such a degree of intensity that continued support of system transformation within the "old" boundaries may not only be ineffective but could well lead to further intensification of ethno-national mobilization, provoking a violent escalation of the conflict.[102] Still, the actual decision to switch strategies lies beyond the mandate of either the Bank or the Fund.

In sum, there are four sets of strategies by which IFIs could contribute to the prevention of ethno-national conflict. The following sections discuss each of these strategies and their operational significance for IFIs in more detail. Greater emphasis is placed on the active strategies because they establish IFIs as primary actors in the prevention of ethno-national conflict.

Passive Strategies

Before discussing some of the options that IFIs have in preventing conflict under circumstances where the territorial integrity of a country can no longer be preserved, a note of caution is in order. The attention to passive strategies should by no means imply that they are the first or best option to deal with the political, economic, and social instabilities during the process of system transformation. To the contrary, it would be a major setback if the international community was forced to rely on passive strategies alone.

The disintegration of the international political and economic system based on the nation-state without any alternative legitimate structures and mechanisms in place does not bode well for its continued stability.[103] All efforts should be made to preserve the territorial integrity of a country, which makes the early and *active* involvement of IFIs so important. At the same time, it would be dangerous to ignore a situation where peaceful disintegration has become the only viable alternative to its violent companion. The central challenge for IFIs and the rest of the international community is to prevent such a path from becoming the norm for coping with ethno-national mobilization.

INDIRECT-PASSIVE. Indirect-passive involvement by IFIs is probably the least important strategy and has the fewest policy and organizational implications. To begin with, it assumes that either the Bank or the Fund are operating in a country whose territorial integrity is no longer sustainable or that has been involved in large-scale violent ethnic conflict but where peacekeeping operations have led to an interruption of hostilities and to international mediation. In such circumstances, an indirect-passive strategy requires that IFIs assess their activities in the country (or countries) and ensure that they do not in any way adversely affect the ongoing mediation process. In addition, IFIs should consider carefully whether to begin any new activities based on the sovereign territory as currently defined. In fact they may even want to halt ongoing projects or financial support, depending on the type of project, its location, and so on. If projects are not interrupted, IFIs face the difficult task of ensuring that their financial support does not free up domestic resources that can be diverted in support of one group's aspirations and thus contribute to a shift in the balance of power among the warring factions, leading to a change in the negotiating positions and possibly even a resumption of violence.

If, as is often the case, another country is impeding the negotiations toward a peaceful settlement or advocating either overtly or covertly the use of violence to resolve the conflict, IFIs could use their activities in that country to encourage the cessation of such policies. Again, close cooperation with other international organizations is a precondition for success. In its strongest form such efforts include IFI support of sanctions imposed by the United Nations, assuming of course that sanctions will actually promote the goal of peaceful disintegration.[104] Finally and as discussed in detail elsewhere, IFIs should join international efforts to contain the proliferation of weapons and weapons-related technology into areas of tension.[105]

DIRECT-PASSIVE. Although IFIs continue to play only a secondary role, their direct-passive involvement can be of considerable importance to the peaceful resolution of a conflict. In essence, IFIs would provide economic backing for a politicomilitary solution. The resources of the IFIs, especially the Bank's, could help to make a financially and economically unattractive but otherwise acceptable settlement—including the division of a country—more attractive. For example, IFIs could promise the prospective new states not just membership in their organizations but a continuation of their support of system transformation. In fact, there are indications that the Washington Accords of April 1994 that led to the creation of the Muslim-Croat federation were backed by IFI commitments. Within a few months of the accord, the World Bank approved a $128 million loan to Croatia.[106] This was followed in October by a $192 million credit facility extended by the IMF.[107]

Indeed, on numerous other occasions not related to ECE and the FSU, both the Bank and the Fund have supported the peaceful resolution of an ongoing or threatening conflict long before the political settlement was actually reached. For example, both the Bank and the Fund, the latter in the context of an article 4 consultation, sent missions to South Africa in early 1991.[108] This was almost four years before the first free elections in South Africa, at a time when the apartheid regime was beginning to disintegrate but when the future direction of the country was by no means clear and racial tensions were high. In July 1993 the Bank reported that it planned to lend up to $1 billion a year for five years once a new, democratically elected government was in place.[109] In September 1993, one day after the Transitional Executive Council—a multiparty, multiracial body—was created to oversee preparations for South Africa's first universal suffrage election, the country received an $850 million loan from the IMF for repayment relief on drought-related debt. Since the elections in April 1994, the international community has bestowed unaccustomed praise on the IFIs for their role in South Africa's move to a market-oriented economic policy. In addition to the IMF loan, the International Finance Corporation (the World Bank affiliate that lends to the private sector) announced in October 1994 that it would create a $375 million fund to make loans and equity investments to black South Africans who want to buy franchises. As of the end of 1994, the World Bank remained eager to assist South Africa, and awaited only the new government's final decisions on appropriate projects.

Another example of IFIs supporting the peaceful resolution of a conflict is the Bank's involvement in the Middle East peace process. Although financial support was officially pledged only in October 1993, about two weeks *after* the historic peace accord between Israel and the PLO, a World Bank mission had visited the region nine months before the agreement. The purpose of the mission, which took place during the height of negotiations, was to assess the "development needs and prospects of the economies of the West Bank and Gaza."[110] As a result of these early initiatives, the Bank in May 1994 published its Emergency Assistance Program for the Occupied Territories. The report, developed in collaboration with the Palestinians and designed to channel the support pledged in October 1993, outlined a three-year, $1.2 billion program focusing on priority investments and technical assistance.[111] Yet another case can be found in Haiti. For several months before President Aristide was restored to power in October 1994, the World Bank had been working closely with him on plans for restoring the Haitian economy, the poorest in the western hemisphere. In August 1994 an informal conference of donors organized by the World Bank convened in Paris to develop a broad plan for Haiti in anticipation of Aristide's return, and arrived at a formula that provided Haiti with about $1 billion over the next five years. By the end of 1994 the Bank had been able to organize three commitments to provide $226 million worth of assistance.[112]

The principal mechanism through which such arrangements are made is a so-called consultative group. The request for such a meeting comes from the recipient country but needs the approval of the major donor countries, who therefore have great influence in the design of an aid package and the financial incentives that it contains. At first sight it may seem that such a mechanism is not readily applicable to many situations in the FSU because in many cases sovereignty and territory itself are in question. The Bank's involvement in Haiti, Gaza, and the West Bank demonstrate, however, that sovereignty and territorial integrity are not preconditions for forming a consultative group. What is necessary is an international consensus to support a political settlement that incorporates IFIs.

Another potential example of direct-passive engagement is support for a settlement that requires the resettlement of ethnic groups. As discussed earlier, the Bank has accumulated considerable experience in the implications of the displacement of people in the context of economic development. This expertise as well as the financial resources to provide incentives could, if necessary, be put to use in ECE and the FSU.[113]

Finally, there is a precedent for IFI involvement in mitigating real or potential economic implications of conflict for countries not directly involved. To alleviate any negative consequences of the Gulf War, the Fund amended the conditions for access to or duration of seven of its instruments. This included, among others, a modification and rephasing of finance available to members; suspension of some borrowing limits; increased ESAF financing and a fourth year of ESAF support; and a change in the Compensatory and Contingency Financing Facility (CCFF) conditions.[114]

The above discussion has both intra- and interinstitutional implications. For passive strategies to succeed, IFIs would have to ensure that projects are examined with regard to their contributory potential to delay or impede a peaceful settlement of an ethnic conflict. This should be done first when a project is being considered but needs to be repeated regularly as the political negotiations unfold. In the Bank, for example, such a guideline would have to be injected into the project cycle discussed earlier. A project could be first evaluated for its contributory potential during the identification and preparation phase. Subsequently, the implementation and supervision phases of the project cycle would include regular reexaminations of a project based on its conflict potential. In each case a brief evaluation by the country desk could discuss the anticipated or current implications of the proposed project based on the actual political and security conditions on the ground. If there is concern about the project's "insensitivity" to the ongoing politicomilitary situation, the design could be altered during the negotiation phase. If the concern arises ex-post, that is, during implementation, the Bank should consider the interruption or even termination of the project.

In addition to establishing such a procedure within the Bank, IFIs should cooperate to exchange information on such issues and develop joint positions, regardless of whether the passive engagement is indirect or direct.

Here the Policy Framework Paper (PFP) lends itself as a useful coordinating mechanism.[115] The PFP is currently used to coordinate Bank and Fund operations in the context of SAF and ESAF, and could be expanded with a few modifications to include the aspect of passive prevention. Moreover, collaborating on this issue within the context of the PFP would avoid duplication and save resources.

Finally, close cooperation is required between IFIs and the various political and military organizations that are mediating a conflict (for example, the UN, the Organization for Security and Cooperation in Europe [OSCE], NATO). Ultimately it is those organizations that require and request IFI support of peaceful conflict resolution, and they should continue to be the primary coordinators of third-party support. This support is not restricted to IFIs, but could also come from other regional or international organizations, including regional development banks, the European Union, individual countries, NGOs, and others. In fact, given the scarce resources available to IFIs, it may be prudent not to burden IFIs with direct-passive activities. As stated earlier, prevention of ethno-national conflict through active strategies is the first and best policy approach. It does not call into question the territorial integrity of a country, nor does it risk the escalation of violence. Given the important and instrumental role that IFIs play in the design and implementation of active strategies, they may wish to leave direct-passive engagement to others and focus on active strategies.

Active Strategies

INDIRECT-ACTIVE. Active engagement is indirect if it focuses on what has been referred to as the "traditional" operations of IFIs. IFIs ensure that their activities in countries where there is a threat of ethno-national conflict are checked against their potential to heighten ethnic tensions.

Taking first the Bank as an example, it is possible to rely on the experience it gained in integrating environmental protection as an enabling condition into its mandate and operations. As part of its increasing attention to the environment in the early 1980s, the Bank adopted Environmental Assessment (EA) procedures.[116] The purpose of the Bank's EAs is to ensure that projects under consideration are environmentally sound and sustainable, and that any negative environmental consequences are detected *early* in the project's development stage.[117] EAs are said to be a flexible procedure, varying in depth, breadth, and type of analysis depending on the type and purpose of the project. These procedures usually include an environmental impact screening of the project in question, environmental categorization of the project, identification of the issues, interagency consultations, a list of recommendations, solutions, or alternatives, a mitigation plan, a management plan, and a monitoring plan.

The Bank has designated the environmental assessment process as the responsibility of the borrower, and the outcome of these assessments are said to be considered heavily by the Bank in its lending policies and in the selection of project sites and design. The Bank's country desks as well as the Regional Environmental Division assist and monitor the EA process. Because environmental issues usually affect national, regional, and local government agencies, the Bank requires that interagency meetings be held during key points in the assessment cycle.[118] The Bank expects the borrower to take the views of those groups and NGOs affected by the project into consideration.

The use of an assessment procedure by the Bank in ensuring that its lending policies do not intensify or instigate the outbreak of ethno-national conflict is a feasible proposition which would not require any major organizational change or the creation of additional institutions. Such an assessment plan would allow the Bank to ensure that projects under consideration are sensitive to the ethnic conditions in the borrower country and that any negative ethno-national impact is detected early in the project's development stage. The rationale and legitimacy for an ethnic assessment plan is derived from the fact that IFIs need to secure the proper enabling environment for system transformation in ECE and the FSU.

An ethno-national assessment (ENA) should be a flexible procedure with varying levels of analysis depending on a country's degree of ethnic stratification, the degree of ethno-national mobilization, and the purpose of the project. It may be helpful to distinguish further between two types of ENAs: first, *project-specific* ENAs, used to asses the ethno-national impact of a particular project; and second, *regional or sectoral assessments,* employed when a number of significant projects with potentially cumulative impacts are planned for a particular region of a country. The latter are likely to detect potential sources of conflict that several individually conducted ENAs may fail to detect. A detailed ENA modeled in part on the EA is currently being prepared in the context of another research project (see also direct-active strategies below).

The ENA would take place in the early phases of the project cycle discussed earlier (especially phases 1–3: identification, preparation, and appraisal). Among other elements, it would include the identification of key ethno-national issues (current and historical),[119] a recommendation of the type of ethno-national analysis that is required (the type or types of ethno-national manifestations, their stages, the level of mobilization and its causes), and a preliminary ENA schedule or timeline. In most cases an ENA should form part of a project's feasibility study so that the results can be directly integrated into the initial project design. The borrower should submit the ENA report to the Bank and all interested parties before Bank appraisal of the project.

The so-called Executive Project Summary should detail the ENA's status and describe how major ethno-national issues have been resolved or are to be addressed. The Bank, during its appraisal, should review the procedural and substantive elements of the ENA with the borrower, resolve any outstanding issues, assess the adequacy of the institutions charged with the management of the ENA's findings, and determine if the ENA's recommendations are properly addressed in the project design. Environmental Assessments have been correctly criticized for a lack of transparency and access. Both aspects are of central importance in the case of an ENA because ethnic groups and minorities must be involved in both the ENA itself and the subsequent implementation of an ENA-customized project.

Turning to the Fund, its programs, which focus more on macroeconomic aspects of system transformation, may for the most part not be very well suited for a project-specific ENA. One exception to this, however, would be its support for transforming the financial systems of ECE and the FSU. A financial system lies at the core of a market economy, providing intermediary services for savers and investors. Whatever the particular structure of the financial system, all market economies in the West, albeit with varying degrees of success, have special legal and institutional arrangements to ensure access by minority groups to credit. Universal individual or group access to credit is one of the central preconditions for taking advantage of the economic opportunities that a transforming and growing economy offers.

As of the summer of 1995, the IMF did not consider the question of ethnic minority access to credit when designing reform programs for the financial system of ECE and the FSU, even though the structure of the financial system is usually mentioned in the context of IMF activities relating to good governance.[120] An assessment procedure that would sensitize these IMF activities to the potential for ethno-national mobilization would guard against the Fund inadvertently contributing to ethno-national mobilization. In the context of its technical assistance program, and in particular with respect to the legal framework program, the Fund could advise countries on developing banking regulations and prudential supervision sensitive to ethnic minorities.[121] With help from its Central Banking Department and the IMF Institute,[122] as well as the IMF training center established in the fall of 1992 in Vienna, the Fund could also train regulators about enforcement of minority legislation as well as bankers about minority banking itself.[123]

Such an effort would address several potential sources of ethno-national conflict. By making credit accessible to ethnic minorities the Fund could reduce societal sociopsychological sources of conflict and counter arguments advanced by right-wing nationalist elites and their press, which have described the IMF as a "Jewish world conspiracy."[124] In addition, it would increase the legitimacy of state institutions as they are able to respond to the interests of a wider spectrum of society.

However, as has been the case with Environmental Assessments, project-level and to a lesser degree regional ENAs could be criticized because they deal only with project-level mitigation issues, and do not consider ethnic issues from a long-term planning perspective. In other words, indirect engagement alone may not be sufficient to steer a country toward a form of social organization that is characteristic of cross-patterned reticulation and ensure the success of system transformation.

DIRECT-ACTIVE. As discussed above, if active engagement is direct, IFI engagement relies on a strategy that specifically targets potential causes of ethno-national conflict, be they systemic or societal, institutional or socio-psychological, or any combination thereof. Active strategies presume the continued territorial integrity of the state and are formulated so as to encourage the establishment of cross-patterned reticulation, deemphasizing ethnic identities and encouraging alternative modes of identification characteristic of a system governed by political democracy and an economy based on market principles.

As in the case of indirect engagement, it is helpful to sketch a blueprint for ethno-national conflict prevention by considering IFI experience and practice in securing other enabling components. However, rather than scrutinizing projects for their "ethnic sensitivity," direct active engagement develops strategies for conflict prevention that address the causes of ethno-national conflict themselves. Among current Bank practices, the poverty reduction strategy provides a good model. The strategy, which was first outlined in the World Development Report of 1990 and is now a component of every Country Assistance Strategy, "involves supporting policies that promote broad-based growth and increase the productivity and economic opportunities for the poor as well as policies and institutions that provide the poor with better access to social services."[125]

A central plank in this strategy is a country-specific analysis of poverty to determine which elements of the strategy are most relevant to the prevailing country circumstances; often this is achieved by way of a poverty assessment (PA). Formally, the PA is described as an "assessment that quantifies the extent and nature of poverty and identifies the policy, public expenditure, and institutional issues, that constrain effective poverty reduction and that develops recommendations for government action aimed at reducing poverty."[126] In practice, the type and scope of the PA required by the Bank varies widely across countries depending on the internal situation, commitment by the government, and the data available for that country. The PA usually begins with a poverty profile of a country. This profile, depending on the country's circumstances, normally: (1) analyzes the effectiveness of economic management in promoting labor-intensive growth; (2) evaluates the ability and adequacy of government efforts to develop human resources for the poor; and (3) examines the existence and effectiveness of the country's social safety nets in protecting the most vulnerable groups and the very poor. Based on the profile, the PA develops a country poverty strategy that recommends actions (for example, phased programs of policy reform, public expenditures, institutional development) to strengthen the country's governmental policies and efforts toward poverty reduction. All recommendations are required by the Bank to incorporate sensitivity toward the social organization, traditions, and values of the local inhabitants.[127] Finally, the country PA includes a list of targets and social indicators to help convey the broad dimensions of what the proposed effort is likely to achieve.

In terms of actual lending, poverty concerns are reflected most clearly in projects that fall under the Program of Targeted Interventions (PTI). Classification in the PTI is limited to projects that have a specific mechanism for targeting the poor or demonstrate that the proportion of poor people among project beneficiaries is significantly larger than the proportion of the poor in the total population. (In recent years the Bank has also begun to include only those projects in which components targeted at poverty reduction total more than 25 percent of the loan amount.) By definition, PTI projects establish a notable precedent by targeting specific and identifiable groups or subgroups in the population, either to the exclusion of other parts of the population or benefiting them disproportionately. In fiscal year 1994, PTI lending comprised roughly 21 percent of total Bank lending.[128]

In conjunction with PAs, and as part of its poverty reduction strategy, the Bank has identified traditional noneconomic issues that hamper poverty reduction, such as gender disparity. In response to these issues, it has targeted specific subgroups and developed programs to assist them. For example, the Bank's gender development program attempts to reduce economic disparities and enhance women's participation in the economic development of their countries through the design of "gender sensitive" policies. Such policies include: the integration of gender considerations in country assistance programs; the design of programs to ensure that the overall impact of development is equally beneficial for both men and women; the identification of gender barriers; the review and if necessary modification of legal and regulatory frameworks to improve women's access; and the training of country officials in gender analysis and gender sensitivity.

As part of the gender development program, the Bank has also encouraged and promoted collaboration with international, national, and local nongovernmental agencies in implementing gender-specific Bank-financed projects. To analyze gender issues in a country, the Bank relies on country poverty assessments, economic sector work, and country dialogue. The gender analysis and strategies are incorporated into the country assessment strategies.[129]

The poverty reduction strategy, particularly the PA, could be used as a model for developing projects specifically tailored to address any of the four causes of ethno-national conflict. For example, just as the PA has led to the design of gender-specific projects, a similar process could be used to design an assessment policy for a particular ethnic group. The type and scope of the assessment required by the Bank would vary widely across countries depending on the existing system of ethno-national stratification, the degree of ethno-national mobilization and its causes, the type of ethnic manifestations, and commitment by the government to system transformation, ethnic pluralism, or both. The assessment should then be used to develop a country-specific ethno-national profile identifying the possible causes for ethno-national conflict. Based on this profile, a series of strategies could be developed to reduce the potential for conflict and thus enable the continuation of the Bank's efforts in the country—system transformation.

It should be obvious that, from an operational perspective, this type of assessment can and should be merged into the ENA outlined in the context of indirect-active IFI engagement. Not only is the same expertise required for each of the assessments, but in many cases a direct strategy may be appended to a larger project that failed an initial ENA. A single integrated ENA assessment process that can respond to the requirements of both indirect- and direct-active Bank engagement avoids unnecessary duplication, keeps the bureaucratic and organizational ramifications to a minimum, and saves costs. Monitoring and evaluation of the implementation of an integrated ENA's recommendations should be an essential aspect of the overall project assessment. In general, the monitoring and evaluation system needs to be able to provide information for assessing progress in achieving the project's target—reducing the potential for ethno-national conflict.

Many of the necessary policy responses are already being practiced by the Bank in the context of the enabling conditions discussed earlier. What is not being done, however, is the consideration of the ethnic dimension of development in general and the potential for ethno-national mobilization during the process of system transformation in particular. In fact, the Bank's emphasis on poverty reduction is the principal policy response when dealing with the sociopsychological sources of ethnic conflict. Targeting ethnic groups in the reduction of deprivation or integrating a multicultural curriculum into the Bank's educational programs are just two of the more obvious examples, the latter of which could easily be applied at the elite level as well. While not specifically related to ethnic conflict, the Bank has in fact targeted elites in its efforts to improve the performance of a country's bureaucracy.[130]

Similarly, in the context of good governance, institution building or institutional reform programs at both the systemic and societal level could be used to reduce the tendencies toward ethno-national mobilization. Good governance essentially implies the presence of political democracy in the context of a market economy, both of which have been identified as the central constituent elements of cross-patterned reticulation.

Finally, a strong emphasis on participatory development is required. In the context of an ENA-based strategy for conflict prevention, it would help to provide incentives for ethnic groups to join the process of system transformation by increasing their influence and share in the control over development initiatives, decisions, and resources. The incentives created by a participatory approach to development improve the chances that system transformation will be successful. For the strategy of system transformation itself, this implies much greater emphasis on decentralization. In the countries of ECE and the FSU, it requires a greater focus on local and regional actors for the Bank. Greater involvement by NGOs would also be helpful, especially in those areas where the Bank has little practical experience.

Direct-active engagement of the IMF is likely to be more limited. Still, as in the case of the Bank, the Fund's recent emphasis on poverty reduction creates the possibility for sensitizing Fund activities in ECE and the FSU to the potential for ethnic conflict. The Fund Board recently stated that "some [of its] policy measures may have important distributional implications [and] that such distributional effects can undermine public support for the reforms."[131] To counter such tendencies, "Fund staff, in discussions with program countries, should continue to analyze the implications of reform measures for vulnerable groups and to advise the authorities on how to integrate social safety nets and their financing into the programs."[132]

Given the analytical linkage between system transformation and ethno-national mobilization established above, and the Fund's recognition that "vulnerable groups" can "undermine reform,"[133] an ENA for the Fund's poverty policy is the logical next step. However, the above statement by the Board also states that the Fund should draw on the resources of the World Bank whenever possible.[134] It could therefore rely on the Bank's ENA findings for sensitizing its own structural adjustment program to the ethnic tensions in a target country. This could be done in three ways. First, the Fund could endorse a more gradual application of measures that might have a negative impact on a particular ethnic group. This is likely to be the least preferred option. Second, the Fund could seek additional aid from other international institutions or donors. A direct-active engagement by the Bank would seem an appropriate response to such a request. Third, in developing an adjustment program, the Fund could target government expenditures more directly at the needs of a particular ethnic minority and ensure their access to social safety nets.

Conclusion

In the wake of the end of the cold war, new global challenges, and escalating criticism from national governments and NGOs, IFIs have witnessed a growing debate over their goals and mandates. This is especially true for the World Bank and the International Monetary Fund, commemorating their fiftieth anniversary, but also for other institutions such as the regional development banks.

This chapter began by showing that IFIs have demonstrated—albeit reluctantly and only after considerable external criticism—a capacity to adjust to a new and still changing international environment, in particular the unprecedented socioeconomic and political transformation of the former East bloc, and to changing notions of growth and development and how they can best be achieved. By paying particular attention to the role of ethnicity, the analysis conceptualized system transformation in ECE and the new republics of the FSU as a transformation of a society characterized by vertical hierarchy to one structured by cross-patterned reticulation. Though for very different reasons, both of these forms of social organization were shown to exhibit a relatively high degree of societal integration where the level of ethnic mobilization is low and conflict unlikely.

Societal integration, does not remain high as countries transform their political and economic systems from vertical ethnic stratification toward societies structured by cross-patterned reticulation. Rather, a period of societal disintegration may intervene, caused by the sudden delegitimization of the entire social system and a process of ethno-national mobilization. While the strong resurgence of ethnic identities becomes the principal basis of societal integration, it is also the principal manifestation of the emergence of internal conflict. The sources of internal violence, however, are rapidly disintegrating social structures and institutions and the lack of new ones to take their place. This leads different ethnic segments of society to compete to redefine political, economic, and cultural boundaries along ethnic lines. In a multi-ethnic state and in the absence of well-established and legitimate forums to mediate interests, such competition is prone to conflict resolution by violence rather than compromise, as competing groups attempt to divide what not long ago seemed indivisible and was considered common to all—territory *and* property alike.

Given their deep involvement in system transformation, IFIs cannot divorce themselves from the pressures for ethno-national mobilization and the likelihood that it might turn violent. In fact, as this chapter has shown, system transformation is the critical link between IFIs and ethno-national conflict and they must therefore be sensitive to the four sources of ethno-national conflict, discussed above. This requires first of all a strong emphasis on institution building, both at the systemic and societal level, to support the establishment of a framework within which cross-patterned reticulation can take place. Second, system transformation must ensure both the participation and support of a country's elites and their supporters. This presupposes a relatively broad identification among the population with the emerging structure of democracy and a market economy.

The proposed ethno-national assessment procedure, derived from the IFIs' previous experience with enabling conditions such as environmental protection and poverty alleviation, would keep the bureaucratic and organizational, that is, intra-institutional, ramifications of IFI involvement to a minimum. Of equal or even greater importance for conflict prevention are a set of interinstitutional implications. First, IFIs should cooperate among each other to exchange information for the ENA procedure and develop joint policy positions. The Policy Framework Paper could become a useful mechanism for closer coordination. Second, closer cooperation on a regular basis is required between IFIs and the various political and military organizations that are involved in ECE and the FSU. Only when such an institutional network is firmly in place, ready to cooperate and geared toward the early recognition of ethnic tensions, can the outbreak of internal conflict be prevented.

Finally, although this analysis has focused on ECE and the FSU, the discussion of the dynamics of ethno-mobilization and the sources of ethno-national conflict lend themselves to a broader application in other regions, such as in Africa, Asia, or elsewhere. All of them are undergoing fundamental socioeconomic and political change as they are no longer constrained by the bipolar global structure. Of course the circumstances in each country or region differ and thus require different emphasis by IFIs.

This chapter has aimed to establish the conceptual linkage between ethno-national conflict and IFIs in the particular context of the former East bloc. Ultimately its value will be judged by its ability to stimulate debate and further research applicable to all regions of the world where internal conflict has and continues to destroy life.

Notes

1. On Fund lending to Yugoslavia, see David Driscoll, *What Is the International Monetary Fund?* (IMF, 1993), p. 15. As for the Bank's involvement in Yugoslavia, while it is admittedly difficult to identify what proportion of its lending has been affected by the ongoing hostilities, the case of infrastructure financing presents a telling picture. Beginning in 1963, Bank-funded projects played a major role in the expansion and modernization of Yugoslavia's infrastructure; indeed, between 1963 and 1991 the Bank lent in excess of $700 million for roads and railway projects in the former Yugoslavia (historical cost basis). By the time of the cease-fire between Croatia and Serbia in November 1991, it was estimated that almost 40 percent of all main roads in Croatia had been damaged by fighting. Estimates of damage to the Croatian railway system were put at about $300 million (figures from the Ministry of Reconstruction of the Republic of Croatia). In Bosnia-Herzegovina, the UN

High Commissioner for Refugees expected the costs of restoring the railway system there to exceed $150 million (*UNHCR Information Notes on Yugoslavia,* January 1994). Given the destruction wrought on Bank-supported infrastructure projects, it is somewhat ironic that one of the first loans to have been approved for Croatia is an $80 million disbursement, initialed at the beginning of 1995, to aid in the rehabilitation and modernization of the Croatian transport sector.

2. For a discussion of system transformation in ECE and the FSU that emphasizes not only economic but also political and social-psychological aspects, see Wolfgang Reinicke, *Building a New Europe: The Challenge of System Transformation and Systemic Reform* (Brookings, 1992), and the literature cited therein.

3. IMF Annual Report, 1994.

4. *IMF Survey,* January 9, 1995.

5. World Bank annual reports.

6. The Keynesian approach favored a more structured world economy, with intergovernmental institutions, such as the abortive International Trade Organization (ITO), and rules regulating currencies, investment, and trade. The more traditional approach preferred to let market forces dominate, with limited governmental interference and few or no international organizations. Margaret Garritsen de Vries, *The IMF in a Changing World* (IMF, 1986), p. 8.

7. World Bank Info Briefs, A.02.4–94.

8. Raymond Mikesell, *The Bretton Woods Debates: A Memoir* (Princeton University Press, 1994), p. 58.

9. Ibid., p. 8.

10. Ibid., pp. 8–9.

11. Catherine Gwin, *U.S. Relations with the World Bank, 1945–92* (Brookings, 1994), p. 3.

12. Criticism has come from a broad spectrum of actors, including powerful member countries, NGOs, academics, and IFI staff members who have left the institution.

13. A. W. Hooke, *The International Monetary Fund: Its Evolution, Organization and Activities* (IMF, 1982), p. 9.

14. The Board of Governors is the senior decisionmaking body in the World Bank. Each member appoints one governor and one alternate to the Board. Because the size of the Board makes it unwieldy, general operations of the Bank are conducted by the executive directors, five of whom are appointed by the five largest stockholders, with the remaining seven positions elected by the remaining members. A majority of the executive directors, exercising 50 percent or more of the total voting power, constitutes a quorum. The president of the Bank is elected by the executive directors and serves as their chairman. The president is chief of the operating staff of the Bank and subject to the review of the directors on matters of policy.

15. Briefly, area departments are responsible for maintaining operational relationships. Among other duties, they develop plans for loans and missions, review loan applications, and follow economic developments in and assess credit worthiness of member countries.

16. *The International Bank for Reconstruction and Development: 1946–1953* (published for the IBRD by Johns Hopkins University Press, 1954), p.14; Hooke, *The IMF,* p. 9.

17. Bruce Rich, *Mortgaging the Earth* (Beacon Press, 1994), p. 58.

18. Discussions are currently under way to adapt the project cycle to what is perceived as "the increasingly risky, volatile, and participatory framework of development assistance today." Robert Picciotto and Rachel Weaving, "A New Project Cycle for the World Bank?" *Finance and Development* (December 1994).

19. Driscoll, *What is the IMF?*, p.5.

20. Hooke, *The IMF,* p. 2.

21. See IBRD, Articles of Agreement, article 1.

22. IBRD, 1954. Early critics of the Bank, such as U.S. senator Robert A. Taft, claimed that the professed purpose of the Bank was misleading; it was not a relief organization but a "permanent institution involving [the United States] in a permanent policy." He argued that if relief and reconstruction for war-torn Europe were the goals, then a temporary organization for funneling assistance would be more appropriate. See Rich, *Mortgaging the Earth,* p. 61.

23. One of the biggest obstacles was the government guarantee requirement. The Bank would often try to work around this problem by extending credits to private projects through a local development bank, but this was seen as inadequate.

24. Mikesell, *Bretton Woods Debates,* p. 61.

25. Another cycle that led to a radical change in the donor agenda started in 1980 when the Bank moved away from project-driven loans and focused its efforts on reforms of economic policies. For an excellent discussion of these issues, see Joan Nelson, *Global Goals, Contentious Means: Issues of Multiple Aid Conditionality* (Overseas Development Council, 1993).

26. See, for example, the Wapenhans Report, *Effective Implementation: Key to Development Impact,* September 22, 1992.

27. See also "Mr Preston Makes Poverty His Judge," *Financial Times,* May 11, 1992.

28. World Bank, *Poverty Reduction,* Operational Directive, 1992.

29. See "Resettlement and Development: The Bankwide Review of Projects Involving Involuntary Resettlement 1986–1993," Environment Department, World Bank, April 1994.

30. World Bank, *Development and the Environment,* World Development Report 1992, Executive Summary, p. 14.

31. Ibid.

32. World Bank, *Governance and Development,* 1992.

33. Carol Lancaster, "Governance and Development: The Views from Washington," *IDS Bulletin,* vol. 24, no. 1 (1993); see also Mick Moore and Mark Robinson, "Can Foreign Aid Be Used to Promote Good Governance?" *Ethics and International Affairs,* vol. 8 (1994), pp. 141–58.

34. For the role of these elements in the constitution of democracy, see Michael Coppedge and Wolfgang H. Reinicke, "Measuring Polyarchy," *Studies in Comparative International Development,* vol. 25 (Spring 1990), pp. 51–72.

35. The following discussion draws on Wolfgang H. Reinicke, "Cooperative Security and the Political Economy of Nonproliferation," in Janne E. Nolan, ed., *Global Engagement: Cooperation and Security in the 21st Century* (Brookings, 1994), pp. 175–234.

36. World Bank, *Poverty Reduction,* Handbook and Operational Directive, 1992.

37. *The World Bank and Participation* (draft), 1994.

38. The World Bank, *NGO 1993 Progress Report.*

39. NGO Operational Manual, Mutual Transmittal Memorandum, OD 14.70.

40. The Articles of Agreement had been amended once before, to create the SDR in 1969. Driscoll, *What Is the IMF?*, p. 19.

41. Ibid., p. 10.

42. Manuel Guitian, "The IMF as a Monetary Institution: The Challenge Ahead," *Finance and Development,* vol. 31 (September 1994), p. 11.

43. In 1975 the IMF created the Oil Facility, which enabled members with payment problems due to the rise in oil prices to borrow additional IMF funds. In addition to that it established the Oil Facility Subsidy Account. It was the first facility designed exclusively for developing countries. The account provides assistance in the form of a subsidy on interest charges paid by members on purchases under the 1975 oil facility.

44. *Bretton Woods Commission,* 1994, p. B-9

45. Mikesell, *Bretton Woods Debate,* p. 62. The Compensatory and Contingency Financing Facility (CCFF) was created in February 1963. It was intended mainly for exporters of primary products to compensate for large fluctuations in commodity prices or other factors largely beyond the member's control. As with other Fund facilities, members are expected to make early repurchases if their balance of payments and reserve position improve sufficiently. Repurchases are made in three and one-quarter to five years. The Buffer Stock Financing facility, created in June 1969, makes finance available for the support of arrangements designed to dampen export price fluctuations. Repayments are made in three and one-quarter to five years. This facility has been inactive for nine consecutive years.

46. *IMF Survey,* January 9 and July 31, 1995.

47. IMF Annual Report, 1991; see also John Starrels, *Assisting Reform in Central and Eastern Europe* (IMF, March 1992), p. 3.

48. Omotunde Johnson and Joanne Salop, *Distributional Aspects of Stabilization Programs in Developing Countries* (IMF, March 1980).

49. IMF Annual Report, 1990.

50. Jacques J. Polak, "The Changing Nature of the IMF Conditionality," *Essays in International Finance* (September 1991), no. 184, p. 27; see also "Appendix G: Poverty (IMF)," in *International Finance,* Annual Report of the Chairman of the National Advisory Council on International Monetary and Financial Policies to the President and to the Congress for Fiscal Year 1990, p. 201.

51. "Appendix D: The IMF and the Environment," in *International Finance,* Annual Report of the Chairman of the National Advisory Council on International Monetary and Financial Policies to the President and to the Congress for Fiscal Year 1990, p. 175.

52. IMF Annual Report, 1991.

53. Polak, "The Changing Nature," pp. 24–29.

54. Ibid.

55. Note, however, that this may not necessarily result in an actual decline of a country's military arsenal. This work shows that military expenditures divert resources from other areas, such as social and economic services. In addition, military spending has tended to exhibit resilience during the implementation of adjustment programs that have emphasized fiscal tightening. This implies that the share of military expenditures as a percentage of total expenditures has actually risen as a result of IMF policies. Paula de Masi and Henri Lori, "How Resilient Are Military Expenditures," *IMF Staff Papers,* vol. 36, no. 1 (1989), pp. 130–65; Daniel

Hewett, "Military Expenditure: International Comparison of Trends," Working Paper WP/91/54 (IMF, May 1991), and "Econometric Testing of Economic and Political Influences," Working Paper WP/91/53 (IMF, May 1991).

56. For some of the classics, see Anthony Smith, *The Ethnic Revival* (Cambridge University Press, 1981) and *Ethnonationalism in Comparative Perspective* (University of Nevada Press, 1991); Joseph Rothschild, *Ethnopolitics: A Conceptual Framework* (Columbia University Press, 1981); Donald Horowitz, *Ethnic Groups in Conflict* (University of California Press, 1985); Hurst Hannum, *Autonomy, Sovereignty, and Self-Determination* (University of Pennsylvania Press, 1990); Andrew Greely, *Ethnicity in the United States* (New York: John Wiley Press, 1974); John Armstrong, *Nations before Nationalism* (University of North Carolina Press, 1982); Peter Alter, *Nationalism* (Frankfurt-am-Main: Suhrkamp Verlag, 1985); Hans Kohn, *The Ideal of Nationalism* (Macmillan, 1967); Karl Deutsch, *Nationalism and Social Communication* (MIT Press, 1953); John McGarry and Brendan O'Leary, *The Politics of Ethnic Conflict Regulation* (London: Routledge, 1993); Frank Chalk and Kurt Jonassohn, *The History and Sociology of Genocide: Analyses and Case Studies* (Yale University Press, 1990); and Barbara Harff, "Recognizing Genocide and Politicides," in *Genocide Watch* (Yale University Press, 1992). Some of the more recent literature on ethnic relations in the FSU and ECE include Bogdan Denis Denitch, *Ethnic Nationalism: The Tragic Death of Yugoslavia* (University of Minnesota Press, 1994); John F. Stack, Jr., *The Primordial Challenge: Ethnicity in the Contemporary World* (University of California Press, 1993); Gerhard Simon, *Nationalism and Policy toward the Nationalities in the Soviet Union* (Boulder, Colo.: Westview Press, 1991); Clifford Geertz, ed., *Old Societies and New States* (Yale University Press, 1963).

57. Vojislav Stanovcic, "Problems and Options in Institutionalizing Ethnic Relations," in *International Political Science Review,* vol. 13, no. 4 (1992), p. 376, no. 1.

58. Smith, "The Ethic Revival," p. 66.

59. Ibid.

60. Kohn, *Nationalism.*

61. Ted Gurr, *Minorities at Risk: A Global View of Ethnopolitical Conflicts* (Washington: United States Institute for Peace Press, 1993), p. 21.

62. Janusz Bugajski, "The Fate of Minorities in Eastern Europe," *Journal of Democracy,* vol. 4, (October 1993), p. 89.

63. Ibid.

64. Hannum, *Autonomy,* pp. 4–13.

65. Ibid.

66. Ibid.

67. Kumar Rupesinghe, "Theories of Conflict Resolution and Their Applicability to Protracted Ethnic Conflicts," *Bulletin of Peace Proposals,* vol. 18, no. 4 (1987), pp. 527–39.

68. The literature on ethnic mobilization generally distinguishes between two approaches—primordial and instrumental. The former are evolutionary theories that view ethnicity either as primordial sentiments reactivated in a modern society, often in defense of the threat of being replaced by some other more modern basis for mobilization. Instrumental approaches to ethnic mobilization argue that ethnic mobilization is not simply the inevitable result of primordial differences that generate unique or revitalized ethnic identifications and organizations. Rather, the

essence of ethnic mobilization in both old and new nation-states is dependent on the way in which ethnicity is "situationally determined." See Joanne Nagel and Susan Olzak, "Ethnic Mobilization in New and Old States: An Extension of the Competition Model," *Social Problems* (December 30, 1982), pp. 127–43; Fredrik Barth, ed., *Ethnic Groups and Boundaries* (Little, Brown, 1969). For a discussion of different theories of ethnic mobilization, see Stack, *The Primordial Challenge,* pp. 5–8.

69. Rothschild, *Ethnopolitics,* pp. 67–69.

70. This by no means implies that all ethnic segments are of equal strength. See Rothschild, *Ethnopolitics,* pp. 67–135. It is noteworthy that Rothschild, writing in 1981, characterized Yugoslavia as moving in that direction.

71. Note that a low level of mobilization does not by itself imply a low level of ethnic awareness or identity. The case of blacks in South Africa or that of Jews in the FSU comes to mind.

72. Ellen Jones and Fred Grupp, "Modernization and Ethnic Equalization in the USSR," *Soviet Studies,* vol. 36 (April 1984), pp. 159–84.

73. Rothschild, *Ethnopolitics,* p. 118.

74. S. W. R. de A. Samarasinghe and Reed Coughlan, *Economic Dimensions of Ethnic Conflict* (St. Martin's Press, 1991), pp. 1–15.

75. Stanley Lieberson, "Stratification and Ethnic Groups," in Anthony Richmond, ed., *Readings in Race and Ethnic Relations* (Pergamon Press, 1972), pp. 199–209.

76. The population of the former Czechoslovakia has remained throughout its seventy years of existence ethnically polarized. According to the 1991 census, the last census taken in the former Czechoslovakia, the ethnic breakdown in the Czech Republic was 81.2 percent Czech and only 3.1 percent Slovak. In the Republic of Slovakia 85.7 percent of the population was Slovak and 1.1 percent Czech.

77. On the role of institutions, see Peter Evans, Dietrich Rueschemeyer, and Theda Skocpol, *Bringing the State Back In* (Cambridge University Press, 1985); John Hall and G. John Ikenberry, *The State* (University of Minnesota Press, 1989); Sven Steinmo, *Structuring Politics: Historical Institutionalism in Comparative Analysis* (Cambridge University Press, 1992); R. Kent Weaver and Bert Rockman, eds., *Do Institutions Matter: Government Capabilities in the United States and Abroad* (Brookings, 1993).

78. Daniel Bell, "Ethnicity and Social Change," in Nathan Glazer and Daniel P. Moynihan, eds., *Ethnicity, Theory and Experience* (Harvard University Press, 1975), p. 169.

79. For a general discussion on this see Milton J. Esman, *Ethnic Conflict in the Western World* (Cornell University Press, 1977), pp. 12–15.

80. Victor Azarya, "Reordering State-Society Relations: Incorporation and Disengagement," in Donald Rothschild and Naomi Chazan, eds., *The Precarious Balance: State and Society in Africa* (Boulder: Westview Press, 1988), pp. 3–21.

81. Victor Azarya, *Aristocrats Facing Change* (Sage Press, 1976); Kumar Rupesinghe, *Internal Conflict and Governance: The Disappearing Boundaries* (St. Martin's Press, 1992). According to Geertz, *Old Societies,* it is the very process of state formation, among other things, that stimulates sentiments of parochialism, communalism, racialism and so on because it introduces into society a valuable new prize over which to fight and a "frightening new force with which to contend."

82. The desire for autonomy and separateness during times of fundamental political and economic change is not restricted to ethnic groups. The debate over national identity and greater independence and the calls for subsidiarity in the European Union attest to that.

83. Richard Staar, *Transition to Democracy in Poland* (St. Martin's Press, 1993).

84. On the limits of institutions, see Walter Powell and Paul DiMaggio, *The New Institutionalism in Organizational Analysis* (University of Chicago Press, 1991), pp. 63–82.

85. Elites are defined here as a group of individuals who exercise an inordinate amount of power and authority in society. For a general discussion of the role of elites in society, see Peter Bachrach, *Political Elites in a Democracy* (Atherton Press, 1971), especially chapter 1 and the literature cited therein.

86. On the role of elites in ECE see Hans-Ulrich Derlien and George Szablowski, "East European Transitions, Elites, Bureaucracies, and the European Community," *Governance,* vol. 6 (July 1993), pp. 304–24; Joachim Jens Hesse, *Administrative Transformation in Central and Eastern Europe: Towards Public Sector Reform in Post-Communist Societies* (Oxford, 1993). For the FSU, see above and in addition Mary McAuley, "Politics, Economics and Elite Realignment in Russia: A Regional Perspective," *Soviet Economy,* vol. 8, no. 1 (1992), pp. 46–88; David Lane, *Russia in Flux* (Edward Elgar, 1992), pp. 3–23; Martha Brill Olcott, "The Future of Central Asia," *The Harriman Institute Forum,* vol. 6, (October 1992), pp. 1–10.

87. *RFE/RL Report,* vol. 1 (October 1992); *Christian Science Monitor Global Report,* June 29, 1994.

88. On the concept of ethnic core, see Anthony Smith, *The Ethnic Revival* (Cambridge University Press, 1991).

89. See K. M. de Silva, *A History of Sri Lanka* (Hurst and Co., 1981), pp. 8–16.

90. Smith, *The Ethnic Revival.* Smith further states that locating such ethnic cores is important because it can "reveal a good deal about the subsequent shape and character of nations—if (and when) such nations emerge."

91. Aleksander Gella, *The Intelligentsia and the Intellectuals* (Sage Publications, 1976).

92. This is not to say that such defusion is "better," only that it is less likely to lead to conflict.

93. Martin Marger, *Elites and Masses: An Introduction to Political Sociology* (Van Nostrand Press, 1977), pp. 12–15.

94. Esman, *Ethnic Conflict in the Western World.*

95. Richard Rose, "Post-Communism and the Problem of Trust," *Journal of Democracy,* vol. 5, no. 3 (July 1994), pp. 18–30.

96. J. Dollard, *Frustration and Aggression* (Yale University Press, 1939), pp. 42–49.

97. Reinicke, *Building a New Europe,* pp. 23–43.

98. Ibid.

99. Take the example of the former Czechoslovakia. Despite the relatively high degree of Czech and Slovak segregation, there are other minorities in each of the new republics. In the Czech Republic: 13.2 percent Moravian and 2.5 percent divided between Polish, German Silesian, Roma, and Hungarian. The Republic of Slovakia: 10.7 percent Hungarian, 1.4 percent Roma, 1.1 percent Czech, and the

remaining 1.1 percent is divided among Ruthenian, Ukrainian, German, Polish, and Russian.

100. This is due to the fact that IFIs are there even before ethno-national mobilization starts because of system transformation.

101. For an argument that IFIs contributed to disintegration, see Susan Woodward, *Balkan Tragedy: Chaos and Dissolution after the Cold War* (Brookings, 1995).

102. Again the example of Yugoslavia and the Czech and Slovak Federal Republic (CSSR) comes to mind.

103. Wolfgang Reinicke, *Global Public Policy: A Challenge for International Finance and Trade* (Brookings, forthcoming).

104. Lori Fisler Damrosch, "The Collective Enforcement of International Norms through Economic Sanctions," *Ethics and International Affairs,* vol. 8 (1994), pp. 59–75; RFE/RL Daily Report, 5/21 and 8/27, 1993.

105. Reinicke, "Cooperative Security," pp. 175–234.

106. Monthly Operational Summary, 17/8, 1994.

107. IMF Survey, October 31, 1994.

108. On the Fund's mission, see *IMF Occasional Paper 91,* 1992.

109. The aid was to target housing, education, electrification, and so on.

110. *Developing the Occupied Territories: An Investment in Peace,* September 1993; see also Stanley Fischer, Dani Rodrik, and Elias Tuma, *The Economics of Middle East Peace: View from the Region* (MIT Press, 1993); *Executive Summary,* PLO, Department of Economic Affairs and Planning, September 1993.

111. As of the end of 1994, only about $80 million of the $720 million pledged for the year had been disbursed with another $350 million committed. *Financial Times,* November 30, 1994.

112. Forty million dollars would come from the Bank's International Development Association, which lends to the poorest countries in the world under highly favorable terms. The United States and nine other countries would provide $82 million to settle Haiti's outstanding debts to the IFIs. (Haiti made a contribution toward settling these arrears.) Finally, the World Bank released $104 million that was committed but not disbursed for programs frozen in 1991, when Haiti's elected government was ousted. *Wall Street Journal,* December 12, 1994.

113. For a proposal to use financial incentives for settlers in the West Bank, see William Quandt and others, *Washington Post,* May 29, 1994.

114. IMF Annual Report, 1991.

115. Jacques Polak, *The World Bank and the IMF: A Changing Relationship* (Brookings, 1994), pp. 28–37.

116. Three reasons are usually given for the introduction of EAs: the entry of the Bank into conditioned policy lending; the rise of the Bank as the leader of the international donor community; and the rise of the environmental protection movement and the emergence of environmental NGOs.

117. Operational Directive 4.01: Environmental Assessment, October 1991; Operational Directive 4.00, Annex A: Environmental Assessment, 1989.

118. Interagency meetings can include agencies of the national government, agencies of the governments of the affected region, NGOs both local and international with an interest in the country or region, affected national and regional groups such as indigenous people, trade based groups, and so on.

119. This reflects the continued theoretical debate over the role of primordial vs. material sources or causes of ethno-national conflict.

120. For a detailed discussion of the nature of IMF activities, see IMF Workings Papers 3/1994, 75/93, and 23/93.

121. On IMF technical assistance, see *Bretton Woods Commission,* 1994.

122. The IMF Institute was established in 1964. The topics for discussion are jointly determined by the country authorities and the Institute in coordination with the Fund's concerned area department.

123. Currently seminars and training programs are geared toward a variety of issues, including market economics, tax policy, tax and customs administration, treasury systems, budgetary accounting, social safety nets, and social security.

124. Paul Hockenos, *Free to Hate: The Rise of the Right in Post-Communist Eastern Europe* (London: Routledge, 1993), chapter 8.

125. *Poverty Reduction and the World Bank: Progress in Fiscal 1994.*

126. *Implementing the World Bank's Strategy to Reduce Poverty: Progress and Challenges,* 1993.

127. See Operational Directives OD 4.15 and OD 4.20.

128. *Poverty Reduction and the World Bank: Progress in 1994.*

129. See World Bank Operational Policies OP 4.20; and Bank Policies BP 2.11 Annex A.

130. In Guyana, Bank efforts include $12 million to improve basic public services by establishing a longer-term salary structure (thus enabling the government to attract and retain essential staff) and the support of a related recruitment program. World Bank Annual Report, 1993, p. 158.

131. IMF Annual Report, 1994.

132. Ibid.

133. IMF OD on Political Sustainability.

134. IMF Annual Report, 1994.

SEVEN

Conflict Prevention in Transition Economies: A Role for the European Bank for Reconstruction and Development?

Melanie H. Stein

INTERNATIONAL lending for development and the parceling of foreign aid are two subjects fueling a heated debate among elected officials, bureaucrats, pundits, and scholars. Two issues are the crux of the debate: the return on foreign economic assistance, measured in terms of contribution to long-term security interests, and the value of "political conditionality," the contemporary proclivity to link access to soft loans, grant funds, trade privileges, and similar benefits to adherence by the recipient to human rights norms or principles of "civil society" established by donor states.[1] The fury that preceded the continuance of most favored nation trade status for China, the heated exchanges on aid to Turkey in the face of its war on the Kurds, and the post–election day 1994 hostility to the very notion of foreign economic assistance bear ample witness.

This paper has been undertaken in the author's personal capacity. All thoughts, reflections, and views expressed herein are attributable solely to the author and are in no way intended to represent the views of the Board of Directors or management of the European Bank for Reconstruction and Development. The author wishes to thank the Ford Foundation for support provided in 1991 in the form of a Public International Law Research Fellowship which led to a position at the EBRD and ultimately the writing of this paper.

Accusations, rhetoric, and bold statements on foreign aid reverberate against a backdrop of carnage in the former Yugoslavia, heightened nationalist fervor in post–cold war Europe, the destruction of Grozny in Chechnya, and a remote but perceptible threat of an Islamic fundamentalist insurgency in central Asia. Aside from a few outliers, there is a consensus that economic assistance and increased trade links are fundamental to political stabilization in central and eastern Europe and the former Soviet Union. Yet few agree on the optimal form, scope, and means of channeling economic assistance. Should funds be used primarily to shore up foundering governments; to build institutions of civil society; to empower economically disadvantaged groups; or to promote democracy? Varying perceptions of the causes of ethno-national conflict give rise to discordant responses. The tension between political stabilization and democracy building, goals not easily reconcilable in the short to medium term, further complicates matters.

Two things are clear. U.S. and European strategic aims in the post-cold war era include political stabilization and the crystallization of democratic values in central and eastern Europe and the former Soviet Union. Large-scale economic assistance is fundamental to the realization of these aims, and the means by which such assistance is allocated and expended, whether through bilateral or multilateral institutions, conditionally or unconditionally, in periodic sizable installments or one-shots, alone or in association with private investment partners, substantively influences the scope and nature of its impact. How might the international community better manage and check, in a manner consistent with international norms and principles, the conflicting aims and aspirations of the diverse ethno-national groups of central and eastern Europe and the former Soviet Union? Could the international financial institutions (IFIs) working in the region, by redefining their lending strategies and adopting a more strategic approach, assist in reducing or stifling burgeoning ethno-national conflicts in the jurisdictions of central and eastern Europe and the former Soviet Union?

Sights are turned to the European Bank for Reconstruction and Development (EBRD), the regional IFI founded by forty states, the Commission of the European Economic Community, and the European Investment Bank in May 1990 on the heels of the collapse of communism in central Europe.

The Basics

The EBRD's purpose is to assist the former East bloc in the transition to market economies. What role might the EBRD play in securing and preserving ethno-national peace in central and eastern Europe and the former Soviet Union?[2]

Purpose and Charter

The purpose of the EBRD is enshrined in Article 1 of the Agreement Establishing the EBRD, the international treaty that is the constitutive document of the Bank and serves as its charter:

> In contributing to economic progress and reconstruction, the purpose of the Bank shall be to foster the transition towards open market-oriented economies and to promote private and entrepreneurial initiative in the Central and Eastern European countries committed to and applying the principles of multiparty democracy, pluralism and market economics.

The EBRD fulfills this stated purpose by extending loans and guarantees to enterprises in central and eastern Europe engaged in productive projects, investing equity in local private enterprises or state-owned enterprises in the process of privatization, and providing technical assistance, advisory services, and training to assist its recipient member countries to implement structural and sectoral economic reforms, including demonopolization, decentralization, and privatization.

The Agreement distinguishes the youngest member of the family of international financial institutions from its elder siblings in three important ways.

—First, the Agreement trains the institution's sights squarely on the private sector. At least 60 percent of the EBRD's total committed loans, guarantees, and equity investments must be channeled to the private sector. The reconstruction or development of infrastructure is to be financed only if necessary for private sector development and the transition to a market-oriented economy. Consistent with this private sector mandate, whereas the International Bank for Reconstruction and Development (IBRD) is required by its charter in each instance to obtain a sovereign guarantee, the EBRD is free of any such restraint in respect of its public as well as private sector activities.

—Second, the Agreement places upon the EBRD an affirmative obligation to safeguard the environment.

—Third, the Agreement orients the EBRD politically. Article 8 is proscriptive: "The Bank may conduct its operations in countries from Central and Eastern Europe which are proceeding steadily in the transition towards market-oriented economies and the promotion of private and entrepreneurial initiative, and which apply, by concrete steps and otherwise, the principles as set forth in Article 1 of this Agreement."

Countries not proceeding steadily in the transition toward market-oriented economies and the promotion of private and entrepreneurial initiative and not applying the principles of multiparty democracy, pluralism, and market economics may not benefit from EBRD resources. This stands in fundamental opposition to the principles underlying the IBRD and its affiliates the International Development Agency (IDA), International Finance Corporation (IFC), and Multilateral Investment Guarantee Agency (MIGA) (collectively, the World Bank Group), and the other regional multilateral development banks, the African Development Bank, the Asian Development Bank, and the Inter-American Development Bank. The charters of each of these institutions include provisions dictating neutrality as to the political and economic systems of borrowers.[3]

This latter distinction, like the emphasis on private sector development and environmental concerns, was intentional. John Major, prime minister of the United Kingdom, in his inaugural address at the first meeting of the Board of Governors of the EBRD in April 1991, made it clear: "The European Bank is unique in having an explicit political aim; to bolster democracy in Eastern Europe."[4] President François Mitterrand of France sounded a similar theme in his inaugural address, reminding the governors that the fragility of the new democratic institutions of central and eastern Europe had been one of the motivations in establishing the EBRD: "It will be for this Bank which has just been born not only to help in rebuilding the economy but also to encourage the progress of democracy. That is not its direct role but it is what inspires and will continue to inspire its leadership."[5]

Membership

Forty states, including the G7 advanced industrialized states, the several states comprising the European Union (EU), the newly independent states of central and eastern Europe, the Union of Soviet Socialist Republics (USSR), and two institutions, the European Community (represented by the Commission of the EU) and the European Investment Bank (EIB), founded the EBRD in May 1990. The member states of the EU, together with the Commission of the EU and the EIB, own a majority interest. The United States and Japan hold 10 and 8.5 percent interest respectively.

At the time of its founding, the EBRD's recipient members numbered eight: Bulgaria, Czechoslovakia, the German Democratic Republic,[6]

Hungary, Poland, Romania, the (USSR), and the Socialist Federal Republic of Yugoslavia (SFRY). To ensure that the EBRD would in its first years make the lion's share of its investments in central Europe, liberated from the iron curtain the year before, it was agreed that the USSR's right to assistance would be limited for an initial period of three years. By the terms of article 8.3 and annex 4 of the Agreement, the EBRD could provide financing for projects in the jurisdiction of the USSR in an aggregate amount not to exceed the total amount of the cash disbursed and promissory notes issued by the USSR for its shares of the EBRD. Following the dissolution of the Soviet Union, the Board of Governors of the EBRD, the highest governing body of the Bank, resolved that the limitation on financing and operations applicable to the USSR was "no longer meaningful" and not applicable to the member states formerly comprising the USSR.

The end of the communist regime in Albania, the dissolution of the Soviet Union, the division of Czechoslovakia, and the splintering of Yugoslavia had profound consequences for the EBRD's membership. Within two years the ranks of the EBRD's recipient members swelled from eight to twenty-six. Albania, the first to accede to the Agreement Establishing the EBRD, joined on October 4, 1991. Soon after came the breakaway Baltic republics of Estonia, Latvia, and Lithuania. Armenia, Azerbaijan, Belarus, Georgia, Kazakhstan, Kyrgyzstan, Moldova, the Russian Federation, Tajikistan, Turkmenistan, Ukraine, and Uzbekistan followed close behind. The peaceful division of Czechoslovakia in late 1991 brought more changes. Effective January 1, 1992, the membership of Czechoslovakia was terminated, and both of the new republics became members.

The pace of change continued into 1992. On October 9, 1992, a resolution of the Board of Governors recognized the dissolution of the SFRY and held that as a result of such dissolution the SFRY had ceased to exist and ceased to be a member of the EBRD and that each of the countries previously forming part of the SFRY was eligible to apply for membership in the EBRD. On that same day the Board of Governors approved Slovenia's membership in the EBRD. Croatia followed on January 15, 1993, and the former Yugoslav republic of Macedonia on February 13, 1993.[7]

As of January 1, 1995, the EBRD's recipient member states numbered twenty-five. Of the original eight listed in annex 2 to the Agreement, only four—Bulgaria, Hungary, Poland, and Romania—remained intact.

Organization

As noted above, the EBRD's Board of Governors, comprising the finance ministers or central bank governors of member states, is the highest governing body of the Bank. Beneath the Governors sits a sizable resident Board of Directors with the exclusive competence to authorize investments made from the EBRD's ordinary capital resources or Special Funds established under article 18 of the Agreement. Investments are proposed to the Board by the president, following passage through three stages of review. The first is Concept Clearance, which occurs at the departmental level, followed by Initial Review and Final Review, both of which require participation of the full Operations Committee at which all divisions are represented.

The dissolution, rending asunder, and regrouping of the EBRD's recipient member states in its first years of operation paved the way for upheaval, regrouping, and restructuring of the institution itself. In April 1991, when EBRD opened its doors for business with an initial share capital of 10 billion ecu, it had a bifurcated structure. The Merchant Banking Vice Presidency, divided into sector teams, had responsibility for all private sector initiatives, and the Development Banking Vice Presidency, comprised of Infrastructure and Environment, Financial Institutions, and the Country Advisory Department, had responsibility for all activities in the public domain. The President's Cabinet, serving President Jacques Attali, presided over both operational divisions, the Administration, Finance, and Operations Evaluation Vice Presidencies, the Offices of the Chief Economist, General Counsel, and Secretary-General, and the Political Unit, which was responsible for initiatives in the political sphere.

Less than three years later, in an effort to grapple with the sizable and rapid increase in the ranks of its recipient member countries and to rid itself of the inefficiencies and duplications inherent in its bifurcated structure, the EBRD reorganized along a regional divide. The private and public investment and lending activities were merged, and the two operational Vice Presidencies, Banking North and Banking South, were distinguished on geographic terms. For reasons discussed below, the Political Unit was disbanded at this time. Following a second restructuring several months later, a single unified operational division divided into ten regional and eight sector teams emerged. It is this unified structure that exists today.

Operations

As of December 30, 1994, that is, three and three-quarter years from commencement of operations, the EBRD had signed two hundred operations, representing an EBRD commitment, in aggregate, of 4.4 billion ecu. These operations mobilized additional resources, that is, funds to be invested or provided alongside the EBRD, in the amount of 8.23 billion ecu. The cumulative commitment of technical cooperation funds administered by the EBRD at year end stood at 218.8 million ecu. Disbursements, it should be noted, lag substantially behind commitments. As of December 31, 1994, roughly 1.2 billion ecu of ordinary capital resources and 94.6 million ecu of technical cooperation funds had been disbursed.[8]

EBRD investments to date are concentrated, in terms of both numbers and total value of projects, in seven countries, which account for nearly 75 percent of approved projects: the Czech Republic, Hungary, Poland, the Russian Federation, Romania, the Slovak Republic, and Slovenia. Substantial efforts are under way to broaden the geographic scope of EBRD operations, by increasing local presence through an expanding network of local offices and the engagement of local representatives.

Industry concentration is also to be noted. At the time of writing, nearly 25 percent of EBRD investments are in the financial institutions sector. The telecommunications, transport services, roads and bridges, and oil and gas production sectors combined claim another 50 percent.

As of December 31, 1994, approximately 62 percent of funds committed were for private sector projects and 38 percent for state sector projects. Roughly 15 percent was to be invested in the form of equity.[9]

Political Attributes—Political Mandate?

At the dawn of the new world order, the charter of the first multilateral institution of the post–cold war era appeared to give birth to a new form of international institution: a quasi-financial institution with a distinct political purpose. The states and organizations that joined together to establish the EBRD as the East bloc crumbled broke rank with the principle of "political neutrality" generally applied to multilateral institutions.

Defining Parameters

The political attributes of the EBRD, as crystallized in its Charter, prompt discussion of the EBRD's potential role in reducing or stifling ethno-national disputes in central and eastern Europe. While the text of the Agreement incontestably endows the institution with political attributes, it offers no formal guidance on how those attributes are to be used.[10] The institution clearly has a political orientation. And it is indisputably meant to act politically when not to do so would put it at odds with its charter. But does it have a legitimate claim to act politically in a proactive sense? Does the emphasis placed on multiparty democracy and pluralism in the Agreement, combined with the citations to the rule of law and respect for human rights found in the preamble to the Agreement, justify involvement by the EBRD in conflict-avoidance exercises or attempts to intervene proactively in brewing disputes to defray potentially more serious conflicts?

Certain limits of permissible EBRD political activity and apoliticism may be deduced from its charter. The purpose and objectives of EBRD as set forth in its charter make it clear that the EBRD may not engage in conflict prevention activities that subvert the democracy ideal. Stability is not to be pursued at any cost. Equally fundamentally, the EBRD may not be interventionist in a corporal sense. The EBRD is a financial institution. Its mandate does not include conflict prevention as classically conceived. There are no peacekeepers, experts trained in dissipating conflicts, or statesman skilled in mediation of ethno-national disputes among its ranks. The EBRD is comprised of bankers, economists, lawyers, and accountants. Its tools are financial instruments.

At the same time, the EBRD cannot be wholly apolitical. Since the Agreement makes access to the Bank's ordinary capital resources conditional on a continued commitment to the principles of multiparty democracy, pluralism, and market economics, the EBRD has a duty to monitor and assess each recipient member's continued commitment to these principles. The spirit of the Agreement also suggests a duty of moral suasion or disciplinary action in the event a member purposefully abrogates or subverts the fundamental principles set forth in article 1. Unimpeachable evidence of wide-ranging state-sponsored torture of dissidents would, for example, seem to compel the Board of Directors to recommend to the governors that the offending member's access to funds be suspended.

The limits are defined, but the territory between only roughly mapped: where on the spectrum the EBRD should be sited between *de minimus* and *de maximus* political activity in enforcing article 1, and whether or not the EBRD may concern itself with conflict-prevention goals, remain unresolved.

The Attali Era

Conceived to facilitate the transfiguration of the West and East into a united Europe, the EBRD was for Jacques Attali, François Mitterrand's former aide and the EBRD's controversial first president, far more than a bank applying political conditionality. "A poetical vision of the integration of all European countries,"[11] it had a "political mandate" to promote democracy actively and purposefully. The first promotional brochure, released in the weeks leading up to the EBRD's April 1991 inauguration, reflected this construct. Opening with the words of Jean Monnet on preserving world peace and the creation of solidarity, it portrayed the EBRD as an institution concerned not only with integrating the former command economies into the international economy, but also with strengthening democratic institutions, and encouraging commitment to human rights and environmentally sound practices.[12] Attali summed up his position at the inauguration of the EBRD:

> The European Bank's mandate is both political and economic. . . . It will help [the countries of central and eastern Europe] to consolidate democratic political life and to promote freedom of the press and respect for human rights . . . and will create among them the instruments of a market economy that are needed in order to develop a competitive private sector that will respect both the environment and social justice. . . . As the first institution of the new world order, the European Bank will be, at one and the same time, a political, economic and financial institution. By its very existence it will demonstrate that nowadays no economic development is possible anywhere in the world without respect for human rights, in the hope that this lesson will be heard far beyond the confines of Europe.[13]

The notion of an affirmative political mandate formally emerged in a policy paper presented to the Board of Directors of the EBRD in May 1991, one month after the Bank's inauguration. This paper promotes the view that articles 1 and 3 (which permit the Bank to operate only in countries making steady progress toward market economies) are key. Taken together with the preamble of the Agreement, which records the contracting parties' commitment to multiparty democracy, the rule of law, respect for human rights and market economics, they confer upon the institution a political competence. The political aspects of the EBRD's mandate are interpreted as extending to all elements of the EBRD's purpose set out in article 1. By this construct, the EBRD has an obligation not only to monitor, but also to encourage its recipient members' progress toward democracy and the rule of law as part of the process of assisting the transition to market economies.[14]

To implement the "political mandate," Attali established a separate department within the Bank, the Political Unit. This unit, headed by one of the two professional members of his cabinet, operated independently of the divisions responsible for developing the Bank's pipeline of projects and bringing transactions to fruition. Its principal task was to implement the political conditionality attached to access to EBRD funds, and to monitor, together with the Country Advisory Department in the Development Banking Vice Presidency, the recipient members' continued commitment to the principles enshrined in article 1. In monitoring each recipient member's compliance with article 1, the Political Unit liaison met regularly with a range of international agencies and nongovernmental organizations charged with promoting and safeguarding civil and political rights, including the Council of Europe, the United Nations Commission on Human Rights, the Conference on Security and Cooperation in Europe (CSCE), and Amnesty International, in an effort to assess a host of factors: whether a representative government had been elected in free elections; whether the executive was accountable to the elected legislature or the electorate; the degree to which the government and public authorities acted in accordance with the constitution and law; the availability of redress against administrative decisions; the separation between the state and political parties; the independence of the judiciary; whether there was equal protection under the law, including for minorities; fair criminal procedure; freedom of speech, including the media, of association, and of peaceful assembly; freedom of conscience and religion; freedom of movement; the right to private property; and the right to form trade unions and to strike. The conclusions of the Political Unit, cast in diplomatic hue, were incorporated in the country-by-country strategies presented to the Board of Directors on an annual basis, as required by article 11.2 of the Agreement. In the intervening months, decisions were made, and actions taken, ad hoc, as situations unfolded. There were no precise rules stipulating when, in what manner, and according to what timetable, dissatisfaction with a country's commitment to the principles enshrined in article 1 should be conveyed to the Executive Committee and then to the Board. The proximity of the Political Unit to the Office of the President, the daily interplay between the two, and the president's keen interest in political affairs made it possible for EBRD responses or statements, when deemed desirable, to be quickly formulated and distributed.

   In contrast to Attali, who was far from reticent and expressed opinions in a bold manner, the Political Unit functioned in a consultative, facilitative, nonconfrontational fashion, its focus largely on institution building. In addition to carrying out its monitoring responsibilities and handling (in close cooperation with the Office of the General Counsel and the Office of the Secretary-General) new membership issues, the Political Unit actively promoted the Bank's "political mandate" through discussion and debate and the preparation and publication of reports.[15] Through the Political Unit the EBRD became involved in the organization and sponsorship of conferences, workshops, seminars, and technical assistance programs on parliamentary processes, constitutional drafting, and human rights protection.

The first such event was a closed conference on Baltic minorities and citizenship issues, jointly organized with the Council of Europe, which was held at EBRD headquarters in October 1991. This was followed by a workshop on "Parliaments, Prime Ministers and Presidents: Relations among Branches of Democratic Governments," organized in cooperation with the East-West Parliamentary Practice Project and the Council of Advisors to the Parliament of Ukraine, held in Kiev in March 1993. A conference on the role of government in the economy, jointly organized with Project Liberty of the John F. Kennedy School of Government at Harvard University, was held at Bank Headquarters in London in June 1993. A workshop of parliamentary procedures organized at the request of the Speaker of the Albanian Parliament, took place in Tirana in July 1993. And a seminar on legal and democratic aspects of transition in Uzbekistan was convened in Tashkent in October 1993. The objective of the Tashkent workshop, which the EBRD organized in cooperation with the Uzbek University of World Economy and Diplomacy, was to open a dialogue with the Uzbek authorities on respect for human rights and the importance of establishing a proper legal framework for democratic transition and the effective functioning of a market economy.

In the meantime the Office of the President became the Bank's principal political voice. Attali's operative premise was that the financial institution he helped bring to fruition had a legitimate political role to play in central and eastern Europe and that he, as the president, should lead the effort. He claimed, for himself as well as for his institution, an overtly political role. Interventions by pen or spoken word to promote democracy, reduce brewing conflicts, or further human rights were in his view rightly his responsibility. For example, he issued a letter to protest the threatened enactment in Estonia of legislation that would effectively bar ethnic Russians from assuming Estonian citizenship.

Attali's actions during the failed August 1991 putsch that precipitated the splintering of the Soviet Union are indicative of his interventionist media-conscious approach. On August 20, 1991, one day after the Soviet "State Committee" led by Genady Yanayev placed Mikhail Gorbachev and his family under house arrest at their holiday home in the Crimea and ordered tanks into Moscow, Attali issued a personal statement declaring the coup "a clear and outrageous violation of human rights and democracy." He wrote letters to President Gorbachev (of the Soviet Union) and President Yeltsin (of the Russian Republic) and the mayors of Moscow and Leningrad the same day; they quickly found their way into print. Two days later, on August 22, 1991, with Gorbachev back in Moscow and the unsuccessful putschists on the run, and with the Board of Directors of the EBRD having agreed on a statement welcoming the return to legitimacy in the Soviet Union, Attali gave a press conference: "Those who said a week or a month ago that we could focus on Central and Eastern Europe and forget the USSR must now recognize that Europe is a single interrelated continent, and that one country cannot be successful unless the whole global process succeeds."[16]

As the Political Unit monitored compliance with article 1, liaised with other international organizations, and planned workshops and conferences, Attali attempted to marry symbolic to strategic. His proposals to the Board in late July 1992 are illustrative. In an attempt to forge a cohesive strategy for the Balkans, he urged increased attention to minority rights issues, pushed preparation of regional projects that would facilitate the economic integration of the countries in the region, and suggested that the Board, to demonstrate solidarity with those working for peace in the Balkans, convene its meeting scheduled for July 13 in Sarajevo, or, if this was impossible because of security considerations, in Split or some other location in the former Yugoslavia.

In fact, throughout his tenure as president, Attali tried to prod the Board to political action, on the supposition that political speech and resolute interventions were proper and legitimate means of carrying out the EBRD's mandate. He rarely succeeded. His personal style, and what was perceived by some to be an attempt to usurp the traditional role of government-to-government diplomacy, set many shareholders on edge. Indicatively, in response to Attali's Yugoslavia initiative, the Board supported his call for increased attention to multicountry projects, agreeing that economic cooperation between neighboring countries was a crucial element in preserving economic and political stability,[17] but flatly rejected the proposal to convene the July meeting in Sarajevo. Most telling is that in justifying this rejection the directors did not cite considerations of cost, safety, or time, as one might expect, but instead indicated it would be inappropriate to politicize the role of the Board of Directors in the manner suggested.

By June 25, 1993, the day Attali announced his intention to resign amid allegations of lavish spending and mis-stewardship, the political attributes of the EBRD, hailed by statesman, pundits, and scholars in April 1991 at the EBRD's inauguration, had become a cause of derision and concern. The press ridiculed Attali's political agenda.[18] Clients poked fun. Operational staff mocked the workings of the Political Unit, resenting the allocation of scarce resources to a unit that had no role in the assessment, structuring, and implementation of individual investment operations and appeared to make no contribution to the enlargement or betterment of the Bank's portfolio. And shareholders, fearful that resources meant to be used to grow the EBRD's lending portfolio were misguidedly being stretched to cover political activities as well, were disturbed. The host of multilateral and nongovernmental organizations (such as the Council of Europe, CSCE, and Amnesty International) engaged in political and human rights monitoring in central and eastern Europe called into question the value-added of the Political Unit. In short, the political mandate, as conceived and promoted by Attali, was rejected all around.

The Transition Era

On July 16, 1993, Attali departed disgraced. The EBRD, battered by the British press, had lost much of its credibility. To rehabilitate the media-ravaged Bank in the eyes of the public and, more important, its shareholders, some of which, like the United States, were withholding scheduled capital contributions, structural changes were needed. Brought in September with a brief to increase disbursements, cut costs, and put the house in order, Attali's successor, Jacques de Larosière, a former managing director of the International Monetary Fund, took prompt action. His goal was to create for the EBRD the image of a cost-conscious, lean financial institution with a defined list of priorities focused on private sector development. Rightly perceiving the dissolution of the Political Unit as the best means of distancing himself from his discredited predecessor, Larosière eliminated the Unit shortly after his installation at headquarters.[19] More than a symbolic exorcising of the first president, the disbanding of the Political Unit (greeted with welcome applause)[20] was the implementation of a deliberate change in course, a dispensing with the politics of the "political mandate." EBRD initiatives aimed at promoting democracy, human rights, and the

rule of law in central and eastern Europe were quickly wound up. The
EBRD was transformed, virtually overnight, into an operationally apolitical
institution wholly focused on financial transactions.

The adoption of *Operational Policies: Guidelines for the Medium Term*
in February 1994 officially sounded the death knell of the EBRD's role as
promoter of democracy and human rights. Based on the findings of a task
force established by Larosière in October 1993 to survey corporate clients,
senior officials of the Bank's recipient member countries, local entrepreneurs, staff, staff of other international financial institutions, and members
of the Board of Directors, *Operational Policies* provides that the political
aspects of the Bank's mandate should not constitute "a separate 'proactive'
task for the Bank."[21] Unless the Board otherwise agrees, the Bank is not to
carry out any activities in the political field other those forms of monitoring
and information gathering necessary to ensure compliance with article 1.

The official record of the Third Annual Meeting of the Board of Governors of the EBRD, held in April 1994 in St. Petersburg, reflects this mood
of political retrenchment. In contrast to the events of three years earlier,
only two governors saw cause to comment on the political aspects of the
EBRD's mandate or its role in encouraging adherence to the principles of
multiparty democracy and the rule of law.[22] In 1991 the EBRD's explicit
political aim was heralded; in 1994 it was rendered a nonissue.

The EBRD today operates fully in accordance with the medium-term
guidelines adopted by the Board. The focus is on banking. There is no
attempt to assume the role of political interlocutor. Technical assistance
activities have continued unabated, but the sights have narrowed. Technical
assistance is provided to further specific investment projects or groups of
projects or when it can be shown that such assistance will have a direct
impact on private sector development.

The EBRD's 1994–95 program of technical cooperation for Tajikistan,
adopted by the Board of Directors in June 1994, evidences the Bank's
new-found approach. In June 1994 Tajikistan emerged from a two-year
civil war with a substantial number of citizen-refugees, its economy in free
fall, and its prospects for political stability grim. Political upheaval prevented rigorous reform toward a market-based economy. Tajikistan could
not be considered as conforming with article 1 of the EBRD charter.[23]
Consequently, it was ineligible for investment of the Bank's ordinary capital resources, within the meaning of article 7 of the Agreement Establishing
the EBRD. In view, however, of the government's initiation of negotiations
with the opposition abroad, the publication of a draft constitution, and the

declared intention to hold presidential and parliamentary elections, the EBRD decided to provide a modest amount of assistance in the form of technical cooperation. The basis for this decision was the notion that an international financial institution presence in Tajikistan and the provision of limited forms of assistance might tip the balance toward political stability.[24]

In deciding whether to begin activities in Tajikistan, the EBRD, aware of its antecedent political attributes, consciously factored into its decision consideration of the potential salutary impact of its intervention, not only in economic but also in political terms. Yet, at the same time, in setting the parameters and scope of technical assistance to be provided, management made certain to avoid creating any perception of a return to the "political mandate." The technical assistance package to be made available by the EBRD under the Action Plan, shaped to conform to the responsible professionals' view of what was "sellable" to shareholders, is dedicated exclusively to activities that, if economic and political stability in Tajikistan are achieved, could constitute "the logical foundation for Bank investment projects proper": business advisory services, joint venture promotion, financial sector development, reform of the agribusiness sector to strengthen agricultural input and output distribution system, and telecommunications services.[25]

Should the attempt to weigh in on the side of democracy in Tajikistan through support of private sector activity, combined with disciplinary measures when required, be the paradigm for utilization by the EBRD of its political attributes? Does the "political mandate" debacle of the Attali era preempt any other course of action?

Rethinking the Political Mandate in the Context of Conflict Prevention

Attali's forced departure had a perceptible chilling effect on discourse relating to the uses, purposes, and meaning of article 1. Post-Attali, the EBRD's political attributes, to the extent they are invoked, are invoked as limitations on corporate power, that is, as a reminder that in certain situations the EBRD is proscribed by its charter from disbursing funds.[26] Political conditionality, and the notion that the EBRD should actively engage itself politically, are wholly out of vogue.

It can be argued that this intellectual abandonment of the uses and meaning of article 1, and the silence shrouding the EBRD's political attributes, are to the detriment of the long-term interests of the institution, its recipient member countries, and its shareholders. To the extent that conflict-prevention efforts are consistent with article 1 principles, a reluctance to engage politically and invest strategically could translate into a lesser contribution to regional stability than might otherwise be, and more costly write-offs for the EBRD and its shareholders. Moreover, if one accepts that over time political freedom entrenches economic freedoms by making them more stable and more credible, and that political freedom in this way makes a contribution in its own right to economic growth, the abandonment of article 1 could impact adversely on long-term economic growth.

In Naples in 1994 the G7 cited the need "to take up the challenge of integrating the newly emerging market democracies across the globe" in 1995,[27] integration being considered the key to economic growth and pros-perity and hence stability. Wound up in the challenge of integration is the challenge of conflict prevention. To what extent may the EBRD, an instru-ment of the international community constituted to serve an avowedly political objective but fundamentally financial in character, serve the G7 in meeting these challenges?[28]

The EBRD indisputably has a self-interest in reducing the incidence of ethno-national conflict in central and eastern Europe and the former Soviet Union: portfolio protection. Conflicts and conflagration often impair, if not destroy, commercially viable projects, triggering defaults on loans, dra-matic downturns in the worth of equity investments, and calls on guaran-tees. Since the EBRD, in lending to the private sector in line with its mandate, generally assumes political risks, conflicts may mean projects remain unrealized although loan proceeds have been fully disbursed. Public sector transactions, especially if not accompanied by a sovereign guarantee, also have associated risks. Sectarian violence that renders the underlying project nonviable or unduly impedes implementation could result in a default. The EBRD's stake in avoiding violent conflicts, even if not a sum certain, is quantifiable.

To date, EBRD operations in the areas under siege, such as Georgia or Azerbaijan, have been either nonexistent or nascent, and the Bank has not sustained any losses arising from ethno-national conflict. Nor has the EBRD had to consider suspending *existing* operations in the jurisdiction of a recipient member deemed not in compliance with article 1. Simply refusing to process projects in jurisdictions of members whose commitment to article 1 could be questioned, as was the case for a time with Croatia, has been action enough, both in terms of sound operational practice and politi-cal acceptability. Following the disintegration of the USSR in autumn 1991, the EBRD faced elephantine tasks with scarce resources. In these circumstances it made absolute sense to sit out the difficult-to-fully-analyze and impossible-to-predict civil wars plaguing Tajikistan and Georgia, and instead concentrate efforts and resources on establishing lending programs in recipient member countries ready to provide attractive conditions for investment. As the EBRD expands its operations to the territories of all recipient member countries across all sectors and builds its portfolio of investments, it will find the palliative option of sitting on the sidelines increasingly remote.

Instead of being shunted aside, the prominence afforded multiparty democracy and pluralism in the EBRD charter should be reconsidered anew in a thoughtful, prudent, and pragmatic manner. The rejection of the "political mandate" as conceived and promoted by Attali need not be seen as an a priori eschewing of a political agenda in any form. Had the political mandate been less hyped and Attali less hubristic, the characterization of the EBRD as a quasi-bank with a limited political role might have proven more acceptable and of value.

With the support of its shareholders and in cooperation with the other institutions active in eastern Europe, the EBRD could work to develop a strategy that combats two oft-identified causes of ethno-national conflict: socioeconomic imbalances between coexisting groups and deficiencies in the institutions of "civil society" serving such groups. The EBRD can create economic incentives for diverse peoples to cooperate through judicious application of the financial tools at its disposal. Free to conclude agreements with private enterprises, local governments, municipalities, joint ventures, and sovereigns alike, it has the instruments to promote democracy at the grass-roots level, among the entrepreneurial class. In short, the EBRD's corporate powers permit implementation of a strategy reflecting the convictions and priorities at the heart of the process of European integration. These hold that forging economic links among peoples of diverse ethno-national character, while insisting on adherence to liberal democratic norms and creating relative parity of peoples in terms of wealth, is the surest path to long-term peace and stability.

In the context of a possible reinvigoration of the EBRD's article 1 attributes and a potential contribution by the EBRD to the field of conflict prevention, it is important to recognize that in certain instances the EBRD's interests as commercial lender and assumer of political risks will be difficult to reconcile in the short-term with its interests as promoter of democracy. This is particularly true where the pursuit of democracy objectives threatens short-term stability. In such a situation the EBRD's commercial interest in the nonoccurrence of any political event that might jeopardize its portfolio would presumably be subordinated to its article 1 charter commitment. In other words, the EBRD could not intervene to stymie an impending confrontation if by doing so it would imperil democracy gains.

But other than in this limited context, article 1 enhances the EBRD's justification for adopting a strategic lending initiative to further conflict-prevention objectives. Carried out over time, a continued commitment to multiparty democracy, pluralism, and market economics should increase overall prosperity, reducing incidences of violent ethno-national conflict.

Identifying the EBRD's proper niche among the institutions operating in the political sphere and agreeing on a set of workable forms and methods of intervention is crucial to the rehabilitation of the EBRD's political attributes beyond its present monitoring role.

Modes of Engagement

Two broad categories of engagement are available to the EBRD by which it could potentially play a role in proactively reducing risks of all-out conflicts in the countries in which it operates. The first is through disciplinary action in the form of threatened or actual impairment of a member state's ability to access EBRD resources. The second is through the creation of incentives deliberately designed to bridge divides. Both routes of engagement have inherent limitations. And pursuit of either runs the danger of turning specific grievances into political causes at great cost to foreign investors and local entrepreneurs willing to accept the commercial risks of investing in central and eastern Europe. Nevertheless, both merit consideration.

The Disciplinary Regime

The political conditionality built into the EBRD's charter lays the groundwork for a disciplinary regime that could, in theory, be used to induce member states to confront and resolve certain types of low-intensity imbroglios before they rise to the level of intractable conflicts. As previously noted, article 8.2 of the Agreement mandates the EBRD to conduct its operations only in those countries proceeding steadily in the transition toward market-oriented economies and the promotion of private and entrepreneurial initiative, and which apply the principles of multiparty democracy, pluralism, and market economics. Article 8.3 articulates procedures to be followed in the event a recipient member implements policies at variance with the principles enshrined in article 1. It contemplates, at the discretion of the Board Governors, the suspension or modification of a member's right to access EBRD resources should the situation so warrant.[29] There is also article 38, which authorizes the Governors of the Bank, by supermajority vote, to suspend from membership any member in breach of its obligations to the EBRD. Although this latter provision was probably not intended to be invoked solely in connection with a member's refusal to abide by the principles of in article 1, and was probably meant to apply more to failure of a member to pay-in its capital contributions, there is no reason, from a strictly legal point of view, why a suspension of a member's access to funds could not lead, eventually, to a suspension of its membership.[30]

Together these articles offer a panoply of potential means of asserting influence in an effort to prevent simmering disputes from rising to the level of intractable conflicts. At one end of the spectrum are the nonconfrontational options, such as confidential communiqués protesting the member's failure to honor the principles set forth in article 1, unpublicized decisions by management to redirect human resources and investments from the jurisdiction of offending members to the jurisdictions of members demonstrating clear commitment to the principles underpinning the EBRD's mandate, and informal arrangements under which the government of the member concerned agrees not to submit further requests for disbursement in respect of state sector loans until the problem situation is appropriately resolved.[31] At the other end of the spectrum is full remedial action, such as, for example, suspension of loans to the offending member and enterprises that it owns or controls, the acceleration of loans partially or fully disbursed, and, in the most drastic scenario, the threat or actual suspension of loans to private enterprises established in the jurisdiction of the member state.[32] Midway between are actions designed to exert pressure on the offending state without wreaking havoc. Board decisions to refrain from considering for approval new projects in the offending member state's jurisdiction until settlement of a simmering dispute would be in this category. So, too, would be a tempered communication warning that suspension of disbursements under some or all of the EBRD's existing loans to the member and enterprises owned or controlled by it might be justified.[33] Once considerations of practicality and politics are factored into the equation, however, the prospect of the EBRD's availing itself of the full range of remedies at its disposal becomes exceedingly remote.[34]

PRACTICAL LIMITATIONS, POLITICAL CONSIDERATIONS. First and foremost, since disciplinary action requires the authority imposing the sanctions to take sides, using disciplinary action and sanctions is assertedly not an appropriate means of nipping a burgeoning conflict in the bud. In the embryonic stages of a dispute, clear-cut rights and wrongs and readily identifiable solutions are rarely evident. Often both parties are somewhat in the right and somewhat in the wrong, making it difficult for independent parties to reach a definitive decision on which side deserves support. In addition, a premature recourse to disciplinary action could needlessly exacerbate a tense situation better handled through mediation, and at the same time limit the imposing authority's options for further action. For these reasons, in the early stages of a dispute, particularly where violence is either nonexistent or at a minimum, mediation and negotiation are more useful means of intervention.

As a practical matter, it is unlikely that the EBRD, staffed by bankers, investment specialists, and economists, would be able to muster the skills, information, and expertise needed to analyze properly the background of the dispute in question and the arguments of the parties, to weigh the relative merits of each party's stance, to devise an acceptable solution, and to lead the way forward. Recourse to article 8.3 and in the extreme situation threats of recourse to article 38, both aimed at the relevant member state, would also do little to help reduce conflicts between nonstate actors. For this reason, recourse to political conditionality will in many instances be a nonviable option if the objective is ethno-national conflict prevention.

Moreover, the EBRD, however novel, is a financial institution, moderate and cautious by nature. It is also an intergovernmental institution, political to the core. Betwixt the two, even assuming disciplinary action by the EBRD aimed at tempering conflict would be possible from a practical viewpoint and on balance be in the interest of the "common good"—both highly doubtful for the reasons discussed above—it is unlikely that the EBRD could muster the cohesiveness of vision and unwavering resolve required to thwart conflicts through proactive disciplinary action.

Practice to date in the context of actual ongoing warfare or civil unrest in the jurisdictions of the EBRD's recipient member states emphasizes the political limitations of using disciplinary action to coax belligerent parties to settle disputes peacefully. Civil wars in Georgia and Tajikistan, protracted fighting between Azerbaijan and Armenia, the conflagration in

Bosnia-Herzegovina, and countless accusations of discrimination being leveled by diverse minority and ethnic groups against various recipient members have compelled the Board of Directors to consider issues of belligerency, war, conflict, and discrimination of minorities on a number of occasions. Rarely have such discussions resulted in a unified view or formal decision. To be sure, there are instances where the Board of Directors has taken a public stance, the most notable being the statement concerning the Balkans issued on July 3, 1992, at Attali's behest, expressing "deep concern" about the worsening situation in the former Yugoslavia and quoting Attali's call for the maintenance of internationally recognized borders and the protection of rights of minorities. Statements of this kind must, however, be distinguished from both proactive interventionist statements and statements made in response to less egregious wrongs. Violations of principles of *jus cogens*—that is, reports of mass rapes, "ethnic cleansing," and genocide—compel expressions of moral outrage; this chapter concerns itself with how to quell disputes *before* they give rise to crimes against humanity.

In fact, public statements in connection with disputes not compelling universal outrage in which the government of a member is involved could well generate charges of undue interference in the internal affairs of a sovereign state.[35] For this reason, and in the interests of the shareholders they represent, where territorial claims have been an issue, directors have been careful to place the adjudication of such claims and the determination of whether a particular war is "just" outside the ambit of the political conditionality tied to membership by virtue of article 1. The record of the Board of Directors meeting of December 1992, when the Board took up the 1993 Strategies for Armenia (at war with Azerbaijan) and Georgia (self-destructing), is instructive. At that meeting both Armenia's and Georgia's commitment to article 1 were called into question from the viewpoint of political eligibility, in the case of Armenia due to its maintenance of territorial claims and continuing high military expenditures, and in the case of Georgia due to continuing reports of internecine strife and civil war. The directors also discussed the appropriateness, from the viewpoint of sound financial judgment, of making loans and investments in a belligerent country. Ultimately they agreed that while belligerency and civil strike were relevant to the decisionmaking process for purposes of sound banking practice and staff safety, it was not for the EBRD to take a position on whether territorial claims are justified or to decide whether a war is "just." What is important for purposes of article 1 is the degree to which external or internal armed conflict affects the internal decisionmaking processes, pluralism, or freedom of the press and broadcasting in the relevant country or undermines the rule of law or the accountability of the government thereof.[36] Consistent with this approach and the post-Attali operational apoliticism of the EBRD, and mindful of the relative powers of shareholder states, directors have not made the winter 1994–95 Russian assault on Chechnya a subject of Board discussion.

Worth noting is that any attempt by the EBRD to intervene in brewing disputes could give rise to charges of over-reaching by western governments and political-security international institutions engaged in the field. If not properly coordinated, EBRD attempts at intervention would be swiftly checked by bilateral diplomatic efforts and institutions such as the United Nations, CSCE, or the Council of Europe. Shareholders' keen desire to ensure international bureaucracies remain subordinate must also be borne in mind.

OPERATIONAL CONSIDERATIONS. More important, even assuming EBRD action was judged worthwhile and possible from an institutional perspective, any systematic attempt to apply disciplinary measures to reduce risks of conflict (as opposed to sanctioning atrocities in progress, state-sponsored terrorism, or the like) might cause more harm than good. Bit by bit, the EBRD's recipient member countries are (re)establishing relations with the international banking community. Disciplinary actions by the EBRD aimed at conflict prevention could throw a wrench into this process, leading commercial lenders to halt their move into the region.

In addition, politically motivated disciplinary measures would undoubtedly lead to a downturn in demand for EBRD services. Hinging approval or the continued financial support of individual investment projects on the democratization or human rights record of the member in whose jurisdiction the project is to be carried out, or making the EBRD's support for individual projects open to potential interruption for reasons of unrelated ethno-national conflicts, would have a chilling affect. Potential private sector borrowers would be loathe to approach the EBRD for financing, fearing the vagaries inherent in the financing process.

Costs of public sector projects financed by the EBRD and the amounts of cofinancing made available to EBRD borrowers would likewise be negatively affected due to a certain plunge in supplier interest in public works contracts financed by the EBRD. A precipitous decline in supplier bids caused by an unwillingness to accept the prospect of suspensions for nonproject-related reasons would result in a concomitant increase in the price of contracts awarded.[37] These considerations suggest that EBRD disciplinary action in any but the most extreme situations might in fact be impermissible under the EBRD's charter. Article 13 (i) of the Agreement requires the Bank to apply "sound banking principles" to all its operations. This provision is meant to ensure efficient and economic use of funds and satisfactory identification, appraisal, monitoring, implementation, and ex-post evaluation of all projects. Disciplinary measures applied for political ends that jeopardize implementation and result in interrupted or stalled projects would run counter to sound banking practices.

Strategic Investing

As a financial institution with a political objective networked to a diverse range of multilateral, bilateral, and nongovernmental institutions, the EBRD is well placed to launch a strategic investing initiative that promotes democracy and pluralism and aims at long-term peace yet remains centered on commercially viable projects. The EBRD could develop commercially sound projects and programs meeting a broader political goal through judicious use of information, analyses, and recommendations which could be made available to it by diplomatic, political, and strategic institutions of Europe with which it cooperates. Such projects and programs could then be implemented through selective channeling of funds to defined sectors, localities, or groups of prospective recipients.

As used herein, "strategic investing" means the systematic extension of credits and guarantees and the investment of equity in accordance with procedures and processes consciously designed to achieve, either at the individual project level or at the aggregate level, specified political goals, in particular a reduction in violent ethno-national conflict. As will be seen below, the EBRD is in fact already engaged in several high-transition impact projects and programs that have a strategic as well as commercial end goal, albeit not one necessarily directly related to the prevention of ethno-national conflict. They are not, however, consciously grouped into or perceived as forming a coherent whole. This minimizes the overall impact. Developing a system of strategic investing, or perhaps less ambitiously, a systematic way of examining and evaluating projects with strategic objectives, would better ensure that the sum equals more than the parts. The intent, to be clear, is not to limit EBRD operations to projects motivated by strategic as well as commercial concerns, but rather to give a focus to the EBRD's guiding principles and marketing and promotional activities.

There are, broadly speaking, two channels of strategic investing. The first includes initiatives designed to forge economic links between two or more groups. The purposeful financing of joint ventures involving transnational intergroup alliances or regional projects involving cross-border alliances would be two examples. In the other category belong initiatives aimed at creating parity among geographical regions or diverse groups or rectifying entrenched imbalances. Targeting funds to localities or groups deemed "disadvantaged," either directly or through credit lines to financial intermediaries, would be an example. Means of implementing either strategy of investing could vary. High-profile public championship would be one approach; quiet but resolute targeting of funds another. Any combination of purely private enterprises, state-private joint ventures, state enterprises, or municipal-owned entities could be brought into either strategy.

CONCERNS AND CONSTRAINTS. Creativity must be tempered by pragmatism. In the area of strategic investing there are a slew of predictable criticisms and external and internal limitations that must be acknowledged and weighed.

Whenever funds or opportunities are targeted at specified groups, even on a nonexclusive basis, charges of "undue advantage" or "unjustifiable favoritism" may arise. These stem from the explicit or implicit evaluations of "entitlement" and "merit" that form the backdrop to any such program. Accusations of this nature raise special problems for strategic investing aimed at conflict minimization as the means of achieving this goal, that is, the channeling of financing to select groups, may, by creating new causes of conflict, end up directly undermining that goal.

The willingness of financial institutions that are not part of the strategic investment initiative or that do not share the goal of conflict minimization to provide financing any which way they can may impose another significant external constraint. This will to a certain degree be minimized by the fact that many commercial lenders are unwilling to lend to the less advanced newly independent states. Inter-IFI rivalries and competition between international financial institutions do, however, need to be taken into account. So does shareholder intransigence, which could well derail any strategic investment initiative not well founded and promoted in advance of launch.

Geography also imposes a constraint in terms of potential effectiveness. Whereas targeting resources and creating economic incentives may offer identifiable possibilities for small multicultural countries such as Kyrgyzstan and Macedonia, the potential impact is greatly reduced in large economies such as Russia.

In addition to these external constraints, there are internal constraints, imposed by the EBRD's charter. The requirement that the EBRD operate in accordance with sound banking principles is an example. Consider an investment strategy for Georgia designed to create parity among geographic regions. The Ajeria region of Georgia, with close ties to Russia, is the wealthiest region of the country. It is also the most stable. If the EBRD were to pursue a strategic investing initiative aimed at creating parity, it would presumably seek to invest funds in regions other than Ajeria, that is, in the more economically disadvantaged and relatively less stable areas. In contrast, sound banking principles might guide the EBRD, at least in the initial stages of its lending in Georgia, to center its attentions on the more stable, more advantaged areas.

A similar tension exists between the EBRD's raison d'être of promoting competition and strategic investing. Successful implementation of a coherent plan for strategic investing would require cooperation among financiers, and in particular international financial institutions, leading to a corresponding reduction in benefits derived from competition. Of graver consequence, privileging certain groups or categories of entities by making it easier to access financing, if pursued on a significant scale, could, by influencing the profiles of new entrants to the market, lead to reduced competition.

Added to these concerns are a host of operational hazards and limitations. Most troublesome and elemental is the actual identification of appropriate commercially viable projects. To properly identify and prepare projects with strategic end goals, the EBRD would need substantially more human resources "on the ground." To bridge divides through the creation of economic incentives there must be a keen understanding of, and sensitivity for, local culture, political trends, and national values. The present plan to decentralize EBRD activities and expand the capacity of the Bank's local offices is a step in this direction.[38] But pursuit of strategic initiatives might well require an even greater team in the field than is presently intended. It is extremely time-intensive to prepare and develop local projects that do not have strong western partners. In such instances the EBRD is often called upon to provide financial, administrative, and managerial know-how to the company that is supposed to be providing the information required to shepherd the project through the internal review and approval process.[39] Finally, and of gravest concern, is the risk that pursuit by the EBRD of a strategic investing strategy would result in an overpoliticized process of making investments which retards investment and stymies growth.[40]

PRACTICE TO DATE, ROOM FOR GROWTH.   Under its first president, Jacques Attali, the EBRD early on embarked on a range of initiatives that had at their core clear political and stabilization objectives. *Regional Cooperation: Countries of Central and Eastern Europe including the Former Soviet Union,* an overview of regional cooperation efforts in the EBRD's area of operations published by the Bank in March 1993 at Attali's impetus, describes the regional initiatives undertaken by the EBRD in its first two years of operations. These are defined to include any activity that would substantially assist the economic development or integration of several countries, including significant bilateral arrangements with states or regions outside the Bank's recipient member countries and single-nation infrastructure projects such as transportation corridors with a regional impact. Among them are motorway, railway, and shipping regional transport initiatives, the financing of improved telecommunications links and the construction of new network routes, the expansion of the Eurovision Network, and a range of projects in the field of environment and nuclear safety. *Regional Cooperation* suggests that fostering interdependence, by increasing the costs of conflict and maximizing gains from cooperation, is one of the best means of engendering cooperation and discouraging disruption.

In this spirit, in addition to pushing regional infrastructure and environmental projects, Attali fought to make increased trade, both among recipient member countries and between the newly independent states and their western European neighbors, a G7 priority and an EBRD occupation. He also pushed support to small and medium-size enterprises, crucial to the development of an entrenched entrepreneurial class, and an excellent means of promoting democratic values. Nuclear safety was the fourth integral component of Attali's integrated political-economic-environmental strategic investing agenda.

Attali's efforts to use economic incentives to reduce risks of ethnic conflict and promote democracy had limited institutional resonance beyond his tenure. This is in part due to the fact that few directors shared his vision or, perhaps more accurately, his view of how to proceed. The noncommercially oriented projects he pushed—such as the proposal that the EBRD finance housing developments in Russia for troops stationed in the Baltics to encourage Russia to withdraw its forces in accordance with the agreed timetable—never even earned Board approval.[41] Nonetheless, the shift in emphasis away from strategic planning following Attali's departure played a significant role in the waning of commercial projects with strategic end goals.

Following Attali's departure, the EBRD continued to augment its portfolio of regional projects and to develop techniques for enhancing inter- and intraregional trade and intraregional cross-investment. The sovereign loan made available in April 1994 for Brest-Minsk-Russian border highway improvements and the facility made available to foster Czech-Slovak trade are two examples. Another interesting case is the May 1994 transaction in which the EBRD provided full cover of nonpayment risk to recognized foreign banks acting in a commercial corespondent capacity on behalf of Komercijalna Banka A.D., Skopje, with the objective of increasing Komercijalna Banka's capacity to provide financing for imports into Macedonia (primarily related to goods needed for production leading to re-exports) in convertible currencies on a regular documentary credit basis. Under the leadership of Larosière, projects of this sort are developed, presented, and pursued in a nonpolitically conscious manner. The spotlight is on product lines designed to increase volume while decreasing per project costs. Wholesale banking techniques and industry lines have been brought to the fore, outstaging strategic investing initiatives.

Larosiere's emphasis on efficiency, productivity, and resource mobilization, to be realized through wholesale banking and industrial lines, is wholly consistent with shareholder concerns. Yet it would be unfortunate if the goal of volume lending was to engender a total abandonment of a politically aware approach to investment decisions. Adequate support for political as well as economic reform, sensitivity to the competing claims of diverse peoples of central and eastern Europe, and intense efforts at building institutions of democratic civil society are critical to the long-term realization of the EBRD's mandate.

Institutional Links

The success of any EBRD strategic investment initiative will largely be a function of the scope and strength of its links with the other institutional players active or substantially influencing developments in central and eastern Europe. In this context, it is not only the EBRD's ties to the family of IFIs to which it belongs by reason of structure, purpose, history, law, and psychology[42] that are important. Its links to the diverse political-diplomatic, military-security, and human rights-oriented institutions saturating twentieth-century fin de siècle Europe may be of even greater consequence. The EBRD's potential contribution to conflict-prevention efforts is in large part dependent on the degree to which it may affirmatively complement and reinforce the activities of organizations such as the CSCE, Council of Europe, and United Nations.

INSTITUTIONAL COOPERATION. There is interinstitutional cooperation that impacts decisions made in the context of the political conditionality associated with membership in the EBRD and access to EBRD funds. Such interactions indicate there may be a significant value in developing interinstitutional initiatives for positive action aimed at conflict reduction. Particularly instructive is the institutional networking that influenced the EBRD's actions with respect to the former Yugoslavia described below—at the time of its dissolution and thereafter, when Slovenia, Croatia, and Macedonia applied for membership.

On May 18, 1992, Yugoslav director Branimir Pajkovic resigned from the Board of Directors of the EBRD, stating that since the country that had nominated him and that he represented had effectively ceased to exist, it was impossible for him to carry out his duties. This gave rise to certain questions under article 26 of the Agreement, the article governing the composition of the Board of Directors. By the terms of article 26.5, if the office of a director becomes vacant more than 180 days before the end of his term, a successor is to be chosen for the remainder of the term by the governors who elected the former director. The Socialist Federal Republic of Yugoslavia had, however, been reduced to the Serbian-controlled rump state of Yugoslavia. What was to be done? President Attali decided not to proceed with the election of a new director in view of the uncertainties regarding the representative status of the different authorities concerned. The Board approved this decision and requested that the competent international parties and other multilateral organizations be consulted. Among those the EBRD turned to for advice were the secretary-general of the United Nations, the head of the Bretton Woods institutions, Lord Carrington, then Chairman of the European Community (EC) Peace Conference for Yugoslavia, and R. Badinter, then president of the Conseil Constitutionel of France and adviser to the EC Peace Conference for Yugoslavia on succession issues. The Board's ultimate conclusion was that the SFRY, an EBRD founding member, had been dissolved and no longer existed, and therefore had ceased to be a member of the EBRD, and that none of the countries resulting from the dissolution of the SFRY could be regarded as the continuation of the SFRY or the sole successor of its membership in the Bank.[43]

Several months later, as the Board prepared to make a decision on membership of the states that had formerly comprised the Socialist Federal Republic of Yugoslavia, outside advice was again sought. In October 1992

Lord Owen briefed the EBRD Board on the status of the Peace Conference, proposing that the Bank link its decision on membership to progress in two key areas: mutual recognition of boundaries and constitutional protection of ethnic groups. Voting later that same year to recommend membership of Croatia to the Board of Governors—with the understanding that the Bank would not commence investment operations in Croatia until its commitment to article 1 could be further confirmed—the Board relied substantially on the advice of the two Peace Conference chairmen, Lord Owen and Cyrus Vance. With their support, Croatia was eventually admitted to membership in January 1993.[44]

Institutional cooperation and consultation in enforcing the EBRD's political conditionality continues to this day. The history of the EBRD's Air Navigation Project for Croatia is another case in point. In developing the project and identifying the goods it would finance, the EBRD consulted the International Civil Aviation Organization (ICAO), requesting confirmation that the project was of a civilian nature, and that the military value of equipment to be purchased under the project was not significant. The project proposals were also submitted to the United Nations Sanctions Committee on the Former Yugoslav Republics by the ICAO. In an April 13, 1993, letter, this committee indicated to the government of Croatia that it had no objection to the project. Around the same time, following consultation with the Peace Conference chairmen, Jacques Attali notified the prime minister of Croatia that he would refrain from presenting any projects in the jurisdiction of Croatia to the Board of Directors for decision until he had a clearer picture of events in the region, particularly the circumstances surrounding the fighting in Bosnia-Herzegovina. The project was placed on internal hold, pending further analysis of Croatia's commitment to article 1. Two agreements reached in March 1994 formed the basis for the resumption of operational activities in Croatia: the "Washington Agreement" of March 18, which ended hostilities between Bosnian Croat and Muslim forces and established the principle of a federation between Croats and Muslims in Bosnia, and the comprehensive cease-fire negotiated in Zagreb on March 30 for those areas of Croatia outside government control (Krajina and Slavonia). The EBRD's Board of Directors ultimately approved the Air Navigation Project in August 1994.

Institutional networking in the form related above is critical to the EBRD's ability to monitor efficiently and effectively the continuing commitment of its recipient members to the principles of multiparty democracy, pluralism, and market economics. In this the EBRD relies on the institutions whose primary activity is information gathering and reporting. It is important to note, however, that this reliance is voluntary in nature, and the response it engenders advisory. The EBRD at all times maintains a right of independent action. Neither the UN, nor the CSCE, nor the Council of Europe can dictate whether the EBRD suspends a member's access to funds or bars a country from membership. Their advice is influential but not binding.

Such limits to interinstitutional coordination are unavoidable due to the differing shareholder bases of the various institutions, which is important to bear in mind when evaluating the possibility for cooperative efforts. The CSCE is pan-European–North American, the Council of Europe is limited to Europe, the UN is global. The EBRD is pan-European and pan-G7, but excludes the greater part of the less developed world. Because any institution's ability to make political statements or take certain kinds of political actions is equally a function of its shareholder base as of the provisions of its charter, it is possible that the EBRD, acting in what it considers the interests of the "international community," will be unwilling to follow the same line as the European Union, Council of Europe, or OSCE.

The admission of the Former Yugoslav Republic of Macedonia (FYRM) to membership in the EBRD in February 1993 is a case in point. Jacques Attali began pressing for Macedonia's admission to membership as early as August 1992, recognizing that Macedonia, if welcomed into the community of nations quickly, could become a stabilizing presence in the region. In response to those opposed to Macedonia's admission to the EBRD, in particular Greece, Attali circulated an opinion of the general counsel of the EBRD which advanced the view that since it was generally agreed that Macedonia met the four requisite characteristics of statehood (defined territory, stable population, a government with authority over such population, and the capacity to enter into relations with other international legal persons), and public international law did not appear to bar the Bank from admitting as a member an entity lacking a universally recognized name, it was permissible for the Board of Governors to admit the Former Yugoslav Republic of Macedonia as a new member provided that FYRM was willing to accept such a name for the purposes of its relations to the Bank. The governor of the EBRD for Greece promptly submitted a written objection on the following grounds: that FYRM had not yet been recognized as an independent state by the international community; it had yet to comply with the conditions set by the Declaration of the EC Foreign Ministers on December 16, 1991, as well as those set by the European Council on May

2, 1992, in Lisbon; and that FYRM had not yet filed a formal application for membership in the United Nations.

It was not until January 1993 that the EC directors indicated their support for Attali's recommendation on Macedonia. On February 13, 1993, the Former Yugoslav Republic of Macedonia was admitted to membership in the EBRD with the proviso that the designation "Former Yugoslav Republic of Macedonia" would be used provisionally until the Board of Directors determines that a name has been agreed between the members and the Bank. In the case of the FYRM, the fact that the EBRD's shareholder base was wider than that of the EU, for instance, and the EBRD made the decision according to a different set of basic concerns than would have dominated among EU members—where reaching a unified policy through consensus would be paramount—allowed the EBRD to deal with the question of the FYRM in the face of the Greek resistance that has paralyzed the EU on this issue.

The potential of the institutional network, of which the EBRD is a part, for uniting Europe politically, economically, socially, and strategically, remains to be fully realized. To date, apart from cofinancing arrangements agreed with other IFIs in the context of specific investment projects, co-operation has largely been limited to the joint provision of technical assistance, exchange of information, and consultation for purposes of ensuring continued commitment to the principles of multiparty democracy, pluralism, and market economics and taking action when it seems a member is not acting in conformity with these principles. With gargantuan tasks and limited resources, and under immense pressure to sign deals and disburse, the EBRD cannot afford to carry out detailed fact-finding missions of the sort generally conducted by political-diplomatic multilateral organizations. It instead relies on reports of international organizations such as the UN, CSCE, and Council of Europe and nongovernmental organizations such as Amnesty International and Human Rights Watch. Efforts aimed at better exploiting each institution's comparative advantage and increasing inter-institutional reliance could create synergies leading to the development of a coherent plan aimed at minimizing conflict in central and eastern Europe. Considered in this context, the EBRD, whose primary purpose is to extend loans and invest equity, with or without a political end goal, becomes an economic link in the network of multilateral diplomatic, financial, cultural, and security institutions supporting and influencing the economies in transition.

Just as the EBRD turns to political-diplomatic institutions for advice on substantive political matters, diplomatic, strategic, and political institutions could refer potentially viable commercial projects (with political end goals) in need of finance and politically contentious issues of economic content in need of attention to the EBRD and its cofinancing partners. Consider, for example, the continuing dispute between Albania and Greece over the treatment of the Greek minority in Albania and the Albanian minority in Greece, which has attracted the attention of the Council of Europe, the CSCE, and NATO, or the simmering ethno-national disputes in Macedonia which prompted the stationing of a precautionary UN peacekeeping force. If the CSCE, Council of Europe, NATO, and the UN, in the course of their activities, were to become aware of potentially viable projects that would create economic incentives for members of diverse national groups to cooperate, they could refer such projects onward. To be sure, this is not the way to generate projects in bulk. It could, however, be a way of reinforcing diplomatic efforts and serving conflict-minimization goals.

Another possibility would be for the EBRD, in cooperation with specialist agencies, to promote, perhaps through its local offices, the establishment of private commercial dispute panels tailored to the needs of the local community, with membership in such panels open to all financial institutions, professional firms, private enterprises, and individuals resident in the relevant community. It could be argued that commercial disputes spawning low key ethno-national conflicts, being too inextricably tied to deeper historical and political issues, are best handled in diplomatic-political (that is, Stability Pact round tables) or judicial forums. The development of innovative schemes for community-based private resolution of commercial disputes may, however, be a worthwhile, if limited, means of reducing potential ethno-national conflicts.[45]

Instilling Values, Changing Attitudes

As discussed above, opportunities for the EBRD to engage itself directly in conflict-minimization efforts are limited. Nevertheless there are certain steps that the EBRD could take to better support conflict-minimization goals indirectly while serving the interests of the institution and shareholders alike.

Internal Challenges

The EBRD should seek to create a corporate culture more appreciative of the EBRD's political purpose and cognizant of its limited but valuable contribution in the political sphere. Investment concerns are and should rightly continue to be the core organizing principle. But while the focus on investment is correct, a greater effort should be made to integrate information culled from diplomatic-political organizations and nongovernmental organizations into the organic life of the institution and its operational activities. At present, while the Environmental Unit monitors compliance with the EBRD's public notice and comment policies,[46] and a few souls struggle with questions such as how to measure "multiparty democracy" in a country like Turkmenistan that has a nomadic culture that gives primacy of place to town elders, most staff give little thought to democracy or pluralism issues of any dimension. In fact, a significant portion pay "negative attention," believing all emphasis is best placed on the commercial merits of individual transactions.

Leadership from the top is essential. It is the level of engagement of senior officers that determines what tack the bureaucracy takes and the scope of its accomplishments.

Setting Standards

Creating a corporate culture sensitized to the goal of promoting pluralism and democratic values is important in its potential knock-on effect in terms of new product development, the way in which staff analyze individual investment proposals, and the structuring of projects at the preparation and development stage. Greater emphasis on the multiparty democracy-building aspect of the EBRD's mandate might, for instance, mean that in developing financial intermediary projects, the EBRD would seek to ensure that potential beneficiaries are afforded equal access to financing. Or, in dealing with joint ventures between state entities and private parties, particular attention might be paid to the choice of corporate governance provisions and the rights of specified classes of shareholders. Efforts might also be made to encourage labor practices that promote pluralism, including, for example, equal employment opportunities, adoption of staff rules permitting internal communications in regional dialects where such practices do not impair firm productivity, and policies that recognize staff members' right to celebrate religious and cultural holidays.

A corporate culture sensitive to the EBRD's political attributes would also better equip the EBRD to devise creative solutions to political issues that crop up in a commercial context. The EBRD can already boast certain successes in this area, but gains in consistency could be achieved.

Conclusion

Today the EBRD operates more or less as "plainly and simply a bank,"[47] free of the political rhetoric that characterized its first two years. In response to the turbulence of the Attali era, in part due to the political hype, the EBRD—leaving aside its hybrid public-private lending authority—has become less like the novel new form of institution it was initially thought to be and more like "just another IFI." In light of the EBRD's rocky start, this caution is probably well placed. Yet the costs of overcautiousness and nonintervention argue against long-term pursuit of a conservative status quo approach. Only by fostering *political* as well *economic* reform, and by providing intellectual and political leadership through investments that are oriented strategically as well as commercially, will the EBRD distinguish itself from commercial lenders engaged in project finance in the former East bloc and best serve the interests of its shareholders in the long run.

Notes

1. Political conditionality is to be distinguished from conventional conditionality, meaning a link between access to funds and demonstrated commitment to a package of agreed macroeconomics policies designed to stabilize the recipient state's economy. Macroeconomic conditionality was the cornerstone of the U.S.'s Marshall Plan for Europe and of the Bretton Woods system established in July 1944. It remains the central feature of International Monetary Fund policy.

2. The Agreement Establishing the EBRD establishes the geographic mandate of the EBRD to be "Central and Eastern Europe." Following the dissolution of the USSR in autumn 1991, the shareholders of the EBRD agreed that each newly independent state previously forming part of the USSR, which had been characterized as a central and eastern European country for the purposes of the Agreement Establishing the EBRD and was a recipient member country at the time of its dissolution, was eligible for membership in the EBRD. See Resolution no. 21 of the Board of Governors of the EBRD (March 28, 1992). The actual geographic mandate of the EBRD thus extends to the central Asian republics of Kazakstan, Kyrgyzstan, Tajikistan, Turkmenistan, and Uzbekistan. For this reason, wherever used in this paper, unless otherwise stated, the term "central and eastern Europe" should be read to include all states formally comprising the USSR.

In assessing EBRD's potential contribution to conflict avoidance efforts in central and eastern Europe, it is helpful to consider both the World Bank Group's and the Asian Development Bank's (ADB) activities in the region. All of the countries in which the EBRD operates are now members of the IBRD and IFC. Kazakhstan, Kyrgyzstan, and Uzbekistan are also members of the ADB.

3. The "political mandate" of the EBRD has been the subject of much commentary. See, for example, Ibrahim F. I. Shihata, The European Bank for Reconstruction and Development: A Comparative Analysis of the Constituent Agreement

(1990); D. R. R. Dunnett, "The European Bank for Reconstruction and Development: A Legal Survey," *Common Market Law Review,* vol. 28 (1991), pp. 571–97; P. Saunier and J. Touscoz, *La Banque européenne pour la reconstruction et le développement,* Revue du Marche Common (Paris: 1992); J.-V. Louis, *La Banque européenne pour la reconstruction et le développement: Aspects juridiques,* Collected Courses of the Academy of European Law, vol. 2, book 1, pp. 251–302 (1992).

4. See Inaugural Address by the Right Honourable John Major MP, Prime Minister of the United Kingdom of Great Britain and Northern Ireland, in Summary Proceedings of the Inaugural Meeting of the Board of Governors, London, April 15–17, 1991, p. 11.

5. See Inaugural Address by His Excellency Mr François Mitterrand, President of the French Republic, in Summary Proceedings of the Inaugural Meeting of the Board of Governors, London, April 15–17, 1991, p. 13.

6. Following the unification of the Federal Republic of Germany and the German Democratic Republic on October 3, 1990, the German Democratic Republic, which never deposited an instrument of ratification, was effectively struck from the list of recipient countries; the shares initially allotted to the German Democratic Republic were allocated to unsubscribed capital.

7. For an explanation of the legal basis for the decision to lift the limitation on the USSR and a discussion of issues raised by the former Yugoslav Republic of Macedonia's accession to membership, see "The First Three Years of the EBRD: Legal Issues and Solutions," remarks of Andre Newburg, General Counsel of the EBRD, as delivered at an IMF seminar on Current Legal Issues Affecting Central Banks, Washington, May 16, 1994.

8. Annual Report of the European Bank for Reconstruction and Development (London: 1994).

9. Annual Report of the European Bank for Reconstruction and Development (1994).

10. According to S. Weber, "Origins of the European Bank for Reconstruction and Development, *International Organization,* vol. 48 (Winter 1994), pp. 1–38, at the three intergovernmental negotiating sessions resulting in the multilateral treaty establishing the EBRD, how the political conditionality written into EBRD's charter would be applied in practice was never really addressed.

11. Jacques Attali in "Answering Back: Jacques Attali," an interview produced by Juniper Productions and broadcast on Channel 4 in the United Kingdom in late October 1991. Asked to respond to those opposed to EBRD on grounds of institutional redundancy, Attali, as recorded in the postproduction script made available following the interview, commented: "We certainly don't need another bank; there [are] a lot of banks available in the private sector and [if the purpose] was to create a bank, it was worthless (sic). What we needed, at the beginning of [the] period [following the fall of the Berlin wall] was to create an institution in which all European countries, including the former East and USSR, would be full members, equal partners, in the building of Europe. And it happened to be a bank because bank means money and the best way to have people accept the idea of working together is to hope to find the best use of money. It's why [the EBRD] is a bank. It's a bank because a bank is the best tool for building the first pan-European institutions. But first it's a poetical vision of the integration of all European countries."

12. Brochure entitled "European Bank for Reconstruction and Development," printed by S. W. Sharman & Co. Ltd. (early spring 1991).

13. Address by Mr. Jacques Attali, President of the European Bank for Reconstruction and Development, in Summary Proceedings of the Inaugural Meeting of the Board of Governors, London, April 15–17, 1991, pp. 14–15.

14. "Procedures to Implement the Political Aspects of the Mandate of the EBRD" (BDS91–16), May 28, 1991, p. 3.

15. See, for example, "Ethnic Minorities: A Review of the Main Groups and Areas of Actual and Potential Tension or Conflict in Central and Eastern. Europe, including the Former Soviet Union" (SGS92–526) (unpublished), and "Political Aspects of the Mandate of the European Bank in Relation to Ethnic Minorities" (March 1993) (published in pamphlet form by the EBRD).

16. As quoted in the September 6, 1991, edition of the EBRD's internal newsletter, later named *Blueprint.*

17. See press release of July 3, 1992, concerning the Balkans.

18. See, for example, "Fat and Friendless," an article on the World Bank appearing in the September 1993 issue of *Euromoney,* characterizing the "troubles at the EBRD" as "not just extravagance, but the combination of weird leadership and ill-placed importance."

19. In his first speech to staff, de Larosière noted that he had solicited views on the future of the Political Unit from key shareholders and indicated that they had left the decision to him. The dissolution of the Unit was accomplished during the overall reorganization of the EBRD which took place in autumn 1993 and which resulted in the merger of the public sector and private sector operational divisions.

20. See "European Bank Gets Down to Business: Under de Larosière, Lender to East Eschews Politics," *Wall Street Journal,* March 14, 1994.

21. The Task Force on Operational Priorities was comprised of six EBRD staff and chaired by the Chief Economist. Over the course two months, the Task Force interviewed more than 250 individuals to get their views on how the EBRD might better fulfil its purpose and objectives. The final report of the Task Force, essentially a synthesis of the views expressed by interviewees, recommends that the Bank's political activities not be prominent and be confined to basic monitoring and the knowledge about political conditions necessary for operational purposes.

22. Hailing the new unified structure of the Bank, the governor from Belgium called attention to the importance of monitoring compliance with article 1: "The operational documents for each country of operations should be updated regularly and also catalogue the hurdles to be overcome if the Bank is to enhance its capacity for action in the country concerned. I would remind you in this respect that the Agreement Establishing the Bank requires it to model its operational policy on the commitment of its member countries to the principles of democracy, pluralism and respect for human rights. I therefore feel there should be a special unit responsible for monitoring compliance with that political mandate. In this connection the Bank should be careful to avoid encouraging mafia-like practices whose growth in certain countries is a source of concern."

The governor from Luxembourg seconded the Belgian governor's concerns, but stopped short of calling for a separate unit within the Bank responsible for monitoring compliance. See *Statements by the Governors from Belgium and Luxembourg* printed in *Statements at the Third Annual Meeting of the Board of Governors of the EBRD.*

23. The assessment in the Technical Cooperation Action Plan for Tajikistan that Tajikistan "overall . . . at present cannot be considered as conforming to Article 1 of

the Agreement Establishing the Bank" was not intended as an official recordation of noncompliance with the principles enshrined in article 1 of the Treaty Establishing the EBRD. As reported by the author of the report, the rendering of any such judgment was considered unnecessary since the EBRD, due to the devastated state of the Tajik economy and risks associated with investing in Tajikistan, was not contemplating preparation of investment projects in, and dedication of ordinary capital resources to, the jurisdiction of Tajikistan.

24. In an opinion on the consistency of the Action Plan with the Agreement Establishing the EBRD requested before presentation of the Action Plan to EBRD's Board of Directors, the general counsel concluded that the implementation of the Action Plan, if approved by the Board of Directors, would be consistent with the Agreement provided it was entirely financed from the Technical Cooperation funds of donors administered by the Bank and no proposal was presented to the Board for the provision of financing from the Bank's ordinary capital resources of any operation in Tajikistan until a Strategy Paper for the country has been approved by the Board and the political and economic stabilization process has come to the point where Tajikistan could be considered to conform to article 1 of the Agreement. At the time of the submission of the Technical Cooperation Action Plan for Tajikistan there was already a precedent for the presentation to the Board of an Action Plan in place of a Strategy. In July 1991, before the August 9 coup that led to the splintering of the USSR, management sent to the Board for consideration at the August meeting of the Board a Strategy for the USSR. The Strategy was subsequently pulled and reworked into an Action Plan.

25. Technical Cooperation Action Plan for Tajikistan, BDS/TA/94–1 (June 27, 1994).

26. When the Board of Directors adopted the Strategy for Uzbekistan (BDS/UZ/94–1) in March 1994, they expressed concern about the slow pace of economic reform and lack of progress to multiparty democracy and protection of human rights and stated they would like to see a link made between progress on this front and the Bank's operational strategy. The president undertook to express the directors' concerns to the Uzbekistan government. The need for reform and privatization had in fact already been communicated to the Uzbekistan government two months earlier, in January 1994, in a letter from the president of the EBRD to the governor of the EBRD for Uzbekistan granting a Limited Waiver of the EBRD's Negative Pledge. This expression of dissatisfaction likewise was made at the request of the Board.

27. Naples G7 Summit Communiqué setting the agenda for the 1995 Summit in Halifax.

28. Although the EBRD is situated and operates within Europe and its regional mandate and membership base (the EBRD is majority-owned by the states comprising the EU, the Commission of the EU, and the European Investment Bank) might suggest it is a European institution or instrument of European Union policy, it is as much a vehicle for G7 policy. The United States, which holds 10 percent of its shares, and Japan, which holds around 8.5 percent, are among the key shareholders.

29. Article 8.3 provides: "In cases where a member might be implementing policies which are inconsistent with Article 1 of this Agreement, or in exceptional circumstances, the Board of Directors shall consider whether access by a member to the Bank resources should be suspended or otherwise modified and may make

recommendations accordingly to the Board of Governors. Any decision on these matters shall be taken by the Board of Governors by a majority of not less than two-thirds of the Governors, representing not less than three-fourths of the total voting power of the members."

30. The inclusion within the Agreement of procedures by which a member's access to funds could be suspended in response to nonconformity with article 1 suggests article 38 is meant to address situations other than non-compliance with article, such as; for example, non-payment by a member of all or a portion of its capital subscription.

31. In January 1980 the IDA agreed to such an arrangement with the government of Afghanistan on the grounds that hostilities prevented the IDA from supervising project implementation as originally planned. Disbursements on credits to Afghanistan were subsequently formally suspended.

32. Every loan and subscription agreement executed by the EBRD contains a provision that permits it to suspend its commitment to make disbursements thereunder in the event the governors of the EBRD suspend a member's right to access EBRD funds pursuant to article 8.3 of the Agreement Establishing the EBRD. Loan agreements also permit acceleration in such an event.

33. The possibilities scattered along the spectrum of potential disciplinary actions are not mutually exclusive. They could be invoked sequentially, in order of escalating severity, to engender the desired effect.

34. Looking to the family of IFIs and the Paris Club for insights to how EBRD might best develop its political attributes is of limited utility. Since the charters of the IBRD, IFC, and ADB all bar political considerations from being factored into lending decisions, the IFI family history is on the political front silent, at least when taken at surface value. Decisions to halt funding or liquidate investments are always characterized as commercial decisions motivated by sound financial judgment, even where politics, if not the primary impetus, is a substantial contributing factor. (The IFCs characterization of its liquidation of its investments in Iran in the early 1980s as a "sale of investments" is one example. The IBRD's insistence that credit concerns fully explain its failure to authorize new loans to Chile in the early 1970s, during Salvador Allende Gossens' presidency, is another.) Official export credit agencies and private actors lend no better guidance.

35. With certain exceptions (for example, gross violations of human rights and express acceptance of third-party intervention), traditional public international law does not concern itself with internal armed conflicts. Recent years, however, have shown some movement in this area. In particular, CSCE participating states have begun to consider norms concerning nonrecourse to force within a state.

36. A February 1993 EBRD Staff Paper on War and Democracy observes: "Armed conflicts may, in many instances, constitute a violation of international law and recognised international human rights. On the other hand, not every act will do so nor will necessarily imply a violation of the principles of Article 1 of the Agreement and application of the relevant provisions of Article 8."

37. At present, tender notices for contracts financed by EBRD and other international financial institutions attract extremely competitive bids in part because the involvement of such institutions is perceived by suppliers as reducing the risk of interruption of the awarded contracts or untimely payment for work satisfactorily performed.

38. In December 1994, the EBRD had offices in Almaty, Bucharest, Budapest, Bratislava, Kiev, Minsk, Moscow, Sofia, Prague, Riga, Tallinn, Tashkent, Tirana, and Warsaw; advisers in Dushanbe and Bishkek; regional representatives working in specially targeted cities in the Russian Federation, including St. Petersburg, Volgograd, and Vladivostok; and plans to open an office in Ljubliana and to establish a local presence in Azerbaijan and Croatia in 1995.

39. This is one reason why, in the EBRD's first three years of operations, as it staffed up, its private lending activities were driven largely by the demands of western sponsors who approached the EBRD for financing.

40. Jesus Seade, deputy director-general of GATT, speaking at the EBRD on July 5, 1994, on "The Uruguay Round and the Integration of Eastern Europe and the Former Soviet Union into the World Trade and Financial Systems" made a similar point with regard to the desirability of keeping GATT free of what might best be termed "human rights conditionality."

41. The lack of support had both a political and commercial dimension. There was concern that if the EBRD agreed to the project, it might unwittingly end up creating further excuses on which Russia could rely in not withdrawing its troops (for example, housing complex not fully ready for occupancy). The project was also judged commercially nonviable and thus counter to "sound banking practices."

Attali argued to the Board—entirely unsuccessfully—that initiatives in the social security sector should be considered a priority. In the face of one such rejection, Attali requested that his conviction that the Bank should be active in the social sector and his reminder to the Board that the inability of social security systems in the Bank's countries of operations to cope with rising unemployment could be a major obstacle to the transition process be put on record. It is interesting to consider the Board's total intransigence on this issue as compared to the rigid policy framework imposed on the ADB by the advanced industrialized states as a condition of its fourth general capital increase.

42. Executive and staff cross-fertilization add a psychological dimension. While forging policies and developing operations for their new employer, individuals tend to draw on their past experience in the IMF, IBRD, IFC, or ADB for guidance.

43. See Resolution no. 30 of the Board of Governors of the EBRD (Membership of Countries Previously Forming Part of Yugoslavia) (October 9, 1992)

44. Observing that Croatia's adherence to certain resolutions of the UN Security Council was in doubt, the Board noted that Croatia's adherence to article 1 of the Agreement Establishing the Bank would need to be carefully monitored and confirmed before the Bank launched operations within its jurisdiction.

45. This suggestion is open to criticism on the grounds, among others, that the establishment of commercial dispute resolution panels is not a banking function and thus outside the province of the EBRD. The counterargument is that the EBRD is not just a bank, and should work with the business community on initiatives that promote pluralism and democracy in a commercial context.

46. The Bank's environmental policy provides: "The Bank will ensure that project sponsors provide adequate information on the environmental impacts of projects to governments at all levels and to the general public, especially potentially affected parties, and that the comments and opinions expressed by these parties will be taken into account in the project-approval procedures of the Bank."

Environmental Management: The Bank's Policy Approach (January 1992). For projects requiring a full environmental assessment, the Bank requires the project sponsor to notify citizens, involved government organizations, NGOs, and relevant community organizations of the nature of the project and ensures that the comments and opinions expressed by parties are reflected in the project approval procedures of the Bank. For projects requiring a partial environmental analysis, public participation requirements in the particular country are required to be met.

Due to the nature of the projects considered by the EBRD for funding and the countries in which the EBRD operates, issues related to indigenous people only occasionally arise. Where such issues are potentially of importance, as in the case of oil and gas projects in Siberia and mining projects in central Asia, care is taken to involve nomadic herders and others in project development. Environmental assessments of such projects include a section on effects on indigenous populations.

47. See remarks attributed to Henning Christophersen, vice president of the European Commission ("The EBRD must not be a political institution, but plainly and simply a bank") in "Is What's Good for Jacques Attali Good for the Bank?" *Institutional Investor* (March 1992). In defense of Mr. Attali it should be noted that the EC was riled by Attali's public criticism of EC trade policy toward the central and eastern European Countries and the terms and conditions of the Association Agreements signed with Czechoslovakia, Hungary, and Poland.

Part Four

EIGHT

The Military Perspective on Conflict Prevention: NATO

Antonia Handler Chayes and Richard Weitz

NATO's North Atlantic Council (NAC), its highest decisionmaking body, declared on June 10, 1993: "Conflict prevention, crisis management, and peacekeeping will be crucial to ensuring stability and security in the Euro-Atlantic area in the years ahead. . . . While reaffirming that the primary goal of Alliance military forces is to guarantee the security and territorial integrity of member states, we will contribute actively to these new tasks in order to enhance our security and European stability." On February 28, 1994, NATO aircraft shot down several Serb planes violating a United Nations-declared "no fly" zone over Bosnia-Herzegovina. In subsequent months NATO pilots conducted limited bombing missions against Bosnian Serb military units that had ignored UN-authorized exclusion zones.[1] In late November 1994, NATO bombed a Croatian Serb airfield in Udbina in response to Serb air attacks on the "safe area" of Bihac.[2] These incidents mark both the first use of military force under NATO command in a combat situation and NATO's first experience as an organization performing peace operations.

Yet in May 1995, despite prolonged U.S. pressure for more vigorous military action in the Bosnian conflict, the UN commander for all the former Yugoslavia, Lieutenant General Bertrand Janvier, and the senior UN civilian coordinator there, Yasushi Akashi, denied the request of Lieutenant General Rupert Smith, the UN commander in Bosnia, for NATO air strikes

The authors' views do not necessarily coincide with those of Roles and Missions Commission of the Armed Forces of the United States or any other U.S. government agency.

381

against Serb units shelling civilians in the Bosnian government's capital in Sarajevo.[3] That decision was ultimately reversed, and a Serbian military supply depot was bombed by NATO on May 25. This led to the infamous Bosnian Serb capture of several hundred United Nations Protection Force (UNPROFOR) peacekeepers in retaliation.[4] On August 30, NATO conducted bombing raids on a far larger scale, in response to a documented and bloody shelling of Sarajevo by the Bosnian serbs. It was the largest military operation ever undertaken by the alliance.

These incidents exemplify the uncertain and uncharted path on which the alliance embarked several years earlier. In July 1992 the NATO governments agreed to support Conference on Security and Cooperation in Europe (CSCE, later OSCE) peacekeeping activities.[5] In December 1992 they offered the same assistance to the UN. Documents developing the scope of peace operations were prepared both within NATO and the North Atlantic Cooperation Council (NACC), an advisory body created to include central and eastern European countries, Russia, and many of the former Soviet republics. But events moved so fast that NATO became deeply involved in the Bosnian conflict before it could define its new missions of "conflict prevention, crisis management, and peacekeeping." The former Yugoslavia provided an opportunity to function in peace operations, but the alliance did not enjoy the benefits of a deliberative, detailed planning process, doctrinal development, and the training and practice that such a novel role ideally would entail. Only as the war dragged on, was it able to engage in advance military planning.

This chapter explores the extent to which NATO might serve a useful function in conflict prevention in eastern and central Europe (ECE) and the former Soviet Union (FSU). Part of that inquiry involves the larger examination of a potential military role in conflict prevention, broadly defined. Unfortunately, it is written at a point at which the entire UN operation in the former Yugoslavia has come under strong criticism, and the very parameters of what a peace operation should encompass at the end of the century is in the process of redefinition. It is difficult to step back and assess the future potential of NATO in conflict prevention or peace operations in the present context. Nevertheless, we believe that although NATO's difficult experience in the former Yugoslavia is discouraging, it is not dispositive. Conflict prevention and mitigation will require a significant military dimension. The former Yugoslavia is unlikely to represent the last conflict affecting alliance interests, and NATO, Europe's most robust military organization, is likely to be called upon to contribute to such missions.

However, a number of questions must be answered. Does NATO have a comparative advantage over an ad hoc international effort mounted by the UN? If it does, can the alliance encompass these other missions? Can it acquire credibility and acceptance in its new role while preserving its traditional missions? Does a role in peace operations on behalf of the UN or OSCE mean a transition from a collective defense establishment protecting the North Atlantic community from Soviet aggression to an instrument of collective security and conflict prevention, assuring stability to all Europe? Is that implicit in NATO enlargement?

After describing NATO's early transitional efforts and experience, we address the internal and external obstacles to such a transformation and explore whether they can or should be overcome.

Background

The magnitude of the change required for NATO to become a credible and widely accepted conflict-prevention organization that engages in the full spectrum of peace operations will not be fully understood for some time. NATO policymakers have recognized since the disappearance of the Soviet threat that NATO's historic purpose and membership are no longer appropriate for the new mission of assuring stability in all Europe. They are grappling with the complexity of maintaining old missions, thus providing reassurance of continuing U.S. involvement in Europe, while transforming the alliance and possibly enlarging its membership. At the purely operational level, the nature of the conflict in which NATO might become involved is still unknown. The alliance possesses, through its member states, national knowledge and experience in peace operations conducted elsewhere. But the former Yugoslavia has provided the only experience thus far for NATO as a military organization. NATO's members and affiliates naturally find it difficult to incorporate their disparate conflict-prevention and peacekeeping experiences into a coherent approach and to avoid the tendency to generalize from their limited experience in the former Yugoslavia. Enough is known, however, about peace operations in arenas of internal conflict and state breakup to indicate that they represent neither an entirely different set of tasks from those for which NATO has trained, nor are they merely "lesser included tasks." The real planning process has barely started, and it faces serious obstacles.

At the June 1990 London summit and especially the November 1991 Rome summit, NATO leaders outlined a revised military strategy to reflect the Soviet bloc's collapse. The alliance previously planned to defend its members' territory through the twin strategies of forward defense and flexible response. NATO deployed about half a million troops by national army groups in layercake fashion near West Germany's eastern frontier, aiming to fight close to the inter-German border rather than surrender space for time.[6] The policy of "flexible response" entailed a declaratory commitment to resort to nuclear weapons if necessary to prevent a conventional defeat. This was accompanied by both the requisite training and the deployment of tactical and intermediate range nuclear weapons. The allies believed that flexible response bolstered the alliance's deterrent and assured that the United States would become fully engaged should a Soviet attack occur. Whether or not fully credible, extensive deployments and practice created at a minimum the uncertainty about resort to nuclear weapons that itself provided deterrent power.

The member governments no longer feared a direct military threat to their territories after the cold war, but instability and conflict soon erupted in ECE. NATO policymakers felt uncomfortable about the short- and long-term impact of conflicts that could arise from Europe's serious economic, social, and political difficulties, including ethnic rivalries and territorial disputes. They responded cautiously to the continent's radical changes. Their new military strategy reduced the size of NATO's active duty forces while increasing the flexibility and mobility of the remaining units and endowing them with an assured capacity for augmentation. NATO now had three categories of armed forces: main defense forces, reaction forces, and augmentation forces. A British general commanded a new Rapid Reaction Corps for quick deployment (within five to seven days) in crises. The alliance also fielded more multinational formations to compensate for its members' declining troop contributions. Most controversially, the allies retained some nuclear capacity. Although budgetary pressures prompted members to reduce their defense spending and military forces substantially (the United States now has some 100,000 troops in Europe from a high of 336,000 in 1989),[7] all allies have wanted a robust NATO. They planned to deal with an uncertain security environment by maintaining the collective defense capability at reduced levels, with effective reconstruction capabilities.[8]

So long as nearby conflict might spill over or otherwise disrupt European stability, and so long as uncertainty and substantial military capability exist in the FSU, NATO members perceive a continuing mission for the organization. Even if the alliance's robust military presence provides largely psychological and political reassurance, it gives members the confidence to reduce their military expenditures in a still unsettled continent. Most important, its persistence assures a continuing U.S. commitment to Europe in an era of uncertainty. If NATO were seriously weakened, its members might resort to self-help and renationalization of their armed forces, with likely escalatory and destabilizing effects, particularly if undertaken by Germany. Thus, by its very existence, NATO has a stabilizing effect. This political reassurance is often taken for granted, although it may be the central benefit of NATO's continuation.

The Military Component of Peace Operations

NATO retains its core function, deterrence against direct threats to its members. It probably also has existential credibility against any cross-border aggression that might spill over into its members' territories. But it is hard to imagine the relevance of its military forces in preventing internal conflict that arises from ethno-national issues or state breakdown outside the territory of the member states. Theoretically, the threat of force might deter a government or an organized military group from engaging in wholesale human rights violations or genocide. But if a state is disintegrating, a rational deterrent strategy, which requires a leadership target that both controls its forces and responds rationally to threats, is almost a contradiction in terms.

NATO agreed to consider participating in peace operations if the UN or OSCE requests its assistance. Yet the full range of this undertaking still remains unclear, either in terms of types of operations, duration, or geographical reach. Many military tasks are involved in the full range of peace operations and even in conflict prevention as defined in this volume. Yet one should not overstate the magnitude of the military role in peace operations. Such missions typically have been on a rather small scale—a few thousand troops, as in Egypt, Lebanon, and Namibia. In some cases, such as Somalia and Haiti, they may approach twenty to thirty thousand, although historically that is the exception. Peace operations are not without danger, and do require skill, training, and a high degree of interoperability. But experience does not bear out an "escalation model" of an inexorable progression from diplomacy to economic sanctions to military operations aiming to enforce or impose a settlement.[9] Historically, it has proven difficult to assemble a force with broad legitimacy and sufficient military power in the absence of a threat to the traditionally perceived national interests of the major powers. Forty years elapsed between Korea and the Gulf War. The political dilemmas and vacillation over military policy in Bosnia have underscored this problem.

Nevertheless, the smaller military tasks that may help to prevent or mitigate conflict can be of considerable, even crucial, importance. Military forces may serve as an adjunct to diplomacy, a form of "muscular diplomacy" in which the threat of force hovers in the background, and is used in conjunction with diplomatic efforts and in coordination with a wide variety of civilian tasks. They may prove particularly effective in the very early stages of a conflict when it has not hardened, and compromise and resolution remain possible. This was the experience in the first phase of Somalia, in which civil-military coordination and a minimum show of force permitted a vast increase in the effectiveness of humanitarian assistance.[10] It also was the experience in the early phases of the Haiti operations. The show of force and willingness to use it bought the needed time for the Aristide government to begin rebuilding a democratic society. Although modest, this role may give mediators important credibility and power. The show of military force can buy time and space for nurturing voluntary settlement options.

Such a strategy does not always work. The willingness to use force may be challenged, as it was in the latter phases of Somalia, after the UN decided in June 1993 to pursue Aideed and his supporters. Military necessities may compromise the appearance of neutrality needed for peace operations. Alternatively, the nations cooperating in peacekeeping may prove unwilling to alter the mission to peace enforcement or partisan military support of one of the parties to the conflict, as has been the case, wisely or otherwise, in the former Yugoslavia. However, this dilemma besets peace operations generally, and does not detract from the important role that military forces may play even short of enforcement.

The military role is most limited in preconflict situations. Preventive diplomacy is paramount. But parts of preventive diplomacy, such as negotiation and intermediation, may include a military presence with some military tasks of coordination or symbolic support. A good case in point is a preemptive deployment of troops, such as the UN has performed in Macedonia.[11] Military communications, headquarters, and logistic support also might assist observer missions in a preconflict situation. Military presence or backup can provide reassurance, and perhaps deterrence, even though, if the dog does not bark, establishing that the deployment had preventive value is difficult. This is what makes preventive action so hard to sell. The credibility of potential disaster always appears low.

Once hostilities have broken out, peace operations may require more military support or activity. It is of course a matter of definition whether classic peacekeeping, or any other activity undertaken in the midst of conflict, should be considered a form of conflict prevention, but this volume defines activities undertaken to prevent conflict from spreading as a form of prevention. The provision of headquarters for coordination and communication in a conflict zone, such as NATO established for UNPROFOR in the former Yugoslavia, requires considerable military skill and experience, particularly when it is multinational in character. Other military activities at this stage may include not only the interposition of forces, but a demonstration of force to protect innocent civilians, bolster humanitarian missions, and enforce compliance with agreements.

Humanitarian operations involving the supply of water, food, and medicine have a strong conflict-prevention function. In many cases military organizations can best perform such missions, especially in an early phase of intervention when there is chaos and urgency, as the experience in Rwanda in 1994 has shown. True, once organized and coordinated, nongovernmental organizations and even private businesses often can assume many of these tasks, from providing food and medical assistance to building roads and removing mines. But these services, as recent experience has shown, may require rapid mobilization and complex coordination and communication. The situations in Rwanda, Somalia, and the former Yugoslavia all illustrate the difficulty of protecting humanitarian missions, especially under warlike conditions of anarchy and lawlessness.

A still embryonic and very controversial aspect of peace operations has been the establishment of "safe havens" to protect civilians in conflict situations as part of a conflict-mitigation mission, first in Iraq, then in Bosnia. In Rwanda, French ground forces with UN endorsement also established an exclusion zone to protect threatened civilians. The UN tasked NATO to employ air power to enforce both air and ground exclusion zones in Bosnia. Securing such safe havens has been fraught with military risk, especially when the attacking parties possess sophisticated weapons or when the protected parties exploit the safe havens to regroup their military forces. The "safe haven" concept remains problematic because the degree of military enforcement to protect them may jeopardize any remnant of neutrality, as it has done in Bosnia. The experience in Sarajevo, including the May 1995 hostage-taking of UNPROFOR forces and the later bombing by NATO, has thrown the concept into question. Yet the establishment of safe havens bears strong relationship to interposition forces of classic peacekeeping, and in contemporary internal conflict may be the only means to protect the innocent from slaughter.

The risks and complexity of demonstrating military force in peace operations in the midst of a raging conflict mean that armed peacekeepers require a high degree of specialized military training and practice. The rules of engagement (ROE) need to be worked out in each situation and adjusted with the evolving contingencies on the ground. The peacekeepers must coordinate operations with civilian groups under the most stressful conditions. They often deploy in a region without a clear line of battle. They require special cultural skills and sophistication to interact effectively with the local populace. Although some aspects of these missions resemble past military experiences, the boundaries of peace operations and the way they are carried out is just beginning to be understood under these new conditions of post–cold war state breakdown. The fact that many of these operations have not shown marked success, particularly in the former Yugoslavia, does not mean they cannot succeed when given clear support, workable mandates, and clear ROE. Experts disagree on the philosophy or approach that peacekeeping requires under the diverse circumstances of recent conflicts. UNPROFOR's criteria for self-defense operations have been far more restrictive than those of earlier UN missions such as Cyprus, where the UN force (UNFICYP) received authorization to respond forcefully to attempts to restrict movement, to compel withdrawal, or in general to carry out its mandates, or than the ROE prepared for U.S. forces in Haiti.[12] These new types of peace operations require extensive military planning to assure the force employed corresponds to the mission's objectives, and to prevent an inadvertent transition to an enforcement effort. Intensive debates about these issues now occur frequently within NATO, its member nations, and between NATO and the UN.

Postconflict situations also require military skill and training. A variety of exacting and potentially dangerous missions may be called for immediately after combatants reach an agreement. These include policing an accord and dealing with violations, performing agreed disarmament tasks, patrolling zones of separation, and removing hazardous munitions, mines, and barriers. Simply listing these tasks does not begin to encompass the skills required in performing them nor the issues in deciding whether and when to address them. For example, the question of disarmament may be relatively simple when the combatants actually intend to lay down their arms voluntarily, as occurred in Nicaragua and El Salvador. By contrast, the pressure by the UN secretary-general to disarm the clans in Somalia, where there was no agreement, led to the operation's transformation into a peace enforcement mission, for which the publics in the participating states, especially the United States, were unprepared. In Angola the combatants' failure to disarm led to the conflict's rapid resumption.

The postconflict phase often requires a bewildering array of nation-building (or peace-building) tasks. Each situation presents a different set of challenges. Engineering tasks, including de-mining, have drawn on military experience, but the rebuilding of civil society may be better organized by civilians trained in such areas as police, justice, and education. Nevertheless, the relationship between groups mounting such efforts and the military's endeavors to assure safety, coordination, and orderly withdrawal has created problems in situations such as Cambodia. The risk of recurrence of conflict has proved high, and the presence of military forces able to respond rapidly and decisively may be the best insurance against further conflict.

This recital of military tasks in the range of conflict-prevention measures may not "prove" the importance of the military dimension, but it certainly underscores the reality of the missions for which NATO is preparing. Alliance policymakers proceed on the assumption that the organization enjoys distinct advantages in peace operations over an ad hoc force, in part because of its history and experience in multinational command, control, and communications, and in part because it has practiced military operations as an organization for nearly a half century.[13] If one were to examine discrete (and simple) conflict-prevention or peace operation tasks, it could be argued that they might be performed as well by ad hoc UN forces with some training and the necessary capability and equipment. Where the nations composing a coalition force had prior experience with peace operations, their performance might even prove superior to a NATO contingent that had not jointly exercised such tasks. But the Somali operation illustrates some of the difficulties of developing a fully effective force from elements that have not trained together, lack conceptual and practical interoperability, do not possess a common doctrine, and differ in their concept of operations. Some clear NATO advantages emerge if the operation is complex, with diverse and perhaps changing components, requires military sophistication, and must be mounted quickly. The ability of NATO, as well as a single large power such as the United States or Russia, to perform complex and stressful military operations could make it an effective "subcontractor" for the UN.

In the field of peace operations, however, NATO training and doctrinal development remains rudimentary.[14] The emerging conceptual approach to peace operations is generally consistent with the pronouncements on peace-keeping in its members' literature and the UN, although the author of the British manual "Wider Peacekeeping" argued that NATO's early draft doctrine did not sufficiently emphasize consent of the parties, the linchpin of the British concept.[15] The draft NACC Doctrine for Peace Support Operation emphasizes minimum force, transparency, impartiality, and specifically excludes peace enforcement (such as employed in Korea or Iraq), "which is generally covered by existing NATO or other national doctrine": "Peace support operations are based on the premise that peaceful methods will generally be used to achieve the goal of the mission. Any use of force must be justified and carefully controlled. The unnecessary or irrational use of force will undermine the acceptability of the force and lead to an escalation of violence in the area of operation."[16]

The document, like the various pronouncements of the UN secretary-general, contemplates cooperation and coordination with other organizations in the execution of civil tasks, such as election supervision, temporary law enforcement, training indigenous law enforcement personnel, and the like. These tasks also parallel European national, UN, and academic concepts of peace support.[17]

Political obstacles slowed the development of doctrine and training for NATO peace operations. As discussed below, French policymakers insist on keeping their distance from the alliance's integrated military command structure. And the critically important concept of Combined Joint Task Forces (CJTF) remains embryonic, even though the employment of NATO assets such as regional headquarters for missions involving units from countries outside the alliance's integrated military structure would exploit NATO's superior capability to coordinate forces and organize an operation. Alliance officials themselves wonder, with shrinking budgets, whether they can assume new missions requiring costly training, exercises, and procurement without compromising NATO's capability for collective defense, still considered its primary mission.[18]

For NATO to have operational credibility, intensive training focused on peace operations must begin in earnest. The pool of member knowledge is deep, given the experiences of the British, Canadians, Dutch, and others, including the realistic two-week simulations at the U.S. Joint Readiness Training Center. Yet actions that demonstrate NATO's commitment to develop a capability in peace operations as it has in collective defense must accompany the rhetoric about the alliance's new missions.

The NATO Experience in the Former Yugoslavia

NATO's initial participation in the Yugoslav conflict may have been premature in terms of its preparation and understanding for the new demands and responsibilities of peace operations, but it has provided the opportunity to better comprehend the likely demands and relationships involved in such missions. Moreover, there has been time for preparation and planning for its postagreement peace implementation role.

Early pronouncements about the conflict reflected the alliance's traditional reservations about involvement in out-of-area operations. NATO secretary-general Manfred Wörner explained in November 1991 that the allies had decided to give the European Community (EC) a free hand managing the Yugoslav crisis. He observed that many at NATO questioned whether the alliance should intervene militarily in a conflict within a country when its purpose always had been to defend its members from external attack and to prevent aggression among states.[19] After the EC intervention failed, he maintained that the allied governments properly looked next to the UN to manage the international community's response to the Yugoslav war.[20]

In an interview less than a year later, however, Wörner asserted a wide-ranging alliance role in local conflicts and other dimensions of European security.[21] More important, NATO as an institution had begun by this time to intervene militarily in the former Yugoslavia. Under UN direction, the allies drew on long-standing alliance assets to limit the conflict's destructiveness. For example, UNPROFOR's headquarters in Zagreb used elements from NATO's NORTHAG command. Similarly, the alliance provided communications channels to the dual-headed NATO-Western European Union (WEU) blockade fleet in the Adriatic enforcing UN sanctions against Serbia and Montenegro according to Security Council Resolutions 787 and 820. Since the French, who left the integrated command structure in 1966, had previously exercised bilaterally with the United States and other European nations, the thirteen NATO members participating in "Sharp Guard" managed to establish an effective operation.[22] As of October 21, 1994, the units involved had challenged more than 40,000 merchant vessels, boarded 3,133 of them, and halted or inspected 804 ships suspected of attempting to deliver prohibited items to Yugoslavia.[23]

NATO provided both deterrence and reassurance, discouraging the conflict's horizontal expansion during its early stages. For example, when in 1991 the Serbian government expressed concern about alleged troop movements along its border with Bulgaria, Bulgarian officials invited accredited military attachés from NATO countries to the area to disprove the claim.[24] Somewhat later, after Hungarian authorities permitted NATO surveillance aircraft to use their airspace to monitor developments in neighboring Bosnia-Herzegovina, Serbian planes, which had previously bombed a Hungarian village located near the frontier with Bosnia, stopped violating Hungarian airspace.[25]

NATO aircraft, guided by the alliance's multinational Airborne Warning and Control System (AWACS) aircraft, first monitored and then, starting on April 12, 1993, enforced the no-fly zone established by the UN Security Council in Resolution 816 ("Operation Deny Flight"). In 1993 and 1994, NATO planes flew a number of low-level "practice bombing runs" in an only partially successful effort to quiet Serb artillery batteries around Sarajevo and other Bosnian cities.[26] At their June 1993 meeting in Athens, NATO foreign ministers offered to provide air support to any UN forces in Bosnia-Herzegovina that felt threatened. In August 1993 and January 1994, in coordination with UN Security Council action, NATO threatened air strikes to prevent the "strangulation" of Sarajevo and the obstruction of humanitarian aid to other besieged Bosnian towns. The allies also repeatedly consented to implement a peace agreement in the former Yugoslavia should the UN request it, providing the parties accepted and carried out a comprehensive settlement. In late February 1994, NATO planes for the first time shot down four Serb aircraft that had ignored warnings and bombed a Bosnian government munitions plant. Before then most Serb aircraft had landed or had left Bosnian airspace when challenged by NATO air patrols.[27]

After the shelling of a crowded marketplace in Sarajevo killed sixty-eight people, the Security Council on February 9, 1994, imposed an "exclusion zone" around the city and established a safe haven. Pursuant to this action, the NAC instructed the Serbs to withdraw all heavy weapons— including artillery pieces, missiles, mortars, multiple rocket launches, tanks, and antiaircraft systems—to at least twenty kilometers from Sarajevo or place them under UN control. Any heavy weapons (including those of the Bosnian government) remaining within the exclusion zone and outside UN control after February 20 "along with their direct and essential military support facilities" would become subject to air attack. The NAC also agreed to the UN secretary-general's appeal of February 6 to authorize air strikes even outside the exclusion zone when requested by UN personnel against artillery or mortar positions that the UN identified as attacking civilian targets in Sarajevo. Deputy Foreign Minister Vitaly Churkin, a special Russian envoy, interceded directly with Serb commanders to secure the withdrawal of their heavy weapons from around Sarajevo, thus forestalling the need for the threatened NATO military measures. The Serbs placed 281 tanks, mortars, artillery pieces, and antiaircraft guns under UN control within nine compounds.[28] When in early August 1994 Bosnian Serbs seized some of the heavy weapons they had earlier surrendered to UN control, NATO warplanes launched an air strike. The Serbs promptly returned the weapons.[29]

NATO provided additional military support to the peacekeeping operation in April. Fearing massive casualties following the collapse of Bosnian government defenses in the besieged city of Gorazde, the NAC ordered the Serbs to halt their attack, withdraw their troops three kilometers from the town center, and grant free access to the town to UN observers and humanitarian workers. Wörner protested: "The murderous, barbaric attacks against the defenseless civilians of Gorazde are an outrage. . . . It is now up to the Bosnian Serbs to heed these demands, or they will face serious consequences."[30] The ultimatum came several weeks after NATO warplanes, responding to an UNPROFOR request for close air support to protect its observers in Gorazde, had twice bombed Serbian forces that had disregarded UN instructions to halt their assault. (A third raid failed when the Serbs on April 16 shot down an attacking British Sea Harrier jet.) As in Sarajevo, the NATO threat reduced Serb assaults on the town.[31]

The UN exercised far tighter control over enforcement of the safe havens or exclusion zones than over the no-fly zones. The "dual key" process, whereby NATO could undertake military operations only with UN approval, differs from the subcontracting model employed by the UN as early as the Korean War and as recently as Rwanda and Haiti. The dilemma posed by the Bosnian safe havens such as Sarajevo has been that the military enforcement, which appeared to the United States and some within NATO to be necessary and justified, jeopardized the UNPROFOR forces of other NATO members and were moderated by them and by the UN representatives. Many NATO policymakers found the "dual key" procedure frustrating. U.S. general George Joulwan, then newly appointed as Supreme Allied Commander (SACEUR), complained: "It is very difficult when you don't control the ground to be able to fly in support of those folks on the ground when they don't give you permission to do it or they don't have the observation on the ground when you start dropping bombs. . . . I agree with the perception that we [NATO] are impotent on the ground. But I must tell you when the chain of command runs back to Zagreb to the UN, I don't know if you can hold NATO responsible for that. We feel the heat."[32] U.S.

admiral Leighton Smith, commander-in-chief of NATO Allied Forces, Southern Europe, bluntly warned: "Don't ever have another dual key."[33] A particularly notorious incident occurred in March 1994, when three hours elapsed before senior UN officials approved the request of the UN commander in Bosnia for air strikes to defend French peacekeepers under attack by Serbs near Bihac. By the time NATO received the request, the Serb units had withdrawn.[34] Relations became so poor during the latter months of Sir Michael Rose's tenure as UN commander that NATO officials reportedly denied him access to the alliance's daily flight plans because they worried he would leak the information to the Serbs.[35]

On the whole, NATO has performed its military missions well, without strain on its capacity. The much harder issues have been managing the complex political decision process, both within the alliance and between the alliance and the UN. These two issues are related. The U.S. policy of expressing strong sympathy for the Bosnian Muslims, while refusing to deploy U.S. troops in regions of active conflict, created problems from the beginning. The United States advocated more vigorous NATO air strikes and the lifting of the arms embargo as it applied to the Bosnian government. The U.S. Congress ignored vigorous allied protests and in November 1994 precluded further U.S. participation in the embargo's enforcement.[36] As stated, the British and French, whose ten thousand peacekeepers on the ground in UNPROFOR found themselves increasingly vulnerable to Serb retaliation, wanted enforcement kept to a minimum. Since the UN command structure is primarily British and French, it is somewhat difficult to separate the national from the institutional differences.[37] Playing on their fears, Bosnian Serb leader Radovan Karadzic at the time of the Bihac crisis wrote UN leaders in Zagreb: "If a NATO attack happens, it will mean that further relations between yourselves and our side will be rendered impossible because we would have to treat you as our enemies. All United Nations Protection Force personnel as well as NATO personnel would be treated as our enemies."[38] That threat has been realized by the May 1995 hostage-taking of over three hundred UNPROFOR peacekeepers. And despite vocal frustration at the U.S. pressure for enforcement, by June of 1995 the British, French and Dutch were preparing rapid reaction forces which were subsequently deployed and engaged in the late August enforcement action by NATO.[39] The continuing tension over the military aspects of peace operations reflect not only alliance differences and disappointments over the West's handling of the Yugoslav crisis since it began, but also the inability to forge any policy that would stop the mayhem short of major military involvement.

NATO's mission in the former Yugoslavia was limited and ambiguous while UNPROFOR was there. At the time of writing, planning for post-conflict peace implementation has been finalized and its terms and conditions established. There will be no further "dual key"; unity of command has been accepted by the UN. The experience to date demonstrates that the alliance can function technically even under UN command and efficiently perform its assigned tasks. Compared with war with the Soviet Union, or even participation by its members in the Gulf War, the tasks were of relatively low intensity as this is written, and not demanding to coordinate. The operations have certainly not tested NATO's full power and sophistication, but they have been military in nature, and despite the tensions, many of them clearly benefited from the alliance's expertise. The obstacles to effectiveness have not been military but political. The major powers of NATO, who (along with Russia) also dominate the UN Security Council and the Contact Group trying to mediate a solution to the conflict, have been reluctant to increase the use of force. And as the redefinition of peace operations continues, it may become clearer that even robust peacekeeping and enforcement cannot coexist conceptually. NATO could perform either task, but not both at once.

Problems and Prospects of a Prominent NATO Role in Peace Operations

Serious obstacles must be overcome before NATO might play an effective and extensive conflict-prevention role in ECE and the FSU. Effective alliance intervention requires that the parties to a conflict perceive NATO as legitimate. Legitimacy in this context involves several dimensions. The first is legal: on what basis does NATO perform any peace operation beyond the scope of its collective defense charter in the area of its member states? A more subtle aspect of legitimacy is political: how can NATO continue to provide collective defense for its current members while appearing impartial? The question of membership expansion is crucially important to NATO's credibility and acceptability.

There are also issues internal to NATO itself. Some are as mundane as cost. Others, like the French refusal to extend the integrated command structure to the new peace missions, involve long-standing disagreements in novel contexts. The alliance's credibility as a powerful military institution is also an issue. Allied differences over NATO's appropriate role in the former Yugoslavia highlight that the political consensus forged with difficulty over the nearly fifty years when alliance members confronted the Soviet threat does not easily transfer to the post–cold war context.

Legitimacy of Out-of-Area Operations

The allies have resolved the legal question of how NATO might operate "out of area" by restricting alliance intervention to cases in which it receives a request for assistance from the UN or the OSCE, which itself must obtain Security Council authorization. By itself, the NATO treaty merely establishes collective defense for its members. Article 5 provides that "an armed attack against one or more of them in Europe or North America shall be considered an attack against them all." Article 6, which defines the area covered as the territories of alliance members in North America, Europe, and the Atlantic region north of the Tropic of Cancer, further qualifies the treaty's applicability. Neither substantively nor geographically does the North Atlantic Treaty authorize NATO to conduct peace, support operations in ECE and the FSU. Such activities could conceivably be covered by Article 2, which calls for cooperation "towards the further development of peaceful and friendly international relations by . . . promoting conditions of stability and well-being." However, NATO has been more cautious. Despite the expansiveness of some of Wörner's later statements and the widely publicized pronouncements that NATO would assume the new mission of assuring European stability, the NAC has only agreed to consider participating in peace operations when authorized by the OSCE or the UN.

From the perspective of the UN Charter, actions under article 5 of the Treaty in response to an attack on a NATO member would be justified as an exercise of the inherent right of self-defense against an armed attack. The concept of "self-defense" has been stretched a number of times to justify resort to force beyond a nation's borders. It is possible to imagine situations where the possibility of an out-of-area conflict spreading to a contiguous NATO member was so immediately threatening that the alliance might operate on its own initiative. But beyond that, peacekeeping operations in which the use of force is contemplated, whether in ECE or the FSU or elsewhere, would have to be authorized by the Security Council. Such authorization would come either from article 53, which provides for enforcement action by regional organizations, or under the general power of the Council under chapter 7 to take measures to restore international peace and security.

In the New Strategic Concept developed for the 1991 NATO heads-of-state summit in Rome, the allies laid out the rationale for NATO's involvement in "out-of-area" peace operations:

> Risks to Allied security are less likely to result from calculated aggression against the territory of the Allies, but rather from the adverse consequences of instabilities that may arise from the serious economic, social and political difficulties, including ethnic rivalries and territorial disputes, which are faced by many countries in Central and Eastern Europe. The tensions which may result, as long as they remain limited, should not directly threaten the security and territorial integrity of members of the Alliance. They could, however, lead to crises inimical to European stability and even to armed conflicts, which could involve outside powers or spill over into NATO countries, having a direct effect on the security of the Alliance.

NATO documents thus far state that formal agreement is required between the alliance and the UN or the OSCE about the size of any NATO peacekeeping force, its command structure, the ROE, and the participating nations (including nonmembers).[40]

The UN Charter provides no basis for formal "subcontracting" under chapter 6 or 7, as described by Jarat Chopra and Thomas G. Weiss (see chapter 12 in this volume), but as far back as the Korean War and as recently as Haiti, Rwanda, and Georgia, the UN has been prepared to allow a single nation or alliance to undertake an operation under its aegis. In the case of UNPROFOR, NATO has been asked to assume the specific, discrete tasks described earlier. The OSCE is not a treaty organization, and its authority to conduct and especially contract peace operations remains even hazier. Yet as a regional organization, it could engage in peacekeeping operations with Security Council approval under chapter 8, article 53.

Various proposals have been made for the OSCE to assume a more prominent role in peace operations in ECE and the FSU. Russian policymakers in particular regard the OSCE as far less threatening than their former military antagonist, NATO. Russia is a full-fledged member, with an effective veto based on the organization's loose consensus rule.[41] Russian efforts in the NACC and in the UN to encourage such reliance on the OSCE produced no results in the early 1990s, in part because of U.S. opposition, and in part because the impoverished OSCE was just beginning to organize itself to operate in a conflict-prevention mode in the same geographic area. Moreover, the UN gave little real encouragement for OSCE entry into the arena of active traditional peacekeeping, despite rhetoric about the import-

ance of regional organizations. Their initial enthusiasm for the OSCE dampened, ECE nations soon looked primarily to NATO to bolster their security.[42]

Despite recent enhancements to its role and credibility, the OSCE probably
will not become the most prominent institution for European peace operations,
as Diana Chigas points out (see chapter 1 in this volume). Such a development
would require radical changes in its decisionmaking process. The management
of complex, militarily-intensive peace operations would be difficult to mount
with only a Committee of Senior Officials and a Chair-in-Office who must gain
the approval of more than fifty governments for major decisions. Moreover, it
is hard to imagine who would fund yet another focal point for peace operations.
Finally, even if the OSCE should make gradual entry into that arena, it is
unlikely to rely regularly on NATO, at least at the beginning when it must
establish its own credibility and impartiality. Thus, as much as NATO policymakers resent serving as the UN's "military subcontractor," the UN appears the
most likely organization to call on its capabilities. Policymakers still speak of a
"complementary framework of interlocking, mutually reinforcing international
institutions" involving the UN, OSCE, the WEU, and the European Union
(EU), but peace operations seem to depend on the mantle of the UN, at least for
the near term.

If tasking by the UN (or OSCE) is the legal basis for NATO participation in peace operations "out of area," the question remains how far out it
will go, even with UN tasking. In accordance with NATO's consensus
rule, all alliance members must approve accepting a UN mandate for
military intervention. The Mediterranean members express concern about
threats from the south, especially North Africa.[43] The United States has
sought help from NATO members for Middle East operations, but even the
Gulf War did not fall under the alliance's explicit auspices.[44] We discuss
below the dubious prospects of NATO's involvement in peace operations
in the former Soviet Union. Although an enormous need exists for global
peace operations that NATO could help fulfill, the alliance's peacekeeping
activities likely will remain restricted to the Eurasian region for the foreseeable future. Nor is its political utility there yet established.

Membership: Enhancing Legitimacy through the Involvement of
Eastern Europe and the Former Soviet Union

As long as NATO remains only an alliance of western Europe, the United
States, and Canada, with the former Soviet Union, its traditional enemy, the
object of the continuing collective defense mission, the legitimacy of its

transformation into an institution to ensure peace and stability for all of Europe, much less Eurasia, remains questionable. Uncertainty about the continent's security environment can provide continued justification for NATO's continuing existence, but the absence of an immediate threat combined with a failure to undertake new activities risks institutional erosion and declining member support. Although they remain unwilling to relinquish the alliance's collective defense mission or its tactical nuclear weapons,[45] NATO policymakers recognize these problems and have made strong efforts to improve relations with former adversaries by involving them in cooperative and collaborative efforts.

Some observers argue that NATO's commitment to its collective defense strategy is incompatible with pan-Eurasian conflict prevention and collective security.[46] It would be difficult for combatants to perceive NATO as impartial in an FSU conflict when it also retains as its major function the defense of Europe against the possible revival of a threatening Russian empire. This hedge has been an explicit part of U.S. policy.[47] There has been some sensitivity within NATO to this dilemma, but policymakers have been unable to reach either a formula for reassuring Russians that a more prominent role for NATO in ECE does not threaten their security or an adequate set of political or economic trade-offs.

The United States argues that affiliation with NATO, along with the prospect of ultimate membership in the EU, offers an important inducement for maintaining democracy and a market orientation in the former Soviet bloc. It also encourages these governments to moderate their treatment of minorities and potential foreign adversaries. For example, Croatian president Franjo Tudjman agreed to permit a continued UN peacekeeping force in his country only after the Clinton administration acceded to his request to back Croatia's application to join NATO's Partnership for Peace (PfP) program described below.[48] Western Europe and the United States seek stability and democracy in the region, and believe that involvement in NATO promotes these objectives. ECE policymakers, though expressing impatience about the pace of their integration into NATO, appeared initially satisfied with the benefits PfP provides. But the pressures for membership have intensified in recent months after the Russian government decided to intervene militarily in Chechnya and more stridently express its opposition to NATO enlargement. Polish president Lech Walesa cautioned, "There is no partnership yet. There is Russia, which threatens, the west, which is frightened, and us, in the middle."[49]

The question of NATO expansion has dominated the European security debate since early 1994 when the Clinton administration came out in favor of enlargement. Proponents argue that, if pursued in a measured and transparent way so as not to alarm Russia and those nations not quickly offered membership, NATO expansion would reassure and reward the struggling east European democracies and guarantee NATO's continued relevance to pan-European security issues.[50]

Although proponents present thoughtful arguments, the case against NATO enlargement is very difficult to answer. Unfortunately, the more tightly ECE becomes bound to the West in economic relations, political systems, and security cooperation, the more Russians fear isolation and vulnerability. Likewise, the more Russian officials protest against ECE's incorporation into NATO, the more ECE leaders urgently insist on membership. As described below, Russian policymakers have made quite clear their continued opposition to NATO's granting ECE countries membership while leaving Russia outside the alliance, even though, after much vacillation, they agreed to join the Partnership for Peace in May 1995. The threat of a Russian nationalist backlash remains, and could jeopardize European security more thoroughly than enlargement preserves it. Drawing a line west of Russia might increase other ECE and FSU nations' insecurity, were Russia to try to expand its own sphere of influence westward. Ukrainian president Leonid Kuchma cautioned against a quick expansion of NATO because it would trigger a Russian counterreaction that would place border states like Ukraine in a precarious position.[51] Thus an effort designed to counter feared but latent Russian aggression could become a self-fulfilling prophecy if enlargement undermined Russia's moderate policies in ECE.

Furthermore, there are internal political obstacles within NATO. Members must consent unanimously to membership expansion. There must be national approvals. Unsuccessful ratification debate is a distinct possibility given the costs of the security guarantees associated with membership, and risks gravely damaging the alliance's popular support and embarrassing the member governments. As with the EU, increasing the number of members likely would require reexamining NATO's consensus decisionmaking procedures and the possible adoption of less-than-unanimous voting. Achieving true integration also would require western governments to provide extensive military training and transfer costly military equipment to new members at a time when NATO countries reluctantly fund their own forces.[52]

As Michael Brown argues, if Russia does in fact begin to threaten ECE nations, then NATO could accelerate the offer of membership, including the security umbrella.[53] In the meanwhile, NATO will have the chance to work toward meaningful interoperability, taking the financial commitment that a security guarantee implies in small bites. Moreover, there is the opportunity to work with Russia collaboratively in PfP so as to decrease its anxieties. As described below, NATO policymakers and military planners now work daily on joint tasks with former adversaries on a wide range of issues, and are beginning to understand many of the complexities and costs of full integration. The establishment of NACC and the PfP have measurably improved ECE countries' security environment. More time is needed before NATO member will accept the transformation from a collective defense organization into an instrument of collective security for all of Europe. A step-by-step approach that involves ECE nations and Russia to some extent in training for and executing manageable peace operations may be a useful way to test the waters.

FIRST STEPS. As soon as the political landscape in ECE and the Soviet Union began to change, the alliance made gestures to reassure its former adversaries. At the July 1990 London summit, the NATO heads of government extended a "hand of friendship" and invited all former Warsaw Treaty Organization (WTO) countries to establish "regular diplomatic liaison" with the NATO secretariat.[54] In subsequent months the governments of Bulgaria, Czechoslovakia, Hungary, Poland, and the USSR accredited their ambassadors to Belgium to NATO as well. They received regular briefings at alliance headquarters.

Ties deepened with the creation of a formal institution, the North Atlantic Cooperation Council at the November 1991 Rome summit. The NACC initially included representatives from all the NATO and former WTO countries except Albania, whose government had left the WTO in 1968. After the breakup of the Soviet Union at the end of 1991, the NACC invited all the former Soviet republics (an offer delayed for strife-torn Georgia) to become members. Albania joined in June 1992.

The NACC served as a useful first step toward the former communist bloc's integration into NATO. The participants include defense ministers, their military chiefs of staff, and mid-level officials. They formulate annual work plans dealing with a range of military, economic, political, environmental, and scientific subjects. Their activities encompass cooperation on defense planning, civil-military relations (especially instructing former WTO military establishments about western democratic values), civilian conversion of defense industries, air traffic control, environmental cooperation, and arms control.[55]

In 1993 the NACC established an Ad Hoc Group on Cooperation in Peacekeeping. The group provided a forum for NACC members to exchange ideas and experiences on the concept and practice of peacekeeping.[56] The participants, drawing on the experience of the UN and the individual nations involved in the process, reached agreement on broadly held principles of peace operations: transparency, impartiality, consent, and credibility.[57] The June NACC Report to the Ministers and the Draft Doctrine for Peace Support Operations may have gone quite far in socializing members and nonmembers toward the new mission.

The pressure of the Yugoslav conflict also encouraged examples of immediate military cooperation and rapprochement with ECE countries. Since December 1992 the Albanian government has granted alliance forces access to its airfields, ports, and territorial waters to assist in the enforcement of UN sanctions against Serbia and Montenegro.[58] And since October 1992 Hungarian authorities, with the support of the Austrian government, have allowed NATO AWACS to operate in their airspace to monitor the UN-designated no-fly zone over Bosnia-Herzegovina. Although the Hungarians have requested that these reconnaissance planes halt their mission during any NATO-coordinated use of force in the former Yugoslavia, they also have expressed a willingness to host any NATO-UN peacekeeping mission operating in neighboring Bosnia.[59]

The NACC was clearly a way station. It could not remain very satisfactory to either eastern Europe and the non-Russian republics of the FSU or to Russia. ECE countries wanted a rapid transition to full membership. The Russians wanted a withering away of the collective defense mission and a new military organization for collective security and stability—something like a military adjunct to the OSCE, where their voice was strong and their veto effective. Some of the non-Russian republics, particularly the Baltics and Ukraine, wanted protection. Disappointment was unavoidable.

THE PARTNERSHIP FOR PEACE. In a successful exercise in improvisation and innovation, U.S. officials developed the concept of the PfP just before the January 1994 NATO summit.[60] The ability of nations to find in it what they sought immediately made PfP a kind of Rorschach test. It seemed to offer individual pathways to the desired objectives of each group. Poland and the Czech Republic had been pressing for immediate and full NATO membership. Existing NATO members resisted, in large part because of the security guarantee that goes with membership. They understood that extending the guarantee to ECE nations, especially Poland, would set up an adversarial dynamic with Russia that might lead to its further internal destabilization and the weakening of its fragile democratization process. Absorbing the Czech Republic would involve little risk and cost, but pledging to defend Poland would entail both. The situation required a new approach, and the PfP appeared to provide it. The summit communiqué declared NATO's intention to expand, but remained studiously vague as to timing. Private conversations with high-level U.S. officials apparently reassured the countries most likely to be on a "fast track" to membership.[61]

Despite initial disappointment, ECE countries accepted this new arrangement because it allowed for differential ties with NATO based on a country's willingness and ability to participate in a wide range of activities, and because at least rhetorically it affirmed the alliance's commitment to eventual expansion. PfP is organized around a series of separate agreements between NATO and individual nonmember governments. Participation is open to any OSCE member. Each participant agrees to a standard Framework Document and an individual Partnership Program that specifies its military and political commitments and its level of anticipated collaboration with NATO. PfP governments must agree to ensure the democratic control of their armed forces, promote the transparency of their defense planning, respect the principles of international law, the UN Charter, and the OSCE, and be prepared to participate in peace operations, search and rescue, and humanitarian missions under their auspices.[62] The PfP has its own building, the Partnership Coordination Cell, located in Mons next to the Supreme Headquarters, Allied Powers Europe (SHAPE). PfP participants not belonging to NATO have permanent military representation there to complement their newly acquired permanent political liaison missions at NATO headquarters in Brussels.

Thus far, enthusiasm is matched by frustration in equal doses. The Partnership Coordination Cell is poorly staffed, and the PfP budget is small. Countries are expected to pay their own way, although some western governments provide limited financial assistance to favored partners. But PfP contains interesting features. In particular, the standard agreement commits NATO to engage in consultation with PfP members if they perceive "a direct threat to [their] territorial integrity, political independence, or security." The clause does not require NATO intervention and is not a guarantee, but it does set up a consultative mechanism for parties that may result in publicity and exposure for transgressors—and possibly more.[63] Members can and do express concerns in PfP meetings. For example, the Baltic states raised the question of the delay of the Russian troop withdrawal from their territory, and Moldovan representatives called attention to Russian military actions in their country.[64] The forum has an important preventive potential which has been overlooked in the preoccupation with the expansion debate. The consultation clause can offer early warning of low-level conflicts that might grow in intensity. More important, it can provide informal, mediative discussions at a stage before the stakes are high and when reputational pressures can be brought to bear. Some ECE countries also probably see the consultation process as a step toward a security guarantee.[65]

NATO policymakers recognize that cooperation on peacekeeping issues will be a "primary focus" of PfP.[66] Three military exercises were hastily assembled in late 1994. The first occurred in Poland in September, the second in the Netherlands, and a third, a naval exercise, in the Norwegian Sea, included Russian participants.[67] The exercises involved rudimentary tasks, but PfP planners anticipate a more ambitious program in future years.[68] Cooperation between Hungary and Romania under the PfP's auspices provides an especially noteworthy example of how the program might help overcome ethno-national tensions among ECE countries. The focus in PfP is on interoperability in the functional sense—learning how to operate together at the level of standardized procedures, especially with respect to command, control, and communications. The PfP process has not yet tackled the costly issue of equipment interoperability, which took NATO more than forty years to accomplish.[69]

Joint training, exercises, and the development of some integration in command, control, and intelligence may further enhance the value of NATO over ad hoc forces that the UN might assemble to address a crisis. The heightened involvement of east European and former Soviet officials in NATO activities also may help overcome concerns about the alliance's restricted membership and mandate. Finally, by sharing information about their military intentions and capabilities, European governments reassure one another that they will not exploit ethno-national conflicts to intervene militarily in their troubled neighbors.

But for PfP to have practical value in promoting interoperability and developing peacekeeping capability beyond that of an ad hoc force, the CJTF proposal for multinational operations announced at the January 1994 NATO summit must become a reality. The intention of the CJTF mechanism is to permit allied governments to deploy optimally designed ad hoc force packages from military units of different services and countries to deal with the specific requirements of a given military situation. They would allow WEU members acting outside the alliance or even a mixture of NATO and non-NATO members (such as PfP participants) to draw on NATO's military resources for missions such as peacekeeping.[70] PfP participants also need practice with sophisticated planning and exercises involving stressful scenarios. UN-assembled forces have encountered great difficulties coordinating complex operations such as Somalia with little advanced combined training. U.S. and other national forces exercising peace operations scenarios find the demands challenging and different from those that use more standard warfighting skills.[71] Moreover, it is only through joint planning and exercises that PfP will have the chance to become more than a paper organization or a holding room. Despite the current "24 + 1" approach and the differentiation of individual Partnership Programs, it is bureaucratically infeasible to work out military exercises tailored to individual states. They must be grouped. And the most likely locus for planning is SHAPE. Unfortunately, differences between France and other allies over what role Washington should have in military operations involving NATO (including U.S.) assets but not U.S. troops has slowed the CJTF's development.[72]

The unprepared experience in Bosnia, the first tentative steps in NACC planning, and the rudimentary PfP exercises have given NATO some impetus for the development of real capability in peace operations. The inclusion of eastern European and former Soviet representatives in planning for peace operations, and their absorption of NATO military culture, can bring benefits when these forces deploy in the field. Among the most important benefits are the training and experience gained from working together. Very different military histories and cultures need to be reconciled. And many steps are required before planning translates into capability. If the headlong rush to membership does not collapse the process, the NACC and the PfP, designed as interim measures to sidestep the issue of broader membership, could become the major channel for enhancing NATO's capability in peace operations. Europe would suffer a great loss if the capability, once honed, is unusable because of unresolved national tensions.

THE RUSSIAN RELATIONSHIP. The largest conceptual problem of any new security relationship is reconciling Russian interests with those of ECE countries. Overcoming fifty years of confrontation is difficult enough. That difficulty is now compounded by the idea of imminent NATO expansion. Russian foreign minister Andrei Kozyrev told an OSCE meeting in March 1995: "Whatever one may think of NATO, it's still a military alliance that was created when Europe was divided. It should be replaced by a new model based on comprehensive security."[73] The Russian ambassador to Poland lamented what he called a "feeling of NATO-mania in Eastern Europe."[74] After the January 1994 NATO summit, Russian representatives postponed signing the PfP agreement for several months, insisting in one forum after another on special status. At a June 1994 NACC meeting in Istanbul, Russian representatives forced the deletion of a reference in the communiqué linking PfP to NATO's future expansion.[75] In recent months Defense Minister Pavel Grachev warned that expansion would cause Russia to discard the restrictions imposed by the 1990 Conventional Forces in Europe (CFE) treaty and could lead to other "countermeasures." Other policymakers and analysts have indicated that NATO enlargement could lead Moscow to fail to ratify the SALT II treaty, to slow down nuclear cooperation with the West, and to seek to reestablish a military sphere of influence in ECE and the FSU.[76] Fear that NATO expansion would hurt them domestically preoccupies Russian policymakers.[77] Wary of Russian nationalists, Russia's leaders have sought to distance themselves from the perceived "hyperwesternism" that characterized the Gorbachev and early Yeltsin years.

At the same time, ECE nations fear that any special status for Russia could lead to a great power condominium at their expense. Although NATO formally rejected broad special treatment for Russia in the PfP or special Russian access to alliance deliberations, it did promise more substantial early political consultations under the rubric of "no vetoes, no surprises."[78] When Russia first agreed to enter the PfP in late June 1994, the resulting accord provided for extensive military cooperation and the establishment of NATO missions in Russia and Russian missions at the alliance's political and military headquarters. It also created a telephone hotline between NATO's Supreme Allied Command and the Russian General Staff.[79] Russian forces agreed to participate in the third of the PfP exercises. Yet in early December, Kozyrev surprised the assembled NATO dignitaries in Brussels by further postponing Russia's formal adherence to the PfP. Immediately before the scheduled ceremony, NATO had adopted a timetable to develop membership guidelines for PfP participants.

NATO policymakers have groped for a solution that would satisfy both sides. ECE countries are pushing for an accelerated timetable for membership, which has concerned Russian officials as they face new elections against increasingly strident nationalists. Stability in the former Soviet Union remains a paramount alliance concern. Aiding Russia's transition to a stable market democracy has been a linchpin of allied policy to ensure that a Soviet-type threat never again arises. In addition, a key element of U.S. policy in particular has been to reduce the threat of proliferation of weapons of mass destruction from Russia and other former Soviet republics. The orderly drawdown of the former Soviet nuclear arsenal also has been of crucial concern to the entire NATO alliance. Russian leaders signaled early in 1994 that if NATO expanded, their willingness to cooperate with the West on these issues might decline precipitously. START II, already in trouble, would face an additional obstacle. The United States does not want to act to undermine the positive developments that are under way, yet many analysts think NATO enlargement will do exactly that. Russian concerns came to a head at the December 1994 OSCE summit in Budapest, when President Yeltsin accused President Clinton of sowing mistrust and risking a "cold peace" just days after Russia suspended involvement in the PfP. At their May 1995 summit, Yeltsin reportedly spent the first forty minutes of his discussion with Clinton arguing against NATO expansion.[80]

Fundamental policy differences between Russia and alliance members have emerged over Bosnia, and this has soured the relationship with the West as well. Historic Russian sympathies toward the Serbs clash with allied perceptions of Serb aggression. Throughout 1993 and 1994 Russian representatives complained about a lack of consultation on western enforcement actions against the Serbs. In particular, they expressed resentment at NATO's unexpected air strikes around Gorazde, with Yeltsin himself indicating that in response Russia might curtail military cooperation with NATO members.[81] And during the Bihac crisis of November 1994, Kozyrev argued against additional NATO air strikes by maintaining that the Bosnian government had provoked the situation to ensure foreign military intervention on its behalf.[82] These differences over peace operations have continued. Russian analysts fear "the emphasis of the West on NATO as a main instrument in the crisis management in the former Yugoslavia . . . [will be] interpreted in Russia as a shift towards unilateralism which might revive the past East-West confrontation."[83]

Russian policymakers admittedly have not opposed all enforcement. Russian diplomats, frustrated by their inability to curb Bosnian Serb attacks on Gorazde, expressed support for NATO's ultimatum there with its threat of air strikes.[84] Moscow's diplomatic interventions and willingness to deploy Russian peacekeepers under UN auspices have allowed the Serbs a face-saving way to accept UN-NATO ultimatums.[85] Nor has Russia exercised its Security Council veto on Bosnian matters, and it remains an active participant in the UN Contact Group seeking an acceptable peace plan for Bosnia. And although Moscow might have voiced strong objections, its criticisms of the large scale airstrikes of August 1995 were muted. Yet the disagreements over Bosnia have negatively affected Russian views of NATO's other policies.[86]

The violent conflicts raging in the FSU drain Russia's economy and hinder its transition to a stable democracy. They have been a constant worry to the Yeltsin government and a distraction from democratization and denuclearization. Russia's possible disintegration is nearly as threatening to European security as a hostile Soviet Union was during the cold war. Russia needs the breathing space and support that effective international conflict-prevention and conflict-mitigation efforts would offer. Ideally, NATO could be a partner in the conflict-reduction process. But the tensions created by the alliance strategy of NATO expansion to the Visegrad nations, and the differences over Bosnia have made that unlikely for a while. No simple formula exists to ease Russian concerns about an expanded NATO, although perhaps Russian entry into the PfP opens some new possibilities and some joint participation in Bosnian post-conflict peacekeeping, an even greater opportuniuty. Until then, Yeltsin appeared unmoved by various allied proposals for an enhanced security dialogue, partial NATO membership, or a nonaggression pact. Russian assurances that there will be no deployment of nuclear weapons in former WTO states also has had little effect.[87] Enormous obstacles will continue to burden efforts to reconcile Russian policymakers to an evolving collective security role for NATO. Nor are the obstacles to the alliance's evolution limited to the East. Both the experience in Bosnia and the attempt at NATO's reconceptualization have opened old wounds within the alliance itself.

The French Perspective

Since withdrawing from the integrated military command in 1966, the French have presented a special set of issues for NATO. Tensions erupted anew after 1989 when other members advocated the alliance's assuming new missions such as peace operations. Whereas the British and U.S. governments, and to a lesser extent the Germans, wanted the alliance to remain Europe's preeminent defense institution, French policymakers desired to limit NATO's role in post–cold war Europe as a way of curtailing U.S. influence. Accordingly, they wanted the EU to assume the broader European security function, with the WEU as its security arm. They also favored a strengthened OSCE involved in peace operations.

The French government initially advocated a strict separation between the activities of NATO and those of the OSCE. After a Dutch proposal to allow the OSCE to request help from NATO for its peacekeeping operations gained widespread support among the other allies, French representatives approved the plan but still insisted on certain conditions for its implementation. In particular, they demanded that, as in the Gulf War, individual alliance members rather than NATO as an institution provide the assistance in a manner worked out at the time among the participating states. Besides emphasizing that the WEU too could become involved in the resulting operations and denying that NATO had acquired a new mission, Minister of Defense Roland Dumas called on the alliance to manage its peacekeeping missions on an ad hoc basis under the NAC's guidance rather than within its standard integrated military structure. He also insisted that, "The CSCE must be in a position to retain control over, and real responsibility for, the operations decided by it."[88]

The French government's approach toward peacekeeping operations in the former Yugoslavia demonstrated its institutional preferences. French policymakers strongly supported the EC's early conflict-prevention efforts. They subsequently sought to deploy an EC or WEU peacekeeping force to the region. They also indicated they would provide troops only for a WEU-commanded military operation, not one led by NATO. They insisted on a WEU component for the UN-sanctioned naval embargo against Serbia and Montenegro, and declined to assign any of their ships to NATO's parallel operation. After the UN and NATO became more involved in the Yugoslav crisis, French representatives initially insisted they would partic- ipate in the alliance's enforcement of the no-fly zone over Bosnia and contribute troops to a planned NATO peacekeeping force only if the UN clearly ran these campaigns. They also unsuccessfully urged that an ad hoc planning unit and not the alliance's regular chain of command should direct these missions.[89]

By 1993, French policymakers had grudgingly accepted that the surpris- ingly virulent conflict in the former Yugoslavia and the unexpected difficul- ties plaguing the European integration process left NATO as the best available institutional instrument for managing ethno-national conflict in eastern Europe.[90] UNPROFOR, for which France provided the largest contingent of ground troops, had proved unable to halt the fighting or guarantee humanitarian assistance to besieged towns. Like the other allies, they tacitly stopped referring to potential prohibitions against NATO oper- ations "out-of-area."[91] More significantly, they began to urge increased alliance military operations in the former Yugoslavia. By working through NATO, French policymakers may have expected to gain greater U.S. partic- ipation in international peacekeeping efforts in Bosnia.

But French officials have remained unready to accept the integrated command structure as the vehicle for peace operations. While denying that they seek a parallel command structure for "non-Article V" actions, they prefer ad hoc arrangements rather than the integrated command for NATO peace operations, even though they recognize that certain operations require a strong U.S. military contribution. French representatives continue to complain that NATO has not sufficiently changed to reflect Europe's transformed security situation following the cold war. They speak of the flexibility required for new missions, and the strong political component of peace operations that needs to be addressed differently from NATO's traditional military planning process.[92]

Although France participated for the first time since 1966 in an informal Defense Ministers' meeting in September 1994, the tensions over the integrated command structure will likely slow NATO's preparation for and involvement in peace operations. French concerns already have delayed the development and exercise of CJTFs with ECE countries. Admiral Jacques Lanxade, chief of defense staff, warned that his government "might well not participate in CJTFs if they are based on a virtually unreconstructed IMS [Integrated Military Structure]. Ad hoc arrangements would then be made with the French armed forces for particular operations."[93] French pressures for a greater UN role in UNPROFOR's possible evacuation from Bosnia and Croatia delayed final approval of NATO's withdrawal plan.[94] At the same time, French policymakers desire to strengthen the WEU and the EU's Common Foreign and Security Policy by drawing on NATO assets. Therefore, they hesitate to block all progress.

The Costs of Transition

NATO will not and should not relinquish its traditional missions and become an institution primarily designed for peace operations. The alliance therefore will require additional funds to carry out any nontraditional missions it assumes or to pay for upgrading PfP participants' armed forces to make them functionally interoperable. It is hard to believe that NATO members will agree to assume all the costs of near-term integration of the Visegrad countries—a far greater cost.

It is doubtful that the costs of transition to a collective security organization have begun to be estimated with any precision. The costs of NATO's present involvement in Bosnia have already been a matter of concern.[95] Moreover, there is worry that NATO's increased involvement in peace operations will decrease the alliance's military readiness for its collective defense mission by draining already reduced funds and manpower. (Many analysts make the same argument about the U.S. armed forces.) Admittedly, the major peacekeeping interposition force in Bosnia would prove expensive and leave significant gaps in NATO's force structure given its ongoing manpower and budget reductions. Nevertheless, the absence of a near-term military threat to NATO means that it can safely divert forces to a post-conflict Bosnia.

Making the required attitudinal adjustments may prove even harder than these operational changes. The process of state disintegration raises a set of issues that NATO has not dealt with conceptually or operationally. The alliance developed to combat military aggression against member states with a side glance at restraining Germany's military resurgence. The founding governments did not envision NATO as a mechanism to deal with internal conflict within its membership. As an organization, the alliance remained largely aloof from the struggle in Northern Ireland, the Kurdish issue in Turkey, or the Basque dispute. When the member governments of Greece and Turkey approached direct military conflict in 1974, it was the UN that assumed the peacekeeping mission in the contested island of Cyprus, even though NATO previously offered its own assistance.[96]

Harmonizing Relations with the UN and Other Institutions

Given the sources of legitimacy for NATO out-of-area operations, institutional cooperation and coordination is a precondition to alliance participation in peace operations in ECE and the FSU. Paramount are relations with the UN. The experience in the former Yugoslavia has made it clear that failure to clarify roles and relationships can lead not only to frustration and ineffectiveness, but also to exploitation by the parties to the conflict.[97] The basic legal fact, poorly understood by the public, is that unless alliance members can claim a legitimate case of article 51 self-defense under the UN Charter, they can legally take enforcement action only with the Security Council's authorization. NATO operations in the FSU and ECE would require such approval unless justified by the hard-to-prove threat of spillover.

Before 1992, NATO and the UN had little institutional contact.[98] The seminal UN publication *Agenda for Peace* made no reference to the alliance in its discussion of how regional organizations could assist UN activities in the area of conflict prevention. NATO's decision in December 1992 to offer the UN military assistance with European peace operations, case by case and in accordance with alliance procedures, created the basis for a relationship. NATO subsequently posted a liaison officer from the International Military Staff to New York.[99] In the former Yugoslavia, the alliance has diligently and effectively implemented its UN-assigned tasks—clearly demonstrating that NATO can work under another institution's mandate. NATO officials also repeatedly provided their UN counterparts with detailed contingency plans for the protection of UN-designated safe areas in Bosnia and for the implementation of any UN-approved peace plan.[100]

But tensions have been evident for a variety of reasons. From the beginning the institutions' conceptions of the appropriate use and levels of force differed. After stepping down as commander of UN forces in the former Yugoslavia, French lieutenant general Bertrand de Lapresle observed: "The two organizations have completely different natures. I was a general with no enemy to fight, and no victory to win. But NATO is structured to engage a very clearly defined enemy, and to identify a victory to win."[101] Akashi explained that the UN always interpreted its mission in largely humanitarian terms and not as a party to the conflict: "We are in a war, but not at war."[102] In defending his opposition to an aggressive NATO operation to deter Serb assaults against Bihac, Akashi explained the overarching dilemma of the UN peacekeeping operation in the former Yugoslavia: "If we do not act, UNPROFOR will be considered incompetent and spineless. If we act too vigorously and aggressively, we may create a situation in which there is escalation leading to most tragic consequences. We tried to tread this narrow path."[103]

On the other hand, NATO commanders lament the disunity of command and their lack of influence over developments on the ground. A former NATO commander characterized the UN leadership as having a "Chapter VII mandate, but a Chapter VI mentality."[104] Planning officer Michael Ruehle complained that in the Yugoslav conflict, "NATO was relegated to a supporting role only, publicly perceived as a sub-contractor with little influence on the policy pursued." Ruehle acknowledged that NATO staff found it difficult to operate when the alliance had "to perform military action but . . . have the scope of action determined by a third party whose expertise and judgment were debatable."[105] Reflecting on the lessons of Yugoslavia, Secretary-General Willy Claes concluded, "It is of primary importance . . . that NATO maintain its autonomy as a sovereign organization: we support the UN, but we are not its sub-contractor. In the final analysis, we must preserve the Alliance's credibility. It is our most valuable asset, and it remains essential to the preservation of peace in the wider Europe."[106]

The leading UN and NATO members' divergent perceptions and preferences have complicated relations between the two organizations (as well as troubled transatlantic ties within NATO itself). A U.S. policymaker correctly observed, "The issue is not a UN-NATO issue, it is that NATO countries disagree among themselves."[107] The French and British provide the largest number of lightly armed peacekeeping troops, and have repeatedly expressed concerns about their safety. Furthermore, while U.S. policymakers have depicted the Serbs as aggressors, Russian and UN officials have suggested Bosnian government forces deliberately provoke the Serbs in order to trigger NATO air strikes.[108] Indeed, UN staff members intimated in early 1995 that NATO (that is, the United States) has covertly permitted weapons deliveries to the Bosnian government.[109] In contrast, U.S. officials worried that the repeated UN refusals to authorize air strikes in the face of Serb defiance undermined NATO's credibility.[110]

The tensions partly arise from the ambiguity and messiness of the peace effort in the former Yugoslavia. It has simultaneously involved sanctions, negotiations, large-scale humanitarian efforts, and enforcement. Reconciling or even separating these strands may be an impossibility. Disagreements among the five permanent Security Council members and the inconsistency and vagueness of many of the Council's resolutions have compounded matters. Not only is the NATO-UN relationship being built in the killing fields, but as pointed out above, the very concept of appropriate peace operations is being developed on the basis of trial and error. Had there been more time to develop the doctrinal underpinnings of NATO's new involvement in peace operations, some of the tension might have been anticipated and avoided. The former Yugoslavia provided unpleasant and dangerous on-the-job-training, but it underscores the need for intensive training and concept development now.

Institutional cooperation might improve over time as the allies focus on the nature of peace operations in a more deliberate manner than participation in the former Yugoslavia has thus far allowed. There remain large differences between close allies—the Americans and British, for example—in attitudes toward appropriate peacekeeping behavior.[111] Alliance leaders also better recognize that "we must achieve a more structured relationship with the United Nations in order to generate the conditions which are essential for future crisis management—namely, a clear-cut mandate, a better coordination between humanitarian and peacekeeping/peacemaking missions, and a unitary chain of command."[112] All allied governments accept that the UN Security Council legitimized NATO's intervention, and indeed provided its legal basis, as no other institution could have. The recent U.S. decision to commit sufficient forces to rescue UNPROFOR may permit the mission to continue with less friction. At the same time, planning for a forced evacuation will provide U.S. policymakers with a better appreciation of the concerns of those nations whose citizens serve as vulnerable ground troops.[113]

Relations between NATO and OSCE have been more distant and less engaged. So long as OSCE focuses on the diplomatic side of conflict prevention, NATO's role can be supportive, providing logistics, communications, and some minimum protection. The alliance can still make forces available to OSCE under its 1992 decision, and the possibilities for preventive deployments subordinate to preventive diplomacy remain an unused potential. A key question is how long before the rhetoric of commitment to the principle of "interlocking institutions" evolves into a satisfactory division of labor. Western policymakers acknowledge that no single institution possesses sufficient resources and mandate to manage all European crises, but the concrete requirement of NATO cooperation with the UN, and perhaps the OSCE and WEU, needs to become a comfortable reality.

Conclusion

NATO's difficulties in Bosnia do not portend a deep rift in the alliance. As long as uncertainty persists about the future European security environment, the allies will manage their differences and continue to work together. Potential alternatives such as the OSCE and the WEU may enlarge the available options, but they will not replace NATO so long as its members perceive a need for a powerful transatlantic military force. They lack the financial resources to duplicate NATO's military capabilities and the necessary political backing.

Alliance policymakers have evidently concluded that if attempting to prevent a Serbian victory in the Bosnian conflict would risk destroying NATO, then alliance solidarity must receive priority. U.S. secretary of state Warren Christopher commented: "The Bosnian crisis is about Bosnia, but the NATO alliance is far more enduring, far more important than the Bosnian crisis."[114] Claes similarly observed, "Maybe I'm a little bit brutal in saying this, but NATO, ladies and gentlemen, is more than Bosnia."[115] Even those most dissatisfied with the Bosnian experience stress the need to retain a robust alliance. After visiting Brussels to meet with important NATO and PfP policymakers, U.S. senator Robert Dole said, "There is a preoccupation with Bosnia, but the message I will take back to Congress and the people of the United States is that the investment we've made in NATO has paid off for America."[116]

Yet NATO's painful experience in the former Yugoslavia during the hostilities may discourage future alliance peace operations, particularly those linked to a parallel UN humanitarian or traditional peacekeeping operation. After the Bihac fiasco, Claes observed: "It is very difficult, maybe impossible, to reconcile a peace mission on the ground with a kind of peace enforcement from the air. We've learned several lessons, and before accepting a new peace mission, we will look very carefully at the rules."[117] In early 1995 alliance members quickly dismissed a Croatian request that NATO supplant the UN and deploy its own troops along Croatia's border with Serbia.[118]

For now, apart from the former Yugoslavia, potential conflicts in ECE do not appear sufficiently grave to warrant a militarily intensive solution. By contrast, the FSU suffers from many conflicts where both traditional and innovative peace operations may involve military forces. But without significant efforts by NATO to win Russian confidence, the appropriate authorities in the FSU are unlikely to seek alliance involvement. Even if the governments of Russia or of the other former Soviet republics really wanted NATO to intervene militarily in the FSU, it is questionable whether alliance members would accept the burdens and risks such operations likely would entail. These uncertainties militate against a significant financial diversion by NATO into preparing or procuring for expanded peace operations. Doctrinal development, realistic training, and institutional innovations such as the CJTP warrant the highest priority.

In the end, NATO's potential for peace operations is not a military but an intensely political question. It will depend on NATO's ability to develop effective working relations with both the UN and Russia. This in turn will require fundamental change in NATO's traditional attitudes toward both. Adequate preparation and joint planning after Bosnia may help forge a workable NATO-UN relationship. But it will not be easy, perhaps impossible, to develop a comfortable relationship with both Russia and ECE nations who are pressing for membership within the context of NATO alone.

The frame of reference must widen. All the governments involved in NATO seek security, stability, and prosperity. Most recognize that economic growth promotes security, and that the EU can best promote democratization and economic development in ECE and the FSU. The power of an economic strategy for preventing conflict appears throughout this volume.

It has special relevance to the NATO dilemma. To avoid placing the principal burden on the alliance and the security dimension, policymakers should exploit the synergistic impact of the whole panoply of powerful western institutions, including the international financial institutions, to prevent ethno-national conflict in ECE and the former FSU.

Notes

1. For more on these incidents, see Elizabeth Neuffer, "NATO Planes Strike Bosnian Serb Position," *Boston Globe,* August 6, 1994, p. 1.

2. John Pomfret, "Serb Response to NATO Raid: More Attacks," *Washington Post,* November 23, 1994, p. 15.

3. U.S. Ambassador to the UN Madeline Albright said the Clinton administration was "baffled" by the decision, which resembled earlier disputes between the UN and NATO, and within the alliance itself, over the appropriate use of force in the Yugoslav mission. Barbara Crossette, "UN Overrules New Calls for Air Strikes against Serbs," *New York Times,* May 9, 1995, p. 8.

4. Steven Greenhouse, "U.S. and NATO Demand Quick Release of the Hostages," *New York Times,* May 31, 1995, p.8.

5. The name changed in December 1994 from "Conference" to "Organization."

6. In 1985 Norway, Denmark, West Germany, Luxembourg, Belgium, France, Britain, the United States and the Netherlands had 877,000 ground forces deployed in Europe with 1,738,000 ground force reserves. The International Institute for Strategic Studies, *The Military Balance, 1985–1986* (London, 1985), p. 186.

7. Robin Knight, "From the Ashes of War," *US News & World Report,* May 8, 1995, p. 49.

8. For a description of NATO's new command structure, see David Miller, "New Look for European Command," *International Defense Review* (May 1994), pp. 30–32; and Daniel R. Schroeder, "Forward Presence and Crisis Response: The Role of America's Army," in Robert L. Pfaltzgraff, Jr., and Richard H. Shultz, Jr., eds., *Ethnic Conflict and Regional Instability: Implications for US Policy and Army Roles and Missions* (Carlisle, Pa.: US Army War College, 1994), p. 270.

9. Chayes and Chayes, "Alternatives to Escalation," in *The United States and the Use of Force in the Post Cold War Era* (Queenstown, Md.: Aspen Institute, 1995), pp. 191–220, develops this point.

10. See John L. Hirsch and Robert B. Oakley, "Challenge and Confrontation," in *Somalia and Operation Restore Hope* (Washington: United States Institute of Peace Press), pp. 115–48.

11. For a discussion of the composition and mission of this Macedonian requested deployment, which since January 1993 has involved about 1,200 military observers, infantry battalions, and civilian police from Canada, the United States, and various Nordic countries, see Julie Kim and Carol Migdalovitz, *Macedonia: Former Yugoslav Republic of Macedonia Situation Update* (Washington: Congressional Research Service, February 18, 1994), pp. 9–10.

12. See *Report of the Secretary-General to the Security Council on the United Nations Operation in Cyprus,* September 10, 1964, 19 UN SCOR, July–Sept 1964

at 280, UN Doc. S 5950 (1964). The Force was already authorized to interpose "where specific arrangements accepted by both communities have been, or in the opinion of the commander on the spot are about to be, violated, thus risking a recurrence of the fighting or endangering law and order."

13. For a discussion of how these advantages will aid NATO peace operations, see Bernd A. Goetze, "Peacekeeping and Crisis Management from an Alliance Perspective," in Pfaltzgraff and Schultz, eds., *Ethnic Conflict and Regional Instability*, p. 197; and Joseph Kruzel, "Peacekeeping and the Partnership for Peace," in Dennis J. Quinn, ed., *Peace Support Operations and the US Military,* (Washington: National Defense University Press, 1994), pp. 96–97.

14. For comparison see the evolution of U.S. Army Peacekeeping Doctrine over its successive drafts of FM 100–23 during 1994, until it became final in 1995. See also Joint Chiefs of Staff publication, "Joint Tactics, Techniques, and Procedures for Peacekeeping Operation," Joint pub. 3–07.3 (Washington: April 29, 1994). Given the expectation of continuing peace operations, the U.S. Army has accelerated efforts to develop an encompassing doctrine. Interviews with senior U.S. Army military officers in November and December 1994.

15. Charles Dobbie, "A Concept for Post Cold War Peacekeeping," *Survival,* vol. 36 (Autumn 1994), pp. 121–49. Dobbie is the author of the British manual.

16. See "NATO and Peacekeeping: The Doctrine for NATO Military Involvement in or Support of Peacekeeping, Conflict Prevention, and Humanitarian Missions" (Brussels: NATO Headquarters, May 31, 1993).

17. See *The Army Field Manual Volume 5,* HMSO, 1995.

18. For a discussion of the difficulties involved in NATO out-of-area military operations, see Sir Richard Vincent, "The Brussels Summit—A Military Perspective," *NATO Review,* vol. 42 (February 1994), p. 8.

19. "Die Deutschen wollen keine Verbände aus der Nato lösen," *Die Welt,* November 2, 1991, p. 4. For more on NATO's early attitudes toward the Yugoslav conflict, see the speech of James P. McCarthy, Deputy Commander in Chief, U.S. European Command, reprinted in *Vital Speeches of the Day* (November 15, 1992), p. 67.

20. Manfred Wörner, "NATO's Role in a Changing Europe," in *European Security after the Cold War: Part I,* Adelphi paper no. 284 (Brassey's and the International Institute for Strategic Studies, January 1994), p. 99.

21. NATO Press Service, lecture at Chatham House, London, cited in Grzegorz Kostrzewa-Zorbas, "NATO Regional Peacekeeping Center in Central and Eastern Europe: A Proposal," *European Security,* vol. 2 (Winter 1993), p. 595.

22. David Rohde, "US Commander Speaks on New Role for NATO on its Southern Flank," *Christian Science Monitor,* March 14, 1995, p. 7. See pp. 443–45 in Huntington chapter which outlines some of the early coordination problems

23. U.S. Naval Institute, "Periscope" database, October 21, 1994. In November the Pentagon stated that the patrols had found only three ships to be delivering arms to Bosnia (Bradley Graham and William Drozdiak, "Bosnia Hails Arms Ban Shift by US," *Washington Post,* November 12, 1994, p. 1).

24. Rolf Hallerbach, "Jeliu Schelews NATO-Visite: Sofias Plan zum Trialog mit Athen und Ankara," *Europäische Sicherheit* (January 1992), p. 7.

25. Alfred A. Reisch, "Central Europe's Disappointments and Hopes," *RFE/RL Research Report,* vol. 3 (March 25, 1994), p. 20.

26. See, for example, Joel Brand, "NATO Planes Quell Clashes in Sarajevo," *Washington Post,* November 8, 1994, p. 13; John F. Burns, "NATO Planes Fly Sarajevo Sortie," *New York Times,* October 18, 1993, p. 5; Michael R. Gordon, "G.I.'s to Relieve Scandinavians for Bosnian Duty," *New York Times,* March 11, 1994, p. 7; and John Kifner, "Serbs Apparently Use Sarajevo Arms on Two Cities," *New York Times,* March 1, 1994, p. 12.

27. R. W. Apple, Jr., "Playing Down Getting Tough," *New York Times,* March 1, 1994, p. 13.

28. Reuters, August 3, 1994 (Mead Data Service, NEXIS). Observers differ in their estimates of how many heavy weapons the Serbs retained for their use.

29. For a review of this incident, see John Pomfret, "Bosnian Drive Riled Serbs, Who Then Provoked NATO," *Washington Post,* August 9, 1994, p. 14.

30. Cited in Craig R. Whitney, "NATO Warns Serbs to Cease Attacks or Face Bombings," *New York Times,* April 23, 1994, p. 1.

31. NATO's military threats also appeared to have deterred Croat attacks in Bosnia. Croat leaders apparently feared that NATO would threaten them if their forces, like those of the Serbs, continued to assault those Bosnian government towns such as Mostar they besieged (William E. Schmidt, "Truce in Bosnia's Other War Quiets Guns in Another City," *New York Times,* February 25, 1994, p. 8).

32. "Supreme Allied Commander Sketches Challenges of 'New NATO,'" *Defense Week* (February 6, 1995), pp. 10, 11.

33. "The Jane's Interview," *Jane's Defence Weekly* (January 28, 1995), p. 32. Smith explained "it has not been easy to work under this dual key and two separate chains of command. I would not make that mistake again." Richard Holbrooke, assistant secretary of state for European and Canadian Affairs, described the "horrendous dual-key arrangement" as "a dual veto in practice [that] inhibits us severely" (cited in Ben Barber, "NATO Bombing 'Viable' in Bosnia," *Washington Times,* May 2, 1995, p. 1).

34. Michael R. Gordon, "Serbian Gunners Slip away as US Planes Await UN Approval," *New York Times,* March 14, 1994, p. 8.

35. David Rohde, "US Commander Speaks on New Role for NATO on Its Southern Flank," *Christian Science Monitor,* March 14, 1995, p. 7.

36. *The Economist* lamented: "Never before had a NATO member declared it would cease to carry out an agreed NATO policy" ("It Can't Be Done Alone" [February 25, 1995], p. 19).

37. French foreign minister Alain Juppé complained about "governments that want to give us lessons when they have not lifted a little finger to put even one man on the ground. Alan Riding, "French Successfully Bluff Their Allies on Bosnia," *New York Times,* December 13, 1994, p. 8. See also William Drozdiak, "Airstrike Fails to Mend Split between US and Europeans," *Washington Post,* November 23, 1994, p. 16.

38. Cited in Roger Cohen, "Fighting Rages as NATO Debates How to Protect Bosnian Enclave," *New York Times,* November 25, 1994, p. 16. For more on how the Bihac crisis aggravated relations between the United States and other NATO allies, see William Drozdiak, "Airstrike Fails to Mend Split between US and Europeans," *Washington Post,* November 23, 1994, p. 16.

39. Steven Greenhouse, "Allies Resolve to Bolster UN Peacekeeping in Bosnia; U.S. Weighs a Ground Role," *New York Times,* May 30, 1995. p. A1.

40. For a description of the procedure how the CSCE or the UN would authorize a NATO peacekeeping operation, see "NATO and Peacekeeping: The Doctrine for NATO Military Involvement in or Support of Peacekeeping, Conflict Prevention, and Humanitarian Missions" (Brussels: NATO Headquarters, May 31, 1993), p. 6.

41. For a clear and official statement of Russia's preference for the NACC and the OSCE, see Andrei V. Kozyrev, "Russia and NATO: A Partnership for a United and Peaceful Europe," *NATO Review,* vol. 42 (August 1994), p. 4. See also Yeltsin's statements cited in R. W. Apple, Jr., "The Growth of NATO: Will Moscow Go Along?," *New York Times,* May 11, 1995, p. 10.

42. Richard Holbrooke aptly states the US position: "The OSCE can in no way be superior to NATO; the functions of the two organizations are and shall remain entirely different" ("America, A European Power," *Foreign Affairs,* vol. 74 [March–April 1995], pp. 48–49).

43. William Drozdiak, "NATO Seeks Talks with N. Africa, Mideast States on Islamic Militants," *Washington Post,* February 9, 1995, p. 26; and Martin Sieff, "NATO Looks South to Secure Partners, Block New Threats," *Washington Times,* March 9, 1995, p. 15.

44. Analysts nevertheless agree that past involvement with NATO enhanced allied operations in the Gulf conflict; see, for example, Richard L. Kugler, *Commitment to Purpose: How Alliance Partnership Won the Cold War* (Santa Monica, California: The RAND Corporation, 1993), pp. 500–501.

45. Interviews with NATO policymakers in Brussels, September 1994. In May 1994, NATO's Defence Planning Committee and Nuclear Planning Group "reaffirmed the essential role of nuclear forces, including sub-strategic forces widely deployed in Europe at the minimum level necessary to preserve peace and stability" (communiqué reprinted in *NATO Review,* vol. 42 [June 1994], p. 33).

46. Celeste Wallander, "Assessing Security Missions after the Cold War: Strategies, Institutions and the Limits of a Generalized Approach," paper presented at the conference "The Role of International Organizations," of the Carnegie Project on Conflict Prevention in Eastern Europe and the Former Soviet Union, at the Brookings Institution, Washington, D.C. September 26–28, 1994. According to Wallander, the "features that afford NATO its effective collective defense capabilities severely limit its capacity for fulfilling other security tasks." She relies less on NATO's history or its limited membership than the inherent characteristics of the missions, arguing that collective defense is incompatible with neutral peace operations.

47. In February 1994 U.S. secretary of defense William Perry said the West could use PfP to protect ECE if things go wrong in Moscow (Thomas W. Lippman, "NATO Peace Partnership's New Look: A Protective Shield against Moscow," *Washington Post,* February 8, 1994, p. 11).

48. Steven Greenhouse, "Clinton Meets with Bosnian and Croatian Chiefs," *New York Times,* March 17, 1995, p. 9.

49. Cited in Steven Erlanger, "East Europe Watches the Bear, Warily, " *New York Times,* October 21, 1994, p. 10.

50. See, for example, Ronald D. Asmus, Richard L. Kugler, and F. Stephen Larrabee, "NATO Expansion: The Next Steps," *Survival,* vol. 37, (Spring 1995), pp. 7–33; Zbigniew Brzezinski, "A Plan for Europe," *Foreign Affairs,* vol. 74 (January–February 1995), pp. 26–42; Holbrooke, "America, A European Power,"

pp. 42, 44–48; and Joseph S. Nye, Jr., "NATO's Vital New Role," *Boston Globe,* March 16, 1995, p. 13. NATO's Senior Political Committee has identified a range of principles to guide NATO enlargement; for a summary, see Marc Rogers, "Principles Emerge for Enlarging Membership," *Jane's Defence Weekly* (March 4, 1995), p. 4.

51. R. Jeffrey Smith, "Danger Is Seen in Rapid NATO Expansion," *Washington Post,* November 23, 1994, p. 16. The need to draw a line somewhere became obvious when U.S. secretary of defense William Perry told Congress in early February 1995 that many PfP participants "will never qualify for NATO membership" (cited in Dana Priest, "Not All Partners Will Join NATO, Perry Concedes," *Washington Post,* February 9, 1995, p. 26); on this matter, see also Warren Christopher and William J. Perry, "Foreign Policy, Hamstrung," *New York Times,* February 13, 1995, p. 19.

52. Cogent arguments against NATO enlargement appear in Michael E. Brown, "The Flawed Logic of NATO Expansion," *Survival,* vol. 37 (Spring 1995), pp. 34–52; Paul Cook, "Extending Borders for a New NATO," *Insight* (March 13, 1995), pp. 6–8; Michael Mandelbaum, "Preserving the New Peace: The Case against NATO Expansion," *Foreign Affairs,* vol. 74 (May–June 1995), pp. 9–13; and John Pomfret, "NATO Worries about East European Armies Meeting Standards," *Washington Post,* February 19, 1995, p. 45. These analysts correctly note that should a Russian threat to ECE emerge, NATO can always decide to expand at that point. There is no need to rush.

53. Brown, "Flawed Logic," p. 35.

54. For more on the elements and rationale of NATO's early strategy of rapprochement, see Stephen J. Flanagan, "NATO and Central and Eastern Europe: From Liaison to Security Partnership," *Washington Quarterly,* vol. 15 (Spring 1992), pp. 144–46.

55. With respect to this last function, the NACC played an important role in the difficult task of apportioning among the newly independent Soviet republics the CFE Treaty's equipment quotas for the former USSR. Its success in this regard prevented potential conflicts among these countries that could have resulted from a process of competitive rearmament. For more on the NACC's activities, see Rosser Baldwin, Jr., "Addressing the Security Concerns of Central Europe through NATO," *European Security,* vol. 2 (Winter 1993), pp. 554–56; and Guido Gerosa, "The North Atlantic Cooperation Council," *European Security,* vol. 1 (Autumn 1992), pp. 273–94.

56. In November 1993 high-level civilian and military personnel also met for four days at the George C. Marshall European Center for Security Studies in Garmisch, Germany, to participate in a U.S.-sponsored workshop on peacekeeping operations among NACC members. In January 1994 Hungary hosted a seminar on the humanitarian aspects of peacekeeping. In addition, the NATO School in Oberammergau, Germany, held several courses for staff officers and their civilian counterparts from nonalliance members on various aspects of peacekeeping.

57. NACC-AHG-D(93)9 (Revised), June 7, 1993. See also NATO Press Release M-NACC 1(93)40, June 11,1993, Press Release M-NACC 2 (93)73, December 3,1993; and John Kriendler, "NATO's Changing Role—Opportunities and Constraints for Peacekeeping," *NATO Review,* vol. 41 (June 1993), p. 20.

58. Kjell Engelbrekt, "Southeast European States Seek Equal Treatment," *RFE/RL Research Report,* vol. 3 (March 25, 1994), p. 40.

59. Rosser Baldwin, Jr., "Addressing the Security Concerns of Central Europe through NATO," *European Security,* vol. 2 (Winter 1993), p. 551. For more on the east European and former Soviet republican governments' reactions to NATO's increased military involvement in the Yugoslav civil war, see Stan Markotich, "Former Communist States Respond to NATO Ultimatum," *RFE/RL Research Report,* vol. 3 (February 25, 1994), pp. 6–12.

60. For a review of these efforts, see Michael Mihalka, "Squaring the Circle: NATO's Offer to the East," *RFE/RL Research Report,* vol. 3 (March 25, 1994), pp. 2–4. For reviews of the summit itself, see Les Aspin, "New Europe, New NATO," *NATO Review,* vol. 42 (February 1994), pp. 12–14; Mihalka, "Squaring the Circle: NATO's Offer to the East," pp. 4–5; and Manfred Wörner, "Shaping the Alliance for the Future," *NATO Review,* vol. 42 (February 1994), p. 4.

61. Interviews with selected ECE ambassadors to Belgium and NATO, September 1994.

62. The PfP Framework Document is reprinted in *RFE/RL Research Report,* vol. 3 (March 25, 1994), pp. 22–23. For more on the benefits and obligations of PfP participants, see Willy Claes, "NATO and the Evolving Euro-Atlantic Security Architecture," *NATO Review,* vol. 43 (December 1994–January 1995), pp. 4–5; Paul E. Gallis, *Partnership for Peace* (Washington: Congressional Research Service, August 9, 1994), especially pp. 2–3; and Gebhardt von Moltke, "Building a Partnership for Peace," *NATO Review,* vol. 42 (June 1994), pp. 3–7. According to von Moltke, a typical Presentation Document "lists the steps that have been, or will be, taken to promote transparency in national defense planning and budgeting processes, and to ensure the democratic control of defense forces. It also contains an indication of the kind of cooperative activities of interest to the partner, and the military forces and other assets that it might make available for Partnership activities. The Document not only addresses short-term possibilities for cooperation but also covers longer-term planning factors that could affect a partner's future involvement, such as changes in the structure of the armed forces or the setting-up of special peacekeeping units" (pp. 5–6).

63. A representative of the Czech Ministry of Defense wrote that, "From our perspective, a key aspect of Partnership for Peace is the possibility to consult with the Alliance on a 16 + 1 basis in case we perceive a direct threat to our territorial integrity, political independence or security" (Jaromir Novotny, "The Czech Republic—An Active Partner with NATO," *NATO Review,* vol. 42 [June 1994], p. 12). See also Gebhardt von Moltke, "Russia and NATO," *The RUSI Journal* (February 1995), p. 10.

64. Interview with policymakers at NATO headquarters, September 1994.

65. Interviews with American policymakers at NATO headquarters, September 1994

66. Von Moltke, "Building a Partnership for Peace," p. 7. He notes that PfP's Political-Military Steering Committee will gradually assume the responsibilities of the NACC Ad Hoc Group on Peacekeeping.

67. For more on these exercises, see Robin Beard, "Defence Procurement Cooperation with Central and Eastern Europe," *NATO Review,* vol. 42 (August 1994), p. 23.

68. General George Joulwan, NATO's new Supreme Allied Commander, antic-ipated between ten and twenty PfP exercises in 1995. "Supreme Allied Commander Sketches Challenges of 'New NATO,'" *Defense Week* (February 6, 1995), p. 9.

69. In the words of Gebhardt von Moltke, NATO's assistant secretary-general for political affairs, "The concept of inter-operability in peacekeeping is aimed at ensuring compatibility in approaches and procedures, not at common or standard-ized equipment" ("Building a Partnership for Peace," p. 5).

70. A month before the January 1994 NATO summit, U.S. secretary of state Warren Christopher said establishing CJTFs "would allow new flexibility for organizing peacekeeping and other tasks. It would enable NATO to take effec-tive action in contingencies that do not evoke Article V of the North Atlantic Treaty." Warren Christopher, U.S. Department of State, Office of the Spokes-man, Excerpts of NAC Intervention, NATO Headquarters, Brussels, Belgium, December 2, 1993, p. 4, cited in British American Security Information Coun-cil, *NATO, Peacekeeping, and the United Nations* (London, September 1994), p. 14. For more on the CJTF concept, see "It Can't Be Done Alone," *The Economist* (February 25, 1995), pp. 20–21; and John D. Morrocco, "NATO Struggles to Refine Joint Task Force Concept," *Aviation Week & Space Tech-nology* (March 20, 1995), p. 54.

71. For example, the Cortina peace enforcement scenario developed by the Joint Readiness Training Center of the US Army at Fort Polk, Louisiana.

72. Interview with a French policymaker at NATO headquarters in September 1994, who stated that it was acceptable for Americans to command an operation only if their assets were critical to its success. For more on this dispute, see Robert Grant, "US, France Close the Strategic Gap," *Defense News* (May 16, 1994), p. 19; and Robin Knight, "From the Ashes of War," *US News & World Report* (May 8, 1995), p. 47.

73. Cited in Rick Atkinson, "Russia Warns NATO on Expansion," *Washington Post,* March 21, 1995, p. 14. See also Yeltsin's various comments, cited in Bernard Gwertzman, "Yeltsin to Alter Parade on V-E Day to Draw Clinton," *New York Times,* March 17, 1995, p. 1; and in an interview he gave to *Time,* "Heading for the Summit" (May 8, 1995), p. 75.

74. Cited in John Pomfret, "Brawl Delays Russian Premier's Visit to Poland," *Washington Post,* November 4, 1994, p. 35.

75. Ian Black, "Nato and Moscow Squabble over 'Peace Partnership,'" *The Guardian,* June 11, 1994, p. 13; and Brooks Tigner, "Russia, NATO Grope toward Political Compromise," *Defense News* (June 13, 1994), p. 3. For more on Russia's truculent behavior toward PfP, see Daniel Vernet, "La Russie veut faire reconnaître son statut de grande puissance, *Le Monde,* May 24, 1994, p. 1.

76. R. W. Apple. Jr., "The Growth of NATO: Will Moscow Go Along?," *New York Times,* May 11, 1995, p. 10; and Bill Gertz, "Russia Rebuffs US on Reactor Sales to Iran," *Washington Times,* April 4, 1995. For additional Russian warnings against NATO expansion, see Judy Dempsey, "Nato Warned over Eastward Expan-sion," *Financial Times,* January 24, 1995, p. 2; and Carey Schofield, "Moscow General in Warning to Nato," *The Times,* April 19, 1995, p. 10.

77. In accounting for his belligerent stance at the Istanbul meeting, Kozyrev allegedly told an American official "my problem is not so much what is in the communiqué as what is not there. I'll go home and they'll say to me, 'Where is

Russia in the communiqué?'" Cited in Elaine Sciolino, "Russia Pledges to Join NATO Partnership," *New York Times,* June 11, 1994, p. 3. See also Martin Sieff, "NATO Growth Could Aid Russian Ultranationalists," *Washington Times,* February 7, 1995, p. 1.

78. For more on the origins and meaning of this phrase, see "Address by Mr. Hurd, The Foreign Secretary, to the WEU Assembly," June 14, 1994, reprinted in British Foreign & Commonwealth Office, *Arms Control and Disarmament Quarterly Review,* no. 34 (July 1994), p. 6. See also von Moltke, "Russia and NATO," *The RUSI Journal* (February 1995), pp. 11–12.

79. Associated Press, "Heisser Draht zwischen Moskau und der Nato," *Neue Zuercher Zeitung,* June 29, 1994, p. 3.

80. Ann Devroy and Fred Hiatt, "US, Russia Cite Discord at Summit," *Washington Post,* May 11, 1995, p. 1. Although the participants failed to resolve their differences over NATO enlargement, they did express their support for a stronger OSCE, the ECE countries's sovereignty, and the goal of not isolating Russia. Yeltsin also agreed to resume participation in the PfP.

81. Celestine Bohlen, "Russia Faults NATO Step," *New York Times,* April 12, 1994, p. 10; and Lee Hockstader, "Yeltsin Vents Anger at NATO," *Washington Post,* April 13, 1994, p. 19. His deputy prime minister called the air strike a blow to Russia's prestige and claimed a target was "the internal political situation in Russia" (cited in Steven Erlanger, "Anti-Western Winds Gain Force in Russia," *New York Times,* April 17, 1994, section 4, p. 4). See also Daniel Sneider, "Russians React to NATO Airstrikes," *Christian Science Monitor,* April 15, 1994, p. 1.

82. Roger Cohen, "Fighting Rages as NATO Debates How to Protect Bosnian Enclave," *New York Times,* November 25, 1994, p. 16.

83. Nadia Arbatova, "Horror Mirror: Russian Perceptions of the Yugoslav Conflict," unpublished draft chapter in Chayes, Chayes, and Olson, eds., *Managing Internal Conflict in the Former Soviet Space* (working title, forthcoming).

84. Fred Kaplan, "Russia, in a Reversal, Backs NATO's Threat to Bomb Bosnia Serbs," *Boston Globe,* April 24, 1994, p. 11; and Michael Specter, "Moscow Withdraws Its Objections to NATO Strikes near Gorazde," *New York Times,* April 24, 1994, p. 13.

85. In addition to its Sarajevo intervention, Russian diplomacy and its offer to deploy observers to the crisis in Tuzla helped resolve the impasse there over the delivery of food and medicine. Nor has Russia absolutely refused to sanction NATO's use of force. Russian officials did approve of NATO's downing in February 1994 of the four aircraft that violated the UN no-fly zone over Bosnia. Michael Specter, "Russia Backs NATO," *New York Times,* March 1, 1994, p. 13.

86. See Andrei Kozyrev, "Don't Threaten Us," *New York Times,* March 18, 1994, p. 29. For information on Russian policymakers' complex position toward NATO involvement in the Yugoslav conflict, see Justin Burke, "Russia's Ambitions Pose Test for NATO Program," *Christian Science Monitor,* April 27, 1994, p. 2; Lee Hockstader, "Divided Russian Officials Publicly Squabble over Pro-Serb Policy," *Washington Post,* April 24, 1994, p. 26; and Allen Lynch, "After Empire: Russia and Its Western Neighbors," *RFE/RL Research Report,* vol. 3 (March 25, 1994), pp. 10–11. For information on possible differences between Yeltsin and the more moderate Kozyrev on this issue, see Bruce

Clark, "Nato Pressed to Shelve Enlargement," *Financial Times,* March 23, 1995, p. 3.

87. Bruce Clark, "Nato Balks at Swallowing Russian 'Sweeteners,'" Financial Times, February 27, 1995, p. 4; and Michael Shields, "Perry Wants Russia Consulted, Informed as NATO Moves East," Washington Times, February 6, 1995, p. 11. Some of Yeltsin's subordinates appeared more willing to strike a deal; see, for example, R. Jeffrey Smith and Daniel Williams, "Russia Intends to Pursue Guarantees from NATO," *Washington Post,* March 11, 1995, p. 21.

88. Roland Dumas, "Security and Defence of France—French Foreign Policy," *NATO's Sixteen Nations,* vol. 37, no. 3 (1992), p. 12. See also Karl Feldmayer, "Im Wechsel Bewahren," *Frankfurter Allgemeine Zeitung,* December 22, 1992, p. 12; "Folgerungen aus dem Balkankrieg erwartet," *Frankfurter Allgemeine Zeitung,* May 25, 1993, p. 7; Herbert Kremp, "Die Nato würde, wenn," *Die Welt,* June 6, 1992, p. 2; Winfried Muenster, *Sueddeutsche Zeitung,* "Frankreich sieht sich im Abseits," December 19, 1992, p. 7; Winfried Muenster, "Stillschweigend reiht sich Frankreich wieder ein," *Sueddeutsche Zeitung,* April 16, 1993, p. 7; "NATO Diary," *NATO's Sixteen Nations,* vol. 37, no. 2 (1992), p. 74; and Claire Trean, "L'élargissement des compétences de l'OTAN continue d'alimenter la polémique entre Français et Américains," *Le Monde,* June 6, 1992, p. 4.

89. Commenting on the proposed NATO mission, a French representative observed, "It must be a UN-controlled operation, not a NATO-controlled operation with a United Nations blessing" (cited in Frank J. Prial, "Key Issue for US and UN: Who Leads the Peacekeepers," *New York Times,* May 6, 1993, p. 16). For more on French policies toward peacekeeping in the former Yugoslavia, see Leonard Doyle and Andrew Marshall, "UN May Urge WEU to Take on Peace Role," *The Independent,* April 30, 1992, p. 6; Karl Feldmeyer, "Neue Aufgabe, gemischte Gefuehle," *Frankfurter Allgemeine Zeitung,* April 10, 1993, p. 10; Walter Goldstein, "Europe after Maastricht," *Foreign Affairs,* vol. 71 (Winter 1992–93), p. 126; and Reuters and Associated Press, "France to Ask WEU to Weigh Sending Force to Yugoslavia," *International Herald Tribune,* August 6, 1991, p. 1.

90. Interview with a French policymaker, March 1994. See also Reuters, "Paris Appears Primed for Larger Role on 'Renovated' NATO Military Team," *International Herald Tribune,* January 31, 1995, p. 2.

91. On the demise of the "out-of-area" taboo, see Laszlo Valki, "A Future Security Architecture for Europe?," *European Security,* vol. 2 (Winter 1993), pp. 531, 532. Wörner remarked in late 1993 that "The slogan 'out-of-area or out-of-business' is out of date. NATO *is* acting out of area and it *is* very much in business." Manfred Wörner, "NATO's Role in a Changing Europe," in *European Security after the Cold War: Part I,* Adelphi paper (Brassey's and the International Institute for Strategic Studies, January 1994), p. 102; emphasis in original.

92. Interview with a French policymaker at NATO headquarters, September 1994. See also "It Can't Be Done Alone," *Economist* (February 25, 1995).

93. Cited in Carey Schofield, "France as the Wild Card in NATO?," *International Defense Review,* vol. 27 (July 1994), p. 21. The article offers a comprehensive summary of French complaints since the January 1994 NATO summit.

94. Bruce Clark, "Warning as Bosnia Plan Eludes Nato," *Financial Times,* April 6, 1995, p. 3.

95. Brooks Togner, "Bosnia Effort Recasts NATO Buying Plan," *Defense News* (April 17, 1995), p. 4. As of yet, however, the alliance has not requested members to procure equipment solely for peacekeeping operations. NATO military leaders assume that if their units retain excellence in their core military competencies, they can effectively undertake peace operations. General Rose explained, "We are more concerned now with nations maintaining force levels and readiness" (cited in Morrocco, "NATO Struggles to Refine Joint Task Force Concept," p. 54).

96. For more on NATO's involvement in that crisis, see Monteagle Stearns, *Entangled Allies: US Policy toward Greece, Turkey, and Cyprus* (New York: Council on Foreign Relations Press, 1992). On NATO's past practice of not confronting governments' internal policies, see Charles William Maynes, "NATO's Tough Choice in Bosnia," *New York Times,* July 27, 1994, p. 21.

97. On this problem, see Wilhelm Höynck, "CSCE Works to Develop its Conflict Prevention Potential," *NATO Review,* vol. 42 (April 1994), p. 21.

98. Mats Berdal, "Peacemaking in Europe," in *European Security after the Cold War, Part I,* p. 60.

99. French policymakers have insisted that each such rotation receive NAC approval and that the officer cannot represent NATO policy to the UN. Instead, he or she can only report back to Brussels on operational matters pertaining to UN-authorized peacekeeping operations. Bruce George and John Borawski, "Sympathy for the Devil: European Security in a Revolutionary Age," *European Security,* vol. 2 (Winter 1993), p. 480.

100. Michael Ruehle, "Crisis Management in NATO," *European Security,* vol. 2 (Winter 1993), pp. 495, 496. For a discussion of possible conflicts between NATO and the UN over the command and control of UN-authorized operations, see Kofi A. Annan, "UN Peacekeeping Operations and Cooperation with NATO," *NATO Review,* vol. 41 (October 1993), pp. 6–7. The UN's decision to grant NATO military operations wide discretion has helped avoid many of these potential problems.

101. Cited in Frank Viviano, "UN Learns Hard Lessons on Peacekeeping," *San Francisco Chronicle,* March 28, 1995, p. 1.

102. Cited in Reuters, June 29, 1994 (NEXIS, Mead Data Central).

103. Cited in John Pomfret, "NATO Jets Bomb Serb Airfield," *Washington Post,* November 22, 1994, p. 25. For more on these UN-NATO differences over the use of force in Bosnia, see Christopher Bertram, "Irreconcilable Partners," *Washington Post,* November 2, 1994, p. 23; Roger Cohen, "Serbs Lagging in Complying, UN Asserts," *New York Times,* May 4, 1994, p. 13; Michael R. Gordon, "UN Blocks NATO's Call to Hit Serbs," *New York Times,* April 24, 1994, p. 12; Paul Quinn-Judge, "Serbs Begin to Pull out of Gorazde," *Boston Globe,* April 24, 1994, p. 1; Paul Lewis, "US Says UN Officers in Balkans Lack the Will to Block Serbs," *New York Times,* May 2, 1994, p. 7; and John Pomfret, "Hope Erodes for Muslims in Bosnia," *Washington Post,* November 28, 1994, p. 20.

104. Interview, October 1994.

105. Michael Ruehle, "Crisis Management in NATO," *European Security,* vol. 2 (Winter 1993), pp. 495, 496, 500. Ruehle correctly urges that, when acting under a

mandate from the UN or any other international organization, the relevant authorities should allow NATO staff to become involved much earlier in the politico-military planning process to expedite NATO contingency planning and enhance the coherence of the mandating body's response to the crisis.

106. Claes, "NATO and the Evolving Architecture," pp. 5–6. See also the comments of German defense minister Volker Ruehe, cited in "Germany Sets Criteria for Foreign Missions," *International Defence Review* (March 1995), p. 5.

107. Cited in Daniel Williams, "US Deploys Marines off Bosnian Coast," *Washington Post,* November 26, 1994, p. A20.

108. Major Rob Annink, spokesperson for UNPROFOR, asserted the Bosnian government's forces sought to provoke Serb attacks to trigger airstrikes: "It seems to be their hope that NATO will come to their rescue" (cited in John Pomfret, "Bosnian Serbs Seeking to Thwart US, Allies," *Washington Post,* August 2, 1994, p. 19).

109. Roger Cohen, "NATO Disputes UN Reports of Possible Arms Airlift to Bosnia," *New York Times,* March 1, 1995.

110. See, for example, Clinton's statement at the January 1994 summit, cited in Reuters, August 3, 1994 (NEXIS, Mead Data Service).

111. See Dobbie, "A Concept for Post Cold War Peacekeeping," *Survival,* vol. 36 (Autumn 1994), pp. 121–49.

112. "Speech by Mr. Manfred Wörner, Secretary General of NATO, to the National Press Club," Washington, October 6, 1993, reprinted in British Foreign & Commonwealth Office, *Arms Control and Disarmament Quarterly Review,* no. 32 (January 1994), p. 10.

113. For a review of NATO's plans to rescue UNPROFOR and the diverse political, military, and legal complexities involved, see Rick Atkinson, "Reveille for NATO Rapid Reaction Corps," *Washington Post,* March 19, 1995, p. 28; Bruce Clark and Laura Silber, "Bosnia's Nightmare Brew of Problems," *Financial Times,* April 28, 1995, p. 13; and David Fairhall, "Hard-hitting Nato Troops Head Rescue Team," *The Guardian,* May 10, 1995, p. 11. In general, NATO policymakers anticipate using some 60,000 troops under ROE that permit an easier resort to force than current guidelines authorize. They also want the UN to pay for the evacuation, despite NATO's plans to assume full command of the operation.

114. "US Has Useful Role in Russian Reform," *Washington Times,* January 17, 1995, p. 12. On another occasion, Christopher told reporters, "The crisis in Bosnia is about Bosnia and the former Yugoslavia. It is not about NATO and its future. The United States is staying in Europe . . . and so NATO remains the foundation for our American role in Europe" (cited in Daniel Williams, "In Policy Switch, US Puts Bosnia Aside to Preserve Alliance," *Washington Post,* November 30, 1994, p. 32). Another administration official more bluntly said, "We are favoring NATO unity over what we have long believed the course in Bosnia ought to be" (cited in Daniel Williams and Ruth Marcus, "US Favors Making Concessions to Serbs," *Washington Post,* November 29, 1994, p. 18).

115. Cited in Daniel Williams, "NATO Chief Warns That Arming Bosnian Muslims Will Endanger Peacekeepers," *Washington Post,* November 22, 1994, p. 24. British foreign secretary Douglas Hurd likewise commented: "Bosnia is not

a test. NATO was not born to solve the Bosnia problem" (cited in Elaine Sciolino, "US and NATO Say They Have Settled Dispute on Bosnia," *New York Times,* December 2, 1994, p. 1).

116. Cited in William Drozdiak, "Dole Places Bosnia Atop Senate Agenda," *Washington Post,* November 30, 1994, p. 30.

117. Cited in Craig R. Whitney, "Adversarial Allies: Sparring over Bosnia and NATO Membership," *New York Times,* December 2, 1994, p. 14.

118. Davor Huic, "Croatia Rethinks Ouster of Peacekeepers," *Washington Times,* March 9, 1995, p. 15.

NINE

A Peacekeeping Role for the
Western European Union

David S. Huntington

LONG DISMISSED as an obscure and inconsequential bureaucracy, the nine-nation Western European Union (WEU) seems to have found a new legitimacy in the post–cold war era.[1] With the signing of the Maastricht Treaty on European Union in 1991, the WEU was formally designated as the defense arm of the European Union; and in January 1994 it was recognized by the North Atlantic Treaty Organization (NATO) as the European "pillar" of the Atlantic Alliance. The organization has now taken steps to expand its operational capabilities and redirect itself to newly emerging threats to European security, including the problem of ethno-national conflict in eastern Europe and the former Soviet Union. The member states have broadened the legal mandate of the WEU to allow for military operations outside of western Europe and have pledged to undertake "the effective implementation of conflict-prevention and crisis management measures, including peacekeeping activities."[2] The organization has now carried out a series of limited military actions including naval operations in the Adriatic Sea and on the Danube River to enforce United Nations sanctions against the former Yugoslavia.

In spite of these developments, the WEU continues to suffer from an identity crisis that has prevented it from implementing this new agenda and becoming actively involved in the field of peacekeeping. The central problem is that its members are not in agreement on the role that the WEU should play within the European security system. Certain states, notably France, have traditionally viewed the organization as an independent European alternative to NATO. For these states, the central purpose of the WEU is to enable the Europeans to take responsibility for their own security, outside of the U.S.-dominated framework of NATO. Other members of the WEU, principally Britain, have seen the organization as a threat to NATO and have downplayed its independence from the Atlantic Alliance. For these "Atlanticist" states, NATO is still the only effective European defense organization, and to the extent that the WEU plays any role at all in European security, it should do so as a subsidiary component of NATO.

This divergence within the WEU is compounded by the fact that it is a "defense" organization without any military capabilities of its own. The WEU has no permanent military structures and therefore must rely on ad hoc contributions from the forces of its members states, forces that have been earmarked, first and foremost, for use by the NATO alliance. Indeed, the organization must rely directly on NATO for certain specialized military assets, such as early warning aircraft and communications facilities, which are not possessed individually by any European nations. Although the Atlantic Alliance has recently pledged to make its military assets available to the WEU, the arrangement is problematic because the European states most interested in seeing a greater role for the WEU, particularly France, are not eager to cooperate closely with NATO.

The WEU's lack of a clear identity has translated into ineffectiveness in practice. In the former Yugoslavia, the organization has struggled to find a place for itself, but has ultimately failed to overcome the deep-rooted political divisions between its members. The French have advocated a greater role for the WEU in the Balkans, while Britain and others have preferred to leave peacekeeping in the hands of the United Nations and NATO. The WEU has managed to carry out limited naval sanctions enforcement operations but has lacked the political will to contribute in a peacekeeping capacity. At times the organization has even played a counterproductive role by competing for political visibility with the United Nations and NATO, and adding to the international institutional confusion surrounding the former Yugoslavia.

The question posed in this chapter is whether the WEU realistically has a new role to play in peacekeeping, specifically in eastern Europe. The assumption is that in the spectrum of possible conflict-prevention measures, there will be an ongoing need for a military component, what is loosely termed here as "peacekeeping." This component consists of a range of different peace operations: traditional peacekeeping, humanitarian and protection operations, sanctions enforcement, and in some cases peace enforcement. The chapter is divided into three parts; the first presents an overview of the history and institutional structure of the WEU and describes the organization's current place within the European security system; the second part takes a close look at the WEU's past military operations in the Persian Gulf and Yugoslavia in an effort to identify some of the practical obstacles facing the WEU as a military organization; the final part examines the future potential of the WEU as a peacekeeping organization. It focuses on the relationships between the WEU and three key institutional actors—NATO, the United Nations and the European Union—in an effort to understand what kind of future peacekeeping role the organization might play within the "architecture" of European security and to understand some of the political obstacles keeping the organization from fulfilling that role.

The Western European Union and the "Architecture" of European Security

The WEU began modestly in the immediate aftermath of World War II. Its development in the post–cold war environment, however, may turn out to be considerably more ambitious.

Origins of the Western European Union: 1948–54

The Western European Union has its origins in the Brussels Treaty of 1948, which established a collective self-defense alliance between Britain, France, Belgium, Luxembourg, and the Netherlands.[3] The first such alliance of its kind in western Europe, the Brussels Treaty bound the five signatories to defend each other in the event of an armed attack against any one of them and created an organization known as the "Western Union" or "Brussels Treaty Organization" to facilitate consultations among the members. In 1954 the Treaty was modified through a series of protocols, known as the Paris Agreements, to incorporate West Germany and Italy and to establish a formal international organization called the Western European Union. The cornerstone of the modified Brussels Treaty remained the commitment to collective defense as set out in article 5: "If any of the High Contracting Parties should be the object of an armed attack in Europe, the other High Contracting Parties will, in accordance with the provisions of Article 51 of the Charter of the United Nations, afford the Party so attacked all the military and other aid and assistance in their power."[4] The self-defense formulation enabled the member states to act defensively as an organization without prior authorization from the United Nations, but it provided only a limited mandate with respect to threats arising outside the territory of the member states. As to such "out-of-area" threats, the Treaty authorized the members of the WEU to "consult with regard to any situation which may constitute a threat to peace, in whatever area this threat should arise, or a danger to economic stability"; however, it sanctioned the use force only in the event of an "armed attack in Europe."[5]

The principal organ of the new Western European Union was its inter-governmental Council, comprised of representatives from the member states and endowed with the power to make decisions by unanimous vote. Situated in London, the Council was to meet regularly at both the permanent representative level and at the foreign and defense minister level, and was to be assisted by a secretary-general and any other subsidiary bodies as might be necessary. The other major organ of the WEU was the Parliamentary Assembly, comprised of representatives of the Brussels Treaty Powers to the Consultative Assembly of the Council of Europe. Located in Paris, the Assembly was entitled to consider matters relevant to the Treaty and to receive an annual report from the Council. However, the Assembly was given no formal decisionmaking powers within the framework of the WEU.

The aim of the Paris Agreements was to create an organization that could provide a true European security dimension. Because the parties did not want to duplicate structures already being developed by the Atlantic Alliance, however, the modified Brussels Treaty did not call for the formation of any kind of military staff or integrated military command. Indeed, the Treaty explicitly stated that the WEU would "rely on the appropriate military authorities of NATO for information and advice on military matters."[6] Thus, in its earliest conception, the WEU was an organization lacking a clear identity. Although designed as a "defense" organization, it had no military capabilities of its own and from the outset was overshadowed by NATO.

Cold War Years: 1954–84

From 1954 to 1973 the WEU functioned principally as a high-level forum for consultation between its members. Its most significant contribution was providing a link for political discussions between Britain and the continental states. Between 1957, when the Treaty of Rome was signed, and 1973, when the United Kingdom finally acceded to the European Communities, the WEU was the only forum in which the six continental states plus Britain could meet on a regular basis. In addition, in 1955 the WEU played an important role in the resolution of the postwar Franco-German dispute over the Saar region. In October of that year, with the consent of both France and Germany, the WEU organized a successful referendum in which the Saarlanders voted to return to Germany. The WEU organization also continued during this period to contribute to arms control, through the ongoing work of its Agency for the Control of Armaments (ACA) and Standing Armaments Committee (SAC).

Between 1973 and 1984 the WEU fell into disuse. It was no longer needed as a link between the United Kingdom and the continent, and as a result no meetings were held at the ministerial level during this period. While the Assembly continued to call for the development of an independent European security dimension, the Council remained content to keep the organization in the shadow of NATO.

Reactivation: 1984–94

The WEU was reactivated in 1984 in response to several emerging security concerns in Europe. President Reagan's announcement of the Strategic Defense Initiative (SDI) in 1983 raised fears in western Europe that the United States might divide the NATO alliance into separate security zones. At the same time, disagreements within NATO over the deployment of U.S. nuclear missiles in western Europe further weakened the cohesion of alliance. Both developments suggested a need for a stronger European security dimension. The renewed interest in the WEU was also linked to the failure of the European Community to extend European Political Cooperation (EPC) to defense matters, because of resistance from Denmark, Greece, and Ireland. The initial impetus for reactivation of the WEU came from the French government, which circulated a proposal in 1984 calling for regular meetings of the Council of Ministers and an increased role for the organization in the field of European security.

During the past ten years, the WEU has developed as an organization on four different levels: first, the WEU has expanded its legal mandate through a series of quasi-constitutional texts adopted by its members; second, it has developed its institutional structure with an eye toward improving operational capabilities; third, it has enlarged its membership substantially; and finally, through a series of out-of-area military operations, the WEU has begun to assume a role in implementing European defense policy. The evolution of the WEU has not always been smooth. The French-led "Europeanists" have continued to push for the establishment of an independent European defense system built around the WEU, while the British-led

"Atlanticists" have strongly resisted such a notion as a threat to NATO. The result has been an uneasy process of compromise between the two factions under which the WEU has been identified on the one hand as the European "pillar" of the Atlantic Alliance and on the other as the defense arm of an integrated European Union.

"CONSTITUTIONAL" DEVELOPMENTS. Beginning in Rome in 1984, the Council of Ministers of the WEU adopted a series of quasi-constitutional texts designed to reactivate the WEU as an instrument of security policy in Europe;[7] and by 1991 the WEU was formally linked to the process of European integration through the Maastricht Treaty on European Union. The treaty established a framework for a common foreign and security policy among the members of the Union, and requested "the Western European Union (WEU), which is an integral part of the development of the Union, to elaborate and implement decisions and actions which have defence implications."[8] This language represented a compromise between France, which wanted to incorporate the WEU into the European Union, and Britain, which resisted the idea of European defense integration and was reluctant to refer to the WEU at all in the Maastricht Treaty.[9]

The Council of Ministers of the WEU first addressed itself to the problem of peacekeeping at a meeting in Bonn in June 1992. The Petersberg Declaration asserted that the WEU was "prepared to support, on a case-by-case basis and in accordance with our own procedures, the effective implementation of conflict-prevention and crisis-management measures, including peacekeeping activities of the CSCE [Conference on Security and Cooperation in Europe] or the United Nations Security Council." In calling for the strengthening of the WEU's operational role, the ministers declared that "military units of WEU member States, acting under authority of WEU, could be employed for: humanitarian and rescue tasks; peacekeeping tasks; tasks of combat forces in crisis management, including peacemaking."[10] The Petersberg Declaration effectively removed the internal legal constraints on out-of-area WEU military operations, and represented an important political commitment of the organization to assume a role in peacekeeping and conflict prevention.

The current position of the WEU within the European security system was articulated at the NATO Summit of January 1994. The NATO leaders formally recognized the WEU as both the European "pillar" of the Atlantic Alliance and as the defense component of the European Union and pledged to make the collective assets of the alliance available to the WEU for operations undertaken by the European allies in pursuit of their common foreign and security policy.[11] The declaration had enormous practical significance in that the WEU now has access to the military assets necessary to conduct effective peacekeeping operations. It also had political significance as a partial resolution of the ongoing conflict between the Europeanist and Atlanticist members of the organization.

INSTITUTIONAL DEVELOPMENTS. The last ten years have witnessed a significant development of the institutional structure of the WEU. Most important, the adoption of the Rome Declaration led to the reactivation of the Council as a forum for high-level intergovernmental consultation and coordination. The Council now meets weekly at the permanent representative level and meets at least twice a year at the foreign and defense minister level. In 1993, at the urging of Britain and over the resistance of France, the Council and Secretariat moved from London to Brussels to facilitate military and political cooperation with NATO and the European Union. France strongly opposed the move, fearing greater NATO influence over the WEU. A majority of WEU states, however, including West Germany, Italy, and Spain, as well as Britain, believed that the WEU would benefit from closer proximity both to NATO and to the European Political Cooperation mechanism. In the end a compromise was struck whereby the Council was moved to Brussels and a new Institute for Security Studies was established in Paris.[12]

Further modifications came in 1992, when, in an effort to strengthen the WEU's military capacity, the Council established a Planning Cell consisting of some forty military experts. The Planning Cell has been charged with identifying forces available to the WEU, preparing contingency plans for the deployment of forces under WEU auspices, and serving as an advisory and coordinating body in times of military crisis.

The Parliamentary Assembly of the WEU continues to meet twice a year in plenary session in Paris, where its permanent seat is located. As the only European parliamentary body with competence in the area of defense, the Assembly functions as a democratic forum for debate on defense issues. The Assembly carries on an institutional dialogue with the Council and has generally been a strong advocate of expanding the activities of the WEU. However, the Assembly still has not formal decisionmaking powers within the WEU.

ENLARGEMENT. The WEU has now enlarged its membership to include, through varying types of status, all of the European members of NATO and the European Union. In 1988 Spain and Portugal joined as full members, and in 1992 Greece signed a protocol of accession, which has yet to be ratified by all of the other member states. The remaining members of the European Union—Denmark and Ireland—were admitted as "observers" to the WEU in 1992. Austria, Finland, Norway, and Sweden will be able to join the WEU as observers once they have become members of the European Union. The remaining European members of NATO which do not belong to the European Union—Norway, Iceland, and Turkey—were admitted in 1992 as "associate members" of the WEU, and may become full members only after joining the European Union. Both observers and associate members are permitted to take part in meetings of the WEU Council, and associate members may participate in WEU military operations. However, neither observers nor associate members have any formal decision-making powers in the Council.

In 1992 the WEU further broadened its potential membership through the establishment of a Forum for Consultation between the members of the WEU and those eastern European and Baltic states that had signed, or were on the way to signing, association agreements with the European Union. The participating states are Bulgaria, Estonia, Hungary, Latvia, Lithuania, Poland, Romania, Slovakia, and the Czech Republic. The idea of the Forum was to facilitate military cooperation and information exchanges between eastern and western Europe, with the aim of developing a future capacity to carry out joint military activities, including peacekeeping. During the past two years, the Forum has met at both ministerial and ambassadorial levels to discuss various defense-related problems of mutual concern.

In May 1994, in response to NATO's Partnership for Peace, the WEU Council of Ministers decided to offer "associate partner" status to all of the Forum for Consultation countries. The arrangement permits the new associate partners to participate in WEU Council and workings group meetings, establish links with the WEU Planning Cell in Brussels, and join in peacekeeping, humanitarian, rescue, or intervention operations carried out under WEU auspices. The arrangement does not, however, provide any security guarantees to the new partners or grant those countries any decisionmaking powers within the WEU. The associate partner arrangement goes further than the NATO Partnership for Peace in that it provides for regular contacts at a relatively high official level (that is, ambassadorial level). In addition, by limiting the scheme to those countries that have a prospect of joining the European Union, the WEU has created a smaller group than the NATO Partnership that may prove easier to work with, especially given that Russia is not included in the group.

Military Operations of the Western European Union

Since 1987 the WEU has authorized and carried out three different military operations—a minesweeping mission in the Persian Gulf during the Iran-Iraq War, a sanctions enforcement operation against Iraq during the Gulf War, and the ongoing sanctions enforcement operation against Serbia and Montenegro—each of which has involved the "coordinated" deployment of naval forces of the WEU member states. Overall, these operations have been heralded as successes for the newly reactivated WEU, but a closer look reveals serious problems of political and military coordination. The membership of the WEU has been divided on the role that the organization should play in crisis situations as well as on substantive issues of policy. When the WEU has acted, its missions have been operationally inefficient because the organization lacks a permanent command structure and other standing military capabilities. A further problem has been a lack of coordination between the WEU and the other international organizations engaged in military activities, notably NATO and the United Nations.

"Operation Cleansweep": 1987–88

The WEU's first attempt at coordinated military action came in 1987 during the Iran-Iraq War. In response to U.S. pressure for greater military burden-sharing in the Middle East, five WEU members—Britain, France, Italy, Belgium, and the Netherlands—dispatched naval units to the Gulf to protect their own countries' maritime traffic and to sweep the area for mines. The Council of Ministers of the WEU authorized "Operation Cleansweep" pursuant to article 8 (3) of the modified Brussels Treaty, which permits the Council to "consult with regard to any situation which may constitute a threat to peace, in whatever area this threat should arise, or a danger to economic stability."

The operation, which lasted nearly two years, served to enhance the visibility of the WEU as a workable forum for European military cooperation; however, the level of actual coordination between naval forces in the Gulf was quite limited. To carry out the mission, the Council established a three-tier framework for consultations between participating members: high-level meetings between experts from foreign and defense ministries; contacts between officers within the various admiralties; and on-the-spot consultations between task force commanders in the Gulf. In spite of this framework, there was no unified command and control for the operation, nor were there uniform rules of engagement for the various naval detachments. The British, Belgian, and Dutch navies cooperated closely in practice, but the French and Italian operations remained independent and entirely under national command and control.

The Gulf War: 1990–91

The second Gulf operation in 1990–91 suffered from a similar lack of coordination. Three weeks after Iraq's invasion of Kuwait on August 2, 1990, the WEU Council of Ministers met in extraordinary session, at the behest of the French presidency, to coordinate the member states' participation in the naval blockade of Iraq. The meeting was held pursuant to article 8 (3) of the modified Brussels Treaty and article 3 (4) of the Hague Platform which called on states to "concert . . . policies on crises outside Europe in so far as they may affect our security interests." On August 27 the Chiefs of Defense Staff of the WEU met in Paris to establish a three-tier working mechanism similar to the framework employed in the 1987 operation. However, the new procedures went beyond those used in 1987 in several respects, covering definition and performance of missions, definition of areas of action, coordination of deployments, exchange of information, mutual protection of shipping in the area, and logistic and operational support.[13] In the following weeks, seven of the nine WEU members deployed naval vessels to participate in the embargo against Iraq.

A closer look at the WEU naval operations, however, again reveals dangerous problems of coordination among forces from different member states. As of early September, the WEU had not resolved the fundamental issue of command and control. The French government pushed to establish a separate command and control under WEU auspices, leaving the non-European forces (U.S., Australian, and Canadian) to coordinate among themselves. The British, on the other hand, preferred closer cooperation with the United States. When the French plan was adopted in mid-September, the British departed to join forces with their English-speaking allies under U.S. command.[14]

The discord continued throughout the first months of the crisis. According to a Congressional Research Service report, western naval forces in the Gulf were still acting under national command at the end of December, and there was still "no formal command arrangement; a situation that would not suffice in the event of armed conflict."[15] The same report criticized the limited coordinating role played by the WEU, pointing out that the organization had not established an operational command arrangement.[16] The

Assembly of the WEU issued a similarly critical report, noting that the WEU forces did not possess an accepted tactical command structure and had not achieved coordination of national rules of engagement or logistic support functions.[17] The WEU operations suffered an additional setback on January 9, when the Dutch government decided to place its frigates under U.S. command in the event of war. This left the French with operational control over only Belgian and Spanish ships, in addition to their own.[18]

The effectiveness of the WEU operation in the Gulf was further hindered by the erosion of political consensus among members of the European Community and the WEU. As the use of force against Iraq became imminent, the members of the WEU split into two factions: an "Atlanticist" minority, notably Britain and the Netherlands, which was willing to stand behind the U.S. demand for unconditional Iraqi withdrawal from Kuwait; and a "Europeanist" majority, led by France, which was reluctant to use force in Kuwait and willing to consider a broader regional settlement with Iraq. When the Gulf War finally came, the Europeans fell in line with the U.S.-led coalition, but the divergence of views on the need for forceful intervention had undermined their solidarity. The British, French, and Italian forces, which ultimately participated in the air and ground campaigns, did so not as "WEU" forces, but as individual members of a UN-sanctioned coalition under joint U.S.-Saudi command.

The Former Yugoslavia: 1991–94

The story of the WEU's involvement in the former Yugoslavia is one of an inexperienced institution struggling to assert itself in the face of deep political divisions among its members. At various stages in the conflict, certain member states, most notably France, have pushed to give the institution a greater role and visibility in the context of a broader international response to the crisis. To a limited extent, these efforts have been successful, as the WEU is currently involved in sanctions enforcement operations in the Adriatic Sea and on the Danube River. More generally, however, the WEU has found itself unable to play a role because of the reluctance of Britain and other Atlanticist members to promote the WEU at the expense of other international organizations. In the end, when the time has come for air and ground operations, the international community and the Europeans themselves have turned to the more experienced United Nations and NATO for military and political leadership, leaving the WEU wholly removed from the peacekeeping and humanitarian operations in the region.

CONFLICT IN CROATIA: 1991–92. When war first broke out in Yugoslavia following the declarations of independence in Croatia and Slovenia in June 1991, the European Community (EC) was quick to fashion a response to the crisis. The European Council immediately dispatched a mediating mission to Yugoslavia, initiating an EC-sponsored peace process that would continue, largely in vain, throughout the summer and fall of 1991. At several different times during this period, European Community members discussed sending peacekeepers to Yugoslavia under WEU auspices, the idea being that the WEU would function as an implementing arm of the Community. As the peace process continued to falter, however, the WEU was unable to reach a consensus on the deployment of peacekeepers, and the responsibility ultimately fell to the United Nations, which sent the first peacekeeping forces to Croatia in March 1992.

The first concrete proposal for WEU involvement in the Yugoslav crisis came from the secretary-general of the WEU, Willem van Eekelen, in mid-July 1991. Van Eekelen suggested sending military observers to Croatia to replace a group of approximately forty civilians that had been sent by the Community to stabilize an agreed cease-fire. He argued that armed military observers would be both safer and more effective than civilians, and recommended sending a force of several hundred military personnel under the auspices of the WEU. At the time, however, the initiative received little support from EC foreign ministers.

At the end of July, France introduced a proposal for a full-scale peacekeeping force in Yugoslavia. The idea was to send a "European interposition force" under WEU auspices to act as a buffer between Croatians, Serbian guerrillas inside Croatia, and the Yugoslav army. The proposal received a mild endorsement from Luxembourg's foreign minister, Jacques Poos, who commented in early August: "We might need to consider some military interposition forces. . . . Up to now our mission was diplomatic and psychological. . . . But maybe the moment is not too far away when we have to go a step forward and even if the European Community does not have military forces at [its] disposal I could imagine we use the Western European Union for that purpose."[19]

There was little agreement, however, when EC foreign ministers met on August 6 to discuss the proposed WEU force. There were a variety of objections, but the strongest opposition to the proposal came from the British, who rejected any kind of armed intervention as long as the war continued. As one British minister commented, "you can't have peacekeepers if there's no peace to keep."[20] The result of the meeting was that the issue of military deployment was set aside for further study. The president of the European Community, Jacques Delors, credited the failure to reach a decision on peacekeeping to the Community's lack of maturity: "The Community is like an adolescent facing the crisis of adulthood. If the Community were 10 years older, there would have been an intervention force."[21]

The idea of a European peacekeeping force reemerged in mid-September at the urging of the Netherlands, France, and Germany. In early September, Dutch foreign minister van den Broek floated a proposal to send a "lightly armed" contingent of about five thousand troops to Yugoslavia under WEU auspices.[22] On September 18 France and Germany adopted a joint declaration seeking a more extensive peacekeeping force to establish buffer zones in Yugoslavia and calling on the United Nations to provide a mandate for such a force. The declaration was unclear as to which international organization would assume operational responsibility for the force, but the French later suggested that the WEU could play a leading role. The issue of a legal mandate was of particular importance to Germany, which viewed a Security Council resolution as a legal prerequisite to intervention as long as the fighting continued in Yugoslavia. German foreign minister Hans-Dietrich Genscher reasoned: "According to international law, the WEU would only have been able to become active with the unanimous agreement of all affected parties . . . [whereas] the UN Security Council can make decisions that are binding for all."[23] For France, however, the issue of a Security Council mandate was not legally conclusive. In an effort to keep European options open, President Mitterand publicly maintained that an EC or WEU force could be sent into a warring Yugoslavia even without such a mandate. According to Mitterand, a "political decision by the 12 [EC states] at the very highest levels" could authorize a WEU force in the absence of a UN mandate.[24]

At a meeting of EC and WEU foreign ministers on September 19, the Franco-German peacekeeping initiative was derailed almost single-handedly by British foreign minister Douglas Hurd. Hurd rejected the proposal outright, citing the dangers of ill-conceived military adventures and calling on his colleagues not to "exaggerate" what the European Community could achieve in Yugoslavia.[25] He added that even the active consideration of a peacekeeping force was unwise because it created the impression that an intervention was imminent when everybody knew that the conditions made it impossible. Denmark and Portugal also strongly opposed the peacekeeping idea, and the Netherlands, in spite of its own proposal for limited intervention in Yugoslavia, in the end appeared to side with the British. Italy was the only other WEU member to endorse the Franco-German proposal. The result of the meeting was a commitment by the WEU ministers not to intervene militarily in Yugoslavia without first achieving a durable cease-fire and the agreement of all Yugoslav parties, and a decision to convene an ad hoc working group of senior officials from the foreign and defense ministries of the WEU states to consider the practical conditions under which such an initiative could take place.[26]

By the end of September the members of the European Community turned to the United Nations for leadership. On September 25, at the urging of its European members, the Security Council imposed an arms embargo on Yugoslavia, and two weeks later, secretary-general Perez de Cuellar appointed former U.S. secretary of state Cyrus Vance as his special envoy to the region. At the end of October the secretary-general submitted a report to the Security Council calling the Yugoslav conflict a "threat to international peace and security," and from this point on, the United Nations assumed the leading role in the international peace process.

In early November, Serbia and Croatia finally both agreed to the deployment of international peacekeeping forces in Yugoslavia; however, Serbia made it clear that it would accept forces only from the United Nations, and not those from the European Community or the WEU.[27] Presumably this was because some members of the European Community, notably Germany, had alienated Serbia by suggesting recognition of the breakaway republics of Croatia and Slovenia. In spite of the position of the Serbs, the French government continued to advocate a central and visible role for the WEU in any force deployed to Yugoslavia.[28] Most of the other delegations disagreed, however, stating their preference for participation in UN peace-keeping on an individual country basis.

As the peace process accelerated during the next several months, the WEU faded quietly in the shadow of increasing United Nations involvement. On November 23 Cyrus Vance negotiated the first cease-fire in Yugoslavia with UN involvement. The Security Council authorized a force of some twelve to thirteen thousand UN peacekeepers on February 14, and deployment began on March 8. The United Nations retained full operational command over the forces, and the role of the WEU consisted of nothing more than the contributions of its member states.

CONFLICT IN BOSNIA: 1992–94. In spite of its failure to act in Croatia, the WEU again became a focus of attention following the outbreak of war between Serbs, Croats, and Muslims in Bosnia in April 1992. A week after the violence erupted, the WEU Assembly called on the member states of the organization to send a peacekeeping force to Bosnia under WEU auspices. By the end of April, France and Germany had circulated a proposal for such a force among their EC and WEU allies.[29] At the same time, the question of a WEU peacekeeping force was being raised in the United Nations. Under strong pressure from France, UN secretary-general Boutros-Ghali agreed to consider an arrangement whereby the task of peacekeeping in Bosnia could be "subcontracted" by the United Nations to the WEU, pursuant to article 53 of the UN charter, which allows for the use of "regional arrangements" to maintain international peace and security.[30]

The idea of a WEU force predictably met with opposition from several member states, notably Britain, and the United Nations rejected the idea of peacekeepers as long as the war continued.[31] WEU secretary-general van Eekelen was outspoken in his disappointment: "We recognised [the break-away republics] but at the same time we are not prepared to defend those countries. . . . Countries don't have the political will to intervene. . . . I can only express regret that my organisation was not used earlier."[32]

At the end of May the proponents of military action in Bosnia refocused the debate, calling for limited action short of full-scale peacekeeping. In Lisbon on May 24, western governments discussed the idea of sending international forces to reopen the airport in besieged Sarajevo and to establish Kurdish-style "protective enclaves" for civilians in Bosnia. Several weeks later Italy floated another proposal for military intervention, calling on its WEU partners to prepare for a naval and air blockade of Yugoslavia.[33] Seizing on the newly adopted Petersberg Declaration, which provided authority for the WEU to engage in crisis management and peace-making, the Italians stated their intention to seek Security Council authorization for military action against Serbia. The Italian proposal received a mild endorsement from German foreign minister Klaus Kinkel, but in the end, predictably, the proposal was blocked by Britain, which insisted that the Yugoslav conflict was under the jurisdiction of the United Nations and not appropriate for WEU action. At the time, senior British officials maintained that the Petersberg Declaration commitment to peace-making was "theoretical rather than practical."[34]

The members of the WEU finally reached a consensus in mid-July when they announced a decision to send warships and maritime patrol aircraft to monitor shipping in the Adriatic Sea as a means of enforcing the UN sanctions against Serbia and Montenegro. Although the Council stated that the operation would be "open to the participation of other allies and coordinated in cooperation with NATO," the decision was taken without formally consulting NATO.[35] NATO secretary-general Manfred Wörner immediately called a meeting in which the alliance announced its own decision to conduct "surveillance" operations in the Adriatic. In the following weeks, the WEU and NATO deployed two separate naval forces to the Adriatic, each with its own patrol aircraft overhead and each with its own command structure.[36] The two organizations established a sharing arrangement whereby the area to be monitored was divided into a north region and a south region, with the two forces taking turns patrolling each region. Under the terms of both missions, naval vessels and reconnaissance planes were to observe and report naval activity along the Yugoslav coast without authorization to take military action against violators of the sanctions.

Although hailed as an important success for the WEU, operation "Sharp Vigilance" in many respects exemplified the inadequacies of the international response to the crisis in Bosnia. In the first place, the operation failed to address effectively the problem of sanctions violations. Neither NATO nor the WEU had any powers of enforcement beyond surveillance, and, more important, the vast majority of the sanctions violations were occurring overland and on the Danube River, not in the Adriatic. Indeed, by the end of July it was estimated that Serbia was still carrying as much as 50 percent of its presanctions trade, mostly through leaks along the Danube and across Serbia's border with Greece.[37] A second problem was that the dual nature of the mission, with separate fleets and command structures, introduced dangerous and unnecessary operational inefficiencies. Although the WEU and NATO appointed a joint coordinating officer for each day (to ensure the "transparency and complementarity" of the operation), it was unclear what would have happened if a crisis had required the officer to seek orders from above and those orders had been different.[38] The needless inefficiency of this arrangement is evident if one considers, as defense analyst Lawrence Freedman pointed out at the time, that militarily there was little difference between the two forces: "The WEU in military terms is no more than a subset of NATO, without the latter's command and control structures, so in order to contrive this symbolic cooperation NATO forces and personnel are masquerading as WEU forces."[39] A third problem with the Adriatic operation was that it exacerbated an institutional tension between the WEU and NATO. Notwithstanding official assurances of perfect cooperation between the two organizations, the WEU mission was an assertion of European independence from NATO and, as such, represented something of a challenge to the alliance. At least one commentator suggested that this institutional competition may have precluded more forceful sanctions enforcement measures: "The armada is meaningless so long as it does not have the power to stop and search suspect vessels. For it to have that, we would need another UN resolution. And we do not want to have another UN resolution because we would then have to decide who should be mandated by the UN to do it. The WEU? NATO? The EC? The French would want the WEU mandated, while the British do not want to let go of NATO's role, and neither do the Americans, but the Americans don't want to have a row with the French."[40] The WEU's Adriatic mission can thus be viewed as an obstacle to effective international military action in Yugoslavia. In launching the mission, the WEU managed to demonstrate to a limited extent its independence from NATO. The result, however, was a stalemate situation in which it was politically impossible, at least in the short term, for either NATO or the WEU to take steps to enforce effectively the sanctions against Serbia.

As the fighting in Bosnia intensified during the summer of 1992, the international community turned its attention to securing humanitarian relief deliveries to Sarajevo and other besieged Bosnian cities, and initially it appeared that the WEU would rise to the challenge. At its meeting on July 10, the WEU Council endorsed the idea of a military operation to establish overland "humanitarian corridors" from Adriatic ports into Bosnia, and on July 31 the WEU ad hoc group of defense and foreign office officials met in Rome to draw up plans for such an operation. In early August, as the UN Security Council began to consider a resolution authorizing the use of force to secure humanitarian aid in Bosnia, the WEU's van Eekelen proposed that such a mission be run by the WEU and backed by U.S. air power. Van Eekelen suggested that NATO would not take charge of such an operation because of political differences among its members, presumably referring to the reluctance of the United States to commit ground troops to Bosnia. At the same time, the secretary-general of the United Nations was firmly opposed to any deeper UN involvement in Yugoslavia, arguing that scarce UN resources should not be spent on Yugoslavia at the expense of the situation in Somalia.[41] Boutros-Ghali thought that the European Community should take the lead in Bosnia, and he formally recommended that the Security Council "seek the help of European regional arrangements in meeting the demands for peace-keeping in the former Yugoslavia."[42] On August 13 the Security Council adopted a resolution authorizing the use of force to secure the delivery of humanitarian aid to Bosnia, and on the same day the WEU Council instructed its group of military experts to draw up detailed plans for the kind of ground forces and air cover an armed escort would require. Four days later the WEU Assembly called on Italy, which held the presidency of the organization, to convene an urgent meeting of the Council of Ministers to discuss WEU contributions to implementing the resolution.[43]

When the time came to implement its military plans, however, the WEU once again failed to reach a consensus. France and Italy were initially committed to finding a role for the organization in securing humanitarian aid deliveries, but other WEU members were slow to come forward with offers of military participation. By the end of August there was a growing sentiment that the operation should not be organized by either the WEU or NATO, but should be left to the United Nations. According to one NATO source, the reasoning was that a UN operation would be politically more acceptable to the warring factions in Bosnia.[44] Dutch foreign minister Hans van den Broek was more critical of the decision, however, suggesting that the move to the United Nations was because neither the WEU nor NATO had been able to get its act together.[45] One problem may have been Britain, which pledged 1,800 troops but earmarked them exclusively for use by the United Nations. In the end the task of protecting humanitarian aid convoys in Bosnia fell to the United Nations, which began deploying UNPROFOR II in September. The force consisted of 7,500 troops with the largest contributions from France, Britain, Spain, and Canada.

Unable to reach agreement on further direct military intervention in Bosnia, the UN Security Council voted on November 16 to tighten economic sanctions against Serbia and Montenegro. Resolution 787 called on states "acting nationally or through regional agencies or arrangements" to take necessary measures to stop shipments on the Adriatic and the Danube which would violate the UN-imposed economic sanctions and arms embargo.[46] On November 20 the WEU and NATO responded by imposing a full naval embargo against Serbia and Montenegro in the Adriatic. Under the new rules of engagement, the two allied fleets could stop and search vessels suspected of violating the sanctions, and could fire warning shots across the bows of ships that did not cooperate.[47] Soon after it came into effect, the embargo was heralded as a successful example of cooperation between the WEU and NATO. "Nothing can get through," commented the commander of the NATO Standing Naval Force, Admiral Enrico Martinotti, "the filter is so strict."[48]

The winter of 1992–93 witnessed continued disagreement among western allies on military strategy in Bosnia. In December the United States called for the aggressive use of air power to enforce a no-fly zone in Bosnia, but met with firm resistance from Britain and other states who were worried about the safety of their UN troops on the ground. At the same time, the WEU Assembly advocated a full-scale military intervention in Bosnia.[49] Secretary-general van Eekelen echoed the concerns of the Assembly: "Our credibility today is zero politically because we are just not doing anything. . . . What I am advocating . . . is that we limit our objectives but at least do credibly those things we say we want to do—that means the embargo, the humanitarian effort and the safe havens."[50] Van Eekelen went further to say that the WEU should act independently if necessary: "In principle, the WEU should maintain some autonomy. . . . If the U.N. couldn't act, I don't exclude some autonomous action."[51] In the end, however, the proposals of both the Assembly and the secretary-general were rejected out of hand by the members of the Council, most of whom maintained that Europe should wait patiently for the United Nations to take the lead on Bosnia.

Tensions between the WEU and NATO resurfaced during the spring of 1993, as western allies discussed proposals for implementing a peace plan developed by mediators Cyrus Vance and Lord Owen, which called for the division of Bosnia into seven to ten largely autonomous regions. Following an announcement by the United States of its willingness to commit ground troops to monitor the plan, the UN undersecretary-general for peace-keeping, Marrack Goulding, agreed in principle that NATO could act as a "subcontractor" to enforce an eventual peace plan under overall UN author-ity. In an apparent effort to preserve a role for itself in the Vance-Owen plan, the WEU Council decided to draw up its own plans for sending thousands of peacekeepers to Bosnia and for establishing a "safe haven" in Sarajevo. As both NATO and the WEU developed their plans during the following months, the issue of command and control of a future peacekeeping force became the subject of some disagreement. The United States and Britain, supported by NATO secretary-general Manfred Wörner, wanted NATO to have clear, overall control of the operation, acting as a subcontractor to the United Nations.[52] France, however, resisted the idea of full NATO control, arguing that a special UN coordinator should be appointed with responsibil-ity for the military operation, and that the WEU should have a role in the operation.[53] In the end the Vance-Owen plan was rejected by the Bosnian Serbs, and it faded from international discussion after the United States lost interest during the summer of 1993. Had it been accepted, however, the western allies would have faced the extraordinary task of implementing a complex agreement between enemies in Bosnia, while at the same time struggling to overcome their own deep-rooted divisions as to which institution should carry out the task.

In spite of the disagreements over peacekeeping, the WEU did manage to reach a consensus on expanding its role in sanctions enforcement. In April 1993, in response to requests from Romania, Bulgaria, and Hungary, the WEU Council of Ministers decided to send a "police and customs" mission to the Danube River to help enforce the sanctions against Serbia and Montenegro. The mission was to consist of at least eight speedboats and some three hundred armed police and was to be carried out under the auspices of the CSCE, which was coordinating sanctions enforcement on the Danube. Operations were to be undertaken in cooperation with Romania, Bulgaria, and Hungary, with joint teams of police and customs officers from WEU countries and the three riparian states. The controllers were authorized to stop and inspect barges but were to do so "without recourse to force."[54] The first WEU team arrived in Bulgaria in early June and the operation started soon thereafter.[55]

At the same time, the WEU's operational role in the Adriatic mission was reduced considerably. At the end of April 1993, NATO and the WEU agreed to strengthen the rules of engagement for their fleets in the Adriatic, after a Liberian ship laden with oil had tricked its way through the blockade and entered the Montenegrin port of Bar. Under the new rules, allied ships were permitted to pursue merchant vessels into coastal waters and to shoot holes in them as a last resort. Soon after the new rules came into effect, NATO military authorities proposed that the alliance take over full command of both fleets, arguing that a unified command was vital to ensure the safety of the ships and a quick response in the event of a threat. The proposal predictably met with resistance from the French. The disagreement was finally resolved on May 28 when NATO announced a "compromise" arrangement, under which the alliance would take over full command of the two fleets, but that command would report to the political authorities of both the WEU and NATO.[56] Secretary-general van Eekelen summed up the essence of the new arrangement: "This means that NATO will take over the job but that my organisation will maintain some visibility."[57]

The WEU's other notable role in Bosnia was the preparation and the implementation of a joint WEU–EU administrator for the city of Mostar. The administrator was deployed as part of an agreement to end fighting between the Bosnian Croats and Muslims. Unfortunately, the results of the administration in Mostar are inconclusive to date.

This part explores the future potential of the WEU as a peacekeeper in light of these realities of European politics. It focuses on the relationship between the WEU and three other institutional actors—NATO, the United Nations, and the European Union—in an effort to understand how the WEU might work more effectively with these other organizations and what kind of future peacekeeping role it might play.

Coordination with NATO

A key issue for the WEU will be the coordination and clarification of its heretofore uneasy relationship with NATO. If the WEU can cooperate more closely with NATO, both politically and militarily, then it potentially has a significant role to play as the European "pillar" of the Atlantic Alliance. Given some of the recent changes in the European security environment, there may well be situations in the future in which NATO is considered a politically inappropriate channel for military action—either because the United States is not prepared to intervene, or because Russia is unprepared to accept NATO forces in eastern Europe, or because the parties to a particular conflict are unwilling to accept NATO peacekeepers. In such cases the WEU could function as a more politically acceptable framework for military action involving NATO forces, assets, and command structures. Such an arrangement would allow the members of the WEU to act as a unified European force without duplicating NATO military structures and without competing with NATO on a political level. The main problem at this point is that the French have strongly resisted closer cooperation between the WEU and NATO, viewing such an arrangement as a subordination of the WEU to the U.S.-dominated Atlantic Alliance.

MILITARY COOPERATION AND COMBINED JOINT TASK FORCES. The most obvious limitation of the WEU is that it lacks a structured and effective military capability. When the WEU has acted, it has done so by hastily patching together forces from contributing countries, with the result that important issues of command and control have been blurred and confused. Thus far it has limited itself to naval operations, which are generally easier to coordinate and execute than air and ground operations, and yet it has still fallen short on a military operational level. Even the Adriatic mission, which has been heralded as a great success for the WEU, ultimately had to be turned over to the more experienced and efficient NATO command. Any attempt to carry out peacekeeping or protection operations on the ground in Yugoslavia would have suffered from the same command and control confusions, with the added problem that the WEU does not possess the communications and other support systems necessary to conduct such an operation.

The WEU Planning Cell in Brussels is currently working to improve the organization's procedures for military deployments. However, there has been no attempt as yet to move to the next level of military planning through integrated command structures or jointly held "WEU" military assets. The principal task of the Planning Cell has been to develop a database of all "forces answerable to the Western European Union" (FAWEUs). These forces should more correctly be termed forces "potentially available" to the WEU, as participation in an out-of-area WEU operation is still a decision to be made by each member state on a case-by-case basis. In the event that the Council decides on military action, the Planning Cell will assemble an appropriate force with units from participating member states. The idea is that the force will then be put under the command and control of a "lead nation," which will emerge as the political leader of the operation. The Planning Cell thereafter serves as a liaison between the Council and the lead nation command, but plays no direct role in the execution of the operation. The problem with this arrangement is that the WEU is still functioning in an ad hoc mode. The Planning Cell has made it easier for the WEU to assemble forces once a crisis has erupted, but it has not overcome the hurdle of military integration and the need for some sort of permanent military command structure.

If the WEU is to play a role in peacekeeping, it needs to improve its military capabilities in two respects. First, the organization needs to gain access to the basic military assets necessary to carry out effective peacekeeping operations. These include not only highly mobile air, ground, and naval forces from its members states, but also an array of transportation, intelligence, and communications support systems, many of which are not presently possessed by the WEU states. Second, the WEU needs to acquire a permanent integrated command and control structure specifically designed for peacekeeping. Future peacekeeping forces will consist of bits and pieces of existing larger force structures, and what is needed is a means of putting those bits and pieces together *before* a crisis erupts. The key to this type of coordination is command and control. A permanent structure will eliminate many of the operational confusions inherent in an ad hoc process and enable the organization to respond more rapidly to future conflict situations.

As a result of the NATO Summit in January 1994, both of these military objectives can be achieved by the WEU through closer cooperation with

NATO. The summit provided an important breakthrough in terms of military assets, as NATO agreed to make the full range of its collective assets available for WEU operations. NATO heads of state endorsed the concept of "separable but not separate" capabilities, whereby NATO forces and other assets could be separated out for use by the WEU, but would otherwise remain integral components of the alliance security structure.[58] The alliance pledged not only those assets operated by national forces from NATO countries (which have been used by the WEU in the past), but also those systems pooled by member states and operated by NATO itself. Among the most important assets are a fleet of early warning aircraft (AWACs) with mixed crews from different countries (including the United States) on each plane, fuel pipelines to allow for rapid deployment of armored and mechanized forces, communications facilities, real-time satellite information systems, and specialized staffs. It is likely that the WEU will also have access to NATO's long-range transport aircraft with air-to-air refueling capabilities, which the Europeans currently lack and which are especially important for out-of-area peacekeeping operations. With proper planning and coordination, the WEU's newly granted access to these assets could enable the organization to carry out effective air and ground operations, in addition to the more limited naval operations it has already conducted.

The 1994 NATO summit also provided a breakthrough in terms of developing a permanent command and control structure for peacekeeping, as the alliance decided to develop Combined Joint Task Forces (CJTFs) specifically designed for peacekeeping operations. The idea of the CJTFs is to create mobile and rapidly deployable integrated military units, with participation from both NATO and non-NATO countries, which could be used for peacekeeping and other conflict-prevention operations. As with other NATO assets, the CJTFs are to be implemented in a manner that would permit deployment under the auspices of NATO, the WEU, or the United Nations.

The concept of the CJTFs thus gives the WEU its first realistic opportunity to contribute positively to the cause of peacekeeping in eastern Europe. The "double-hatting" arrangement of the CJTFs would allow the WEU to deploy NATO peacekeeping forces under "WEU" auspices, with a European commanding officer, in cases where NATO (that is, the United States) is unprepared to act or where NATO is considered a politically unacceptable actor. The members of the WEU could take action through a unified European force without duplicating NATO military structures or competing politically with the Atlantic Alliance.

It seems unlikely, however, that the WEU will take advantage of the CJTFs in the near future, largely because of resistance from France. Although the French initially approved the NATO Summit declaration establishing the concept of the CJTFs, they have since effectively blocked implementation of the task forces. During the spring and summer of 1994, France held up discussions within NATO on the CJTFs and prohibited members of the WEU Planning Cell from participating in NATO meetings in Brussels concerning the task forces. In one such meeting, French political officials went so far as to demand the departure of several WEU military planners who had attended with the intention of developing an inter-institutional dialogue on the CJTFs.[59] The fear among French policymakers has been that participation in the integrated task forces would signal a realignment of France with the broader integrated military structures of NATO. France has been unwilling to be drawn back into a U.S.-dominated NATO and unwilling to allow the WEU to be subordinated to the Atlantic alliance through a "double-hatting" arrangement controlled by the Alliance.

POLITICAL COORDINATION. Implicit in the idea of a "double-hatting" arrangement such as the CJTFs is the notion that the actions of the WEU and NATO will be coordinated at the highest political levels. In the past the problem of political coordination between the WEU and NATO has been a source of considerable confusion. In the former Yugoslavia the relationship several times degenerated into an outright institutional rivalry. The WEU and NATO acted simultaneously in the Adriatic, with the absurd result that there were two separate command structures controlling ships from the same participating countries. Again, in the context of planning for the implementation of the Vance-Owen peace plan, the simultaneous participation of both institutions introduced potential operational inefficiencies as well as counterproductive political debates over the precise roles of the respective organizations.

The 1994 NATO Summit Declaration has proven an important conceptual step forward in harmonizing the relationship between NATO and the WEU; however, it has clearly not resolved some of the deeper political disagreements between the Atlanticist and Europeanist members of the two organizations. The Declaration set out a new design for the architecture of European security, defining the WEU both as the European "pillar" of the Atlantic Alliance and as an essential component of an emerging "European Security and Defense Identity."[60] This theoretical balancing act represents a compromise between the Atlanticists and Europeanists—in essence, it has been viewed as a French step toward NATO and a British acceptance of a future role for the WEU. The compromise established an important political link between the WEU and NATO in that it defines the WEU for the first time as a compatible "pillar" of NATO, rather than as an independent alternative to NATO. At the same time, however, there is an inherent tension in this dual definition, a tension that continues to fuel uncertainty about the relationship between NATO and the WEU within the architecture of European security.

The NATO Summit has also helped to improve the day-to-day political cooperation between the two organizations. Welcoming "the close and growing cooperation between NATO and the WEU that has been achieved on the basis of agreed principles of complementarity and transparency," the NATO heads of state decided that "in future contingencies, NATO and the WEU will consult, including as necessary through joint Council meetings, on how to address such contingencies."[61] The two organizations have established a regular mechanism for information exchange, and the two Councils have now met jointly several times at the ambassadorial level. The NATO Summit has also led to an important change in French policy toward NATO. France has now suggested that it would participate in some NATO defense ministers' meetings for the first time in nearly thirty years. As noted in the previous section, however, there are still serious problems of political coordination between NATO and the WEU. The fact that the French continue to block cooperation on the CJTFs clearly suggests that France is not yet truly committed to transparency and complementarity between the organizations.

The most important issue that has yet to be resolved is the question of which organization will have priority to act in a given situation. The prevailing view among NATO officials and most members of the alliance is that NATO should enjoy a right of first refusal in any situation requiring the deployment of allied military forces. If NATO chooses not to act—in the event, for example, the United States is not prepared to intervene directly— then the problem will pass to the WEU, which will generally have access to the full range of NATO assets. This view of the primacy of NATO has been endorsed by the United States, Britain, Germany, and the Netherlands, among others.

As the Yugoslavia experience illustrates, however, this hierarchical model of the WEU-NATO relationship has not been shared by all of the allies. France, in particular, has maintained that the WEU is free to act independently of NATO and that it can preempt NATO in a given situation. The French view is problematic because it opens the door to the kinds of operational and political confusions experienced in the former Yugoslavia, and because the WEU does not presently have the military capability to carry out certain peacekeeping operations without NATO support. Given that France remains outside of the NATO military planning structure, it is unlikely that it will agree in the near future to a model in which NATO retains the right of first refusal. At the same time, the fact that Britain and Germany have endorsed such a model will hopefully ensure that the WEU Council does not act independently of NATO. Still, in this unresolved issue there is lurking potential for future political and institutional gridlock.

Coordination with the United Nations

Lack of coordination between the WEU and the United Nations is another stumbling block. Two UN-related issues in particular need to be reexamined and resolved if the WEU is to contribute in the area of peace-keeping. The first concerns the legal relationship between the two organizations, and specifically, the extent to which a UN mandate should be a prerequisite for WEU operations. The second concerns the operational relationship between the WEU and the United Nations within the context of UN-sponsored peacekeeping missions.

The question of the legal requirements for WEU action was an issue of some debate during the conflict in Croatia in 1991. Britain and Germany, among others, argued that legal authorization from the UN Security Council was an absolute prerequisite to the WEU sending troops into a potentially hostile situation in the former Yugoslavia. France, on the other hand, maintained that the WEU could deploy troops even in the absence of a Security Council resolution, and even where those troops would be engaged in quasi-peace-making activities, such as establishing buffer zones between warring factions. French president Mitterand implied at the time that the WEU could rely on the legal authority of the European Community for such action. This disagreement created an institutional tension between the WEU and the United Nations, with some states pushing to assert the independence of the WEU and others looking to the United Nations for leadership. This institutional tension in turn had the effect of diverting attention away from the underlying political and strategic problems faced by the international community in the Balkans.

One solution to the legal problem would be for the WEU to establish formal links with the United Nations by declaring itself a "regional arrangement" within the meaning of chapter 8 of the UN Charter. Article 52 of the

Charter endorses the existence of "regional arrangements or agencies for dealing with such matters relating to the maintenance of international peace and security as are appropriate for regional action." Article 53 goes on to establish limits on the use of regional arrangements: "The Security Council shall, where appropriate, utilize such regional arrangements or agencies for enforcement action under its authority. But no enforcement action shall be taken under regional arrangements or by regional agencies without the authorization of the Security Council." There are at least two advantages to formally defining the WEU as a chapter 8 "regional arrangement." First, it would clarify the confused legal relationship between the two organizations and thereby preclude the kind of intra-WEU debate that occurred during the first Yugoslav conflict. In cases requiring out-of-area enforcement or peace-keeping operations, the WEU would always look first to the Security Council for authorization. Second, the requirement of Security Council authorization under article 53 would ensure that the WEU had clear authority for its actions under international law.

There are disadvantages, however, to linking the WEU and the United Nations in this manner. The principal legal problem is that such an arrangement could limit the scope of permissible actions that the WEU could take in the absence of a Security Council resolution. If the WEU were to declare itself a "regional arrangement" under chapter 8, then it would be defining itself as an instrument of the United Nations, with principal responsibility to the Security Council. The implication would be that the WEU could act only in very extreme cases without the authorization of the Security Council. If, on the other hand, the WEU continued to define itself as a collective defense organization independent of the UN, then it would arguably have greater legal and political leeway to take military action in "self-defense." For example, the WEU might justify intervening in Yugoslavia without UN authorization on the basis of a doctrine of collective self-defense. Such an argument would be more difficult to make if the WEU were formally linked to the UN as a "regional arrangement."

There are also political problems with defining the WEU as an instrument of the United Nations. The commitment of the Europeanist states to an independent European defense identity will not realistically permit the kind of subordination of the WEU to the United Nations that an article 52 regional arrangement entails. France, in particular, is not likely to accept an arrangement that gives the United States or any other permanent member of the Security Council a veto over WEU actions. One possible solution would be for the WEU to refrain from drawing formal links to the United Nations under chapter 8, but adopt a policy whereby it always looks first to the United Nations for authorization for military action. If the Security Council declines to consider a given situation, or if its decisionmaking process breaks down, then the WEU could proceed independently, but only in accordance with international law. A formal policy along these lines would go a long way toward clarifying the legal relationship between the WEU and the United Nations and would eliminate some of the disagreements that arose over action in the former Yugoslavia. Unfortunately, such a solution still might not satisfy the desire of the Europeanists for a truly independent European defense identity.

The second issue that needs to be addressed is what kind of operational role the WEU might play in peacekeeping missions once they have been authorized by the United Nations. At several different points during the Bosnian conflict, the WEU came forward with offers to participate in UN-sponsored operations, only to defer in the end to the operational control of the United Nations and NATO. In the summer of 1992 the WEU Council offered to establish humanitarian corridors in Bosnia after the idea had been approved by the Security Council; and in the spring of 1993 the WEU submitted its own plans for implementing the Vance-Owen peace plan. Again, in the fall of 1993, the WEU considered plans for humanitarian aid corridors in Bosnia. In each instance there was a faction within the WEU pushing for greater "visibility" for the organization, while other members argued that the task should be left to the United Nations (or in the case of the Vance-Owen plan, to NATO, acting at the request of the United Nations). While there is nothing inherently wrong with the WEU functioning as an implementing arm of the United Nations—indeed, during the summer of 1992, many in the United Nations would have been pleased if the WEU had been willing to carry out a humanitarian corridors operation—problems have arisen when certain states have tried to thrust the WEU into a UN peacekeeping operation that could otherwise be carried out more efficiently under a unified UN or NATO command. This kind of pressure for visibility, which was clearly evident during preparations for the Vance-Owen plan, has served only to cause confusion in military planning and to create needless institutional tensions between the WEU on one hand and the United Nations and NATO on the other.

The question, then, is how the WEU can make a positive contribution to UN peacekeeping operations while avoiding interinstitutional competition and confusion. There are at least three different scenarios in which the WEU could play a valuable role in UN-sponsored peacekeeping operations, assuming that it had the military capabilities to carry out such operations.

First, in cases where the United Nations has provided a mandate for military action but is not prepared to carry out the action itself, such as the mandate for the sanctions operation in the Adriatic, a regional organization like the WEU could function as a de facto implementing arm of the United Nations.

Second, in situations where the United Nations is considered by the parties to a conflict to be a politically inappropriate channel for peacekeeping action, either because of past problems with the United Nations in a particular region or perhaps because of resistance to U.S. or Russian influence on the Security Council, the WEU might be viewed as a more neutral and politically acceptable peacekeeping actor.

Third, there may be situations in which it is appropriate to establish a division of labor among peacekeeping organizations. One of the serious problems with the UN operation in the former Yugoslavia has been the divergence of interests between UN negotiators on the ground, UN military commanders, NATO decisionmakers, and individual NATO units, all of which come under the UN umbrella in Yugoslavia. NATO has generally had an interest in being forceful with the Serbs and thereby maintaining its credibility as a viable post–cold war defense organization. The United Nations, on the other hand, has had a strong institutional interest in not appearing to take sides in the war. Problems have arisen, in Goradze for example, where NATO issued an ultimatum to the Serbs, but left the United Nations with the decisionmaking power to enforce the ultimatum. The result of this arrangement has been political and military confusion and embarrassing inaction. One possible solution to the problem would be to effect a division of labor between the United Nations on one hand and regional organizations like NATO and the WEU on the other. The United Nations could address itself primarily to political negotiations and traditional peacekeeping, that is, neutral blue helmets sent into a situation after a peace agreement and cease-fire have been achieved. Other more aggressive tasks, such as sanctions enforcement and peace-making (such as the NATO ultimata and air strikes in Sarajevo and Goradze) could be carried out by NATO and the WEU. Given that future situations are likely to require elements of both carrot and stick, the WEU might find a role for itself as an occasional wielder of the stick, while leaving the more neutral United Nations to handle the carrot.

If the WEU is to play any kind of role as an implementing arm of the United Nations, what is needed is a coherent decisionmaking framework that would allow the member states of both organizations to determine when the WEU should participate in a given UN operation and in what capacity. Such a framework need not be hierarchical, but it should provide a clear mechanism for consultations between the WEU and United Nations on issues of peacekeeping and should set out clear guidelines for reaching decisions on those issues.

In the current European political environment, it is unclear whether this kind of framework for WEU-United Nations coordination is a realistic possibility. On one hand, the rivalry between the WEU and the United Nations has not been as politically volatile as that between the WEU and NATO. It may well be possible for the key actors—France, Britain, Germany, and the United States—to sit down and work out a rational blueprint for cooperation between the two organizations. On the other hand, the experience in the former Yugoslavia has not been encouraging. The competition between institutions for political visibility is still very much a preoccupation of European policymakers, even at the expense of a more effective response to ethnic conflict in eastern Europe. Moreover, it is clear that the issue of WEU-United Nations coordination is closely intertwined with the problem of WEU-NATO relations. The WEU will find a coherent role for itself within the UN framework only if it can overcome some of the hurdles preventing closer military and political cooperation with NATO.

The WEU and the European Union

The future potential of the WEU as a peacekeeper in eastern Europe will also be shaped in large part by its relationship with the European Union. While the WEU may have a role to play as a pillar of NATO or as an implementing arm of the United Nations, it might also play a very different role as the defense component of the European Union. The Europeanist members of the WEU envision the organization not merely as a political "label" for NATO or UN operations, but rather as the foundation of a truly independent European Security Community. Under this conception, the WEU would develop an integrated military capability of its own and would eventually be incorporated into the political framework of the European Union. The WEU would thus acquire an enhanced political status and would be neither militarily nor politically dependent on NATO. With the development of a common foreign and security policy within the European Union, the WEU would be in a much stronger position to take responsibility for peacekeeping in eastern Europe.

In several respects the groundwork is being laid for the WEU to become an effective defense component of the European Union. The British and French have agreed to take part in preparations for a common European defense policy to be introduced in the 1996 Intergovernmental Conference on the European Union, and there have been discussions of incorporating the WEU into the European Union at that time.[62] It is unlikely that a formal merger of the WEU and the European Union will take place as early as 1996 because Denmark and Ireland are not full members of the WEU and because security is still a sensitive question in the new accession countries. Still, there is a sense in Europe that the WEU will eventually become a part of the European Union.

The members of the WEU have also taken steps to develop a European military capability outside of the framework of NATO. The WEU's principle multinational military asset is the Eurocorps, an integrated European army corps established by France and Germany in 1992. The Eurocorps is in the process of being built up around a Franco-German brigade of 4,200 troops and is slated to have a force of 50,000 troops fully operational by 1995. Belgium, Spain, and Luxembourg have now joined, and Italy and the Netherlands have expressed interest. Hailed as the nucleus of a future European army, the Eurocorps has made itself available for peacekeeping and humanitarian missions under both WEU and UN auspices.

In addition to the Eurocorps, there have been other efforts to develop force structures and assets specifically designed for peacekeeping operations. In March 1994 French defense minister François Léotard proposed that the WEU set up a multinational European "intervention" force comprised of integrated air, land, and sea units and commanded by a European general staff. Linking his plan to an existing one for the creation of a French-Spanish-Italian aero-naval force, Léotard suggested that the new WEU intervention force could carry out peacekeeping operations with joint participation from eastern European states.[63] Also, in May 1994, France and Germany agreed to move ahead with the development of a military transport aircraft for the year 2000 which would enable European armed forces to carry out long-distance peacekeeping or humanitarian missions without being dependent on U.S. military aircraft.[64] The WEU in turn has commissioned a feasibility study on the need for such an aircraft to replace current military transports.

It is unlikely, however, that any of these military initiatives will provide the WEU with an effective peacekeeping capability in the foreseeable future. The Eurocorps is the closest thing in existence to a WEU army, and yet it is ill equipped to carry out peacekeeping or peace-making operations, which generally require highly mobile and rapidly deployable forces. At present the Eurocorps is a burdensome, defense-oriented force designed to fight a cold war battle, without any air or naval forces of its own. Moreover, the Eurocorps suffers from political divisions among the western allies. Viewed as an attempt by the French and Germans to circumvent NATO (which, essentially, it was), the Eurocorps initially elicited strong opposition from Britain and the United States. The tension was eased somewhat in early 1993, when Germany brokered a compromise whereby the Eurocorps would come under NATO command in the event of a war in Europe. Still, the British continue to be skeptical of the Eurocorps and have made no attempt to join.

There are also obvious problems with the idea of developing a WEU "intervention" force, which is essentially an attempt to create a combined joint task force outside of the framework of NATO. It is highly unlikely that the British would agree to the development of such a force, especially while the French continue to block the implementation of the CJTFs within NATO. In addition, it would be both costly and inefficient to duplicate structures that are already being developed by NATO and that will be available for use by the WEU.

More generally, there are a number of problems with the Europeanist conception of the WEU as an integral component of the European Union standing independent from NATO. Many of the Atlanticist states are still reluctant to develop military structures outside of the NATO context, and other states, such as Denmark and Ireland and the new accession states, are opposed to the very idea of a common defense policy. In addition, on an institutional level, the WEU and the European Union have not yet learned to coordinate their activities effectively. The WEU is not represented at meetings of the European Council when security relations are discussed, although it is represented at NATO Council meetings, and in general it has been noted by Secretary-General van Eekelen that present relations between the WEU and EU are "less satisfactory" than those between the WEU and NATO.[65]

In sum, the processes of European integration are likely to keep moving ahead, and there is a possibility that the WEU will be incorporated into the European Union, which would give it enhanced political clout and perhaps a greater role in peacekeeping. This kind of development would make it more difficult for the organization to function as a political subsidiary of NATO. Given the existing political situation, however, and the slow pace of integration and the problems of European political capabilities, it seems unlikely that the WEU will be able to play a peacekeeping role independent of NATO and the UN in the near future.

Conclusion

This chapter is based on the assumption that there will be a need for a peacekeeping component in the broader processes of conflict prevention, and it has focused on the question of whether the WEU can and should play a role in providing that component. The underlying problem, which is addressed only peripherally, is the issue of substantive policy in situations of ethno-national conflict, that is, how the international community, and specifically the western Europeans, reach substantive decisions on the need for peace operations in conflict situations. Before the WEU, NATO, the United Nations, or any other organization can carry out an effective peace-keeping mission, there needs to be a substantive decision on the political and military objectives of the mission. With the United States less willing to provide superpower leadership in eastern Europe, the burden of making that decision is now falling on the Common Foreign and Security Policy mechanism of the European Union. In the end the effective deployment of a peacekeeping component will depend on the extent to which the western Europeans can use this mechanism to coordinate their substantive policies in eastern Europe.

Notes

1. The nine members are Britain, France, Germany, Italy, Belgium, the Nether-lands, Luxembourg, Spain, and Portugal. Greece has signed a Treaty of Accession, which has yet to be ratified by all of the other members of the WEU.

2. Western European Union Council of Ministers, *Petersberg Declaration on WEU and European Security,* Bonn, June 19, 1992.

3. Treaty of Economic, Social and Cultural Collaboration and Collective Self-Defence, March 17, 1948.

4. Treaty of Economic, Social and Cultural Collaboration and Collective Self-Defence, signed at Brussels on March 17, 1948, as amended by the 'Protocol Modifying and Completing the Brussels Treaty,' signed at Paris on October 23, 1954 (hereafter Modified Brussels Treaty), article 5.

5. Modified Brussels Treaty, article 5.

6. Modified Brussels Treaty, article 6.

7. See Rome Declaration of October 27, 1984, and Platform on European Security Interests, The Hague, October 27, 1987.

8. Article J4, Maastricht Treaty on European Union.

9. At the time the Treaty was signed, the WEU ministers issued their own declaration in support of its provisions: "WEU Member States agree to strengthen the role of the WEU, in the longer term perspective of a common defence policy within the European Union which might in time lead to a common defence, compatible with that of the Atlantic Alliance." *Declaration of the Member States of the Western European Union,* Maastricht, December 10, 1991.

10. Western European Union Council of Ministers, *Petersberg Declaration on WEU and European Security,* Bonn, June 19, 1992.

11. *Declaration of the Heads of State and Government Participating in the Meeting of the North Atlantic Council Held at NATO Headquarters, Brussels, on 10–11 January 1994, Europe Documents,* no. 1867, January 12, 1994 (hereafter 1994 NATO Summit Declaration).

12. See Mathias Jopp and Wolfgang Wessels, "Institutional Frameworks for Security Cooperation in Western Europe: Developments and Options," in Mathias Jopp, Reinhardt Rummel, and Peter Schmidt, eds., *Integration and Security in Western Europe: Inside the European Pillar* (Boulder: Westview Press, 1991), pp. 25, 32.

13. Willem van Eekelen, "WEU and the Gulf Crisis," *Survival,* vol. 32 (November–December 1990), pp. 519, 526.

14. See Thomas-Durrell Young, *Preparing the Western Alliance for the Next Out-of-Area Campaign: Linking NATO and the WEU* (Strategic Studies Institute, U.S. Army War College, April 15, 1991), p. 10.

15. Steven R. Bowman, *Iraq-Kuwait Crisis: Summary of U.S. and Non-U.S. Forces,* CRS Report for Congress, No. 90–639 F, December 27, 1990, p. 19, as quoted in Young, *Preparing the Western Alliance,* p. 11.

16. Ibid.

17. Assembly of the Western European Union, *Consequences of the Invasion of Kuwait: Continuing Operations in the Gulf Region, Report, Document 1248,* Paris, November 7, 1990, p. 14.

18. Young, *Preparing the Western Alliance,* p. 11.

19. "European Military Intervention Possible in Yugoslavia, Poos Says," *Reuters,* August 1, 1991.

20. "Europe and Yugoslavia," *Economist,* August 10, 1991.

21. "Failure to Send Force to Yugoslavia Shows EC Immaturity—Delors," *Reuters,* September 2, 1991.

22. Michael Evans, "Western European Union Split on Special Mission to Yugoslavia," *The Times,* September 18, 1991.

23. *Der Standard,* September 24, 1991, p. 2 (FBIS-WEU-91–185, September 24, 1991, p. 7), cited in James B. Steinberg, *The Role of European Institutions in Security after the Cold War: Some Lessons from Yugoslavia* (Santa Monica, Calif.: Rand, 1992), p. 24.

24. Alexander Ferguson, "Mitterand Wants U.N. Mandate for Yugoslavia Force," *Reuters,* September 19, 1991.

25. Andres Wolberg-Stok, "EC Backs Off On Yugoslavia Troops But Sheds Weakling Image," *Reuters,* September 20, 1991.

26. "WEU Lays Down Very Stringent Conditions for Sending Forces into Yugoslavia to Protect the European Observers," *Agence Europe,* September 21, 1991.

27. Ian Traynor and Hella Pick, "UN Peace Force Possible if Fighting Stops," *Reuters,* November 15, 1991.

28. "WEU to Present a Report on Yugoslavia on 2 December," *Agence Europe,* November 19, 1991.

29. Tony Barber and Tim Jackson, "French Push for Action over Yugoslavia," *Independent,* May 2, 1992.

30. Leonard Doyle and Andrew Marshall, "United Nations Secretary-General May Urge Western European Union to Take Peace Role," *Independent,* April 30, 1991.

31. *Further Report of the Secretary-General Pursuant to Security Council Resolution 749* (1992), UN Doc. S/23900, (1992).

32. Andres Wolberg-Stok, "WEU Chief Chides EC for Lack of Will to Use Force," *Reuters,* May 21, 1992.

33. Peter Almond and Tony Catterall, "WEU Agrees to Form Troubleshooter Force," *Daily Telegraph,* June 20, 1992.

34. John Eisenhammer, "Fight over Role of WEU in Yugoslavia," *Independent,* June 20, 1992.

35. *WEU Council Decision, Extraordinary Meeting of WEU Council of Ministers on the Situation in Yugoslavia, Helsinki,* July 10, 1992.

36. "WEU Assembly Calls for Plans for a European Military Operation in Bosnia-Herzegovina," *Agence Europe,* December 4, 1992.

37. "When Will They Call It Peace?," *New York Times,* August 1, 1992, p. 37.

38. "WEU Versus NATO in the Adriatic—When Europeans Unravel," *Economist,* August 1, 1992.

39. Nicholas Doughty, "What Are the West's Warships Doing Near Yugoslavia?," *Reuters,* August 5, 1992.

40. Annika Savill, "The Real Game Has Little to Do with Balkan Conflict," *Independent,* July 22, 1992.

41. Paul Lewis, "U.S. and Allies Divided over Role of U.N. Forces," *New York Times,* August 9, 1992, p. 12.

42. Anthony Goodman, "U.N. Likely to Leave Bosnia If Use of Force Approved," *Reuters,* August 7, 1992.

43. "WEU Assembly Calls for Ministers' Meeting on Yugoslavia," *Reuters,* August 17, 1992.

44. Nicholas Doughty, "NATO to Discuss Military Plans for Yugoslavia," *Reuters,* August 24, 1992.

45. Ibid.

46. S.C. Res. 787, 3137th mtg., U.N. Doc. S/RES/787 (1992). The resolution was adopted pursuant to chapter 7 and chapter 8 of the UN Charter.

47. "Rules of Engagement to Reinforce Embargo in the Adriatic," *Agence Europe,* November 21, 1992.

48. John Phillips, "NATO Answers Critics with Sea Blockade Success," *The Times,* December 3, 1992.

49. "WEU Assembly Calls for Plans for a European Military Operation in Bosnia-Herzegovina," *Agence Europe,* December 4, 1992.

50. "West Has Zero Credibility in Bosnia—WEU's Van Eekelen," *Reuters,* December 8, 1992.

51. Nicholas Doughty, "WEU, in Yugoslavia Row, Holds First Brussels Meeting," *Reuters,* January 19, 1993.

52. Nicholas Doughty, "NATO Worried by Confusion over Command for Bosnia Force," *Reuters,* March 1, 1993.

53. Ibid.

54. "WEU Council to Take Part in 'Police and Customs' Operations Along Danube," *Agence Europe,* April 6, 1993.

55. WEU Says It Now Helping Police Danube Traffic," *Reuters,* June 9, 1993.

56. Nicholas Doughty, "NATO Agrees It Could Use Air Power to Defend Bosnia Zones," *Reuters,* May 28, 1993.

57. Nicholas Doughty, "NATO Expected to Take Command of Adriatic Naval Force," *Reuters,* May 27, 1993.

58. 1994 NATO Summit Declaration, para. 5–6.

59. Interview with a member of the WEU Planning Cell, May 1994.

60. 1994 NATO Summit Declaration, para. 5–6.

61. Ibid., para. 5.

62. John Palmer, "Britain Joins Defence Policy Talks," *Guardian,* May 10, 1994.

63. Bernard Edinger, "Léotard Suggests Wider European Intervention Forces," *Reuters,* March 3, 1994. Italy had floated a similar proposal in 1993.

64. "Paris, Bonn Press Ahead with Military Transport Plane," *The Reuter European Community Report,* May 31, 1994.

65. "French Defense Minister Léotard Proposes Summit Meeting of WEU," *Agence Europe,* March 5, 1994.

Part Five

TEN

The Role of the United Nations in European Peacekeeping

Shashi Tharoor

FEW EUROPEAN analysts of international affairs at the end of the 1980s would have predicted that, at the end of 1994, a majority of the peacekeepers deployed by the United Nations across the world would be based in Europe, nor that the world organization would be spending more money on peacekeeping in Europe than in all the other continents put together.

And yet that is precisely where the United Nations finds itself today. It has three peacekeeping operations in Europe—the United Nations Peace-Keeping Force in Cyprus (UNFICYP), the United Nations Protection Force (UNPROFOR) in the former Yugoslavia, and the United Nations Observation Mission in Georgia (UNOMIG)—employing, as of October 31, 1994, a total of some 40,000 infantry, 730 military observers, more than 730 civilian police, and 4,200 civilian staff. (One might suggest that in fact the correct total of operations should be five, because UNPROFOR, by far the largest peacekeeping operation in the history of the United Nations, is arguably three distinct and different operations labeled as one.) The United Nations plans to spend some 70 percent of its estimated $3.3 billion global peacekeeping budget on these three operations. And other European conflicts appear to be, if not quite on the anvil, edging ominously close to it.

The views expressed in this chapter are personal and do not necessarily represent the views of the UN. This chapter was originally presented as a paper at the conference on "Peacekeeping in Europe—Assessing UN and Regional Initiatives" (November 17–18, 1994), organized by NUPI (the Norwegian Institute of International Affairs) as a part of the institute's Ford Foundation program on Second Generation Peacekeeping Operations. A version of this chapter was also published in *Survival,* vol. 37, (Summer 1995), pp. 121–34, under the title "The United Nations and Peacekeeping in Europe."

This phenomenon raises a number of questions. What are the character-istics of United Nations peacekeeping in Europe? What issues arise from the contemporary United Nations experience in that continent? What are the challenges the United Nations confronts as it grapples with these issues? This chapter attempts to address each of these questions in turn.

Characteristics of United Nations Peacekeeping in Europe

Peacekeeping is defined by the United Nations as "a United Nations presence in the field (normally including military and civilian personnel), with the consent of the parties, to implement or monitor the implementation of arrangements relating to the control of conflicts (cease-fires, separation of forces etc.) and their resolution (partial or comprehensive settlements), and/or to protect the delivery of humanitarian relief."[1] The last element of this 1994 definition is new; the rest can fairly be described as reflecting what has come to be called "traditional peacekeeping." But traditional peacekeeping is only one of the activities that today's United Nations peacekeepers have been called upon to undertake. For the purposes of this chapter, I would argue that United Nations peacekeepers in Europe are engaged in five different, though sometimes overlapping, kinds of activity:

—*Traditional peacekeeping* (UNFICYP, UNOMIG, and UNPROFOR in Croatia): the monitoring of cease-fire arrangements, including through patrolling, observation, and interposition between hostile armies, pending a negotiated political settlement to the conflict.

—*Preventive deployment* (UNPROFOR in the former Yugoslav Repub-lic of Macedonia): the deployment of peacekeepers to perform observation functions in order to deter rather than to help resolve conflict.

—*Observation of a non-UN peacekeeping force* (UNOMIG): the de-ployment of United Nations military personnel tasked to observe the func-tioning of a peacekeeping force established outside United Nations auspices (in this case, by the Commonwealth of Independent States) in order to monitor and verify the implementation of a cease-fire agreement.

—*Humanitarian relief* (UNPROFOR in Bosnia and Herzegovina): the deployment of United Nations peacekeepers to ensure and protect the delivery of humanitarian aid to civilians in the midst of an ongoing conflict, not necessarily with the consent of the parties through whose territories the aid must be delivered.

—*Conflict mitigation* (UNPROFOR in Bosnia and Herzegovina): the deployment of United Nations peacekeepers tasked to mitigate the nature and course of an ongoing conflict by limiting the parties' recourse to certain military means (in this case, maintenance of an interdiction on the use of aircraft for combat purposes) or to attacks upon certain cities (protection of "safe areas"), in both cases backed by the threat of military force provided by a regional organization (NATO).

Two of these activities, preventive deployment and what I have called conflict mitigation,[2] are unique to Europe; of the other three, two have been practiced only to a limited extent elsewhere (UNOMIL observes a regional peacekeeping force, ECOMOG, in Liberia, and UNOSOM has till recently protected humanitarian relief deliveries in Somalia). The tasks undertaken by United Nations peacekeepers in Europe are therefore at the forefront of the evolution, and indeed the ongoing redefinition, of United Nations peacekeeping as an activity of the world organization.

The context in which the United Nations conducts peacekeeping operations in Europe includes the following distinctive elements.

Existence of regional organizations and arrangements. Europe is richly endowed with groupings of states, capable of playing a significant role in the implementation of a peacekeeping mandate: NATO, the European Union, the Western European Union, the Organization for Security and Cooperation in Europe, and the Commonwealth of Independent States (CIS). The presence of these entities and their willingness to engage, to a greater or lesser degree, in activity on the ground both supports and delimits United Nations action.

Involvement of regional powers. The traditional United Nations reluctance to permit the participation of neighboring states or states with special interests in United Nations peacekeeping operations has proved difficult to uphold in Europe. It has not been possible for the United Nations to find an adequate number of troops sufficiently trained, equipped, and politically willing to participate in these operations, whereas European states themselves have sought eagerly to serve. Britain, which as the former colonial power maintains sovereign bases in Cyprus, is a key member of UNFICYP, Turkey of UNPROFOR, and Russia of UNOMIG (not to mention the CIS forces monitored by it), all despite obvious national and historical interests in these issues.

Situations of civil war or internal conflict. All three operations are deployed within the borders of sovereign states recognized by the international community and members of the United Nations. The conflicts in all cases involve civilians who have lived together in a single society in the past and who have been pitted against each other in the course of warfare fought for political ends. They also involve opposing military forces organized largely along ethnic lines, which enjoy some degree of external support, and the presence of a mixture of both governmental and nongovernmental factions, many with little military experience, training or discipline.

Strong presence of public pressure and media interest. All these operations, and in particular UNPROFOR, involved considerable local and international media attention at their start, which contributed to the perception by international decisionmakers that they were obliged to respond, and which limited the options of the international community.

High political and diplomatic stakes. The public visibility of the crises in which these operations were deployed has helped raise the political and diplomatic stakes of the major powers involved, with direct consequences for these operations, crucial aspects of which (for example, the proclamation of "safe areas" in UNPROFOR) were primarily predicated upon political–diplomatic rather than military–operational considerations.

Limited or no progress toward an overall political solution. In all these cases, the political solution of the overall conflict, which might bring the peacekeeping operation to an end, has proved remote or elusive. Though the operations have been conducted with a view to maintaining peace or promoting its restoration pending the outcome of political negotiations, the absence of a clearly visible political "end-game" has clouded the functioning and prospects of all these operations.

Issues Arising from UN Peacekeeping in Europe

As recently as two years ago, it was fashionable to speak of a "renaissance of peacekeeping," as the end of the cold war brought about an unprecedented degree of agreement in the Security Council. As the superpowers authorized the United Nations to intervene in situations and in areas to which they would never have admitted the world body in the past, its secretary-general, Boutros Boutros-Ghali, spoke of a "crisis of too much credibility." In implementing many of these new operations, however, the United Nations has found itself confronting a crisis of mandate (over the tasks it has been called upon to perform), a crisis of method (over the manner in which it has attempted to fulfill these tasks), and a crisis of means (over the resources needed to execute them). As a result, and particularly as a result of its operation in Bosnia and Herzegovina, the United Nations once again confronts a crisis of credibility, this time of too little, rather than too much.

In the process, some of the fundamental principles of United Nations peacekeeping have been called into question. While it is difficult to disentangle issues arising from, say, the UN's experience with UNPROFOR from those that emerged in the course of the UN's parallel efforts in Somalia and Rwanda, it is fair to suggest that the UN's current experience in Europe throws into sharp relief problems clustering around three major axes: what one may call the "United Nationsness" of peacekeeping, the UN's relations with the parties, and the issue of the use of force.

The "United Nationsness" of peacekeeping was traditionally derived not only from the establishment of UN operations by a UN body, usually the Security Council, but also from several of the arrangements that underpinned such operations: collective financing by member states of the United Nations as an activity of the Organization, the deployment of troops from a variety of UN member states with a wide geographical spread, and, perhaps most important, the fact that these troops were under the operational command of the secretary-general. Recent experience in Europe has involved significant exceptions to all these arrangements. UNPROFOR in Bosnia and Herzegovina was, for several months, financed by the participating states themselves, with lingering consequences for the command and control of the Force.[3] Until very recently, the Force in Bosnia and Herzegovina was constituted overwhelmingly of troops from west European countries (though the size of their majority has been diluted in the course of 1994 by the arrival of a large number of troops from Muslim countries). In Georgia the United Nations has left the bulk of the peacekeeping burden on the shoulders (and on the soldiers) of the Russian Federation. In Cyprus the Force was, for nearly three decades, financed by voluntary contributions alone; only recently, and that too after an initial Russian veto, has the Security Council agreed to finance the operation under the standard United Nations scale of assessments. But even here a substantial portion of UNFICYP's costs are provided by voluntary contributions, not least by the government of Cyprus. Finally, the absence of the great powers—the five Permanent Members of the Security Council—from United Nations peacekeeping operations was itself a sign of "United Nationsness," often seen as the nonthreatening military intervention of middle and smaller powers under an international flag. All three United Nations peacekeeping operations in Europe, however, feature the active (and sometimes predominant) involvement of Permanent Members of the Security Council. In Europe, more so than in any other continent, the notion of the "United Nationsness" of peacekeeping seems strained.

This is exacerbated in the case of UNPROFOR by its relations with, and reliance upon, NATO. Whereas a handful of United Nations military observers located at an assortment of airfields monitor the no-fly zone on the ground, the interdiction of violators, and the enforcement of the Security Council's ban on flights, is actually undertaken by NATO. So are the attacks from the air that, on five occasions so far, have been called in by UNPROFOR. Though Council resolutions speak of NATO acting in "support of UNPROFOR in the performance of its mandate,"[4] NATO has made it clear that, in the words of its new secretary-general, it is not a "sub-contractor of the United Nations"[5] and has its own credibility to be concerned about. Indeed, the North Atlantic Council has on two occasions proclaimed heavy weapon "exclusion zones" around Bosnian towns which the United Nations troops on the ground have helped maintain, even without any explicit Security Council authorization for the concept. The problem of competing credibilities is a particularly serious one between an organization designed to fight war and another dedicated to keep peace. Differences publicly aired between NATO and the United Nations about the nature and extent of the use of air power in Bosnia and Herzegovina have inevitably questioned the degree to which the United Nations can, in these circumstances, expect to control the military environment within which its forces are functioning. While common ground has so far been found, the principle of United Nations primacy remains to be fully endorsed by all concerned.

The second cluster of issues concerns relations with the parties to the conflicts in which United Nations peacekeepers intervene. Traditionally, peacekeeping operations upheld, monitored, or implemented agreements between or among warring parties, and where such agreements were not available, functioned on the basis of agreements by the parties as to their presence and role; United Nations peacekeepers worked with the legal consent and the practical cooperation of all sides to the conflict; they acted with impartiality, and without prejudice to the rights and claims of any side. United Nations peacekeepers in UNPROFOR have found that this traditional anchor has dragged and the peacekeeping ship has slipped its moorings. There are no lasting agreements in Bosnia and Herzegovina, and when ad hoc agreements are reached, they are violated as routinely as they are signed. The Force has never enjoyed the explicit consent of the Bosnian Serbs to its composition[6] or activities, and receives at best the grudging cooperation of the parties; obstruction of UNPROFOR by all sides is common, and attacks upon it are frequent. While it seeks to be impartial, some of its mandates place it in the position of thwarting the military objectives of only one of the parties. (As the government of Bosnia and Herzegovina mounts successful attacks upon the Bosnian Serbs which the latter may be unable to counter without incurring UN-mandated NATO air strikes, this impartiality is likely to look increasingly threadbare.)

In any case, international opinion, including that of many members of the Security Council, gives short shrift to UNPROFOR's impartiality; analysts and editorialists demand how UNPROFOR can be impartial between "aggressors" and their victims, between "ethnic cleansers" and terrorized civilians, between a recognized government and its reviled besiegers. Impartiality is essential for peacekeepers, but it is not easily maintained when there is no peace to keep, and ongoing events demand daily responses. In the context within which it functions, UNPROFOR cannot credibly claim that its work is entirely without prejudice to the claims and aspirations of the Bosnian Serbs; yet many of its humanitarian tasks cannot be performed without their active day-to-day cooperation. As calls mount for it to take "robust" action against violations of Security Council resolutions and respond in a "muscular" manner to obstructions of its humanitarian relief efforts, the basic assumptions about how peacekeepers function in relation to the parties are stretched to the breaking point.

Linked to this conundrum is the third set of problems, concerning the use or, more appropriately in peacekeeping, the nonuse of force. United Nations peacekeepers are traditionally either unarmed observers or lightly armed infantry who use force only in self-defense, who have no enemies and are deployed not to win a war but to help warring parties end one. In UNPROFOR, however, their equipment, including tanks and machine-gun-mounted armored personnel carriers (APCs), vastly exceeds that of any prior peacekeeping force except that in Somalia; and some battalions in Bosnia and Herzegovina have not hesitated to use their weapons, particularly to eliminate snipers. What I have termed conflict mitigation has for the first time made force an explicit part of a peacekeeping mandate, with the threat of its use central to the peacekeepers' ability to fulfill their responsibilities. The use of air power has brought in an additional dimension, unprecedented in peacekeeping elsewhere. Whether such threat (and use) of force is compatible with existing peacekeeping principles is debatable; what is clear is that the United Nations is walking a very taut (and swaying) tightrope between peacekeeping, which requires consent,[7] and peace enforcement, an ill-defined concept practically indistinguishable from warfighting.[8] But wars are not (and cannot effectively be) fought in blue helmets and out of white-painted APCs; so in its newfound capacity to be forceful, UNPROFOR has constantly to be careful not to trip over the fine line that separates peace from war and peacekeeping from disaster.

It has been suggested by some that such doctrinal confusion is unnecessary, and that conflict-mitigation tasks, involving the use of force, are simply not peacekeeping and do not need to be reconciled with it.[9] The problem is, however, that the Security Council has given such tasks to *peacekeepers,* as part of an operation in which they have also been given tasks that require them to cooperate closely with all parties. To suggest that peacekeeping rules need not apply to nonpeacekeeping tasks is somewhat sophistical if those tasks are allocated to peacekeepers in a peacekeeping operation whose very viability could be undermined by the pursuit of peace-enforcement methods.

To summarize, the United Nations' experience in peacekeeping in Europe has thrown fundamentally into question the existing principles and practices relating to United Nations control, financing, and composition of peacekeeping operations; to the traditional requirement for the consent and cooperation of the parties, and for United Nations impartiality between them; and to the nonuse of force to achieve the ends established by the mandate. These are crucial developments that are bound to have a profound effect on the nature of United Nations peacekeeping worldwide in the years to come.

The Challenges for United Nations Peacekeeping in Europe

In reacting to the problems identified above, the United Nations may be said to be facing a series of challenges that I would describe as "the eight c's." These challenges are all interconnected; they overlap and reinforce each other; and in my view, they are central to the efforts of the United Nations to cope with the demands of peacekeeping in a changing world. These "eight c's" are the challenges of capacity, cooperation, command, coercion, choice, credibility, contributions, and the common cause.

The challenge of capacity relates to the ability of the United Nations to deploy and manage peacekeeping operations, in Europe or elsewhere, to the satisfaction of the Security Council and the troop-contributing nations. Large and complex operations require to be supported, supplied, and spoken up for in international councils; the difference from the past is not just one of degree but of kind. The Secretariat has taken several significant steps in the last two years to enhance its capacity, notably through the establishment of a twenty-four-hour-a-day, seven-day-a-week Situation Center to maintain constant communications with, and instant responsiveness to, the field; the creation of new units for planning, training, and logistics support; the merger into the Department of Peacekeeping Operations of the former Field Operations Division of the Department of Administration and Management, thus largely eliminating a dual chain of command from Headquarters to the field; and the creation of a Standby Forces roster of troops and equipment available for peacekeeping (though governments with earmarked assets still have to agree to make them available when required, and in the case of Rwanda all those who had theoretically offered standby forces declined to provide them).

The challenge of cooperation is particularly relevant in Europe, which offers so many entities with which to cooperate. There is no doubt that the United Nations—despite the general authorizations granted in articles 24 and 39 of the Charter that grant it predominance over any regional organizations,[10] and despite the improvements in its capacity—will continue to need partners, particularly to help ease the financial and resource burden it bears. The European institutions mentioned at the beginning of this chapter are also likely to be able both to respond more quickly to problems in Europe and to bring special insights to bear upon them. The newly rebaptized Organization for Security and Cooperation in Europe (OSCE) could, in future, serve as the instrument of first resort in meeting European peacekeeping challenges. Cooperation between the United Nations and the European Community Monitoring Mission in the former Yugoslavia has been exemplary; that with NATO has involved a few hiccups, related primarily to differing organizational cultures and mission perceptions, but the few problems that have arisen have been resolved without undue difficulty. Indeed, NATO secretary-general Manfred Wörner predicted a future of "frequent and close co-operation between the UN and NATO."[11] Cooperation with the CIS in Georgia is still in its embryonic stages but has so far occurred smoothly. Provided that cooperation is in all cases conducted under the authority of the Security Council and in accordance with its resolutions, the "challenge of cooperation" is one to which it is in the interests of the United Nations to rise.

Of course, there is certainly a danger that some regional organizations may be too close to the problems they seek to resolve and may be unable to bring to bear the advantages of detachment and impartiality that characterize United Nations involvement. In such cases there is a risk that a regional organization could either become a vehicle for a new hegemony or that its intervention might make it a party to the conflict rather than a means to its resolution.[12] The United Nations has a valuable role to play in cooperation with such regional organizations to ensure that international standards are met and that the larger interests of the world community take precedence over more narrowly defined priorities. But such a proposition is fraught with pitfalls, as will be readily apparent to anyone who attempts to read the three preceding sentences twice, with a different organization (say, NATO and the CIS) in mind each time.

The challenge of command is a more complex matter. For decades the United Nations Secretariat assumed, almost without needing to say it, that troops provided for its peacekeeping operations were under the command and control of the secretary-general. This proposition was even conveyed to the General Assembly in the text of a Model Agreement with Troop Contributing Countries.[13] Subsequently, however, member states have found it more convenient to speak of granting "operational control" to the secretary-general of troops provided to him for peacekeeping operations.[14] The debate has gone beyond that point: a former senior Secretariat official has recently argued that the business of commanding troops belongs not to the Secretariat but, according to the Charter, to member states and specifically those on the Security Council and the Military Staff Committee.[15] In practice, it is fair to say that the Secretariat has tended largely to leave command in the hands of the commanders in the field, providing guidance of a primarily political nature; but that as United Nations peacekeeping operations have increased in complexity and risk, member states have strengthened their lines of communication to their contingents in United Nations service. The entry of the big powers into United Nations peacekeeping, a phenomenon not confined to Europe but most visible there, has in practice limited the extent to which command is, or can be, exercised by the Secretariat. The challenge for the United Nations today is to combine the need to pay due heed to the legitimate concerns of governments who are politically accountable to their publics for the risks taken by their soldiers, with the need to maintain force cohesion as well as the integrity and legitimacy of international command and control of troops wearing blue helmets and serving under the United Nations flag.

In Europe the challenge of command is further complicated by the relationship with NATO, that provides air power in support of UNPROFOR. This innovation has raised issues of command and control that are unprecedented in United Nations peacekeeping and have led to intensive discussions between the two organizations, in the course of which much common ground has been found, in particular through a "dual key" arrangement in which both organizations must grant prior approval of specific actions. NATO's imposition of exclusion zones around the safe areas in Bosnia and Herzegovina, in furtherance of Security Council resolutions but not specifically authorized by them, also requires close coordination between the two organizations, whose priorities may not always coincide, given the different mission cultures involved. The experience of NATO-UN cooperation has on the whole proved positive, while also providing a valuable learning process for both.

The challenge of coercion involves the issues relating to the use of force which have been fully discussed in the preceding section. Can the United Nations expect to mix peacekeeping and coercion, as it has sometimes been obliged to do in Bosnia and Herzegovina? When public opinion and political rhetoric outstrip both the mandate and means given to the United Nations, the challenge acquires a larger dimension. UNPROFOR has, in particular, been blamed for failing to do things it was never mandated, staffed, financed, equipped, or deployed to do. Many of its critics would have liked it to take sides in the conflict; others wanted UNPROFOR to intervene more directly on behalf of some of the war's many victims; yet others blame UNPROFOR for not ending the war. These are not the functions of a peacekeeping force. Most of UNPROFOR's critics seem to think that UNPROFOR ought to be resisting or repelling "aggression." But the answer to aggression is not a peacekeeping operation; it is Desert Storm. In responding to the complex origins of the Yugoslav tragedy, the Security Council chose not to take military sides in the conflict, but rather to use a peacekeeping operation as a means to alleviate the consequences of the conflict—feeding and protecting civilians, delivering humanitarian relief, and helping create conditions conducive to promoting a peace settlement. As a result a large number of people are alive, and housed, and safe today who would have been killed, or displaced, or in peril had UNPROFOR not been deployed.

Should UNPROFOR have jeopardized these achievements by a greater use of coercive force? Such a question points to a central dilemma in those situations where the United Nations deploys peacekeepers when there is no peace to keep. Impartiality is the oxygen of peacekeeping: the only way peacekeepers can work is by being trusted by both sides, being clear and transparent in their dealings, keeping lines of communication open. The moment they lose this trust, the moment they are seen by one side as the "enemy," they become part of the problem they were sent to solve. This is reflected in UNPROFOR's pattern of deployment in a variety of dispersed locations, loosely configured across all the battle lines, full of unarmed or lightly armed observers and relief workers, and traveling in highly visible white-painted vehicles. For such a vulnerable force to take sides through the use of force might be morally gratifying, at least briefly, but it would also be militarily irresponsible. Furthermore, no single Security Council resolution on Bosnia can be read in isolation from the others. Even in those resolutions that allowed for the use of force, the Security Council reaffirmed its previous resolutions on UNPROFOR; in other words, it did not want UNPROFOR to abandon its existing mandates in order to undertake new ones. UNPROFOR thus has the difficult challenge of reconciling its authority to use force with its obligation to perform all the other tasks mandated by the Security Council, tasks that require the cooperation of, and deployment among, all parties to the conflict. The purpose of UNPROFOR's deployment is, in the last analysis, to help extinguish the flames of war, not to fan them.

The challenge of choice is a moral one: what should the United Nations choose to do in peacekeeping, and where? As the world's television screens bombard the international conscience with new and potent images of injustice and suffering, there is an instinctive tendency to want to respond to each problem, and an inevitable countertendency to say that, since the United Nations cannot put out all the fires, it will tackle none of them (beyond the ones it is already attempting to douse). The world needs the United Nations to fulfill the first purpose enshrined in its Charter, the maintenance of international peace and security. But if the United Nations is to achieve any success in this task, it needs to be given both mandate and means by its member states. There must be recognition that peacekeeping is not a panacea for every headline-grabbing case of international disorder; and at the same time there must be acceptance of its potential in solving certain kinds of problems, providing it is given the resources to do so. Both the determination of mandates, and the resources to implement them, can only come from member states. The fundamental question is: "what kind of United Nations do we want?" A vital part of the answer lies in establishing the tasks and methods that member states are ready and willing to approve, support, and pay for.

To some degree, peacekeeping has been a victim of its own success. For years during the cold war, peacekeeping worked well, within the limitations imposed upon it by superpower contention—well enough, at any rate, to win the 1988 Nobel Peace Prize. Then, when the cold war ended, the limitations evaporated, and everything seemed possible: there was no more talk of "superpower paralysis," as former adversaries found themselves on common ground, able to agree with ease and rapidity on common approaches to global crises. At the same time, the new transcendence of the global media added a sense of urgency to these crises: it is a striking coincidence that the reach and impact of CNN and its imitators peaked precisely at this time of post–cold war concordance. Television showed that action was needed, and the end of the cold war meant that action was possible. As the great clamor went up to a newly united Security Council to "do something" in a number of crises, member states found in peacekeeping the "something" that the UN could do. Operations that one superpower or the other might not have agreed to establish in the old days were launched with self-congratulatory ease. United Nations peacekeeping was thrust into a breathtaking phase of rapid and profound evolution.

In the process the international community has been making policy on the run. United Nations peacekeepers have intervened in crises without finding the time to elaborate, or agree upon, the doctrinal justifications, the conceptual issues, or the overall strategy behind each new mandate (or modification of mandate). In the continuing debate about whether peacekeeping operations belong properly under chapter 6 or 7 of the Charter, we have often found ourselves at sixes and sevens.[16] Member states have found themselves announcing model criteria and then proposing operations that met few, if any, of these criteria. There are no simple answers; the challenge remains to acknowledge that choice is inevitable, but to make the choices in ways that reaffirm the integrity of the institution making it.

Which brings me to *the challenge of credibility,* a key concept in the continued viability of United Nations peacekeeping operations. I am often reminded of Stalin's line about the moral authority of the Catholic Church: "how many divisions has the pope?" One might well ask, how many divisions has the United Nations? At one level, none: we have no standing army, no reserve stocks, not even a replenished Working Capital Fund. But at another level, we have all the "divisions" we can possibly want, because there is nothing required by United Nations peacekeeping that member states cannot provide, if they want to. For member states to want to support and strengthen United Nations peacekeeping, it is obviously important both that *we do the right thing,* and that *we do the thing right.* We have to mount the "right" operations, those that are worth doing because, they respond to a real threat to international peace and security, and because, an equally important consideration, they *can be done* well. We also have to ensure sustained political and popular support in member states for these worthy peacekeeping operations. And to merit that support, we have to earn it. We must develop the capacity to plan, mount, support, and manage such operations better than ever before, and to combine the "gifted amateurism" and inventive idealism of the traditional days of peacekeeping with the technological sophistication, the modern communications and logistics, and the will to win of the great powers.

This cannot be done unless the United Nations surmounts the perennial *challenge of contributions,* or more accurately (if less alliteratively) the challenge of resources. The enormous costs associated with United Nations peacekeeping in Europe have highlighted the endemic problem of the enormous gap between mandates and means. The General Assembly routinely exhorts member states to pay their assessed contributions for peacekeeping operations "on time and in full," but in practice only a handful of states send in their contributions within the stipulated thirty days after the issuance of a letter of assessment (which itself comes at the end of a lengthy process of budget preparation and review by two different governmental bodies, and a vote by the General Assembly). Recent experience has been that, three months after assessments are levied, barely 50 percent of the required funds have come in. The result is to tie the operational hands of the United Nations—which frequently has to deal with commercial contractors, and in some cases government providers, who want cash "up front" before providing goods and services to peacekeeping operations—and, equally troubling, limits the ability of the Secretariat to reimburse troop-contributing countries. In the case of developing countries, this can cause serious hardship, particularly since governments with hard-currency problems tend to await United Nation's reimbursement *before* paying their troops. The resulting problems of morale in missions like UNPROFOR, where soldiers subsisting on the UN's daily allowance of $1.25 a day serve side by side with western troops earning hardship bonuses in addition to their much higher regular salaries, have contributed to serious operational difficulties on the ground.

The problem is all the more ironic when seen against the comparative costs of other military activities—two days of "Operation Desert Storm," for instance, would have paid for all of the United Nations peacekeeping operations that calendar year (1991)—and even against the kinds of military expenditures national governments are usually willing to contemplate out of their defense budgets. An instructive indication of this came in 1993 when NATO planners, asked to prepare for a possible operation to implement a peace settlement in Bosnia and Herzegovina, estimated its annual cost at $8.3 billion—by ironic coincidence the exact figure, at that point, of the UN's cumulative expenditure on all peacekeeping operations since 1948. The challenge of cash is not one that the world organization must be constantly obliged to rise to, especially given that the sums involved globally each year are still lower than those spent annually by the New York City fire and police departments.

Which leads, ineluctably, to the final challenge, *the challenge of the common cause.* If there is one danger in the recent evolution of United Nations peacekeeping in Europe, it is that we might lose sight of the universality that has for so long been a crucial characteristic of United Nations peacekeeping. It was no accident that the first commander of the first United Nations operation on the European mainland was an Asian, nor that his forces (in those days, in Croatia alone) were predominantly non-European: that was what the United Nations was all about. This has changed, for reasons that are well understood. But United Nations peacekeeping operations must, to paraphrase President Clinton, "look like the United Nations"; and that can only remain the case if the membership at large feels involved in, and supports, these operations, and if the complex interaction of duty and obligation means that each participating state does what it must to sustain the others' commitment to the cause.

All this requires, perhaps, a ninth challenge, one that I will not add to our list of "eight c's" because it is a challenge for both the United Nations and Europe. This is the challenge of creativity, of finding creative solutions to the dilemmas posed above, on a continent that was not expected to be the prime site of United Nations peacekeeping activities in the last decade of the twentieth century. It is always easier to ask questions than to find answers; always simpler to identify challenges than to rise to them. But that is what we must do, together, if the problems of conflict today are to become the peacekeeping solutions of tomorrow.

Notes

1. "Improving the Capacity of the United Nations for Peace-keeping: Report of the Secretary-General," A/48/403, para. 4(c).

2. This term could also arguably be applied to some of the activities of the United Nations Operation in the Congo (ONUC) in 1961–63 and the United Nations Interim Force in Lebanon (UNIFIL) since 1978. However, the tasks as I have defined them above relate specifically to UNPROFOR's current experience.

3. See the secretary-general's reports to the Security Council (S/24848, paras. 36 and 50, and S/25264 paras. 31–33).

4. Security Council Resolution 836, operative para. 10.

5. NATO secretary-general Willy Claes, quoted by Reuters, October 27, 1994.

6. Indeed, the Bosnian Serbs explicitly opposed the deployment in Bosnia and Herzegovina of troops from Muslim countries and particularly from Turkey; their objections were ignored, though contact between such troops and the Bosnian Serbs is avoided to the extent possible.

7. This is the central element identified in the British Army Field Manual, "Wider Peace-keeping," *The Army Field Manual Volume 5, Operations other than the war,* Part 2, HMSO, 1995, perhaps the most comprehensive statement of peacekeeping doctrine ever produced.

8. "Peace-enforcement" has been defined by the United Nations as "action under Chapter VII of the Charter, including the use of armed force, to maintain or restore international peace and security in situations where the Security Council has determined the existence of a threat to the peace, breach of the peace or act of aggression" [A/48/403, para. 4(d)]. It is a technique that "may be needed when peaceful means fail," that is, another term for war.

9. See, for instance, the letter from Noel Malcolm and others in *The Times,* London, November 7, 1994, responding to the assertion of the contrary view by Lt. Gen. Sir Michael Rose of UNPROFOR.

10. For an interesting discussion of the respective authorities of the United Nations and regional organizations, see Alan K. Henrikson, "The Growth of Regional Organizations and the Role of the United Nations," unpublished paper, The Fletcher School of Law and Diplomacy, 1994, especially pp. 30–33 on Europe.

11. Manfred Wörner, "A New NATO for a New Era," speech at the National Press Club, Washington, October 6, 1993. The UN is similarly positive: see Kofi Annan, "UN Peace-keeping Operations and Co-operation with NATO," *NATO Review,* vol. 41, (October 1993), pp. 3–7.

12. Such concerns are addressed by the United Nations secretary-general, Mr. Boutros Boutros-Ghali, "Beleaguered Are the Peacekeepers," *New York Times,* October 30, 1994, p. E15.

13. A/46/185.

14. See, for instance, Statement by the President of the Security Council (S/PRST/1994/22). Similar language is used in the unpublished text prepared by a number of governments in the context of follow-up to the Ottawa Consultations on Peace-Keeping.

15. Giandomenico Picco, "The U.N. and the Use of Force," *Foreign Affairs,* vol. 73 (September–October 1994), pp. 14–18.

16. The debate about the use of force in Bosnia and Herzegovina is a case in point. While critics may disagree with the Security Council's chosen approach, the Council resolutions represent what the international community is prepared to do, to authorize, to pay for, and to supply troops for.

ELEVEN

Strategies of Enhanced Consent

Michael W. Doyle

UNFULFILLED EXPECTATIONS and escalating violence in Somalia and Bosnia, together with a growing awareness of the complexity of intervening in ethnic and civil wars, have given rise to an impetus to rethink and retrench UN operations. It is time to step back and examine those aspects of UN peace operations that not only will continue to be necessary to assure international stability, but that also reveal how the UN has succeeded in being quite successful and very innovative. They encompass not only the traditional areas of peacekeeping requiring the interposition of force after a truce has been reached, but a far more ambitious group of second generation operations that rely on the consent of parties. These operations involve factions, not all of which are clearly identifiable and few of which are stable negotiating parties. They intrude into aspects of domestic sovereignty and internal conflicts once thought to be beyond the purview of UN activity under article 2 (7). Enforcement remains a difficult issue, addressed by the secretary-general, by scholars, and in this volume by Jarat Chopra and Thomas G. Weiss. After

This paper draws on research supported by Princeton's Liechtenstein Research Program on Self-Determination, the Ford Foundation, and the International Peace Academy and on *The UN in Cambodia: UNTAC's Civil Mandate* (Boulder, Colo.: Lynne Rienner, 1995) and "Managing Global Security," to be published by the American Assembly in a volume edited by C. William Maynes and Richard Williamson. I would like to thank Mr. Yasushi Akashi and Dr. Ramirez-Ocampo and many members of UNTAC and ONUSAL. Ms. Antonia H. Chayes, Ambassador Emilio Cardenas, Ambassador Ibrahim Gambari, Professor Jeffrey Herbst, Mr. Ian Johnstone, Mr. Jeffrey Laurenti, Mr. F. T. Liu, Mr. C. William Maynes, Professor Clovis Maksoud, Professor Ali Mazrui, Ambassador Hisashi Owada, Mr. Laurence Pearl, and Professor John Waterbury offered valuable advice, but none of them bear responsibility for the views advocated in this paper.

outlining the problems of peace enforcement, this chapter focuses on some of the accomplishments of the secretary-general and the international community and outlines how the UN has succeeded in enhancing its traditional strategies of peace by consent.

Limitations of "First" and "Third" Generation Peace Operations

Following on the costly and frustrating experiences of chapter 7 peace enforcement in Somalia and Bosnia, old precepts, painfully learned, from the early days of UN peacekeeping seem newly relevant. The emergence of a working consensus on the Security Council in favor of a more interventionist international order, however impartial those actions may now be, does not remove the other reasons to be wary of forcible intervention.

In order to explore those reasons in a UN context, it is helpful to think in terms of three categories of peace support operations. In traditional peacekeeping, sometimes called "first generation peacekeeping," unarmed or lightly armed UN forces were stationed between hostile parties to monitor a truce, troop withdrawal, or buffer zone while political negotiations went forward.[1] They provided transparency (an impartial assurance that the other party was not violating the truce). They also raised the costs of defecting from and the benefits of abiding with the agreement by the threat of exposure, the potential resistance of the peacekeeping force, and the legitimacy of UN mandates.[2] The virtues were obvious; their costs, as in the long Cyprus operation, were often paid in conflicts delayed rather than resolved.

The second category, called "second generation" operations by the secretary-general, involves the implementation of complex, multidimensional peace agreements. In addition to the traditional military functions, the peacekeepers are often engaged in various police and civilian tasks, the goal of which is a long-term settlement of the underlying conflict. I will return to this rapidly growing category below.

"Peace-enforcing," that is, warmaking, missions are the third generation, which extend from low-level military operations to protect the delivery of humanitarian assistance to the enforcement of cease-fires and when necessary assistance in the rebuilding of so-called failed states. Like chapter 7 UN enforcement action to roll back aggression, as in Korea in 1950 and against Iraq in the Gulf War, the defining characteristic of "third generation" operations is the lack of consent to some or all of the UN mandate.[3]

With all of Minerva's usual sense of timing, insightful doctrine for these peace-enforcing operations appeared just as Somalia and Bosnia exposed their limitations. Recent studies have thoughtfully mapped out the logic of the strategic terrain between traditional UN peacekeeping and traditional UN enforcement action.[4] Militarily these operations seek to deter, dissuade, and deny.[5] By precluding an outcome based on the use of force by the parties, the UN instead uses collective force (if necessary) to persuade the parties to settle the conflict by negotiation. In the former Yugoslavia, for example, the UN following this strategy could have established strong points to deter attacks on key humanitarian corridors. (It did, but the Serbs bypassed them.) Or it could threaten air strikes, as was done successfully around Sarajevo in February 1994, to dissuade a continuation of the Serb shelling of the city. Or, it could have denied (but did not) the Serb forces their attack on Dubrovnik in 1992 by countershelling from the sea or bombing from the air the batteries in the hills above the city.

This terrain is murky. Forcing a peace depends on achieving a complicated preponderance in which the forces (UN and local) supporting a settlement acceptable to the international community hold both a military predominance and a predominance of popular support, which together permits them to impose a peace on the recalcitrant local military forces and their popular supporters.

This strategy, however, is likely to encounter many of the problems interventionist and imperial strategies have faced in the past and discover fresh problems peculiar to the UN's global character. The UN showed itself to be ineffective in imposing order by force, whether to disarm factions in Somalia or provide humanitarian protection in Bosnia. Instead it became complicit in a record of inadequate protection, mission creep, seemingly unnecessary casualties, Vietnam-like escalation, on the one hand, and 1930s-style appeasement on the other. UN warmaking suffers from severe disabilities, some a product of the incapacity of the organization, others a product of the kind of wars the UN has tried to address.

Although the UN seems to have the advantage of global impartiality, which should and often does win it more local acceptance when it intervenes, this is not universally the case. Israel maintains a suspicion of UN involvement dating back to the UN General Assembly's notorious anti-Zionism resolutions of the 1970s. In Somalia, Egypt's support for Siad Barre seems to have tainted the role that Boutros-Ghali, a former Egyptian minister of state for foreign affairs, sought to play as impartial secretary-general. And there is lingering distrust of the UN in other parts of Africa due to its role in the Congo.[6] Many smaller, nonwestern states, moreover, have begun to distrust the use of the Security Council by the great powers, and particularly the western "P-3" (France and the United Kingdom, led by the United States), to impose a selective vision of world order on weaker states.[7]

The UN is particularly poorly suited to interventionist strategies involving the strategic employment of coercive force. The political roots of the UN's "command and control" problems are twofold. On the one hand, countries with battalions in UN peace operations are reluctant to see their (often lightly armed) troops engaged in combat under UN direction, distrusting that a UN force commander of any nationality other than their own will take due care to minimize risks. Countries with seats on the Security Council, on the other hand, pressured to achieve a response to civil war crises and unwilling to confront the UN's ongoing shortage of resources, assign missions to UN peace operations without providing adequate means to achieve those missions. On top of this, the UN's traditional ideology (despite recent practice) is highly protective of national sovereignty, and (to its credit) it lacks the callousness or psychological distance required to inflict coercive punishment on political movements with even the smallest of popular support.[8] "Peace-forcing fatigue" is afflicting the UN's contributing countries, whether new or old. States are rarely willing to invest their resources or the lives of their soldiers in war other than for a vital interest (such as oil in the Persian Gulf). But if states have a vital national interest in a dispute, they are not likely to exercise the impartiality a UN peace operation requires. Nor are they likely to cede decisionmaking control over or command of their forces to the UN.

The very act of intervention, even by the UN, can mobilize nationalist opposition against the foreign forces. In Somalia it contributed to a significant growth of support for Aidid's Somali National Alliance. Aidid's supporters soon roundly condemned UN "colonialism."[9] The strategic balance is not static. Military intervention tilts two local balances, improving the military correlation of forces but often at the cost of undermining the more important political balance.

Coercively intervening for eventual self-determination, as J. S. Mill noted more than a century ago, is very often a self-contradictory enterprise.[10] If the local forces of freedom, self-determination, and human rights cannot achieve sovereignty without a foreign military intervention, then they are very unlikely to be able to hold on to power after the intervention force leaves. Either the installed forces of freedom will collapse, or they themselves will employ those very coercive methods that provoked and justified the initial intervention. The Kurds, for example, won widespread sympathy for their resistance to Saddam Hussein and benefited from a UN-endorsed U.S.-French-British intervention in the aftermath of the war against Iraq. Now the Kurdish factions are so divided that they appear incapable of establishing law and order in their territory. Instead, three factions have divided the region and have begun to fight among themselves. None appear capable of sustaining themselves against whatever attempts to reincorporate Kurdistan that Saddam Hussein may make. The international community has thus placed itself in the awkward position of either adopting Kurdistan as a long-term ward or returning it to the not-so-tender mercies of Saddam Hussein.[11]

The United Nations presents an almost textbook case of multiple strategic incapacity. The United Nations, of course, is nothing more than the collective agent of its member states. Many of the UN's organizational incapacities could be readily cured by additional resources from its members states, who devote but a tiny fraction of what they spend on national security to collective action under the United Nations. But encountering strategic problems while intervening in ethnic and civil wars is not unique to the United Nations. The Multi-National Force in Lebanon created even larger catastrophes of misdirected, overly violent and intrusive intervention in 1983. Even with national-quality command and control, the United States failed to impose peace in Vietnam in the 1960s; the Soviets failed in Afghanistan.

Strategies

The UN's deficiencies as a warmaker suggest the value of innovating within UN traditions to develop a superior form of "peace-making" that recognizes the continuing political significance of national sovereignty. The UN should seek out a consensual basis for a restoration of law and order in domestic crises and try to implement its global human rights agenda in a way that produces less friction and more support.

It has often been remarked that chapter 6 of the UN Charter presents the United Nations with too little authority and chapter 7 offers too much; and that chapter 6 is associated with too little use of force and chapter 7 with too much. Recent "second generation" UN operations, however, taking a substantial step beyond "first generation" operations in which the UN monitors a truce and keeping a significant step short of the third generation "peace-enforcing" operations in which the UN uses force to impose a peace, are multidimensional operations, based on consent of the parties. But the nature of and purposes for which consent is granted are qualitatively different from traditional peacekeeping. In these operations the UN is typically involved in implementing peace agreements that go to the roots of the conflict, helping to build long-term foundations for stable, legitimate government. As Secretary-General Boutros-Ghali observed in *An Agenda for Peace,* "peace-making and peace-keeping operations, to be truly successful, must come to include comprehensive efforts to identify and support structures which will tend to consolidate peace . . . these may include disarming the previously warring parties and the restoration of order, the custody and possible destruction of weapons, repatriating refugees, advisory and training support for security personnel, monitoring elections, advancing efforts to protect human rights, reforming or strengthening governmental institutions and promoting formal and informal processes of political participation."

UNTAC in Cambodia, for example, was based on the consent of the parties, as expressed in the Paris Agreements, but it moved beyond monitoring the actions of the parties to the establishment of a Transitional Authority that actually directly implemented crucial components of the mandate. Moreover, its scale was vastly larger than all but the enforcement mandates, and, for a variety of reasons, it found itself operating without the continuous (in the case of the Khmer Rouge) or complete (in the case of the other factions) cooperation of the factions.

The UN has a commendable record of success in second generation, multidimensional peacekeeping operations as diverse as those in Namibia (UNTAG), El Salvador (ONUSAL), and Cambodia (UNTAC).[12] The UN's role in helping settle those conflicts has been threefold. It served as the *facilitator* of a peace treaty among the parties; as the *enhancer* of fragile agreements supervising transitional civilian authorities; and as the *organizer* of a new basis for peace, implementing human rights, national democratic elections, and economic rehabilitation.

Though nonenforcing and consent-based, these operations are far from harmonious. Consent is not a simple "bright line" demarcating the safe and acceptable from the dangerous and illegitimate. Each function will require an enhanced form of consent if the UN is to help make a peace in the contentious environment of civil strife. We need, therefore, to focus on new ways to design peace operations if the UN, in the face of likely resistance, is to avoid having to choose between either force or withdrawal.

Facilitating Agreement

The conflicts characteristic of ethnic and civil wars result from fundamental differences of political ideology or national identity. The combatants have compounded initial competition with reciprocal acts of violence whose memory erodes a rational calculation of advantages and generates bitterness and desire for revenge. Each party, moreover, often judges that a victory for its side can be achieved only if it displays the requisite fortitude. Leaders rarely control their followers and, indeed, fear that peace will undermine their influence. The very identity of the factions is fluid, as changes in the balance of forces raises, lowers, and sometimes eliminates parties with an effective role in the dispute. Conflicts in these circumstances are rarely "ripe for resolution."[13]

Achieving the peace treaty will therefore often require a difficult and lengthy process characterized by heavy persuasion by outside actors. In Cambodia the process began in 1982 with contacts between the secretary-general's special representative, Raffeeudin Ahmed, and the Phnom Penh authorities. Ahmed succeeded in establishing an independent diplomatic identity as a Secretariat representative separate from the UN General Assembly's condemnation of the Phnom Penh and recognition of the rival Sihanoukist and Khmer Rouge forces on the Thai border. Although he explored the parameters of peace, Ahmed lacked the influence that achieving a negotiated agreement would require. Indonesia and Australia then attempted a regionwide approach in a series of informal meetings in Jakarta. They, too, though enhancing mutual understanding of the factions' concerns, failed to produce an agreement. Only when the negotiations were pushed up to the global level, with the end of the cold war, were the needed carrots and sticks made available. In Paris negotiations in 1989 and finally, effectively, in 1991, the USSR and China let their respective clients in Phnom Penh and the Khmer Rouge know that ongoing levels of financial and military support would not be forthcoming if they resisted the terms of a peace treaty that their patrons found acceptable. The United States and France and then Japan conveyed similar messages, together with promises of substantial financial aid for economic development, to the Sihanouk faction.[14]

Peace treaties thus may themselves depend on prior sanctions, threats of sanctions, or loss of aid, imposed by the international community.[15] The construction of an agreed peace, however, is more than worth the effort. The process of negotiation among the contending factions can discover the acceptable parameters of peace that are particular to the conflict. Peace negotiations can mobilize the support of local factions and of the international community in support of implementing the peace. And an agreed peace treaty can establish new entities committed to furthering peace-keeping and peace-building.

The UN has developed a set of crucially important innovations that help manage the making of peace on a consensual basis. First among them is the diplomatic device that has come to be called the "Friends of the Secretary General." This brings together multinational leverage for UN diplomacy to help make and manage peace. Composed of ad hoc, informal, multilateral diplomatic mechanisms that join together concerned states in support of initiatives of the secretary-general, it legitimates with the stamp of UN approval and supervision the pressures interested states can bring to bear to further the purposes of peace and the UN.

For Cambodia the "Core Group," or "Extended P5," played a "Friends" role in the negotiation and the management of the peace process. Composed of the Security Council "Permanent Five"—the United States, France, USSR, China, and the United Kingdom—and "extended" to include Australia, Indonesia, Japan, and other concerned states, it took the lead in the construction of the Paris Agreements. It provided key political and financial support to the United Nations Transitional Authority in Cambodia (UNTAC), and helped organize International Committee on the Reconstruction of Cambodia (ICORC) aid (almost $1 billion), while providing special funds for various projects. But the Extended P5 lacked a fixed composition. It, of course, included the P5 but then included or excluded others on an ad hoc basis, depending on the issue and topic covered and the "message" the group wished to send. For example, Thailand was excluded from certain meetings in order to send a signal of concern about its lack of support for the restrictions imposed on the Khmer Rouge. In Cambodia, moreover, there was not a sovereign government to monitor or support. Much of the Extended P5's diplomacy was therefore directed at UNTAC itself, protecting, for example, the interests of national battalions. It also served as a back channel for Special Representative Akashi to communicate directly to the Security Council.[16]

In El Salvador the Four Friends of the Secretary-General were Venezuela, Mexico, Spain, and Colombia. Frequently joined by a "fifth friend," the United States, they together played a crucial role in negotiating and implementing the peace accords.[17] The first informal version of this process was developed to further the peace for Namibia where the "Contact Group" composed of Britain, Canada, France, Germany, and the United States engaged the "Front Line States" composed of Angola, Botswana, Mozambique, Tanzania, Zambia, and Zimbabwe. The Contact Group was designed to deliver South Africa when the Front Line States could deliver Southwest Africa People's Organization (SWAPO). Beginning in 1977 the diplomatic minuet taxed the patience of all involved, but eventually ten years later produced a comprehensive peace agreement for both Namibia and Angola.[18] The "Core Group," another "Friends" mechanism, played a valuable role in Mozambique. Hopes now center on the "Contact Group," including Russia, the United States, France, Germany, and the United Kingdom, for the former Yugoslavia. Informal diplomatic support groups have also been active in Haiti, Namibia, Nicaragua, Georgia, Afghanistan, and Guatemala.[19]

Playing a crucial role in the secretary-general's peacemaking and preventive diplomacy functions, these groupings serve four key functions. First, the limited influence of the secretary-general can be leveraged, multiplied, and complemented by the Friends. The UN's scarce attention and even scarcer resources can be supplemented by the diplomacy and clout of powerful, interested actors. The Security Council now overwhelmed by the range of global crises, benefits from the focused attention of powerful member states with a special interest in the dispute.[20] The second value is legitimization. The very act of constituting themselves as a group, with the formal support of the secretary-general, lends legitimacy to the diplomatic activities of interested states that they might not otherwise have.[21] It allows for constructive diplomacy when accusations of special and particular national interest could taint bilateral efforts. The third value is coordination. The Friends mechanism provides transparency among the interested external parties, assuring them that they are all working for the same purposes, and when they are doing so, allowing them to pursue a division of labor that enhances their joint effort. It ensures that diplomats are not working at cross-purposes because they regularly meet and inform each other of their activities and encourage each other to undertake special tasks. And fourth, the Friends mechanism provides a politically balanced approach to the resolution of civil wars through negotiation. It often turns out that one particular "Friend" can associate with one faction just as another associates with a second. In the Cambodian peace process, China backstopped the Khmer Rouge, just as France did Prince Sihanouk and Russia (with Vietnam) did the state of Cambodia. The Friends open more flexible channels of communication than a single UN mediator can provide. They also advise and guide the UN intermediaries, although the process tends to work best when they support rather than move out in front of the UN.

Enhancing Fragile Agreements

Even consent-based peace agreements fall apart. In the circumstances faced by "failed states" or partisan violence, agreements tend to be fluid. In the new civil conflicts, parties cannot force policy on their followers and often lack the capacity or will to maintain a difficult process of reconciliation leading to a reestablishment of nationality sovereignty.[22]

Peace treaties and their peacekeeping mandates thus tend to be affected by two sets of contradictory tensions. First, in order to get an agreement, diplomats assume all parties are in good faith; they cannot question the intentions of their diplomatic partners. But to implement a peacekeeping and peace-building operation, planners must assume the opposite, that the parties will not or cannot fulfill the agreement made. Moreover, diplomats, who design the peace treaty tend to think in legal (authority, precedent), not strategic (power, incentives) categories. Treaties thus describe obligations; they tend to be unclear about incentives and capacities.

All these militate against clear and implementable mandates. Diplomats seek to incorporate in the treaty the most complete peace to which the parties will agree. UN officials seek to clarify the UN's obligations. Knowing that much of what was agreed to in the peace treaty will not be implementable in the field, the officials who write the secretary-general's report (which outlines the implementation of the agreement) contract or expand the mandate of the peace operation.[23] Confused mandates are an inevitable result of this tension.

A second tension also shapes the peacekeeping mandate. The mandate, like a natural resource contract, is an obsolescing bargain. When a country begins a negotiation with an oil company for the exploration of its territory, the company holds all the advantages. The costs of exploration are large, while the possibility of oil is uncertain. The country must therefore cede generous terms. As soon as oil is discovered, the bargain shifts as discovered oil is easy to pump, and any oil company can do it. The old bargain has suddenly obsolesced.[24] So with a UN peacekeeping operation. The spirit of agreement is never more exalted than at the moment of the signing of the peace treaty, the authority of the United Nations is never again greater. Then the parties assume that the agreement will be achieved and that all are cooperating in good faith. They depend upon the UN to achieve their various hopes. Although the UN has put some of its diplomatic prestige on the line, it as yet has no investment in material resources. The UN, in short, holds most of the cards. But as soon as the UN begins its investment of money, personnel, and operational prestige, then the bargaining relationship alters its balance. The larger the UN investment—these multidimensional operations represent multibillion-dollar investments—the greater the independent UN interest in success and the greater the influence of the parties becomes. As the parties control an essential element in the success of the mandate, their bargaining power rapidly rises. So, in the late spring of 1993 as the crucial elections approached, UNTAC chief Akashi acknowledged, "I cannot afford not to succeed."[25] Both the Khmer Rouge and the state of Cambodia were allowed to proceed through the peace process with less and less reference to the actual terms of the Paris Agreement.

This dual tension in designing peacekeeping operations emphasizes that time is critical. The UN should be ready to implement the mandate as soon after the peace treaty is signed as is practicable. UNTAC suffered a large decrease in authority in early 1992 as time passed and expectations of the factions and the Cambodian people were disappointed. In the former Yugoslavia we see each successive agreement, including the recent Carter Agreement, reflect more and more closely not the interests of the international community, but the actual distribution of military forces on the ground.

These tensions also explain how the ideal framework (both legal and political) of a treaty can dissolve in days or months, as the Cambodian peace agreements did, and how the provisions of peace accords become so general, ambiguous, or unworkable that many of the details have to be worked out in the implementation process. To be minimally effective under those circumstances, the UN must innovate.

The UN thus needs a flexible political strategy to win and keep popular support and create (not just enjoy) the support of local forces of order. In a failed state, as was the case in a society subject to colonial rule, what is most often missing is modern organization. This was what colonial metropoles supplied, in their own self-interest, as they mobilized local resources to combat local opposition. Over the longer run, "native" forces, the Zamindars, the King's Own African Rifles, and other locally recruited battalions, not metropolitan troops, were the forces that made imperial rule effective, that preserved a balance of local power in favor of metropolitan influence— and that kept it cheap. Learning from the history of imperial institution building (while avoiding imperial exploitation and coercion), an effective and affordable strategy for UN peace operations faces a greater challenge. It needs to discover ways to generate *voluntary* cooperation from divided local political actors and mobilize existing local resources for *locally legitimate,* collective purposes.[26] And it must do so *rapidly.*

Recent peacekeeping experience has suggested a second peacekeeping innovation: an ad hoc, semisovereign mechanism designed to address those new challenges by dynamically managing a peace process and mobilizing local cooperation. The value of these ad hoc, semisovereign artificial bodies is that they provide a potentially powerful, political means of encouraging and influencing the shape of consent. Indeed, these semisovereign artificial bodies can help contain the erosion of consent and even manufacture it where it is missing. Created by a peace treaty, they permit the temporary consensus of the parties to be formally incorporated in an institution with regular consultation and even, as in the Cambodian Supreme National Council, a semi-autonomous sovereign will. These mechanisms have proved crucial in a number of recent UN missions. They can represent the once-warring parties and act in the name of a preponderance of the "nation" without the continuous or complete consent of all the factions. They can both build political support and, in a legitimate way, with the consent of the parties, adjust the mandate in order to respond to unanticipated changes in local circumstances.

In the *Agreements on a Comprehensive Political Settlement of the Cambodian Conflict,*[27] the parties agreed not only to the terms of a cease-fire and the disarming of the factions, but also to the maintenance of law and order, the repatriation of refugees, the promotion of human rights and principles for a new constitution, the supervision and control of certain aspects of the administrative machinery by a UN body, and, most significantly, the organization, conduct, and monitoring of elections by the UN. The parties to the Agreements created two institutions in order to implement the peace: the Supreme National Council (SNC) and UNTAC.[28] The Agreements defined a transitional period running from the entry into force of the Agreements, October 23, 1991, to the time when an elected constituent assembly established a new sovereign government of Cambodia, anticipated to occur around the end of August 1993.[29] During that period, the Supreme National Council, a committee composed of the four factions, was to "enshrine" the legal sovereignty of Cambodia; and UNTAC, an authority established by the Security Council in February 1992, was to implement the agreed-upon peace.

During the early stages of the peace negotiation process, the Cambodian factions flatly rejected the proposal that national reconciliation be achieved through an interim quadripartite government. As an alternative to Cambodian "power-sharing," the establishment of UN administration required the creation of a legitimate sovereign entity to delegate the required authority to the UN, as the UN is precluded by article 78[30] from adopting a "trusteeship" role over a member state. The Cambodian parties and the international community therefore devised the concept of the Supreme National Council, composed of representatives of the four main factions, to serve as the unique and legitimate source of authority for Cambodia: the "unique legitimate body and source of authority in which throughout the transitional period the sovereignty, independence and unity of Cambodia are enshrined."

In addition to Prince Sihanouk, the SNC had twelve members; six from the state of Cambodia faction and the other six divided among the Coalition Government of Democratic Kampuchea (CGDK) and the Khmer Rouge. Prince Sihanouk was given authority as president of SNC, in recognition of his role as former monarch and prime minister, and as the only leading figure acceptable to all Cambodian parties and the five Permanent Members of the UN Security Council. The Security Council endorsed the formation of the SNC, giving it a degree of international recognition and legitimacy which further supported its primary purpose of delegating all necessary authority needed to implement the settlement plan to UNTAC.

The actual status of the SNC as the legitimate sovereign authority of Cambodia during the transition period was problematic, in both design and practice. On the one hand, the SNC, in its capacity as a sovereign entity, has signed two international human rights conventions that will bind successor governments.[31] The Agreements, moreover, authorized the SNC to act as an "advisory" body to UNTAC. UNTAC thus had to abide by a unanimous decision of the SNC, so long as it was in keeping with the objectives of the Agreements. Whenever the SNC reached an impasse, Prince Sihanouk had the authority to give advice to UNTAC. On the other hand, the Special Representative of the secretary-general was the final arbiter of whether a decision of the Council adhered to the intent and meaning of the Paris Agreements. The Agreements also gave UNTAC and the Special Representative a wide discretion, where necessary, to act independently and to make major binding decisions, whenever the SNC reached a deadlock. In practice, much influence was exercised over SNC decisionmaking by the Permanent Members of the UN Security Council and other interested states acting through their Phnom Penh support group of local diplomatic representatives accredited to the SNC (the Extended P5, Cambodian version of the Friends mechanism). The SNC was a part—indeed the symbolically vital Cambodian part[32]—of the circle of authority in Cambodia; it lacked the resources or coherence it would have needed to have a decided effect.

What, then, did the Council accomplish? Composed of the four factions and chaired by Prince Sihanouk, it offered a chance for these parties to consult together on a regular basis and endorse the peace process. It also lent special authority to Prince Sihanouk, who was authorized to act if the SNC failed to achieve a consensus. Beyond that, it empowered the United

Nations, represented by Special Representative Yasushi Akashi, to act in the interests of the peace process, if Sihanouk failed to do so. Artificially created, the SNC thus established a semisovereign legal personality designed to be responsive to the general interests of Cambodia (even when a complete consensus was lacking among all the factions) and to the authority of the United Nations Special Representative. Acting in the name of Cambodia, as a step in the implementation of the Paris Agreements, the SNC acceded to all the major human rights conventions (including the first and second Covenants on Human Rights), and it authorized the trade embargo against illegal exports of logs and gems. It was the forum that endorsed the protracted and sensitive negotiations over the franchise. It legitimated the enforcement of certain elements of the peace, without the unanimous consent of the parties and without the necessity of a contentious debate at the Security Council. It could have exercised greater authority, perhaps even designing an acceptable scheme for rehabilitation, if Prince Sihanouk or Mr. Akashi had been both willing and able to lead it in that direction.

The Commission on the Peace (COPAZ) in El Salvador played a related, although much less authoritative, role in the Salvadoran peace process. Lacking even formal sovereign authority, it nonetheless served as a forum for consultation among the Frente Faribundo Marti para la Liberacion Nacional (FMLN), the government, and the other political parties that did not play a role in the negotiation of the peace treaties. Designed to monitor and establish a forum for the participation of civilian society in the peace process, it was the only political institution that embodied the full scope of Salvadoran politics, the only institution that after a decade of bitter civil war could legitimately speak for "El Salvador." That its role in the peace process proved to be minimal was unfortunate. In Somalia the "Transitional National Council" was designed to perform a similar function, but its failure to obtain support from the leading actors was perhaps the single most disturbing problem in the peace-making process, one that seriously eroded the attempt to create a peace.

In designing these semisovereign, artificial bodies, the UN should try (to the extent that its freedom of negotiation allows) to "preview" the peace that the parties and the international community seeks. For the Paris Peace Agreements for Cambodia, seeking a "pluralist democracy" should have meant supplementing the Supreme National Council with other bodies, such as one for civil society. It might have included, for example, Buddhist monks, nongovernmental organizations, and other representatives of society outside the state. These supplementary bodies, it should be noted, need not perform executive or legislative functions. The important point is that civil society participate in the decisionmaking process, at a minimum through formally recognized consultative channels.[33]

The UN must avoid the trade-offs between too much force and too little. The dangers of chapter 7 enforcement operations, whether in Somalia or Bosnia, leave many observers to think that it is extremely unlikely that troop-contributing countries will actually show up for such operations. The risks are much more costly than the member states are willing to bear for humanitarian purposes. But when we look at chapter 6 operations, we see that consent by parties easily dissolves under difficult processes of peace. UN operations in the midst of civil strife have often been rescued by the timely use of force, as were the operations in the Congo, when Katanga's secession was forcibly halted, and as was the operation in Namibia, when SWAPO's violation of the peace agreement was countered with the aid of South African forces. But both resulted in grave political costs. Given those options, the semisovereign artificial bodies offer the possibility of mid-course adjustments and "nationally" legitimated enforcement. They artificially but usefully enhance the process of consent in the direction of the promotion of peace while avoiding the dangers associated with attempts to implement a forced peace.

Organizing a Transformation

Multidimensional, second generation peacekeeping pierces the shell of national autonomy by bringing international involvement to areas long thought to be the exclusive domain of domestic jurisdiction. If a peace-keeping operation is to leave behind a legitimate and independently viable political sovereign, it must help transform the political landscape by building a new basis for domestic peace.

The parties to a multidimensional peace agreement, in effect, consent to limitation of their sovereignty for the life of the UN-sponsored peace process. They do so because they need the help of the international community to achieve peace. But acceptance of UN involvement in implementing these agreements is less straightforward than, for example, consenting to observance of a cease-fire. Even when genuine consent is achieved, it is impossible to provide for every contingency in complex peace accords. Problems of interpretation arise, unforeseen gaps in the accords materialize, and circumstances change. The original consent, as the Salvadoran peace process, suggests, can become open-ended and in part a gesture of faith that later problems can be worked out on a consensual basis. In the process the international community, represented by the United Nations, exercised a monitoring pressure to encourage progress on the reform of the judiciary, the expansion of the electoral rolls, and the operation of a free press.

Traditional strategies of conflict resolution, when successful, were designed to resolve a dispute between conflicting parties. Successful resolution could be measured by: (1) the stated reconciliation of the parties; (2) the duration of the reconciliation; and (3) changes in the way parties behaved toward each other.[34] But successful contemporary peace-building not merely changes behavior but, more important, transforms identities and institutional context. More than reforming play in an old game, it changes the game.

This is the grand strategy General Sanderson invoked when he spoke of forging an alliance with the Cambodian people, bypassing the factions. Reginald Austin, electoral chief of UNTAC, probed the same issue when he asked what are the "true objectives [of UNTAC]: Is it a political operation seeking a solution to the immediate problem of an armed conflict by all means possible? Or does it have a wider objective: to implant democracy, change values and establish a new pattern of governance based on multi-partism and free and fair elections?"[35]

The UN's role, mandated by these complex agreements rather than chapter 7, includes monitoring, substituting for, renovating, and in some cases helping to build the basic structures of the state. The UN is called in to demobilize and sometimes to restructure and reform once-warring armies; to monitor or to organize national elections; to promote human rights; to supervise public security and help create a new civilian police force; to control civil administration in order to establish a transitional politically neutral environment; to begin the economic rehabilitation of devastated countries; and, as in the case of Cambodia, to address directly the values of the citizens, with a view to promoting democratic education.

Going beyond the monitoring of a cease-fire or the interposition of a force, UNTAC undertook a multidimensional set of responsibilities in human rights, civilian administration, election organization, refugee repatriation, and economic rehabilitation. The international community charged the UN, for the first time in its history, with the political and economic restructuring of a member of the UN, as part of the building of peace in which the parties would then (it was planned) institutionalize their reconciliation. The roots of the Cambodian conflict lay in the collapse of both the domestic and the international legitimacy of the Cambodian state. The multidimensional strategy of peace embodied in the Paris Agreements lay in the UN's stepping in to help rebuild the legitimacy of the state, after the parties had failed to achieve a reconciliation of their own.

The Paris Agreements granted extraordinary power to the UN during the transition period.[36] UNTAC was required to supervise a military stand-down, including verification of the withdrawal of Vietnamese troops and the cessation of external arms supply. It also undertook to supervise de-mining and to canton and disarm the forces of the four parties, which then would be followed by the demobilization of 70 percent of the factions' troops. But the true complexities of the security mission arose later, when the military component had to step in to provide security and logistical support for a faltering civilian effort to organize the national elections.

UNTAC also added key new civilian duties: (1) to control and supervise crucial aspects of civil administration; (2) to organize and monitor the elections, as a first step to a "system of liberal democracy, on the basis of pluralism"; (3) to coordinate with United Nations High Commissioner for Refugees (UNHCR) the repatriation of more than three hundred and fifty thousand refugees living in camps on the Thai side of the border; (4) to foster an environment in which respect for human rights and fundamental freedoms is ensured; (5) and to help plan and raise funds for the social and economic rehabilitation of Cambodia.

On the civilian side, the Paris Agreements focused on two key issues. First, they specified five essential areas of UNTAC control in the sphere of *civil administration,* in order to achieve the "neutral political environment" that would be conducive to the holding of "free and fair" elections. The areas specified for the strictest level of scrutiny and control over *each* of the four factions were defense, public security, finance, information, and for-eign affairs. A lesser degree of scrutiny was required over other governmen-tal functions, such as education, public health, agriculture, fisheries, energy, transportation, and communications. These levels of scrutiny and control were anticipated as necessary to ensure a politically neutral environment in which no faction (especially that of the predominant state of Cambodia, controlling 80 percent of the country) would be able to employ state resources to tilt the electoral contest in its favor. The secretary-general's Special Representative also had the apparent (but unexercised) authority to appoint UNTAC officials within the factional administrations and to re-move officials who did not respond to his directives.

Second, one of the Paris accord's most striking civilian features was that the international community and *all* the Cambodian factions agreed to "a system of *liberal democracy,* on the basis of pluralism" as the basis for the

Cambodian constitution. While it remains to be seen whether the Cambodians will embrace the principles and practice of constitutional democracy, the parties to the negotiation process (with the encouragement of the international community in general) explicitly agreed to a peace plan that required them to establish constitutional democracy in Cambodia. What was unique about this process was the UN's role in guaranteeing democracy. The Agreements specified all the elements necessary for a constitutional democracy: periodic and genuine elections; freedom of assembly and association, including that for political parties; due process and equality before the law; and an independent judiciary. Indeed, the right of self-determination of the Cambodian people through free and fair elections became the hallmark and linchpin of the Paris Agreements.

For the first time, unlike UN operations in Namibia, Nicaragua, Haiti, and Angola, the entire organization and supervision of the elections was left to the UN. UNTAC's responsibilities included: establishing electoral laws and procedures, invalidating existing laws that would not further the settlement, setting up the polling, responding to complaints, arranging for foreign observation, and certifying the elections as free and fair. The creation of laws and procedures was a critical legislative function granted to UNTAC regarding elections. This authority to draft legislation was not a power provided to UNTAC in other areas of civil administration, and signified an innovative and intrusive role for the UN in the internal affairs of a member state.

UNTAC thus helped create new actors on the Cambodian political scene: the electors, a fledgling civil society, a free press, a continuing international and transnational presence. The Cambodian voters gave Prince Ranariddh institutional power, and the Khmer Rouge was transformed from an internationally recognized claimant on Cambodian sovereignty to a domestic guerrilla insurgency. The peace-building process, particularly the election, became the politically tolerable *substitute* for the inability of the factions to reconcile their conflicts.

Authentic and firm consent to a peace treaty, in the aftermath of severe civil strife such as that which Cambodia endured, is rare. The international negotiators of a peace treaty and the UN designers of a mandate should, therefore, first attempt to design in as many bargaining advantages for the UN authority as the parties will tolerate. Even seemingly extraneous bargaining chips will become useful as the spirit of cooperation erodes under the pressure of misunderstandings and separating interests. The UN counted upon the financial needs of the Cambodian factions to ensure their cooperation and designed an extensive rehabilitation component to guarantee steady rewards for cooperative behavior.[37] But the Khmer Rouge's access to illicit trade (with the apparent connivance of elements of the Thai military along the western border) eliminated this bargaining chip. And the suspicion of State of Cambodia's (SOC) rivals prevented a full implementation of rehabilitation in the 80 percent of the country controlled by the SOC.

Second, the architects of the UN operation should therefore also design into the mandate as much independent implementation as the parties will agree to in the peace treaty. In Cambodia the electoral component and refugee repatriation seem to have succeeded simply because they did not depend on the steady and continuous positive support of the four factions. Each had an independent sphere of authority and organizational capacity that allowed it to proceed against everything short of the active military opposition of the factions. Civil administrative control and the cantonment of the factions failed because they relied on the continuous direct and positive cooperation of each of the factions. Each of the factions, at one time or another, had reason to expect that the balance of advantages was tilting against itself, and so refused to cooperate. A significant source of the success of the election was *Radio UNTAC,* a UN radio station established by the operation. It gave UNTAC the ability to speak directly to the potential Cambodian voters, bypassing the propaganda of the four factions and invoking a new Cambodian actor, the voting citizen. But voters are only powerful for the five minutes it takes them to vote, if there is not an institutional mechanism to transfer democratic authority to bureaucratic practice. Now, lacking such a mechanism in Cambodia, the voters are vulnerable to the armies, police, and corruption that take over after the votes were tallied.

In these circumstances the UN should try to create new institutions to make sure votes in UN-sponsored elections "count" more. The UN needs to leave behind a larger institutional legacy, drawing, for example, upon the existing personnel of domestic factions, adding to them a portion of authentic independents, and training a new army, civil service, police force, and judiciary. These are the institutions that can be decisive in ensuring that the voice of the people, as represented by their elected representatives, shape the future. This is exactly the task that lies ahead in Haiti, following the permissive takeover by the United States negotiated in September 1994.

In the end these difficulties highlight the crucial importance of risk-spreading multidimensionality itself. The UN should design in as many routes to peace—institutional reform, elections, international monitoring, economic rehabilitation—as the parties will tolerate. Yet none of these alternative strategies will eliminate the formidable challenges of making, keeping, and building peace in the midst of protracted civil wars. Some crises will not find their solution. But today as the United Nations is under attack in the United States and elsewhere, we should not neglect its authentic peace-making potential. Employing strategies of enhanced consent, the United Nations can play a constructive role in the forging of peace and reconstruction in those areas of the world in need of assistance. Avoiding the dangerous and often counterproductive effects of armed imposition, whether unilateral or multilateral, the UN can be the legitimating broker in the making, keeping, and building of peace that takes the first steps toward the opening of political space for human rights and participatory communal self-expression.

Notes

1. Traditional peacekeeping is a shorthand term that describes many but by no means all cold war peacekeeping missions, the most notable exception being the Congo operation of 1960–64. For a cogent analysis of different types of peacekeeping, see Marrack Goulding, "The Evolution of United Nations Peacekeeping" *International Affairs,* vol. 69, no. 3 (July 1993), pp. 451–64.

2. In game theoretic terms, they solved variable sum, "coordination" problems, where both parties have the same best outcome, and will reach it if they can trust each other, and "prisoner's dilemma" problems, where the parties have an incentive to cheat. The peacekeepers provide the missing transparency in the first and alter the payoffs in the second, making the prisoner's dilemma into a coordination game. First generation operations include both sorts of games.

3. Other recent categories include "preventive deployments" intended to deter a possible attack, as in Macedonia today. There the credibility of the deterring force must ensure that the potential aggressor knows that there will be no easy victory. In the event of an armed challenge, the result will be an international war that involves costs so grave as to outweigh the temptations of conquest. Enforcement action against aggression (Korea or the Gulf), conversely, is a matter of achieving victory—"the decisive, comprehensive and synchronized application of preponderant military force to shock, disrupt, demoralize and defeat opponents"—the traditional zero sum terrain of military strategy. See John Ruggie (below, n. 4), who draws on "A Doctrinal Statement of Selected Joint Operational Concepts," Office of the Joint Chiefs of Staff, Department of Defense, Washington, November 23, 1992.

4. Categories of action are effectively examined in John Mackinlay and Jarat Chopra, *A Draft Concept of Second Generation Multinational Operations 1993* (Providence, R.I.: Thomas J. Watson Jr. Institute for International Studies), and John Ruggie, "The United Nations: Stuck in a Fog between Peacekeeping and Enforcement," in *Peacekeeping: The Way Ahead?* McNair Paper 25, Institute for National Strategic Studies (Washington: National Defense University, 1993) pp. 1–11.

And also see John Mackinlay's update, "Problems for US Forces in Operations beyond Peacekeeping," in the McNair Paper 25, pp. 29–50.

5. See the Ruggie and Chopra and Mackinlay articles cited above for further discussion.

6. Recently this distrust has given way to a sense of urgency about Africa's conflicts, in which UN involvement is seen as necessary. See *The OAU and Conflict Management in Africa*. Report of a Joint OAU/IPA Consultation, Addis Ababa, May 1993 (1995).

7. See the panel discussion among UN permanent representatives at the "UNHCR/IPA Conference on Conflict and Humanitarian," reported in *Conflict and Humanitarian Action* (UNHCR/IPA, 1994) by Michael Doyle and Ian Johnstone.

8. An added problem is that the use of force in civil wars frequently causes casualties among civilians, opening the UN and its members to accusations of neocolonialism and brutality. Adam Roberts, *The Crisis in Peacekeeping* (Oslo, Norway: Institutt for Forsvarsstudier, 2/1994), p. 24.

9. Mr. Abdi Hassan Awale, an Aidid adviser in Mogadishu, complains, "the UN wants to rule this country. They do not want a Somali government to be established. The UN wants to stay and colonize us." *New York Times* March 2, 1994.

10. For a classic discussion of these problems see J. S. Mill, "A Few Words on Nonintervention" (1859), in Gertrude Himmelfarb, ed., *Essays on Politics and Culture* (Garden City, N.Y.: Anchor, 1962).

11. Chris Hedges, "Quarrels of Kurdish Leaders Sour Dreams of a Homeland," *New York Times,* June 18, 1994, p. A 1.

12. Before the UN became involved, during the cold war when action by the Security Council was stymied by the lack of consensus among the P5, the international community allowed Cambodia to suffer an autogenocide and El Salvador a brutal civil war. Indeed, the great powers were involved in supporting factions who inflicted some of the worst aspects of the violence the two countries suffered. We should keep this in mind when we consider the UN's difficulties in Somalia and Bosnia.

13. I. William Zartman and Saadia Touval, *International Mediation in Theory and Practice* (Boulder, Colo.: Westview Press, 1985).

14. See, for sources, Michael Doyle, "Making a Peace," chapter 2 of *The UN in Cambodia: UNTAC's Civil Mandate* (Boulder, Colo.: Lynne Rienner, 1995).

15. The Governor's Island Accord, which produced the first (ineffective) settlement of the Haitian conflict, resulted from economic sanctions on arms and oil imposed by the UN and OAS on Haiti as a whole. Sanctions targeted on the perpetrators (the military elite and their supporters) might have been much more effective (and were later imposed in the summer of 1994). Restrictions on the overseas private bank accounts and air travel of the ruling elite would have been both more just and perhaps more effective than general economic sanctions, whose impact was most severe on the most vulnerable and from which the elite may actually have benefited.

16. Yasushi Akashi, "UNTAC in Cambodia: Lessons for UN Peace-Keeping," The Charles Rostow Annual Lecture (Washington: SAIS, October 1993), and Doyle interviews in Phnom Penh, March 1993, and New York, November 1993.

17. Ian Johnstone and Mark LeVine, "Lessons from El Salvador," *Christian Science Monitor,* August 10, 1993.

18. See the U.S. side of these negotiations told in Chester Crocker, *High Noon in Southern Africa* (W.W. Norton, 1992).

19. The group of "Friends" for Haiti consisted of France, the United States, Canada, and Venezuela.

20. Some members of the Security Council have begun to express a concern that excessive independence by the "Friends" will undermine the authority of the Council.

21. For a good discussion of the UN's, and especially the secretary-general's, potential strength as a diplomatic legitimator, see Giandommenico Picco, "The U.N. and the Use of Force," *Foreign Affairs,* vol. 73 (September–October, 1994), pp. 14–18. The "Friends" mechanism seems to answer many of the objections to UN mediation expressed by Saadia Touval, "Why the UN Fails," *Foreign Affairs,* vol. 73 (September–October 1994), pp. 44–57.

22. See Adam Roberts, "The United Nations and International Security," *Survival,* vol. 35 (Summer 1993), pp. 3–30; William Durch, ed., *The Evolution of UN Peacekeeping* (St Martins, 1993); Mats Berdal *Whither UN Peacekeeping? Adelphi paper* 281 (London: IISS, 1993); and Thomas Weiss, "New Challenges for UN Military Operations," *Washington Quarterly,* vol. 16 (Winter 1993), pp. 51–66.

23. I first heard a variation on this point from Edward Luck.

24. See Raymond Vernon, *Sovereignty at Bay* (New York: Basic Books, 1971), pp. 46–59.

25. Yasushi Akashi, interview in "Peace in the Killing Fields," part 3 of *The Thin Blue Line,* BBC Radio 4, released May 9, 1993.

26. It is interesting in this light to note that some key, early UN experts in peacekeeping were eminent decolonization experts, deeply familiar with the politics of colonial rule, as was Ralph Bunche from the UN Trusteeship Division. See Brian Urquhart, *Ralph Bunche, An American Life* (Norton, 1993), chapter 5, and for a discussion of imperial strategy, Michael Doyle, *Empires* (Cornell, 1986), chapter 12. But there are key differences. Empires were governed primarily in the interests of the metropole; UN peace operations explicitly promote the interests of the host country. And what made imperial strategy work was the possibility of coercive violence, the over-the-horizon gunboats that could be and often were offshore. That, for good and bad, is what the UN usually lacks, unless it calls in the enforcement capacity of the major powers. Rehabilitation assistance is sometimes an effective carrot, but not the equivalent of the Royal Navy.

27. October 23 1991, UN document A/46/608-S/23177; 31 I.L.M. 183 (1992).

28. See Steven Ratner, "The Cambodia Settlement Agreements," *American Journal of International Law,* vol. 87 (1993), pp. 1–41, and his "The United Nations' Role in Cambodia: A Model for Resolution of Internal Conflicts?" in Lori Damrosch, ed., *Enforcing Restraint* (Council on Foreign Relations, 1993), pp. 241–73.

29. The new Cambodian government would be and was created when the Constituent Assembly elected in conformity with the Agreements approved the new Cambodian Constitution and transformed itself into a legislative assembly.

30. Article 78 of the Charter provides that "The trusteeship system shall not apply to territories which have become Members of the United Nations, relationship among which shall be based on respect for the principle of sovereign equality."

31. The SNC signed instruments of accession to the International Convention on Civil and Political Rights and the International Convention on Economic, Social and Cultural Rights on April 20 1992.

32. The lack of even this minimally formal authority in Somalia leaves UNOSOM without a symbolic interlocutor that could serve to legitimate its actions. See the letter to the *New York Times* of September 15, 1993, by Issa Ahmed Nour.

33. For a model of this kind of process developed for the possible Bosnian peace process, see Abram Chayes and Antonia Handler Chayes, "After the End: A Preliminary Appraisal of Problems of Keeping the Peace in Bosnia If and When It Comes," in Richard Ulman, ed., *The World and Yugoslavia's War* (Council on Foreign Relations, forthcoming).

34. For a good account of traditional views of reconciliation, see A. B. Fetherston, "Putting the Peace Back into Peacekeeping," *International Peacekeeping*, vol. 1 (Spring 1994), p. 11, discussing a paper by Marc Ross.

35. Dr. Reginald Austin (UNTAC, 1993).

36. See appendix 1 for the complete UNTAC Mandate, pp. 17–22, of *Agreements on a Comprehensive Political Settlement of the Cambodia Conflict* (DPI, 1992).

37. This link was drawn explicitly by Deputy Secretary Lawrence Eagleburger at the Conference on the Reconstruction of Cambodia, June 22, 1992, Tokyo, where he proposed that assistance to Cambodia be "through the SNC—to areas controlled by those Cambodian parties cooperating with UNTAC in implementing the peace accords—and only to those parties which are so cooperating" (Press Release USUN-44–92, June 23, 1992). Disbursing the aid through the SNC, however, gave the Khmer Rouge a voice, as a member of the SNC, in the potential disbursement of the aid.

TWELVE

The United Nations and the Former Second World: Coping with Conflict

Jarat Chopra and Thomas G. Weiss

THE END of the cold war seemed to promise a millennial era of international peace and cooperation. But the reality of the transition to democratic governments and market economies soon belied that hope in the former second world, that is, the former Soviet Union and the countries of eastern and central Europe.[1] Of the twenty-seven successor states that together constituted the former Muscovite bloc, close to half are in the throes of armed conflict, and many of the remainder are contending with violent disorder of one kind or another. The symbiotic forces of too little order, as in Somalia, Rwanda, and Cambodia, and too much authority, as in the countries of Central and South America, are no longer the monopoly of the third world. Fragmentation and chaos, suppression and resistance, proliferating warlords—sovereign and not—and internecine violence are global trends and characteristic of the conditions in eastern Europe and the former Soviet Union. This chapter assesses whether there are ways for the international community as represented by the United Nations to cope with armed conflict there.

During the cold war, pundits, parliamentarians, and the public juxtaposed on the geopolitical compass the "East," consisting of the former second world, with the North Atlantic "West." Developing countries in the

---

An earlier version of this chapter appeared as "Prospects for Containing Conflict in the Former Second World," *Security Studies* 4 (Spring 1995), pp. 552–83.

"South" categorized both East and West as parts of the "North." The North-South axis crystallized with the eventual incorporation of Soviet successor states and Moscow's former clients from eastern Europe into the Conference (since January 1995, the Organization) on Security and Co-operation in Europe (CSCE). But this geographic sleight-of-hand cannot obscure the harsh fact that nine of its fifty-three members are actively participating in shooting wars. Moreover, their economies have more in common with the vast majority of developing countries than with the advanced industrialized members of the Organization for Economic Co-operation and Development (OECD).

Since the signing of the United Nations Charter fifty years ago, it has been recognized, if not fully realized, that peace anywhere is in the interest of the international community everywhere, and that conflict somewhere is a threat to the community as a whole.[2] Nevertheless, the imperatives of the cold war effectively precluded the UN from responding to a broad range of conflicts: internal violence, disputes within superpower spheres of influence, and wars in their areas of proxy competition. This narrowed the opportunities where the UN could exercise its function of maintaining international peace and security, principally in parts of the third World and then only on the rare occasions when the two superpowers could agree.

Within this narrow geographic scope, and in the absence of a UN standing force, peacekeeping emerged as a response to the need for something more than the voluntary pacific settlement of disputes enjoined by article 33 of the Charter. Not originally envisioned in the Charter, it was developed largely under the aegis of former UN secretary-general Dag Hammarskjöld, who referred to it as a kind of "chapter 6½." Although peacekeeping maintained much of the consensual nature of chapter 6, it was more than the purely voluntary and bilateral form of settlement referred to in article 33. Nonetheless, it resembled more the peaceful settlement of disputes than the "action" contemplated under chapter 7 for countering "a threat to the peace, breach of the peace or act of aggression."

Over time the practice of peacekeeping developed certain basic principles:

—The force had to be established by resolution of the Security Council and continuously supported politically.

—It would be deployed only with the consent of the parties in conflict.

—Command and control would be vested in the secretary-general and a force commander, under the authority of the Security Council.

—The force would be composed of troops supplied voluntarily by member states on request from the secretary-general and would represent a wide geographic spectrum, although by convention the Permanent Members of the Security Council were excluded.

—The troops would be lightly armed, and could use force only in self-defense.

—The force would be impartial as among the parties to the conflict.[3]

With the ascent of Mikhail Gorbachev to power and the end of the cold war, new possibilities for preventing conflict and responding to violence emerged.[4] As bipolar tensions waned, the Security Council began to cooperate routinely, though still not quite as had been anticipated by the framers of the UN Charter. At the same time, there was a dramatic increase in the number of conflicts, particularly within states, demanding attention even in areas once considered the bulwark of stability, such as the former Yugoslavia. As a result, the UN has deployed increasingly complex operations in noninternational armed conflicts, including those in the spheres of influence of the former superpowers.

The initial excitement after the end of the cold war provided a second chance for the United Nations to realize more fully the aims originally imagined by its founders. Great power collegiality in the Security Council helped breach traditional barriers of state sovereignty. Issues that had been formerly regarded as exclusively domestic under Charter article 2 (7) were now deemed matters of international concern. An expanded notion of security at the first summit meeting of the Security Council took account of nontraditional sources of conflict,[5] providing what Stanley Hoffmann called an "all-purpose parachute" because it could justify action in the absence of military aggression, if the Security Council nevertheless considers the situation a threat to international peace and security. This summit led to a request for the then new secretary-general to outline his vision for strengthening the security capacity of the United Nations. His response was published as *An Agenda for Peace* in June 1992.[6]

Since then, UN reactions to humanitarian emergencies, human rights abuses, and other nonmilitary crises have been labeled as responses to threats to international peace and security. In dramatic ways—for example, through the use of chapter 7 for operations in northern Iraq, Somalia, and Bosnia-Herzegovina, or through the establishment of a War Crimes Tribunal for the former Yugoslavia—the UN has become increasingly intrusive in enforcing collective decisions regarding issues beyond traditional notions of military security. Although these operations have not always been as muscular as UN rhetoric implies, at least at times Security Council resolutions have been backed by the might of the great powers.[7]

In a departure from past practice, the UN now routinely negotiates directly with insurgent forces or factions. These groups have different characteristics from the perhaps intransigent but nonetheless more coherent governments that the UN has dealt with in the past. In a collapsed state such as Somalia,[8] structures of authority are nonexistent or very poorly defined. Leaders of the myriad parties in the dispute who sit at negotiating tables in New York, Geneva, or elsewhere often are neither accountable to anyone other than themselves nor do they comply with the rule of international law. Above all they cannot with any assurance exercise control in the field over local leaders who comprise their factions but who are largely autonomous.[9] This development represents a significant new challenge to the United Nations.

In addition to its new jurisdictional and geographic range, the UN has entered a new operational environment. The Security Council assumed responsibility for increasingly complex tasks, well beyond traditional observer missions and peacekeeping operations of the type that had been fielded for forty years.[10] The UN has deployed soldiers to prevent the spread of conflicts, demilitarize areas and demobilize combatants, organize elections and transfer government power, ensure humanitarian access, protect human rights, and guarantee and deny movement.

After a period of short-lived euphoria, a more realistic assessment of the problems and prospects for multilateralism has emerged in the wake of failed UN missions in the former Yugoslavia and Somalia, and the complexities of Haiti and Rwanda. However, there should be no illusions about the UN as "utopia lost."[11] A definitive psychological shift to "multilateralism" has never occurred among peoples and their governments: as with realist and neorealist scholars, western constituencies have not accepted the human and financial costs of international action as investments in their own self-interest. There is still a good-Samaritan-in-distant-lands perspective, while substate anarchy proliferates throughout the world, fragmenting further Hedley Bull's anarchical society of states.[12] As states and governments collapse, outrage at famine in Somalia or slaughter in Rwanda leads to the demand to "do something!" But as casualties and costs mount, many of the same individuals ask, "Why are we there?"

Furthermore, no commensurate change in operational concepts was developed within the Secretariat for the "second generation" of UN operations in spite of prodding by scholars and national governments,[13] as is now recognized at least implicitly by the UN secretary-general in a recent progress report on the occasion of the world organization's fiftieth anniversary.[14] To conduct these tasks successfully, a range of capabilities needs to be developed within the UN system. In particular, an enhanced military competence is required instead of the moral authority that was relied upon during the cold war. Hostilities have increased dramatically in areas of UN operations because consent from belligerents is less forthcoming and often absent. Disparate components of multifunctional operations—military forces, civilian elements, humanitarian action, and diplomatic negotiations—are not orchestrated jointly and coordinated with UN specialized agencies and nongovernmental organizations (NGOs). Complex operations require better-established headquarters facilities as well as clearer chains of command and procedures for control.

Attempts at these and other reforms, however, have been outstripped by the pace of events. Even if the most politically unrealistic proposals had been implemented—such as an international army, the resuscitation of the Military Staff Committee, or the supranationalization and democratization of the United Nations—the world organization would not have been able to respond to the scale of current international crises. As it is, the UN remains an essentially diplomatic organization on to which some military resources have been awkwardly grafted. Operations with too much of a diplomatic strategy and a weak military presence, such as in Cambodia or Angola, proved ineffective. When military imperatives dominated, operations tended to be either unaccountable, as during the Persian Gulf War, or uncontrollable, as in Somalia.

Inability to respond effectively to a seemingly endless number of more and more gruesome crises has led to devastating fatigue among UN officials and government delegations as well as to negative public reactions throughout the western world. As a result, accumulated regular budget and peacekeeping arrears in mid-1994 of some $3.3 billion were about three times the annual regular budget of the UN, and member states continue to be reluctant to commit substantial new resources to UN operations. Half of the shortfall was Washington's responsibility, and although the United States found cosmetic measures to reduce its debt in the short run, there is still no definitive solution to financial troubles.[15] Meanwhile, major powers began taking charge of some missions, with official UN approval but only minimal accountability to the international community. The self-proclaimed roles of Washington in Haiti, Moscow in Abkhazia and Ossetia, and France in Rwanda were manifest in mid-1994.

Through complex and special arrangements employing great power assets as part of an overall political framework, the UN may be able to address the largely unfamiliar environment of the former second world. This is a limited but practical response to the problems presented by the combination of strained UN resources and the special circumstances of internal conflict in the region. As subcontracts raise serious issues of legitimacy and accountability to international norms and standards, a mechanism for international oversight is required.

The turmoil in the former second world creates an acute security challenge, particularly in what Russia now labels the "near abroad" of newly independent Soviet republics. Moscow's commitment to stability in the near abroad is represented by some 200,000 Russian troops stationed there. However, the Kremlin was back in the headlines beginning in mid-December 1994 for military action on its own territory—using troops, heavy artillery, and air power in an attempt to crush Chechnya's separatists. Boris Yeltsin's use of force, even if on Russia's own soil, drew as much domestic as international criticism and jeopardized the legitimacy of Moscow's "peacekeeping" deployments in the near abroad. A Russian parliamentary delegation stated that "thousands of innocent people have died, tens of thousands made homeless, and hundreds of servicemen have died."[16] A former Ukrainian minister of defense wrote with concern for his own country's future, "It's getting hard to tell Russia from the Soviet Union."[17]

Both partisans and critics of Russia's deployments now agree that efforts to contain conflict and keep the peace are expanding on the territory of the former Soviet Union and are likely to continue to do so. Commentators also agree that, with burgeoning crises worldwide and fatigue among donors, it is unlikely that western soldiers and humanitarians—the backbone of UN efforts—will readily aid many of these conflict-ridden areas. The question arises, to cite Lenin out of context, "What is to be done?"

Relying on Moscow's ability and willingness to use its military forces to maintain stability in parts of the former second world may be the only option. There is an essential and missing dimension, which would help distinguish these operations from both the Soviet machinations of the past as well as from nineteenth-century gunboat diplomacy by other great powers. Russian or Commonwealth of Independent States (CIS) peacekeeping must be held accountable if it is to be accepted as legitimate.

The opportunity for doing so may help develop a model that can be applied to operations by other permanent members of the Security Council or other regional powers. Subcontracting the implementation of international decisions to powerful states could be accounted for by joint control mechanisms composed of belligerents, regional states, multilateral and nongovernmental organizations, as well as interested and disinterested states to provide leverage and a modicum of confidence in peace processes. A political framework of this kind could include observers deployed throughout the command structure of the forces of the major power that dominates a particular field operation.

We wish to make clear in the beginning that this is not a neoimperialist or neocolonialist essay seeking to justify and facilitate great power manipulation, but rather an attempt to offer a realistic mechanism to mitigate subnational violence that plagues the post–cold war era. The old order is crumbling, but the international community does not yet have the means to stave off violence and minimize life-threatening suffering. With conflicts proliferating around the globe and with the unabashed return to national-interest calculations—not as a balance of power but as a kind of survival of the fittest—minimal assurances of an internationalist agenda need to be guaranteed.

Because states generally lack a commitment to collective machinery to settle conflicts, and because of the looming specter of what the U.S. representative at the UN, Madeline Albright, has called "sphere-of-influence peacekeeping," the only possibility in the short term is to ensure greater accountability of great powers operating under international mandates in specific cases. Through the direct and indirect collective engagement required in the functioning of such accountability, however, the overall system of international peace and security in turn can be strengthened by fostering limited but genuine commitments to international rather than solely national interests.

But what are the prospects? We answer this question first by providing an overview of UN involvement in the former second world and then proposing in this context, and more generally, subcontracting with accountability. In the final sections of this chapter, we consider the likelihood of such a development.

The UN in the Former Second World

There is a prevailing perception throughout the former Soviet Union, indicated to the authors in a series of interviews in the last year and a half, that the experience of the United Nations in the third world is not directly applicable. The second world's problems were said to be unique: the West was not expected to understand them; and the UN was considered incapable of solving them. And there is some basis for this position. Although for some time analysts have been calling for an expanded outside role in the region,[18] the UN had no operational experience in the former Soviet sphere of influence until the 1991 quagmire of the former Yugoslavia.[19] The United Nations, like governments and nongovernmental organizations, lacks country and language specialists in the Secretariat and has virtually no previous experience on the ground.

The critical factor affecting UN efforts to cope with armed conflicts in the former second world, however, is the prevalence of Russian troops deployed in its former republics where some 25 million ethnic Russians reside. Moscow's sphere of influence is not receding despite the new independence of these republics, but rather evolving as distinctions are drawn between the "near" and "far abroad." The countries of the former Soviet Union remain interdependent economically to a considerable degree. Most are beset by political, economic, and social instabilities that inevitably affect the security of Russia itself. They are members of the CIS, the political and economic dimensions of which are still developing.

Therefore, Russia's role in the region cannot be ascribed merely to resurgent imperial tendencies but is firmly rooted in common security interests. As the dominant regional power and a veto-wielding permanent member of the Security Council, Russia cannot be divorced from UN operations deployed to the area. And it is no more comfortable than the United States with the UN's performance in the former Yugoslavia or the Secretariat's incapacity to organize and supervise similar dangerous missions. Russia's activist role in the region and its importance at the UN distinguishes the terrain of the second world from that of the third.[20]

Nevertheless, issues demanding attention in the former second world are similar enough to those of the third world to be considered not only within the jurisdiction of but also familiar to the UN. The dictum of traditional peacekeepers that no two conflicts are the same can be overstated. Its applicability was to some degree a feature of a system that could respond only in an ad hoc fashion because it lacked established institutions that could act consistently to prevent conflict in a manner similar to a national government within its borders. Although UN forces were deployed in various types of armed conflicts, the tasks assumed by the UN were similar enough for the international community to develop over time rules and procedures governing the conduct of peacekeepers as impartial referees.[21]

In spite of obvious differences, parallels can be drawn between the tasks assumed earlier by the UN in the third world and the threats that many citizens in the former second world believe represent instability. A list of potential sources of armed conflict looks much the same in both: fragmentation, emergence of national minorities, boundaries in flux, human rights abuse, movements of peoples, nuclear dangers, environmental hazards, economic conditions; and loss of control over the armed forces.[22]

There are more specific conditions manifest in the former second world that have caused conflict in the past and suggest the potential for future violent clashes.[23]

—The economic crisis has led to attacks against minorities as scapegoats.

—The privatization of state property has resulted in fights over the division of land and resources, such as in the Baltics where restrictive citizenship laws have been used to disenfranchise ethnic Russians.

—The weakness of civil society has been unable to resolve disputes peacefully.

—The disorientation of a collectivist psychology in the transition from the Soviet era has been met by reliance on ethnic exclusivity.

—A threatened *nomenklatura* has orchestrated military attacks against opponents in central Asia and in the formation of the "Trans-Dniester Republic."

—Ethno-territorial autonomy in state construction has led to conflict between titular ethnic groups and other minorities and majorities.

—The militarization of the male population from conscription and the availability of weapons have meant armed and trained individuals and groups are willing to fight outside regular armed forces.

—Clashes within ethnically based states have arisen from the breakdown of multiethnic states. The new states tend to have heterogeneous populations with large communities of minorities, especially Russians as in Tajikistan. Group leadership tends to be associated with ethnic identity in the former Yugoslavia, Moldova, the Baltics, and the Transcaucasus. The legitimacy of boundaries tend to be in question in such places as Moldova and the Caucasus. New states can collapse altogether, as in Tajikistan, or be weakened by further breakup, as in Georgia.

—Traditional social and political structures have been placed under stress, in Tajikistan and the Caucasus, as a result of shifts in population and depletion of resources since the pre–Soviet era.

—New conflicts threaten as a result of struggles between political factions, like that in Moscow in 1993, and the prospect of civil war and the fracturing of larger states like Russia, as demonstrated by Chechnya. As an opposing force to fragmentation, armed struggle calling for imperial reconstitution could result from support of secessionist movements in Abkhazia, Ossetia, and Dniestria.

These factors are prevalent throughout the area. But after the breakup of the Soviet Union, they erupted into violent conflict in Tajikistan, the Caucasus and Transcaucasus, and Moldova. In addition, of course, the war in the former Yugoslavia has dominated central and eastern Europe. The Crimea has been simmering with secessionist claims. The republics of the North Caucasus are disputing boundaries with each other, and in some cases—Chechnya is at present the most violent—claiming independence from the Russian Federation. The struggle over Nagorno-Karabakh continues. The central Asian republics of Uzbekistan and Kyrgyzstan are menaced by the potential expansion of the Tajik conflict. And Russian ethnic claims may yet develop into secessionism in Kazakhstan and Ukraine. There was even violence between extremists and moderates in Moscow in October 1993.

The response to date by the United Nations has been extremely limited. The Security Council has issued resolutions condemning aggressors in Armenia and Abkhazia and condoning some Russian peace efforts. It has sent representatives to Tajikistan and Abkhazia to foster negotiations, and appealed for humanitarian assistance in the former. In both Tajikistan and Abkhazia, it has deployed small numbers of unarmed observers who were largely isolated from events.

Russia itself has tried to cope with the conflicts within its territory and the near abroad. Either on its own or under the aegis of the CIS, it has deployed five "peacekeeping" operations in Moldova, Georgia-Ossetia, Georgia-Abkhazia, Ossetia-Ingushetia, and Tajikistan; and a similar operation is proposed for Nagorno-Karabakh.[24] In each of these cases, there has been only limited contact between Russia and the United Nations, sometimes in conjunction with the renamed Organization for Cooperation and Security in Europe (OCSE). The process to date has been very much trial and error, but it suggests both possibilities and pitfalls for the future.

Tajikistan

In Tajikistan one round of fighting between a Russian-backed, Soviet-style regime and a Tajik opposition ended in late 1992, but social and political fragmentation continued throughout the countryside. The violence has led to probably 50,000 deaths, displaced at least 500,000 people, and forced another 60,000 to flee to northern Afghanistan. The UN launched an urgent preliminary appeal for $20.4 million in humanitarian assistance. And in August 1992 the Security Council appealed to the Tajik government to accept the need for a political solution, including a cease-fire and national reconciliation. Instead, clashes continued. The UN secretary-general appointed a special envoy for Tajikistan, first Ismat Kittani and later Ramiro Piriz-Ballon, who visited neighboring countries in August 1992 and much later in May 1994 to foster inter-Tajik talks.

From the outset it was clear that political, military, and humanitarian issues needed to be addressed simultaneously. Like the North Atlantic Treaty Organization (NATO) and the UN Protection Force (UNPROFOR) in the former Yugoslavia, and the Economic Community of West African States (ECOWAS) and the UN Observer Mission in Liberia (UNOMIL), Tajikistan represents a possible model, though much more fragmented, of an effort at regional and UN cooperation in a comprehensive response. In November 1992 the central Asian states and Moscow adopted the Alma Ata Declaration in which they agreed to take joint steps in Tajikistan. Troops were deployed along the Tajik-Afghan border, the UN secretary-general sent a good offices mission, and the Office of the UN High Commissioner for Refugees (UNHCR) began to try to promote conditions that would permit refugees and internally displaced persons to return home. However, not only did the UN and the CIS function separately, but Russian generals and contingents sometimes operated independently of Moscow.

The secretary-general himself raised the issue of UN action at the Security Council in late 1993. In addition to his special representative, a handful of UN observers finally were deployed to Dushanbe as the UN Military Observer in Tajikistan (UNMOT). They had freedom of movement and contact with Russian and CIS forces in the area but no access to their various decisionmaking hierarchies. In June 1994 a "Joint Commission," chaired by High Commissioner for Refugees Sadako Ogata, met to address the plight of those left homeless by the conflict. Although she recognized that the human rights situation was "fragile" and that a "shortage of funds may force us to curtail our activities," Mrs. Ogata nonetheless judged that the attempted "integrated approach in Tajikistan has helped to contain the crisis and also to encourage an early search for political solutions."[25]

A fourth round of peace talks was arranged by the UN secretary-general between the government of President Imamali Rakhmonov and insurgents on May 22, 1995. Beforehand, China, France, the United Kingdom, the U.S.,

Germany, the Czech Republic, and Italy issued a joint statement at the Security Council urging progress amongst the parties. UNMOT consists of G7 individuals, including thirty-six military observers from ten countries that monitor the cease-fire. They will effectively legitimate CIS peacekeepers, although there is no mandate to genuinely account for the Russian-led operation.

Georgia

The UN involvement in Georgia has been its most extensive and visible to date within the former Soviet Union, but the impact on the course of events is yet to be determined. Through a de facto institutional division of labor in Georgia, the UN monitored the Russian-backed secession in Abkhazia, while the CSCE covered South Ossetia. After fighting erupted in Abkhazia in August 1992, the UN secretary-general dispatched two fact-finding missions, in September and October. The UN's Department of Humanitarian Affairs (DHA) organized an interagency mission that visited the area in early 1993, and by March the UN issued a consolidated appeal for $21 million to cover the needs of the affected population. In May, Boutros Boutros-Ghali appointed a special envoy, Edouard Brunner, to review the peace process. After a cease-fire agreement in July brokered by the Russians, the Security Council in August approved the deployment of ten UN military observers. Security Council Resolution 858 established the UN Observer Mission in Georgia (UNOMIG) in late August. In January 1995 the Security Council extended the mandate of this 134-member observer group.

In September 1993 fighting broke out again, possibly with the involvement of Moscow, or at least of Russian troops in the area. Georgian forces were routed at the siege of Sukhumi. In several resolutions between September and December, the Security Council expressed concern about the renewed fighting; demanded the withdrawal of Abkhaz forces; affirmed the sovereignty and territorial integrity of the Republic of Georgia; condemned the Abkhazians for their cease-fire violation; and welcomed the efforts of the special envoy, the CSCE, and the Russian Federation in the peace process. In December the parties concluded a memorandum of understanding, and later in the month the Security Council authorized the phased deployment of fifty additional observers.

UN-sponsored peace talks continued in Geneva, New York, and Moscow in 1994 and led to agreement on UN and CIS peacekeeping operations. The combatants were separated by a 24-kilometer security zone along the Inguri River, where Russian forces were deployed. The CIS operation was separate and independent of the UN mission, but the two were to coordinate. UN observers constitute an international presence of sorts in the area. There are regular meetings at the highest command levels, but the observers do not have the kind of access to the Russian forces that would constitute an adequate form of accountability. The issue was further complicated in July 1994 when the Security Council approved the CIS operation in Resolution 937. The decision was generally seen as a *quid pro quo* for approving the French chapter 7 operation in Rwanda and the U.S. invasion of Haiti through Resolutions 929 and 940. And the proximity of the decisions, after months of saying no to the Russian request for a UN imprimatur, seems to indicate that the timing was more than fortuitous.

Both UN and CSCE observers agree that Russian troops, either on their own or under the umbrella of a CIS mandate, have had to manage double objectives in the area. At times they have favored the separatists, but Moscow also had to fulfill its CIS obligations toward Georgia once it became a member after its defeat in the field. This tension may have resembled impartiality, but even Russian spokesmen admitted that their interests were at stake. And it was fair that these should be secured, as is the prerogative of any state. Consequently, to obtain CIS bases in Georgia where Russian troops would be stationed, Russia curtailed support for the nascent Abkhaz and Ossetian regimes.

Moscow's heavy hand pushed the right political buttons locally and ensured that peace and order were maintained on an even keel. A calm environment was in Russia's interest, but this was ensured in the offices of local separatist officials and without the direct participation of the United Nations. Other arrangements, such as negotiations for the repatriation of refugees, were conducted by Russia directly with Abkhazia and Georgia without consulting UNHCR.

In March 1995 Georgians repatriating themselves led to violent reprisals by Abkhaz authorities. The UN did not act, and the Russian response was limited. But as events in Chechnya evolve, the Kremlin may require the collaboriatuon of the Georgian government, and this will affect the balance of "peacekeeping" in the Caucasus.

The March 22 agreement in principle between Russia and Georgia remains in the balance as twenty-five-year rights to Georgia military bases and cooperation on the Chechnyan issues are measured against restoring Georgian jurisdiction over breakaway areas and shifting assistance for

Abkhazia to Georgia. Meanwhile, in mid-April 1995 Russia agreed to an OSCE observer mission in Grozny. Peace has remained elusive to Chechnya despite intermittent negotiations, while the Georgian parliament approved in August 1995 wider powers for the President. This increases Sheverdnadze's freedom to bargain with Russia despite Georgian extremists who feel he has not been as harsh as they wished with separatists in Abkhazia and South Ossetia.

Nagorno-Karabakh

Nagorno-Karabakh is an enclave once populated mostly, now entirely, by Armenians and surrounded by Azerbaijan. Jurisdiction over the enclave was given to Azerbaijan in 1923 on Lenin's orders, and tensions between the two Soviet republics of Armenia and Azerbaijan began almost at once. A shooting war broke out well before the dissolution of the Soviet Union and has gone on more or less continuously since then, with Armenia gaining the upper hand and occupying 20 percent of Azeri territory, in part forming a corridor to the enclave.

In early 1993 both the UN and the CSCE became seized of the Armenian-supported secession of Nagorno-Karabakh from Azerbaijan. Security Council Resolution 822 in April demanded the immediate cessation of hostilities and the withdrawal of Armenian forces from Azerbaijan. In late July Security Council Resolution 853 affirmed the sovereignty and territorial integrity of Azerbaijan, reaffirmed the inviolability of international boundaries and the inadmissibility of the use of force to acquire territory, and condemned the Armenian occupation of parts of Azerbaijan. In the meantime, the CSCE's "Minsk Group," under the leadership of former UN undersecretary-general Jan Eliasson, assumed responsibility for fostering negotiations to resolve the conflict. Eliasson's prior post is perhaps a coincidence, but the Swedish diplomat's long experience in New York, both as his country's permanent representative and as a senior UN official, facilitated an informal collaboration between the two organizations.

The Conference (now Organization) on Security and Cooperation in Europe tried to establish for Nagorno-Karabakh what may be the first genuinely joint Russian-international peacekeeping effort. The operation was to have placed CSCE observers within the Russian military command structure, which was to be within the CSCE political framework. However, the fifty-two-nation summit meeting on European security on December 6, 1994, in Budapest could only agree on continuing to plan for a three thousand-strong multinational force. Despite persisting attempts by Russia to dominate the force, the United States and other governments made clear their intention to keep the Russian contribution below 50 percent. The CSCE had originally wanted an international force with not more than 30 percent supplied by any single nation. In any case, although the exact composition of the force is yet to be determined, the majority of the units are likely to be supplied by CIS member states.

In Nagorno-Karabakh the OSCE is groping to find an appropriate mechanism for balancing the regional power's interests with international accountability. The OSCE is a continuation of the CSCE, which was less a military organization than one concerned with human rights, security norms, and preventive diplomacy within highly consensual operating procedures. Nevertheless, combined CSCE military and civilian monitors have been on the ground in parts of the former second world for some time, particularly the 120 sanctions monitors under the direction of Swedish general Bo Pellnas on the borders of Serbia and Montenegro. But the deployment of peacekeeping forces in Nagorno-Karabakh is quite another matter. Eighteen months of negotiations for some sort of arrangement capable of sanctioning and monitoring third-party peacekeeping to ensure compliance with international standards has not yet been finalized, primarily because of Moscow's refusal to permit meaningful monitoring of its troops on the ground. But if Russian hostility to the idea increasingly erodes and softens within the OSCE context, that organization may take a place beside the Security Council as a source of authorization for accountable forms of intervention.

Whether or not there will be sufficient troops forthcoming from OSCE member states remains to be seen, particularly given the demand of the president of Georgia, Eduard Shevardnadze, that this be a "real mission" and that "If this proves to be just the same as peacekeeping under the United Nations aegis, it will have no result."[26] Also, the U.S. initiative that changed the name from "conference" to "organization" was specifically aimed to enhance the OSCE's stature and establish it as a mechanism for responding to ethnic and regional conflicts in Europe.

Planning continues with what could be an important precedent, but serious political questions ranging from the nature of the cease-fire and the concept of operations to the exact composition of the force and its command and control remain. If extensive commitments are unacceptable to potential troop-contributing OSCE member states, the combination of international observers as part of a Russian command may have to be accepted by both Russia and others. On July 24, 1995, the OSCE resumed another round of negotiations near Vienna between the parties to end the conflict. But the UN remains only indirectly engaged, approving peace efforts from afar.

Moldova

The fourth main region of conflict in the former Soviet Union, Moldova, has not been addressed by the United Nations to any significant degree. While the UN Development Programme (UNDP) maintained a presence in Kishinev, the CSCE mission was preoccupied with gaining access to the Joint Control Commission that directed the Russian-led separation of Moldovan troops from the forces of the separatist "Trans-Dniester Republic." The CSCE also had to contend with the formidable Lieutenant-General Alexandr I. Lebed commanding the 14th Army, which supported the separatists, whether with or without Moscow's approval. This force has now been directed to withdraw over a three-year period.[27]

The trilateral buffer force, comprising Russian, Moldovan, and Trans-Dniester elements, has effectively prevented violent exchanges since its deployment in July 1992, but the underlying causes of the conflict are still unresolved. In particular, Moldovans are unlikely to be satisfied with anything short of the reincorporation of the "Trans-Dniester Republic" within their borders. Yet something of a Cyprus scenario is developing, with de facto permanent division, which the OSCE is better placed to arrest than is the UN.

Bosnia

The main experience of the world organization in the former second world has been in the former Yugoslavia. Before the breakdown of the tenuous cease-fire on May 1, 1995, and the reconfiguration of UN troops in Croatia, UNPROFOR had an annual budget approaching $2 billion, 6,000 civilian personnel and some 40,000 soldiers and police officers from thirty-six countries, of which 24,000 were posted in Bosnia-Herzegovina. UNHCR's annual expenditures in the former Yugoslavia remain about $500 million. Another billion dollars are spent annually by other governmental, intergovernmental, and nongovernmental organizations. This constitutes probably the most expensive, dangerous, and volatile operation ever undertaken by the international community, and with, at best, limited results. Although there has been plenty of rhetorical support for tough action, it has not been backed by sufficient military and political resolve to find a solution among the parties.

For example, November 1994 witnessed a new twist in Balkan violence. After unexpected victories in the Bihac pocket by the Bosnian government army, nationalist Serbs counterattacked. Artillery, tanks, and finally aerial bombardment were especially embarrassing for the United Nations because attacks were staged from the Udbina airfield in the Serbian-controlled vicinity of Krajina, an area of Croatia supposedly patrolled by UN troops. The spectacle of a UN safe area first being used to mount an offensive and then being strafed with cluster bombs and napalm from planes based in another UN-protected area epitomized the feebleness of international efforts. Bihac was a microcosm of long-standing military-political dynamics. The futility of traditional peacekeeping was obvious. Yet the absence of NATO forces on the ground and the limits of its mandate prevented NATO from damaging the Serbian ability to wage war and pushing them to negotiate seriously.

The present chapter is not the place to provide a full account of the UN effort and failures in Yugoslavia. The story has been told and retold,[28] and other authors in this volume address the Yugoslav case in detail. But it is worth mentioning that this area has hosted the first experiment with UN preventive deployment, in Macedonia. If it is to be an effective deterrent, soldiers on the ground require contingency plans and reserve firepower for retaliation. This would amount to an advance authorization for chapter 7 action should the symbolic preventive force be challenged. No such ultimatum has been presented in Macedonia in spite of the presence of some 350 U.S. soldiers among the 1,000-man force. Rather than retaliation, in the event of a serious battle the more likely response will be withdrawal, as western troops did in Beirut in 1982, or indeed as the UN did in the Sinai in 1967.

Although credible reinforcements would not be easy to assemble, and the specter of the combined forces of the Yugoslav National Army (JNA) and the Bosnian Serbs would be difficult to intimidate, it is absolutely essential. Otherwise, the currency of UN preventive action is devalued to such an extent that it should not be attempted. Empty saber-rattling is as dangerous for the credibility and viability of the United Nations as it is for governments.

Subcontracting and the Need for Accountability

After 1989, as the UN's operational landscape became considerably more complicated, the principles of traditional peacekeeping have been challenged. With UN operations increasingly deployed in conflicts within rather than between states, the consent of the parties, which had been a precondition of traditional peacekeeping, was not always forthcoming, was usually ambiguous when given, and was sometimes withdrawn. In the absence of reliable consent, Security Council decisions could not be implemented without considering the use of force, which required a military capability that only the armed forces of permanent members of the Security Council possessed. Inclusion of contingents from these countries in militarily challenging operations in turn raised acutely the issue of command and control. The principle of impartiality also evolved as UN forces attempted to implement Security Council decisions without local consent. A second generation of operations had come into being, beyond peacekeeping but still short of enforcement.

This new category of UN military operations—neither traditional interpositional peacekeeping nor high intensity action against interstate aggression as in the Korean and Gulf Wars—accounts for most of the UN military activity since 1989. These operations are wide-ranging and attempt to prevent and mitigate violence as well as help to assure that conflict does not recur once some kind of settlement has been reached. They include preventive deployment to deter the outbreak of hostilities, as in Macedonia; internal conflict resolution measures in the course of underwriting a multiparty cease-fire within a state, as in Mozambique and El Salvador; assistance to interim civil authorities, as in Namibia and Cambodia; protection of humanitarian relief operations; or guarantee or denial of movement and the protection of safe havens established by the Security Council. These last two have been the principal UN missions in the former Yugoslavia. UN operations of this magnitude are unlikely contingencies in the former second world. The international community is unwilling to provide either the finance or personnel for such undertakings. And in any case it is unlikely that Russia would permit intrusive military measures by outsiders in its former dominions.

In a number of cases, action has been taken by powerful states independently or in coalitions with other member states, nominally under the UN banner but with varying degrees of accountability. Prominent examples of this development include the U.S.-led Unified Task Force in Somalia (UNITAF or Operation Restore Hope), the French in Rwanda (*Opération Turquoise*), the United States in Haiti (Operation Uphold Democracy), and Russia in Tajikistan and Georgia. Such actions have antecedents in UN practice. Both the Korean and the Gulf wars were fought not by multilateral

UN forces but by U.S.-led coalitions under carelessly broad Security Council resolutions authorizing the use of all necessary means to repel the invasion. The Security Council authorized the use of British naval vessels to interdict the passage of oil into Southern Rhodesia to enforce previously ordered economic sanctions. In Korea and Rhodesia, at least the form and sometimes the substance of UN supervision was maintained. The Security Council authorized the Korean force to fly the UN flag and the United States to designate its commander. The force was formally responsible to headquarters in New York, though with a reporting procedure that first passed through Washington. The "Beira Patrol," was a kind of "article 41½" operation, for which Britain was explicitly responsible to the authority of the UN. In the Gulf War, however, although the Security Council authorized an attack on Iraqi forces and imposed the onerous cease-fire terms, there were charges of unaccountability and disproportionate use of force.

On a parallel track, historically there were a number of clearly independent military operations conducting unlawful interventions or genuine peacekeeping-like tasks from which the UN was clearly dissociated. The British-led Commonwealth Monitoring Force (CMF) in Rhodesia-Zimbabwe was a successful arrangement of this kind, though principally designed to remove the issue from Prime Minister Margaret Thatcher's agenda.[29] The Multinational Force and Observers (MFO) in the Sinai was established when Israel refused to accept a replication of the predecessor UN Emergency Force II (UNEF II).[30] The Indian Peacekeeping Force (IPKF) in Sri Lanka was deployed in a peacekeeping posture but rapidly escalated its force structure to contend with the demands of counterinsurgency operations.[31] The Arab League force in Lebanon was entirely dominated by Syria, and the Organization of African Unity (OAU) intervention in Chad proved ineffective.[32] The United Nations did not officially approve any of these missions. Whatever the conclusions about their international legal character,[33] these operations should be judged separately according to the nature of the objectives and the effectiveness in achieving them.

The recent UN practice has developed a kind of subcontract under which a single nation or group of states can be authorized to implement UN decisions. On the one hand, this may be a creative response to the limitations on the institutional resources and resolve of the United Nations. On the other, the practice raises the possibility that governments conducting operations independently could obtain fig-leaf resolutions that convey the legitimacy of UN approval but without sufficient monitoring by the Security Council to assure that the troops meet UN standards of impartiality or that their modus operandi has the approval of the international community in whose name they operate.

Moreover, the requirement to coordinate UN humanitarian and other activities with those of deployed regional forces raises questions about the exact nature of the UN's relationship to non-UN operations. For example, a UN observer mission in Liberia supervises the Nigerian-led Economic Community of West African States Monitoring Group (ECOMOG), while international humanitarian assistance is coordinated through another UN office. To date this has hardly been a model for collaboration.[34] The issue of coordination with non-UN actors, especially with nongovernmental organizations, has become critical in humanitarian assistance in UN areas of operation.[35]

Assuring the legitimacy of independent military activity through standard setting, monitoring, and coordination is likely to become more crucial in the near future as a means of accountability for UN-approved but independently conducted operations in the former second world. Beginning in 1993, Russia sought UN blessing and financing to arbitrate disputes in the former Soviet Union, which would have given these efforts in effect the status of UN peacekeeping operations. For some this amounted to dressing traditional Russian hegemony in the guise of CIS peacekeeping.[36]

Until the summer of 1994, these approaches were consistently rejected. Indeed, in April the secretary-general informed President Boris Yeltsin during a meeting in Moscow that Russia could not receive a UN imprimatur for its military deployments. Later he summed up the position: "a [UN] peacekeeping operation . . . must have multinational forces under direct UN control," if not direct UN command.[37] But this seemed somewhat ambitious in light of UN overstretch and Russia's geopolitical interest in stability in the new states contiguous to it.

Whatever their perceived deficiencies in April, Russian requests were soon viewed differently. Between late June and late July 1994, the Security Council approved three resolutions authorizing intervention of three different Permanent Members of the Security Council in civil wars: a Russian proposal to deploy more troops in Georgia to end the three-year-old conflict there; the French intervention in Rwanda to help stem three months of genocidal conflict; and the U.S. plan to spearhead a force to reverse the military coup in Haiti.

After the initial experiences of the early post–cold war era, the secretary-general has straightforwardly recognized the world organization's poor performance. Even he has been influenced by the new great power activism and UN ineffectiveness. In his first press conference of 1995, he stated "that the United Nations does not have the capacity to carry out huge peace enforcement operations, and that when the Security Council decides on a peace enforcement operation, our advice is that the Security Council mandate a group of Member States, [that] have the capability."[38] This statement reflected the hard realization—based largely on the blurred distinctions between chapters 6 and 7 in Somalia and Bosnia—that was also expressed in his new *Supplement to An Agenda for Peace*. Peacekeeping and enforcement, he said, "should be seen as alternative techniques and not as adjacent points on a continuum."[39]

This thinking reverts back to the black-and-white options that were the root causes of failed experiments with the use of force and indicates a failure to learn the lessons of the last several years.[40] Instead, in this chapter we have sought, as a middle ground between UN ineffectiveness and great power self-help, to make a virtue of the vice of Russian domination over military peacekeeping in the former second world. The crucial element of this middle ground is "accountability."

The Nature of Accountability

Charles William Maynes has argued that big powers inevitably resort to military intervention to pursue their interests, but that they do not necessarily subject themselves to international scrutiny, and hence are not necessarily accountable for their actions. His proposal to move forward with "benign realpolitik" straightforwardly acknowledges the desirability of recognizing this reality, which comes close to a revival of spheres of influence, albeit with UN oversight.[41] Although he later dubbed the concept "benign spheres of accountability," it is not so much regional institutions or international approval that count but regional powers. By endorsing requests from Russia, France, and the United States to take matters into their own hands, the Security Council seemed to be experimenting with a novel type of great power politics that the United Nations had originally been founded to end. As Boutros-Ghali has recently written about such operations: "They may herald a new division of labour between the United Nations and regional organizations, under which the regional organization carries the main burden but a small United Nations operation supports it and verifies that it is functioning in a manner consistent with positions adopted by the Security Council."[42]

Recent decisions have indicated the growing acceptance of the idea of military intervention by major powers in regions of their interest. Mutual consent by permanent members of the Security Council to each other's ventures could be a means of responding to problems that the United Nations is itself unable to manage. But it could also seriously harm the organization. The switch from multilateral toward national execution of international decisions could further slow the development of UN capabilities, fragment collective responses to problems demanding more resources than single nations can or are willing to muster, increase the selectivity of cases, decrease accountability, and subordinate international interests to national imperatives.

Therefore, if subcontracting is to be acceptable, stringent criteria must be articulated and developed to ensure its legitimacy. At the very least:

—It should be clear that the state or group of states are agents of and acting on behalf of the UN and that the link between the two is direct and continuing.

—Although the command of the operation is not functionally part of the UN's administration, instructions from the organization to its agent must be clear, specific, and incontestable.

—The agents must be responsible to the authority of the United Nations and held accountable on an ongoing basis for their actions taken in the name of the international community.[43]

These conditions were approximated during Britain's Beira Patrol. There was certainly U.S.-UN cooperation of a kind in Somalia during UNITAF from December 1992 to May 1993, and subsequently until the withdrawal of U.S. troops in March 1994. Similar cooperative arrangements were envisioned for Haiti both in 1993 before the original mission was aborted and again in the U.S. action in 1994.

The principal instrument for ensuring accountability thus far has been the UN observer mission. Although these missions have reported on conditions in the field, they tend not to have adequate access to the organizational structure of the power in command of an operation. For example, the first UN military observers in Tajikistan did not even speak Russian. In Georgia, in spite of nominal cooperation through regular meetings, both UN and CSCE observers are treated as guests of the powerful and have had only limited exposure to Russian intentions, decisionmaking, mission functioning, and force organization. This problem has been exacerbated in Abkhazia by the decision to move UN headquarters from the Russian base at Sukhumi to Kutaisi outside the area of Russian operations. If UN observers are to become genuine agents for enhanced international accountability, they should operate much more intimately with the regional power or organization that is the UN agent.

In these contexts, what would be a meaningful definition of accountability? Accountability means the ability to ensure that a mission subcontracted by the international community to a powerful state reflects collective interests and norms and not merely the national imperatives and preferences of the subcontractor. There are of course very limited means to ensure lawful behavior and compliance by states generally. However, the issue of ensuring accountability is more acute when a powerful state seeks international approval of an intended or an ongoing military deployment in its backyard. Here the decisionmaking organ is in a position to refuse approval and hence can demand that specific conditions be met—pertaining to the character, size, timing, and goals of an operation and continuing arrangements to ensure accountability—before the potential subcontractor is given an international stamp of approval. Ensuring accountability consists of three elements: an effective mechanism in the field; meaningful content to restrictions governing the behavior of the subcontractor's troops; and costs associated with noncompliance.

The power to withhold approval by itself is not enough. An operational political framework such as a joint monitoring commission must be established in the field. A workable framework consists of two components: a multinational and interorganizational political directorate, to which a force commander or other national civilian officials are responsible; and the physical deployment of outside military and civilian observers within the command structure of the respective military forces and national civilian institutions, also responsible to the political directorate via a subdirectorate or headquarters. This political framework in the field must be linked directly to the international organization that approves the operation, such as the UN or OSCE; it must therefore report independently and not through the subcontractor deploying the majority of military forces.

The political directorate and observers must also ensure that international standards of behavior are respected. The subcontractor's military forces should be expected to adhere to the specifics of the Geneva Conventions and Additional Protocols, to respect the principles of necessity and proportionality in the use of force, and to allow free access by outside humanitarian agencies and the media. Ensuring respect for these conditions entails, in addition to outside military officers, international civilian observers to monitor human rights, the delivery of humanitarian aid, local civilian administration, police and legal systems, as well as relations between local authorities and the intervening force.

The greatest problem of any international regime is enforcement in cases of noncompliance, and this proposal is no exception. If a major power intends to serve national interests that diverge significantly from its proclaimed international role, the only recourse for the decisionmaking body is to refuse approval to the subcontractor. If the subcontractor's performance diverges from agreed standards after the international approval is granted, the observers and the political directorate can only hope to function as whistle-blowers. Such a monitoring body obviously will be most effective when the great power is sincerely motivated. Intransigence of the subcontractor in the face of adverse comments and recommendations will be a strong indicator of ulterior motives. This can then be reported directly to the authorizing body, which maintains the ability to remove its blessing (although withdrawal of Security Council approval granted to a Permanent Member would be subject to veto). This limited leverage to condemn a subcontractor may not stop an illegitimate operation, but it should at least serve to prevent the international organization from being dragooned into national service.

There is some practical experience with similar models for ensuring accountability. The UN Transition Assistance Group (UNTAG) was initially conceived as an exclusive authority in Namibia during a transition period. It was to conduct and organize an election as part of the decolonization of the territory. South Africa, however, was reluctant to surrender so much authority to its nemesis during the transition, and UNTAG effectively became one half of a joint administration of the territory. The UN and the local administration cooperated closely in developing the electoral rules and conducting the registration and balloting processes. UNTAG officials could appeal to the secretary-general and Security Council if the South African administrator-general was intransigent. Another reviewing body was the Joint Monitoring Commission (JMC) composed of the belligerent parties—Angola, Cuba, and South Africa—and of observers from the Soviet Union and the United States, with UN officials acting as experts. This mechanism helped provide confidence in the ongoing peace process and leverage when disagreement emerged. Carefully deployed UN observers in operational structures, with access to the secretary-general and Security Council, as well as a cooperative mechanism like the Namibian JMC as a reviewing body, could serve as effective instruments of accountability generally.[44]

In Cambodia, the Supreme National Council (SNC), composed of the warring factions, exercised interim sovereignty until the election of a national government. Prince Sihanouk held a tie-breaking vote, but if he refused to act, an appeal lay to the UN special representative. The flaw in this arrangement was that the UN was not adequately integrated into the joint mechanism but participated only loosely in the process.[45] The absence of a joint mechanism including the factions and the UN at the operational level meant that each new administrative issue assumed political proportions and led to the UN negotiating rather than exercising its wide powers. Such an operational mechanism apparently had been envisioned by the UN negotiator of the peace plans, Rafeeudin Ahmed, but his replacement with Yasushi Akashi as Special Representative of the secretary-general just before deployment of the operation led to the loss of this unwritten understanding, the fracturing of the SNC at the political level, and the overall dysfunction of the operation.

Another model is to be found in the design of Russia's own operations in the near abroad. Russian forces have had to develop radically new instruments for military challenges faced not far away but close to home. A concept of "peacekeeping-plus" has evolved, which has been applied in the near abroad. The mechanism that coordinates political goals and military forces in peace missions is the Joint Control Commission (JCC). The instrument developed gradually. In Moldova the JCC was composed of the two parties, Moldova and the breakaway regime of the "Trans-Dniester Republic," with Russia as a "big brother" and first among equals. A so-called peacekeeping mission was deployed in a buffer zone between the two belligerent forces. Checkpoints were manned by Russia and the belligerents themselves, and monitored by "observers" responsible to the JCC. Russia provided heavy armaments and therefore an enforcement element of the mission. Nearby General Lebed's 14th Army provided a deterrent capability and ensured a cease-fire that has held since its inception.

Since the CSCE was never permitted access to the body, it could not ensure impartiality. In fact, the JCC in Moldova proved to be an effective means by which Russia could manipulate the parties to suit its interests. Nevertheless, a forum of this kind, if it were internationally accountable, could be a means of controlling recalcitrant political and military leaders whose participation is necessary in a peace process, if they begin to challenge international law and UN authority. A similar mechanism is pending in South Ossetia with the full participation of the OSCE, but it is yet to be realized.

In the initial proposal for Nagorno-Karabakh, also, OSCE observers and Russian forces were to operate under a JCC-like framework with OSCE chairmanship. This could still develop into a realistic and flexible mechanism generally applicable in light of limited international resources, overall fatigue, and the need to provide accountability for great power action. The Nagorno-Karabakh proposal can be distinguished, in principle, from the Abkhazia model where the overall diplomatic framework for negotiations in Geneva under UN chairmanship cannot provide the kind of confidence and leverage that is required for genuine accountability in the field.

Russian operations in the near abroad may be designed to secure Russian interests, whether of the ministry of defense, of President Boris Yeltsin, or in some cases of the general in the field. However, with an adequate mechanism to ensure that they also serve genuinely international interests, they could provide a valuable model and set of lessons for UN operations.

Conclusions

What little the UN has done in the former second world starkly contrasts not only with the scope of UN operations that were required but also with the number of tasks envisioned at present. At the same time, the United Nations is unlikely to deploy in the near future large-scale operations that are independent of Russia or of its regional institution, the Commonwealth of Independent States. In the face of this dilemma—a range of conflicts that it cannot contend with itself but that are too important for it to ignore—the question remains: what is possible for the UN?

Conceptual progress about multilateral military operations is taking place, as is apparent in the secretary-general's *An Agenda for Peace* and *Supplement*, in the veritable cottage industry of analyses about peace-keeping, and in new thinking in many staff colleges and defense ministries.[46] Yet there have been few operational improvements within the United Nations and certainly not enough for the militaries of major or middle powers to feel at ease about the United Nations commanding combat missions.

The kinds of requirements in the former second world are shared in a variety of armed conflicts worldwide. Yet the dominant position of Russia in the region along with the limitations of the UN dictate that an alternative strategy should be considered. In our view, the United Nations should develop its capabilities for a special type of deployment in the former second world. Russia as the regional power would be the main troop-contributing nation rather than a "partner" in a coalition, while the United

Nations would provide an overall political framework. The Security Council would endorse the operation subject to the criteria of legitimacy outlined above. UN observers deployed throughout the command structure of the operation would ensure international accountability.

Indeed, the concept has broader applications. International organization and UN peacekeeping has focused, particularly since the end of the cold war and the collapse of the Soviet Union, on developing an international enforcement capability. But the evident gap between international capacities and the increasing demands for help could be filled by something less in the immediate future. Subcontracting to major regional powers is not a sufficient response to the problems of donor fatigue and UN "strategic overstretch" of the kind that Paul Kennedy attributes to empires.[47] But it may be that reinforced UN observer forces jointly operating with a regional power, hegemon, or even local parties are the best available means to ensure concrete action in the face of internal violence that is feasible, effective, and legitimate.

In principle, major powers with a long democratic tradition are more likely to be embarrassed by criticisms of their aberrant behavior under a subcontract from an international authority than are authoritarian governments. However, all major powers require effective oversight. There has been a significant development in world politics regarding the need for international legitimation of interventions by major powers in the post–cold war era. During the age of empires, imperial masters openly intervened when and where they wished. Then in a second phase, as a result of decolonization, major powers increasingly opted for less noticeable economic and political arm-twisting to foster their interests by proxy rather than for more obvious military force. But when they made use of their armed forces, there was no requirement to seek and no advantage arising from international approval. Finally, in the last half decade we have seen what appears to be a third phase, the increasing importance major powers attach to securing an international imprimatur for their military interventions. The felt necessity of the acting powers to seek Security Council approval for interventions in the Persian Gulf, Somalia, Rwanda, Haiti, Liberia, and Georgia represents a crucial change in international relations and provides important precedents for international decisionmaking.

Official Soviet rhetoric began to change beginning with Mikhail Gorbachev's highly publicized September 1987 *Pravda* article and fully reflects the temper of the post–cold war period. But Moscow's policies to date toward its former republics have largely been reminiscent of those by other major powers during decolonization. This impression has been heightened by Moscow's behavior toward the insurrection in Chechnya. Although this conflict is within the boundaries of Russia, the disregard for international commitments affects any design for an appropriate joint mechanism in Russia's former republics. In the "code of conduct" from Budapest in December 1994, governments pledged not to assign their military to internal security except in accordance with constitutional procedures. In particular, "The armed forces will take care to avoid injury to civilians or their property." Yet hundreds of civilians were killed and homes and means of economic livelihood destroyed when Grozny was leveled. As Christopher Smith, the new Republican chair of the Congressional subcommittee on human rights in Europe stated, "the eradication of a people and its territory is not an internal matter."[48] Moreover, CSCE treaties of 1990 and 1992 set limits for NATO and Warsaw Pact armies. These agreements contain provisions that call for prior notice when more than 9,000 troops or 250 tanks are relocated and for invitations to outside observers when more than 13,000 troops are deployed. There are at least that many soldiers participating in the Chechnya operation (most estimates are 40,000), but no notice was given by President Yeltsin nor was there any invitation to OSCE member states to observe actions on the ground.

Yet we end where we began. With a growing gap between the mushrooming demand for outside help in war zones and the available resources and political will in the West, there is no plausible alternative in the near future to more military interventions by major powers. Because no intervention is impartial,[49] there may be less difference between UN-approved and non-UN efforts than is sometimes thought to be the case.

The utility of a blue or another multilateral-colored decision for outside interventions affords some leverage in the contemporary world disorder. Skeptics will no doubt argue that this is a slender reed on which to rely while the international community takes a next step toward the better maintenance of international peace and security. But it appears to be the only feasible alternative to help contain conflict in the former second world in the foreseeable future.

Major powers, although they inevitably flex their muscles when their geopolitical interests are at stake, do not inevitably subject themselves to international monitoring and law. The struggle, which is an ongoing one in the UN and has just begun in the OSCE with deliberations about its efforts in Nagorno-Karabakh, will be to ensure that subcontractors are held internationally accountable for the actions they undertake on behalf of a wider community of states. As part of a larger and more integrated political and operational framework, the United Nations could join forces with other intergovernmental and nongovernmental organizations, disinterested outside and interested regional states, and the belligerents themselves to provide the confidence and leverage to avoid, mitigate, or even start to resolve violent disputes in the former second world and beyond.

Notes

1. See, for example, Jonathan Dean, *Ending Europe's Wars* (New York: Twentieth Century Fund, 1994), and Valery Tishkov, *Nationalities and Conflicting Ethnicity in Post-Communist Russia* (Geneva: UNRISD, March 1994 working paper).

2. See a set of essays on this subject in Thomas G. Weiss, ed., *Collective Security in a Changing World* (Boulder, Colo.: Lynne Rienner, 1993). For a discussion of the new dimensions of UN security efforts, see Thomas G. Weiss, David P. Forsythe, and Roger A. Coate, *The United Nations and Changing World Politics* (Boulder, Colo.: Westview Press, 1994), pp. 17–100.

3. See Brian Urquhart, "Beyond the Sheriff's Posse," *Survival,* vol. 32 (May–June 1990), pp. 196–205.

4. See Thomas G. Weiss and Meryl A. Kessler, eds., *Third World Security in the Post-Cold War Era* (Boulder, Colo.: Lynne Rienner, 1991).

5. "Note by the President of the Security Council," UN document S/23500, January 31, 1992.

6. Boutros Boutros-Ghali, *An Agenda for Peace: Preventive Diplomacy, Peace-making and Peace-keeping* (United Nations, 1992).

7. See Thomas G. Weiss, "The United Nations and Civil Wars," *Washington Quarterly,* vol. 17 (Autumn 1994), pp. 139–59.

8. For a general discussion of this phenomenon, see Gerald B. Helman and Steven R. Ratner, "Saving Failed States," *Foreign Policy,* vol. 89 (Winter 1992–93), pp. 3–20. For a more detailed case study, see Mohamed Sahnoun, *Somalia: The Missed Opportunities* (Washington: U.S. Institute of Peace Press, 1994); and John G. Sommer, *Hope Restored? Humanitarian Aid in Somalia 1990–1994* (Washington: Refugee Policy Group, 1994).

9. For a further discussion of these issues, see Jarat Chopra, "United Nations Civil-Governance-in-Trust," and John Mackinlay, "Military Responses to Complex Emergencies," in Thomas G. Weiss, ed., *The United Nations and Civil Wars* (Boulder, Colo.: Lynne Rienner, 1995).

10. For discussions, see *The Blue Helmets* (United Nations, 1990), and Alan James, *Peacekeeping in International Politics* (London: Macmillan, 1990).

11. Rosemary Righter, *Utopia Lost: The United Nations and World Order* (New York: Twentieth Century Fund, 1995).

12. Hedley Bull, *The Anarchical Society: A Study of Order in World Politics* (Columbia University Press, 1977).

13. See John Mackinlay and Jarat Chopra, *A Draft Concept of Second Generation Multinational Operations, 1993* (Providence, R.I.: Thomas J. Watson Jr. Insti-

tute for International Studies, Brown University, 1993). UN secretary-general Boutros Boutros-Ghali has affirmed the second generation concept in his public statements and his September 1993 report on the work of the Organization. See UN Press Releases SG/SM/4920 of February 2, 1993 and SG/SM/4985 of April 28, 1993. See also British Army Field Manual, "Wider Peacekeeping," Third Draft, January 1994; U.S. Army FM 100–23, "Peace Operations," Version 6, January 1994; North Atlantic Treaty Organization, "NATO Doctrine for Peace Support Operations," February 28, 1994.

14. Boutros Boutros-Ghali, *Supplement to An Agenda for Peace: Position Paper by the Secretary-General on the Occasion of the Fiftieth Anniversary of the United Nations,* January 3, 1995, document A/50/60, S/1995/1.

15. For a discussion of these issues and some possible solutions, see the report of an independent advisory group chaired by Paul Volcker and Shijuro Ogata, *Financing an Effective United Nations* (New York: Ford Foundation, 1993).

16. Michael Specter, "Rebels Beat Back a Russian Force," *New York Times,* January 3, 1995, p. A3.

17. Kostantin Morozov, "The Grasp of Empire," *New York Times,* January 5, 1995, p. A27. See also Galina Starovoitova, "Reforms Fail Test in Chechnya," *Moscow News,* no. 51, December 23–29, 1994, pp. 1–2.

18. Kurt M. Campbell and Thomas G. Weiss, "The Third World in the Wake of Eastern Europe," *Washington Quarterly,* vol. 14 (Spring 1991), pp. 99–108.

19. See Thomas G. Weiss, "Collective Spinelessness: UN Actions in the Former Yugoslavia," in Richard H. Ullman, ed., *The World and Yugoslavia's Wars* (forthcoming 1996).

20. See Mohammed Ayoob, *The Third World Security Predicament: State-Making, Regional Conflict, and the International System* (Boulder, Colo.: Lynne Rienner, 1995).

21. For an additional discussion, see Thomas G. Weiss and Jarat Chopra, *UN Peacekeeping: An ACUNS Teaching Text* (Hanover, N.H.: Academic Council on the United Nations System, 1992).

22. Richard Smoke and Jan Kalicki, *Final Report of the Security for Europe Project* (Providence, R.I.: Thomas J. Watson Jr. Institute's Center for Foreign Policy Development, 1994).

23. The authors are grateful to Stephen Shenfield for his help on this categorization. See his "Armed Conflict in Eastern Europe and the Former Soviet Union," in Weiss, ed., *The United Nations and Civil Wars,* pp. 31–48. See also Michael E. Brown, ed., *Ethnic Conflict and International Security* (Princeton University Press, 1993); and Ted Robert Gurr and Barbara Harff, *Ethnic Conflicts in World Politics* (Boulder, Colo.: Westview Press, 1994).

24. For a discussion, see Andrei Raevsky and I. N. Vorobev, *Russian Approaches to Peacekeeping Operations,* Research Paper 28 (Geneva: UN Institute for Disarmament Research, 1994)

25. Sadako Ogata, "Humanitarianism in the Midst of Armed Conflict," speech at the Brookings Institution, May 12, 1994, p. 5.

26. Cited in "No Unity on Balkans at Europe Summit," *New York Times,* December 7, 1994, p. A12.

27. "Russian Troops Quitting a Hot Spot in Moldova," *New York Times,* October 28, 1994, p. A12.

28. For an up-to-date discussion, see Ullman, ed., *The World and Yugoslavia's Wars.* See also Lawrence Freedman, "Why the West Failed," *Foreign Policy,* vol. 97 (Winter 1994–95), pp. 53–69; Larry Minear and others, *Humanitarian Action in the Former Yugoslavia: The UN's Role, 1991–1993,* Occasional Paper 18 (Providence, R.I.: Thomas J. Watson Jr. Institute for International Studies, 1994); and Thomas G. Weiss, "UN Responses in the Former Yugoslavia: Moral and Operational Choices," *Ethics & International Affairs* no. 8 (1994), pp. 1–22. A succinct depiction of the military problems of UNPROFOR is Åge Eknes, "The UN's Predicament in the Former Yugoslavia," in Weiss, ed., *The United Nations and Civil Wars,* pp. 109–26.

29. See John Mackinlay, "The Commonwealth Monitoring Force in Rhodesia-Zimbabwe," in Thomas G. Weiss, ed., *Humanitarian Emergencies and Military Help in Africa* (London: Macmillan, 1990), pp. 38–60.

30. See John Mackinlay, *The Peacekeepers* (London: Unwin Hyman, 1989).

31. Rajesh Kadian, *India's Sri Lanka Fiasco: Peacekeepers at War* (New Delhi: Vision Books, 1990); and Shankar Bhaduri and Afsir Karim, *The Sri Lankan Crisis* (New Delhi: Lancer International, 1990).

32. See F. T. Liu, "The Significance of Past Peacekeeping Operations in Africa to Humanitarian Relief," in Weiss, ed., *Humanitarian Emergencies,* pp. 24–37.

33. Jarat Chopra, "Military Peacekeeping outside International Organisations," LL.M thesis, Cambridge University, 1988.

34. See Margaret A. Vogt and A. E. Ekoko, eds., *Nigeria in International Peace-keeping, 1960–1992* (Lagos: Malthof Press, 1993); Margaret A. Vogt, ed., *The Liberian Crisis and ECOMOG: A Bold Attempt at Regional Peace-keeping* (Lagos: Gaboumo Publishers, 1992); and Colin Scott with the collaboration of Larry Minear and Thomas G. Weiss, *Humanitarian Action and Regional Security in Liberia: Problems and Prospects,* Occasional Paper 20 (Providence, R.I.: Thomas J. Watson Jr. Institute for International Studies, 1995).

35. This is a major theme in Larry Minear and Thomas G. Weiss, *Mercy under Fire: War and the Global Humanitarian Community* (Boulder, Colo.: Westview Press, 1995), and *Humanitarian Politics* (New York: Foreign Policy Association, 1995).

36. See "Moscow Counts on Itself to Stem Conflicts in CIS," *Peacekeeping Monitor,* vol. 1 (May–June 1994), 4–5, 12–13.

37. Cited in *Keesing's Record of World Events,* April 1994, p. 39969.

38. Boutros Boutros-Ghali, "Transcript of Press Conference," Press Release SG/SM/5518, January 5, 1995, p. 5.

39. Boutros-Ghali, *Supplement,* para. 36.

40. See Jarat Chopra, Åge Eknes, and Toralv Nordb, *Fighting for Hope in Somalia* (Oslo: Norwegian Institute of International Affairs, 1995); Thomas G. Weiss, "Overcoming the Somalia Syndrome—Operation Restore Hope?" *Global Governance,* vol. 1 (May–Aug. 1995), pp. 171–87.

41. Charles William Maynes, "A Workable Clinton Doctrine," *Foreign Policy,* vol. 93 (Winter 1993–94), pp. 3–20.

42. Boutros-Ghali, *Supplement,* para. 86.

43. For a discussion, see Weiss and Chopra, *United Nations Peacekeeping: An ACUNS Teaching Text,* pp. 24–30.

44. See further on the application of this concept, Jarat Chopra, "Breaking the Stalemate in Western Sahara," *International Peacekeeping,* vol. 1 (Autumn 1994), pp. 303–29.

45. See Janet E. Heininger, *Peacekeeping in Transition: The United Nations in Cambodia* (New York: Twentieth Century Fund, 1994); Michael Doyle and Nishkala Suntharalingam, "The UN in Cambodia: Lessons for Complex Peacekeeping," *International Peacekeeping,* vol. 1 (Summer 1994), pp. 117–47; and Jarat Chopra, *United Nations Transition Authority in Cambodia* (Providence, R.I.: Thomas J. Watson Jr. Institute for International Studies, 1994), Occasional Paper 15; and Steven R. Ratner, *The New UN Peacekeeping* (St. Martin's, 1995).

46. Some good examples of the growing analytical literature are: William J. Durch, ed., *The Evolution of UN Peacekeeping: Case Studies and Comparative Analysis* (St. Martin's, 1993); Paul Diehl, *International Peacekeeping* (Johns Hopkins University Press, 1993); Mats R. Berdal, *Whither UN Peacekeeping?* Adelphi Paper 281 (London: International Institute for Strategic Studies, 1993); John Mackinlay, "Improving Multifunctional Forces," *Survival,* vol. 36 (Autumn 1994), 149–73; and Adam Roberts, "The Crisis in Peacekeeping," *Survival,* vol. 36 (Autumn 1994), pp. 93–120.

47. Paul Kennedy, *The Rise and Fall of the Great Powers* (Random House, 1987).

48. Quoted in "In Brussels Urgent Talks on Chechnya," *New York Times,* January 10, 1995, p. A11.

49. See Richard K. Betts, "The Delusion of Impartial Intervention," *Foreign Affairs,* vol. 73 (November–December 1994), pp. 20–33.

Part Six

THIRTEEN

Fragile Stability and Change: Understanding Conflict during the Transitions in East Central Europe

Keitha Sapsin Fine

The final chapter takes us back to the nature of the conflicts that have devel-oped in the post-Communist world and offers an alternative perspective on them. It gives a vivid portrait of some of the human struggles and chaos common to communities in transition. It reminds us that in many situations where ethnically based violence—even state disintegration—is a possible out-come of local conditions, NGOs operating close to problems at the grassroots level can play a key role in helping to resolve low-level conflict before it becomes violent and intractable. At the least, NGOs, often underfunded, under-staffed, and forced to respond to the agendas of others outside, are beginning to help, barnacle-like, to educate and build the skills for civil societies that can manage conflict through their own institutions.

The Editors

THIS CHAPTER is dedicated to exploring the context for conflict prevention or reduction by various kinds of nongovernmental organizations (NGOs) in east central Europe (ECE), during the difficult and diverse processes of change from authoritarianism to something else, as yet undefined. The several kinds of transitions and the highly differentiated realities of daily life in the countries of east central Europe and the former Soviet Union (FSU) make the subject as complicated, and as open-ended, as the events that have given birth to it. The chapter comprises a thematic discussion, addresses the possibilities for successful local initiatives of various kinds during transitions, and concludes with several broad reflections.

In Place of an Introduction

The past four years have amply demonstrated that no single approach to making a transition from authoritarian practices and mentalities, active or passive, can alone repair long-lived economic-structural, political-social, or individual dysfunctionality. The weakness and corruption of national elites, the continuing presence of the old bureaucratic class, the absence of universal agreement about either the terms of or the transition itself, unpreparedness for emerging problems once central planning and social control disappear, the early fragmentation of oppositions, and inexperience with and misunderstanding of the sphere of so-called civil society was almost universal in ECE. Neither inside nor outside attempts to facilitate development based on economic and political renewal, foreign aid or intervention, lessons in "democracy" or constitutionalism can successfully avoid the outbreak of catastrophe whose origins are either structural and ongoing or irrational, often inexplicable, and ultimately irrelevant to their resolution. In such situations international negotiation, mediation, and conventional conflict-resolution techniques—the conventional tools of international diplomacy—have a patchy record. The scenario remains a gloomy one.

This chapter was prepared with additional support from the Carnegie Project on Conflict Prevention, under the auspices of the Consensus Building Institute and of the Soros Foundation, under the auspices of the Research Support Scheme of the Central European University. Research assistance and translation was provided by Stephanie Baker, Filip Donner, Neven Petrovic, Misa Petrovic, Elena Siderenko, Matyas Szabo, and Irene Zemenova. I am grateful for their enthusiasm and hard work and for our lively discussions. Warm thanks also to Andrii Palianytsia, codirector of the Project on Migration in the Czech Republic, and to Ivan Fiala, regional director of PHARE, for good colleagueship, and to the directors and staff of the numerous NGOs for their generous help.

It is now evident that postcommunist governments, whose officeholders have little experience in the practical matters of governing, whip the long-held grievances of ethnic minorities and others into conflicts by errors of both omission and commission. Once begun it is difficult to resolve conflicts that result from deliberate neglect, ignorance, willful violence, or a human "imbalance" with or within a fixed environment. "Spontaneous combustions" in the authentic sense—that is, conflagrations that, however comforting the phrase, defy our attempts at explanation and often also at remediation—are peculiarly intractable either to conventional or unconventional resolutions.

Most ethnically based conflicts also have underlying historical causes or are a function of undeveloped new social relations. Transitional periods are fertile fields for spontaneous combustions. Peoples struggling for the ethnic identity denied to them quickly become political groups demanding territory or the social and linguistic concession they believe will enhance their security for all time. The absence of a usable past and a viable present, widespread xenophobia, and the non- or shaky existence of viable nation-states (however different in origin and practice) around them, almost guarantee the emergence of ethnic nationalism—cultural and political—on the part of neglected minorities and old and newly enfranchised majorities. This has been particularly the case during the transitions in ECE and the FSU.

In environments fraught with conflicts, there are certain functions that some kinds of local nongovernmental organizations seem best fit to undertake. NGOs that are devoted to conflict prevention or resolution can open doors and windows to dialogue between some perpetrators and victims of endemic hatreds, bear public witness to grievances, and introduce new ideas and occasionally new techniques to break political and verbal logjams. They can work to educate local populations and the next generation about everyone's human and civil rights, and teach some skill sets: how to spot signs of trouble and what to do when "hate comes to town." They can also train community leaders, design a number of projects that mixed populations in local communities can work on together, and mount creative media projects to help spread the word.

But no NGO—international, national, or local—can prevent an ethnic conflict or bring about its resolution in the absence of a political, economic, and civil environment that honors at least some major rules of law and practices the rudiments of public discourse. Millions of dollars and countless efforts have gone down the drain because foreign governments, major funders, and overzealous activists have neglected to understand that transitions do not emerge with fully developed civil societies in tow. The rhetoric of transitions no more creates democratic practices than does the scheduling of elections. These are hard but essential truths. When beginning this project I recalled and reread Primo Levi's marvelous essay "Stable/Unstable" in *Other People's Trades*. Let me quote from the last paragraph here:

> The contours of . . . fragile stability which chemists call metastability are ample. Included in them, besides all that which is alive, are also almost all organic substances, both natural and synthetic; and still other substances, all those that we see change their condition of a sudden, unexpectedly: a serene sky, but secretly saturated with vapor, which in a flash becomes clouded; a quiet stretch of water which below zero freezes in a few instants if a pebble is thrown into it. But the temptation is great to stretch those contours even further, to the point of enclosing in them our social behavior, our tensions, all of today's mankind, condemned and accustomed to living in the world in which everything seems stable and is not, in which awesome energies (I am not speaking only of the nuclear arsenals) sleep a light sleep.

What I write about NGO work in regard to ethnically based conflicts, any recommendations I make, any conclusions I reach, are reassuring only to the extent that another "spontaneous combustion" does not consume them or great power politics fan a casual spark into a bonfire. I begin then with this disclaimer and continue by raising some salient issues.

Antecedent Regimes: "The Old Is Not Yet Dead; the New Cannot Be Born"

In any example we can pose, antecedent regimes inevitably have a much longer reach on hearts and minds, habits and practices, vision and experience during transitions than most people are prepared to admit beforehand.[1] A number of characteristics carry over from antecedent regimes into transitional periods. The form of the authoritarianism—one-party regime, personal or military dictatorship—subtly frames expectations about post-transition politics. The existence and extent of systemic and systematic use of violence by the state to enforce its rule and the extent to which a high level of violence was also internalized (and hence legitimated) by both the opposition and the populace can appear again in new guises. The deliberate confusion of dissidence with criminality by the old regime, the suppression of ethnic minorities, and the identification of criminality with a minority group such as the Roma also carry over into public response toward democratic opposition and minority claims in the new regime. National myths about the past used by the old regime, its strength, and the extent to which negotiations became part of the immediate transition period all help set the stage for how conflicts are handled in the post-transition period.

It is important to underscore that in almost no transition are former political, economic, and military elites and bureaucratic structures, including the various police, ever completely stripped of power or function. If they were, who would run the remnants of the former states?[2] The prior state may loose its old monopoly over violence, but the new state rarely abandons some forms of violence as an agent of social control; it cannot. Neither new norms nor practices nor the rule of law have been internalized, and outside elements also disrupt the fragile status quo. Clearly, a high level of violence before and during a transition does not bode well for quickly developing norms of democratic behavior or a universal rule of law.[3] The form and kind of police activity before the shift in combination with prior judicial structures that remain in place and the absence of reformed legal training also ensure that some "business" goes on as usual. Responses to the new state, both by criminals—domestic and foreign—and by "normal" people, are remarkably similar to practices in the past: don't provoke it; try to ignore it.

The existence of an imperial or "colonial" past prior to the antecedent regime is also an important indicator of the politics to come. On rare occasions it may be the only prior form of government that is referred to as a model. High degrees of social and economic inequality correlate with high degrees of intolerance and hence with high degrees of state and private violence toward specific groups. There is no sane reason to expect these practices to cease overnight. Moreover, no matter how harsh the preconditions, in almost no instance did everyone, participant or witness, agree that a revolution or evolution was desirable or necessary. Various oppositions are built in to every transition unless one form of authoritarian government is simply to be replaced with another.

The Uneven Character of Transitional Processes

The literature on transition theory, on the transitions themselves, on nationalism, on ethnicity, on religious and other fundamentalisms, on conflicts and their resolution, on civil society and its discontents is growing by leaps and bounds. No doubt reflecting a new academic industry fueled by the so-called end of the cold war. Strangely absent is a full consideration of the effects of the antecedent regimes and the character of a given transition on all manner of ensuing social organization and conflict. I cannot here do justice to this theme, but want to draw several points, beginning by noting that transitions are notoriously periods of uneven development.

The character of transition is seemingly the easiest to address, if one can trust the huge literature in the burgeoning field of "transitionology." Its volatility rests on an unstable bedrock of dedication, illusion, ambition, confusion, and a powerful if inchoate desire to leave the past behind. Some transitions are in effect revolutions; others evolutions; still others seem to run in place. Some occur according to ruling plan, others escape the faltering grasp of authoritarianism, pushed over the edge by a small core of dedicated members of an opposition who often have no taste for, interest in, or sustained capacity for rule. Sometimes their opponents, the former rulers, simply have to conduct "business as usual" to upset the new apple cart. The ECE transitions have a mixed history in these regards as in others, specifically: (a) the manner in which the various transitions either integrated or (mostly) discarded the oppositional generation; (b) who succeeds the dissident generation; and (c) how new regimes deal with their own pasts. The last is a subject around which much NGO activity has already occurred, but it is hard to measure how much impact "watch-dogging" has had on treatment of old regime actors. Not every communist was "bad"; not every noncommunist "good" is how one member of the former opposition put it.

Actors

All the recent transitions contained from the beginning their own antitheses, built in opposition to the putative changes they promised. The conservative opposition (including surprisingly large numbers of former Communists) can later become a dangerous source of intransigence on the path to democratization—even or especially because it usually manages quickly to control key sectors of the old and new economy and later enters the government. Another group becomes wildly opportunistic, given the right circumstances in their pasts and the chaos of the present (corruption, insider knowledge, outside aid, geographical proximity to power, resources, markets, and so on). If they are successful, over time they turn peculiarly helpful to those they once might have opposed. In the second phase of the transition, economic success leads many members of the former regime and opportunistic nomenclature to throw their weight behind renewed calls for stability and "normalization." They, too, soon try to enter the government.

The solidification of strata of new economic and political conservatives also encourages the emergence of political forces to their right. A variety of nationalist and economically conservative political parties emerge rapidly. Although their representation in the new parliaments is small, some become sectarian. The most extreme practice extraconstitutional "politics," dabbling in destabilization tactics, and become an ongoing thorn in the side of the early generations of political leaders. Their presence on the political scene helps ensure that both the public elites of the major new parties and the private elites in the business world remain relatively closed groups. The narrowness of the new elites creates an environment in which a culture of real and perceived exclusion continues to prevail, further exacerbating old social divisions and grievances and creating a widespread conviction that "nothing has really changed."

In this climate, newly permeable to myriad outside influences, criminal and social violence, often highly politicized, can and does emerge. Some of this violence is, sad to say, "normal" in western terms, and probably intractable. But the new nation-states must still confront it, must still grapple with the issue of how much disorder, how much violence and in which venues, is morally and practically tolerable. A first response is often to limit the range of emerging civil liberties.

The prior existence of a moderately competent and ambitious educated class who, while not classical "dissidents," did not actively oppose change, is crucial for the success of any transition. In combination with the opportunistic nomenclature from the previous regime, with whom they frequently overlap, they help keep the transition alive after the exhilarating first weeks and months wear thin, rationalizing and articulating the new directions in the face of the inevitable popular withdrawal from politics. This is a particularly important group because its members acquired sufficient skills under the prior regimes to perform valuable functions in and for the new state. However, significant sectors of the general population, especially groups that feel particularly betrayed or disenfranchised by the changes, find them too redolent of the old order. Resentment can build quickly over the rapidity with which the "opportunists" legitimate themselves, acquiring power and fortunes in the process. Yet, in the strange way in which the familiar is often preferred to the new, unless their behavior is scandalous, they are almost never replaced by the members of the old opposition movements, who are perceived as too radical or too "visionary" to accomplish day-to-day tasks.

Despite their foreign contacts and good press abroad, after each transition, many from the dissident generation are relatively quickly pushed out of or remove themselves from public office. If such individuals remain in public life, they are quickly marginalized unless they shift ideology and strategy. At best, they eventually form the nucleus of a new democratic opposition, which tries to rescue the vestiges of social welfare politics from the rush to marketize politics as well as the economy. But often they remain better known abroad than at home. The smartest and most committed become journalists, academics, and heads of NGOs—all positions from which they can either watchdog the new regime or mount a new opposition to it. In almost every case the new political cleavages that emerge exacerbate old resentments and provide the basis for a new competitiveness. They also ensure that those who have the most to lose, those with the fewest political skills, or those with no taste for rapid maneuvering are the most rapidly marginalized.

Timing within Transitions

Timing within the phases of each transition is another key variable. By the end of the first year the slow pace of change and the erosion of the widespread illusion that foreign nation-states that had been the loudest sworn opponents of the authoritarian regimes (at least in the wars of propaganda) would be the guarantors of a new social and economic cushion, and through heavy investment the savior of the inevitable economic crisis, dissipates a lot of goodwill. The groundswell of economic insecurity undermines popular enthusiasm for the transition, and a wave a demoralization sets in. Moreover, on practical grounds alone, the amount of time that continues to be devoted to family production chills interest in political participation.

The slow death of illusions, the withdrawal of many of the most competent bureaucrats from the public sector, a gradual exodus by talented youth, the impact of global forces (social, economic, political) all increase new regime fragility to internal violence and external manipulation. At this point, somewhere in the first year of a transition, two groups of important internal conflicts surface: (a) old unresolved grievances based on ethnicity or minority status and the unfinished business from the past, and (b) new ones based on the realignment of social forces. The former frequently encompass quarrels around a broad range of citizenship rights, issues around transborder migration, around repatriation of fellow nationals long in residence elsewhere, immigration and refugee problems, and restoration of material goods and political status to those injured by previous regimes. The latter include problems of youth, pensioners, social welfare, and issues of civil liberties. In particular how the new regime and the population at large deals with the past—both past abuses of segments of the population and the social costs of repression—is a crucial turning point in the development of any transition. (At such moments the role of certain NGOs can become very useful for ensuring regime continuity, if not regime probity or stability.) Where a "thick line" has not been drawn, as in most cases, the propensity for an increase in social violence is heightened. And in the course of all this, politics becomes increasingly "ethnified."

After the first two phases of a transition, if a transition is "lucky" (Poland, Hungary) a segment of the old communist core and precommunist democratic socialists join some members of the oppositionalist generation to resurrect progressive social welfare politics. Assuming a thermidor has been avoided, this coalition serves as an antidote to the extremes promulgated by the "conservative" governments that usually emerge and can also address popular discontents. At the second round of elections, this faction sometimes manages to reenter the formal political arena by means of a variety of coalitions. The period after the second round of elections is usually another time of great political and social confusion as well as great economic uncertainty. During the long "third phase" of a transition, new regimes must survive both domestic and international trade and investment controversies; the regularization of numerous forms of the new economy; continuous political squabbling, the claims of minorities for redress and justice, the consequences of new economic and social inequities generated by the transition (for example, sharp increases in costs for education). They must simultaneously learn to function in new domestic and foreign environments. Under these conditions, the new Communists and social democrats become in fact a stabilizing force. At best this is also a phase in which NGO activity—both service projects and attempts to mobilize legislatures around new policies—could increase, providing sufficient human and capital resources are available. But in most cases resistance to broadening the sphere of the social and the political remains high; civil interventions are difficult to accomplish.

Where this trajectory occurs only partially (as in the Czech Republic)— that is, the social democratic coalition enjoys wide popularity but few seats in parliament and no government posts—or not at all (Slovakia, Romania), the development of civil aspects of the transition is slowed, and the propensity for social violence increases. In these instances, many members of the new states become convinced that nothing much has changed except names and faces and that their economic and social well-being, already in decline, is newly at risk. During this period, which can be quite a long one, new social factions resurrect old grievances and levy new demands on the state. Some of these are stimulated by the evidence of increasing inequities in daily life chances; other issues are fueled and funded by partisan outsiders. In either case the complaints can easily be perceived as demands for new forms of privilege, particularly if they come from minority ethnic groups. And in each case various local and international mafias have stoked criminality and contributed to escalating violence as well as a range of illicit activities that frequently accompany instability.

There are partial exceptions to the above trajectory. In countries where the social democratic opposition has played an increasingly active role in constructing the agenda of the transitions (Poland, Hungary), the propensity for new heights of social violence—for example, by youth or against the Roma or refugees, excepting criminal activity—has been quite limited. The former East German state is an exception to many of the political and economic aspects of transitions elsewhere, but not to the escalation of social violence. In Romania the "transitional" government itself continues to play an instrumental role in fomenting discord and a high level of social violence. The Bulgarian transition, on the other hand, contained a curious mix of protowestern-type politics and economics, a heavy dose of centralized planning and state supports, along with a continuation of repressive state politics toward the significant minority populations: Turks, Roma, Pomacks, and ethnic Greeks. However, it is also a place where the concerted activities of a small number of organized human rights activists has gradually led to changes in state policy and even behavior.

Ethnic Identity and Interethnic Conflict

In extensive discussions with a variety of east central Europeans and former citizens of the Soviet Union, I have been struck over and over again by how often and vehemently people in minority groups, as well as members of majorities, deny the very suggestion that it is ethnicity (or religion or language) per se that lies at the basis of a given conflict. The conversations go something like this.

No, it is not the ethnicity of "X" (individual or group) that is the problem, it is their desire to have their own (that is, "our") territory for themselves (or: their insistence that we speak their language, and so on) that engenders the strife, a member of an ethnic minority tells me. We have never had a chance to have our own ethnic identity; central planning was as hard on us as it was on the economy—the old "majority" didn't care about us and neither does the new one. We're still a minority. Even when we have our own political party, and members in new parliaments, we're still a minority. How can you expect us to want to again acquire a new national identity that's not our own? Attempts to force us to assimilate or integrate remind us of the past: the state's telling us what to do again! [If the new state is particularly weak or particularly strong, it can actually provoke rather than help resolve simmering or incipient conflicts.] If we each had our own country, our own state, maybe we wouldn't have to fight over the allocations of the past or over the inequities of the present.

You can talk about resolving ethnic or racial conflict, people would add, because you live in a political system that works, and you have enough economic resources for everyone (sic!). But when you don't have a functioning political system, and normal people can't make a living, they are going to fight over controlling an entire autonomous nation-state or pieces of it. Everyone wants to be part of a ruling majority—just like in the United States. And no amount of western reasoning or sanctions or human rights talk will convince us otherwise.

Okay, I'd respond, but there just aren't enough empty countries to go around, and giving up territory—or privilege—is not exactly the most popular game in town. I know the transitions are imperfect—to say the least. So what would help cool passions? Lead to integration—not assimilation—and the acceptance of pluralism? Economic aid, was the answer, lots and lots of economic aid. [Ethnic minorities often immigrate, or want to, for economic reasons.] Pause. Maybe. And education. Pause. Maybe. Giving us our rights. [Collective rights, I note, not individual ones.] And time. Lots and lots of time.

When I spoke with members of majorities about the "minority" problem, the conversations were remarkably similar, with some additions: We're not responsible for how they were treated under communism, people told me. We're the largest group with a historical claim to this region, this country. It simply makes sense that everyone follows the same rules and speaks the same language—ours—inside the same political borders. We're too poor a country to have programs and education in more than one language. Or, referring mostly to the Roma, I was told: They're okay if they work and obey the rules like everyone else. The problem is they don't; even the Communists couldn't make them conform—how can we?

In regard to the increasingly large numbers of asylum seekers and refugees who are being supported by the Czech and Slovak and Hungarian governments as best they can (in and out of camps), local populations express ambivalence. They sympathize with the trauma induced by loss of place, home, identity, yet are simultaneously fearful that the wars elsewhere will spill over their borders, that the newcomers will be a tremendous drain on the budget, that they "won't fit in." They say: If people don't want to obey our rules, they shouldn't come here in the first place. Anyway, most of them don't really want to stay here; they just use us to try to go west any way they can. They know they can't go home. What is happening in . . . Yugoslavia, Russia . . . is awful; we know that. If they want to stay here and work and learn our language and apply for citizenship, become like us, that's another story. But most don't. And we can't support them forever. . . . I don't know what I would do differently, except not let them in. How can they think otherwise? Recently, even the major human rights groups are reluctantly engaging in discussions designed to limit the numbers of refugees and asylum seekers, in part to ward off future conflicts.

Ethnicity can simply be a matter of belonging to an ethnic group, knowing it and saying so. It can also be a matter of political self-definition, an ascriptive category subjectively supplied by others, a chosen behavior, a belief structure, or simply a reflection of the perception of others. It does not in itself connote power status. People often act seamlessly as both individuals who happen to be members of an ethnic group and as "ethnics"—members of a group whose attributes happen to make them "different" from "others" (the "majority") with a clear agenda. In either case, negotiating life as an "ethnic" and as a member of a "minority" is very different from transiting life as a member of a hegemonic majority—which might also be ethnically coherent. Members of ethnic minorities are never free of certain problems, the burden of perceptions, of stereotyping. Obviously, it is particularly difficult to work with majority and minority populations under these conditions.

It is tempting to believe that ethnic group identity does not have to turn automatically into minority politics, minority politics into ethnocentrism or ethnic nationalism, and ethnic nationalism into a struggle for a unitary, culturally and linguistically coherent nation-state. But there are certain conditions that belie optimism: conditions where the collapse of a centralized power put the "monopoly of legitimate violence," the enforcement of social order, up for grabs; instances where popular movements worldwide have legitimated xenophobia; where old forms of social relations swiftly become unstable; where some new states are weak, other "ethnic groups" too weak to form states or nations, and a broad range of other insecurities characterize daily life, then realizing one's group identity linguistically, culturally, as a new political unit—a homogeneous nation-state—becomes more and more compelling.[4] Even where the possibility of achieving an actual nation-state—or at lesser levels, a second official language, or concessions such as state-supported religious or cultural education, or street signs in two languages—is remote or nonexistent, ethnicity has become the dominant cleavage in ECE, replacing class with a far less malleable social and economic category than class once offered.

Yet there is no such thing as a single form of ethnic identity or one type of struggle for it. Ethnic identity contains both subjective and objective elements; it can be "inherited" culturally or it can reflect a deliberate choice, an opportunistic response to perceived benefits. Post–World War II history has provided numerous instances of protracted ethnically based conflicts—initiated by minorities and majorities both—that have been resistant to all conventional forms of intervention. Sometimes they die down, sometimes the cost is so great that one or the other side makes concessions; sometimes the pressure of externalities, mostly economic factors, makes the stakes so high that the stronger side will move to stem the conflict. People fighting against those they consider historical oppressors or undesirable compatriots are not easily convinced that there is anything left to bargain over. They fight on, retreat, go underground, nurse wounds and defeats, and gather strength for the next time. In ECE they can do this because of the crazy-quilt pattern of ethnic settlement in the region, and because national ethnic majorities are rarely also majorities at all local levels.[5] Locally, majority-minority distinctions can be reversed by wealth, status, function. Conflicts in the former Yugoslavia illustrate this all too well, despite "multicultural" family and regional structures.

I cannot help but believe that the conditions about which I have just written were exacerbated by the "successful" example of the Slovene secession and thoughtless western responses to many elements of the transitions, as well as to the tragic unfolding of a new terror in Croatia, Bosnia, and Serbia. The continuing horror in the former Yugoslavia and steady eruptions in the near and far reaches of the former Soviet Union serve to raise anxieties and to rub salt in many small wounds elsewhere. I emphasize, then, that the various long historical routes to the unified nation-states of western Europe, which included both "revolutions" and evolutions resulting in religious and linguistic accommodation, in the transformation of labor markets, in the development of modern administrative and military structures, in the emergence of a common culture, and so on[6] are now moot in regard to ECE and the FSU.

When two or more unequal groups have been equally oppressed by a common authoritarian power, the collapse of central power provides the "freedom" to indulge historic hatreds and newfound interests. In ECE, in fact, some who were "oppressed" by an "outside" power were also the former ruling local power. That did not help make them a popular majority or minority in the postauthoritarian period. Nor do their members feel secure in the newly won "freedom." Now, one respondent of such an ex-ruling majority told me, we are free to carry a gun, just like you are. It's dangerous here now. If someone attacks me or my family, I have to be able to protect myself.

That's what the police and a legal system are for under western forms of government, I remark, even when they work imperfectly. People laugh. You've got too much crime, they say; under the Communists we didn't have very much criminality, now we do. The mafias—Chinese, Russian, Italian—are all over the place; so are the smugglers and the gypsies. And the police are corrupt too, just differently than before. It's better, but it's more dangerous. Who are your enemies, I ask. Foreigners, they answer, Russians and gypsies and immigrants; we don't like them. They are not like us. What about "Y" minority, I'd ask. You've lived together in the same state for years. Are they enemies too? Yes and no, was the usual answer. Things have changed. You never can tell. Then they'd tell me where to buy the guns and knives and trained attack dogs that are commonplace in more and more households.

Perhaps needless to say, I have had parallel conversations with members of former minority groups—who believe they always did and still have the most to fear from the ex-ruling group, many of whose members still control essential resources. Under conditions of fear, and with horrible wars raging out of control in the Balkans and the eastern reaches of the former Soviet Union, issues of criminality and ethnicity are easily confused. Everyone who is "other" becomes a criminal, an enemy. We should not be surprised.

Ethno-political identity and the groups that embrace it come in all sizes, shapes, colors, languages, histories. Some long-lived conflicts between ethnic groups can be contained within a prevailing political and legal system. They rankle and stimulate ill will, feelings of discrimination and isolated cases of violence, but rarely ignite a destabilizing civil war between the French and English spatting against the Quebecois, and between the Basques and the Spanish state. These are often, but not always, local in origin and geographically bounded. Other ethnic conflicts are national in scope and intention, demanding power, rights, recognition, benefits but more rarely spill over into wholesale intractable violence (involving the Native American and Latino populations in the U.S., and the Welsh in Britain). Still others are at least partially organized and conceive of their rights and needs in the context of an international arena; depending in part on state response, a violent struggle may or may not emerge (such is the case regarding the Kurds, Palestinians, Irish, African Americans). Still other violent ethnic (and racial) conflicts are stoked by years of abuse, repression, or neglect of minority populations by majorities (as in South Africa, and the FSU). If leadership is strong enough, a few of these die down; in others the form shifts from conflicts with the state to intergroup conflicts that do not threaten the integrity of the state.

To westerners, the outbursts of ethnic nationalism in ECE and the FSU appear as artifacts of transitions from authoritarianisms, a consequence of manipulations by unscrupulous regional power brokers, and as a confused response to the collapse of public order. They are also, clearly, unwoven remnants of the collapse of earlier empires, long buried in subsequent ones, lost in the inevitably unhappy divisions of territory following on two world wars. But, in addition, we need to be clear that fierce ethnic identity in ECE—tragic, seemingly irrational, economically counterproductive—appears rational to its adherents. We need to understand the strength of these identities in terms of the sharp disassociation with the old regimes, and in terms of a very particular use of myth to create a new security in the face of collapse. In these circumstances, ethnic identity and identity politics offer a "clean" new identity, without reference to previous roles or status.[7] And ethnic nationalism offers a counterweight to the right-wing coalitions of former communist elites and extremist nationalists who are determined to resist modernization and political change.[8]

Clearly, then, in the current context there is no absolute right to self-determination based on race or ethnicity either on the part of majorities or minorities. The context sketched above suggests that it remains to be seen if either intergroup relations between ruling majorities and minorities *or* transfers of populations and resources can occur peacefully within the region as a whole and particularly across its many troubled border areas. This is surely another area for creative work on the part of local and international NGOs.

The New Demography—New Conflicts

East central Europe as a whole, not just the Balkans, is a crowded region of the world overpopulated by people of many languages, religions, and cultures crammed into small, territorially artificial nation-states. Population groups have been shifted back and forth across borders for most of this century. Thanks in large part to the Soviet policy about ethnicity, all the countries behaved as if they were completely homogeneous (while collecting statistics about the behavior of their minorities, particularly the Roma) at long-lived cost to ethnic identity. Most remain fiercely attached to a majority identity, to the extent of seriously entertaining plans for sending "home" the "foreign" populations that have lived inside their borders for years. The extent of the attachment is no better revealed than in the behavior and policies that have emerged toward people expelled from territories after World War II by the Communists, and toward members of the majority ethnic group who found themselves on the other side of their own border after the war. In neither case have ruling majorities rushed toward their excompatriots or coethnics with open arms. Neither Sudaten Germans nor hyphenated Czech-Ukrainians are welcome in the Czech Republic; Slovak-Hungarians are *not* welcome in Slovakia; Hungarian-Romanians are *not* welcome in Hungary, and so on.

When we put repatriation efforts, the violent conflicts in the Balkans and the former Soviet Union on hold, what immediately appears most worrisome is the long-term effects in ECE and the West of the new movements of people originating further east and south. The first stop to the west is often either Prague or Budapest, the new "buffer zones" between East and West.[9] The thousands of people on the move, legal and "illegal" and mostly unwelcome, create situations fraught with potential conflicts. Their ranks are many: young people fleeing "westward"; refugees and asylum seekers from the wars; waves of young men and women immigrants seeking work; extended families of Roma fleeing situations engendered by the new politics; single men traveling in search of a new life; young westerners looking for adventure, for a cheap place to live, for themselves (and for drugs); prostitutes and their "controls"; smugglers of various ilks; traders and carpetbaggers of every stripe coming and going.

At the other end of the spectrum, dark-suited industrialists, consultants, and putative investors (mostly but not exclusively westerners and Middle Easterners) rub elbows in the lobbies of the $200 a night hotels, at the tables of the Euroclass restaurants. The ubiquitous mafias—Italian, Russian, Chinese (dealing in drugs, goods, and money)—and hordes of tourists complete the picture.[10] In various mixes, they fill the streets and cafés of center cities, overflow into old fixed neighborhoods, spill out of the refugee camps into the surrounding villages.

The new immigrants both complement and distort the old economies and traditional social order. Undeniably a certain new cosmopolitanism is emerging. But on the other hand, car thefts escalate, housebreaking and purse snatching become shockingly common, and women hesitate to travel alone at night. New social divisions emerge along economic and foreign-native lines, between rich and poor, fanning local feelings of economic and social insecurity. Ethnic and racial incidents appear from nowhere, among students, in pubs, around wage differentials in hiring. In extreme instances the behavior of the interior and police departments seems strikingly enough like "before" to provoke, either by default or bad behavior, suspicion on all sides concerning their "neutrality" and hence to raise the level of free-floating anxiety. In fact, then, the rapid emergence of new ethnic labor markets within the "buffer zone" has fanned new sets of resentments: here familiarity is breeding contempt.

Given the range of the phenomena sketched above—from the relatively low-level conflicts that have appeared between, for example, "foreign" Hungarians and "host" Slovaks or Romanians, the Baltic peoples and the Russians, the Russians and the Ukrainians, to the holocaust in the former Yugoslavia and the ethnically defined wars in the FSU—lesser disputes must be kept in perspective, even as resolutions to them are neither easy to come by nor obvious. I must emphasize that over time responses to perceptions of ethnic disloyalty have become harsher throughout the greater region, as witnessed by recent Russian behavior in Chechnya. (In fact, the strife between Muslim Chechnya and Orthodox Russia is ancient.) There are, then, fewer and fewer "classic" conflicts subject to peaceful resolution, even if the local political systems were so inclined.

We have seen that in ECE so-called "classic" ethnic issues can quickly escalate into violent ethno-national conflict.[11] Included among issues that easily produce sparks if not flames are resistance by newly enfranchised majorities to the demands of newly disenfranchised minorities, as in the Baltics or the Transcaucasus; a group's insistence on the "correctness" of its

own interpretation of a shared past; the deliberate refusal to accept as
legitimate the behaviors and demands of others in regard to the public
sphere; the insistence of majority ethnic control over all or part of the
educational and cultural institutions; what priority to give to individual
citizen rights rather than to collective group rights. In addition, there are
also a number of very real secondary demands that need to be addressed if
they are not to grow into major long-lasting conflicts. They include demands for local control, for official language rights, for "affirmative"
treatment to redress prior neglect, for bi-lingual education, for restitution,
for state aid for churches, for public signs in dual languages. The high
stakes of membership in the European Union and western aid or investment
will force compliance with "western" norms around some of these issues,
but many remain open questions.

The New Racism

If the instances outlined above were the only kinds of conflicts in which
ethnicity were central, the tasks of reconciling needs and interests would be
difficult enough. But there are also other kinds of conflicts that involve
ethnicity, race, and politics: random violence against fellow countrypeople,
deliberate attacks on foreigners and on certain political minorities, and
against the Roma by the new neofascists and skinheads. The Roma, of
course, also suffered discrimination during the communist period, were
widely castigated for their antisocial behavior, and were arrested then and
now in disproportionate numbers. In addition, for a complicated set of
reasons, they are now subject to new inequities under the new citizenship
laws in several countries. The ad hominem attacks that have appeared
against "strangers"—people who are dark like Roma (Latins, for example),
Asians, or Africans, even westerners—are not yet addressed in the language
of "racism," but the character of the attacks suggests that a new racism is
emerging alongside the refusal to admit to an ethnic, as distinct from a
national, basis for both social violence and for ethnically based conflict.

In the West we no longer debate the appearance of racism both in de jure
(legal) and de facto (ascriptive and social) forms; we accept that racism can
and has become, in effect, a social relation.[12] In ECE racism is associated,
historically, with anti-Semitism. Will it, like ethnicity, remain in the minds
of people in ECE subsidiary to nationalism, or will it achieve an independent momentum, in part stimulated by the reemergence of neofascism and
the new right in the region? In the face of the emergence of racism in ECE,

there is cold comfort in the recollection that in classical Nazism, the racial project overwhelmed the national one, only far too late, after millions died, leading to its defeat.

Racial signifiers like "Jew" or "Muslim" and "gypsy" or "nigger" transcend national boundaries in order to elicit transnational sympathies and solidarities. The ahistorical usage of the terms has already appeared in ECE without remark. Fully garbed neonazis, beating African students in a tram in Bratislava, screamed "Die, Jew, Die. You should have died in the ovens!"; Slovak youth, beating Latin American students outside a pub, scream "Dirty Gypsy Go Home!" Nationalism as an ideology standing alone may be insufficient to achieve the creation of a nation-state, but we have again seen that a vicious politics of identity under the umbrella of ethnicity can achieve a considerable portion of such a project. In the Balkans, in the eastern most reaches of the FSU, identity politics has become conflated with ethnic cleansing and a continuance of ethnically based authoritarianism. Under these conditions, it is hard to believe that a racialized politics is far away.

The countries of ECE have yet to discover what level, if any, of discrimination based on ethnicity and racism is "morally tolerable." One reason for this is that people in the so-called new democracies have remarkably few legal, political, and civic skills; they hold deep-seated prejudices and an enormous reservoir of anxiety about the future. They have as yet little willingness to reconceptualize their prejudices or anxieties in language familiar to westerners. Their primary concerns remain material—economic and social. Their main ways of functioning are holdovers from the past. Issues of "rights"—human and civil—hold little interest. They are learning that the price of "freedom" is conflict; we who live in adversarial cultures should not be shocked by their discords—they bear more than faint resemblance to our own.

This said, the most pressing problems in ECE have less to do with classic forms of ethnic nationalism per se (that is, those that demand territory and nation-state status) or with the endemic low-level conflicts expressed in terms of racism or ethnic privilege that, sadly, plague every political order, than with three other matters.

—The extent to which ethnically based conflicts and the rise of racism are specific consequences of the transitional processes under way in various ECE countries. In this sense the historical, political, and economic origin of a specific conflict with an ethnic component and its appearance as part of the collective memory of a group, are only part of the problem. We must be cognizant of the ways in which the new structures, and perhaps agendas, of the transitional governments exacerbate all levels of social conflict. An obvious corollary to the impact of transitions on ethnic conflict is the comparable effect of the vast population movements throughout the region.

—The ways in which ethnicity and, slowly but surely, racism—the first legislated out of existence by the old regimes, the second barely acknowledged—are addressed or ignored by troubled governments and peoples of states in "transition." A combination of types of denial, ascribing racism and ethnocentrism to the West or to fascist and communist pasts, respectively, or to the current rapid influx of foreigners, has created enormous confusion and exacerbated social tensions. The conflation of these issues with that of legal citizenship both for old minorities (especially the Roma) and new immigrants has compounded both legal and social problems. The patterns of behavior that individuals carry with them from the old regime into the new, and their inexperience in handling the new complex environment, complement government ineptitude and malfeasance.

Hannah Arendt pointed out that the Nazis' use of racism turned its irrational core into ordinary behavior, made it the function of ordinary institutions. Balibar asks whether there is not a cycle of historical reciprocity between nationalism and racism "which is institutionalized in the domination of the system of nation states over other social formations." The same points apply to the extreme exercise of ethnocentrism, even short of an all-out war. It suggests that where ethnic politics seeks its resolve in a nation-state, racism is its inevitable companion, a situation beginning to appear throughout ECE. It also suggests that racism by any name can also destabilize transitional societies, making the emergence of a "civil society" much more difficult. Arendt's work helps us understand how "normal" this has again become.

—Finally, the third new aspect we must remark on is the patent inability of conventional instruments of western politics and legal systems to function effectively in ECE in the aftermath of the conventional cold war. Western polities have been able neither to predict, prevent, nor resolve dangerous conflicts. An approach to these conflicts based on pure human rights or the techniques of conventional conflict resolution can never generate a zero-sum or neutral outcome, for there is never an equal amount of rights or territory or benefits to go around. In situations of extreme ethnic conflict only the extent of abuses, not the abuses themselves, can be bargained over. Without a history of and practice in participatory politics, warring groups have little incentive to negotiate, which requires a commitment to compromise. Mediation or conflict resolution, or both, are only embraced, if at all, after the damage has been done and there are clear winners and losers. Flirtation with issues around rights, compromise, mediation, conflict resolution become, first, tactics in the conflict and then a strategic move toward recalibrating a relationship with the West. Sadly, Bosnia is an overworked example of this scenario.

The remarks above point to why carving up territory and drawing new boundaries cannot satisfy national wars conducted by ethnic groups in ECE. Territory is a crucial issue, religion can become one, but borders are not. After months, sometimes years, of frustrating attempts to resolve ethnically based conflicts, international organizations are sometimes willing to turn to NGOs to "fly low," as one recent report put it (in language redolent of spy games!), to watchdog hot spots, to intervene (how is never specified) before an explosion occurs, and occasionally to play other than a service role after one has occurred. Are there new kinds of local activity that might prove useful to inhibit the outbreak of violent conflict between ethnic groups? Perhaps. But first we must know something more about the context.

The Generation Gap: Neo-Fascists, Skins, Youth

The uncertainties of the past four years, ensuing economic crises, and the spillover effect from wars in the Balkans and the FSU have exacerbated traditional ethnic conflicts, and stoked the fires of anti-Semitism and attacks on the Roma peoples almost everywhere. This much was perhaps predictable. Less so was the way the entire climate of the transition—including the rapid-fire embrace of "lustration" in various forms—would aid the development of the new fascist and skinhead movements, some western in origin, some indigenous. Once upon a time communism was seen as a viable weapon against fascism; now, in the absence of democratic traditions, certain sectors embrace neofascist movements to combat both the communist past and the uncertain, unknowable "democratic" (capitalist) future. The failure to come to term with the past, the polarization of almost every issue, has helped to give birth to neoconservatives with a national agenda, and they in turn have engendered new monsters on the far right.

In the Czech Republic and Slovakia, the soil for planting new extremisms was fertilized by the publication of STB (the Czechoslovakian secret police) lists of supposed "collaborators" in the right-wing journal *Red Cow.*

The release of thousands of names referenced (for many different reasons) in the files rekindled massive suspicion and distrust among neighbors, even though the lists were notoriously inaccurate, prepared originally by hardly disinterested STB agents.[13] There was little faith that neutral judicial processes could sort out the truth—after all, many members of the judiciary were themselves compromised by their own pasts. And the long-ingrained practice of arriving at judicial decisions on the basis of politics and connections ensured that reform would not occur overnight. At the height of the frenzy against supposed agents, one of the most principled human rights activists of the older dissident generation in ECE said, with sad irony: Lots of bad things are happening to good people; and people everyone knows collaborated are making fortunes. I wouldn't be surprised if someone suggested that the entire oppositional generation (many of whom were former members of communist parties) be put on trial!

In the former East Germany, admitted collaborators seem to be rehabilitated more quickly than their victims; in other countries, officials of the hated interior departments hold important posts in the private and public sectors. Those who think about the issue know that the crimes of the secret police in all countries were so ubiquitous that, once painted with its brush, however falsely the scarlet letter is applied, rehabilitation is as difficult now as it was under Stalin. In no case has a society fully realized a process to come to terms with the past—and move on. (Hungary alone has made an attempt to draw some kind of "thick line.") Judging by the ease with which neofascism has made a reappearance, time may or may not heal the new wounds.

In ECE, neofascists have found plenty of space to indulge in effective random violence against individuals and property, and more calculated attacks on "ethnics," Roma, Jews, foreigners, and "others." As in the West, pubs, concerts, and football games serve as favorite venues. A growing number of active groups of neofascists and skinheads now meet regularly, within and across borders of former east and west.[14]

The groups are active, organized, funded internationally, and sometimes linked to the drug and smuggling trades. They are composed for the most part of dislocated, alienated, poorly educated youth (communist-style: membership in youth organizations was held up to the age of thirty-five), casualties of the transitions, whose futures are grim. Members are bonded, competitive, distinct, and combative, offering a node for attachment to young people who have little if any models or motivation for constructing a "free" world, or for dealing with "normal" levels of insecurity. At least a dozen magazines across the region carry messages of hatred to bored and impressionable youth—mixed with news of the hard and acid rock music scenes and the best place to buy discarded U.S. military camouflage clothing and the variously colored steel-tipped "Doc Maartens" that identify the different groups. Their message of hatred and blame and disillusionment, of group solidarity, of a hedonism of sorts, is welcomed by many youth who simply hate and distrust any form of politics.

The groups differ from western gangs by their instrumental use of violence and the breadth of their intentions—to destabilize the existing fragile order and reestablish a (poorly understood) fascist authoritarianism, free of "strangers." The explicitly political agenda, however confused its ideological underpinnings, sharply distinguishes them from western gangs and "soccer hooligan." Very few (one articulate young east German comes to mind) have seen the error of their ways and spoken out.

When violence erupts, the police are still rarely in the right place in time. Many speculate that while they may disapprove the association with fascism, they tacitly approve the attacks on Roma and other foreigners, populations that present the police with another set of dilemmas. Others say that the violence perpetrated by the rapidly growing neofascist and skinhead groups is a convenient distraction from corruption, inflation, and faltering transitions. Moreover, the Roma, now "fair game" for new perpetrators of violence against the "socially undesirable," were also regularly victimized by the old regimes. Two generations brought up to believe that enemies were everywhere can easily find new ones in strange-looking and behaving foreigners, in "hippies," in "undesirable" ethnic neighbors who are easily blamed for perverting both traditions and the transitions.

Human rights and special interest groups do their best in fragile self-absorbed environments to raise concerns, develop awareness, protect the interests of foreigners; but they must, for many reasons, work within the constraints of local laws, little changed from the previous regimes. The very few small spontaneous groups that have organized against neofascist activity work hard, mostly documenting cases of racial and ethnic abuse, and following them through the legal process. A few are trying to connect with counterparts in other countries. (HOST, in the Czech Republic, is one of the better groups.) But so far they are not developing into social or political movements against fascism. Apathy and fear are deep-seated; the levels of silent sympathy for anti-ethnic activity are hard to gauge; and, perhaps most important, people are not used to organizing in their own defense. The lessons have been painful ones: neither transitions nor elections make "democracy"; and the old activists, venerable though they might have been, did not create the core of a new civil society.

On the streets, in the schools, in the pubs and villages my young collaborators and I hang out, ask questions. We talk, drink, joke around, try to stay out of trouble. (Skins and neos in fatigues are visible almost everywhere.) More and more young people have begun to carry weapons to defend themselves, our respondents tell us. From whom, I ask? From everyone, they tell me. You can never tell. It's dangerous out here.

What Can a Concept of Civil Society Mean in ECE? What Are the Prevailing Attitudes toward Everyday Life?

Civil society is a subject that potentially can include almost everything and the proverbial kitchen sink.[15] To simplify: for purposes of this discussion, I mean by civil society that conceptual "space" and metaphorical "place" between the private and the public arenas where a broad array of system confirming, sustaining, and developmental (change) activities take place.

Civil society requires a certain "social mutuality,"[16] a notion of community, shared ethics, behaviors in most spheres of political and economic as well as social life. Each of these spheres must be separate (theoretically) from the state at the same time that it is interconnected with it. The forms of these interactions, which are invariably dependent and even interdependent, must be located within a shared system of values and norms, which in turn need to be quite elastic. In addition, civil society requires a "fit," however loosely, between individual and group identities and that of the whole. Under the best of circumstances, a "normal" level of social conflict, that which I have termed "morally tolerable disharmony,"[17] is contained, and resolved, within the boundaries of common norms. Mechanisms to prevent or resolve conflicts often use the instruments of state but without thereby obliterating the institutions or diverse practices of civil society. No such system is or can be perfect—that is *not* the point. Eighteenth- and nineteenth-century theory aside, civil society has been realized only imperfectly everywhere. It must only be able to sustain dissent and differences—some of them vast.

Civil society is, by all accounts, the least developed area under a communist form of authoritarianism, yet it is inaccurate to claim that no aspects of it existed under the former regimes. Rather, both its parameters and its perimeters were sharply delimited, and the functioning within them distorted by the ever-present fear of repression. The opposition movements clearly constituted one of the most active areas of civil society under the previous regimes; alternative cultural initiatives, theater and music in particular, and perhaps religious activities constituted others. Each of these areas, however, existed "underground." The extreme privatism—in the family, for example—that was used to protect oneself from the state and public spheres introduced peculiar distortions into psyche and functioning alike. The family was the one realm of relative "freedom," the only place one could possibly relax, not look over one's shoulder. Communication and a modicum of trust inside it was possible; outside it was not. Public behavior conformed to a quite rigid set of expectations. When it did not, it was because everyone understood that a certain amount of "functional corruption" and "deviant behavior" was what kept the system ticking.

Many of the unwritten rules that guided social interactions still persist. "That the old is not yet dead, and the new has not yet been born" makes daily life much more confusing, choices problematic. The character of a transition, and the habits and patterns of behavior that individuals carry with them from the old regime into the new are, of course, connected. One dimension concerns the outer environment, with its inherent propensity for conflagration. Another comprises a combination of attitudes about the processes of change and the existence of sufficiently elastic inner (social-psychological) resources with which to integrate dramatic new experiences into hitherto sharply proscribed life frames. Two areas that still suffer from "post-traumatic stress" are the ability to communicate ideas in public and a residual disbelief in the power of words and deeds, in new behaviors to make changes. Yet some modes of living are slowly changing, and new norms are also emerging.

It is important to underscore that the problems in ECE will be complicated for a long time by the fact that cold war rhetoric created sets of expectations on both sides that can never be met. If everything the Communist party said was patently false, if daily life under communism consisted of straddling a sharp disjuncture between words and lived reality, then everything on the other side must be perfect. Every once in a while I still meet people who say to me: It's not true, is it, that black people are discriminated against in America? or, conversely, looking at the new phenomenon of homelessness or unemployment in ECE, who remark somewhat sadly, if more wisely, that in these respects the communist propaganda was right after all. Now that it has become possible to look at the "other side," people have begun to understand that life there often fails to pass the litmus test of their dream for a post-communist future. Increasingly, despite the magnet of material abundance, people mention, a bit wistfully, that they feel something about the quality of life they knew and loved is being lost in the "rush to market."

The societies that are emerging, and people in them, had very little actual experience with daily life in a civil society as we in the West think of it. Ingrained patterns of thought, response, and behaviors required for daily survival under authoritarianism are often simply dysfunctional or counter-productive under more "open" societies. Inner integrity became highly malleable, adaptable, a component in the struggle for survival. The numbing effect of years of quite regimented daily life wears off slowly. Even the seemingly most cosmopolitan of colleagues will have, upon long acquaintance, an Achilles heel of past practices that is not simply a cultural difference or one of style or taste. It is interesting and painful to watch the generation gap about these matters emerge; intergenerational conflict within the family has begun to be a major social problem in ECE. The overall cultural scene has changed; in particular, young people have embraced a new music scene, full of Latin, Brazilian, and African sounds and lyrics that carry quite a different message than acid rock. Cross-cultural communication is much easier in theory than accepting the stranger next door. These kinds of changes will take more time to internalize than the inside and outside pushes and pulls of the transitions, and western agendas, normally allow: a generation at least.

A well-known social psychologist, a member of the oppositional generation, repeats to me often: You think we are "normal," but we are not. The distortions to the human personality were too deeply ingrained. Look at all the madness that's emerged over coming to terms with the past; good people's lives are being ruined—just like they always were. And the worst criminals go free. Look at the suspicious way some of us respond to questions, requests for help or collaboration that would be normal anywhere else. Look at the cut-throat competition between colleagues to get ahead or to get out, to make it in western terms. We're afraid we're going to be the new "third world." Even intellectuals. It's almost impossible for us not to be paranoid, suspicious. It's hard to trust anyone. Most people don't tell the truth, either to each other or to westerners. And most people are still terribly afraid—of each other, of anyone and anything new and of the future. It will take two generations at least to recover. Look at my family: it seems that we function wonderfully, yet underneath . . . I hope the children can recover. We're at least trying.

We go on to talk about intellectual interests, children, possible vacations. She tells me that they hope to get to Croatia to the beach, like in the old days. (Croatia was a traditional "watering place" for many central Europeans. Many are now braving war for a taste of the sea again.) Then she laughs: See, she said, a vacation on the beach with war raging around us. We can become accustomed to anything. I told you we weren't normal!

During transitions, publics are exposed to foreigners, to other ethnic groups through press and television reports about their needs, their complaints, their criminality, the impossibility of granting citizenship to everyone who asks, their drain on the state budget, and so on. The effect of the mass media, however still subject to massive amounts of "self"-censorship, is extraordinarily powerful and manipulative. (This is another area in which to expand NGO work.) Governing parties couch ethnic dislike in the language of economic necessity. Taking a cue from their western counterparts, the new quite conservative parties appeal to people's self-protective instincts (law and order) to push restrictive legislation. On the flip side, the new coalitions of moderately progressive parties, where they exist, appeal for votes on the basis of the oft-quoted sentiment that despite the many other things that were wrong in the past, "we didn't have unemployment, we didn't have criminality [sic!], and we didn't have these problems with foreigners under communism."

Local Initiatives: Place—Space—Politics

Inevitably, issues around domestic minorities, ethnicity, the location and status of segments of one's own population abroad, the spillover effects of foreign wars, citizenship and borders, generation gaps, and so forth become salient, are located in new places. Structural and functional connections between urban and rural life remain, still essential for most to sustain a reasonable standard of living. But the empty villages of communist times are now emptier still. The enormous population shifts discussed above have provided a broad new venue for class, ethnic, and racially based conflicts— the cities.

Hastily and ill-conceived local policies, or the lack of them, combined with the shifts in population, have helped turned the central cities of the region into oddly configured boom towns. New construction vies for attention with abandoned skeletons of communist construction or neglect. Local markets bump against new bazaars; bordellos, refuges for the displaced, pockets of growing homelessness, bars full of under- and unemployed nestle side by side with upscale shops, foreign vendors, and myriad tourist attractions. Local private enterprise, foreign economic entrepreneurs, and western money from governments anxious to secure their borders coexist a bit uncomfortably, whether in Warsaw, Prague, or Budapest, Bucharest, Bratislava, or Sofia. And the tourists are fair game for a whole new generation of petty and not-so-petty thieves.

In this entrepreneurial context the "western" attributes of class and ethnicity collapse into each other, are subsumed by the market. Race, however, remains race: mysterious, poorly understood, something that engenders problems elsewhere. All thieves are Roma; all Roma are thieves. All illegal money laundering is done by the Chinese in their many almost empty restaurants; all Chinese are money launderers. All quasi-legal laundering is handled by the Italian mafia, via their connection with the banks; all Italians (and banks) have mafia connections. All smugglers are Russian; all Russians are smugglers. If you want something cheap, go to the Vietnamese; the Vietnamese have cheap goods. Western-type economic ethnic enclaves have arrived in force. And so have the resentments that accompany them. Populations accustomed to polarizing their lives to sustain the habits of another kind of survival, automatically polarize their responses to the unknown.

"Normal" people often find the phenomenon of so many strangers among them a bit intimidating, sometimes frightening. Two generations of indoctrination about international brotherhood did not help to dispel the shock of actually having to deal with foreigners. Neither east central European societies nor their cities are (yet) cosmopolitan centers. What the Communists had told them about criminality and racial conflict in the West—which was disbelieved at the time—seems to have come home to roost. Fears about their economic futures may make some adults swallow hard and deal with widely disliked Germans or Russians or boorish North Americans in ways similar to those with which they dealt with communist authorities: few words, few truths, few personal contacts. Take the money, go home, keep your mouth shut. This degree of contact is a lot, compared with opportunities for interaction with foreigners by most people outside the center.

Other groups—Roma, the remnant of Vietnamese workers now street merchants, resident non-nationals, and all groups tolerated by dictate under the former regime—are viewed ambivalently, even when they are patronized. Refugees and asylum seekers, housed mostly in rural camps, mingle with village populations in matters of petty commerce or in pubs (opportunities for employment are few); they report increases in everyday kinds of discrimination, in fist fights, and some fatal knifings. Yet it would be wrong to exaggerate these kinds of incidents, or to claim they are any different from similar events in the west.[18]

To complicate matters, all European government policies toward refugees, asylum seekers, and formerly welcome *gastarbeiter* from the East and South are increasingly restrictive, at worst downright oppressive. Western European policies hardly provide an emulation model for those of ECE. Members of the European Union actively pressure the countries of the "buffer zone" to keep people from crossing through them into the West. In central Europe government officials are afraid the "hordes of less-educated," "lower-class people" from the East will invade them, absorb scarce resources, take jobs, increase the strain on paltry pension funds and social welfare budgets. This, they know, will also jeopardize their chances for admission to the European Union, so they redouble vigilance on eastern and southern borders. Among the population at large, there is little experience with, and little public discourse about, the phenomenon of strangers in their midst or other difficult issues. Public discussion, such as it is, emphasizes the problems immigrants and refugees pose. Self-censorship by still-wary editors, sharp editorial pencils, and the fundamentally conservative environment in the region ensure that little open discussion occurs about the problems newcomers face.

Human rights activists—usually members of the dissident generation, a few young people and outsiders like the author who talk about such matters—are portrayed as liberal do-gooders or reform communists out of touch with reality. With the exception of the too few agencies dealing with the service aspects of social problems and a handful of journalists, discussions about individual or collective rights and needs of "others" are met with open dismissal, except when foreign funders or politicians are within earshot. It is also true that funds are short, know-how lacking, and cultural pride on the defensive. Ingrained habits and bureaucratic obstinacy can combine with them to defeat the best of intentions. It is reasonable to ask from where in the immediate future the voices and new activists are going to come in sufficient numbers to raise sensitive issues and forge a meaningful polity.

With few exceptions, the once dissident generation finds that it was much easier to be in opposition than to govern or even to remain dissidents. Principles sometimes go down the drain in the face of a chance for a modicum of "power" or opportunity long denied. Populations accustomed to a certain order, however resentful of it they had been, find familiar routines comforting in the face of so much change. New freedoms quickly lead to disorder, corruption, instant fortunes, and complete collapse; the gild on the exotic "other" soon tarnishes. Those who had been most determined to provide the preconditions for an escape from authoritarianism—the "old" oppositions—and the others who in unconscious concert with them opened the floodgates to the future, have already become a first generation of "founding fathers" and followers in astonishingly short order. With few exceptions, they were as ill equipped as the many to transform euphoria into measured leadership, ideals into workable institutions, passivity and bad practices into the rudiments of participatory democracy. Naiveté, poor leadership skills, confusion, and so on all encouraged the emergence of conservative, even reactionary, new parties whose adherents now populate governments almost everywhere.

Not only is the experience of functioning openly if competitively within a civil society limited, but so is the habit of interacting publicly on the basis of shared norms, trusting that a disagreement will not make instant enemies. Outside the family, social interactions still occur within deliberately narrow circles, usually connected to work rather than to shared interests or personal preference. Speaking with a stranger is still almost never done without a personal, preferably family-linked, introduction. Telling the whole truth, or an entire story, outside the tight family circle is rare. With the exception of a few courageous and outstanding journalists and intellectuals, communicative competencies are still developing. Of course, some individuals and families have slowly and gingerly begun experimenting with new lifestyles; so far, they do so by enlarging the sphere of the private rather than by relocating themselves in a public space. Clearly, it will take time to develop a new political generation, a functioning civil society.

NGOs: The Wages of Methodological Inelegance
Are Circularities

Viable roles for NGOs or other group actors almost anywhere throughout the greater region—by definition, organizations that require individual initiative, vision, sustained energy (as well as financial resources)—are proscribed by how well and widely the very concepts of civil society, of public space, of democracy, of a political system that encourages and validates participation and values tolerance are understood, given priority, or remain anathema. Fortunately, there is also in each country a small but growing number of dedicated people, committed to developing a tolerant, functional civil society by way of NGO work. However, this kind of work is frustrating in the best of circumstances, and a slow but steady trickle of local activists is draining west.

Whether any NGO—local, national, international—can function in such a way as to inhibit the outbreak of ethnic conflicts during a transition from authoritarianism depends on many factors outside its immediate control. To review, these include, among other things:

—the character of the antecedent regime;

—the history of the opposition before and after the immediate transition;

—the character of the transitional processes;

—the kinds of interventions and support foreign governments and private actors—industries, foundations—mount in the postauthoritarian period;

—respect and support for the policies of the opposition once they become post-transition elites;

—who is immediately most successful at manipulating the volatile environment in his or her own interest;

—the role of pretransition elites in the immediate post-transition period;

—the rapidity and success with which structural changes can be introduced;

—the health of the economy;

—the legal and financial environment;

—attitudes toward strangers and "foreign" ideas;

—how deeply embedded in the past the mentalities and practices of daily life remain;

—whether there are outbreaks of ethnic and racial violence;

—whether there are opportunities to create a common feeling of hopefulness and trust among inevitably suspicious populations;

—the rapidity with which political movements, foreign money, or both penetrate and disrupts local life.

On a brighter note, despite serious constraints, new social groups—businesspeople, for example, staking claims to legitimacy—have begun to support social change and to work with local groups in areas where cross-cutting interests are clear. Controversies over the formal legal organization of the states and the private institutions within them have encouraged contact between the business and "nonprofit" worlds in regard to regularizing their relationships to the state. Thousands of NGOs have appeared in the last four years, proliferating literally right and left. (Two thousand are registered in the Czech Republic, more than one thousand in Hungary and eight hundred in Slovakia.) Most of them, while technically "registered" with the state, exist in a legal gray area. Without overall tax reform—a subject of major interest to foreign investors and the newly privatized industries—and nonprofit status, they are subject to the enormously high taxes the new regimes have imposed on all enterprises and salaries (36 percent in the Czech Republic, for example).

A variety of organizations registered as NGOs have appeared: (a) international and local foundations, which function as conduits for money that goes to others; (b) institutes or similar organizations that collect data, produce research, and generally try to catalogue what's going on; (c) special interest and service organizations, which work in and around human rights, citizenship, immigrant, and refugee issues. Small local agencies have also formed around specific problems such as unemployment, Roma issues, ecology, the press, low-level ethnic and community conflicts. In combination, NGOs undertake a broad array of activities properly belonging to civil society, but also many that in more evolved societies exist in concert with the public sector or are properly reserved for the public sphere.

Since the initial boom period in 1990–91, when foreign foundations rushed in with open hands (and people who had never possessed $200 found themselves managing—or mismanaging—thousands), the monies are flowing less freely. Like their counterparts in the West, legitimate NGOs must now compete to raise money even as they are learning how best to use it. On the other hand, bluntly put, many were and a few remain players in the opportunistic games that transitional periods encourage. Affiliation with an NGO can provide access to the West as well as to hard currency. Quick learners who also happen to possess good language skills can rapidly become part of the new NGO "circuit" and have ready access to travel, conferences, and funding. It is very difficult for western funders to sort out who is sincere and who is simply trying to advance a career. Inevitably, costly mistakes will be made.

The above helps to explain why some NGO activities seem to have emerged only in response to the funding agendas of the big western foundations and intergovernmental agencies, which are anxious to solidify transitions in the direction of "democratic" market societies. Where this has been the case, there may certainly result a limited redistribution and circulation of funds at a local level, but skills development and real contributions to social improvement remain at a minimum. With the remarkable exception of one U.S. foundation that has worked in the field with local staff for many years, and some of the smaller U.S. and European granting agencies, the ability of U.S. funders, European and North American governments, international organizations, and banks to adequately assess local needs and capacity, and fund accordingly, has been strikingly limited. Western funders need to learn something about the various ECE cultures in order to assess local capabilities realistically before simply pouring money into underdeveloped situations where they can do more harm than good.

By now, for example, almost everyone in ECE knows that projects structured around the needs of the Roma, or containing elaborate plans for reeducation or containing the catchwords "civil society" or "rights" or "democracy" will receive funding. Where public sector resources are as impoverished as they remain in ECE, and where there is little consensus about their use, one cannot just blame local NGOs (or unscrupulous individuals) for tailoring projects to meet the requirements of funders without also facing the dilemmas that have been created by the outside world. The practice of "shotgun" funding ensures that monies will dry up before the ability to use them is developed. It also encourages the erroneous belief that western funders will "insure" the transitions via grants. A tertiary effect of this kind of funding is that it also provides an excuse for transitional governments to delay structuring reasonable policies concerning such matters as social welfare, education, and human rights, and makes it even harder for NGOs to function effectively over the long run. Overall, good agencies receive little local support, and foreign support can be contradictory, naive, and bumbling.

With the best of intentions—and sometimes the worst—legions of foreign consultants and advisers have unintentionally rebuilt walls between East and West, their insistence on certain "western" procedures, styles, and programs engendering more resistance and negativity than constructive change. They misunderstand local norms, have no idea of the cultural dimensions that must develop for change to occur, do not appreciate how difficult it is to recruit and train people to think and act in new ways in an environment where so much of the past governs daily life. Directors of two well-known agencies mentioned repeatedly how much time it takes to "entertain" and explain their work to foreign visitors. Spare me another visit by Mr. "Y," one director said to me in response to my asking how I could be of help. Why do you agree to see so many foreigners, I asked, conscious of my own intrusion. It is hard not to, was the response; besides, every once in a while foreign funds or a good contact results from the meetings or I learn something. Of course, the cultural misunderstandings and massive miscommunications go both ways; learning about the "other" is never a one-way process. There is much to learn on both sides about the other and about how to work most effectively during choppy transitions.

It is to their credit that many NGOs in ECE are learning to operate in a world of grant-getting and cross-cutting interests on their own terms. While most of the new organizations do not yet function at a high level of efficiency or efficacy, many do provide a modicum of the social welfare services that exist. By example, they also initiate some of the preconditions, however faint, required to build a civil society in the western sense. With the exception of the international human rights organizations, such as the International Helsinki Committees and umbrella organizations like the Helsinki Citizens' Assembly, only a few NGO's conceive of themselves as part of an attempt to initiate projects and create coordinated if not coherent local social movements. Most simply try their best to respond to local issues. This is an item for a future agenda, as is finding a way for NGOs to create for themselves an effective niche between public and private sectors.

This said, under the best of circumstances, confusion often abounds, and NGO staff find it difficult to distinguish among service, legal, and policy functions. Mountains of paperwork—much of it left over from the old regimes, much of it representing "add-ons" from the new governments which conceive of governing as promulgating more and more rules and regulations, many of them circular in effect—consume half the days. One staffer, working with refugee and asylum seekers, told me: I fill out form after form, application after application, for people whom I am sure will be turned down. It is frustrating work. Surely there is something else I could do that would have better results for them. But what?

Or again, poor telephone service encourages people to communicate in person, spending hours on public transportation between meetings that are longer and more elaborate than they need to be. (In the past, "official" lunches, seminars, conferences in remote castles were "perks" in an otherwise dreary work life.) The habit of writing decisions down, as a way of demonstrating agreement as distinct from merely generating a record, is not yet widespread—and is often resisted. (This may help explain why written agreements, so dear to westerners trying to resolve conflicts, are so easily abrogated.) Curiously, the fax machine, which often seems to work when the telephone does not, is proving to be a godsend in places where no such thing as rapid mail or messenger services exists. One colleague actually carries a small one with him when he is working in remote areas and needs to access information quickly. (E-mail is still too tricky outside university centers.)

Heads of good agencies are overwhelmed by the numbers and kinds of problems appearing daily, literally at the door. One director of a human rights agency asked, rhetorically: How do I turn away Mrs. or Mr. "X" who have traveled many miles to see me because they have no one else to turn to? Their problem (something about village water mains and a struggle with a neighbor over a right of way) is not properly about human rights at all; it should be handled locally, by the mayor; they probably need an honest local lawyer. We both know that the municipality doesn't care, and that getting good representation is impossible. They have no water, they have seen me on television, so they come to me. We try to explain the issues and find them a decent lawyer nearby. Sometimes, if there is an egregious abuse of civil rights (for example, the eviction by eminent domain of an elderly woman from her lifelong housing, without providing her another comparable dwelling), we send one of our staff to talk to the local officials. It's all very frustrating and time-consuming. We must spend half our time on such matters. Another quarter of my time is spent arm-twisting people in the government. Meanwhile we are desperately backed up on human rights cases, and our commitments to review new legislation, to initiate human rights and legal education projects, to lobby for judicial reform and modification of the new citizenship laws get badly neglected. The director added: I really do not see a way out of this dilemma in the short run.

Too-thin resources are spread between service goals to client populations, the pressing need to initiate long-lasting political and legal change, and the equally important goal of educating the public about salient issues. NGOs are also pulled between the demands of foreign funders for western-style accountability and eastern-style work norms. Another director of one of the most active agencies in ECE commented that even communist bureaucracy had not prepared them for the number of forms they had to fill out to get and stay funded by a major U.S. foundation. The staff laughed. We are sure, they said, that in the United States it is very important for each report to include a statistical profile of the agency staff: how many women, how many men, how many minorities, everyone's age, and so on. As for us, look around! We agree that it is not good that mostly women do this work! We would love to hire more men and more members of "minorities"— please, feel free to recruit some! And then, please, be so kind as to train them! (It is still a commonplace in ECE that women do most of the hard work of organizing, while men do the talking!) They also complain that, given how difficult it is to start something new in ECE, western funding cycles are so short that just when a project is finally off the ground, it is time to file a report or apply for an extension.

The shortage of well-trained, hard-working staff is perhaps one of the greatest inhibitions to effective work. It has no immediate remedy. The uneven work norms remain a highly charged subject, even though many who choose NGO work put in longer hours than their counterparts in government or elsewhere. For many committed individuals, too much of the workday is still spent trying to get something done while simulta- neously taking care of a personal matter that cannot be solved before or after working hours. The latter problem reflects how little patterns of everyday life have changed, and is surely not restricted to those who work for NGOs.

How to interest, recruit, quickly train, and retain staff (and bright young scholars in the academies) is one of the thorniest problems. Promising young people are quickly snapped up at high salaries by international corporations. A funding strategy recently adopted by a few NGOs is to apply for grants for staff recruitment and training along with a western partner; those accepted for training must commit themselves to work for the agency for a given period after completing the training. It is clear that staff recruitment, training, and retention is a subject that needs concerted devel- opment by almost all NGOs.

All in all, NGO staff are very short on models and also exhausted by the intensity of interpersonal quarrels—in the office, with the government, among themselves—that are in part another residue of the past. Getting anything out of the government still has a lot to do with who knew whom back then. Networking in the western sense is still largely absent. It is rare for different organizations doing similar kinds of work to meet jointly. I find myself carrying information between organizations only a few blocks apart. Visiting NGOs, working with them, I am continuously reminded of how much time everything takes, of the once-intentional, now-unintentional costs of so much inefficiency, of the ways in which daily life—let alone the paucity of resources—conspires to defeat the best intentions, wears us out.

Can I work differently from other outsiders, I ask myself daily? Avoid the worst errors? Make a difference in the long run? We don't do things that way, I've been told numerous times, in one way or another. It is not possible. What do you really know about us anyway? Maddeningly little, I sometimes feel. Of course there are days where local activists communicate openly and some modicum of personal trust and common goals evolve. I roll up my sleeves, draft letters to funders, help edit proposals, "brainstorm," all the while learning the cultural codes, the minutia of working in a country, a region, a city. Occasionally project planning occurs together or a major grant application is drafted, discussed, revised, and months later receives funding.

A former member of the opposition, now an academic, and I meet for dinner; the conversation drifts to problems of high unemployment, particularly of women (40 percent) and single men, in a multi-ethnic region packed with collapsing heavy industry. All of a sudden we look at each other and realize that we could work together to design local self-help and unemployment programs that might have a secondary effect of bringing together unemployed people from different ethnic groups. We agree to try. Another time, I am speaking openly with a friend about the difficulties of working in her country. My complaint concerns the absolute refusal of a major human rights figure, well known in and abundantly funded from the West, to ever work collaboratively. His overarching egoism ensures that only "his" "horses" eat well, at the expense of the local "sparrows." What else must I do, say, know, I ask, to move things along, to help build a new generation of human rights activists? She laughs at me. Be patient. You are right, but too western. Two generations of life under communism means two generations of recovery! I retort: two generations is a short time, I agree, but long enough to throw the baby out with the bath water, and then be sorry afterwards. Then what? She shakes her head at me, then shrugs. The problem is unavoidable, but we at least understand each other.

Often, I simply trust that the connections I make among local NGOs will sooner or later be useful, and my technical skills at least a route to badly needed hard currency. If I succeed, the learning and mutual adaptations, real collaborations, training, and organizational inputs will evolve later. (Visiting agencies and projects, I am reminded of the sixties in the United States, when every social work and social policy school in the country sent its naive graduate students into the "ghettos" to "study" and make recommendations concerning the putative processes of change!) There is surely room here for better practice on all sides. There is waiting an arena in which to develop substantive and collaborative projects (as distinct from travel junkets) across East-West borders, with a focus on nurturing the variety of organizational and technical skills appropriate to myriad local cultures. Without this, many well-meaning interventions will continue to be perceived as unwanted western imports, and firmly resisted. Others will be embraced blindly, and too few "notables," even among the activists, will continue to control access to funds and knowledge.

In Place of a Conclusion: What to Do and Where to Do It

In sum, I hold that work at the grass-roots level—which means working with and through local NGOs—is essential for anyone interested in conflict prevention. I do not here refer to the role of NGOs under conditions of war, nor to those situations where ethnic conflicts continue to be rubbed raw for political reasons and are beyond anyone's control. I assume such work occurs with a goal of arriving at a "morally tolerable disharmony," in an imperfect world with imperfect people. It goes almost without comment that it also requires a reasonable level of goodwill by all parties and enough healthy skepticism to separate the wheat from the chaff during the process.

A number of the recent "low-level" conflicts in ECE—random attacks on local youth, on Latins, on Africans, sharp local struggles over bilingual education or street signs and official forms in two languages, issues of police-community relations, the demonstrations over high local unemployment, and even those over citizenship, immigration rights, and property that straddles borders—exemplify the common character of everyday problems across the region. All the substantive issues contained in such conflicts are not easily remediable via political solutions proposed by governments that populations do not trust.

It is essential, therefore, that NGOs develop the capacity to work locally. NGOs that are committed to local populations, and are capable of acquiring new skills, can play constructive roles in the prevention of potential conflicts and the resolution of ongoing ones. Under the proper circumstances, it can also be helpful if the approach of a given NGO is legitimated by a major foreign foundation or organization. But staff must above all be competent and perceived as committed and knowledgeable.

There is no question that most NGOs throughout the region still need to improve greatly their organizational and managerial competence. To work effectively they need to develop specific skill sets, particularly those around conflict resolution, problem solving, and resource acquisition and allocation. They still must develop the habit of approaching every situation with an "open book" in hand. And they need to be politically sophisticated at the same time staff must retain strict political neutrality. The latter is critical. Ongoing work on a given conflict will abruptly halt if members of local NGOs adopt a partisan stance toward any local or national issue. Just such a circumstance emerged in Ukraine, where a resolution of a cross-border conflict was aborted when a hitherto highly effective activist, skilled at local interethnic communication, embraced what was perceived as a nationalist position in regard to another matter. The local work was compromised beyond repair, and the conflict escalated. In addition, the NGO was discredited, making it more difficult for others to develop trust.[19]

Fortunately, a growing number of people throughout the region—largely sociologists, social psychologists, and health workers long connected to service delivery—are determined *not* to become embroiled in local or national politics while working with local NGOs to resolve conflicts. They have begun developing diverse skill sets in small group work with multiethnic populations from a variety of perspectives. They use materials and methods from the fields of psychiatry, social and clinical psychology, sociology, human rights (law and ethics), and conflict resolution. Moreover, they have also, slowly, begun to recognize the need to acquire expertise in those organizational and management skills that will provide credibility in the long run: not only grant writing, but recruiting and training committed organizers and facilitators. NGOs and their western supporters must continuously invent new ways to further these aims.

As noted above, there are many local situations where appropriate NGO intervention would be beneficial, and I encourage the continued development of projects to address them. But in the long run, my research also suggests the need for an intensive focus on two areas from which it is reasonable to predict new conflicts will spring: (1) the implications of the massive voluntary and involuntary demographic shifts for ethnic and racial conflicts, including how the new demography is presented to various publics, particularly in urban and border areas; and (2) the specific problems and concerns of youth, and how they are manifested, both overall and with specific attention to those who have been displaced by the war in the Balkans. Both issue areas concern the many people who are and will remain caught between the upper jaw of the transition and the lower one of resistance to it, those who have left the past without perceiving or being able to enjoy the prospect of a viable future, those who are prime candidates for the role of perpetrator or victim of violence. A useful next step for NGOs in the region and their western collaborators would be to think ahead about these subjects, and to design a range of new projects with which to address them.

I conclude by underlining that in the context of transitions, by definition unstable environments, successful NGO work depends on quite specific factors: absolute independence, even when an NGO draws on outside resources; an approach based on a foundation of developing trust and collaborative work with local groups; the willingness to involve in the project of prevention or resolution both local public officials and representatives of each side in a conflict; a commitment to complete political neutrality in regard to a broad range of issues; and flexibility and the resources—human and material—to undertake regular monitoring and follow-up in each situation. When these conditions have been met, it is because a given NGO has made a commitment to remain an active player in the process of social reconstruction.

The past half decade in east central Europe has thrown into sharp relief Primo Levi's words to the effect that the "human condition is incompatible with certainty," that there are no prophets who can reveal the future, that [humankind] must "build . . . tomorrow blindly, gropingly; build it from its roots without giving into the temptation to recompose the shards of the old shattered idols and without constructing new ones." It is this alone that can provide grounds for cautious optimism in the long run.

Notes

1. Guillermo O'Donnell, Philippe Schmitter, and Lawrence Whitehead, *Transitions from Authoritarian Rule: Prospects for Democracy; Southern Europe; Latin America: Comparative Perspectives; Tentative Conclusions about Uncertain Democracies,* 5 vol. (Baltimore: Johns Hopkins University Press, 1991); Paulo Sergio Pinheiro, "Social Violence of Transitions: Comparative Perspectives in New Democracies," Center for the Study of Violence, Universidade de São Paulo; Maria Celia Paoli, "Citizenship, Inequalities, Democracy and Rights: The Making of a Public Space in Brazil," *Social and Legal Studies,* vol. 1 (1992), pp. 143–59.

2. Alfred Stepan, "Ethnic Conflict in Romania," ms. Central European University, Prague, 1994; Douglas A. Chalmers, ed., *The Right and Democracy in Latin America* (New York: Praeger, 1992). See also Pinheiro, "Social Violence of Transitions: Comparative Perspectives in New Democracies."

3. Eva Etzione-Halevy, *The Elite Connection: Problems and Potential of Western Democracy* (Cambridge, Mass.: Polity Press, 1993); and Anthony Giddens and David Held, eds., *Classes, Power and Conflict* (University of California Press, 1982).

4. Ernest Gellner, *Nations and Nationalism* (Cornell University Press, 1992); E. J. Hobsbawn, *Nations and Nationalism Since 1870* (Cambridge University Press, 1990); Benedict Anderson, *Imagined Communities: Reflections on the Origin and Spread of Nationalism* (New York: Verso, 1991); and Anthony D. Smith, *The Ethnic Origin of Nations* (New York: Basil Blackwell, 1988).

5. Miroslav Hroch, *Social Preconditions of National Revival in Europe* (Cambridge University Press, 1985).

6. Anthony D. Smith, *The Ethnic Origin of Nations* (New York: Basil Blackwell, 1988).

7. Claus Offe, "Ethnic Politics in Eastern European Transitions," in J. Jensen and F. Mistiritz, eds., *Paradoxes of Transition* (Szombathely: Savory University Press, 1993), pp. 11–39.

8. Ibid.

9. Claire Wallace, Oxana Chmuliar, and Elena Sidorenko, "The Eastern Frontier of Western Europe: Mobility in the Buffer Zone." ms., Forced Migration Project, Central European University, Prague, 1995.

10. Andrii Palyanitsya and Claire Wallace, "Migration in the Czech Republic" (February 1994), "Transit Migration in the Czech Republic" (March 1994), ms., Central European University, Prague. Final report to the International Organization for Migration, Geneva.

11. Matyas Szabo, "The Social Psychology and Political Life of Ethnic Hungarians in Romania," ms. Central European University, Prague, 1994.

12. Etienne Balibar and Immanuel Wallerstein, *Race, Nation, Class: Ambiguous Identities* (New York: Verso, 1991).

13. Lawrence Weschler, "A Reporter at Large; The Velvet Purge: The Trials of Jan Kavan," *The New Yorker,* vol. 68, no. 35 (October 19, 1992).

14. Paul Hockenos, *Free to Hate: The Rise of the Right in Post-Communist Eastern Europe* (New York: Routledge, 1993).

15. Jean Cohen and Andrew Arato, *Civil Society and Political Theory* (MIT Press, 1992); John Keane, *Democracy and Civil Society* (New York: Verso, 1998); John Keane, ed., *Civil Society and the State: New European Perspectives* (New York: Verso, 1988); Zbigniew Rau, *The Emergence of Civil Society in Eastern Europe and the Soviet Union* (Boulder, Colo.: Westview Press, 1991); Adam Seligman, *The Idea of Civil Society* (New York: Free Press, 1992); and Paul G. Lewis, ed., *Democracy and Civil Society in Eastern Europe* (New York: St. Martin's Press, 1992).

16. Seligman, *The Idea of Civil Society.*

17. Terry K. Aladjem, "Argument, Agreement and Anxiety over Difference in Democratic Discourse: Figures of Truth in Mill, Rorty, Habermans and Foucault," ms., Harvard University, 1993.

18. Elena Sidorenko, "Analysis of Articles about Inter-Ethnic Conflicts in the Czech Mass Media January–May 1994," ms.; "Representation of NGO and Roma Issues in the Czech Press January–May 1994," ms., Central European University, Prague, 1994.

19. Stephanie Baker, "The Role of Civil Groups in Conflicts in Eastern Europe," ms., London School of Economics, 1994.

Contributors

Abram Chayes is the Felix Frankfurter Professor of Law Emeritus at the Harvard Law School, where he teaches international law. His area of research is international law, especially environmental and trade issues, peacekeeping, and conflict prevention. He has been on the faculty since 1955, with one interruption to serve as legal advisor in the Department of State in the Kennedy administration, 1961–64. In the 1980s he represented Nicaragua in its World Court case (attacking the Reagan administration's policy of support for the contras) against the United States.

Antonia Handler Chayes is a senior advisor at Conflict Management Group and a consultant at JAMS/Endispute. She served as a commissioner with the Commission on Roles and Missions of the Armed Forces of the United States (CORM). During the Carter administration she served as under secretary of the U.S. Air Force. She is a director of United Technologies Corporation.

Diana Chigas is director of Conflict Management Group's Project on Preventive Diplomacy in the OSCE, focusing on supporting the High Commissioner on National Minorities in developing methodologies for preventive diplomacy and managing ethnic tension.

Jarat Chopra is research associate and lecturer in international law at The Thomas J. Watson Jr. Institute for International Studies, Brown University. He has published widely on the subject of UN operations and is currently developing a concept of "peace-maintenance."

Michael W. Doyle is professor of politics and international affairs at Princeton University.

Keitha Sapsin Fine is an associate professor of political science at the University of Massachusetts, Boston, and a director of the East European Cultural Endowment, Ltd. Her research focuses on comparative political development, and she writes in the fields of comparative communism, ethnic conflict, and comparative urban affairs.

David S. Huntington holds a J.D. (Harvard Law School, 1995) and is an associate with Cleary, Gottlieb, Steen and Hamilton.

Christophe Kamp is a program assistant at Conflict Management Group where his work focuses on inter-ethnic relations, international organizations, and preventive diplomacy.

Jean E. Manas wrote his chapter in his capacity as a visiting fellow at the European Law Research Center, Harvard Law School, and a consultant to the Carnegie Project. He is now an Associate at J.P. Morgan, New York.

Elizabeth McClintock, a consultant at Conflict Management Group, works in the fields of race relations, intercultural mediation, and preventive diplomacy.

John Pinder is a visiting professor at the College of Europe, Bruges, and chairman of the Federal Trust. He served as director of the Policy Studies Institute, London, 1964–85.

Wolfgang H. Reinicke is a member of the senior research staff in the Foreign Policy Studies program at the Brookings Institution, with which he has been affiliated since 1988. His areas of expertise include system transformation in Eastern Europe, European integration, international banking and finance, and global public policy.

Reinhardt Rummel is a member of the reasearch staff of Stiftung Wissenschaft und Politik, Ebenhausen, Germany. He has been a visiting scholar at the Wilson Center for International Scholars, Washington, D.C., and at the Center for International Affairs, Harvard University, and a lecturer at the Bologna Center, The Johns Hopkins University.

Melanie H. Stein is counsel for the European Bank for Reconstruction and Development. She holds a B.A. (Princeton University, 1986) and a J.D. (University of Michigan Law School, 1990).

Shashi Tharoor is the special assistant to the United Nations under-secretary-general for Peace-keeping Operations.

Thomas G. Weiss is associate director of the Watson Institute and executive director of the Academic Council on the United Nations System (ACUNS). He is on the editorial boards of *The Washington Quarterly, Third World Quarterly,* and *Global Governance.*

Richard Weitz is a professional staff member at CORM. He recently received his Ph.D. in government from Harvard University, where he wrote his dissertation on state behavior in NATO after the cold war.

Mario Zucconi is a political scientist based at the Center for International Political Studies in Rome and a lecturer at the University of Urbino.

Index

585